Y0-EQE-282

WITHDRAWN

CONCORDIA UNIVERSITY
3 4211 00125 9905

An Index of Gregorian Chant, Volume II

An Index of Gregorian Chant

Volume II: Thematic Index

Compiled by John R. Bryden and
David G. Hughes

Harvard University Press, Cambridge, Massachusetts, 1969

KLINCK MEMORIAL LIBRARY
Concordia Teachers College
River Forest, Illinois 60305

© Copyright 1969 by the President and Fellows of Harvard College
All rights reserved
Distributed in Great Britain by Oxford University Press, London
Library of Congress Catalog Card Number 71-91626
SBN 674-44875-8
Printed in the United States of America

93972

INTRODUCTION TO VOLUME II

The second volume of this Index contains largely the same information, and follows the same rules as the first. For full particulars, the user is referred to the general introduction, Volume I, pp. vi-xv. The following paragraphs deal with those matters in which Volume II differs from Volume I.

1. Content. Volume II contains all the entries of Volume I except those that for any reason appeared there without melodic incipit.

2. Order. The order of entries in Volume II is determined by the eight figures of the melodic incipit in algebraic sequence (i.e. -5, -4, -3, -2, -1, 0, 1, 2, etc.). Entries having the same melodic code are arranged in alphabetical order of their texts. If the texts are also the same, then the order is by the textual incipit of the main chant (if the entries are for verses), or the page number or item number in the first source cited (e.g., of two Kyrie with identical melodic incipit, MEL #184 would precede MEL #185).

3. Arrangement of the entries. In the first column there appears the starting pitch of the chant. As in Volume I, this is for information only, and has no effect on the filing order. There follows the eight-number melodic code. Then the final is given, except in the case of verses. The text incipit appears next, followed by the sources, the category, and the mode (the last also omitted for verses).

4. Discrepancies between the two volumes. In general, the entries in Volume II duplicate exactly those in Volume I, even at the cost of occasional minor incongruities. Thus, for example, the entries for an Alleluia and its verse, separated by hundreds of pages in Volume I, are here often brought directly together, making it evident that the text incipit has been carried out to different lengths in the two entries (e.g. "Alleluia: benedicamus patrem ... laudemus," followed at once by its verse, "Benedicamus patrem et filium cum ... laudemus"). This is natural, since the amount of text used was determined by the need to achieve clarity in the alphabetical arrangement of Volume I. There seemed to be no need to impose an artificial uniformity on such cases in Volume II--indeed, there was some risk that to do so would invite error or obscurity.

A somewhat different problem is presented by the indication of mode. It seems at least odd to find a group of entries, all with the same melodic incipit and final, of which some are assigned to mode 2 and others to mode 1. In fact, however, identical incipits do not by any means guarantee that the entire melodies are the same: difference in modal assignment may merely be the result of different melodic continuations. Even when the melodies are substantially the same, the sources may unequivocally disagree and assign one to the authentic and another to the plagal form. Only in the case of the hymns from ST--where the modal designations are the compilers' own--has it been thought occasionally desirable to impose uniformity, if only for appearance's sake. The few changes thus made have all been from authentic to plagal of the same maneria, or the reverse, and they have not been carried back into Volume I.

5. Appearance of textual variants. The re-ordering of the cards for Volume II brought to light a number of cases of variant text-beginnings that conceal the identity of apparently different chants. Thus, for example, Huic dum eremum turns out to be substantially the same, in both text and music, as Qui dum eremum--an identity that passed unperceived so long as the two entries were many pages apart in Volume I, but became evident when the melodic filing of Volume II brought them to successive pages. In order to make use of such disclosures, however, to enlarge the number of cross-references in Volume I, the compilers would have needed either to produce a duplicate set of cards, so that both orders could be consulted at once, or to effect very extensive revisions in the final typescript of the first volume. Neither of these was financially possible.

ML102.C45 B8 V.2 Ref.

Sigla Used for the Sources

(for full titles, see Vol. I, pp. xiii-xv)

AM	*Antiphonale monasticum*
AR	*Antiphonale Romanum* (or *Liber antiphonarius*)
BOS	Bosse, *Untersuchung . . . Gloria*
GB	*Graduel de Bénévent* (Pal. mus. XV)
GR	*Graduale Romanum* (or *Liber gradualis*)
GS	*Graduale Sarisburiense*
LA	*Antiphonaire monastique . . . de Lucques* (Pal. mus. IX)
LR	*Liber responsorialis*
LU	*Liber usualis*
MEL	Melnicki, *Das einstimmige Kyrie*
OHS	*Officium hebdomadae sanctae*
OTT	Ott, *Offertoriale*
PM	*Processionale monasticum*
SCH	Schildbach, *Das einstimmige Agnus Dei*
ST	Stäblein, *Die Hymnen*
SYG	*Graduel de Saint-Yrieix* (Pal. mus. XIII)
THAN	Thannabaur, *Das einstimmige Sanctus*
VP	*Variae preces*
WA	*Antiphonaire . . . de Worcester* (Pal. mus. XII)

Abbreviations for Categories of Chant

al	Alleluia
alv	Alleluia verse
an	antiphon
anv	antiphon verse
co	Communion
cov	Communion verse
gr	Gradual
grv	Gradual verse
hy	hymn
int	Introit
intv	Introit verse
inv	invitatory
of	Offertory
ofv	Offertory verse
re	great responsory
rev	verse of great responsory
sr	short responsory
tr	Tract
trv	verse of Tract

Other Abbreviations

inc illeg	incipit (either textual or musical) illegible
ir	tonus irregularis
nm	no music
sup	supplement
tp	tonus peregrinus
var	variant

A N I N D E X O F G R E G O R I A N C H A N T

THEMATIC INDEX

a	-7	-9	-7	-5	-4	-5	-7	-9	D	Et in terra	BOS #14		
a	-7	-9	-4	-2	0	2	0	-4	D	Agnus Dei	SCH #54		1
a	-7	-9	0	-2	3	2	5	3	D	O admirabile pretium	WA 215 *SYG 140	an	1
d	-7	-5	-2	0	-2	0	3	5	b	Postquam surrexit Dominus a coena	WA 213 *GS 97	an	4
d	-7	-5	-2	0	2	0	2	-2	d	Verbum supernum prodiens a patre	ST 408	hy	2
G	-7	-5	2	4	2	0	2	4	D	Ad manus autem illum	LA 342 WA 262 (inc illeg)	an	1
G	-7	-5	2	4	2	0	2	4	D	Impetum fecerunt unanimiter	LA 41	an	1
a	-7	-4	-5	-7	0	2	-2	0	a	Jesu decus angelicum	AR 302 AM 281	hy	1
a	-7	-4	-5	-7	0	2	-2	0	a	Jesu dulcis memoria	AR 300 LU 452 AM 278	hy	1
c	-7	-3	0	2	0	2	4	5	F	Ordo sanctorum militum	ST 128	hy	5
a	-7	0	-2	-4	-5	-2	0	1	D	O nata lux de lumine	ST 161	hy	1
d	-7	0	-2	-3	-2	0	-2	0	G	Et si ingenua es	WA 273	an	7
G	-7	0	-2	0	-7	-5	-2	0	G	Laudem dicite Deo nostro	WA 396	re	8
a	-7	0	2	-2	0	2	3	2	D	Quem terra pontus aethera	ST 131	hy	1
G	-7	0	2	0	2	4	5	4	G	Signum crucis mirabile	ST 389	hy	8
D	-5	-7	-5	-3	-2	0	-2	0	D	Collegerunt pontifices	GR 166 *GB 105^{v} *GS 84	re	2
e	-5	-4	-2	-9	-12	-11	-7	-9	E	Et in terra	BOS #46		
e	-5	-4	-2	-9	-7	-9	-4	-5	E	Et in terra	BOS #44		
F	-5	-3	-5	-3	0	2	0	2	F	Domine in auxilium meum respice	GR 364 OTT 106 LU 1046 SYG 91 GB 80^{v} GS 53 160	of	6
d	-5	-3	-2	0	-2	0	2	0	G	Omnes de Saba venient ... laudem	LR 76 *LA 70 *WA 53	re	7
D	-5	-3	-2	0	2	0	-2	0	D	Aeterne rerum conditor	ST 2	hy	2
D	-5	-3	-2	0	2	0	2	-2	[D]	Agnus Dei	SCH #240		2
G	-5	-3	-2	0	2	0	2	0	E	Deus dum egredereris	GR 300 LU 892 SYG 186 GB 191^{v} GS 139	int	3
G	-5	-3	-2	0	2	0	2	0	E	Deus misereatur nostri ... nobis	GR [126] LU 1292	int	3
D	-5	-3	-2	0	2	0	2	0	D	Me etenim de die	AR 361 AM 335 *LA 126 *WA 85	an	2
G	-5	-3	-2	0	2	0	2	5	G	Admonitus in somnis Joseph	LR 308	an	8
G	-5	-3	-2	0	2	0	2	5	G	Valde honorandus est	AR 279 LU 421 *AM 255	an	8
d	-5	-3	-2	0	2	0	3	0	G	Accedite ad eum et illuminamini Immittet angelus	OTT 102 GB 71 *SYG 79	ofv	
c	-5	-3	-1	0	-1	-3	-1	-3	E	Peccavi super numerum	LA 270 *WA 166	re	3
F	-5	-3	-1	0	-1	0	-3	0	E	Benedicite Dominum omnes angeli	GR 608 LU 1654 *GB 168 *GS 197	gr	3

F	-5	-3	-1	0	-1	0	-3	0	E	Exaltabo te Domine quoniam suscepisti ... Domine Deus	GR 160 *SYG 113 *GB 101 GS 75	gr	3
F	-5	-3	-1	0	-1	0	-3	0	E	Exsurge Domine non praevaleat	GR 123 LU 553 *SYG 93 *GB 82 GS 54	gr	3
F	-5	-3	-1	0	-1	0	2	-1		Propterea benedixit te Deus Constitues eos	OTT 131 *GB 206v *SYG 203	ofv	
c	-5	-3	-1	0	-1	0	2	0	E	Rogavi Dominum meum	LA 321 *WA 246	re	3
F	-5	-3	-1	0	-1	2	-1	2	E	Eripe me Domine de inimicis	GR 152 LU 570 *SYG 109 *GB 97v GS 71	gr	3
F	-5	-3	-1	0	-1	2	-1	2	E	Salvos fac nos Domine	GR 51 LU 447	gr	3
F	-5	-3	-1	0	-1	2	0	-1		Benedicamus patrem et filium cum ... laudemus Benedictus sit	OTT 81 *GB 215 *SYG 262	ofv	
c	-5	-3	0	-3	-5	0	-5	0		Ego vero orationem meam Improperium exspectavit	OTT 49 *GB 110v *SYG 123	ofv	
c	-5	-3	0	-1	0	2	0	-1	E	Corona aurea super caput	LR 158 *LA 524 *WA 417	re	3
F	-5	-3	0	-1	0	2	4	0	F	Cor contritum et humiliatum	AR 170	an	6
F	-5	-3	0	-1	0	2	4	2	E	Ab Oriente adducam semen	GR (4)	gr	3
F	-5	-3	0	-1	0	2	4	2	E	Confiteantur Domino misericordiae	GR 631 LU 1694	gr	3
F	-5	-3	0	2	0	-5	-3	0	F	Splendor paternae gloriae	ST 253 270	hy	6
F	-5	-3	0	2	0	2	0	-5		Laetificabis eum in gaudio Desiderium animae	OTT 153 SYG 215 *GB 53v	ofv	
c	-5	-3	0	2	0	2	0	4	a	Christe cunctorum dominator alme	ST 14	hy	1
F	-5	-3	0	2	0	2	4	2	F	Gaude visceribus mater in intimis	ST 434	hy	6
F	-5	-3	0	2	0	2	4	2	F	Nullis te genitor blanditiis trahit	AR 682	hy	6
F	-5	-3	0	2	0	2	4	2	F	Regali solio fortis Iberiae	AR 680	hy	6
F	-5	-3	0	2	0	2	4	7	F	Puer Jesus proficiebat	AR 289 LU 437 AM 267	an	6
F	-5	-3	0	2	0	2	5	7	G	Collegerunt pontifices	WA 210 *SYG 117	an	2
F	-5	-3	4	2	0	2	4	0	D	Misso Herodes spiculatore	AR 828 LU 1618 *AM 1025 *WA 363 *LA 454	an	1
F	-5	-3	4	5	4	2	-1	0	D	Traditor autem dedit eis	AR 434 OHS 406 LU 658 *AM 420 *WA 120 *LA 194	an	1
F	-5	-3	4	5	4	2	0	2	D	Ave Maria gratia plena ... benedicta	AR 252 668 872 [139] LU 1416 1679 *AM 228 862 1073 *WA 301 *LA 6 376	an	1
F	-5	-3	4	5	4	2	0	2	D	Ave Maria gratia plena ... sancta Maria	AR 123* LU 1861	an	1
F	-5	-3	4	5	4	2	0	2	D	Canite tuba in Sion quia prope	AR 250 LU 356 *AM 226 *WA 24 *LA 21	an	1
F	-5	-3	4	5	4	2	0	2	D	Canite tuba in Sion vocate	LR 396 *LA 18 WA 22	re	1

F	-5	-3	4	5	4	2	0	2	D	Exclamaverunt ad te Domine	GR 488 LU 1465A *SYG 172 *GB 163v GS 185	int	1
F	-5	-3	4	5	4	2	4	0	D	Tecum principium in die virtutis	AR 270 LU 412 *AM 245 *WA 32 *LA 38	an	1
F	-5	-3	4	5	4	2	4	2	D	Appropinquabat autem dies	AR 419 LU 1100 *AM 397 *WA 110 *LA 174	an	1
F	-5	-3	4	5	4	2	4	2	D	Assumpsit Jesus Petrum	AR 805 LU 1588	an	1
F	-5	-3	4	5	4	2	4	2	D	Reddite ergo quae sunt Caesaris	AR 573 LU 1073 *AM 614 *LA 319	an	1
F	-5	-3	4	5	4	2	4	5	D	Iste est Joannes	AR 282 LU 420 *AM 257 *WA 42 *LA 56	an	1
F	-5	-3	4	5	4	2	4	5	D	Isti sunt sancti qui pro Dei	AR 744 *AM 929 *LA 513	an	1
F	-5	-3	4	5	4	2	4	5	D	Ostendit mihi Dominus fluvium	AR 849	an	1
F	-5	-3	4	5	4	2	4	5	D	Quaerite primum regnum Dei	AR 566 810 LU 1040 1591 *AM 605 1004 *LA 316 *WA 189	an	1
F	-5	-3	4	5	4	2	4	5	D	Sanctificavit Dominus tabernaculum ... quia haec	AR [106] LU 1242 *AM 696	an	1
F	-5	-3	4	5	4	7	4	2	D	Subiit ergo in montem	AR 400 LU 564 *AM 376 *LA 163	an	1
G	-5	-2	-3	-5	0	-2	-7	-5	G	Surgens Jesus imperavit	WA 71 *LA 107	an	8
G	-5	-2	-3	-5	0	7	5	4	G	Kyrie	MEL #89		
G	-5	-2	-3	-2	0	-2	0	-5	G	Agnus Dei	SCH #107		2
G	-5	-2	-3	-2	0	2	0	-2	G	Febres fugat tactu	WA 249	an	8
G	-5	-2	-3	-2	0	2	0	-2	G	Nonne vides quanta sit	WA 343	an	8
D	-5	-2	0	-2	0	-2	0	2	D	Ego sum resurrectio et vita	SYG 237	co	2
D	-5	-2	0	-2	0	-2	0	2	D	Gloria et honore coronasti ... Domine Deus	SYG 214	co	2
G	-5	-2	0	-2	0	2	-2	0	G	Propter nomen tuum	AR 170	an	8
D	-5	-2	0	-2	0	2	0	2	D	Qui in sancta ecclesia	WA 315	an	1
D	-5	-2	0	-2	0	2	0	3	D	Domine rex Deus	WA 231	an	2
D	-5	-2	0	-2	0	2	3	0	D	Infantiae primordia	WA 311	an	2
D	-5	-2	0	-2	0	2	3	0	D	Intravit Maria in domum Zachariae	AR 771 LU 1541 AM 954	an	2
D	-5	-2	0	-2	0	2	3	0	D	Kyrie	MEL #206		
D	-5	-2	0	-2	0	2	3	0	D	Omnes qui in Christo baptizati	GR 261 OHS 829 LU 807 SYG 162 GB 144v GS 124	co	2
D	-5	-2	0	-2	0	3	0	-2	D	Benedicamus Domino Ia	AR 59* LU 124		2
D	-5	-2	0	-2	0	3	2	0	D	Missus est angelus Gabriel ... ad virginem	AR 648 LU 1400 AM 837	an	2
D	-5	-2	0	-2	0	3	2	3		Semper mortificationem Christo igitur	GR 482	trv	

D	-5	-2	0	-2	0	3	2	3	D	Septies in die laudem	LA 154 WA 99	re	2
D	-5	-2	0	-2	2	0	2	3	D	Sanctus XI	GR 40* LU 47		2
D	-5	-2	0	-2	3	5	2	0	D	Cum redirent remansit puer	AR 652 LU 1406 AM 841	an	2
G	-5	-2	0	2	-2	0	-2	0	G	Dum fabricam sacri Cluniacensis	PM 211	an	8
D	-5	-2	0	2	-2	0	2	3	D	Quando orabas cum lacrimis	GR 556 LU 1563	of	2
G	-5	-2	0	2	0	-5	-2	0	E	Accipite jucunditatem gloriae	GR 298 LU 890 *SYG 185 GB 191^{v} GS 138	int	4
G	-5	-2	0	2	0	-5	-2	0	G	Nec observavimus neque fecimus	GB 154^{v}	an	8
G	-5	-2	0	2	0	-3	-2	-3	G	Cum turba multa esset	AR 557 LU 1103 AM 595 *LA 312	an	8
G	-5	-2	0	2	0	-3	-2	0	G	In medio ecclesiae	WA 52 *LA 56	an	8
G	-5	-2	0	2	0	-3	-2	0	G	Oravit sanctus Hyppolitus	WA 352	an	8
G	-5	-2	0	2	0	-2	-3	-2	G	Alma Dei genitrix succurre	GS s	co	8
D	-5	-2	0	2	0	-2	0	-2	D	Clementissime Christi confessor	LA 537	an	2
G	-5	-2	0	2	0	-2	0	2	G	Alleluia	PM 238	an	8
D	-5	-2	0	2	0	-2	0	2	D	Dominus Jesus ante sex dies	WA 112 GS 83	re	2
G	-5	-2	0	2	0	-2	0	2	G	Homo quidam descendebat	AR 564 LU 1032 AM 603 *WA 189 LA 315	an	8
D	-5	-2	0	2	0	-2	0	2	D	Non relinquam vos orphanos	LR 98 LA 249	re	2
G	-5	-2	0	2	0	-2	0	2	G	Orietur sicut sol	AR 257 AM 234 *WA 26 LA 30	an	8
D	-5	-2	0	2	0	-2	0	2	D	Sanctus	THAN #201		2
G	-5	-2	0	2	0	-2	0	2	G	Sanctus Mauritius legionem	WA 376	an	8
G	-5	-2	0	2	0	-2	0	2	G	Super solium David	AR 232 AM 206 WA 12 *LA 12 384	an	8
G	-5	-2	0	2	0	-2	0	2	G	Tricesimo ordinationis	WA 403	an	8
D	-5	-2	0	2	0	-2	0	3	D	Resplenduit facies ejus	AM 998	an	2
D	-5	-2	0	2	0	-2	0	3	D	Sanctus	THAN #200		2
D	-5	-2	0	2	0	-2	0	3	D	Sonet vox tua	WA 356	an	2
G	-5	-2	0	2	0	-2	0	5	G	A patre unigenite	ST 366	hy	8
G	-5	-2	0	2	0	-2	0	5	G	Almi beati martyris	ST 392	hy	8
G	-5	-2	0	2	0	-2	0	5	G	Christe patris altissimi	ST 373	hy	8
G	-5	-2	0	2	0	-2	0	5	G	Deus piorum gaudium	ST 400	hy	8
G	-5	-2	0	2	0	-2	0	5	G	Festum colentes annuum	ST 402	hy	8
G	-5	-2	0	2	0	-2	0	5	G	Hymnum cantemus Domino	ST 369	hy	8
G	-5	-2	0	2	0	-2	0	5	G	Illuminator omnium	ST 391	hy	8
G	-5	-2	0	2	0	-2	0	5	G	Illuminavit hunc diem rerum	ST 400	hy	8
G	-5	-2	0	2	0	-2	0	5	G	Imperatoris filium	ST 392	hy	8

G	-5	-2	0	2	0	-2	0	5	G	Jam lucis orto sidere	AM 2 81	hy	8
G	-5	-2	0	2	0	-2	0	5	G	Jam lucis splendor rutilat	ST 367	hy	8
G	-5	-2	0	2	0	-2	0	5	G	Martine confessor Dei	ST 401	hy	8
G	-5	-2	0	2	0	-2	0	5	G	Nunc sancte nobis spiritus	ST 360 AM 84 94 109	hy	8
G	-5	-2	0	2	0	-2	0	5	G	Ortu Phoebi jam proximo	ST 402	hy	8
G	-5	-2	0	2	0	-2	0	5	G	Rector potens verax Deus	AM 88 99 114	hy	8
G	-5	-2	0	2	0	-2	0	5	G	Rerum Deus tenax vigor	AM 90 104 119	hy	8
G	-5	-2	0	2	0	-2	0	5	G	Te lucis ante terminum	ST 362	hy	8
G	-5	-2	0	2	0	-2	2	5	G	Ambulabant martyres Christi	WA 378	an	8
G	-5	-2	0	2	0	-2	2	5	G	Celebremus conversionem beati Pauli	LA 346	an	8
G	-5	-2	0	2	0	2	-2	0	G	Omnes sancti quanta passi	AR [41] LU 1153 AM 647	an	8
G	-5	-2	0	2	0	2	-2	2	G	Splendent Bethlehemitici campi	PM 36	an	8
G	-5	-2	0	2	0	2	0	-5	G	Refulsit sol in clypeos	AR 550 LU 994 AM 588	an	8
G	-5	-2	0	2	0	2	0	-3	G	Dum medium silentium ... perageret	AR 288 LU 433 AM 265 WA 48 LA 62	an	8
G	-5	-2	0	2	0	2	0	-2	G	Accinxit fortitudine	PM 238 LR 220 *LA 540 *WA 433	an	8
G	-5	-2	0	2	0	2	0	-2	G	Adducentur regi virgines	GB 45	tr	8
G	-5	-2	0	2	0	2	0	-2	G	Ave Maria gratia plena ... benedicta	GB 55^{v}	tr	8
G	-5	-2	0	2	0	2	0	-2	G	Cum audisset salutationem Mariae	AR 772 AM 955	an	8
G	-5	-2	0	2	0	2	0	-2	G	Dederunt in celebratione	WA 375	an	8
G	-5	-2	0	2	0	2	0	-2	G	Ecce Deus meus	AR 242 AM 217 WA 19 *LA 25	an	8
G	-5	-2	0	2	0	2	0	-2	G	Epistolam ad se	LR 281	an	8
G	-5	-2	0	2	0	2	0	-2	G	Hic caeli terraeque Petro	WA 278	an	8
G	-5	-2	0	2	0	2	0	-2	G	Intende voci orationis meae	AR 70	an	8
G	-5	-2	0	2	0	2	0	-2	G	Martyres sancti quanta passi	WA 423	an	8
G	-5	-2	0	2	0	2	0	-2	G	Omnis qui invocaverit nomen	AR 298 LU 451 AM 276	an	8
G	-5	-2	0	2	0	2	0	-2	G	Paraclitus autem spiritus	AR 514 LU 900 AM 531	an	8
G	-5	-2	0	2	0	2	0	-2	G	Per lignum servi facti sumus	OHS 584 LU 746	an	8
G	-5	-2	0	2	0	2	0	-2	G	Per lignum servi facti sumus	PM 53	an	8
G	-5	-2	0	2	0	2	0	-2	G	Per manus reverendi pontificis	PM 132	an	8
D	-5	-2	0	2	0	2	0	-2	D	Ponis nubem ascensum tuum	PM 84 LR 105 AM 1186 LA 249 WA 149	re	2
G	-5	-2	0	2	0	2	0	-2	G	Propter lignum servi	LA 215	an	8
G	-5	-2	0	2	0	2	0	-2	G	Sanctus Bricius satisfaciens	WA 404	an	8
G	-5	-2	0	2	0	2	0	-2	G	Scriptum est enim in lege	WA 269	an	8

G	-5	-2	0	2	0	2	0	-2	G	Spiritus sanctus in te descendet ... et virtus	AR 667 LU 1414 AM 861	an	8
G	-5	-2	0	2	0	2	0	-2	G	Spiritus sanctus in te descendet ... ne timeas	AR 216 [137] AM 189 WA 7 LA 6 376	an	8
G	-5	-2	0	2	0	2	0	-2	G	Ut vidit beatus Sebastianus	LA 323	an	8
G	-5	-2	0	2	0	2	0	2	G	Conventione autem facta	WA 75	an	8
G	-5	-2	0	2	0	2	0	2	G	Crux fidelis inter omnes ... sustinet	WA 370 SYG 143	an	8
G	-5	-2	0	2	0	2	0	2	G	Cum ortus fuerit sol	AR 262 LU 367 AM 239 WA 27	an	8
G	-5	-2	0	2	0	2	0	2	G	Dum sacrum mysterium cerneret	AR 855 LU 1652 AM 1057 WA 379 LA 464	an	8
G	-5	-2	0	2	0	2	0	2	G	Jesus junxit se discipulis	AR 448 OHS 771 AM 460 *LA 217	an	8
G	-5	-2	0	2	0	2	0	2	G	Martinus Abrahae sinu	AR 918 LU 1749 AM 1116 WA 398 *LA 487	an	8
G	-5	-2	0	2	0	2	0	2	G	Paulus et Joannes dixerunt ad Terentianum	AR 743 LU 1509 WA 324	an	8
G	-5	-2	0	2	0	2	0	2	G	Redemisti nos Domine Deus	AR 899 LU 1729 *AM 1103 WA 397	an	8
G	-5	-2	0	2	0	2	0	2	G	Sacram hujus diei	WA 256	an	8
G	-5	-2	0	2	0	2	0	5	D	Immutemur habitu in cinere	GR 85 LU 523 *GS 30	an	1
D	-5	-2	0	2	0	2	3	0	D	Considera oves tuas	WA 279	an	2
D	-5	-2	0	2	0	2	3	2	G	Cum vidisset Jesus matrem	AR 677 LU 1425 *AM 868	an	8
D	-5	-2	0	2	0	2	3	2	F	Recordare Domine quid acciderit	GB 160	an	6
D	-5	-2	0	2	0	2	3	2	D	Vos vocatis me magister	GS 97	an	2
G	-5	-2	0	2	0	2	4	0	G	Nativitas gloriosae virginis	AR 834 LU 1625 AM 1032 *WA 368 *LA 460	an	8
G	-5	-2	0	2	0	2	5	4	G	Spiritus sanctus docebit vos	GR 298 LU 889 GB 191 *GS 138	co	8
D	-5	-2	0	2	0	3	0	-2	D	Hodie virgo Maria elevatur	WA 358	an	2
D	-5	-2	0	2	0	3	2	0	D	Dum steteritis ante reges	LA 505	an	2
D	-5	-2	0	2	0	3	2	3	D	In columbae specie spiritus	PM 43 LR 71 *LA 68 *WA 58	re	2
D	-5	-2	0	2	0	3	5	7		Quia defecerunt sicut fumus Domine exaudi	GR 191 OHS 324 LU 619 GS 92 GB 114 SYG 127	trv	
G	-5	-2	0	2	0	5	2	0	G	Ad te levavi animam ... Deus ... neque	GR 1 LU 318 SYG 1 GS A	int	8
D	-5	-2	0	2	3	0	-2	0	D	Cotidie apud vos eram	WA 62 117 *LA 188	an	2
D	-5	-2	0	2	3	2	0	2	D	Laudate Dominum quia benignus	GR 140 [138] OTT 40 LU 562 SYG 102 *GB 90 *GS 64	of	2
a	-5	-2	0	2	3	2	0	2		Qui timetis Dominum benedicite Laudate Dominum	OTT 40 *GB 90 SYG 102	ofv	
G	-5	-2	0	2	5	4	2	0	G	Philippe qui videt me	WA 307	an	8

G	-5	-2	0	2	5	4	2	4	G	Benedico te pater Domini ... quia per apostolum	AR 625 LU 1371 AM 808 *WA 276 *LA 363	an	8
G	-5	-2	0	2	5	4	2	4	G	Benedico te pater Domini ... quia per filium	AR 592 604 925 LU 1324 1341 1757 AM 770 786 1141 *WA 255 408 *LA 322 338 494	an	8
D	-5	-2	0	3	0	-2	0	-2		Non secundum peccata nostra Misericors	GR [113] LU 972	trv	
D	-5	-2	0	3	0	-2	0	3	D	Haec virgo sancta	WA 435	an	2
D	-5	-2	0	3	2	0	-2	0	D	O beata trinitas te laudamus	PM 91	re	1
D	-5	-2	0	3	2	0	2	0	D	Ecclesiae sanctae frequentans	WA 242	an	2
D	-5	-2	0	3	2	0	2	0	D	Sanctissima Christi sponsa	AM 1128	an	2
D	-5	-2	0	3	2	3	5	3	D	In splendenti nube	PM 173	re	2
D	-5	-2	0	3	5	3	2	0	D	Loquebantur variis linguis	WA 156	re	2
D	-5	-2	0	3	7	5	3	2	D	Sanctus	THAN #199		1
G	-5	-2	2	-2	0	2	5	7	G	Athleta Christi Vincenti	WA 261	an	8
G	-5	-2	2	-2	0	5	2	5	G	Aeterne rerum conditor	ST 211	hy	8
D	-5	-2	2	0	-2	0	3	5	D	Dimitte Domine peccata	VP 263 *WA 229	an	2
D	-5	-2	2	0	-2	0	5	2	D	Aeterne rerum conditor	ST 26	hy	2
G	-5	-2	2	0	2	0	2	4	G	Exsurgens Maria abiit	AR 771 LU 1540 AM 954	an	8
G	-5	-2	2	0	2	5	4	5	G	Alleluia	PM 231	an	8
G	-5	-2	2	0	2	5	4	5	G	Iste sanctus fecit mirabilia	PM 229	an	8
a	-5	-2	2	0	3	0	-2	0	a	Inimicitias ponam inter te	GR 584 LU 1603	of	2
a	-5	-2	2	0	3	2	3	0	D	Miserere mei Deus et a delicto	AR 341 AM 312 *WA 74 *LA 113	an	1
D	-5	-2	2	0	3	2	3	2	D	In columbae specie Scholasticae	AM 1192 *LR 299	re	2
c	-5	-2	2	0	4	0	2	0	c	Circuibo et immolabo	GR 336 LU 1009 *SYG 243 GB 250^v *GS 147	co	6
G	-5	0	-3	0	5	4	5	2	G	Venite post me faciam vos piscatores	GR 395 LU 1306 *SYG 231 GB 246^v *GS h	co	8
G	-5	0	-2	-5	0	-2	0	-2	G	Quae sunt haec maleficia	WA 246	re	8
D	-5	0	-2	-3	-5	-2	0	2	D	Agnus Dei	SCH #246		2
G	-5	0	-2	0	-3	-2	0	-5	G	Miserere mihi Domine quoniam infirmus	GR 133 *SYG 96 *GB 85^v GS 58	gr	7
d	-5	0	-2	0	-2	-5	-4	-5	D	Kyrie	MEL #1		
D	-5	0	-2	0	-2	0	3	0	D	Immaculatas hostiarum preces	SYG 220	of	2
d	-5	0	-2	0	2	3	5	3	G	Alleluia: exivi a patre et veni	GR 272 LU 831	al	7
D	-5	0	-2	0	3	0	3	2	D	Sicut pastor portat ovem	GB 159^v	an	2
D	-5	0	-2	0	3	2	3	0	D	Dum fabricator mundi	WA 215 SYG 140 GS 103	an	2
D	-5	0	2	-2	-3	-5	-2	0	D	Sanctus	THAN #198		2

G	-5	0	2	0	-3	-2	0	2	G	Aurora surgit aurea	AM 966	hy	8
G	-5	0	2	0	-3	-2	0	2	G	Fit porta Christi pervia	ST 223	hy	8
G	-5	0	2	0	-3	-2	0	2	G	Jesu corona celsior	AR [78] AM 780	hy	8
a	-5	0	2	0	-2	0	-2	0	a	Nihil inquinatum in eam	GR 48**	gr	2
a	-5	0	2	0	-2	0	-2	0	a	Tecum principium in die virtutis	GR 28 LU 393 *SYG 14 GB 13^{v} GS 13	gr	2
G	-5	0	2	0	-2	0	2	5	G	Fit porta Christi pervia	ST 375	hy	8
G	-5	0	2	0	-2	0	2	5	G	Nunc sancte nobis spiritus	ST 173	hy	8
G	-5	0	2	0	-2	0	2	5	G	Vox clara ecce intonat	ST 171	hy	8
a	-5	0	2	0	-2	2	0	-2	[c]	Beatam Aredii animam	SYG 219	gr	
G	-5	0	2	0	2	0	2	5		Et qui sitit veniat Ego sum radix	GR 45**	trv	
G	-5	0	2	0	2	5	4	5		Mihi autem absit gloriari Qui gloriatur	GR 546	trv	
G	-5	0	2	0	2	5	4	5		Non privabit bonis eos Beatus vir	GR 450 LU 1394	trv	
G	-5	0	2	0	2	5	4	5		Quia respexit humilitatem Magnificat anima	GR 50**	trv	
G	-5	0	2	0	2	5	4	5		Quoniam confirmata est super nos Laudate Dominum	GR 110 237 LU 776^{II} OHS 683 *GS 46 115 173 *GB 74 *SYG 83	trv	
G	-5	0	2	4	2	0	2	4	G	Desiderium animae ejus	LA 525	re	8
G	-5	0	2	4	2	5	4	0		Inebriabuntur ab ubertate Filii hominum	GR 55**	trv	
G	-5	0	2	4	2	5	4	0		Quoniam praevenisti eum in benedictione Desiderium animae	GR [5] LU 1131 GS 208 *GB 51^{v} *SYG 52	trv	
G	-5	0	2	4	2	5	4	0		Secundum nomen tuum Deus Suscepimus Deus	GR 113**	trv	
G	-5	0	2	4	2	5	4	5		Quoniam apud te est fons Filii hominum	GR 55**	trv	
G	-5	0	2	4	2	5	7	5		Divites eguerunt et esurierunt Gustate et videte	GR 95**	trv	
G	-5	0	2	4	2	5	7	5		Non abscondi misericordiam tuam Annuntiavi	GR [2^{2}] LU 1122^{4}	trv	
G	-5	0	2	4	2	5	7	5		Prolongaverunt iniquitatem sibi Saepe expugnaverunt	GR 153 LU 571 *GS 72 *GB 97^{v} *SYG 110	trv	
G	-5	0	2	4	2	5	7	5		Quoniam tu Deus exaudisti Factus es spes	GR 424 LU 1353	trv	
G	-5	0	2	4	5	0	-2	0		Quia apud te propitiatio est De profundis clamavi ad te	GR 75 LU 499 *GS 25 GB 56^{v} *SYG 59	trv	
G	-5	0	2	4	5	2	0	2	G	Alleluia: in multitudine presbyterorum	GR 528 LU 1513	al	8
G	-5	0	2	4	5	2	0	4	G	Te lucis ante terminum	ST 6	hy	8
G	-5	0	2	4	5	2	4	5	G	Rogamus te Domine Deus	LA 557	re	8

G	-5	0	2	4	5	2	5	9		Quoniam magnus Dominus Annuntiate inter gentes	GR [128] LU 1295	trv	
G	-5	0	2	5	2	4	2	0		Quid cruciaris quid	WA 246	re	8
G	-5	0	2	5	2	5	7	5		Factus sum infirmis infirmus Ego autem cum mihi	GR 566	trv	
G	-5	0	2	5	2	5	7	5		Oleum effusum nomen tuum Domine Deus virtutum	GR 53	trv	
G	-5	0	2	5	2	5	7	5		Omne quod est in mundo Nolite diligere	GR 22**	trv	
G	-5	0	2	5	2	5	7	5		Trahe me post te curremus Inveni quem diligit	GR (11)	trv	
G	-5	0	2	5	4	2	0	-2		Quod perierat requiram Ego pascam	GR 66**	trv	
G	-5	0	2	5	4	2	5	2		Vindica Domine sanguinem ... super terram Effuderunt sanguinem	GR 42 LU 429 *GB 26^v *SYG 26	trv	
G	-5	0	2	5	4	5	0	-2		In viis justitiae ambulo Meum est consilium	GR 26**	trv	
G	-5	0	2	5	4	5	0	-2		Quoniam magnus es tu Te Deum	GR [84] LU 1273	trv	
G	-5	0	2	5	4	5	2	0		Accepit regnum decoris Induit eum	GR 13**	trv	
G	-5	0	2	5	4	5	2	5		Sacerdotes tui induantur Surge Domine	GR [119] 90**	trv	
G	-5	0	2	5	4	5	2	5		Si iniquitates observaveris De profundis	GR 75 LU 499 GS 25 *GB 56^v *SYG 59	trv	
G	-5	0	2	5	4	5	7	0		Ut ditem diligentes Meum est consilium	GR 26**	trv	
G	-5	0	2	5	7	4	5	2		Propter David servum tuum Surge Domine	GR [119] 90**	trv	
G	-5	0	2	5	7	5	0	2		Dilexisti justitiam et odisti Veni sponsa	GR [52] LU 1217	trv	
F	-5	0	4	2	0	7	0	-1	F	Kyrie	MEL #139		
F	-5	0	5	4	2	0	7	9	F	Kyrie	MEL #138		
a	-4	-2	-7	-9	-7	-4	-7	-4	D	Salus autem justorum a Domino	GR [28] LU 1169 SYG 193 GB 196 GS 211	int	1
b	-4	-2	-6	-7	-9	-4	-2	-6		Victo senatu Vox tonitrui	WA 41	rev	
a	-4	-2	-5	-7	-5	-2	0	[0]	D	Et in terra	BOS #16		
a	-4	-2	-4	-5	-7	-9	-7	-5	D	Vidi Dominum sedentem ... elevatum	PM 201 AM 1204 LR 383 LA 301 WA 183	re	1
a	-4	-2	-4	-5	-4	-2	-4	-2	F	Desiderium cordis ejus	LR 296	re	6
e	-4	-2	-4	-5	-4	-2	0	-2	c	Modo veniet dominator	LA 20 WA 19	re	6
e	-4	-2	-4	-5	-4	-2	0	-2	c	Vidi Dominum facie ad faciem	LA 141 *WA 93	re	6
a	-4	-2	-4	-2	0	-2	-4	0	G	Judica causam meam defende	AR 422 OHS 68 AM 400 WA 113 *LA 181	an	8

a	-4	-2	-4	-2	0	3	5	3	D	Ad te clamant omnes rei O praeclara stella	VP 187	rev	
E	-4	-2	-4	-2	1	3	1	3	D	Laudate nomen Domini	AR 108	an	2
a	-4	-2	-4	0	3	0	2	3	G	Alleluia	AR 119 LU 285 288	an	8
a	-4	-2	-4	0	3	0	3	5	G	Petite et dabitur vobis	LA 243	an	8
a	-4	-2	-4	0	3	2	-2	2	G	Adhaesit anima mea	AR 388	an	8
a	-4	-2	-4	0	3	2	0	3	G	Venite ascendamus ... et videte	AM 1049 *AR 845	an	8
a	-4	-2	0	-4	-5	-7	-5	-4	G	Beati qui lavant stolas	AR 764 LU 1529 *AM 949	an	8
a	-4	-2	0	-4	-5	-7	-4	-2	G	Qui habitat in adjutorio	LR 237 *WA 318 *LA 549	an	8
a	-4	-2	0	-4	-2	-4	-7	-5	G	Salvum me fac Domine	AR 105 OHS 229 LU 285	an	8
B	-4	-2	0	-4	-2	-4	-6	1	[G]	Agnus Dei	SCH #44		7
E	-4	-2	0	-4	-2	0	3	0	D	Laudate Deum caeli caelorum	AR 366 AM 342 *WA 88 *LA 132	an	2
a	-4	-2	0	-2	-4	-5	-7	[0]	D	Et in terra	BOS #49		
a	-4	-2	0	-2	-4	-5	-4	-2	G	Quodcumque ligaveris	AR 600 753 LU 1517 AM 825 937 991 WA 277 LA 420	an	8
a	-4	-2	0	-2	-4	-2	-4	-2	G	Tu Domine servabis ... in	AR 125 OHS 291 LU 289	an	8
a	-4	-2	0	-2	-4	-2	0	-4	G	Beata es virgo Maria quae omnium	AM 1081 *AR 882^2 *LU 1686	an	8
a	-4	-2	0	-2	-4	-2	0	-4	G	Scitote quia prope est	AR 260 LU 365 AM 237 *WA 26 LA 30	an	8
a	-4	-2	0	-2	-4	-2	0	-4	G	Servite Domino in timore et exsultate	OHS 57 (nm) AM 5	an	8
a	-4	-2	0	-2	-4	-2	0	3	G	Sic erunt novissimi primi	AM 318 WA 76 LA 111	an	8
a	-4	-2	0	-2	-4	0	-2	-4	G	Surrexit Dominus de sepulcro	WA 134 225	an	8
a	-4	-2	0	-2	-4	0	2	3	G	Justus ut palma florebit	LR 154 *WA 417	an	8
a	-4	-2	0	-2	-4	0	2	3	G	Post triduum invenerunt Jesum	AR 324 LU 474	an	8
a	-4	-2	0	-2	-4	0	3	0	G	Ab Oriente venerunt	AR 331 AM 297 *WA 56 LA 75	an	8
a	-4	-2	0	-2	-4	0	3	0	G	Christe cunctorum dominator alme	ST 45	hy	8
a	-4	-2	0	-2	-4	0	3	2	G	In veritate tua	AM 74 WA 70 *LA 104	an	8
a	-4	-2	0	-2	-4	0	3	5	G	Et audientes discipuli	AM 1002	an	8
a	-4	-2	0	-2	-4	0	3	5	G	Libera me de sanguinibus	AR 430 OHS 304 *AM 409 WA 117 LA 187	an	8
a	-4	-2	0	-2	-4	0	3	5	G	Occurrunt turbae cum floribus	GR 174 OHS 97 LU 584 *WA 114 209 *LA 183 *GB 107 *SYG 118	an	8
a	-4	-2	0	-2	-4	0	3	5	G	Occurrunt turbae cum floribus ... in excelsis	PM 58	an	8
a	-4	-2	0	-2	0	-4	-5	-7	D	Scio cui credidi	WA 330 LA 422	an	1
a	-4	-2	0	-2	0	-2	-4	-2	G	Casta Columba nidificans	AM 1135	an	8

a	-4	-2	0	-2	0	-2	-4	-2	G	Contritum est cor meum	AR 433 OHS 402 LU 654 AM 416 WA 120 LA 193	an	8
a	-4	-2	0	-2	0	-2	-4	-2	G	Delicta juventutis meae	AR [161] LU 1788 *WA 437 LA 555	an	8
a	-4	-2	0	-2	0	-2	-4	-2	G	Euntes in mundum docete	AR 470 AM 484	an	8
a	-4	-2	0	-2	0	-2	-4	-2	G	Sitivit anima mea ad Deum vivum	LA 556	an	8
a	-4	-2	0	-2	0	-2	-4	-2	G	Vide Domine afflictionem	AR 408 AM 388 WA 108 LA 171	an	8
a	-4	-2	0	-2	0	-2	-4	0	G	Completa oratione	AM 964	an	8
a	-4	-2	0	-2	0	-2	-4	0	G	Quae est ista speciosa	AR 871 LU 1679 *AM 1072	an	8
a	-4	-2	0	-2	0	-2	0	-2	G	Beati qui audiunt	WA 99	an	8
a	-4	-2	0	-2	0	-2	0	-2	G	Nequando rapiat ut leo	AR [157] LU 1784 WA 436 *LA 553	an	8
a	-4	-2	0	-2	0	-2	0	3	G	Tu es vas electionis	WA 264 330 *LA 423	an	8
a	-4	-2	0	-2	2	3	0	-2	G	Excelsus super omnes	WA 63	an	8
a	-4	-2	0	-2	3	0	2	-2	G	Beati qui persecutionem	LR 186 *WA 412	an	1
a	-4	-2	0	-2	3	2	0	-4	G	Joannes est nomen ejus	AR 732 LU 1496 AM 920 WA 323	an	8
a	-4	-2	0	-2	3	2	0	2	a	Egredimini et videte ... regem	GR 11**	int	2
a	-4	-2	0	-2	3	2	0	2	a	Sacerdotes Sion induam salutari	GR 88**	int	2
a	-4	-2	0	-2	3	2	0	3	D	Meditatio cordis mei	GR 148 SYG 107 GB 95 GS 69	int	1
a	-4	-2	0	-2	3	2	0	3	D	Venite filii audite me	GR 589 LU 1615	int	1
a	-4	-2	0	-2	3	5	3	5	c	Exsultate Deo adjutori	GR 368 *SYG 251 GB 257v GS 168	int	6
D	-4	-2	0	-2	3	5	3	5	F	Sacerdotes Dei benedicite ... sancti	GR [7] LU 1132 *SYG 55 GS 220 GB 52	int	6
D	-4	-2	0	-2	3	5	3	7	F	Dicit Dominus ego cogito	GR 386 LU 1074 *SYG 258 GB 264 GS e	int	6
D	-4	-2	0	-2	3	5	3	7	F	In sermonibus Domini opera	GR 622[1] LU 1681[1]	int	6
a	-4	-2	0	1	0	-4	0	3	F	Scande thronum prolis	WA 355	re	5
a	-4	-2	0	1	0	-2	0	-4	G	Beati quos elegisti	WA 412	an	8
b	-4	-2	0	1	0	-2	0	-2		Isti sunt qui venerunt Tradiderunt corpora ... ideo	LA 388	rev	
E	-4	-2	0	1	0	1	3	1	E	Agnum sponsum virginum	WA 430	inv	4
a	-4	-2	0	2	0	-2	0	-2	G	Laurentius bonum opus	AR 814 LU 1597 AM 1006 WA 350 *LA 440	an	8
a	-4	-2	0	2	3	0	-2	-4	G	Beatus quem elegisti	LR 154 *WA 417 *LA 524	an	8
a	-4	-2	0	2	3	0	-2	-4	G	Magister scimus quia verax es	AR 573 LU 1107 *AM 614 *WA 191 *LA 319	an	8
a	-4	-2	0	2	3	0	2	3	G	Alleluia	AM 118	an	8
a	-4	-2	0	2	3	0	2	3	G	Qui habitas in caelis	AR 119 OHS 287 LU 285 AM 116 *WA 66 LA 93	an	8

a	-4	-2	0	2	3	2	0	-2	G	Apertum est os Zachariae	AR 739 LU 1499 AM 926 *WA 323 LA 408	an	8
a	-4	-2	0	2	3	2	0	-2	G	Attendite a falsis prophetis	AR 558 LU 1104 AM 596	an	8
a	-4	-2	0	2	3	2	0	-2	G	Magister quid faciendo vitam	AM 602 *AR 563 *LU 1106 LA 315	an	8
a	-4	-2	0	3	-2	0	-2	3	G	Completi sunt dies Mariae	AR 260 LU 364 *WA 27 *LA 31	an	8
a	-4	-2	0	3	0	2	-2	0	G	Gaudete et exsultate	LR 144 *LA 509	an	8
a	-4	-2	0	3	2	0	-2	0	G	Tristitia implevit cor	AR 476 AM 490 *WA 143 304	an	8
a	-4	-2	0	3	2	0	2	0	G	Laetetur cor quaerentium	WA 70 *LA 103	an	8
a	-4	-2	0	3	2	3	0	-2	G	Magister quod est mandatum	AR 568 AM 608 *WA 190 LA 317	an	8
a	-4	-2	0	3	2	3	0	3	G	Conversus est furor	AR 76 AM 41 WA 64 *LA 89	an	8
a	-4	-2	0	3	2	3	0	3	G	Cum palma ad regna	AR [41] LU 1153 AM 648 WA 423 LA 519	an	8
a	-4	-2	0	3	5	3	2	0		Salve stella maris O decus	WA 356	rev	
b	-4	-2	1	0	-2	-4	0	-4		Justum deduxit ... et ostendit ... regnum	GB 271	alv	
E	-4	-2	1	0	-2	0	-2	-4	D	Ecce Maria genuit	AR 295 LU 444 AM 273	an	2
E	-4	-2	1	0	-2	0	-2	-4	D	Sitivit anima mea ad Deum vivum	AR [169] LU 1795 *WA 437	an	2
E	-4	-2	1	0	1	3	1	0	E	Aeterna caeli gloria	AR 168 AM 72	hy	4
E	-4	-2	1	0	1	3	1	0	E	Ales diei nuntius	AR 109 AM 51	hy	4
E	-4	-2	1	0	1	3	1	0	E	Aurora jam spargit polum	AR 190 AM 80	hy	4
E	-4	-2	1	0	1	3	1	0	E	Jesu corona virginum	ST 105	hy	4
E	-4	-2	1	0	1	3	1	0	E	Lux ecce surgit aurea	AR 148 AM 65	hy	4
E	-4	-2	1	0	1	3	1	0	E	Nox et tenebrae et nubila	AR 128 AM 57	hy	4
E	-4	-2	1	0	1	3	1	0	E	Quid vobis videtur	WA 190	an	4
E	-4	-2	1	0	1	3	1	0	E	Splendor paternae gloriae	ST 86 AR 73 AM 44	hy	4
E	-4	-2	1	3	-2	1	3	1		Annuntiabitur Domino Deus Deus meus	GR 180 OHS 109 LU 594 *GS 86 *GB 109 *SYG 122	trv	
b	-4	-2	1	3	1	-1	1	-1	a	Oculi mei semper ad Dominum	WA 60 *LA 80	an	4
E	-4	-2	1	3	1	0	-2	0	E	Martyr Dei qui unicum	ST 196	hy	4
b	-4	-2	1	3	1	3	5	3	a	Ascendit fumus aromatum	WA 379 *LA 465	an	4
b	-4	-2	1	3	1	3	5	3	a	Caro et sanguis non revelavit	WA 281	an	4
b	-4	-2	1	3	1	3	5	3	a	Custodiebant testimonia ... quae dedit	WA 412	an	4
b	-4	-2	1	3	1	3	5	3	a	Dominus regit me	WA 60 *LA 80	an	4
b	-4	-2	1	3	1	3	5	3	a	Veniet Dominus cum potestate	WA 20	an	4

E	-4	-2	1	3	1	3	5	8	D	Puer Jesus proficiebat	WA 58	an	1
b	-4	-2	1	3	5	3	1	3	G	Ipse praeibit ante illum	AR 732 LU 1496 *AM 920 *WA 321 *LA 403	an	7
E	-4	-2	5	6	5	3	8	5		Misericordiam meam non dispergam Veritas mea	OTT 148 GB 41^v *SYG 38	ofv	
E	-4	-2	5	7	5	3	1	3	D	Beatus Maurus a teneris	AM 779	an	1
E	-4	-2	5	7	5	3	1	3	D	Sanctus Vincentius a pueritia	WA 256	an	1
E	-4	-2	5	7	5	3	5	3		Confitebuntur caeli mirabilia ... et	SYG 172	alv	
E	-4	-2	5	7	5	3	5	7	D	Exiit sermo inter fratres	AM 259	an	1
a	-4	0	-4	0	-2	-4	-5	-7		Spiritus paraclitus docebit	GB 192	alv	
a	-4	0	-4	0	-2	-4	-2	-4		Ecce concipiet et pariet	GR 3**	alv	
a	-4	0	-2	-5	-7	-4	-7	0		Magnus sanctus Paulus	GB 208	alv	
a	-4	0	-2	-5	-4	-7	-9	-7		Isti sunt duae olivae	SYG 199 *GS n	alv	
a	-4	0	-2	-5	-4	7	-9	-7		Vir Domini Benedictus	SYG 207	alv	
a	-4	0	-2	-5	-4	-7	-9	-7		Virga tua et baculus tuus Si ambulem	GR 137 GC 61 GB 88^v SYG 99	grv	
a	-4	0	-2	-5	-4	-7	-5	-7		Perdam sapientiam sapientium Sapientia hujus mundi	GR 475	grv	
a	-4	0	-2	-5	-4	-7	-4	-7		Justus germinabit sicut lilium	GR [40] (42) LU 1192 *SYG 207 *GB 270^v GS 222	alv	
a	-4	0	-2	-5	-4	-7	-4	-5		Ego veritatem dico vobis	SYG 167	alv	
a	-4	0	-2	-5	-4	-5	-7	-9		Ipse est directus divinitus	GR 566 LU 1581	alv	
a	-4	0	-2	-5	-3	-7	-4	-5		Ego rogabo patrem	SYG 185	alv	
a	-4	0	-2	-4	-5	-7	-2	-4	D	Kyrie	MEL #25		
a	-4	0	-2	0	-2	-4	-5	-7	E	Benedicamus Domino	PM 83		
a	-4	0	-2	0	-2	-4	-5	[0]	E	Benedicamus Domino	GR 55* 59* AR 62*		
a	-4	0	-2	0	-2	0	3	0	G	Deus enim firmavit	GR 32 LU 406 OTT 16 *GB 16 *GS F H *SYG 16	of	8
b	-4	0	1	0	-2	-4	-6	-4	E	Sanctus	THAN #38		3
b	-4	0	1	3	5	3	1	0	G	Sanctus	THAN #37		8
a	-4	0	3	0	2	3	5	3	F	In Domino justificabitur	AR 167 *AM 70 71	an	5
a	-4	0	3	0	3	2	3	5	F	Adjutor meus tibi psallam	LA 94 *WA 66	re	5
a	-4	0	3	0	3	5	3	2	F	Qui operatus est Petro	LA 424 *WA 330	re	5
a	-4	0	3	0	3	5	3	5	F	Regem virginum Dominum	LR 211	inv	5
a	-4	0	3	1	0	1	3	5	F	Sanguis sanctorum martyrum	LR 182 WA 421 LA 516	an	5
a	-4	0	3	1	0	1	3	5	F	Vestri capilli capitis	AR 577^{14} [44] LU 2623 1161 AM 650 738 *WA 423	an	5
a	-4	0	3	2	0	-2	-4	-2	F	Ecce Maria genuit	WA 50 *LA 65	an	5

a	-4	0	3	2	0	-2	3	5	F	Audiens ergo Lucianus	WA 346	an	5
a	-4	0	3	2	0	-2	3	5	F	Audiens Joseph quod Archelaus	LR 308	an	5
a	-4	0	3	2	0	-2	3	5		Complacuit per eum reconciliare Vos qui aliquando	VP 186	rev	
a	-4	0	3	2	0	2	3	-2	F	Intret oratio mea ... Domine	AR 209 OHS 50 LU 316 *AM 59 60 *WA 68 *LA 98	an	5
a	-4	0	3	2	0	3	0	-2	F	De necessitatibus meis eripe	WA 70	an	5
a	-4	0	3	2	0	3	5	3	F	Benedictionis tuae Domine	WA 33	an	5
a	-4	0	3	2	0	3	5	3	F	Exsultet spiritus meus	AM 142 WA 66	an	5
a	-4	0	3	2	0	3	5	3	F	Montes et omnes colles	AR 232 LU 338 AM 205 *WA 16 *LA 16	an	5
a	-4	0	3	2	0	3	5	3	F	Propter insuperabilem	WA 38 *LA 49	an	5
a	-4	0	3	2	0	3	5	3	F	Quia respexit Deus	LA 96	an	5
a	-4	0	3	2	0	3	5	8	F	Paratum cor meum Deus	LA 94 *WA 66	re	5
a	-4	0	3	2	3	0	-2	0	F	Gaudebunt labia mea	LA 98 WA 68	re	5
a	-4	0	3	2	3	0	3	5	F	Cumque ad mensam sederent	LR 292	re	5
a	-4	0	3	2	3	2	0	3	G	Attende Domine ad me	OHS 63 (nm) LA 176 *WA 110	re	7
a	-4	0	3	2	3	2	0	3	F	Obsecro Domine mitte	LA 5 *WA 5	re	5
a	-4	0	3	2	3	2	0	3	F	Vidisti Domine et exspectasti	LA 358 *WA 275	re	5
a	-4	0	3	2	3	5	3	5	F	In servis suis miserebitur	AR 194	an	5
a	-4	0	3	2	3	5	3	7	F	Alleluia: faciem tuam Domine	AR 41 LU 247	an	5
a	-4	0	3	2	3	5	7	5	F	Jerusalem luge et exue	LA 202 *WA 125	re	5
a	-4	0	3	2	3	5	7	5	F	Jerusalem surge et exue	OHS 598 LU 757	re	5
a	-4	0	3	5	0	3	5	8	G	Elisabeth Zachariae magnum virum	PM 158 LR 348 LA 401 WA 321	re	7
E	-4	0	3	5	1	3	0	3	E	Laetamini caeli et exsultet terra	LR 341	an	4
b	-4	0	3	5	1	3	5	1	b	Conditor alme siderum	AM 182 ST 30	hy	4
E	-4	0	3	5	1	3	5	1	E	Creator alme siderum	AR 210 LU 324	hy	4
a	-4	0	3	5	3	0	-2	2	F	Insurrexerunt in me viri iniqui	GR [110]	of	5
a	-4	0	3	5	3	0	1	0	F	Adversum me exercebantur	GR 189 LU 614 OHS 279 SYG 126 GB 113^{v} GS 91	co	5
a	-4	0	3	5	3	0	3	5	G	Adoraverunt viventem	LA 58 *WA 46	re	7
a	-4	0	3	5	3	0	3	5	F	Angelus Domini locutus est	LA 208 WA 128	re	5
E	-4	0	3	5	3	1	3	1	E	Nunc sancte nobis spiritus	ST 137	hy	4
a	-4	0	3	5	3	2	3	0	F	Adjuvit eam Deus mane	LR 261	an	5
a	-4	0	3	5	3	2	3	0	F	Caligaverunt oculi mei	OHS 508 LU 712 *LA 203 *WA 123	re	5

a	-4	0	3	5	3	2	3	5	F	Media nocte clamor factus	LR 226	re	5
a	-4	0	3	5	3	2	3	5	F	Paschasius dixit cessabunt	WA 245	re	5
a	-4	0	3	5	3	5	3	0	F	In manu tua Domine	LA 80 *WA 76	inv	5
a	-4	0	3	5	3	5	3	2	F	Angelus Domini apparuit Joseph	AR 649 LU 1401	an	5
a	-4	0	3	5	3	5	3	2	F	Fecit nos Deo et patri suo	AR 894[9] LU 1708 AM 1095	an	5
a	-4	0	3	5	3	5	3	5		Exaltabo te Deus meus rex	GR 54	alv	
a	-4	0	3	5	3	5	3	5	F	Gloria patri genitoque	WA 160	re	5
a	-4	0	3	5	3	5	3	5		Inveniatur manus tua omnibus Desiderium animae	OTT 153 *GB 53^{v} *SYG 215	ofv	
a	-4	0	3	5	3	5	7	5	F	Cum omnibus se fratribus	LR 274	an	5
a	-4	0	3	5	3	5	7	5	F	Dominus Scholasticam	LR 298	an	5
a	-4	0	3	5	3	5	7	5	F	Solvite templum hoc	AR 401 LU 1094 AM 376 *WA 104 *LA 164	an	5
a	-4	0	3	5	3	5	8	7	F	Elisabeth pacis et patriae mater	AR 784 LU 1553	an	5
a	-4	0	3	5	3	5	8	7	F	Erigitur itaque infantium	WA 43	an	5
a	-4	0	3	5	3	7	8	10		Astantes cives clamore Stans in aede	WA 251	rev	
E	-4	0	3	5	7	5	3	5	a	En clara vox redarguit	AR 215	hy	1
a	-4	0	3	5	7	5	3	5	a	Nunc sancte nobis spiritus	AR 217 LU 318	hy	1
E	-4	0	3	5	7	5	3	5	a	Verbum supernum prodiens a patre	ST 70	hy	2
E	-4	0	3	5	7	5	3	5	a	Vox clara ecce intonat	ST 71	hy	2
c	-3	-7	-12	-7	-5	-3	-5	-7	F	Agnus Dei	SCH #31		5
c	-3	-7	-12	-7	-3	-5	-7	-3	F	Agnus Dei	SCH #41		5
c	-3	-7	-12	-7	-3	-5	-7	-3	F	Sanctus	THAN #35		6
c	-3	-7	-5	-7	-3	0	2	0	F	Agnus Dei XVII	SCH #34 GR 57* OHS 145 LU 61		5
c	-3	-7	-5	-7	-3	0	2	0	F	Sanctus	THAN #34		6
c	-3	-7	-5	-3	-5	-7	-3	-5	F	Sanctus IX	GR 34* LU 42 OHS 459 THAN #33		5
c	-3	-7	-5	-3	-2	-3	-5	-7	F	O Christi mater caelica	ST 320	hy	5
G	-3	-7	-5	-3	-2	2	4	5	[F]	Agnus Dei	SCH #110		5
c	-3	-7	-5	-1	-3	-5	-7	-5	F	Agnus Dei	SCH #30		5
c	-3	-7	-3	0	[0	0	0	0]	F	Et in terra	BOS #8		
c	-3	-7	-3	0	2	0	2	4	F	Servus Dei Benedictus	WA 299	re	6
c	-3	-7	-2	-3	-5	-7	-3	-2	F	Credo III	GR 64* LU 68		5
g	-3	-7	-2	-3	-5	-3	-5	-8	b	Sanctus	THAN #1		5
c	-3	-5	-8	-7	-5	-3	-1	-3	G	Gloria X	GR 36* BOS #9 LU 43		8
c	-3	-5	-7	-5	-3	-5	-7	-5	F	Et in terra	BOS #38 GR 29* LU 37		

c	-3	-5	-7	-5	-3	-5	-7	-5	F	Sanctus	THAN #31		5
c	-3	-5	-7	-5	-3	-5	-7	-3	F	Sanctus	THAN #30		5
c	-3	-5	-7	-5	-3	-5	-7	-2	F	Sanctus	THAN #29		5
c	-3	-5	-7	-5	-3	-5	-7	0	F	Gloria VIII	GR 29* LU 37		5
G	-3	-5	-7	-5	-3	-2	-3	-5	G	Sanctus	THAN #94		8
G	-3	-5	-7	-3	-5	-3	-2	-5	C	Sanctus	THAN #93		6
c	-3	-5	-7	-3	-2	0	2	4	F	Kyrie	MEL #5		
c	-3	-5	-7	-3	0	2	0	-3	F	Sanctus XVII	GR 56* LU 61 OHS 145 THAN #32		5
c	-3	-5	-7	-3	0	2	0	-1	F	Gloria	BOS #8		III
c	-3	-5	-7	-3	0	2	0	2	c	Sanctus	THAN #28		8
c	-3	-5	-7	-2	-3	-5	-7	-3	F	Sanctus	THAN #27		5
G	-3	-5	-7	-2	-3	-2	0	-5	C	Agnus Dei	SCH #106		4
c	-3	-5	-7	0	2	0	5	4	[F]	Agnus Dei	SCH #33		5
c	-3	-5	-7	0	5	4	2	0	F	Kyrie	MEL #11		
c	-3	-5	-3	-7	-5	0	2	0	c	Ecce Dominus veniet et omnes ... et erit	GR 12 *SYG 9 GB 8 *GS 7	co	6
c	-3	-5	-3	-5	-7	-8	-10	-8	E	Martyr egregie Deo dilecte	ST 388	hy	3
c	-3	-5	-3	-5	-7	-3	0	2	[F]	Agnus Dei	SCH #29		5
c	-3	-5	-3	-5	-7	-3	0	2	F	Agnus Dei	SCH #32		5
c	-3	-5	-3	-5	-7	-3	0	2	a	Sanctus	THAN #26		4
c	-3	-5	-3	-2	-3	-5	-7	-5	F	Benedicamus Domino II[b]	AR 60* LU 125		5
c	-3	-5	-3	-2	-3	-5	-7	-5	F	Kyrie	MEL #4		
c	-3	-5	-3	-2	-3	-5	-7	-5	F	O Christi mater caelica	ST 49	hy	5
c	-3	-5	-3	-1	0	-3	-7	-5	F	Gloria	BOS #7		III
c	-3	-5	-3	-1	0	-3	-5	-7	G	Gloria	BOS #6		IV
c	-3	-5	-3	-1	0	-3	-5	-3	E	Gloria XIV	GR 48* LU 54		3
F	-3	-5	-3	-1	2	4	2	0	E	Hanc ergo salvator	WA 359	an	4
F	-3	-5	-3	-1	2	4	2	4	E	Florem mundi adolescens	WA 248	an	4
F	-3	-5	-3	-1	2	4	7	6	E	Ave maris stella Dei mater alma	ST 175	hy	4
c	-3	-5	-3	0	-3	-5	-3	0		Kyrie ... pater de caelis	AR 212* GR 233 274		
F	-3	-5	-3	0	-3	-5	0	2	E	Aurea luce et decore roseo	ST 394	hy	4
F	-3	-5	-3	0	-3	-5	0	2	E	Bartholomaee	ST 402	hy	4
F	-3	-5	-3	0	-3	-5	0	2	E	Beate Simon	ST 403	hy	4
F	-3	-5	-3	0	-3	-5	0	2	E	Bina caelestis	ST 402	hy	4
F	-3	-5	-3	0	-3	-5	0	2	E	Jacobe juste	ST 402	hy	4

F	-3	-5	-3	0	-3	-5	0	2	E	Joannes virgo	ST 402	hy	4
F	-3	-5	-3	0	-3	-5	0	2	E	Luca fidelis	ST 403	hy	4
F	-3	-5	-3	0	-3	-5	0	2	E	Luca sancte	ST 403	hy	4
F	-3	-5	-3	0	-3	-5	0	2	E	Matthaee sancte	ST 402	hy	4
F	-3	-5	-3	0	-3	-5	0	2	E	Matthia juste	ST 403	hy	4
F	-3	-5	-3	0	-3	-5	0	2	E	Paule pie sanctorum mitissime	ST 402	hy	4
F	-3	-5	-3	0	-3	-5	0	2	E	Salve crux sancta salve mundi gloria	ST 389	hy	4
F	-3	-5	-3	0	-3	-5	0	2	E	Sancte Luca	ST 403	hy	4
F	-3	-5	-3	0	-3	-1	0	-3	E	Doctor egregie Paule	LR 433	hy	4
F	-3	-5	-3	0	-3	-1	2	7	E	Ave maris stella Dei mater alma	ST 375	hy	4
F	-3	-5	-3	0	-3	0	-3	0		Audi popule meus et loquar In die sollemnitatis	OTT 61 GB 139^{v} SYG 159	ofv	
c	-3	-5	-3	0	-1	-5	-3	0	E	Vivo ego dicit Dominus	AR 81 AM 5 *WA 89	an	3
F	-3	-5	-3	0	-1	-3	-5	-3	D	Sanctus XVI	GR 54* LU 59 THAN #131		2
F	-3	-5	-3	0	-1	-3	-1	-3	D	Averte Domine faciem	WA 82	an	2
F	-3	-5	-3	0	-1	-3	-1	-3	E	Vir angelice puntatis	WA 315	an	4
F	-3	-5	-3	0	-1	-3	-1	0	E	Martyris Christi colimus triumphum	ST 298	hy	4
F	-3	-5	-3	0	-1	0	-1	0	E	Saulus autem tremens	WA 262 (inc illeg) LA 339	an	4
F	-3	-5	-3	0	-1	0	2	0	E	Felix per omnes festum mundi cardines	ST 393	hy	4
F	-3	-5	-3	0	-1	0	2	0	E	Quodcumque vinclis	ST 394	hy	4
F	-3	-5	-3	0	-1	0	2	0	E	Sinite me inquit	WA 404	an	4
F	-3	-5	-3	0	[0	0	0	0]	F	Kyrie	MEL #136		
G	-3	-5	-3	0	2	0	2	5	E	Naufragantis carnis pudor	WA 249	re	3
F	-3	-5	-3	0	2	4	2	0	F	Rex saeculorum quem laudat	WA 301	an	6
F	-3	-5	-3	0	2	4	2	4	F	Bonum doctrinae gratia nomine	ST 311	hy	6
F	-3	-5	-3	0	2	5	4	2	F	Hanc ergo toto corde	WA 335	an	6
F	-3	-5	-3	0	4	2	4	0	F	Omnes gentes plaudite manibus	GR 336 LU 1009 SYG 178 *GB 177 *GS 133 148	int	6
F	-3	-5	-3	0	4	2	4	0	D	Stetit angelus juxta aram	GR 610 OTT 170 LU 1656 *GB 170^{v} GS 197	of	1
F	-3	-5	-3	0	4	2	4	0	D	Stetit pontifex inter mortuos	GR [140]	of	1
F	-3	-5	-3	0	4	2	4	0	D	Tu es Petrus	GR 411 OTT 187 LU 1333 SYG 53	of	1
F	-3	-5	-3	0	4	2	4	0	D	Viri Galilaei quid admiramini	OTT 172 *SYG 180 *GS 133 *GB 180^{v}	of	1
F	-3	-5	-3	0	4	2	4	2	F	Agnus Dei	SCH #154		6

F	-3	-5	-3	0	4	2	4	2	D	Erue Domine animas eorum	OTT 177 SYG 236	of	1
F	-3	-5	-3	4	5	4	2	4	D	Gloria et honor Deo	WA 160	an	1
c	-3	-5	-1	0	-1	-3	0	-1	a	Magnum salutis gaudium	ST 145	hy	2
c	-3	-5	-1	0	2	0	-1	-3		Adoremus crucis signaculum O crux gloriosa	VP 151	rev	
c	-3	-5	-1	0	2	0	-1	-3	G	Kyrie	MEL #10		
F	-3	-5	-1	2	4	2	0	2	E	Conditor alme siderum	ST 271	hy	4
c	-3	-5	0	-5	-3	-5	-7	0	c	Sanctus	THAN #25		8
F	-3	-5	0	-3	-5	0	2	4	F	Venite venite venite filii	GS 94	an	6
F	-3	-5	0	-3	0	2	0	2	D	Etenim sederunt principes	GR 36 LU 414 SYG 21 GB 21 GS 15	int	1
F	-3	-5	0	-1	-3	0	2	0	F	Lucis hujus festa colat plebs honesta	ST 129	hy	6
G	-3	-5	0	2	0	-5	-7	-5	[G]	Alleluia: Vos qui secuti estis me	GB 267^{v}	al	8
G	-3	-5	0	2	0	-5	-3	-5	G	Alleluia: Deus judex justus	GR 328 LU 982 SYG 239 *GB 248^{v} *GS 142	al	8
F	-3	-5	0	2	0	-3	-5	-1	F	Splendor paternae gloriae	ST 270	hy	6
F	-3	-5	0	2	0	-3	-5	0	D	Regina caeli laetare alleluia	PM 257 335	an	1
F	-3	-5	0	2	0	2	4	0	F	Cum respexisset Petrus crucem	PM 161	an	6
F	-3	-5	0	2	0	2	4	0	F	O quam bonus et suavis	AR 4 (sup 2)	an	6
F	-3	-5	0	2	0	2	4	0	F	O quam gloriosum ... gaudent omnes	AR 903 LU 1732 AM 1107 1123 *LA 479	an	6
F	-3	-5	0	2	0	2	4	0	F	O quam metuendus est locus	AR [113] LU 1249 AM 702 *WA 317 *LA 553	an	6
F	-3	-5	0	2	0	2	4	0	F	O quam speciosi pedes	AR 778 LU 1550	an	6
F	-3	-5	0	2	0	2	4	0	F	Quae mulier habens drachmas	AR 538[16] LU 985 AM 573 *LA 311	an	6
F	-3	-5	0	2	0	2	4	2	F	Ego sum Gabriel angelus	AR 662 LU 1408	an	6
F	-3	-5	0	2	0	2	4	2	F	O admirabile commercium	AR 294 LU 442 AM 271 *WA 50 LA 64	an	6
c	-3	-5	0	2	0	2	4	2	c	Pro eo quod non credidisti	LA 409	an	6
c	-3	-5	0	2	0	2	4	2	c	Sancte Michael archangele	LA 468	an	6
c	-3	-5	0	2	0	2	4	2	c	Sanctimonialis autem femina	LA 372	an	6
c	-3	-5	0	2	0	2	4	5	c	Igitur Abraham de nocte	WA 82	re	6
G	-3	-5	0	2	0	2	4	5	G	Sanctus	THAN #92		8
G	-3	-5	0	2	0	2	4	5		Vox turturis audita est	GR 442 LU 1379[1]	alv	
F	-3	-5	0	2	0	2	4	7	F	Gens et regnum quod non servierit	AR 894[7] LU 1706 AM 1093	an	6
G	-3	-5	0	2	0	4	5	7	G	Agnus Dei	SCH #105		8
c	-3	-5	0	2	4	-1	[0	0]	a	Sanctus	THAN #24		2

F	-3	-5	0	2	4	0	-1	-3	F	Et in terra	BOS #40		
G	-3	-5	0	2	4	2	0	2	G	Kyrie	MEL #88		
F	-3	-5	0	2	4	2	4	2	F	Pater fidei nostrae	AR 353 LU 510 AM 326	an	6
c	-3	-5	0	2	4	2	4	5	c	Quam jucunda et suavis	WA 252	an	6
F	-3	-5	0	2	4	2	4	6	F	Kyrie	MEL #137		
c	-3	-5	0	2	4	5	4	2	G	Kyrie	MEL #3		
F	-3	-5	0	4	2	-1	-3	0	D	Angeli archangeli ... Cherubim	GR [89] LU 1277	co	2
c	-3	-5	0	4	2	4	5	4	c	Gloriam martyrum recolamus	LA 392	an	6
G	-3	-2	-5	-3	0	2	-5	2	D	Credo IV	GR 67* LU 71		1
G	-3	-2	-5	-3	0	2	0	-2	E	Credo II	GR 62* LU 66		4
G	-3	-2	-5	-3	0	2	3	2	E	Credo I	GR 59* LU 64 OHS 139		4
G	-3	-2	-5	-3	0	2	3	2	E	Credo V	GR 69* LU 90		4
G	-3	-2	-5	-3	0	2	3	2	E	Credo VI	GR 72* LU 92		4
d	-3	-2	-5	-2	-5	-9	-10	-9	D	Agnus Dei	SCH #13		1
G	-3	-2	-5	-2	2	0	-2	0	G	A patre unigenite	ST 221	hy	8
G	-3	-2	-5	-2	2	0	-2	0	G	Veni sancte spiritus reple	AR 72* LU 1837 *PM 332 VP 158 *WA 157 LA 262	an	8
G	-3	-2	-5	0	2	0	-2	-3	G	Festivis resonent compita vocibus	AM 947	hy	8
G	-3	-2	-5	0	2	0	-2	-3	G	Festum nunc celebre magnaque gaudia	ST 231	hy	8
G	-3	-2	-5	0	2	0	-2	0	G	Festum nunc celebre magnaque gaudia	ST 292	hy	8
c	-3	-2	-3	-5	-7	-3	0	2	F	Agnus Dei	SCH #27		5
G	-3	-2	-3	-5	-7	0	2	0	C	Benedicamus Domino alleluia	AR 447		
G	-3	-2	-3	-5	-3	-5	-2	0	G	Omnes collaudant nomen	OHS 101 LU 588	an	8
G	-3	-2	-3	-5	-3	-5	0	2	E	Elegisti Domine Deus	WA 283	an	3
G	-3	-2	-3	-5	-3	-2	0	-2	E	Gabriel angelus locutus ... ecce	AR 662 LU 1408	an	4
d	-3	-2	-3	-5	-3	-2	0	2	c	Te lucis ante terminum	ST 330	hy	
c	-3	-2	-3	-5	-2	0	-3	-7	F	Ad honorem regis summi	ST 111	hy	5
G	-3	-2	-3	-5	-2	0	2	0	G	Beata Dei genitrix Maria virgo ... alleluia	AM 1138	an	8
G	-3	-2	-3	-5	0	2	0	-2	G	Festivis resonent compita vocibus	AR 760 LU 1537^{v}	hy	8
G	-3	-2	-3	-5	0	2	0	-2	G	Festum nunc celebre magnaque gaudia	ST 292 (var)	hy	8
G	-3	-2	-3	-5	0	2	0	2	G	Zelo Christi succensa	WA 256	an	8
G	-3	-2	-3	-5	0	2	4	2	G	Kyrie	MEL #91		
G	-3	-2	-3	-5	0	2	4	5	G	Sanctus	THAN #91		8

G	-3	-2	-3	-2	0	2	-2	-3	E	Nonne cognoscit Deus	WA 174	re	4
c	-3	-2	0	-3	-5	-7	-5	-3	F	Sanctus	THAN #23		5
G	-3	-2	0	-3	-5	0	2	4	G	Nunc sancte nobis spiritus	ST 155	hy	8
G	-3	-2	0	-3	-2	0	2	0	E	Gratias ago Deo	WA 349	an	4
G	-3	-2	0	-2	-3	-5	-2	0	E	Exequie Martini	WA 404	an	4
G	-3	-2	0	-2	-3	-5	0	-2	D	Ad Christi laudem virginis	ST 435	hy	2
G	-3	-2	0	-2	-3	-5	0	-2	D	Festi sacrati praesulis	ST 432	hy	2
G	-3	-2	0	-2	-3	-5	0	-2	D	Magno canentes annua	ST 428	hy	2
G	-3	-2	0	-2	-3	-5	0	-2	D	Stephano primo martyri	ST 411	hy	2
G	-3	-2	0	-2	-3	-5	0	2	G	Kyrie	MEL #87		
c	-3	-2	0	-2	-3	-5	0	2	c	Maria Magdalene ut cognovit	WA 336	re	6
c	-3	-2	0	-2	-3	-5	0	2	c	Nunc sancte nobis spiritus	ST 204	hy	8
c	-3	-2	0	-2	-3	-5	0	2	c	Sanctus	THAN #22		8
G	-3	-2	0	-2	-3	-5	0	4	E	Herodes enim tenuit	WA 363	an	3
G	-3	-2	0	-2	-3	-5	0	4	E	Quaerentes eum tenere	WA 95	an	3
D	-3	-2	0	-2	3	2	0	2	D	Sacerdotes ejus induam salutari	GB 212 *SYG 209 GS 224	int	2
d	-3	-2	0	2	0	-3	-2	0	G	Beatus Laurentius dixit ego	LA 438	re	7
d	-3	-2	0	2	0	-2	-5	-2	G	Dixi iniquis nolite loqui	OHS 391 LU 646 WA 119 LA 192	an	7
G	-3	-2	0	2	0	-2	-3	-5	D	De patre verbum prodiens	ST 369	hy	2
G	-3	-2	0	2	0	-2	-3	-5	D	Devota mente socii	ST 396	hy	2
d	-3	-2	0	2	0	-2	-3	-5	G	Sit nomen Domini ... in saecula	AR 47 OHS 159 LU 254 AM 127 LA 87	an	7
G	-3	-2	0	2	0	-2	-3	-5	D	Solemnis dies advenit	ST 369	hy	2
G	-3	-2	0	2	0	-2	-3	-5	D	Stephano primo martyri	ST 368	hy	2
d	-3	-2	0	2	0	-2	0	-2	G	Te laudamus Domine	AR 210* *VP 170		7
G	-3	-2	0	2	0	-2	0	2	G	Pulchra facie sed pulchrior	WA 433	re	8
G	-3	-2	0	2	0	-2	2	0	G	Ordines angelorum videntes	WA 57	an	8
G	-3	-2	0	2	0	2	0	-3	E	Qui timet Dominum in mandatis	AR 46 OHS 158 LU 254	an	4
c	-3	-2	0	2	0	2	4	5	c	Sanctus	THAN #21		8
G	-3	-2	0	2	0	2	5	2	G	Serve nequam omne debitum	WA 191	an	8
d	-3	-2	0	2	0	3	2	3	G	Sancti omnes intercedant	AR 53 [129]	an	7
G	-3	-2	0	2	0	5	7	5	E	Regali solio fortis Iberiae	ST 335	hy	3
G	-3	-2	0	2	4	2	0	-2	G	Alleluia: ecce quam bonum et quam jucundum	GR 568	al	8
c	-3	-1	-5	-3	-7	-5	-3	-1	F	Et in terra	BOS #34		
F	-3	-1	-5	-3	-5	0	-1	2	F	Sacris reliquiarum muneribus	LR 280	an	6

F	-3	-1	-5	-3	-1	-3	0	-1	E	Porta Sion clausi portam	PM 268	re	4
F	-3	-1	-5	-3	-1	0	2	4		Ave rex noster tu solus	GR [108]	alv	
F	-3	-1	-5	-3	0	-3	0	2	E	Jesu Christi Domini	WA 372	an	3
c	-3	-1	-5	-3	0	-1	0	-3	a	Exiit sermo inter fratres	GR 40 LU 423 *SYG 25 GS 17 GB 26	co	2
c	-3	-1	-5	-3	0	2	4	0	c	Serve nequam omne debitum	AR 572 LU 1070 AM 613 *LA 319	an	6
F	-3	-1	-5	-1	0	2	4	-1	D	Ave rex noster fili David	OHS 102 *WA 209 *SYG 118 *GS 85	an	1
F	-3	-1	-5	0	2	0	2	4	F	Vox tua o bone Jesu	WA 40	an	6
c	-3	-1	-3	-5	-7	-3	-1	-3	G	Alleluia: Hoc est praeceptum	SYG 194	al	7
c	-3	-1	-3	-5	-7	-3	0	2	F	Agnus Dei	SCH #28		5
c	-3	-1	-3	-5	-3	-5	-7	-3	G	O vos omnes ... sicut	AR 441 PM 189 OHS 623 LU 776^B AM 448 449 WA 127 LA 206	an	8
c	-3	-1	-3	-5	-3	-5	-7	-3	G	O vos omnes ... similis	OHS 610 LU 767 LA 204 WA 125	re	8
F	-3	-1	-3	-5	-3	-5	0	2	D	Quae est ista quae penetravit	VP 204	re	1
F	-3	-1	-3	-5	-3	-1	2	4	E	Conditor alme siderum	ST 364	hy	4
F	-3	-1	-3	-5	-3	-1	2	4	E	Grates tibi Jesu novas	ST 11	hy	4
F	-3	-1	-3	-5	-3	-1	2	4	E	Victor Nabor Felix pii	ST 10	hy	4
F	-3	-1	-3	-5	-3	0	-1	0	E	Lucia virgo judici	WA 245	re	4
F	-3	-1	-3	-5	-3	0	2	0	F	Sidera scansurus terrisque	WA 277	an	6
F	-3	-1	-3	-5	-3	0	2	0	F	Tunc in viscera ejus	WA 247	an	6
b^b	-3	-1	-3	-5	-1	-3	2	4	F	Fons hortorum puteus aquarum	PM 275 LR 250 *WA 354 *LA 456	an	5
c	-3	-1	-3	-5	0	2	4	0	G	Kyrie rex regum	MEL #9		
c	-3	-1	-3	-5	0	2	4	5	c	Agnus Dei	SCH #10		8
F	-3	-1	-3	-5	0	2	4	6	F	Kyrie	MEL #134		
F	-3	-1	-3	-1	-3	-5	-3	4	D	O quam gloriosum ... gaudent omnes	WA 396	re	1
F	-3	-1	-3	-1	0	2	4	2	E	Videntes stellam Magi	PM 40 LA 72 WA 55	re	4 3
F	-3	-1	-3	0	-1	0	2	0	E	Tui sunt caeli	GR 35 OTT 18 LU 410 *SYG 20 *GB 19^v *GS 15	of	4
F	-3	-1	-3	0	2	4	2	4	E	Intret in conspectu tuo	GR [21] LU 1162 *SYG 40 *GB 43^v GS 210	int	4
F	-3	-1	-3	2	4	9	7	6	E	Sancti tui Domine benedicent	GR [18] LU 1149 *SYG 169 *GB 152^v GS 211	int	3
F	-3	-1	0	-5	-3	0	2	0	F	Pacem relinquo vobis ... non	AR 511 AM 527 *LA 266	an	6
c	-3	-1	0	-3	-5	-3	-1	0	a	Pange lingua gloriosi proelium	ST 417	hy	2
c	-3	-1	0	-3	-5	-3	-1	0	a	Urbs beata Jerusalem	ST 423	hy	2

F	-3	-1	0	-3	-1	-3	-5	-3	E	Auro virginum	WA 239	an	4
F	-3	-1	0	-3	-1	0	-1	-3	G	Resurrexit leo fortis	ST 459	hy	8
c	-3	-1	0	-3	0	-3	0	2	F	Parce Domine parce ... quem redemisti	AR 208* *WA 228	an	5
F	-3	-1	0	-3	0	2	4	5	F	Pater manifestavi nomen	AR 490 LU 844 AM 507 LA 244	an	6
F	-3	-1	0	-1	-5	-3	-1	0	E	Rex noster adveniet	LA 10 *WA 12	re	4
F	-3	-1	0	-1	-5	-1	-3	0	D	Quantas sancti corpore poenas	ST 499	hy	1
c	-3	-1	0	-1	-5	0	-1	-3	E	Domine mi rex da mihi	AR 829 LU 1620 *AM 1026 *WA 363 LA 454	an	3
F	-3	-1	0	-1	-5	0	2	0	D	Beatus qui audit me	GR 3**	co	2
c	-3	-1	0	-1	-3	-5	-3	-1	c	Agnus Dei	SCH #39	ø	8
F	-3	-1	0	-1	-3	-5	-3	-1	E	Ibi olim positi fuimus	WA 346	an	4
F	-3	-1	0	-1	-3	-5	0	-1	F	Alleluia Dominus regnavit decorem	AR 2	an	6
F	-3	-1	0	-1	-3	-5	0	2	F	Alleluia	AM 29	an	6
F	-3	-1	0	-1	-3	-5	0	2	F	Ecce lignum crucis	GR 211 OHS 570 LU 735 *WA 215 GS 102	an	6
F	-3	-1	0	-1	-3	-1	2	4	E	Judaea et Jerusalem	AM 1183 *PM 25 *WA 27	re	4
F	-3	-1	0	-1	0	-3	-5	-3	E	Sicut ovis ad occisionem	OHS 596 LU 755 *LR 339 *LA 205 *WA 126	re	4
F	-3	-1	0	-1	0	-1	-3	-1	E	In ferventis olei dolium	AR 706 LU 1462 AM 904 *WA 38 *LA 49	an	4
F	-3	-1	0	-1	0	2	0	-1	E	Justi autem in perpetuum vivent	LR 180 *WA 421 *LA 516	an	4
c	-3	-1	0	-1	0	2	0	2	F	Memor esto congregationis ... possedisti	AR 156 LU 279[N]	an	5
F	-3	-1	0	-1	0	2	4	0	E	Sacerdotes Domini incensum	GR 319 [98] LU 949	of	4
F	-3	-1	0	-1	2	0	-3	-1	E	Aestimatus sum cum descendentibus	OHS 617 LU 772 *LA 205 *WA 126	re	4
F	-3	-1	0	-1	2	4	2	0	E	Contemplativae vitae magna	WA 335	an	4
F	-3	-1	[0	0	0	0	0	0]	E	Kyrie	MEL #135		
F	-3	-1	0	2	-1	-3	0	2	E	Lux perpetua lucebit sanctis	LA 387 391	an	4
F	-3	-1	0	2	-1	0	-3	0	E	Meditatio cordis mei	LR 334	an	4
F	-3	-1	0	2	-1	0	-1	-3	E	Ne derelinquas me ... virtus	AR 181 LU 302	an	4
c	-3	-1	0	2	-1	0	-1	-3	E	O quam mirifica luce coruscas	ST 129	hy	3
F	-3	-1	0	2	-1	0	-1	-3	E	Populus meus ait Dominus	AR 147 AM 63 64	an	4
F	-3	-1	0	2	-1	0	2	4	E	Deus majestatis intonuit	AR 71	an	4
F	-3	-1	0	2	-1	0	2	4	E	Diligante Domine virtus mea	LR 342 *LA 82 *WA 61	re	4
F	-3	-1	0	2	-1	0	2	4	E	Domine audivi auditum tuum	AM 68 69 WA 69 LA 102	an	4
F	-3	-1	0	2	-1	0	2	4	E	Et in servis suis	WA 70 LA 104	an	4

c	-3	-1	0	2	0	-3	-5	-1	b	Domine fac mecum misericordiam	GR 133 OTT 37 *SYG 96 *GB 85^{V} *GS 58	of	4
c	-3	-1	0	2	0	-3	-5	-1	E	Domine vivifica me	GR 92 OTT 31 *SYG 68 *GB 64 *GS 34	of	3
c	-3	-1	0	2	0	-3	-5	-1	E	Ego dilecto meo et dilectus meus	GR 399	of	3
c	-3	-1	0	2	0	-3	-5	-1	b	Quaerite Dominum et confirmamini	GR 110**	of	3
F	-3	-1	0	2	0	-3	0	-1	E	Sanctis qui in terra sunt	LR 177 LA 514 WA 421	an	4
F	-3	-1	0	2	0	-1	-3	-1	E	Fortitudo mea et laus	AR 152	an	4
F	-3	-1	0	2	0	-1	-3	0	E	In aeternum Dominus regnabit	WA 68 *LA 98	an	4
F	-3	-1	0	2	0	-1	0	-3	E	Anxiatus est in me spiritus meus	AR 438 OHS 510 LU 714 AM 438 439 *WA 124. *LA 200	an	4
F	-3	-1	0	2	0	-1	0	-3	E	Exiit qui seminat	WA 79	an	4
F	-3	-1	0	2	0	-1	0	2	E	Maria et flumina	AR 313 LU 464 AM 291 *WA 56 LA 74	an	4
F	-3	-1	0	2	0	-1	0	2	E	Sicut laetantium omnium habitatio	LR 335	an	4
F	-3	-1	0	2	0	1	2	0	E	Tria sunt munera quae	AR 332 *AM 298 LR 75 *WA 56 *LA 69	an	4
F	-3	-1	0	2	0	2	-1	0	E	Justum deduxit ... et dedit	LA 538	an	4
F	-3	-1	0	2	0	2	4	2	E	Aedomans corpus iuvenis	WA 292	an	4
F	-3	-1	0	2	0	2	4	2	E	Innocens manibus et mundo corde	AR 81 LU 279^{A}	an	4
c	-3	-1	0	2	0	4	5	7		Agnus Dei	SCH #38		7
F	-3	-1	0	2	4	0	-3	0	E	Sciens Jesus quia venit	GR 53**	int	4
F	-3	-1	0	2	4	2	0	-1	E	Donet eis Dominus requiem	GB 266^{V}	co	4
c	-3	-1	0	2	4	2	0	-1	F	Sanctus	THAN #20		5
F	-3	-1	0	2	4	2	0	2	E	Pange lingua gloriosi proelium	ST 52	hy	3
F	-3	-1	0	2	4	2	4	0	E	Mox ut vocem Domini	LA 498 WA 233	re	3
F	-3	-1	0	2	4	2	4	2	E	Notum fecit Dominus opus	LR 266	an	4
F	-3	-1	0	2	4	2	4	5	E	Alleluia: ascendit Deus in jubilatione	GR 286 LU 848 GS 135 SYG 180 *GB 177	al	4
F	-3	-1	0	2	4	2	4	5	E	Alleluia: benedic anima mea Dominum	GR 636	al	4
F	-3	-1	0	2	4	2	4	5	E	Alleluia: benedicite Domino omnes virtutes	GR 612 LU 1664	al	4
F	-3	-1	0	2	4	2	4	5	E	Alleluia: Deus virtuum convertere	GR [132]	al	4
F	-3	-1	0	2	4	2	4	5	E	Alleluia: emitte spiritum tuum	GR 293 LU 879 SYG 183 *GB 187^{V} GS M 137	al	4
F	-3	-1	0	2	4	2	4	5	E	Alleluia: excita Domine potentiam	GR 8 LU 336 GS 4 SYG 7 GB 5^{V}	al	4
F	-3	-1	0	2	4	2	4	5	E	Alleluia: fecisti viriliter et confortatum	GR 39**	al	4

F	-3	-1	0	2	4	2	4	5	E	Alleluia: justi confitebuntur nomini	GR 96**	al	4
F	-3	-1	0	2	4	2	4	5	E	Alleluia: lauda Jerusalem Dominum	GR [136] LU 1285 SYG 259	al	4
F	-3	-1	0	2	4	2	4	5	E	Alleluia: laudate Deum omnes angeli	GR 68 LU 486 GS 22 SYG 35 GB 168v	al	4
F	-3	-1	0	2	4	2	4	5	E	Alleluia: laudate Dominum in sanctis ejus	SYG 224	al	4
F	-3	-1	0	2	4	2	4	5	E	Alleluia: qui posuit fines tuos	GR [137] LU 1286 GS f	al	4
F	-3	-1	0	2	4	2	4	5	E	Congregate illi sanctos ejus	GR 63**	int	4
F	-3	-1	0	2	4	2	4	5	E	Post passionem suam	LR 96 LA 245 *WA 147	re	3
F	-3	-1	0	2	4	2	4	6	E	Alleluia: Confitebuntur caeli ... et veritatem	SYG 172	al	4
F	-3	-1	0	2	4	2	4	6	E	Expandi manus meas	LA 502 *WA 236	re	4
F	-3	-1	0	2	4	2	7	4	E	Protector noster aspice Deus	GR 357 LU 1036 *SYG 248 *GB 255 GS 157	int	4
F	-3	-1	0	2	5	4	2	4	E	Salus populi ego sum	GR 375 LU 1059 SYG 97 GB 86 *GS 59 163	int	4
F	-3	-1	0	2	6	2	4	6	E	Dilexit Andream Dominus	LA 503 *WA 236	re	4
F	-3	-1	2	0	-3	-1	0	-5	E	Est secretum Valeriane	AR 924 LU 1754 *AM 1139 *WA 408 *LA 493	an	4
F	-3	-1	2	4	2	0	-1	-3	E	Ecce jam in sublime	WA 258	an	4
F	-3	-1	2	4	2	4	5	4	E	Nuntium vobis fero de supernis	ST 83	hy	4
F	-3	-1	2	4	2	4	6	4	E	Iste confessor Domini colentes	AR [72]	hy	4
F	-3	-1	2	4	2	4	6	4	E	Solis o virgo radiis amicta	AR 3 (sup 3) LU 1600[2]	hy	4
c	-3	0	-5	-3	-7	-8	-10	-8	F	Sanctus	THAN #19		5
c	-3	0	-5	-3	-7	-8	-10	-5	F	Agnus Dei	SCH #37		5
c	-3	0	-5	-3	-5	-7	-5	-10	G	In sole posuit Deus	LR 260	an	8
G	-3	0	-5	-2	-3	-5	0	7	D	Agnus Dei	SCH #109		1
G	-3	0	-5	-2	-3	-5	0	7	D	Sanctus	THAN #90		1
c	-3	0	-5	0	-3	-1	-3	-5	G	Laus angelorum inclita	ST 401	hy	7
c	-3	0	-5	0	-3	-1	-3	-5	G	Lucifer diem inchoat	ST 374 388 404	hy	7
c	-3	0	-5	0	-3	-1	-3	-5	G	Summe largitor praemii	ST 383	hy	7
c	-3	0	-5	0	-3	0	2	-1	G	Surge aquilo et veni auster	LA 543	an	8
c	-3	0	-3	-7	-3	-5	-3	-2	F	Gaudens gaudebo in Domino	GR 77**	int	5
c	-3	0	-3	-7	-3	-2	-5	-7	F	Ecce Deus adjuvat me	GR 342 LU 1016 SYG 244 GB 252 *GS 150	int	5
F	-3	0	-3	-5	-3	-1	0	-1	E	Hoc in templo summe Deus	ST 107	hy	4
F	-3	0	-3	-5	-3	-1	0	-1	E	Urbs beata Jerusalem	ST 106	hy	4

F	-3	0	-3	-5	-3	0	-1	0	E	Ecce jam in sublime	WA 258	re	4
F	-3	0	-3	-5	0	2	4	2	D	Dixit angelus ad Mariam	WA 302	re	1
F	-3	0	-3	-5	0	2	4	2	D	Dixit autem Maria ad angelum ... ecce	WA 302	re	1
c	-3	0	-3	-5	0	4	2	0		Clamor meus in conspectu ejus Populum humilem	OTT 93 GB 95^{v} SYG 107	ofv	
c	-3	0	-3	-1	0	-5	-3	-5	F	Mihi absit gloriari	GR 65**	int	5
F	-3	0	-3	-1	0	-1	-5	0	F	Esto mihi in Deum protectorem	GR 80 LU 511 *SYG 62 *GB 59 *GS 27	int	6
c	-3	0	-3	-1	0	-1	-3	-5	G	Mense septimo festa	GR 372 LU 1055 *SYG 253 *GB 259 *GS 173	co	8
F	-3	0	-3	-1	0	2	0	-1	E	Omnes gentes quascumque fecisti	LR 73 *WA 54 LA 69 *GB 119	an	4
F	-3	0	-3	-1	0	2	0	-1	E	Omnis terra adoret te	LR 70 *WA 53 LA 67	an	4
F	-3	0	-3	-1	0	2	0	-1	E	Pater sancte serva eos	LA 249 252	an	4
F	-3	0	-3	-1	2	4	2	0	E	Hujus amore	WA 277	an	4
c	-3	0	-3	0	-5	-3	-5	-7	F	Hodie nobis caelorum rex	LR 56 LU 375 LA 32 WA 27	re	5
F	-3	0	-3	0	-3	0	2	0		Ipse autem vulneratus Vere languores	GR [108]	trv	
F	-3	0	-3	0	-3	2	0	-1		Ipsi vero consideraverunt Deus Deus meus	GR 180 OHS 109 LU 594 GS 86 GB 109 *SYG 122	trv	
F	-3	0	-3	0	-1	0	2	4	E	Rector potens verax Deus	ST 267	hy	4
F	-3	0	-3	0	2	0	-1	0	E	Lucianus presbyter dixit	WA 343	re	4
F	-3	0	-3	0	2	0	2	0	F	In splendoribus sanctorum	GR 30 LU 395 SYG 15 GB 15 GS E 14	co	6
F	-3	0	-3	0	2	0	2	4		Illuc enim ascenderunt Laetatus sum in his	SYG 101	trv	
F	-3	0	-3	0	2	0	2	4		Omnes qui videbant me Deus Deus meus	GR 180 OHS 109 LU 594 GS 86 *GB 109 *SYG 122	trv	
F	-3	0	-3	0	2	0	2	4		Scuto circumdabit te Qui habitat	GR 95 LU 533 GS 35 GB 65 *SYG 73	trv	
c	-3	0	-3	0	4	2	0	-1	F	Afferte Domino patriae gentium	GR [129] LU 1296	of	5
c	-3	0	-3	0	4	2	0	-1	F	Reges Tharsis et insulae	GR 59 OTT 21 LU 461 *SYG 31 GB 34 GS 19	of	5
c	-3	0	-3	0	4	2	0	2	F	Quis dabit ex Sion salutare	GR 129 *SYG 95 GB 84^{v} GS 57	co	5
G	-3	0	-2	-3	-5	-2	-5	-3	E	Pastis visceribus ciboque sumpto	ST 480	hy	4
G	-3	0	-2	-3	-2	-5	-3	-2	E	Consors paterni luminis	ST 363	hy	4
G	-3	0	-2	-3	-2	-5	-3	-2	E	Nox atra rerum contegit	ST 363	hy	4
G	-3	0	-2	-3	-2	-5	-3	-2	E	Primo dierum omnium	ST 358	hy	4
G	-3	0	-2	-3	-2	-5	-3	-2	E	Rerum creator optime	ST 363	hy	4
G	-3	0	-2	-3	-2	-5	-3	-2	E	Somno refectis artubus	ST 362	hy	4
G	-3	0	-2	-3	-2	-5	-3	-2	E	Tu trinitatis unitas	ST 363	hy	4

G	-3	0	-2	0	-3	-2	0	-5	G	Qui confidunt in Domino	GB 75	gr	8
d	-3	0	-2	0	2	-2	-3	-7	G	Una hora non potuistis	OHS 397 LU 650 LA 192 *WA 119	re	7
c	-3	0	-1	-5	-3	-5	-7	-5	G	Gloriosa dicta sunt	LR 265	an	8
F	-3	0	-1	-5	-3	-5	0	2	D	Domine si iratus fueris	SYG 64	an	1
F	-3	0	-1	-5	-3	-1	0	-5	D	Domine Deus meus in te speravi libera	GR 111 LU 544 SYG 84 *GB 74^{v} *GS 47	co	2
F	-3	0	-1	-5	-3	2	0	-1	E	Constitues eos principes	LA 510	re	4
c	-3	0	-1	-5	-1	-3	-5	-7	F	Ecce Dominus veniet et omnes ... erit	AR 214 [138] LU 324 AM 187 WA 6 LA 6	an	5
c	-3	0	-1	-3	-5	-3	-7	-3	G	Crastina erit vobis salus	AR 256 LU 363 *WA 26 LA 30	an	8
c	-3	0	-1	-3	-5	-3	-7	-3	G	Fulgebat in eo canities morum	PM 150	an	8
F	-3	0	-1	-3	-5	-3	-5	-3	D	Pater manifestavi nomen	WA 146	an	1
F	-3	0	-1	-3	-5	-3	-1	0	E	Kyrie	MEL #122		
F	-3	0	-1	-3	-5	-3	2	0	E	Ecce merces sanctorum	LR 181 *LA 516	an	4
F	-3	0	-1	-3	-5	0	2	4	F	Alleluia	WA 65	an	6
F	-3	0	-1	-3	-1	-3	-5	0	D	Non confundetur dum loquetur	LA 99	an	2
F	-3	0	-1	-3	-1	0	-3	-1	E	A solis ortu usque ad occasum	AR 299 LU 452 *AM 277	an	4
F	-3	0	-1	-3	-1	0	2	0	E	Convocatis Jesus duodecim ... dedit	AR 513 *AM 529 WA 157	an	4
c	-3	0	-1	0	-3	-5	-7	-5	F	Dilexisti justitiam et odisti	GB 226^{V}	co	6
F	-3	0	-1	0	-3	-5	-3	0	E	Ecce jam noctis tenuatur umbra lucis	ST 263	hy	4
F	-3	0	-1	0	-3	0	2	0	E	Dum oraret in obscuro	WA 288	re	4
c	-3	0	-1	0	-3	2	0	-3	F	Justus Dominus et justitias	GR 120 *SYG 89 *GB 78^{V} *GS 51	co	5
F	-3	0	-1	0	-1	0	-1	0	E	Obtulerunt pro eo Domino	WA 269	re	4
F	-3	0	-1	0	-1	0	-1	0	E	Sufficiebat nobis paupertas	LA 289 *WA 176	re	4
F	-3	0	-1	0	-1	0	-1	2	E	Diffusa est gratia in labiis	LR 216 254 *LA 542 *WA 431	re	4
F	-3	0	-1	0	-1	0	2	0	E	Beatus Laurentius oravit et dixit	WA 350	re	4
F	-3	0	-1	0	-1	0	2	0	E	Dum sacramenta offerret	LA 483 WA 399	re	4
F	-3	0	-1	0	-1	0	2	0	E	Insurrexerunt in me viri iniqui	OHS 185 (nm) LA 180 *WA 111	re	3
F	-3	0	-1	0	-1	0	2	0	E	Videbunt gentes justum tuum	LA 25 *382 *WA 23	re	4
F	-3	0	-1	0	-1	0	2	4	E	Christo confixus sum cruci	GR 479 LU 1433	int	4
F	-3	0	-1	0	-1	2	0	-1	E	Interrogabat Magos Herodes	PM 42 LR 77 *LA 70 *WA 54	re	4
F	-3	0	-1	0	-1	2	0	-1	E	O beati viri N.	LR 210 *WA 297	re	4

F	-3	0	-1	0	-1	2	0	-1	E	Simile est regnum caelorum decem	LR 229 *LA 543	re	4
F	-3	0	-1	0	2	-1	[0	0]	E	Kyrie	MEL #133		
F	-3	0	-1	0	2	0	-3	2	E	Stephanus autem plenus gratia	LA 41	re	3
F	-3	0	-1	0	2	0	-1	-3	E	Confitebuntur caeli mirabilia ... et	GR 512	gr	3
F	-3	0	-1	0	2	0	-1	-3	F	O felix obedientia	PM 125	an	6
F	-3	0	-1	0	2	0	-1	0	E	Adoramus te Christe et benedicimus	WA 369	re	4
F	-3	0	-1	0	2	0	-1	0	E	Beati martyres Christi	LA 410 *WA 324	re	4
F	-3	0	-1	0	2	0	-1	0	E	Beatissimus Dionysius Christi	WA 306	re	4
F	-3	0	-1	0	2	0	-1	0	E	Beatus es tu et bene tibi	LA 328	re	4
F	-3	0	-1	0	2	0	-1	0	E	Christo cotidie sedulum	LA 328	re	4
F	-3	0	-1	0	2	0	-1	0	E	Cum esset plenus spiritu	LA 42	re	4
F	-3	0	-1	0	2	0	-1	0	E	Descendet Dominus sicut pluvia	LA 14 380 *WA 15	re	4
F	-3	0	-1	0	2	0	-1	0	E	Eodem vero anno	LA 372	re	4
F	-3	0	-1	0	2	0	-1	0	E	Hodie Maria virgo puerum	LA 353	re	4
F	-3	0	-1	0	2	0	-1	0	E	Joannes baptista arguebat	LA 451	re	4
F	-3	0	-1	0	2	0	-1	0	E	Lapidabant Stephanum invocantem	LA 44 *WA 35	re	4
F	-3	0	-1	0	2	0	-1	0	E	Misso Herodes spiculatore	WA 363	re	4
F	-3	0	-1	0	2	0	-1	0	E	Plantaverat autem ... paradisum	LA 109 *WA 72	re	4
F	-3	0	-1	0	2	0	-1	0	E	Scindite corda vestra	LA 129	re	4
F	-3	0	-1	0	2	0	-1	0	E	Sebastianus vir Christianissimus	LA 325	re	4
F	-3	0	-1	0	2	0	-1	0	E	Usquequo exaltabitur inimicus	LA 167 *WA 114	re	4
F	-3	0	-1	0	2	0	-1	0	E	Utinam appenderentur peccata	LA 283 WA 172	re	4
F	-3	0	-1	0	2	0	-1	0	E	Venite adoremus et procidamus	WA 90	inv	4
F	-3	0	-1	0	2	0	-1	0	E	Videbant omnes Stephanum	LA 42 *WA 34	re	4
F	-3	0	-1	0	2	0	-1	0	E	Vox in Rama audita ... ploratus	LA 59	re	4
F	-3	0	-1	0	2	0	2	4	E	Isti sunt triumphatores	LR 143 LA 508 WA 412	re	4
F	-3	0	-1	0	2	4	0	-5	E	Christe Deus plebem tuam	SYG 230	int	3
F	-3	0	-1	0	2	4	0	-3	E	Sacerdotes tui Domine induant	GR [35] LU 1186 1495 SYG 27 GB 28 GS 220	int	3
F	-3	0	-1	0	2	4	0	-3	E	Suscitabo mihi sacerdotem	GR [117]	int	3
F	-3	0	-1	0	2	4	2	-1		Tunc aperientur oculi Confortamini et iam	OTT 9 *GB 7 *SYG 8	ofv	
F	-3	0	-1	0	2	4	2	0		Misericordias tuas Domine in aeternum Confitebuntur caeli	GR 512	grv	
F	-3	0	-1	0	2	4	2	6	E	Dum perambularet Dominus	LA 498 *WA 233	re	4
F	-3	0	-1	2	0	-3	-1	-3	E	Biennio ante mortem siluit	LR 284	re	4

F	-3	0	-1	2	0	-1	0	-1	E	Inveni David servum meum	LR 198 *LA 532	re	4
F	-3	0	-1	2	0	-1	0	-1	E	Ipso anno quo de hac vita	LR 331	re	4
F	-3	0	-1	2	0	-1	0	-1	E	Locutus est Dominus ad Moysen	LR 411 *LA 156 *WA 100	re	4
F	-3	0	-1	2	0	-1	0	-1	E	Quam pulchra es amica mea	LR 224	re	4
F	-3	0	-1	2	4	0	2	-1	D	Fili quid fecisti ... ego	GR 66 LU 481 SYG 33 *GB 37 GS 21	co	1
F	-3	0	-1	2	4	2	4	7	E	Omnis terra adoret te	GR 67 LU 484 SYG 35 GB 37 GS 21	int	4
c	-3	[0	0	0	0	0	0	0]	a	Somno refectis artubus	ST 163	hy	2
c	-3	0	2	-3	-5	-3	-1	-5	F	Tu es Deus qui facis	LA 97	an	5
F	-3	0	2	0	-5	-3	-5	-3	F	Tu es Petrus	GR 412 534 [2^{4}] LU 1122^{6} 1521 *SYG 54 GB 207 GS 183 *189	co	6
c	-3	0	2	0	-3	-5	-3	-2	F	Tu mandasti mandata tua	GR 377 LU 1062 SYG 98 *GB 87 *GS 60 164	co	5
d	-3	0	2	0	-3	-2	-5	-7	G	Unus militum lancea	GR 326 [116] LU 975	co	7
d	-3	0	2	0	-3	-2	-5	-3	G	Sacerdotes Dei benedicite ... servi	AR [56] LU 1176 AM 658 *LA 536	an	7
d	-3	0	2	0	-3	-2	-3	-7	G	Adjuvabit eam Deus vultu suo	LR 214 247 375 *LA 541 *WA 432	an	7
d	-3	0	2	0	-3	-2	-3	-7	G	De sub cujus pede fons	AR 928 LU 1760 AM 1145 *LA 496	an	7
d	-3	0	2	0	-3	-2	-3	-7	G	Ecce sacerdos magnus qui ... et inventus	AR [55] LU 1176 AM 657 WA 427 *LA 536	an	7
d	-3	0	2	0	-3	-2	-3	-7	G	Fiat Domine cor meum	WA 406 *LA 489	an	7
d	-3	0	2	0	-3	-2	-3	-7	G	Non est inventus similis	AR [56] LU 1176 AM 657 *LA 536 WA 427	an	7
d	-3	0	2	0	-3	-2	-3	-7	G	Strinxerunt corporis membra	WA 348 *LA 436	an	7
d	-3	0	2	0	-3	-2	-3	-7	G	Tu es Petrus	AR 752 800 141* LU 1515 1578 AM 935 990 VP 17 13* WA 280 *LA 420	an	7
d	-3	0	2	0	-3	-2	-3	-7	G	Veni sponsa Christi accipe coronam	AR 577^{20} [96] *LR 219 LU 262^{8} 1214 AM 682 745 WA 434	an	7
d	-3	0	2	0	-3	-2	-3	-7	G	Vidi supra montem agnum	AR 927 LU 1760 AM 1145 *LA 496	an	7
d	-3	0	2	0	-3	-2	0	-5	G	Beatus Martinus dixit Juliano	WA 399	an	7
d	-3	0	2	0	-3	-2	0	-5	G	Ingressa Agnes turpitudinis	AR 603 LU 1340 *AM 786 *WA 255 *LA 338	an	7
d	-3	0	2	0	-3	-2	0	-5	G	Si vere fratres divites	AR 351 LU 509 *AM 323 *WA 79 *LA 119	an	7
d	-3	0	2	0	-3	-2	0	-5	G	Suscipiat vos Christe	WA 8	an	7
d	-3	0	2	0	-3	-2	0	-5	G	Tanto pondere eam fixit	AR 594 LU 1325 *AM 773	an	7
d	-3	0	2	0	-3	-2	0	-3	G	Egredere modo frater	AM 815	an	7

93972

d	-3	0	2	0	-3	-2	0	-2	G	Dexteram meam et collum	WA 253 *LA 332	an	7
d	-3	0	2	0	-3	-2	0	-2	G	Dominus de summo caelo	WA 288	an	7
d	-3	0	2	0	-3	-2	0	-2	G	Haec requies mea	WA 439	an	7
d	-3	0	2	0	-3	-2	0	-2	G	Justus Dominus et justitiam ... aequitatem	LR 150 193 *WA 416 424 *LA 522	an	7
d	-3	0	2	0	-3	-2	0	-2	G	Specie tua et pulchritudine	LR 214 246 375 WA 432 *LA 541	an	7
d	-3	0	2	0	-3	-2	0	-2	G	Vidit Dominus Petrum et Andream	LA 497	an	7
F	-3	0	2	0	-3	-1	-3	-1	E	In ecclesiis benedicite	LA 238 *WA 143	re	4
F	-3	0	2	0	3	-1	-3	0	E	In craticula te Deum	LA 439 *WA 349	re	4
F	-3	0	2	0	-3	-1	-3	0	E	Qui Lazarum resuscitasti	PM 320	re	4
F	-3	0	2	0	-3	-1	-3	0	E	Suscipe verbum virgo Maria	PM 245 LA 14 379 *WA 4	re	4
c	-3	0	2	0	-3	0	-5	-3	F	Iste sanctus pro lege Dei	LR 150 LA 522 *WA 416	re	5
F	-3	0	2	0	-3	0	2	-1	F	Prope est Dominus	GR 21 LU 354 *SYG 8 *GB 7 *GS 6	gr	5
F	-3	0	2	0	-3	0	2	-1	F	Vindica Domine sanguinem	GR 613 *SYG 190 *GB 195 GS 214	gr	5
d	-3	0	2	0	-3	0	2	0	G	Omnes sitientes venite	AR 214 LU 324 *AM 188 WA 7 *LA 6	an	8
d	-3	0	2	0	-2	-3	-7	-2	G	Et me scitis	WA 104	an	7
G	-3	0	2	0	-2	0	-3	-7	E	Nos scientes sanctum nomen	WA 407 *LA 490	an	4
d	-3	0	2	0	-2	0	-3	-2	G	Caritas Dei diffusa ... spiritum	LA 267	an	7
d	-3	0	2	0	-2	0	-3	-2	G	Christus circumdedit me	WA 253 LA 334	an	7
d	-3	0	2	0	-2	0	-3	-2	G	Dignum sibi Dominus computavit	LA 497	an	8
d	-3	0	2	0	-2	0	-3	-2	G	Gratias tibi ago Domine quia	AR 625 LU 1371 *AM 807 WA 276 *LA 363	an	7
d	-3	0	2	0	-2	0	-3	-2	G	Hoc jam tertio	LA 220	an	7
d	-3	0	2	0	-2	0	-3	-2	G	Imposita manu puero	WA 400 LA 485	an	7
d	-3	0	2	0	-2	0	-3	-2	G	In loco pascuae ibi me	WA 437	an	7
d	-3	0	2	0	-2	0	-3	-2	G	Induit me Dominus cyclade	WA 253 *LA 332	an	7
d	-3	0	2	0	-2	0	-3	-2	G	Justum deduxit ... et ostendit ... regnum	WA 428 LA 538	an	7
d	-3	0	2	0	-2	0	-3	-2	G	Nativitas est hodie ... vita	AR 834 LU 1625 AM 1032 WA 368 LA 461	an	7
d	-3	0	2	0	-2	0	-3	-2	G	Non est hic aliud	LR 237 WA 318 LA 547	an	7
d	-3	0	2	0	-2	0	-3	-2	G	Non meis meritis ad vos	AR 927 LU 1760 AM 1145 WA 410 LA 496	an	7
d	-3	0	2	0	-2	0	-3	-2	G	O Hippolyte si credideris	WA 349	an	7
d	-3	0	2	0	-2	0	-3	-2	G	O quam pulchra est casta generatio	LR 213 WA 432 LA 541	an	7
d	-3	0	2	0	-2	0	-3	-2	E	Panis enim Dei est	WA 100	an	3

d	-3	0	2	0	-2	0	-3	-2	G	Posuit os meum Dominus	LR 351 *LA 403	an	7
d	-3	0	2	0	-2	0	-3	-2	G	Recessit igitur scienter	LR 320	an	7
d	-3	0	2	0	-2	0	-3	-2	G	Si coram hominibus tormenta	WA 420 LA 513	an	7
d	-3	0	2	0	-2	0	-2	-7	G	Tu es qui venturus es Domine	AR 229 LU 1083 *AM 201 *WA 13 *LA 12	an	7
c	-3	0	2	0	-2	0	-2	-3	F	Ecce Dominus veniet et omnes ... erit	WA 10	re	5
c	-3	0	2	0	-2	0	-2	-3	F	Ecce Dominus veniet protector	LA 9 WA 10	re	5
c	-3	0	2	0	-2	0	-2	0	G	Veni Domine et noli ... et revoca	LA 14 *WA 15	re	7
d	-3	0	2	0	-2	0	2	0	G	Annulis septem subarrhavit	AM 1131	an	7
d	-3	0	2	0	-2	0	2	0	G	Annulo suo subarrhavit me	AR 603 LU 1340 AM 786 *WA 253 LA 338	an	7
d	-3	0	2	0	-2	0	2	0	G	Et ecce terraemotus	AR 443 OHS 725 766 LU 782 AM 454 WA 127 *LA 214 232	an	7
d	-3	0	2	0	-2	0	2	0	G	Exsultemus in Domino	LA 40	an	7
d	-3	0	2	0	-2	0	2	0	G	Induit eum Dominus stola	LR 275	an	7
d	-3	0	2	0	-2	0	2	0	G	Mecum enim habeo custodem	AM 786 *LU 1340 *AR 603 LA 338	an	7
F	-3	0	2	0	-1	-3	-1	-3	E	Beatissimae virginis Mariae	LA 457 *WA 365	re	4
c	-3	0	2	0	-1	0	-1	-3	F	Ecce veniet Dominus et omnes	LA 8	re	5
c	-3	0	2	0	-1	0	-1	-3	G	Fuit vir vitae venerabilis	LR 318	an	8
F	-3	0	2	0	-1	0	-1	0	E	Hoc signum crucis erit	LA 396 *WA 308	re	4
F	-3	0	2	0	-1	0	-1	0	E	Joannes vocabitur nomen	WA 322	re	4
c	-3	0	2	0	-1	0	2	0	F	Domine pater et Deus	LA 276 WA 169	re	5
d	-3	0	2	0	2	0	-3	-2	G	Cum jucunditate nativitatem	AR 835 LU 1626 AM 1033 WA 368 LA 461	an	7
d	-3	0	2	0	2	0	-3	-2	G	Domine si adhuc populo ... laborem	AR 917 LU 1749 *AM 1115 WA 402 LA 486	an	7
d	-3	0	2	0	2	0	-3	-2	G	Ego signo crucis	WA 399 LA 480	an	7
d	-3	0	2	0	2	0	-3	-2	G	Ego si patibulum crucis	LA 499	an	7
d	-3	0	2	0	2	0	-3	-2	G	In hoc cognoscent omnes	GR 202 OHS 450 LU 674 *SYG 131	an	7
d	-3	0	2	0	2	0	-3	-2	G	Ipsi sum desponsata	LA 334 *WA 254	an	7
d	-3	0	2	0	2	0	-3	-2	G	Jam corpus ejus corpori meo	LA 334	an	7
d	-3	0	2	0	2	0	-3	-2	G	Nos autem gloriari	AR 701 LU 1460 AM 900 1041 WA 371 LA 463	an	7
d	-3	0	2	0	2	0	-3	-2	G	O magnum pietatis opus	AR 700 LU 1459 AM 899 1040 WA 369 LA 462	an	7
d	-3	0	2	0	2	0	-3	-2	G	Propter fidem castitatis	WA 274 LA 360	an	7

d	-3	0	2	0	2	0	-3	-2	G	Quis es tu qui venisti	AM 807 *AR 624 *LU 1370 LA 363 *WA 276	an	7
d	-3	0	2	0	2	0	-3	-2	G	Relicta domo rebusque patris	LR 319	an	7
d	-3	0	2	0	2	0	-3	-2	G	Salve crux pretiosa suscipe	AR 579 LU 1307 AM 755 WA 236 LA 504	an	7
d	-3	0	2	0	2	0	-3	-2	G	Si culmen veri honoris	AR 352 AM 324 *WA 79 LA 120	an	7
d	-3	0	2	0	-2	0	-3	-2	G	Sicut laetantium omnium nostrum	LR 250 LA 350 WA 269	an	7
d	-3	0	2	0	2	0	-3	-2	G	Solve jubente Deo terrarum	AM 993 *WA 328 LA 420	an	8
d	-3	0	2	0	2	0	-3	-2	G	Stans Jesus clamabat	AR 538^{7} LU 977 AM 565	an	7
d	-3	0	2	0	2	0	-3	-2	G	Tamquam aurum in fornace	LR 176 WA 420 LA 513	an	7
d	-3	0	2	0	2	0	-3	-2	G	Vidisti Domine agonem	WA 274 LA 359	an	7
F	-3	0	2	0	2	0	-3	0	D	Me exspectaverunt peccatores	GR [55] LU 1220 SYG 41 GB 44^{v} GS 226	int	2
d	-3	0	2	0	2	0	-2	-5	G	Dirige Domine Deus meus	AR [154] LU 1782 *WA 436 *LA 553	an	7
d	-3	0	2	0	2	0	-2	-5	G	Misit Dominus manum suam	LR 347 WA 320 LA 400	an	7
d	-3	0	2	0	2	0	-2	-5	G	Mittite in dexteram navigii	AR 450 OHS 795 AM 462 *WA 135 LA 219	an	7
d	-3	0	2	0	2	0	-2	-5	G	Unam petii a Domino ... omnibus	GR 334 LU 1005 *SYG 242 GB 249^{v} GS 146	co	7
d	-3	0	2	0	2	0	-2	-5	G	Unus panis et unum corpus	GR [134]	co	7
d	-3	0	2	0	2	0	-2	-3	G	Homo natus est in ea	LR 74 WA 29 LA 64	an	7
d	-3	0	2	0	2	0	-2	-3	G	Si gloriam dignitatis	WA 79	an	7
d	-3	0	2	0	2	0	-2	0	G	Ecce dedi verba mea	LR 347 WA 320 LA 401	an	7
d	-3	0	2	0	2	0	-2	0	G	Omne quod dat mihi Pater	AR [146] LU 1776 AM 1154 WA 438 LA 560	an	7
d	-3	0	2	0	2	0	-2	0	G	Virgo est electus	LA 52	an	7
d	-3	0	2	0	2	0	-2	2	G	Signa eos qui in me credunt	GR 575 SYG 192 *GB 216 GS 193	co	7
d	-3	0	2	0	2	0	[0	0]	d	Splendor paternae gloriae	ST 163	hy	2
F	-3	0	2	0	2	0	[0	0]	F	Tu es Deus qui facis	WA 67	an	6
c	-3	0	2	0	2	0	2	4	F	Benedicta et venerabilis ... quae sine tactu	GR 77**	co	5
d	-3	0	2	0	2	3	2	0	G	Dominus Scholasticae dedit	LR 293	an	7
c	-3	0	2	0	2	4	2	0	[G]	Agnus Dei	SCH #36		7
F	-3	0	2	0	2	4	2	0	F	Si quis sitit veniat ad me	GR [116] LU 975	co	6
D	-3	0	2	0	3	2	0	-2	G	Omne quod dat mihi Pater	GB 266^{v}	co	7
d	-3	0	2	3	0	-5	-2	-3	G	Mens mea solidata	WA 273 *LA 360	an	7

d	-3	0	2	3	0	-3	-2	-5	G	Caro mea requiescit	OHS 593 LU 753 *WA 125 LA 201	an	7
d	-3	0	2	3	0	-3	-2	-5	G	Caro mea vere est cibus	AR 4 (sup 2)	an	7
d	-3	0	2	3	0	-3	-2	-3	G	Me suscepit dextera tua	AR 397 [178] LU 1802 *AM 1163 *WA 438 *LA 559	an	7
d	-3	0	2	3	0	-3	-2	0	G	Voce mea ad Dominum	AR 186	an	7
d	-3	0	2	3	0	-2	-3	-7	G	Liberavit Dominus pauperem	OHS 382 LU 638 WA 118 *LA 190	an	7
d	-3	0	2	3	2	0	-2	-3	G	Proprio filio suo non pepercit	AR 438 OHS 509 LU 712 AM 438 *LA 200 WA 124	an	7
c	-3	0	2	4	0	-2	0	-3	F	Mecum enim habeo custodem	WA 255	an	5
c	-3	0	2	4	0	-1	0	2	F	Non in solo pane	AR 371 LU 538 AM 344 *WA 87	an	5
c	-3	0	2	4	2	0	-1	2	F	Dico vobis gaudium	GR 330 LU 984 *SYG 260 *GB 248^v *GS e	co	5
c	-3	0	2	4	2	0	-1	2	F	Venit sponsus et virgines	GR 106**	co	5
F	-3	0	2	4	2	0	2	4	E	Pastis visceribus ciboque sumpto	ST 480	hy	4
F	-3	0	2	4	2	4	2	0	F	Innocens manibus et mundo corde	GR (37)	co	6
F	-3	0	2	4	5	2	0	-3	F	Sexaginta sunt reginae	WA 163	an	6
G	-3	0	2	4	5	2	0	2	G	Gloria ad lib. I	GR 83* LU 86		8
G	-3	0	2	4	5	2	0	4	G	Te lucis ante terminum	ST 28 AR 60 LU 268 AM 171	hy	8
F	-3	0	2	4	5	4	0	2	F	Jesu redemptor saeculi	ST 325	hy	6
c	-3	0	2	4	5	4	2	0	c	Egressus Jesus de praetorio	WA 123	re	5
F	-3	0	2	4	5	4	2	0	F	Kyrie VIII amator sancte (etc)	MEL #132 GR 81* LU 84		6
F	-3	0	4	2	-1	0	2	0	E	Lauda Jerusalem Dominum quoniam	GR 487 LU 1277^B	of	3
F	-3	0	4	2	0	2	4	2	G	Gaudeo in passionibus	GR 68**	of	8
F	-3	2	-1	-5	-3	0	-1	-5	D	Hic itaque cum jam relictis	LA 369	an	2
F	-3	2	-1	0	2	4	2	4	E	O quantus erat luctus hominum	LA 486 *WA 401	re	4
c	-3	2	0	-1	-3	0	-1	-3		Deus judicium tuum Reges Tharsis	OTT 21 GB 34 *SYG 31	ofv	
F	-3	2	0	-1	0	-1	0	2	F	Ad annuntiandum mane Justus ut palma	OTT 150 *GB 25^V *SYG 24	ofv	
F	-3	2	0	-1	2	4	7	6	E	Nunc scio vere quia misit	GR 532 LU 1518 *SYG 202 *GB 204 GS o 189	int	3
c	-3	2	0	2	0	-1	-5	-3	G	Clamor meus Domine	AR 198 LU 279^S	an	8
F	-3	2	4	0	-1	0	-3	2	E	Alleluia: beati qui habitant in domo	GR 2**	al	3
F	-3	2	4	0	-1	0	-3	2	E	Alleluia: sperent in te qui noverunt	GR 94**	al	3
F	-3	2	4	0	-1	0	-3	2		Beati qui habitant in domo ... in saecula	GR 2**	alv	

F	-3	2	4	0	-1	0	-1	0	E	Ascendit Deus in jubilatione	LR 103 LA 247 *WA 148	re	3 4
F	-3	2	4	2	4	7	6	7	E	Beatus Martinus obitum	LA 484 *WA 399	re	3
F	-3	2	4	7	6	7	4	9		Custodi me Domine ut pupillam Perfice gressus	OTT 90 *GB 58^{v} *SYG 61	ofv	
G	-3	2	5	2	4	5	4	5		Operuisti omnia peccata Benedixisti Domine	OTT 8 *GB 6 *SYG 7	ofv	
F	-3	2	5	2	4	5	4	5		Quam bonus Israel Deus Tenuisti manum	GR 179 OHS 108 LU 593 GS 86 *GB 109 *SYG 122	grv	
F	-3	2	6	2	4	6	7	9	E	Alleluia: Crucifixus surgens	SYG 164	al	3
F	-3	2	7	4	2	7	6	7	E	Ego clamavi quoniam exaudisti	GR 130 *GB 84^{v} GS 57 *SYG 95	int	3
a	-2	-7	0	-2	-4	-5	-7	-5	D	Salve regina misericordiae	WA 352	an	1
d	-2	-5	-9	-7	-12	-9	-12	-14	D	Agnus Dei	SCH #12		1
d	-2	-5	-9	-7	-12	-9	-12	-14	D	Sanctus	THAN #6		1
d	-2	-5	-7	-5	-9	-7	-5	-9	D	Agnus Dei	SCH #8		1
d	-2	-5	-7	-2	-3	-2	0	2		Ego sum panis vivus qui Ego sum panis	LR 128	rev	
a	-2	-5	-7	-2	0	2	0	-2	E	Amor Jesu dulcissime	AM 1000	hy	4
a	-2	-5	-7	-2	0	2	0	-2	E	Jam lucis orto sidere	ST 71	hy	4
d	-2	-5	-7	-2	0	2	0	-2	G	Jam lucis orto sidere	ST 203	hy	7
a	-2	-5	-7	-2	0	2	0	-2	E	Quicumque Christum quaeritis	AM 995	hy	4
D	-2	-5	-7	-2	0	2	3	0		Te sancta Dei crux Protege Domine	OTT 168	ofv	
D	-2	-5	-7	-2	0	2	3	2	D	Amore Christi nobilis	ST 9	hy	2
D	-2	-5	-7	-2	0	2	3	2	D	Hymnum canamus gloriae	ST 390	hy	2
D	-2	-5	-7	-2	0	2	3	2	D	Mysteriorum signifer	ST 13	hy	2
a	-2	-5	-7	-2	0	3	0	-2	E	Agnes beatae virginis	ST 39	hy	4
a	-2	-5	-7	-2	0	3	0	-2	E	Aras nefandi numinis	ST 40	hy	4
a	-2	-5	-7	-2	0	3	0	-2	E	Deus tuorum militum	ST 404	hy	4
a	-2	-5	-7	-2	0	3	0	-2	E	Quem terra pontus aethera	ST 29	hy	4
a	-2	-5	-7	-2	0	3	0	-2	E	Solemnis redit temporis	ST 373	hy	4
a	-2	-5	-7	-2	0	3	2	0	a	Amore Christi nobilis	ST 39	hy	2
a	-2	-5	-7	-2	0	3	2	0	a	Ascendant nostrae protinus	ST 42	hy	2
a	-2	-5	-7	-2	0	3	2	0	a	Aurora solis nuntia	LU 1438	hy	2
a	-2	-5	-7	-2	0	3	2	0	a	Aurora soli praevia	AR 632 VP 69	hy	2
a	-2	-5	-7	-2	0	3	2	0	a	Caelestis aulae nuntius	AR 873 LU 1672 AM 1074	hy	2
a	-2	-5	-7	-2	0	3	2	0	a	In monte olivis consito	LR 448	hy	2
a	-2	-5	-7	-2	0	3	2	0	a	In principio erat verbum	ST 39	hy	2
a	-2	-5	-7	-2	0	3	2	0	a	Jam morte victor obruta	AR 876 AM 1077	hy	2

a	-2	-5	-7	-2	0	3	2	0	a	Jam regina discubuit	AM 1020	hy	2
d	-2	-5	-7	-2	0	3	2	0	d	Jesu nostra redemptio	ST 93	hy	2
a	-2	-5	-7	-2	0	3	2	0	a	Lucis beatae gaudiis	LR 444	hy	2
a	-2	-5	-7	-2	0	3	2	0	a	Memento rerum conditor	AR [133]	hy	2
a	-2	-5	-7	-2	0	3	2	0	a	Mysterium signifer	ST 42	hy	2
a	-2	-5	-7	-2	0	3	2	0	a	Nunc sancte nobis spiritus	AR [124] AM 710	hy	2
d	-2	-5	-7	-2	0	3	2	0	d	O gloriosa domina	ST 87 AM 709 864 1016	hy	2
a	-2	-5	-7	-2	0	3	2	0	a	O gloriosa virginum	AR [122] LU 1314	hy	2
a	-2	-5	-7	-2	0	3	2	0	a	O prima virgo prodita	AR 1 (sup 3) LU 1600	hy	2
a	-2	-5	-7	-2	0	3	2	0	a	Omnis sanctorum concio	AM 984	hy	2
a	-2	-5	-7	-2	0	3	2	0	a	Praeclara custos virginum	LR 259	hy	2
d	-2	-5	-7	-2	0	3	2	0	d	Quem terra pontus aethera	ST 87 184 LR 245 273	hy	2
a	-2	-5	-7	-2	0	3	2	0	a	Succedit nocti lucifer	AM 982	hy	2
a	-2	-5	-7	-2	0	3	2	0	a	Te gestientem gaudiis	AR 880 LU 1680 AM 1079	hy	2
a	-2	-5	-7	-2	0	3	2	0	a	Te lucis ante terminum	AR 61 AM 172	hy	2
a	-2	-5	-7	-2	0	3	2	0	a	Te mater alma numinis	AR 882[4] AM 1083	hy	2
a	-2	-5	-4	-7	-9	-7	-4	-7		Intactae matri reseratur janua Porta Sion	PM 268	rev	
a	-2	-5	-4	-5	-7	-2	0	3	E	Lauda mater ecclesia	VP 191	hy	3
a	-2	-5	-4	-5	-4	-2	-5	-4	D	Alleluia	AR 158 LU 295 298	an	1
a	-2	-5	-4	-2	-5	-4	-7	-5	D	Ecce quam bonum et quam jucundum	AR 158 LU 295 *AM 140 141 *LA 93	an	1
a	-2	-5	-4	-2	-4	-5	-7	-9	D	Clamavi et exaudivit	LA 93	an	2
a	-2	-5	-4	-2	-4	-5	-7	-9	D	Speret Israel in Domino	LA 93	an	1
a	-2	-5	-4	-2	-4	-5	-7	[0]	D	Adjutor in tribulationibus	OHS 297 (nm) WA 65 *LA 90	an	1
a	-2	-5	-4	-2	-4	-5	-7	[0]	D	Expugna impugnantes	WA 63 LA 87	an	1
a	-2	-5	-4	-2	-4	-5	-7	[0]	D	Laudate Dominum de caelis	AR 342 AM 43 313 *LA 114 *WA 75	an	1
a	-2	-5	-4	-2	-4	-2	-7	-9		Dilexit Andream Dominus	GR 393 LU 1305 SYG 231 GB 246 GS g	alv	
a	-2	-5	-4	-2	-4	-2	-7	-9		Dum complerentur dies	GR 305 LU 903 *SYG 183 *GB 187	alv	
a	-2	-5	-4	-2	-4	-2	-7	-9		Misso Herodes spiculatore	GS 196	alv	
a	-2	-5	-4	-2	-4	-2	-7	-9		O quam bonus et suavis	GR 303 LU 898	alv	
a	-2	-5	-4	-2	2	-2	0	-5		Gloria claritas decus Te laudant angeli	WA 28	rev	
a	-2	-5	-4	-2	2	-2	0	-5		Ipsum unicum Dei patris Te laudant angeli	WA 28	rev	

D	-2	-5	-3	-7	-5	-3	-2	0	D	Gaude Maria virgo	GR [78] LU 1266	tr	2
G	-2	-5	-3	-7	-5	-2	0	2	G	Domine Deus virtutum converte	GR 53	tr	8
G	-2	-5	-3	-7	-5	-2	0	2	G	Ecce sic benedicetur omnis	GR [123] LU 1290	tr	8
G	-2	-5	-3	-7	-5	-2	0	2	G	Ego pascam oves meas	GR 66**	tr	8
G	-2	-5	-3	-7	-5	-2	0	2	G	Ego sum radix et genus	GR 45**	tr	8
G	-2	-5	-3	-7	-5	-2	0	2	G	Saepe expugnaverunt me	GR 153 LU 571 SYG 110 GB 97^v *GS 72	tr	8
G	-2	-5	-3	-7	-5	-2	0	2	G	Surge Domine in requiem	GR [119] 90**	tr	8
G	-2	-5	-3	-7	-5	-2	0	2	G	Veni sponsa Christi accipe coronam	GR [52] LU 1217	tr	8
D	-2	-5	-3	-5	-7	-2	0	5	D	Kyrie	MEL #199		
D	-2	-5	-3	-5	-2	2	0	-2	D	Kyrie	MEL #205		
G	-2	-5	-3	-2	-3	-5	-7	-5	G	Amicus meus osculi me	OHS 388 LU 643 LA 191	re	8
G	-2	-5	-3	-2	-3	-5	-7	-5	G	Descendit Jesus cum eis	LR 316	re	8
G	-2	-5	-3	-2	-3	-5	-7	-5	G	Ecce Adam quasi unus	LA 112 *WA 74	re	8
G	-2	-5	-3	-2	-3	-5	-7	-5	G	Isti sunt sancti qui non inquinaverunt	LA 59 *WA 45	re	8
G	-2	-5	-3	-2	-3	-5	-7	-5	G	Jerusalem plantabis vineam	LA 9 *WA 11	re	8
G	-2	-5	-3	-2	-3	-5	-7	-5	G	O bona crux quae decorem	LA 501 *WA 235	re	8
G	-2	-5	-3	-2	-3	-5	-7	-5	G	O mira res filia	PM 252	an	8
G	-2	-5	-3	-2	-3	-5	-7	-5	G	Prolapso in lacum Placido	LR 276	re	8
G	-2	-5	-3	-2	-3	-5	-7	-5	G	Radix Jesse quae exsurget	LA 20 378 *WA 15	re	8
G	-2	-5	-3	-2	-3	-5	-7	-5	G	Salvum me fac Deus	LA 177 *WA 111	re	8
G	-2	-5	-3	-2	-3	-5	-7	-5	G	Specie tua et pulchritudine	LR 217 LA 542	re	8
G	-2	-5	-3	-2	-3	-5	-3	-2	G	Debitas laudes Domino canentes	ST 438	hy	8
G	-2	-5	-3	-2	-3	-2	0	-2	E	Apparuerunt caelestes spiritus	AM 1136	an	4
G	-2	-5	-3	-2	0	-2	0	2	G	Dixit sanctus Vincentius	WA 259	an	8
G	-2	-5	-3	-2	0	2	0	-2	G	Agnetis festum martyris	ST 425	hy	8
G	-2	-5	-3	-2	0	2	0	-2	G	Alias oves habeo	AR 472 *AM 486	an	8
G	-2	-5	-3	-2	0	2	0	-2	G	Alleluia: angelus Domini descendit	GR 245 OHS 775 LU 786 *GS 125 *GB 131 *SYG 159	al	8
G	-2	-5	-3	-2	0	2	0	-2	G	Alleluia: biduo vivens pendebat	SYG 231	al	8
G	-2	-5	-3	-2	0	2	0	-2	G	Alleluia: spiritus sancti gratia	SYG 24	al	8
G	-2	-5	-3	-2	0	2	0	-2	G	Alleluia: venerunt de tribulatione	GR 108**	al	8
G	-2	-5	-3	-2	0	2	0	-2	G	Alleluia: verbo Domini caeli firmati	GR 300 LU 893	al	8
G	-2	-5	-3	-2	0	2	0	-2	G	Archangele Christi per gratiam	PM 154 WA 383 LA 470	an	8
G	-2	-5	-3	-2	0	2	0	-2	G	Aspiciens in caelum	LA 41	an	8

G	-2	-5	-3	-2	0	2	0	-2	G	Caecilia virgo almachum	WA 405 *LA 488	an	8
G	-2	-5	-3	-2	0	2	0	-2	G	Cum esset desponsata ... antequam ... quod	WA 26 LA 31	an	8
G	-2	-5	-3	-2	0	2	0	-2	G	Descendit Jesus cum eis	AR 325 654 LU 474 1407 AM 842	an	8
G	-2	-5	-3	-2	0	2	0	-2	G	Domine Deus meus exaltasti	WA 435	an	8
G	-2	-5	-3	-2	0	2	0	-2	G	Exaltare Domine qui judicas	AR 197 LU 279[S]	an	8
G	-2	-5	-3	-2	0	2	0	-2	G	Haec locutus sum vobis	AR 498 AM 515 LU 858 LA 254	an	8
G	-2	-5	-3	-2	0	2	0	-2	G	Hodie sacratissima	ST 427	hy	8
G	-2	-5	-3	-2	0	2	0	-2	G	Manifeste magnum est	AR 335	an	8
G	-2	-5	-3	-2	0	2	0	-2	G	Oris divini	WA 312	an	8
G	-2	-5	-3	-2	0	2	0	-2	G	Stabunt justi in magna constantia	WA 308	an	8
G	-2	-5	-3	-2	0	2	0	2	G	Ad omnia quae mittam te	LR 346 WA 320 *LA 400	an	8
G	-2	-5	-3	-2	0	2	0	2	G	Convertere Domine et eripe animam	AR [156] LU 1783 *WA 436 LA 553	an	8
G	-2	-5	-3	-2	0	2	0	2	G	Corde et animo Christo	AR 835 LU 1626 AM 1033 WA 368 *LA 461	an	8
G	-2	-5	-3	-2	0	2	0	2	G	Dilexisti justitiam et odisti	LR 289	an	8
G	-2	-5	-3	-2	0	2	0	2	G	Dominus ab utero	LR 347 WA 320 *LA 401	an	8
G	-2	-5	-3	-2	0	2	0	2	G	Dum sacrum mysterium beatus Dionysius	WA 386	an	8
G	-2	-5	-3	-2	0	2	0	2	G	Dum tolleret Dominus Eliam	AR 542 LU 988 AM 578 *LA 275	an	8
G	-2	-5	-3	-2	0	2	0	2	G	Ego sum qui testimonium	AR 407 LU 568 AM 388	an	8
G	-2	-5	-3	-2	0	2	0	2	G	Formans me ex utero	LR 351 WA 321 *LA 403	an	8
G	-2	-5	-3	-2	0	2	0	2	G	Hodie nomen tuum ita	AR 631 LU 1381	an	8
G	-2	-5	-3	-2	0	2	0	2	G	Interrogabat Magos Herodes	AR 333 LU 482 AM 299 *LA 74	an	8
G	-2	-5	-3	-2	0	2	0	2	G	Judaea et Jerusalem	AR 255 LU 358 AM 232 WA 26 *LA 30	an	8
G	-2	-5	-3	-2	0	2	0	2	G	Laetabitur justus in Domino ... laudabuntur	WA 417	an	8
G	-2	-5	-3	-2	0	2	0	2	G	Sic Deus dilexit mundum	AR 510 AM 525 WA 155 *LA 264	an	8
G	-2	-5	-3	-2	0	2	0	2	G	Soror mea Lucia virgo	AR 593 LU 1325 AM 770 WA 246 *LA 322	an	8
G	-2	-5	-3	-2	0	2	0	2	G	Verbum caro factum est ... plenum	AR 323 LU 469	an	8
G	-2	-5	-3	-2	0	2	0	2	G	Verbum caro factum est ... et vidimus	WA 37 *LA 39	an	8
G	-2	-5	-3	-2	0	2	0	2	G	Videns Andreas crucem	PM 118 *WA 234 *LA 499	an	8

G	-2	-5	-3	-2	0	2	0	4	G	Congaudete mecum et congratulamini	AR 604 LU 1341 AM 787 WA 255 LA 338	an	8
G	-2	-5	-3	-2	0	2	0	4	G	Elevare elevare consurge	AR 246 AM 222 WA 18 *LA 17	an	8
G	-2	-5	-3	-2	0	2	0	4	G	Maria virgo assumpta est	AR 820 LU 1606 AM 1014 WA 358 *LA 448	an	8
G	-2	-5	-3	-2	0	2	4	0	G	Venient ad te	AR 334 AM 300 LR 78 *LA 76 *WA 57	an	8
c	-2	-5	-3	-2	0	2	5	4	F	Sanctus	THAN #18		5
G	-2	-5	-3	-2	2	0	-2	2	G	Crucifixus surrexit tertia die	LA 399	an	8
G	-2	-5	-2	-5	-3	-2	0	2	G	Dicit Dominus paenitentiam	AR 253 AM 229 *WA 16 LA 17	an	8
G	-2	-5	-2	-3	-5	-7	-5	-2	G	Baptizat miles regem	PM 44 WA 58 *LA 76	an	8
G	-2	-5	-2	-3	-5	-7	-2	0	G	Inito consilio venenum	WA 297	re	2
G	-2	-5	-2	-3	-2	0	-7	-5	G	Obviam procedunt Cherubim	WA 359	an	8
G	-2	-5	-2	-3	-2	0	-2	0	G	Nomen eorum permanet	AR 642	an	8
G	-2	-5	-2	-3	-2	0	2	0	G	Dabo in Sion salutem	AR 231 LU 330 *AM 204 WA 16 *LA 16	an	8
G	-2	-5	-2	-3	-2	0	2	0	G	Dantur ergo laudes Deo	WA 261	an	8
G	-2	-5	-2	-3	-2	0	2	0	G	Ergo pater sancte	WA 286	an	8
G	-2	-5	-2	-3	-2	0	2	0	G	Jam corpus ejus corpori	WA 254	an	8
G	-2	-5	-2	-3	-2	0	2	0	G	Relicta domo rebusque patris	WA 297 *LA 367	an	8
G	-2	-5	-2	-3	-2	2	0	-2	G	Cibavit nos Dominus	LR 125 LU 935	an	8
a	-2	-5	-2	0	-2	-5	-4	-5		De quacumque tribulatione	GR 486 LU 1441	alv	
D	-2	-5	-2	0	-2	-5	-2	0	E	Kyrie alpha et O	MEL #204		
a	-2	-5	-2	0	-2	-4	-2	0	D	Rector potens verax Deus	ST 164	hy	1
D	-2	-5	-2	0	-2	0	2	3		Loquebar Domine de testimoniis	GR 437 LU 1369	alv	
d	-2	-5	-2	0	-2	0	2	3		Mortem enim quam salvator Lapides torrentes	WA 36	rev	
D	-2	-5	-2	0	-2	0	2	3	D	O beata benedicta	WA 161	an	2
D	-2	-5	-2	0	-2	0	2	3	D	Sancte Paule apostole praedicator ... ad Deum	LA 428 WA 266 (inc illeg)	re	1
G	-2	-5	-2	0	-2	0	2	5	G	Transiens ex hoc mundo	WA 314	re	8
D	-2	-5	-2	0	-2	0	3	2	D	O crux viride lignum	VP 152	an	2
D	-2	-5	-2	0	-2	0	3	2	F	O pietatis Deus qui mundum	GB 158^{v}	an	6
D	-2	-5	-2	0	-2	0	3	2	D	Pater insignis confessor Benedicte	VP 128	re	2
D	-2	-5	-2	0	-2	0	3	5	D	Loquebantur variis linguis ... prout	LR 113	re	2
D	-2	-5	-2	0	-2	0	3	5	D	Nunc dimittis Domine	WA 270	re	2
D	-2	-5	-2	0	-2	2	5	2		Initium sapientiae timor	GR 112**	alv	

D	-2	-5	-2	0	-2	2	5	2		Oculus Dei respexit illum	GR 604 LU 1646	alv	
D	-2	-5	-2	0	-2	2	5	2		Sicut cinnamomum et balsamum	GR 34**	alv	
D	-2	-5	-2	0	-2	2	5	3	E	Beatus es vas electionis	LA 345 *WA 265	re	4
D	-2	-5	-2	0	-2	2	5	3		Spiritus sanctus procedens	GS M 137	alv	
G	-2	-5	-2	0	-2	2	5	4	G	Ecce dedi te in lucem	AR 894^{2} LU 1716 AM 1089	an	8
D	-2	-5	-2	0	-2	3	2	0	D	Alleluia: loquebar Domine de testimoniis	GR 437 LU 1369	al	2
G	-2	-5	-2	0	-2	3	5	3	G	Jam lucis orto sidere	ST 172	hy	2
G	-2	-5	-2	0	-2	3	5	3	G	Verbum supernum prodiens a patre	ST 170	hy	2
D	-2	-5	-2	0	-2	3	5	7	D	Erectus in culmine	WA 285	re	2
G	-2	-5	-2	0	0	2	0	-2	G	Ante sex dies solemnitatis	GS 80	an	8
G	-2	-5	-2	0	2	-2	-5	-2	G	Et recordatae sunt verborum	LA 233	an	8
D	-2	-5	-2	0	2	-2	0	2	D	Sancte Christi confessor audi	VP 258	re	2
G	-2	-5	-2	0	2	0	-2	0	G	Ave praesul gloriose	WA 424	an	8
D	-2	-5	-2	0	2	0	-2	0	D	Christe Deus misericordiarum	VP 117	an	1 2
D	-2	-5	-2	0	2	0	-2	0	D	Christe pater misericordiarum	SYG 69	an	1
D	-2	-5	-2	0	2	0	-2	0	D	Crede mater Agathen	WA 243	an	2
D	-2	-5	-2	0	2	0	-2	0		Domine Jesu Christe judex O pie Deus	OTT 178 *SYG 237	ofv	
D	-2	-5	-2	0	2	0	-2	0	D	Dum adhuc paene vigilaret	WA 342	an	2
D	-2	-5	-2	0	2	0	-2	0	D	Duo seraphim clamabant	AR 179* PM 107 LR 418	re	1
D	-2	-5	-2	0	2	0	-2	0	D	Feliciter virgines vincunt	WA 394	re	2
a	-2	-5	-2	0	2	0	-2	0	E	Nos autem gloriari ... in quo	GB 167^{v}	co	3
G	-2	-5	-2	0	2	0	-2	0	G	O per omnia laudabilem	WA 242	an	8
G	-2	-5	-2	0	2	0	-2	0	G	Propter nimiam caritatem	AR 293 LU 440 AM 270 *LA 40	an	8
D	-2	-5	-2	0	2	0	-2	0	D	Protege Domine plebem tuam	GR 594 LU 1630 OTT 168 SYG 174 GB 167 GS 185 236	of	2
D	-2	-5	-2	0	2	0	-2	0	D	Qui Raphaelem archangelum	WA 292	an	2
G	-2	-5	-2	0	2	0	-2	2	G	Gloriosus confessor ... Benedictus	AM 852 WA 334 LA 374	an	8
G	-2	-5	-2	0	2	0	-2	2	G	Homo erat in Jerusalem	WA 270	an	8
G	-2	-5	-2	0	2	0	-2	2	G	Vox laetitiae in tabernaculis	WA 132	an	8
D	-2	-5	-2	0	2	0	-2	3	D	Postquam domi puerilem	WA 238	an	2
G	-2	-5	-2	0	2	0	2	-2	G	Hodie electorum omnium caput	PM 130 *WA 267 (inc illeg)	an	8
G	-2	-5	-2	0	2	0	2	0	G	Accingimini filii potentes	WA 180 LA 300	an	8
G	-2	-5	-2	0	2	0	2	0	G	Benedictio et claritas	WA 162	an	8
G	-2	-5	-2	0	2	0	2	0	G	Christo datus est principatus	PM 45 OHS 831 WA 57 *LA 77	an	8

G	-2	-5	-2	0	2	0	2	0	G	Elegit Dominus virum de plebe	LA 331	an	8
G	-2	-5	-2	0	2	0	2	0	G	Hic est vir qui non est derelictus	PM 220	an	8
G	-2	-5	-2	0	2	0	2	0	G	Iste est qui ante Deum ... et omnis	WA 294 LA 539	an	8
G	-2	-5	-2	0	2	0	2	0	G	Manum suam aperuit inopi	AR 577^{22} [103] LU 262^{10} 1236	an	8
G	-2	-5	-2	0	2	0	2	0	G	Operamini non cibum	WA 100 *LA 155	an	8
G	-2	-5	-2	0	2	0	2	0	G	Pacificus vocabitur et thronus	AR 894^{1} LU 1715 *AM 1088	an	8
G	-2	-5	-2	0	2	0	2	0	G	Rex pacificus magnificatus	AR 259 LU 364 AM 236 *WA 26 LA 30	an	8
D	-2	-5	-2	0	2	0	2	3	D	Media nocte dominica	WA 402	an	2
D	-2	-5	-2	0	2	0	2	3	D	Quomodo fiet istud respondens	WA 302	re	1
G	-2	-5	-2	0	2	0	2	4	G	Vos vocatis me magister	WA 214 *SYG 133	an	8
G	-2	-5	-2	0	2	0	3	2	G	Qui major est	WA 94	an	8
G	-2	-5	-2	0	2	0	5	4	G	Kyrie ad lib. IX O pater excelse	MEL #86 GR 82* LU 85		8
D	-2	-5	-2	0	2	3	0	2	D	Angelorum esca nutrivisti	AR 530 LU 940 *AM 550	an	2
D	-2	-5	-2	0	2	3	2	0		Animae fidelium quas assumpsisti Domine Jesu Christe	OTT 189 SYG 235	ofv	
D	-2	-5	-2	0	2	3	2	0	D	Venite populi ad collaudandum	WA 262	inv	2
D	-2	-5	-2	0	2	3	5	3	D	Sancte Martine Christi	LA 485	re	2
D	-2	-5	-2	0	2	3	5	3	D	Sanctus	THAN #196		2
D	-2	-5	-2	0	2	3	5	3	D	Sanctus	THAN #197		2
D	-2	-5	-2	0	3	0	-2	0	D	Ecce vere Israelita	LR 195 LA 533 *WA 390	re	2
D	-2	-5	-2	0	3	0	2	0	D	Rex gloriose martyrum	ST 404	hy	2
D	-2	-5	-2	0	3	0	3	2	D	Magno canentes annua	ST 285	hy	2
D	-2	-5	-2	0	3	2	0	-2	D	Operibus sanctis Nicholaus	WA 239	re	2
D	-2	-5	-2	0	3	2	0	2	D	Dilectus meus candidus	AR 674 LU 1423	an	2
a	-2	-5	-2	0	3	2	0	2	D	Kyrie	MEL #19		
D	-2	-5	-2	0	3	2	0	2	D	Sint lumbi vestri ... et vos	PM 228 LR 202 LA 535 WA 430	re	1
a	-2	-5	-2	0	3	2	0	3	G	O beate Joannes corona	VP 210	re	7
d	-2	-5	-2	0	3	2	3	5		Magnus Dominus ... in civitate	GR 340 LU 1014 *SYG 242	alv	
D	-2	-5	-2	0	3	2	3	5	D	Sancte N. confessor	WA 428	re	2
D	-2	-5	-2	0	3	5	3	2	D	Terribilis est locus iste	GR [71] LU 1250 *SYG 263 GB 172^{v} GS 174	int	2
D	-2	-5	-2	0	3	7	3	2	D	Agnus Dei	SCH #239		2
G	-2	-5	-2	0	5	2	0	4	G	Quam felix es Gallia	PM 347	re	8
D	-2	-5	-2	0	5	3	5	7	D	Nomine aeterno haereditavit	WA 251	an	2

D	-2	-5	-2	0	5	7	3	2	D	Kyrie ad lib. VII splendor aeternae	MEL #192 GR 81* LU 84		1
D	-2	-5	-2	0	5	7	3	2	D	Sanctus	THAN #195		2
G	-2	-5	-2	2	-2	0	-2	2	G	Sanctus	THAN #89		8
G	-2	-5	-2	2	-2	0	2	0	G	Sancte Paule apostole praedicator ... ad Deum	AR 598 612 755 LU 1350 AM 796 824 940 *LA 430 WA 266		8
G	-2	-5	-2	2	-2	0	2	4	G	Ista est speciosa electa	WA 365	an	8
G	-2	-5	-2	2	0	-2	0	-2	D	Rector potens verax Deus	ST 162	hy	2
G	-2	-5	-2	2	0	-2	0	2	G	Martyr Dei qui unicum	ST 313	hy	2
G	-2	-5	-2	2	0	-2	0	5	G	Volens Noe scire	WA 77	re	8
G	-2	-5	-2	2	0	2	0	2	G	Iste est de primoribus theologis	WA 291	an	8
D	-2	-5	0	-2	3	0	2	0		Fiant aures tuae intendentes De profundis	OTT 126 *GB 265 *SYG 258	ofv	
G	-2	-5	0	2	0	-2	-3	-5	G	Festum nunc celebre magnaque gaudia	ST 389	hy	8
a	-2	-4	-7	-5	-4	-2	0	-2	G	Jam sol recedit igneus	AR 206 516 LU 312 915	hy	8
a	-2	-4	-7	-5	-4	-2	0	-2	G	Tu trinitatis unitas	AR 520 LU 907	hy	8
a	-2	-4	-7	-4	-5	-4	-2	0	G	Lucis creator optime	ST 86	hy	8
a	-2	-4	-7	-4	-5	-4	-2	0	G	O lux beata trinitas	ST 85	hy	8
a	-2	-4	-7	-4	-5	-4	-2	0	G	Tibi laus perennis auctor	ST 483	hy	8
a	-2	-4	-7	-4	0	-4	-2	0	G	O lux beata trinitas	ST 252	hy	8
a	-2	-4	-5	-9	-5	-2	-4	-5		Benedicamus patrem et filium cum	GR [85] LU 1274	alv	
a	-2	-4	-5	-9	-5	-2	-4	-5		Ego sum pastor bonus et cognosco	GR 47 264 LU 818	alv	
a	-2	-4	-5	-9	-5	-2	-4	-5		Ego sum pastor bonus qui pasco	SYG 165	alv	
a	-2	-4	-5	-9	-5	-2	-4	-5		Haec est virgo sapiens quam	GS 228	alv	
a	-2	-4	-5	-9	-5	-2	-4	-5		Mirabilis Dominus noster	GR 414 GS 216 SYG 176 *GB 268^{v}	alv	
a	-2	-4	-5	-7	-9	-7	-5	-7		Ecce Dominus in fortitudine Ecce Dominus veniet	LA 19	rev	
a	-2	-4	-5	-7	-5	-4	-7	-9		Lacrimosa dies illa Libera me de morte	WA 438	rev	
a	-2	-4	-5	-7	-5	-4	-2	0	E	Agnus Dei	SCH #65		1
a	-2	-4	-5	-7	-4	-7	-9	-7		Stephanus Dei gratia plenus Impetum fecerunt	WA 34	rev	
a	-2	-4	-5	-7	-4	-5	-7	-9		Gloria Deo patri cuncta Impetum fecerunt	WA 34	rev	
a	-2	-4	-5	-7	-4	-2	-4	-5	[D]	Agnus Dei	SCH #64		1
a	-2	-4	-5	-7	-2	0	-2	0	E	Deus deorum Domine	ST 247	hy	4
a	-2	-4	-5	-7	-2	0	-2	0	E	Deus tuorum militum	ST 243	hy	4
a	-2	-4	-5	-7	-2	0	3	0	E	Deus creator omnium	ST 254	hy	4

a	-2	-4	-5	-4	-5	0	2	3	[D]	Agnus Dei	SCH #63		1
a	-2	-4	-5	-4	-2	-7	-5	-4	D	Assunt festa jubilaea	ST 140	hy	1
a	-2	-4	-5	-4	-2	-5	-4	-5	D	Alleluia	AM 43	an	1
a	-2	-4	-5	-4	-2	-5	-2	-5	D	Et omnis mansuetudinis	LA 93	an	1
a	-2	-4	-5	-4	-2	-4	-5	-7	D	Agnus Dei	SCH #53		1
a	-2	-4	-5	-4	-2	-4	-5	-7	D	Dei fide qua vivimus	ST 187	hy	2
a	-2	-4	-5	-2	-4	-5	-7	-9		Iterum videbo vos et gaudebit	SYG 166	alv	
d	-2	-4	-5	-2	0	-2	0	2		Dilexit justitiam et odisti Fuit sacra	WA 433	rev	
a	-2	-4	-5	-2	0	2	0	-7		Quem dilexerat viventem Valde mane	WA 338	rev	
a	-2	-4	-5	-2	0	3	5	3		De medio autem ejus In visione Dei	WA 372	rev	
a	-2	-4	-2	-7	-5	-9	-5	-7		Mixtum rorem balsami Felix Maria	PM 169 *WA 337	rev	
a	-2	-4	-2	-7	-4	-5	-7	-9	D	Clama ne cesses	LA 126	an	1
a	-2	-4	-2	-4	-5	-9	-7	-5		Secundum quod dictum est Quem vidistis	WA 30	rev	
e	-2	-4	-2	-4	-5	-7	-9	-4	a	Ad perennis vitae fontem	ST 463	hy	1
a	-2	-4	-2	-4	-5	-7	-5	-9		Timentibus Deum nihil Deum time	WA 88	rev	
a	-2	-4	-2	-4	-2	0	-2	1	D	Sapientiam sanctorum ... nuntiet	GR [25] LU 1166 SYG 189 GB 194v GS 211	int	1
a	-2	-4	-2	0	-7	-5	-4	-2	G	Kyrie puerorum caterva (etc)	MEL #24		
a	-2	-4	-2	0	-7	-5	-4	-2	G	Kyrie VII rex splendens	GR 25* LU 34		8
a	-2	-4	-2	0	-7	-4	-5	-7	D	Gloriosa magnifici voluntas	WA 287	an	1
a	-2	-4	-2	0	-7	-4	-2	-5	D	Christi miles pretiosus	ST 84	hy	2
a	-2	-4	-2	0	-7	-4	-2	-5	D	Crux fidelis inter omnes ... sustinens	ST 228	hy	2
a	-2	-4	-2	0	-7	-4	-2	-5	D	Pange lingua gloriosi proelium	ST 227	hy	2
a	-2	-4	-2	0	-7	-4	-2	-5	D	Sancte Dei pretiose protomartyr	ST 82	hy	2
a	-2	-4	-2	0	-7	-2	-4	-7	D	Nunc sancte nobis spiritus	AR 461 LU 808	hy	1
a	-2	-4	-2	0	-5	-2	-4	-7	D	Deus tuorum militum	ST 61	hy	2
a	-2	-4	-2	0	-4	-5	-7	-4	D	Caritatis gratia repletus Ecce jam coram te	PM 31 VP 79	rev	
E	-2	-4	-2	0	-4	-2	1	0	E	Factum est ut quaedam	WA 326	an	4
E	-2	-4	-2	0	-4	-2	1	3	E	Facies et pennas	WA 373	re	4
a	-2	-4	-2	0	-2	-5	-4	-7	D	Gloria XIII	GR 45* LU 51		1
a	-2	-4	-2	0	-2	-5	-2	-5	E	Benedicimus Deum caeli	GR 310 LU 912 *SYG 262 *GB 215v GS c	co	4

a	-2	-4	-2	0	-2	-5	-2	-5	E	Si ambulavero in medio umbrae	GR 42**	co	4
a	-2	-4	-2	0	-2	-4	-5	-7	D	Misericordia et veritas praecedent	AR 179 LU 279R	an	1
a	-2	-4	-2	0	-2	-4	-5	-4	D	Gloria	BOS #18		I
a	-2	-4	-2	0	-2	-4	-2	-7	D	Kyrie	MEL #23		
a	-2	-4	-2	0	-2	-4	-2	-4	D	Viri impii dixerunt opprimamus	OHS 184 (nm) WA 116	re	1
a	-2	-4	-2	0	-2	-4	-2	0	D	Gloria laus et honor	ST 484	hy	1
a	-2	-4	-2	0	-2	-4	-2	0	G	Nos autem gloriari ... in quo	SYG 142	an	8
E	-2	-4	-2	0	-2	-4	-2	0	D	Placebo Domino in regione	LA 560	an	2
a	-2	-4	-2	0	-2	-4	0	-2	G	Et dicebant unde huic	AR 325 LU 475	an	8
a	-2	-4	-2	0	-2	-4	0	2	G	Hymnum cantate nobis	LA 96 WA 67	an	8
a	-2	-4	-2	0	-2	-4	0	3	G	Iste sanctus pro lege Dei	AR 334 577[12] [15] LU 262 1123 AM 639 736 LA 521	an	8
a	-2	-4	-2	0	-2	-4	0	3	G	Nocte surgentes vigilemus omnes	ST 250	hy	8
a	-2	-4	-2	0	-2	0	-4	0	G	Vox laetitiae in tabernaculis	PM 221	an	8
a	-2	-4	-2	0	-2	0	-2	-4		Agnus Dei	SCH #62		
a	-2	-4	-2	0	-2	0	-2	-4		Da nobis Domine virtutum Haec tua sunt	WA 316	rev	
a	-2	-4	-2	0	-2	0	-2	-4	G	Exaudi Domine orationem meam	AR [177] LU 1801 AM 1162 *WA 438 LA 559	an	8
a	-2	-4	-2	0	-2	0	-2	0	G	Postquam ergo lavit	SYG 133	an	8
b	-2	-4	-2	0	-2	0	1	0	b	Gloria I	BOS #12 GR 5* LU 16		4
E	-2	-4	-2	0	-2	0	1	3	E	Adoremus crucis signaculum	WA 371 *LA 464	an	4
a	-2	-4	-2	0	-2	0	2	0	D	Gloria	BOS #19		I
a	-2	-4	-2	0	-2	0	3	0	G	Alleluia	AR 31 LU 239 AM 32 87	an	8
a	-2	-4	-2	0	-2	0	3	2		Erat enim valde compatiens Confessor Dei Nicholaus	WA 239	rev	
a	-2	-4	-2	0	-2	0	3	2	G	Lux aeterna luceat eis	GR 102* LU 1815 SYG 236 GB 266v GS 233	co	8
a	-2	-4	-2	0	-2	1	0	3	D	Gloria II	GR 8* LU 19		1
E	-2	-4	-2	0	1	-2	0	-2	E	Magnus Dominus ... et sapientiae	LR 340	re	4
a	-2	-4	-2	0	1	-2	1	0	a	Clamavi et exaudivit	AM 111	an	ir
a	-2	-4	-2	0	1	-2	1	0	a	Et omnis mansuetudinis	AM 139 140	an	ir
a	-2	-4	-2	0	1	-2	1	0	a	Speret Israel in Domino	AM 139	an	ir
E	-2	-4	-2	0	1	0	-2	0	C	Conclusit vias meas	LA 176 *WA 115	re	6
E	-2	-4	-2	0	1	0	-2	1	D	Christe qui lux es et dies	ST 5	hy	2
E	-2	-4	-2	0	1	0	-2	1	D	Te lucis ante terminum	AM 337	hy	2
E	-2	-4	-2	0	1	3	1	0	D	Conserva me Domine	LA 102	an	2

E	-2	-4	-2	0	1	3	1	0	E	Ecclesiae principatum	WA 311	an	4
E	-2	-4	-2	0	1	3	1	0	E	Splendor paternae gloriae	ST 2	hy	4
b	-2	-4	-2	0	1	3	1	0		Ut caelestis regni Miles Christi	WA 391	rev	
E	-2	-4	-2	0	1	3	5	3	E	Sanctifica nos Domine	SYG 142	an	4
a	-2	-4	-2	0	2	0	-7	-5		Requiem aeternam dona eis Domine Congregati sunt	AR 197*	rev	
a	-2	-4	-2	0	2	0	-2	0		Cumque complesset apostolus Apparuit caro	WA 17	rev	
a	-2	-4	-2	0	3	-2	-4	-2		Media nocte clamor factus Audivi vocem	PM 236 *WA 394	rev	
a	-2	-4	-2	0	3	2	0	-2	D	Beati mundo corde quoniam ipsi	WA 414	an	1
a	-2	-4	-2	0	3	2	0	-2	G	Virginis proles opifexque matris	ST 202	hy	8
a	-2	-4	-2	0	3	2	3	2	G	Nunc scimus quia scis	WA 146	an	8
a	-2	-4	-2	0	3	2	3	5	G	Sub altare Dei audivi voces	PM 35 LA 57 WA 43	re	7
E	-2	-4	-2	0	3	5	3	1	E	Agnus Dei X	GR 38* LU 45		4
a	-2	-4	-2	0	3	5	3	1	a	Agnus Dei	SCH #61		5
E	-2	-4	-2	0	3	5	3	1	E	Agnus Dei	SCH #186		4
b	-2	-4	-2	0	3	5	3	1		Ut ad videndam faciem Perfecto corde	WA 336	rev	
E	-2	-4	-2	1	-2	1	0	[0]	E	Et omnis mansuetudinis	WA 66	an	4
E	-2	-4	-2	1	0	-2	0	-2	D	Convocatis Jesus duodecim ... misit ... egressi	WA 371	an	1
E	-2	-4	-2	1	0	1	-2	0	E	Magnus Dominus et magna virtus	WA 159	re	4
a	-2	-4	-2	1	0	1	3	1		Misericors et miserator et juste Rogamus te Domine	VP 241	rev	
E	-2	-4	-2	1	3	1	0	-4	E	Splendor paternae gloriae	ST 183	hy	4
E	-2	-4	-2	1	3	1	0	-2	E	Claris psallendo vocibus	ST 304	hy	4
E	-2	-4	-2	3	5	1	0	-2	D	Ante luciferum genitus ... nasci	WA 29 *LA 37	an	2
a	-2	-4	0	-2	-4	-5	-7	-5	D	Alleluia: Martinus signi potens	SYG 227	al	1
a	-2	-4	0	-2	-4	-2	-4	-5	D	Parce Domine parce ... ne in aeternum	AR 93* LU 1868		1
a	-2	-4	0	-2	-4	-2	0	3	G	Jussu impii Paschasii	WA 245	re	7
a	-2	-4	0	-2	-4	0	-2	0	E	Surrexit enim sicut dixit	WA 138	an	4
a	-2	-4	0	-2	-4	0	3	-2	G	Summe largitor praemii	ST 285	hy	8
a	-2	-4	0	-2	0	-2	0	-2	E	Sanctus	THAN #43		4
a	-2	-4	0	-2	0	1	-2	0	F	Ego sum Raphael angelus	AR 890 LU 1698	an	5
a	-2	-4	0	-2	0	2	3	0		In laetitia et exsultatione Adducentur regi	GB 45	trv	
E	-2	-4	0	-2	0	3	0	-2	E	Omnium Christe pariter tuorum	ST 64	hy	4
E	-2	-4	0	1	3	1	0	-2	D	Sanctus	THAN #155		2

a	-2	-4	0	3	0	-2	0	2		Delicta juventutis meae Congregati sunt	AR 197*	rev	
a	-2	-4	0	3	0	3	-2	-5		Nunc ergo ora pro nobis	GR 39**	alv	
E	-2	-4	0	3	1	-2	-4	-2	E	Deus tuorum militum	AR [25]	hy	4
E	-2	-4	0	3	1	-2	-4	-2	E	Fortem virili pectore	AR [100] LU 1234	hy	4
E	-2	-4	0	3	1	-2	-4	-2	E	Invicte martyr unicum	AR [32]	hy	4
E	-2	-4	0	3	1	-2	-4	-2	E	Jesu corona celsior	AR [80]	hy	4
E	-2	-4	0	3	1	-2	-4	-2	E	Jesu corona virginum	AR [91] LU 1213	hy	4
E	-2	-4	0	3	1	-2	-4	-2	E	Jesu redemptor omnium	AR [60]	hy	4
E	-2	-4	0	3	1	-2	-4	-2	E	Rex gloriose martyrum	AR [27] LU 1145	hy	4
E	-2	-4	0	3	1	-2	-4	-2	E	Te splendor et virtus patris	AR 707 LU 1463	hy	4
a	-2	-4	0	3	1	0	-2	3		Orans jacentem suscitat Servus Dei Benedictus	WA 299	rev	
a	-2	-4	0	3	1	0	1	0	F	Kyrie	MEL #17		
a	-2	-4	0	3	2	-2	0	-2	G	Juravi dicit Dominus	LA 19 WA 23	re	8
a	-2	-4	0	3	2	0	-2	3	F	Adveniente Petro	WA 326	an	5
a	-2	-4	0	3	2	3	0	-2	G	Ecce fidelis servus et prudens	AR 658 LU 1407 AM 846	an	8
a	-2	-4	0	3	5	3	0	-2	F	Agnus Dei	SCH #51		5
a	-2	-4	0	3	5	3	0	1		Divinum munus votum praevenit Unam quam petiit	PM 266	rev	
a	-2	-4	0	3	5	3	0	3	F	Labia eorum salutarem	WA 372	an	5
a	-2	-4	0	3	5	3	0	3	F	O insignissime pater	WA 284	an	5
E	-2	-4	0	3	5	3	1	3	E	Conditor alme siderum	ST 215 255	hy	4
a	-2	-4	0	3	5	3	1	3	F	Dignum namque est	WA 364	an	5
a	-2	-4	0	3	5	3	1	3	F	Ideo petivi inducias	WA 247	an	5
E	-2	-4	0	3	5	3	1	3	E	Jesu redemptor omnium	ST 387	hy	4
a	-2	-4	0	3	5	3	5	3	F	Ascendit haec virga Jessea	WA 359	an	5
a	-2	-4	0	3	5	3	5	7	F	Agnus Dei	SCH #52		5
a	-2	-4	0	3	5	3	5	7	F	Agnus Dei	SCH #60		5
a	-2	-4	0	3	5	3	5	7	F	Merito sanctitatis et gradu	WA 294	re	5
a	-2	-4	0	3	5	3	5	7	F	O sacrum convivium	AR 535 98* LU 959 AM 555 VP 9 4*	an	5
a	-2	-4	0	3	5	3	5	7	F	Te jure laudant	WA 162	an	5
a	-2	-4	0	3	5	3	5	8	F	Ex quo omnia per quem omnia	AR 519 LU 915 AM 536 *WA 159	an	5
a	-2	-4	0	3	5	3	5	8	F	Vincenti dabo manna	AR 531 LU 940 AM 551	an	5
E	-2	-4	0	3	5	7	5	3	a	Cum ambularent animalia	WA 374	re	1
a	-2	-4	0	3	5	7	5	3	F	Unam quam petiit virgo	PM 266	re	5

E	-2	-4	1	3	5	3	1	3	E	Conditor alme siderum	ST 170	hy	4
E	-2	-4	3	1	0	8	3	1	C	Kyrie	MEL #156		
a	-2	-4	3	2	3	5	3	2	F	Confitebor nomini tuo Domine	AR 160 LU 298	an	5
a	-2	-4	3	5	8	7	3	7	F	Pande tuis caelis	WA 277	an	5
d	-2	-3	-7	-5	-3	-2	0	-2		Sancti tui Domine florebunt	SYG 222	alv	
g	-2	-3	-5	-7	-5	-3	0	2		Ex te namque egredietur Dixit autem Dominus ad Abraham	WA 80	rev	
d	-2	-3	-5	-7	-3	-5	-7	-9	D	Jam lucis orto sidere	ST 142	hy	1
G	-2	-3	-5	-7	-2	0	2	0	G	Dixerunt impii opprimamus virum	AR 429 OHS 247 284 *AM 408 *WA 115 LA 186	an	8
d	-2	-3	-5	-7	-2	0	2	0		Jam per terras Magne pater Nicholae	WA 241	rev	
d	-2	-3	-5	-7	-2	0	2	5	[G]	Agnus Dei	SCH #11		7
G	-2	-3	-5	-7	-2	0	3	2	G	Quem terra pontus aethera	ST 298	hy	8
d	-2	-3	-5	-3	-7	-3	-7	-9	F	Sanctus	THAN #5		7
G	-2	-3	-5	-3	-2	-5	-7	-3	D	Tibi Christe splendor patris	ST 399	hy	2
G	-2	-3	-5	-3	-2	-5	-7	-2		Tibi Christe splendor patris	ST 461	hy	
G	-2	-3	-5	-3	-2	-3	-7	-5	G	Agnus Dei	SCH #104		4
G	-2	-3	-5	-3	-2	-3	-5	-7	G	Vox clara ecce intonat	ST 408	hy	8
G	-2	-3	-5	-3	-2	0	-2	2	G	Gloria V	GR 18* LU 28		8
D	-2	-3	-5	-3	-2	0	2	0	[D]	Agnus Dei	SCH #245		2
G	-2	-3	-5	-3	-2	0	2	0	G	Gloria	BOS #25		IV
G	-2	-3	-5	-3	-2	0	2	0	G	Miserere mei Deus secundum	AR 75	an	8
G	-2	-3	-5	-3	-2	2	0	-2	G	Beata Dei genitrix Maria virgo	AR 923 LU 1754 *AM 714	an	8
G	-2	-3	-5	-3	-2	2	0	-2	G	Beata Dei genitrix Maria virgo ... ora	AR [130] *WA 361 *LA 449	an	8
d	-2	-3	-5	-3	0	-7	-2	-3	D	Juste judex Jesu Christe	ST 498	hy	1
c	-2	-3	-5	-3	[0	0	0	0]	E	Kyrie	MEL #7		
G	-2	-3	-5	-2	-5	-3	-2	0	G	Mirabile mysterium declaratur	AR 296 *AM 274 717 *WA 51 *LA 65	an	8
d	-2	-3	-5	-2	0	-2	-5	-7	d	Adstemus mente vigili	ST 376	hy	2
G	-2	-3	-5	-2	0	2	0	2	G	Agnus Dei	SCH #103		8
G	-2	-3	-5	-2	0	2	0	2	G	Domine Deus meus magnificatus	AR 200 LU 279^{T}	an	8
G	-2	-3	-5	-2	0	2	0	2	G	Sanctus	THAN #88		8
G	-2	-3	-5	-2	2	-2	0	2	G	Jam Christe sol justitiae	ST 89	hy	8
G	-2	-3	-5	-2	2	0	-2	0	G	A patre unigenite	ST 81	hy	8
G	-2	-3	-5	-2	2	0	-2	0	G	Christe redemptor omnium ex patre	ST 81	hy	8

G	-2	-3	-5	-2	2	0	-2	0	G	Deus tuorum militum	AM 254	hy	8
G	-2	-3	-5	-2	2	0	-2	0	G	Exsultet caelum laudibus	AM 257	hy	8
G	-2	-3	-5	-2	2	0	-2	0	G	Hostis Herodes impie	ST 180	hy	8
G	-2	-3	-5	-2	2	0	-2	0	G	Intende qui regis Israel	ST 30	hy	8
G	-2	-3	-5	-2	2	0	-2	0	G	Jam ter quaternis trahitur	ST 88	hy	8
G	-2	-3	-5	-2	2	0	-2	0	G	Jesu redemptor omnium	AM 268	hy	8
G	-2	-3	-5	-2	2	0	-2	0	G	Martyr Dei qui unicum	AM 251	hy	8
G	-2	-3	-5	-2	2	0	-2	0	G	Nunc sancte nobis spiritus	AR 268 LU 407	hy	8
G	-2	-3	-5	-2	2	0	-2	0	G	Procedat e thalamo suo	ST 30	hy	8
G	-2	-3	-5	-2	2	0	-2	0	G	Salvete flores martyrum	AM 261	hy	8
G	-2	-3	-5	-2	2	0	-2	0	G	Sic ter quaternis trahitur	ST 188	hy	8
G	-2	-3	-5	-2	2	0	-2	0	G	Signifer invictissime	LR 443	hy	8
G	-2	-3	-5	-2	2	0	-2	0	G	Surgit Jesus a coena	SYG 133	an	8
G	-2	-3	-5	-2	2	0	-2	0	G	Te lucis ante terminum	AR 263 LU 367	hy	8
G	-2	-3	-5	-2	2	0	-2	0	G	Veni redemptor gentium	ST 81	hy	8
c	-2	-3	-5	0	-2	0	-2	-3		Recordatus Dominus Noe Peractis centum	WA 77	rev	
G	-2	-3	-5	0	2	0	2	4	G	Alme dictatis resonante gratis	ST 67	hy	8
c	-2	-3	-5	0	2	0	2	4		Dignis ergo veneremur Praesul Christi	WA 250	rev	
c	-2	-3	-5	0	2	4	2	0	c	Consecrandus ad altare	WA 250	re	6
D	-2	-3	-2	-5	-7	-2	0	3	D	Magno canentes annua	ST 285	hy	2
d	-2	-3	-2	-5	-7	-2	0	3	d	O gloriosa domina	ST 223	hy	2
d	-2	-3	-2	-5	-7	-2	0	3	d	Quem terra pontus aethera	ST 223	hy	2
G	-2	-3	-2	-5	-7	-2	0	3	G	Vox clara ecce intonat	ST 216	hy	2
G	-2	-3	-2	-5	-3	-2	0	2	G	Alleluia: juravi et statui custodire	GR 73**	al	8
G	-2	-3	-2	-5	-3	-2	0	2		Surrexit pastor bonus ... grege	GS 128	alv	
c	-2	-3	-2	-5	-3	0	2	4	c	Ave regina caelorum ave	AR 66 OHS 174 LU 274 AM 175 *WA 360	an	6
G	-2	-3	-2	-5	-3	0	2	4		Juravi et statui custodire	GR 73**	alv	
G	-2	-3	-2	-5	-2	-3	-2	0	E	Benedictus Dominus Deus Israel	AR 75	an	4
G	-2	-3	-2	-5	-2	2	0	-2	G	Benedicamus Domino VI[b]	AR 62*		8
d	-2	-3	-2	-3	-5	-3	-5	-2		Proba me Domine Lavabo inter innocentes	SYG 86	ofv	
G	-2	-3	-2	-3	-5	-3	-5	-2		Quia oblitus sum manducare Domine exaudi	OTT 53 SYG 128	ofv	
G	-2	-3	-2	-3	-2	0	-2	0	G	Rex autem David	WA 165 *LA 275	an	8

G	-2	-3	-2	-3	-2	0	2	0	G	Quem dicunt homines	WA 281	an	8
d	-2	-3	-2	0	-3	-2	-5	0	d	Agnus Dei	SCH #10		7
G	-2	-3	-2	0	-2	-5	-7	-8	G	Apostolorum passio	ST 12	hy	8
G	-2	-3	-2	0	-2	-5	-7	-8	G	Post Petrum primum principem	ST 7	hy	8
G	-2	-3	-2	0	-2	-5	-7	-3	G	Evangelista fulgidus	ST 141	hy	8
G	-2	-3	-2	0	-2	-3	-5	-3	G	Agnus Dei	SCH #108		1
G	-2	-3	-2	0	-2	-3	-5	-3	E	Credo V	GR 69* LU 90		4
d	-2	-3	-2	0	-2	-3	-5	-3	D	Et in terra	BOS #53		
G	-2	-3	-2	0	-2	-3	-5	2	E	Credo VI	GR 72* LU 92		4
G	-2	-3	-2	0	-2	-3	-2	-5	G	Rex Christe factor omnium	ST 228 287	hy	8
G	-2	-3	-2	0	-2	-3	-2	0	C	Ecce nomen Domini Emmanuel	AR 149* PM 29 VP 72	an	5
G	-2	-3	-2	0	-2	[0	0	0]	F	Nunc sancte nobis spiritus	ST 328	hy	6
G	-2	-3	-2	0	-2	0	2	0	G	Domine quando veneris judicare	PM 319 AR [160] LU 1787 LA 554 *WA 437	re	8
G	-2	-3	-2	0	-2	0	2	0	G	Oravit Jacob et dixit	LA 140 *WA 92	re	8
d	-2	-3	-2	0	-2	0	2	0		Precibus tuis sanctis O venerabiliter	WA 238	rev	
D	-2	-3	-2	0	-2	0	2	5	D	Aeterna Christi munera et martyrum	ST 44	hy	2
G	-2	-3	-2	0	-2	0	2	5	G	Gentis Polonae gloria	AR 886 LU 1697	hy	8
D	-2	-3	-2	0	-2	0	2	5	D	Jam surgit hora tertia	ST 35	hy	2
G	-2	-3	-2	0	-2	0	2	5	G	Jesu corona celsior	AR [75] AM 672	hy	8
G	-2	-3	-2	0	-2	0	2	5	G	Matris sub almae numine	AR 640 LU 1388	hy	8
G	-2	-3	-2	0	-2	0	2	5	G	Te deprecante corporum	AR 887	hy	8
D	-2	-3	-2	0	-2	0	2	5	D	Traduntur igni martyres	ST 44	hy	2
G	-2	-3	-2	0	-2	2	0	2		Fac nos innocuam Joseph	GR 486 LU 1441	alv	
D	-2	-3	-2	0	-2	2	5	7	D	Alleluia: architectus Deus fundavit	GB 174	al	2
d	-2	-3	-2	0	-2	3	2	-2	G	Summe Dei confessor	WA 241	re	7
d	-2	-3	-2	0	2	-2	0	-2	G	In tribulatione invocavi Dominum	AR 409 AM 389 WA 108 LA 171	an	7
d	-2	-3	-2	0	2	0	-2	-5	G	Angelus Domini apparuit in somnis Joseph	AR 320 LU 467	an	7
d	-2	-3	-2	0	2	0	-2	-3	G	Agatha laetissime et glorianter	PM 138 LA 356	an	7
d	-2	-3	-2	0	2	0	-2	-3	G	Animam de corpore quam assumpsisti	LA 560	an	7
D	-2	-3	-2	0	2	0	-2	-3	D	Christe sanctorum decus angelorum	ST 119	hy	2
d	-2	-3	-2	0	2	0	-2	-3	G	Si iniquitates observaveris	LA 560	an	7
d	-2	-3	-2	0	2	0	-2	-3	G	Undecim discipuli in Galilaea	AR 451 AM 464 OHS 815 WA 135 LA 222	an	7

d	-2	-3	-2	0	2	0	-2	0	G	Angeli archangeli ... laudate	AR 857 LU 1660 AM 1059 WA 384 LA 472	an	7
d	-2	-3	-2	0	2	0	-2	0	G	Angelus archangelus Michael	WA 380 LA 472	an	7
d	-2	-3	-2	0	2	0	-2	0	G	Fac Deus potentiam	AM 154 *LA 99	an	7
d	-2	-3	-2	0	2	0	-2	0	G	Fecit Deus potentiam	AR 162	an	7
D	-2	-3	-2	0	2	0	-2	0	D	Intende qui regis Israel	ST 8	hy	2
G	-2	-3	-2	0	2	0	-2	0	G	Jam Christe sol justitiae	ST 380	hy	8
G	-2	-3	-2	0	2	0	-2	0	G	Si iniquitates observaveris	AR [144] LU 1779 AM 1152 WA 435	an	8
G	-2	-3	-2	0	2	0	-2	0	G	Ut nox tenebris obsita	ST 384	hy	8
G	-2	-3	-2	0	2	0	-2	2	G	Gaudeamus universi ecclesiae	WA 287	an	8
G	-2	-3	-2	0	2	0	-2	2	G	Peto Domine ut de vinculo	LA 293	an	8
d	-2	-3	-2	0	2	0	2	-2	G	Praecedam vos in Galilaeam	AR 465 AM 478 LA 222 *WA 131 136	an	7 8
G	-2	-3	-2	0	2	0	2	0	G	Multos hic sanavit	WA 293	an	8
G	-2	-3	-2	0	2	0	2	0	G	Non me permittas	WA 237 *LA 500	an	8
G	-2	-3	-2	0	2	0	2	0	G	Pastores dicite quidnam	WA 48 LA 40	an	8
G	-2	-3	-2	0	2	0	2	0	G	Puer quidam parvulus	WA 298 *LA 375	an	8
d	-2	-3	-2	0	2	0	2	0	G	Respice cuncta quia tua sunt	GB 160^v	an	7
d	-2	-3	-2	0	2	0	2	0	G	Sacram praesentis diei	WA 257	re	7
G	-2	-3	-2	0	2	0	2	4	G	Alleluia: nimis honorati sunt	SYG 207 *GS y	al	8
c	-2	-3	-2	0	2	0	2	4	c	Benedicens ergo Deus	WA 78	re	6
c	-2	-3	-2	0	2	0	2	4	c	Elegit eos ex omni	WA 372	an	6
G	-2	-3	-2	0	2	0	2	4		Hodie Maria virgo caelos ascendit	SYG 216 *GS 195	alv	
G	-2	-3	-2	0	2	0	2	4		Modicum et non videbitis me dicit	SYG 166 *GB 273^v *GS 128	alv	
G	-2	-3	-2	0	2	0	2	4	G	Sanctus	THAN #87		8
G	-2	-3	-2	0	2	0	2	5	G	Aeterna Christi munera	ST 16	hy	8
G	-2	-3	-2	0	2	0	2	5	G	Deus tuorum militum	ST 16	hy	8
G	-2	-3	-2	0	2	0	2	5	G	Jam surgit hora tertia	ST 4	hy	8
G	-2	-3	-2	0	2	0	4	2		Nimis honorati sunt amici tui	SYG 207 *GS y	alv	
G	-2	-3	-2	0	2	4	0	2		Sanctus	THAN #86		8
G	-2	-3	-2	2	-2	-5	-2	-3	E	Speret Israel in Domino	WA 66	an	4
G	-2	-3	-2	2	0	-2	0	2	G	O sol salutis intimis	AR 366	hy	8
d	-2	-3	0	-2	-3	0	2	-2	G	Domine labia mea aperies	AR 378 AM 352 WA 93 LA 141	an	7
d	-2	-3	0	-2	-3	0	2	-2	G	Posuit signum in faciem	WA 253 *LA 332	an	7
G	-2	-3	0	-2	-3	0	2	0	E	Semel juravi in sancto meo	GR [6] LU 1132 *SYG 209 *GB 211^v GS 191	co	4

d	-2	-3	0	2	-2	-5	-7	-5	G	Qui vicerit dabo ei	GR 512 LU 1485	co	7
d	-2	-3	0	2	-2	0	-2	-3	G	Dedit pater penitenti	WA 95	an	7
d	-2	-3	0	2	-2	0	-2	0	G	Laetabitur justus in Domino	AR 188	an	7
d	-2	-3	0	2	-2	0	-2	0	G	Laetabitur justus in Domino ... laudabuntur	LR 153	an	7
G	-2	-3	0	2	0	2	-2	0	E	Ego dilecto meo et dilectus meus	GR 629 LU 1692	co	4
G	-2	-3	0	2	0	2	-2	0	E	Feci judicium et justitiam	GR [59] LU 1224 *SYG 40 GB 43v GS 230	co	4
d	-2	-3	0	2	0	2	-2	0	b	Tollite hostias et introite	GR 374 LU 1058 *SYG 255 GB 261 GS 162	co	4
G	-2	-3	0	2	4	5	4	2	G	Sponsae Christi eximiae	ST 353	hy	8
a	-2	0	-7	-9	-5	-4	-5	-7	D	Gloria	BOS #16		I
G	-2	0	-7	-5	-7	-5	-2	0	G	Orbata pontifice	WA 284	re	8
G	-2	0	-7	-5	-2	0	-2	0	G	Clarissimis viris Marcelliano	LA 327	re	8
G	-2	0	-7	-5	-2	0	-2	0	G	Nascetur nobis parvulus	LA 21 382 *WA 24	re	8
G	-2	0	-7	-5	-2	0	2	0	G	Amen dico vobis nisi abundaverit	WA 188	an	8
G	-2	0	-7	-5	-2	0	2	0	G	Beati martyres Christi	WA 377 LA 409	an	8
G	-2	0	-7	-5	-2	0	2	0	G	Ecce concipies et paries	WA 302	re	8
G	-2	0	-7	-5	-2	0	2	0	G	Ecce dies veniunt	PM 20 *LA 10 WA 11	re	8
G	-2	0	-7	-5	-2	0	2	0	G	Ecclesiae sponsum virgo	PM 269	re	8
G	-2	0	-7	-5	-2	0	2	0	G	Fallax gratia et vana	LR 222	re	8
G	-2	0	-7	-5	-2	0	2	0	G	Gabriel angelus apparuit Zachariae	LA 407	re	8
G	-2	0	-7	-5	-2	0	2	0	G	Hi sancti viri ... Dionysii	WA 388	re	8
G	-2	0	-7	-5	-2	0	2	0	G	Hic est vir qui non est derelictus	LA 528 WA 415	an	8
G	-2	0	-7	-5	-2	0	2	0	G	Hic in annis adolescentiae	WA 290	re	8
G	-2	0	-7	-5	-2	0	2	0	G	Hoc est praeceptum meum	LA 510	re	8
G	-2	0	-7	-5	-2	0	2	0	G	Iste est de sublimibus caelorum	VP 259 LA 405	re	8
G	-2	0	-7	-5	-2	0	2	0		Veniant super me miserationes Levabo oculos	OTT 34 GB 67v SYG 76	ofv	
G	-2	0	-7	-5	-2	0	2	4	G	Archangeli Michaelis interventione	LA 470 *WA 383	re	8
G	-2	0	-7	-5	-2	2	0	-2	G	Quid me quaeritis interficere	LR 413	re	8
a	-2	0	-7	-4	-5	-4	-2	0	D	Sanctus	THAN #42		1
a	-2	0	-7	-4	-2	2	3	0	D	Kyrie summe pater rerum	MEL #22		
a	-2	0	-7	-4	0	-2	-5	-7	D	Kyrie	MEL #21		
a	-2	0	-7	0	-2	-4	-5	-4	D	Salve regina mater	AR 68 LU 276 *AM 176	an	1
D	-2	0	-5	-7	-5	-7	-5	-2		Si iniquitates observaveris De profundis	OTT 126 GB 265 SYG 258	ofv	

a	-2	0	-5	-4	-2	0	1	-2		Exaudi Domine justitiam meam Perfice gressus	OTT 90 *GB 58v *SYG 61	ofv	
G	-2	0	-5	-3	-2	0	2	0	G	Quae est ista quae progreditur	GR 399	co	8
d	-2	0	-5	-2	-3	-5	-2	-3	G	Laetare virgo mater alleluia	AR 875 LU 1674	an	7
G	-2	0	-5	-2	0	2	0	-2	G	Benedicamus patrem et filium cum ... laudemus	LA 477 *WA 160	re	8
G	-2	0	-5	-2	0	2	0	2	G	O crux benedicta quia in te	WA 308 *LA 395 *SYG 142	an	8
D	-2	0	-5	-2	0	3	2	0	D	Sanctas primitias offert genitus	PM 267	re	2
G	-2	0	-5	0	-2	0	-2	-3	E	Audi filia ... et obliviscere	PM 270	an	4
a	-2	0	-4	-7	-9	-7	-5	-4		Aemulor enim vos Dei	GS 227	alv	
a	-2	0	-4	-7	-9	-7	-5	-4		Quam magna multitudo	GR 628	alv	
a	-2	0	-4	-7	-4	-5	-7	-4	E	Aegypte noli flere	LA 14 *WA 14	re	4
a	-2	0	-4	-5	-9	-7	-4	-7	E	Ne derelinquas me ... pater	LA 279 *WA 169	re	4
a	-2	0	-4	-2	-7	-2	0	-2	D	Festa praesentis celebret diei	ST 152	hy	2
a	-2	0	-4	-2	0	-7	-4	-2	D	Praebe fili cor tuum	LA 280 *WA 170	re	1
a	-2	0	-4	-2	0	-2	-4	-5	D	Videns Dominus flentes sorores	SYG 108	co	1
E	-2	0	-4	-2	0	1	0	-2	E	Beata nobis gaudia	ST 354	hy	4
a	-2	0	-4	-2	0	1	3	1	F	Rector potens verax Deus	ST 317	hy	6
E	-2	0	-4	-2	0	3	5	3	C	Post Petrum primum principem	ST 424	hy	6
E	-2	0	-4	-2	0	3	5	3	C	Sacratum hoc templum Dei	ST 423	hy	6
a	-2	0	-4	0	-2	-4	-2	-4	D	Da mihi Domine sedium	LA 277 WA 169	re	1
a	-2	0	-4	0	-2	-4	-2	-4	D	Emitte Domine sapientiam	LA 276 WA 169	re	1
a	-2	0	-4	0	-2	-4	-2	-4	D	Peto Domine ut de vinculo	LR 423 LA 288 WA 176	re	1
E	-2	0	-4	0	3	1	0	-2	D	Spiritus qui a Patre procedit	SYG 186	co	2
a	-2	0	-4	0	3	2	0	3	F	Exsultavit spiritus meus	AR 123	an	5
a	-2	0	-4	0	3	5	3	5	F	Dominus aedificet nobis	AR 121 OHS 290 LU 287	an	5
a	-2	0	-4	0	3	5	3	5	F	Exsulta et lauda Floriacum	LR 372	re	5
a	-2	0	-4	0	3	5	3	5	F	Sanctum et terribile nomen	AR 298 LU 451 AM 276	an	5
d	-2	0	-3	-2	-5	-9	-7	-3	G	Ecce panis angelorum	AR 96*		7
G	-2	0	-3	0	-2	0	-2	-3	E	Peccavimus Domine peccavimus tibi	GB 154v	an	4
a	-2	0	-2	-7	-4	-5	-7	-9	D	Benedicamus Domino VIa	AR 62*		1
a	-2	0	-2	-5	-7	-2	0	3	F	Ultimo festivitatis die	GR 291 LU 861 *SYG 182 GB 184v *GS L	co	5
a	-2	0	-2	-5	-4	-5	-4	-2		Laudem Domini loquetur	GR 52 LU 448	alv	
a	-2	0	-2	-5	-4	-2	-5	-4	D	Clamor meus ad te	WA 70 LA 103	an	1
a	-2	0	-2	-5	-4	-2	-4	-7	D	Lauda Jerusalem Dominum	LA 105	an	1
a	-2	0	-2	-5	-4	-2	-4	-7	D	Quia mirabilia fecit	LA 101	an	1

a	-2	0	-2	-5	-4	-2	-4	-7	D	Rectos decet collaudatio	WA 63 LA 87	an	2
a	-2	0	-2	-5	-4	-2	-4	-5	D	Alleluia	WA 64	an	1
a	-2	0	-2	-5	-4	-2	-4	-5	D	Facti sumus sicut consolati	WA 66 LA 93	an	1
a	-2	0	-2	-5	-4	-2	-4	-5	D	In excelsis laudate Deum	LA 89	an	1
a	-2	0	-2	-5	-4	-2	-4	-5	D	Unde veniet auxilium	LA 96	an	1
a	-2	0	-2	-5	-4	-2	-4	-5	D	Ut non delinquam	WA 64 LA 88	an	1
a	-2	0	-2	-5	-4	-2	-4	-2		Ascendit Deus in jubilatione	GR 286 LU 848 GS 135 *SYG 180 *GB 177	alv	
a	-2	0	-2	-5	-4	-2	-4	-2		Laudate Deum omnes angeli	GR 68 LU 486 GS 22 *SYG 35 *GB 168^{v}	alv	
a	-2	0	-2	-5	-4	-2	0	-4	D	Veniet Dominus et non tardabit	AR 231 LU 338 AM 204 WA 16 LA 16	an	1
a	-2	0	-2	-5	-4	-2	2	-2		Et valde devote properantes Cum transisset	WA 129	rev	
d	-2	0	-2	-5	-3	-5	-7	-2	c	Agnus Dei	SCH #9		2
D	-2	0	-2	-5	-3	-5	-7	-2	D	Kyrie	MEL #203		
d	-2	0	-2	-5	-3	-5	-7	-2	C	Sanctus	THAN #4		2
G	-2	0	-2	-5	-3	-2	-3	-5	G	Montes Gelboë nec ros	LA 269 *WA 165	re	8
G	-2	0	-2	-5	-3	-2	0	-2		Loquimur Dei sapientiam Non judicavi	GR 476	trv	
G	-2	0	-2	-5	-3	-2	0	-2		Scapulis suis obumbrabit Qui habitat	GR 95 LU 533 GS 35 *GB 65 *SYG 73	trv	
G	-2	0	-2	-5	-3	-2	0	2	G	Sancti et justi in Domine	AR 577^{12}[36] LU $262^{1}1122^{1}$ AM 637A 736 910 *LA 391	an	8
G	-2	0	-2	-5	-3	-2	2	0	G	Saul et Jonathas amabiles	LA 274	an	8
a	-2	0	-2	-5	-2	-4	-5	-7		Laetamini cum Jerusalem	GR 510 LU 1483	alv	
a	-2	0	-2	-5	-2	-4	-2	0		Benedicamus patrem et filium cum ... in	SYG 261	alv	
a	-2	0	-2	-5	-2	-4	-2	0		Crastina die delebitur	GS 13	alv	
a	-2	0	-2	-5	-2	-4	-2	0		Dextera Dei fecit virtutem	GR 269 LU 827 SYG 254 GB 234^{v} GS 161	alv	
D	-2	0	-2	-5	-2	-3	-2	0		Deus autem rex noster	GR 79**	alv	
D	-2	0	-2	-5	-2	-3	-2	0	D	Memento mei Deus in bono	WA 179	re	2
D	-2	0	-2	-5	-2	-3	-2	0	D	Memento mei Deus quia ventus	AR [164] LU 1791 LA 284 WA 172	re	2
G	-2	0	-2	-5	-2	-3	-2	0	G	Virgo Israel revertere	LA 19 381 WA 23	re	8
D	-2	0	-2	-5	-2	0	-2	0	D	Adjuva nos Deus salutaris noster	GR [131]	tr	2
D	-2	0	-2	-5	-2	0	-2	0	D	Adoramus te Christe et benedicimus	GR [104]	tr	2
D	-2	0	-2	-5	-2	0	-2	0	D	Angelus Domini apparuit in somnis	GR 6**	tr	2
D	-2	0	-2	-5	-2	0	-2	0	D	Angelis suis Deus mandavit	GR [144]	tr	2

D	-2	0	-2	-5	-2	0	-2	0	D	Apud Dominum gressus hominis	GR 528	tr	2
D	-2	0	-2	-5	-2	0	-2	0	D	Audi filia ... quia concupivit	GR [62] LU 1227	tr	2
D	-2	0	-2	-5	-2	0	-2	0	D	Auribus percipe Domine	LA 91 *WA 65	re	2
D	-2	0	-2	-5	-2	0	-2	0	D	Ave Maria gratia plena ... et benedictus	GR 459 LU 1412 GS 183 SYG 57	tr	2
a	-2	0	-2	-5	-2	0	-2	0	D	Beatus Jamaliel doctoris	WA 342	re	1
D	-2	0	-2	-5	-2	0	-2	0	D	Benedicat nos Deus ... filius	SYG 263	tr	2
D	-2	0	-2	-5	-2	0	-2	0	D	Benedicite Dominum omnes angeli	GR [87] LU 1276	tr	2
D	-2	0	-2	-5	-2	0	-2	0	D	Bonum est confiteri Domino	GR 497	tr	2
D	-2	0	-2	-5	-2	0	-2	0	D	Bonum mihi Domine	LA 142 WA 93	re	2
D	-2	0	-2	-5	-2	0	-2	0	D	Christi mater dilectissima	VP 268 WA 303	re	2
D	-2	0	-2	-5	-2	0	-2	0	D	Christo igitur passo in carne	GR 482	tr	2
D	-2	0	-2	-5	-2	0	-2	0	D	Confitemini Domino quoniam bonus	GR 113 LU 547 SYG 86 GB 75	tr	2
D	-2	0	-2	-5	-2	0	-2	0	D	Contristatus sum in exercitatione	GR 622[3]	tr	2
D	-2	0	-2	-5	-2	0	-2	0	D	De necessitatibus meis eripe	GR 102 LU 841[A] SYG 78 GB 69[v] GS 39	tr	2
D	-2	0	-2	-5	-2	0	-2	0	D	Deus Deus meus respice	GR 180 OHS 109 LU 594 SYG 122 GB 109 GS 86	tr	2
F	-2	0	-2	-5	-2	0	-2	0	D	Diffusa est gratia in labiis	SYG 49 GS 228	tr	2
D	-2	0	-2	-5	-2	0	-2	0	D	Dixit Dominus mulieri	SYG 85 GS 47	tr	2
D	-2	0	-2	-5	-2	0	-2	0	D	Domine audivi auditum tuum	OHS 529 GR 206 LU 721 SYG 136 GB 116 GS 98	tr	2
D	-2	0	-2	-5	-2	0	-2	0	D	Domine exaudi orationem meam ... veniat	GR 191 OHS 324 LU 619 SYG 127 GB 114 GS 92	tr	2
D	-2	0	-2	-5	-2	0	-2	0	D	Domine non aspicias peccata	SYG 56	tr	2
D	-2	0	-2	-5	-2	0	-2	0	D	Domine non secundum peccata	GR 89 OHS 209 LU 527 SYG 66 GS 31	tr	2
D	-2	0	-2	-5	-2	0	-2	0	D	Eripe me Domine ab homine malo	GR 208 OHS 534 LU 725 SYG 137 GB 116[v] GS 99	tr	2
D	-2	0	-2	-5	-2	0	-2	0	D	Exaudi me Domine quoniam benigna	GR 9**	tr	2
D	-2	0	-2	-5	-2	0	-2	0	D	Gaudens perenniter felicitas	SYG 238	tr	2
D	-2	0	-2	-5	-2	0	-2	0	D	Gratificavit nos Deus	GR 538	tr	2
D	-2	0	-2	-5	-2	0	-2	0	D	Hostiam et oblationem	GR 61	tr	2
D	-2	0	-2	-5	-2	0	-2	0	D	Ipse invocabit me pater meus	GR 640 LU 1711	tr	2
D	-2	0	-2	-5	-2	0	-2	0	D	Jam hiems transiit ... flores	GR 615	tr	2
D	-2	0	-2	-5	-2	0	-2	0	D	Laetatus sum in his	SYG 101	tr	2
D	-2	0	-2	-5	-2	0	-2	0	D	Magnificentiam gloriae sanctitatis	GR 99**	tr	2
D	-2	0	-2	-5	-2	0	-2	0	D	Miserere mei Domine quoniam	GR [145]	tr	2

D	-2	0	-2	-5	-2	0	-2	0	D	Misericors et miserator Dominus longanimis	GR [113] LU 972	tr	2
D	-2	0	-2	-5	-2	0	-2	0	D	Non judicavi me scire	GR 476	tr	2
D	-2	0	-2	-5	-2	0	-2	0	D	Omnis gloria ejus filiae	GR 104**	tr	2
D	-2	0	-2	-5	-2	0	-2	0	D	Per signum crucis de inimicis	SYG 129	tr	2
D	-2	0	-2	-5	-2	0	-2	0	D	Persequar inimicos meos	GR 463 LU 1420	tr	2
D	-2	0	-2	-5	-2	0	-2	0	D	Propter intolerabiles rerum	WA 288	re	2
D	-2	0	-2	-5	-2	0	-2	0	D	Qui habitat in adjutorio	GR 95 LU 533 SYG 73 GB 65 GS 35	tr	2
D	-2	0	-2	-5	-2	0	-2	0	D	Stabat sancta Maria	GR 471 LU 1634	tr	2
D	-2	0	-2	-5	-2	0	-2	0	D	Tu es Petrus	GR 409 LU 1332 SYG 53 GS 182	tr	2
D	-2	0	-2	-5	-2	0	-2	0	D	Vere languores nostros	GR [108]	tr	2
D	-2	0	-2	-5	-2	0	-2	0	D	Vultum tuum deprecabuntur	GR [64] LU 1229 SYG 28 GB 29 221 GS 231	int	2
D	-2	0	-2	-5	-2	0	2	0	D	Alleluia: Deus autem rex noster	GR 79**	al	2
D	-2	0	-2	-5	-2	0	2	0	D	Non vos relinquam ... veniam	WA 148	re	2
a	-2	0	-2	-5	-2	0	2	3		Deus in nomine tuo salvum Peccantem me quotidie	AR [171] LU 1797 *LA 556 *WA 437	rev	
D	-2	0	-2	-5	-2	0	2	3	D	Impetum inimicorum	LA 296 *WA 181	re	2
D	-2	0	-2	-5	-2	0	3	0	D	Beatus Laurentius dixit ego	WA 349	re	2
D	-2	0	-2	-5	-2	0	3	0	D	Benedictus Dominus Deus Israel	LR 337 *WA 159	re	2
D	-2	0	-2	-5	-2	0	3	2	D	Cornelius centurio vir religiosus	PM 125 *WA 279	re	1
D	-2	0	-2	-5	-2	0	3	2	D	Deletis cunctis substantiis	WA 77	re	2
D	-2	0	-2	-5	-2	0	3	2	D	Reges Tharsis et insulae	LR 72 LA 71 WA 55	re	2
D	-2	0	-2	-5	-2	0	3	2	D	Velum templi scissum est	OHS 488 LU 695 LA 199 WA 123	re	2
a	-2	0	-2	-5	-2	0	3	5	a	Multae tribulationes justorum	GR 515 (20) LU 1507 SYG 199 GB 201 GS m 212	int	2
D	-2	0	-2	-5	-2	0	5	7	D	Circumdederunt me viri mendaces	PM 52 OHS 63 (nm) 303 (nm) LA 183 WA 113	re	2
D	-2	0	-2	-5	0	-2	0	-2	D	Sanctissimi martyris Stephani	WA 36	re	2
a	-2	0	-2	-4	-7	-9	-2	-4	D	Caelitum Joseph decus	AR 690 LU 1879 AM 888 *LR 302	hy	1
a	-2	0	-2	-4	-7	-9	-2	-4	D	Iste confessor Domini colentes	AR [53] LU 1179 AM 656 669	hy	1
a	-2	0	-2	-4	-7	-2	-4	-2	D	Ut queant laxis resonare fibris	ST 295	hy	1
a	-2	0	-2	-4	-5	-9	-5	-2		Domine Deus meus in te speravi salvum	GR 322 LU 962 GB 248 *GS f 167	alv	
a	-2	0	-2	-4	-5	-7	-9	-5	D	O lux beata trinitas	AM 163	hy	1
a	-2	0	-2	-4	-5	-7	-2	-4	D	Iste confessor Domini sacratus	LR 190	hy	1

a	-2	0	-2	-4	-5	-7	-2	-4	D	Quod chorus vatum venerandus olim	VP 103	hy	1
a	-2	0	-2	-4	-5	-7	-2	0	D	Ave maris stella Dei mater alma	ST 133	hy	1
a	-2	0	-2	-4	-5	-7	-2	0	a	Benedicamus Domino IIIb	AR 61* LU 126		2
a	-2	0	-2	-4	-5	-7	-2	0		Sancti immensitas amoris Gloriosa es	WA 335	rev	
a	-2	0	-2	-4	-5	-7	-2	0	D	Summe sacerdos rector et custos	ST 157	hy	1
a	-2	0	-2	-4	-5	-4	-5	-7	D	Alleluia: in omnem terram exivit sonus apostolorum	SYG 209	al	1
a	-2	0	-2	-4	-5	-4	-5	-7	D	Alleluia: ingressus Zacharias templum	SYG 198	al	1
a	-2	0	-2	-4	-5	-4	-5	-7	D	Alleluia: qui confidunt in Domino	SYG 255 *GS 163	al	1
a	-2	0	-2	-4	-5	-4	-2	-5	D	Christe sanctorum decus angelorum	AR 659 857 889 LU 1409 1702	hy	1
a	-2	0	-2	-4	-5	-4	-2	-5	E	Ecce jam tristes abiere luctus	LR 453	hy	4
a	-2	0	-2	-4	-5	-4	-2	-5	E	Laudibus cives resonent canoris	PM 339	hy	4
a	-2	0	-2	-4	-5	-4	-2	-5	E	Non profanorum sinitur vagari	LR 456	hy	4
a	-2	0	-2	-4	-5	-4	-2	-5	E	Quidquid antiqui cecinere vates	LR 317	hy	4
a	-2	0	-2	-4	-5	-2	-5	-4	D	Christe sanctorum decus angelorum	AM 1061	hy	1
a	-2	0	-2	-4	-5	-2	-4	-5	D	Iste confessor Domini sacratus	ST 104	hy	1
a	-2	0	-2	-4	-5	-2	-4	-5	D	Quod chorus vatum venerandus olim	ST 87	hy	1
a	-2	0	-2	-4	-5	-2	0	-7		Recordatus est Deus Ascendens ergo Deus	WA 81	rev	
a	-2	0	-2	-4	-5	-2	0	-2		Deus misereatur nostri ... nos Deus Benedicat nos	WA 158	rev	
a	-2	0	-2	-4	-5	-2	0	-2		Dignissime namque devotis Celebremus solemniter	WA 282	rev	
a	-2	0	-2	-4	-5	-2	0	-2		Quasi trames aquae Quae in sinu	LR 282	rev	
a	-2	0	-2	-4	-5	-2	0	-2		Tibi laus tibi gloria O beata trinitas	PM 91	rev	
a	-2	0	-2	-4	-5	-2	0	1		Clamantes et dicentes advenisti Libera me Domine de viis	AR [173] LU 1798 PM 317 *LA 556 WA 438	rev	
a	-2	0	-2	-4	-5	-2	0	1		Et dum seminat Cum turba plurima	LR 400	rev	
a	-2	0	-2	-4	-5	-2	0	1		Floribus ejus nec rosae Beata vere mater	LR 388	rev	
a	-2	0	-2	-4	-5	-2	0	1		Requiem aeternam dona eis Domine Libera me Domine de viis	AR [173] PM 318 LU 1798	rev	
a	-2	0	-2	-4	-5	-2	0	3		Est ubi vera quies Celebremus diem istum	WA 248	rev	
a	-2	0	-2	-4	-5	-2	0	3		Nam ubi pauperum O acceptabilem	WA 285	rev	

a	-2	0	-2	-4	-5	-2	0	3		Tanto namque feliciores Valerius igitur	WA 257	rev	
a	-2	0	-2	-4	-2	-4	-5	-9		Memor esto congregationis ... adquisisti O pastor apostolice	WA 290	rev	
a	-2	0	-2	-4	-2	-4	-5	-7		Statimque pauci Cum non posset	WA 283	rev	
a	-2	0	-2	-4	-2	-4	-5	-4	E	Ad coenam agni providi	ST 190	hy	4
a	-2	0	-2	-4	-2	-4	-2	-7	D	Exi cito in plateas	AR 538 LU 964 AM 558 *WA 187 *LA 310	an	1
E	-2	0	-2	-4	-2	-4	-2	-4	E	Alleluia: oportebat pati Christum	GR 267 LU 822 GS 126 SYG 155 GB 133^{v}	al	4
E	-2	0	-2	-4	-2	-4	-2	-4		Oportebat pati Christum	GR 267 LU 822 GS 126 SYG 155 GB 133^{v}	alv	
a	-2	0	-2	-4	-2	-4	-2	1	D	O felix Joachim genuisti prolem	PM 182	re	1
a	-2	0	-2	-4	-2	0	-4	-5	D	Erunt primi novissimi	WA 76	an	1
a	-2	0	-2	-4	-2	0	-4	-5	D	Gloria laus et honor	GR 176 OHS 99 LU 586 *WA 210	hy	1
E	-2	0	-2	-4	-2	0	-4	0	E	Haec locutus sum vobis	WA 151	an	4
a	-2	0	-2	-4	-2	0	-4	0	D	O princeps apostolorum	WA 278	re	1
a	-2	0	-2	-4	-2	0	-2	-4	F	Alleluia	AR 165	an	6
a	-2	0	-2	-4	-2	0	-2	0		Adjuvent nos eorum merita Concede nobis	PM 202 *WA 393	rev	
a	-2	0	-2	-4	-2	0	-2	0		Agnus Dei	SCH #59		
a	-2	0	-2	-4	-2	0	-2	0	G	Alleluia: venite ad me sancti mei	SYG 207	al	8
a	-2	0	-2	-4	-2	0	-2	0		Ecce enim ut facta Repleta est spiritu	PM 164	rev	
E	-2	0	-2	-4	-2	0	-2	0	D	Ego te tuli de domo	LA 270 WA 166	re	1
a	-2	0	-2	-4	-2	0	-2	0	D	Erit mihi Dominus in Deum	LA 139 WA 92	re	1
e	-2	0	-2	-4	-2	0	-2	0	F	Gloria VII	BOS #1 GR 25* LU 34		6
a	-2	0	-2	-4	-2	0	-2	0		Qui custos est Domini Fidelis servus	AM 1193 *LR 316	rev	
b	-2	0	-2	-4	-2	0	-2	0	a	Sanctus	GR 169 58* 101* LU 1814 THAN #41		
b	-2	0	-2	-4	-2	0	-2	0	b	Sanctus I	GR 6* OHS 686 LU 18 THAN #154		4
a	-2	0	-2	-4	-2	0	-2	0		Tamquam sponsus Dominus Descendit de caelis Deus	LR 59		
a	-2	0	-2	-4	-2	0	-2	0		Timor et tremor ... super me Domine ne in ira	LR 398 LA 81 *WA 60	rev	
E	-2	0	-2	-4	-2	0	[0	0]	E	Kyrie miserere rex (etc.)	MEL #155		
a	-2	0	-2	-4	-2	0	1	-2	a	In matutinis Domine	AM 372	an	ir
E	-2	0	-2	-4	-2	0	1	0	E	Consul aeterni trabeate regni	ST 468	hy	4

E	-2	0	-2	-4	-2	0	1	3	D	Hymnum dicamus Domino	ST 9	hy	2
E	-2	0	-2	-4	-2	0	1	3	D	Mysterium ecclesiae	ST 7	hy	2
E	-2	0	-2	-4	-2	0	1	3	D	Optatus votis omnium	ST 10	hy	2
E	-2	0	-2	-4	-2	0	1	3	D	Verbum supernum prodiens nec patris	ST 10	hy	2
a	-2	0	-2	-4	-2	0	2	3	G	Alleluia	AR 145	an	8
a	-2	0	-2	-4	-2	0	2	3	G	Jubilate in conspectu	AR 145	an	8
a	-2	0	-2	-4	-2	0	3	0	D	Videns crucem Andreas	LA 502	re	1
E	-2	0	-2	-4	-2	0	3	5	D	Denariorum numero	ST 33	hy	2
E	-2	0	-2	-4	-2	0	3	5	D	Hymnum dicamus Domino	ST 33 386	hy	2
E	-2	0	-2	-4	-2	1	-2	0	E	Quia mirabilia fecit	WA 69	an	4
E	-2	0	-2	-4	-2	1	-2	1	E	Alleluia	WA 69	an	4
E	-2	0	-2	-4	-2	1	-2	1	E	Habitare fratres	WA 66	an	4
a	-2	0	-2	-4	-2	1	-2	1	a	Illumina Domine vultum	AR 107	an	1
a	-2	0	-2	-4	-2	1	-2	1	a	Lauda Jerusalem Dominum	AR 167 *AM 162	an	1
E	-2	0	-2	-4	-2	1	0	-4	D	Agnus Dei	SCH #185		2
a	-2	0	-2	-4	-2	1	0	-2	D	Ecce apparebit Dominus super nubem	LR 393 *LA 13 WA 13	re	1
a	-2	0	-2	-4	-2	1	0	-2	D	O felix Anna peperisti prolem	PM 171	re	1
a	-2	0	-2	-4	-2	1	0	-2	D	O regem caeli cui talia	PM 36 LR 397 *LA 35 *WA 30	re	1
a	-2	0	-2	-4	-2	2	-2	0		Ego sum vestra redemptio Ego sum alpha et omega ... manus	SYG 147 *GS 125	anv	
a	-2	0	-2	-4	-2	3	0	-2	D	Alleluia	WA 66	an	1
a	-2	0	-2	-4	-2	3	0	-2	D	Ite dicite Joanni	WA 15 *LA 10	an	1
a	-2	0	-2	-4	-2	3	0	-2	D	Quam bonus Israel Deus	WA 67	an	1
a	-2	0	-2	-4	0	-4	-5	-7	D	Fuit Dominus cum Joseph	LR 305	re	1
a	-2	0	-2	-4	0	-4	0	3	a	Ut tibi clarum resonemus hymnum	ST 56	hy	2
E	-2	0	-2	-4	0	-2	-4	-2	E	Sanctus	THAN #153		4
a	-2	0	-2	-4	0	1	0	-2	F	Exaltate Dominum Deum ... in monte	AR 164	an	6
a	-2	0	-2	-4	0	2	0	-2	E	Gloria	BOS #15		II
a	-2	0	-2	-4	0	3	0	-2	D	Caesar dixit ad Hippolytum	WA 352	an	1
a	-2	0	-2	-4	0	3	0	-2	D	Lucia virgo venerabilis	WA 243	an	1
a	-2	0	-2	-4	0	3	0	2	D	Vidi Dominum sedentem ... plena	AR 552 LU 995 AM 590 *WA 183 *LA 308	an	1
a	-2	0	-2	-4	0	3	2	0	F	Ecce gens quae	WA 287	an	5
a	-2	0	-2	-4	0	3	2	0	F	Exaudi Deus orationem meam et ne	GR 143 SYG 103 GB 91^v GS 65	int	5

b	-2	0	-2	-4	0	3	5	3	b	Agnus Dei I	GR 7* OHS 715 LU 18		4
a	-2	0	-2	-4	3	5	3	2	F	Adoremus in aeternum sanctissimum	AR 92* LU 1853		5
a	-2	0	-2	-4	3	5	3	2	F	In conspectu angelorum	AM 146 147 *WA 67 384 *LA 96	an	5
d	-2	0	-2	-3	-5	-7	-5	-2		Multa fecisti tu Domine Exspectans exspectavi	OTT 104 GB 92 SYG 104	ofv	
G	-2	0	-2	-3	-5	0	2	0	[G]	Agnus Dei	SCH #102		8
D	-2	0	-2	-3	-2	0	-2	0	D	Laetabimur in salutari tuo	GR 144 SYG 104 GB 92^{v} GS 66	co	2
D	-2	0	-2	-3	-2	0	-2	0	D	Nemo te condemnavit mulier nemo	GS 63	co	2
G	-2	0	-2	-3	-2	0	-2	0	E	Turba multa quae convenerat	AR 423 GR 175 LU 585 *AM 401 PM 58 OHS 73 98 *WA 113 *LA 182	an	4
G	-2	0	-2	-3	-2	0	2	0	E	Forti animo esto Tobia	AR 891 LU 1701	an	4
d	-2	0	-2	-3	-2	0	2	0	G	Virgo est electus	LA 53	re	7
G	-2	0	-2	-3	0	2	0	2	D	Plateae tuae Jerusalem	LA 228 *WA 141	re	1
G	-2	0	-2	-3	0	4	0	2	D	Haec est Jerusalem civitas	LA 228 *WA 142	re	1
a	-2	0	-2	0	-4	0	-2	-4	G	Nunc sancte nobis spiritus	ST 173	hy	8
a	-2	0	-2	0	-4	0	-2	-4	G	Rector potens verax Deus	ST 174	hy	8
a	-2	0	-2	0	-4	0	-2	-4	G	Rerum Deus tenax vigor	ST 175	hy	8
a	-2	0	-2	0	-2	-4	-5	-4	D	Gloria	BOS #17		I
a	-2	0	-2	0	-2	-4	-2	-4	G	Nunc sancte nobis spiritus	AR 84 AM 93 108	hy	8
a	-2	0	-2	0	-2	-4	-2	-4	G	Rector potens verax Deus	AR 89 AM 98 113	hy	8
a	-2	0	-2	0	-2	-4	-2	-4	G	Rerum Deus tenax vigor	AR 93 LU 519 AM 103 118	hy	8
a	-2	0	-2	0	-2	-4	-2	0	a	Alleluia	AM 113	an	ir
e	-2	0	-2	0	-2	-4	-2	0	G	Notas mihi fecisti vias	GR 134 *SYG 97 *GB 86 *GS 59	co	7
a	-2	0	-2	0	-2	-4	0	3	F	Mirum dictu hinc	WA 292	an	5
a	-2	0	-2	0	-2	0	-2	-4	[G]	Agnus Dei	SCH #58		7
a	-2	0	-2	0	-2	0	-2	-4	D	Haec est vera fraternitas	PM 222 LR 187 LA 409 WA 422	re	1
a	-2	0	-2	0	-2	0	-2	-4	E	Qua Christus hora sitiit	ST 319	hy	4
a	-2	0	-2	0	-2	0	-2	3	a	Sanctus	THAN #40		
a	-2	0	-2	0	-2	0	1	0	D	Scio cui credidi	GR 417 LU 1344 *SYG 204 *GB 207^{v} *GS 189	int	1
a	-2	0	-2	[0	0	0	0	0]	G	Nunc sancte nobis spiritus	ST 321	hy	8
E	-2	0	-2	0	1	0	-2	-4	D	Nunc sancte nobis spiritus	ST 27	hy	2
E	-2	0	-2	0	1	0	-2	-4	D	Rector potens verax Deus	ST 28	hy	2
E	-2	0	-2	0	1	0	-2	-4	D	Rerum Deus tenax vigor	ST 28	hy	2

d	-2	0	-2	0	2	0	-2	-3	G	Vox in Rama audita ... ploratus	GR 44 LU 430 SYG 27 *GB 28 GS 18	co	7
d	-2	0	-2	0	2	0	-2	0	G	Aspiciens a longe ecce video	PM 18 *LA 2	re	7
a	-2	0	-2	0	2	0	-2	0	D	O pater sancte mitis atque pie	ST 456	hy	2
a	-2	0	-2	0	2	0	-2	0	D	Tibi laus tibi gloria	WA 161	an	2
G	-2	0	-2	0	2	0	2	4	G	Clamaverunt justi et Dominus	GR [29] LU 1170 *GS 213 SYG 188 *GB 194	gr	7
D	-2	0	-2	0	2	0	3	2	D	Haec mulier sancta	WA 335	an	2
D	-2	0	-2	0	2	3	0	-2	D	Immolabit haedum multitudo	AR 114* LR 122 LU 926	re	1
D	-2	0	-2	0	2	3	0	2	D	Alleluia: nuptiae factae sunt	SYG 35	al	1
D	-2	0	-2	0	2	3	2	0	D	O magni meriti Maria	WA 335	re	2
D	-2	0	-2	0	2	3	5	3	D	Caeli enarrant gloriam Dei ... quia	WA 410	re	1
G	-2	0	-2	0	2	5	2	5	G	Igitur Lucianus de revelatione	WA 345	re	8
D	-2	0	-2	0	3	0	-2	0	D	In circuitu tuo ... ubi constituisti	WA 423	re	2
D	-2	0	-2	0	3	0	-2	0	D	Magnificavit eum in conspectu	LA 534 *WA 427	re	1
D	-2	0	-2	0	3	0	-2	0	D	Non enim misit Deus	LA 265	an	1
D	-2	0	-2	0	3	0	-2	3	D	Domine Jesu Christe rex gloriae	GR 100* LU 1813 *SYG 235 *GB 266 *GS 232	of	2
D	-2	0	-2	0	3	0	3	2	D	Martinus igitur obitum	SYG 225	of	1
d	-2	0	-2	0	3	0	3	2		Praestet nobis gratiam Summae trinitati	WA 161	rev	
d	-2	0	-2	0	3	2	0	-2	G	Haec virgo sancta	WA 433	re	7
D	-2	0	-2	0	3	2	0	2	D	Psallite Domino omnes	WA 396	re	2
D	-2	0	-2	0	3	2	0	3	D	Carnales viriliter edomuit	WA 289	an	2
D	-2	0	-2	0	3	2	3	5	D	Instabat enim precibus	WA 287	an	2
a	-2	0	-2	0	3	2	3	5		Qui cogitaverunt supplantare Custodi me	OTT 52 *SYG 126	ofv	
G	-2	0	-2	0	3	2	3	7	G	Fuit sacra virgo	WA 433	re	7
D	-2	0	-2	0	3	5	3	5	D	O mirum et magnum miraculum	VP 190	re	1
G	-2	0	-2	2	5	2	0	2		Propterea unxit te Deus Dilexisti	GR [52] LU 1216 GS 226 GB 4 SYG 5	grv	
D	-2	0	-2	3	2	0	-2	3	D	Astra polorum super ascendit	ST 350	hy	2
D	-2	0	-2	5	7	5	7	9	G	Kyrie	MEL #202		
E	-2	0	1	-2	-4	0	1	3	E	Existimo omnia detrimentum	AR 849 LU 1647	an	4
E	-2	0	1	-2	-4	0	1	3	E	Sanctus	THAN #152		4
E	-2	0	1	-2	0	-2	-4	0	E	O beata anima quae meruit	AM 1131	an	4
E	-2	0	1	0	-4	-2	0	-2	E	Mane surgens Jacob	LA 553	an	4

B	-2	0	1	0	-2	0	-2	-4	[G]	Agnus Dei	SCH #43		7
a	-2	0	1	0	-2	0	-2	-4		Esto tuis clemens cui Christus Apparuit Dominus	PM 176	rev	
a	-2	0	1	0	-2	0	-2	-4		Lauda anima mea Dominum Redemptor meus vivit	LA 560	rev	
a	-2	0	1	0	-2	0	-2	-4		Oculi tui sicut columbae Pulchra es o virgo	PM 263	rev	
E	-2	0	1	0	-2	0	3	5	E	Kyrie	MEL #159		
E	-2	0	1	0	1	-2	0	-2	E	Venite exsultemus Domino	LA 87	inv	4
E	-2	0	1	3	1	0	1	0		Ne timeas Zacharia ... deprecatio	SYG 198	alv	
E	-2	0	1	3	1	3	1	0		Propter veritatem ... et deducet Diffusa est gratia	SYG 49	trv	
E	-2	0	1	3	5	3	5	3	E	O nimis felix meritique celsi	AM 926	hy	4
d	-2	0	2	-2	-3	-7	-5	-2	G	Signum magnum apparuit	PM 120 LR 268	re	7
a	-2	0	2	-2	0	-2	-4	-2		Cantabant sancti canticum	SYG 26	alv	
D	-2	0	2	-2	0	3	5	3	[D]	Agnus Dei	SCH #244		2
G	-2	0	2	0	-3	-2	0	2	G	Fontes aquarum sanctificati	WA 59 *LA 76	an	8
a	-2	0	2	0	-2	-4	-5	-4	G	Alleluia: benedicta tu inter mulieres	SYG 216	al	8
a	-2	0	2	0	-2	-4	-5	-4	G	Alleluia: ite nuntiate fratribus	SYG 163	al	8
a	-2	0	2	0	-2	-4	-2	0	D	Agnus Dei	SCH #57		1
G	-2	0	2	0	-2	-3	-2	-5	G	Haec autem scripta sunt	LA 230	an	8
D	-2	0	2	0	-2	-3	-2	0	D	Jam lucis orto sidere	ST 73	hy	2
a	-2	0	2	0	-2	0	-2	-4		Interrogabat Magos Herodes	SYG 31 GB 33^v	alv	
a	-2	0	2	0	-2	0	-2	-4		Requiem aeternam dona eis Domine Redemptor meus vivit	LA 560	rev	
a	-2	0	2	0	-2	0	-2	0	E	Gloria ad lib IV	GR 89* LU 88		4
D	-2	0	2	0	-2	0	-2	0		Spiritus qui a Patre procedit	GB 191^v	alv	
G	-2	0	2	0	-2	0	-2	2		Viriliter agite et confortetur	GR (36)	alv	
G	-2	0	2	0	-2	0	2	0	G	Ad hanc vocem Christi ... Dionysius	WA 387	an	8
D	-2	0	2	0	-2	0	2	0	D	Inveni David servum meum	GR [3] LU 1130 SYG 37 GB 41 GS 221	gr	1
D	-2	0	2	0	-2	0	2	3		Initio cognovi de testimoniis	GR 82**	alv	
D	-2	0	2	0	-2	0	2	3	D	Sancta Maria clemens et pia	WA 357	re	1
G	-2	0	2	0	-2	0	3	2	G	Aurora lucis rutilat	ST 419	hy	2
G	-2	0	2	0	-2	0	3	2	G	Solemnis dies advenit	ST 412	hy	2
D	-2	0	2	0	-2	0	3	2	D	Viri autem qui comitabantur	LA 341	an	1
D	-2	0	2	0	-2	2	-2	0	C	Aurora lucis rutilat	ST 229	hy	6

G	-2	0	2	0	-2	2	4	5		Iste sanctus digne in memoriam	SYG 226 *GS 207	alv	
G	-2	0	2	0	-2	2	5	0	G	Subiit ergo Jesus in montem	WA 104	an	8
G	-2	0	2	0	-2	2	5	4	G	Sacerdos Dei Martine pastor	WA 400 *LA 483	an	8
G	-2	0	2	0	2	0	-2	-3	G	Dum aurora finem ... dixit	WA 408	an	8
c	-2	0	2	0	2	0	-2	2	c	In sudore vultus tui	WA 206	an	6
G	-2	0	2	0	2	0	-2	2	G	Sanctus quidem	WA 240	an	8
G	-2	0	2	0	2	0	2	0		Venite ad me sancti mei	SYG 207	alv	
G	-2	0	2	0	2	0	5	4		Spiritus omnia scrutatur	SYG 186	alv	
D	-2	0	2	0	2	3	2	0	D	Ecce ego mitto vos	LA 512	an	1
d	-2	0	2	0	2	3	5	3		Venite justi ad prandium	SYG 44	alv	
G	-2	0	2	0	2	4	0	2	G	In illa die stillabunt	AR 213 LU 323 AM 187 WA 6 LA 6	an	8
G	-2	0	2	0	2	4	5	4	G	Testis mihi est Deus	GR 544 LU 1544	gr	7
G	-2	0	2	0	2	5	4	5	G	Tradiderunt corpora sua propter ... ideo	LA 388	re	8
D	-2	0	2	0	3	0	-2	0	D	Venit enim princeps mundi	LA 266	an	1
D	-2	0	2	0	3	2	3	5	D	Felix Maria unxit	PM 169	re	2
d	-2	0	2	0	5	3	2	0	G	Alleluia: venite justi ad prandium	SYG 44	al	7
a	-2	0	2	3	-2	0	2	3	D	Agnus Dei	SCH #56		1
D	-2	0	2	3	-2	0	2	3	GG	Agnus Dei	SCH #243		3
a	-2	0	2	3	-2	0	2	3	D	Kyrie	MEL #20		
a	-2	0	2	3	-2	0	2	3	D	Sanctus	THAN #39		1
D	-2	0	2	3	-2	0	2	3		Sanctus	THAN #194		
D	-2	0	2	3	0	-2	0	2	D	Ascendens Jesus in navim	AR 555 LU 1103 *AM 593 *WA 187 *LA 311	an	1
D	-2	0	2	3	0	-2	0	3	D	Te sanctum Dominum in excelsis	AR 196* *PM 109 VP 216 *WA 382	re	1
D	-2	0	2	3	0	-2	0	3	F	Te unum in substantia	WA 158	an	6
D	-2	0	2	3	0	-2	3	5	D	Passer invenit sibi domum	SYG 94	co	1
D	-2	0	2	3	0	[0	0	0]	D	Kyrie	MEL #197		
D	-2	0	2	3	0	2	-2	0	D	Ad occasum vergens	WA 251	re	1
D	-2	0	2	3	0	2	-2	0	D	Eripe me de inimicis meis Domine	AR 165	an	2
a	-2	0	2	3	0	2	0	-2	G	Ad coenam agni providi	ST 387	hy	8
D	-2	0	2	3	0	2	0	-2	D	Apparuit caro suo	WA 41	re	2
D	-2	0	2	3	0	2	0	-2	D	Aspice Domine quia facta	AR 552 LU 996 AM 590 LA 308	an	1
a	-2	0	2	3	0	2	0	-2	G	Aurora lucis rutilat	ST 387	hy	8

D	-2	0	2	3	0	2	0	-2	D	Ecclesia virtute roboratur	WA 401	re	1
D	-2	0	2	3	0	2	0	-2	D	In medio carceris stabat	LA 455	an	1
a	-2	0	2	3	0	2	0	-2	G	Ortu Phoebi jam proximo	ST 439	hy	8
a	-2	0	2	3	0	2	0	-2	G	Rex aeterne Domine	ST 386	hy	8
D	-2	0	2	3	0	2	0	-2	E	Sanctus	THAN #193		4
D	-2	0	2	3	0	2	0	-2	D	Valde mane die	WA 338	re	1
D	-2	0	2	3	0	3	0	-2	D	Auctor salutis unicus	ST 386	hy	2
D	-2	0	2	3	0	3	0	-2	D	Audi benigne conditor	ST 381	hy	2
D	-2	0	2	3	0	3	0	-2	D	Caeteri tantum cecinere vatum	ST 393	hy	2
D	-2	0	2	3	0	3	0	-2	D	Gloria dignos colimus triumphos	ST 393	hy	2
D	-2	0	2	3	0	3	0	-2	D	O pater sancte mitis atque pie	ST 391	hy	2
D	-2	0	2	3	0	3	0	-2	D	O veneranda trinitas laudanda	ST 392	hy	2
D	-2	0	2	3	0	3	0	-2	D	Ut queant laxis resonare fibris	ST 393	hy	2
D	-2	0	2	3	0	3	0	2	D	In Wulstano cujus aetas	WA 248	an	2
D	-2	0	2	3	0	3	5	7	D	Immaculatam conceptionem virginis	PM 121	an	1
D	-2	0	2	3	2	0	-2	0	D	Alleluia: psallite Domino	GB 182	al	2
D	-2	0	2	3	2	0	-2	0	D	Alleluia: spiritus sanctus in te	SYG 2	al	1
D	-2	0	2	3	2	0	-2	0	D	Multa sunt Domine peccata	GB 156^{v} *WA 229	an	2
D	-2	0	2	3	2	0	-2	0	D	Nunc autem ad te venio	LA 254	an	2
D	-2	0	2	3	2	0	-2	0		Psallite Domino qui ascendit	GB 182	alv	
D	-2	0	2	3	2	0	-2	0	D	Quae sunt in corde hominum	LA 280 *WA 170	re	2
D	-2	0	2	3	2	0	-2	0	D	Redemptor meus vivit	LA 560	re	1
D	-2	0	2	3	2	0	-2	0	D	Sanctus	THAN #192		2
D	-2	0	2	3	2	0	-2	3	D	Abiit Jesus trans mare	WA 103	an	1
D	-2	0	2	3	2	0	-2	3	D	Foderunt manus meas	GR [111]	co	2
D	-2	0	2	3	2	0	2	-2	D	Kyrie	MEL #195		
D	-2	0	2	3	2	0	2	0	D	Alleluia: regi autem saeculorum	SYG 262	al	1
D	-2	0	2	3	2	0	2	0		Animae eorum in bonis Domine Jesu Christe	OTT 189 SYG 235	ofv	
D	-2	0	2	3	2	0	2	0	D	Iste confessor Domini colentes	AM 668	hy	2
D	-2	0	2	3	2	0	2	0	D	Potum meum cum fletu	GR 194 OHS 346 LU 624 SYG 128 GB 115 GS 93	co	2
D	-2	0	2	3	2	0	2	3	D	Comedetis carnes et saturabimini	LR 123 LU 927	re	2
D	-2	0	2	3	2	0	2	3	D	Infirmus fui et visitastis	GR 553 LU 1560	co	1
a	-2	0	2	3	2	0	2	3	G	Iste quem laeti colimus fideles	AR 654 181* AM 844 VP 126	hy	8
D	-2	0	2	3	2	0	2	3	D	Kyrie conditor rerum alme	MEL #191		

D	-2	0	2	3	2	0	2	3	D	Multitudo languentium et qui ... ad eum	GR 416 LU 1337 *SYG 41 *GB 44v *GS 218	co	2
D	-2	0	2	3	2	0	2	3	D	Multitudo languentium et qui ... ad Jesum	GR 69**	co	2
D	-2	0	2	3	2	0	2	3	D	Stirps Jesse virgam produxit	AR 129* PM 186 WA 303	re	2
D	-2	0	2	3	2	0	3	-2	F	Diem festum virginis	GB 50v	of	6
D	-2	0	2	3	2	3	0	2	D	Salvator mundi salva ... sancta	LA 474	an	1
D	-2	0	2	3	5	2	3	0	D	Christianissimus Francorum rex	LR 283	re	2
D	-2	0	2	3	5	2	3	0		Posui vos ut eatis	GR 568	alv	
d	-2	0	2	3	5	2	5	3		Exivi a patre et veni	GR 272 LU 831	alv	
D	-2	0	2	3	5	2	5	7	D	Omnis qui se exaltat	WA 189	an	1
D	-2	0	2	3	5	2	5	7	D	Significavit Dominus Petro	WA 332	an	1
D	-2	0	2	3	5	3	0	-2	D	Bonum certamen certavi	WA 331 LA 422	an	1
D	-2	0	2	3	5	3	0	-2	D	Magi videntes stellam obtulerunt	WA 57	an	1
D	-2	0	2	3	5	3	0	-2	D	Mensuram bonam	WA 187	an	2
D	-2	0	2	3	5	3	0	2		Nunc Christe te deprecor Libera me Domine de morte	LA 557	rev	
D	-2	0	2	3	5	3	0	2		Plangent se super se Libera me Domine de morte	LA 557 *WA 438	rev	
D	-2	0	2	3	5	3	0	2	D	Vos amici mei qui secuti	WA 331	an	1
D	-2	0	2	3	5	3	0	2	D	Vos qui secuti ... sedebitis ... dicit	AR 611 757 PM 217 AM 794 942	an	1 2
D	-2	0	2	3	5	3	0	2	D	Vos qui secuti ... sedebitis ... dicit	GR 588 LU 1614 GS z 203	co	2
D	-2	0	2	3	5	3	2	0	D	Alleluia: benedictus es Domine Deus patrum ... superexaltatus	SYG 261	al	1
D	-2	0	2	3	5	3	2	0	D	Alleluia: specie tua et pulchritudine	SYG 41	al	2
D	-2	0	2	3	5	3	2	0		Benedictus es Domine Deus ... superexaltatus	SYG 261	alv	
D	-2	0	2	3	5	3	2	0	D	Confessor Domini Maure	ST 424	hy	2
D	-2	0	2	3	5	3	2	0	D	Deus a Libano veniet	AR 243 AM 218 WA 19 LA 26	an	1
D	-2	0	2	3	5	3	2	0	D	Dicebat enim intra se	AR 573 LU 1108 AM 615 WA 191 LA 320	an	1 2
a	-2	0	2	3	5	3	2	0	D	Dixerunt impii apud se	OHS 302 (nm) LA 179 *WA 116	re	1
D	-2	0	2	3	5	3	2	0	D	Dixit Dominus Simoni	WA 338	an	2
D	-2	0	2	3	5	3	2	0	D	Ecce in nubibus caeli Dominus	AR 224 LU 331 AM 195 WA 12 20 LA 11 377	an	1
D	-2	0	2	3	5	3	2	0	D	Ecce in nubibus caeli filius	WA 16	an	1
D	-2	0	2	3	5	3	2	0	D	Fuit vir vitae venerabilis	WA 296 LA 366	an	1

D	-2	0	2	3	5	3	2	0	D	Hoc genus daemoniorum	AR 547 AM 584	an	1
D	-2	0	2	3	5	3	2	0	D	In nomine Jesu Christi	WA 340 LA 412	an	2
D	-2	0	2	3	5	3	2	0	D	In patientia vestra	AR [4] LU 1112 AM 623 WA 414 LA 511	an	1
D	-2	0	2	3	5	3	2	0	D	Juste et pie vivamus	AR 232 LU 339 AM 205 WA 16 62 LA 16	an	2
D	-2	0	2	3	5	3	2	0	D	Justus ut palma florebit	LA 524	an	2
D	-2	0	2	3	5	3	2	0	D	Levabit Dominus signum	AR 230 AM 203 WA 11 LA 12	an	1
D	-2	0	2	3	5	3	2	0	D	Levate capita vestra	AR 260 LU 365 AM 237 WA 26 LA 30	an	1
D	-2	0	2	3	5	3	2	0	D	Lex per Moysen data	AR 239 AM 214 *WA 17 *LA 23	an	1
a	-2	0	2	3	5	3	2	0	a	Magnum haereditatis mysterium	AR 297 LU 444 AM 275 716 *WA 51 LA 66	an	2
D	-2	0	2	3	5	3	2	0	D	Multiplicabitur ejus imperium	AR 244	an	1
D	-2	0	2	3	5	3	2	0	D	Nemo in eum misit manum	AR 402 LU 1094 AM 377 WA 104	an	1
D	-2	0	2	3	5	3	2	0	D	Patefactae sunt januae	LA 47	an	2
D	-2	0	2	3	5	3	2	0		Qui confidunt in Domino	GB 266^{v}	alv	
D	-2	0	2	3	5	3	2	0	D	Relictis retibus suis	LA 497	an	2
D	-2	0	2	3	5	3	2	0		Specie tua et pulchritudine	SYG 41	alv	
D	-2	0	2	3	5	3	2	0	D	Tribus miraculis ornatum	AR 318 LU 466 AM 296 LA 79	an	1
D	-2	0	2	3	5	3	2	0	D	Tulerunt lapides Judaei	AR 414 LU 574 AM 392 LA 172	an	1
a	-2	0	2	3	5	3	2	0	D	Veni hodie ad fontem	LA 122 *WA 83	re	1
D	-2	0	2	3	5	3	2	0	D	Vox in Rama audita ... plorans	AR 284 AM 261 *WA 46 LA 61	an	2
D	-2	0	2	3	5	3	7	10	G	Emitte spiritum tuum	GR 290 OTT 77 LU 860 *SYG 182 GB 184 *GS L	of	8
D	-2	0	2	3	5	7	5	3	D	Deus qui mundum crimine jacentem	ST 377	hy	2
D	-2	0	2	3	5	7	5	3		Dies sanctificatus illuxit nobis	GR 34 LU 409 GB 17^{v} *GS G SYG 19	alv	
D	-2	0	2	3	5	7	5	3		Domine diligo habitaculum	LU 1623^{D}	alv	
D	-2	0	2	3	5	7	5	3		Gaudens in verbo sed turbata virgo	ST 378	hy	1
D	-2	0	2	3	5	7	5	3		Gustate et videte quoniam	GR 616	alv	
D	-2	0	2	3	5	7	5	3		Hic est discipulus ille qui testimonium	GR 39 LU 422 *GS 17 GB 24^{v} SYG 24	alv	
D	-2	0	2	3	5	7	5	3		Hic est sacerdos quem coronavit	GR [8] [34] LU 1184	alv	
D	-2	0	2	3	5	7	5	3		Hic est vere martyr quem coronavit	SYG 226	alv	
D	-2	0	2	3	5	7	5	3		Inveni David servum meum	GR 514 LU 1489 *GS 222 *SYG 38	alv	

D	-2	0	2	3	5	7	5	3		Justum deduxit ... et ostendit ... regnum	GB 271	alv	
D	-2	0	2	3	5	7	5	3		Justus non conturbabitur	GR 573 *GS 208 SYG 34 GB 270	alv	
D	-2	0	2	3	5	7	5	3		Martialis magnus precibus	SYG 208	alv	
D	-2	0	2	3	5	7	5	3		Oculis ac manibus in caelum	GB 242^v	alv	
D	-2	0	2	3	5	7	5	3		Ora pro nobis beate Clemens	GB 245	alv	
D	-2	0	2	3	5	7	5	3		Posui adjutorium super potentem	GB 272	alv	
a	-2	0	2	3	5	7	5	3		Potens in terra erit semen	GR 585	alv	
D	-2	0	2	3	5	7	5	3		Sancti tui Domine benedicent	GR 415 LU 1336 *GS 215 GB 269^v SYG 40	alv	
D	-2	0	2	3	5	7	5	3		Saturninus pontifex magnus	SYG 230	alv	
D	-2	0	2	3	5	7	5	3		Tu es Petrus	GB 202^v	alv	
D	-2	0	2	3	5	7	5	3		Tu puer propheta ... praeibis ... Dominum	GR 524 LU 1501 *GS 1 188 GB 197^v *SYG 196	alv	
D	-2	0	2	3	5	7	5	3		Video caelos apertos	GR 37 LU 416 *GS 15 GB 21^v SYG 22	alv	
D	-2	0	2	3	5	7	5	3		Vidimus stellam ejus ... et venimus	GR 58 LU 460 *GS 19 GB 33^v SYG 31	alv	
D	-2	0	2	3	5	7	5	10	[D]	Agnus Dei	SCH #238		1
D	-2	0	2	3	5	7	9	10	D	Ascendit Deus in jubilatione	GR 287 LU 849 OTT 75 *GS 136 *SYG 179 GB 177	of	1
D	-2	0	2	3	5	7	10	9	D	Tunc Valerianus in conspectu	WA 352	an	1
D	-2	0	2	3	5	8	5	3	D	Christi factus sum ego	GR 622^5 LU 1681^3	of	1
D	-2	0	2	3	5	8	5	3	D	Repleti sumus mane	GR (19) OTT 175 *SYG 171 *GS 209 *GB 163	of	1
D	-2	0	2	3	7	5	2	3	D	Opes decusque regium reliqueras	AR 782	hy	1
G	-2	0	2	4	0	2	0	2	G	Inundaverunt aquae super caput	AR 426 OHS 190 AM 405 *WA 114 *LA 184	an	8
G	-2	0	2	4	2	0	2	0	F	Domus mea domus orationis	GR [74] LU 1253 *SYG 265 GB 176^v GS 175	co	5
G	-2	0	2	4	5	2	0	-3	G	Gloria	BOS #24		IV
G	-2	0	2	4	5	4	5	7	G	Agnes beatae virginis	ST 15	hy	8
G	-2	0	2	4	5	4	5	7	G	Apostolorum supparem	ST 13	hy	8
G	-2	0	2	4	5	4	5	7	G	Jesu corona virginum	ST 16	hy	8
G	-2	0	2	4	5	7	5	4	G	Vox exsultationis et salutis	LA 390	re	8
G	-2	0	2	5	2	0	-2	0	G	In ecclesiis benedicite	WA 66 *LA 93	an	8
G	-2	0	2	5	4	0	4	5	G	Jesum qui crucifixus est	LA 223	an	8
G	-2	0	2	5	4	2	0	-3	G	Soror nostra parvula	WA 163	an	8
G	-2	0	2	5	4	2	5	4	G	Sancti Dei dedit vobis	WA 393	re	8
G	-2	0	2	5	4	5	7	5	G	Agathae sacrae virginis	ST 41	hy	8

G	-2	0	2	5	4	5	7	5	G	Apostolorum supparem	ST 42	hy	8
G	-2	0	2	5	4	5	7	5	G	Conscendat usque sidera	ST 396	hy	8
G	-2	0	2	5	4	5	7	5	G	Fit porta Christi pervia	ST 280	hy	8
G	-2	0	2	5	4	5	7	5	G	Gaude sacrata meritis	ST 401	hy	8
G	-2	0	2	5	4	5	7	5	G	Jacebant sancta corpora	ST 396	hy	8
G	-2	0	2	5	4	5	7	5	G	Jesu corona virginum	ST 44	hy	8
G	-2	0	2	5	4	5	7	5	G	Jesu sacrator mentium	ST 382	hy	8
G	-2	0	2	5	4	5	7	5	G	Nunc tempus acceptabile	ST 381	hy	8
G	-2	0	2	5	4	5	7	5	G	Post triduum jussus tamen	ST 42	hy	8
G	-2	0	2	5	4	5	7	5	G	Quem in superna patria	ST 377	hy	8
G	-2	0	2	5	4	5	7	5	G	Quod seminavit lacrimans	ST 377	hy	8
G	-2	0	2	5	4	5	7	5	G	Rex Christe factor omnium	ST 386	hy	8
G	-2	0	2	5	4	5	7	5	G	Sisti jubet martyram	ST 41	hy	8
G	-2	0	2	5	4	5	7	5	G	Zeno pontifex inclite	ST 387	hy	8
a	-2	0	3	-2	-4	-7	-5	-4	G	Jesu salvator saeculi	ST 144	hy	8
D	-2	0	3	-2	2	0	-2	0	D	Holocausta medullata laudationis	SYG 230	of	2
a	-2	0	3	0	-7	-2	-4	-2	G	O Christi mater caelica	ST 355	hy	8
D	-2	0	3	0	-5	0	-2	0	D	Deus qui quosvis eligis	ST 234	hy	2
D	-2	0	3	0	-5	0	-2	0	D	O sancta mundi domina	ST 236	hy	2
a	-2	0	3	0	-2	0	-2	-5	C	Caeli cives applaudite	ST 351	hy	5
a	-2	0	3	0	-2	0	-2	0		Exaudi me in tua justitia Eripe me	OTT 51 *GB 111^{v} SYG 125	ofv	
D	-2	0	3	0	-2	0	-2	0	D	Nunc sancte nobis spiritus	ST 4	hy	2
D	-2	0	3	0	-2	0	-2	0	D	Rector potens verax Deus	ST 5	hy	2
D	-2	0	3	0	-2	0	-2	0	D	Rerum Deus tenax vigor	ST 5	hy	2
D	-2	0	3	0	-2	0	-2	0	D	Sicut dies verni	WA 359	an	2
a	-2	0	3	0	-2	0	-2	0		Velociter exaudi me Eripe me	OTT 51	ofv	
D	-2	0	3	0	-2	0	3	0	D	Dum intraret Jesus	AR 564 LU 1106 *AM 604	an	1
D	-2	0	3	0	-2	0	3	0	D	Os justi meditabitur	GR [38] LU 1191 SYG 206 GB 53 GS 204	gr	1
D	-2	0	3	0	-2	0	3	2	D	Martyres Christi ad praesidem	WA 378	an	1
D	-2	0	3	0	-2	0	3	5	D	Apparuit Dominus Jesus	PM 175	re	1
D	-2	0	3	0	-2	0	3	5		Sitivit in te anima mea Deus Deus meus	OTT 66 GB 147^{v} SYG 165	ofv	
D	-2	0	3	0	-2	2	3	5		Habet in vestimento	GR 641 LU 1712	alv	
D	-2	0	3	0	-2	2	3	5		Non dilexerunt animas suas	GR 109**	alv	

D	-2	0	3	0	-2	2	3	5		Quae est ista quae progreditur	GR 75**	alv	
D	-2	0	3	0	-2	3	0	3	D	Montes Gelboë nec ros	AR 540 LU 986 *AM 576 WA 164 *LA 274	an	1
D	-2	0	3	0	-2	3	5	3		Eructavit cor meum Afferentur regi ... post eam	OTT 163 SYG 5 *GB 4^{v}	ofv	
D	-2	0	3	0	-2	3	5	3	D	Jam lucis orto sidere	ST 148	hy	1
D	-2	0	3	0	-2	3	5	7	D	Concede nobis Domine quaesumus	PM 202 WA 393	re	1
E	-2	0	3	0	1	0	-2	0	G	Alleluia: beata Agathes ingressa	SYG 51	al	3
E	-2	0	3	0	1	0	-2	0		Beata Agathes ingressa carcere	SYG 51	alv	
D	-2	0	3	0	2	-2	0	3	D	Audiebam sonum alarum	WA 375	re	1
D	-2	0	3	0	2	-2	0	3	D	Simon Barjona tu vocaberis	WA 341	re	1
D	-2	0	3	0	2	-2	2	0	D	Alleluia: auditui meo dabis	GR [142]	al	1
D	-2	0	3	0	2	-2	2	5	E	Fluminis impetus ... Scholasticam	LR 290	an	4
D	-2	0	3	0	2	0	-2	0	D	Assumptus ex eculeo	WA 261	an	1
D	-2	0	3	0	2	0	-2	0	D	Audi filia ... et obliviscere	VP 250 WA 433	re	1
D	-2	0	3	0	2	0	-2	0	D	Confide filia quia fides	WA 191	an	1
D	-2	0	3	0	2	0	-2	0	D	Cum sublevasset oculos	AR 398 LU 1093 *AM 373 WA 191 *LA 162	an	1
D	-2	0	3	0	2	0	-2	0	D	Cum turba plurima convenirent	LR 400	re	1
D	-2	0	3	0	2	0	-2	0	D	Ex ejus tumba marmorea	PM 118 VP 61 *WA 241	re	1
D	-2	0	3	0	2	0	-2	0	D	In velamento clamavi	AR 348 *AM 320	an	2
D	-2	0	3	0	2	0	-2	0	D	O beati martyres	WA 377	re	1
D	-2	0	3	0	2	0	-2	0	D	O claviger regni caelorum	VP 182 WA 280 (inc illeg)	re	1
D	-2	0	3	0	2	0	-2	0	D	Per unum hominem peccatum	LR 262	re	1
D	-2	0	3	0	2	0	-2	0	D	Pretiosus martyr Vincentius	WA 260	re	1
D	-2	0	3	0	2	0	-2	0		Quod ego miserrimus Libera me Domine de morte	LA 557	rev	
D	-2	0	3	0	2	0	-2	0	D	Rerum Deus tenax vigor	ST 175	hy	2
D	-2	0	3	0	2	0	-2	0	D	Unus panis et unum corpus	AR 113* LR 129 VP 16	re	1
D	-2	0	3	0	2	0	-2	0	D	Valerius igitur episcopus	WA 257	re	1
D	-2	0	3	0	2	0	-2	0	D	Vir inclitus Dionysius	WA 387	re	1
D	-2	0	3	0	2	0	-2	3	D	Alleluia: dignus es Domine accipere	GR 540	al	1
D	-2	0	3	0	2	0	-2	3		Dignus es Domine accipere	GR 540	alv	
D	-2	0	3	0	2	0	-2	3	D	Domine praevenisti Saturninum	SYG 229	int	1
D	-2	0	3	0	2	0	-2	3	D	Hi qui amicti sunt	AR 763 LU 1528 *AM 948^{B}	an	1
D	-2	0	3	0	2	0	-2	3	C	Magnum salutis gaudium	ST 418	hy	6
D	-2	0	3	0	2	0	-2	3	D	Rex Christe tu mirificas	ST 99	hy	2

D	-2	0	3	0	2	0	-2	3	D	Sustinuimus pacem et non venit	LA 309	an	1
D	-2	0	3	0	2	0	3	5	D	Visitavit nos oriens	WA 68	an	2
D	-2	0	3	0	2	3	2	0	D	Non in solo pane	LA 130	an	1
D	-2	0	3	0	2	3	2	0	D	Omnium sanctorum chori	LA 478	an	1
d	-2	0	3	0	2	3	5	3		Ista est speciosa inter filias Haec virgo sancta	WA 433	rev	
D	-2	0	3	0	2	3	5	3	D	Tu quae in columbina	LR 300	re	1
a	-2	0	3	0	3	-2	-4	0		Deus meus pone illos ut rotam Sciant gentes	GR 78 LU 506 GS 26 GB 58 *SYG 60	grv	
D	-2	0	3	0	3	0	-2	0	D	Audi benigne conditor	ST 283	hy	2
D	-2	0	3	0	3	0	-2	0	D	Oppressit me dolor	AR 847 LU 1642 AM 1051	an	2
D	-2	0	3	0	3	0	-2	0	D	Sancta Dei genitrix moesta comitata	ST 347	hy	2
D	-2	0	3	0	3	0	3	0		Et concupiscet rex Diffusa est gratia	SYG 49	trv	
D	-2	0	3	0	3	2	0	2		Viribus corporis cepit Martinus igitur obitum	SYG 225	ofv	
D	-2	0	3	0	3	2	3	5	D	Domare cordis impetus	AR 781	hy	1
d	-2	0	3	0	3	2	3	5		Omnia quaecumque voluit ... in caelo Laudabile miraculum	WA 289	rev	
D	-2	0	3	0	3	5	0	3		Subiecit populos nobis et gentes Ascendit Deus	OTT 75 SYG 179 GB 177	ofv	
a	-2	0	3	0	3	5	3	0		Eructavit cor meum Filiae regum	OTT 157 GB 43 SYG 39	ofv	
D	-2	0	3	0	3	5	3	2	D	Martinus ecce migrat	WA 398	inv	2
D	-2	0	3	0	3	5	3	5	D	O nimis felix meritique celsi	AR 738	hy	1
D	-2	0	3	0	3	7	5	7	D	Mulier amicta sole	AR 630 LU 1380	an	1
a	-2	0	3	1	-2	0	-2	-4		Datiano frustra cogitante Pretiosus martyr	WA 260	rev	
E	-2	0	3	1	0	-2	0	-4	E	Kyrie	MEL #158		
E	-2	0	3	1	0	-2	0	3	E	O verbum fidelissimum	ST 236	hy	4
E	-2	0	3	1	0	3	5	3	E	O quam glorifica luce coruscas	ST 398	hy	3
D	-2	0	3	2	-2	2	0	2	D	Angeli Dei qui nobis	VP 225	re	1
D	-2	0	3	2	-2	2	0	2	D	Salvasti nos Domine	AR 119 LU 279[H]	an	2
D	-2	0	3	2	-2	2	0	3	D	Ite missa est XIII	GR 47* LU 53		1
D	-2	0	3	2	-2	2	0	3	D	Kyrie XIII stelliferi conditor	MEL #194 GR 44* LU 51		1
D	-2	0	3	2	-2	2	3	0	D	Beata es virgo Maria Dei genitrix	AR 874 LU 1674 AM 1074	an	1
a	-2	0	3	2	-2	3	0	-2		Ora pro hiis ovibus Simon Barjona	WA 341	rev	
a	-2	0	3	2	-2	3	0	2		Hic venit in testimonium Inter natos	LR 355 *WA 323	rev	

a	-2	0	3	2	0	-2	0	-7		In omnem terram exivit sonus eorum O quam pulchri	VP 252	rev	
D	-2	0	3	2	0	-2	0	-2	D	Intempestae noctis hora	LR 328 LA 371 WA 334	re	1
D	-2	0	3	2	0	-2	0	-2	D	Inter natos mulierum	LR 355 LA 406 *WA 323	re	1
D	-2	0	3	2	0	-2	0	-2	D	Interrogatus Joannes	LA 451	re	1
a	-2	0	3	2	0	-2	0	-2	D	Ite missa est IV	GR 18* LU 28		1
a	-2	0	3	2	0	-2	0	-2	a	Kyrie IV cunctipotens genitor	MEL #18 LU 25 GR 15*		1
D	-2	0	3	2	0	-2	0	-2	D	Nunc sancte nobis spiritus	ST 77 266 AM 84		2
D	-2	0	3	2	0	-2	0	-2	D	Rector potens verax Deus	ST 78 267 361 AM 87	hy	2
D	-2	0	3	2	0	-2	0	-2	D	Rerum Deus tenax vigor	ST 78 AM 90	hy	2
D	-2	0	3	2	0	-2	0	-2	D	Rogamus te virgo	WA 354	an	1
D	-2	0	3	2	0	-2	0	2	D	Operarii qui de illius fama	LR 282	re	2
D	-2	0	3	2	0	-2	0	2		Requiem aeternam dona eis Domine Domine Jesu Christe	OTT 189 *SYG 235	ofv	
D	-2	0	3	2	0	-2	0	3	D	Adjuro vos filiae	WA 353	an	2
D	-2	0	3	2	0	-2	0	3	D	Benedicam Dominum qui mihi	WA 70	an	2
D	-2	0	3	2	0	-2	0	3	D	Cujus pulchritudinem sol	WA 254 LA 334	an	2
D	-2	0	3	2	0	-2	0	3	D	Inventor rutili dux bone luminis	ST 479	hy	2
D	-2	0	3	2	0	-2	0	3	D	Martinus signipotens	WA 405	an	1
D	-2	0	3	2	0	-2	0	3	D	Pulchrae sunt genae tuae	WA 162	an	2
D	-2	0	3	2	0	-2	0	3	D	Quod chorus vatum venerandus olim	ST 222	hy	2
D	-2	0	3	2	0	-2	0	3	D	Sacris solemniis juncta sint gaudia	AR 109* GR 154* LU 952 ST 346	hy	1
D	-2	0	3	2	0	-2	0	3	D	Sancti per fidem vicerunt	AR [47] LU 1156 AM 652 WA 420	an	2
D	-2	0	3	2	0	-2	0	3		Vera fides geniti	GS u	co	2
D	-2	0	3	2	0	-2	0	3	D	Virgo Dei genitrix ex qua	WA 303	an	1
D	-2	0	3	2	0	-2	2	3	D	Exsultet omnium turba ... Benedicti et eorum	AM 1120	an	1
D	-2	0	3	2	0	-2	2	3	D	Exsultet omnium turba ... Benedicti laetentur	AM 850 963 *LA 366	an	1
D	-2	0	3	2	0	-2	2	3	D	Exsultet omnium turba ... in transitu	WA 296	an	1
D	-2	0	3	2	0	-2	2	3	D	Exsultet omnium turba ... Scholasticae	AM 814	an	1
D	-2	0	3	2	0	-2	2	3	D	Sanctus	THAN #191		1
D	-2	0	3	2	0	-2	2	3	D	Tu autem Domine scis omne	AR 431 OHS 307 347	an	1
D	-2	0	3	2	0	-2	2	5	D	Kyrie ad lib. III rector cosmi pie	GR 77* LU 81		2
D	-2	0	3	2	0	-2	2	5	D	Kyrie unus omnipotens (etc)	MEL #198		
a	-2	0	3	2	0	-2	3	-2	G	Aurora lucis rutilat	ST 92	hy	8

a	-2	0	3	2	0	-2	3	-2	G	Rex aeterne Domine	ST 92	hy	8
D	-2	0	3	2	0	-2	3	5	D	Ancilla dixit Petro	AR 432 OHS 358 AM 411 *LA 187	an	1
D	-2	0	3	2	0	-2	3	5	D	Auferte ista hinc	WA 104	an	1
a	-2	0	3	2	0	-2	3	5	G	Christe sanctorum decus angelorum	ST 57	hy	7
D	-2	0	3	2	0	-2	3	5	D	Christi miles pretiosus	WA 259	re	1
D	-2	0	3	2	0	-2	3	5	D	Ejicientes eum extra civitatem	LA 41	an	1
D	-2	0	3	2	0	-2	3	5	D	Gloriosi Domine testis	WA 260	re	1
D	-2	0	3	2	0	-2	3	5	D	Justi confitebuntur ... et habitabunt	AM 980 WA 394 LA 473	an	1
D	-2	0	3	2	0	-2	3	5	D	Majorem caritatem nemo habet	AR [2] LU 1111 AM 622 WA 414 LA 511	an	1
D	-2	0	3	2	0	-2	3	5	D	Ne discedas a me	AR 174 LU 279[O]	an	2
D	-2	0	3	2	0	-2	3	5	D	Prophetae praedicaverunt nasci	AR 240 AM 215 LA 24 377 WA 18	an	1
D	-2	0	3	2	0	-2	3	5	D	Respondens autem Petrus	AM 999	an	1
D	-2	0	3	2	0	-2	3	5	D	Rogabo patrem meum	LA 246 WA 148	an	2
D	-2	0	3	2	0	-2	3	5	D	Sede a dextris meis	WA 63	an	2
D	-2	0	3	2	0	-2	3	5	D	Tunc surrexerunt omnes virgines	PM 237 WA 434 LA 546	an	1
D	-2	0	3	2	0	-2	3	7	D	Ego sum panis vivus qui	AM 553	an	1
D	-2	0	3	2	0	2	-2	3	D	O quam pulchri super montes	VP 252	re	1
D	-2	0	3	2	0	2	0	-2	D	A porta inferi erue Domine	AR 441 [179] OHS 622 LU 776[A] 1802 AM 447 448 1164 *WA 127 *LA 206 559	an	2
D	-2	0	3	2	0	2	0	-2	D	Antra deserti teneris sub annis	ST 95	hy	2
D	-2	0	3	2	0	2	0	-2	D	Auditu auris audivi	LA 287	an	1
a	-2	0	3	2	0	2	0	-2	D	Beati mundo corde quoniam ipsi	GR 650 LU 1727	co	1
a	-2	0	3	2	0	2	0	-2	D	Beati servi illi quos cum venerit	GR 97**	co	1
D	-2	0	3	2	0	2	0	-2	D	Beatus Stephanus jugi legis	WA 33	an	1
D	-2	0	3	2	0	2	0	-2	D	Beatus vir qui suffert tentationem	LA 528	an	1
D	-2	0	3	2	0	2	0	-2	D	Christe cunctorum dominator alme	ST 107	hy	2
D	-2	0	3	2	0	2	0	-2	D	Christe sanctorum decus angelorum	ST 97	hy	2
D	-2	0	3	2	0	2	0	-2	D	Confessor Domini Benedicte	WA 334	an	1
D	-2	0	3	2	0	2	0	-2	D	Cum pervenisset beatus Andreas ... exclamavit	AR 582 LU 1308 AM 758 WA 237 LA 504	an	1
D	-2	0	3	2	0	2	0	-2	D	Daemonis saeva perit hic rapina	ST 107	hy	2
D	-2	0	3	2	0	2	0	-2	D	Deus de caelis qui es pius	GB 157[v]	an	1
D	-2	0	3	2	0	2	0	-2	D	Dominus dabit virtutem	AR 76	an	1
D	-2	0	3	2	0	2	0	-2	D	Dum vero adhuc penderet	WA 239	re	1

D	-2	0	3	2	0	2	0	-2	D	Erat Jesus ejiciens	WA 99	an	1
D	-2	0	3	2	0	2	0	-2	D	Gaudeat ecclesia festa colens annua	ST 159	hy	2
D	-2	0	3	2	0	2	0	-2	D	In regeneratione cum sederit	AM 1125 WA 332 LA 432	an	1
D	-2	0	3	2	0	2	0	-2	D	Iste confessor Domini colentes	AR [68] LU 1196	hy	2
D	-2	0	3	2	0	2	0	-2	D	Laetus hoc festum colat universus	ST 192	hy	2
D	-2	0	3	2	0	2	0	-2	D	Multi ab oriente	WA 71	an	1
D	-2	0	3	2	0	2	0	-2	D	Nunc sancte nobis spiritus	AR 25 LU 235	hy	2
D	-2	0	3	2	0	2	0	-2	D	O beate Oswalde	WA 392	an	1
D	-2	0	3	2	0	2	0	-2	D	O beati viri Benedicti	WA 301	an	1
D	-2	0	3	2	0	2	0	-2	D	O beatum virum qui spreto	AM 777	an	1
D	-2	0	3	2	0	2	0	-2	D	O felicem virum beatum Joseph	AR 183* PM 143 VP 126	an	1
D	-2	0	3	2	0	2	0	-2	D	O laudanda sancti Benedicti	LR 326	re	1
D	-2	0	3	2	0	2	0	-2	D	O nimis felix meritique celsi	ST 95	hy	2
D	-2	0	3	2	0	2	0	-2	D	O quam glorifica luce coruscas	AR 134* PM 180 LU 1864 VP 43 ST 41 96 193	hy	2
D	-2	0	3	2	0	2	0	-2	D	Psallite Deo nostro	LR 70 WA 53 LA 66	an	1
D	-2	0	3	2	0	2	0	-2	D	Quod autem cecidit	WA 79	an	1
D	-2	0	3	2	0	2	0	-2	D	Quod chorus vatum venerandus olim	ST 257 276	hy	2
D	-2	0	3	2	0	2	0	-2	D	Rerum Deus tenax vigor	ST 138	hy	2
D	-2	0	3	2	0	2	0	-2	D	Servivit Domino beatus Oswaldus	WA 282	an	2
D	-2	0	3	2	0	2	0	-2	D	Sic patres vitam peragunt	AR 638	hy	2
a	-2	0	3	2	0	2	0	-2	a	Stabat mater dolorosa	ST 336	hy	2
D	-2	0	3	2	0	2	0	-2	D	Supra pectus Domini	WA 38 LA 48	an	2
D	-2	0	3	2	0	2	0	-2	D	Ut queant laxis resonare fibris	ST 94	hy	2
G	-2	0	3	2	0	2	0	3	G	O venerabiliter pia	WA 338	re	7
D	-2	0	3	2	0	2	3	-2	D	Lapides pretiosi omnes	AR [107] LU 1247 AM 698 *WA 319 LA 552	an	1
D	-2	0	3	2	0	2	3	0	D	Gaudete justi in Domino alleluia	GR [20] LU 1152 *GS 218 *GB 153 SYG 169	co	1
D	-2	0	3	2	0	2	3	0	D	Hodie nobis beata illuxit	PM 41	an	1
D	-2	0	3	2	0	2	3	0	D	Laudemus Dominum quem laudant	AR 865 LU 1665 AM 1067 *WA 381 *LA 467 477	an	2
D	-2	0	3	2	0	2	3	0	D	Libera me Domine de morte aeterna	AR [174] GR 102* LU 1767 PM 321 *LA 557 *WA 438	re	1
D	-2	0	3	2	0	2	3	0	D	O sancta mundi domina	ST 300	hy	2
D	-2	0	3	2	0	2	3	0	D	Sit nomen Domini ... ex hoc	LU 1825	an	2
a	-2	0	3	2	0	2	3	0	E	Te poli cives super astra Christe	ST 150	hy	3

D	-2	0	3	2	0	2	3	2	C	Splendor paternae gloriae	ST 2	hy	5
D	-2	0	3	2	0	2	3	5	D	Veni redemptor gentium	ST 273	hy	2
D	-2	0	3	2	0	3	-2	0	D	Splendor paternae gloriae	ST 26	hy	2
D	-2	0	3	2	0	3	-2	3	D	Laudate pueri Dominum	GR 550 *SYG 206 *GB 211 GS 190	int	1
D	-2	0	3	2	0	3	0	-2	D	Doleo super te	WA 165 LA 274	an	1
D	-2	0	3	2	0	3	0	-2	D	Domine Deus noster qui cum patribus	PM 46 VP 107	an	2
D	-2	0	3	2	0	3	0	-2	D	Hortus conclusus es ... quam pulchra	WA 361	an	1
D	-2	0	3	2	0	3	0	-2	D	In visione Dei	WA 372	re	1
D	-2	0	3	2	0	3	0	-2	D	Inclyta stirps Jesse	PM 183	an	1
a	-2	0	3	2	0	3	0	-2	a	Laus angelorum inclita	ST 340	hy	2
D	-2	0	3	2	0	3	0	-2	D	Principes sacerdotum consilium	AM 397 *AR 420 *LU 1101 *WA 110 LA 174	an	1
D	-2	0	3	2	0	3	0	-2	D	Principes sacerdotum et pharisaei	OHS 631 LU 776[G]	an	1
D	-2	0	3	2	0	3	0	-2	D	Sacerdos Domini Oswaldus	WA 283	an	2
D	-2	0	3	2	0	3	0	7	D	Gaudete justi in Domino alleluia	LR 174	re	1
D	-2	0	3	2	0	3	2	-2	D	In velamento clamabant	AR [29] LU 1120 AM 633 *LA 386 391	an	2
a	-2	0	3	2	0	3	2	-2	D	Virginis proles opifexque matris	ST 162	hy	1
D	-2	0	3	2	0	3	2	0	D	Hortus conclusus es ... hortus ... surge	LA 446 *86	an	2
D	-2	0	3	2	0	3	2	0		Reddet Deus mercedem	SYG 191	alv	
D	-2	0	3	2	0	3	2	3	D	Vox clara ecce intonat	ST 272	hy	2
D	-2	0	3	2	0	3	5	3	D	Beatissimae virginis Mariae	WA 364	an	2
D	-2	0	3	2	0	3	5	3	D	Beatus es care Dei	WA 315	re	1
D	-2	0	3	2	0	3	5	3	D	Diligite Dominum omnes sancti	LR 385 WA 395 LA 475	an	2
D	-2	0	3	2	0	3	5	3	D	Nunc sancte nobis spiritus	AM 244 554	hy	2
a	-2	0	3	2	0	3	5	3	a	Nunc sancte nobis spiritus	ST 174	hy	2
D	-2	0	3	2	0	3	5	3	D	Te lucis ante terminum	AM 549	hy	2
D	-2	0	3	2	0	3	5	3	D	Veni redemptor gentium	ST 217	hy	2
D	-2	0	3	2	0	3	7	5	D	Hoc audito furore	WA 378	an	2
D	-2	0	3	2	0	3	7	5	D	Sanctus	THAN #190		1
D	-2	0	3	2	0	5	3	2		Concaluit cor meum intra me	GR 502 LU 1473	alv	
D	-2	0	3	2	3	0	-2	0	D	Herodes enim metuebat Joannem	LA 451	re	1
D	-2	0	3	2	3	0	-2	0	D	Oramus te virgo virginum	PM 279	an	1
D	-2	0	3	2	3	0	2	-2	D	Beatus Wulstanus Domini	WA 250	re	2

D	-2	0	3	2	3	0	2	0	D	Alleluia: loquebantur variis linguis	GR 297 LU 888 GS 139 *GB 193 *SYG 184	al	1
D	-2	0	3	2	3	0	2	0	D	Audi benigne conditor	ST 32 88 AR 362 LU 539 AM 337	hy	2
D	-2	0	3	2	3	0	2	0	D	Crux Jesu Christi adaperiat	SYG 130	co	2
D	-2	0	3	2	3	0	2	0	D	Cum ascendisset Petrus	WA 327	an	2
D	-2	0	3	2	3	0	2	0	D	Cum sederit filius ... coeperit	SYG 70 *WA 206	an	1
D	-2	0	3	2	3	0	2	0	D	Ingrediente Domino	GR 177 PM 60 OHS 104 LU 590 LA 181 *WA 112 GS 85	re	2
D	-2	0	3	2	3	0	2	0	D	Libenter gloriabor	WA 265	re	1
D	-2	0	3	2	3	0	2	0		Per te omnes gentes Tu es vas	GR 420 LU 1346 *GS 178 *SYG 44	trv	
D	-2	0	3	2	3	0	2	0	D	Tu principatum tenes in choro	PM 32 *WA 35 *LA 40	an	1
D	-2	0	3	2	3	0	2	3	D	Terribilis est locus iste	LR 235 WA 317	re	1
D	-2	0	3	2	3	0	3	0	D	Audi benigne conditor	ST 225	hy	2
d	-2	0	3	2	3	2	0	-2		Memento Domine filiorum Edom Super flumina	OTT 119 *GB 102[v] *SYG 115	ofv	
D	-2	0	3	2	3	2	0	2	D	Homo quidam erat dives qui ... qui jacebat	LA 309	an	1
D	-2	0	3	2	3	5	2	0		In Deo salutare meum	GR 622[4]	alv	
D	-2	0	3	2	3	5	2	0		Salvabo populum meum Israel	GR [140]	alv	
D	-2	0	3	2	3	5	2	0	D	Sanctus	THAN #189		1
D	-2	0	3	2	3	5	2	3	D	Annuntiate de die in diem	LR 337	an	2
D	-2	0	3	2	3	5	2	3		Dolens ego pro meis Libera me de morte	WA 438	rev	
D	-2	0	3	2	3	5	2	5		Quoniam declinaverunt in me Contristatus	GR 622[3]	trv	
D	-2	0	3	2	3	5	3	0	D	Benedicamus Domino IIa	AR 60* LU 125		2
D	-2	0	3	2	3	5	3	0	D	Cum audisset turba quia venit	WA 112	re	1
a	-2	0	3	2	3	5	3	0		Et apparuerunt apostoli Factus est repente	GB 192	ofv	
D	-2	0	3	2	3	5	3	0	D	Regina mundi dignissima	GR 552 LU 1558	co	1
D	-2	0	3	2	3	5	3	2		Beatae de proelio Feliciter virgines	WA 394	rev	
D	-2	0	3	2	3	5	3	2	D	Beatus Stephanus levita	WA 38 LA 47	an	1
D	-2	0	3	2	3	5	3	2	D	Diligite Dominum omnes sancti	GR 93**	gr	1
D	-2	0	3	2	3	5	3	2	D	Ecce vidi agnum stantem	WA 47	an	1
D	-2	0	3	2	3	5	3	2	D	Hic dum matris adhuc	WA 238	an	2
D	-2	0	3	2	3	5	3	2	D	Hortus conclusus es ... surge	LR 255	an	1
D	-2	0	3	2	3	5	3	2	D	Misericordia tua Domine ante oculos	AR 133 LU 279[J]	an	1

D	-2	0	3	2	3	5	3	2	D	Non enim loquetur a semetipso	LA 242	an	2
D	-2	0	3	2	3	5	3	2	D	Positis genibus beatus Stephanus	LA 41	an	1
D	-2	0	3	2	3	5	3	2	D	Psallite Domino qui ascendit	GR 287 LU 849 SYG 180 GB 182 GS 136	co	1
D	-2	0	3	2	3	5	3	2	D	Quinque autem ex eis	WA 430	an	2
D	-2	0	3	2	3	5	3	2	D	Sanctitate quoque insignis	WA 256	an	2
D	-2	0	3	2	3	5	3	2	D	Sanctus antistes Cuthbertus	WA 293	an	1
D	-2	0	3	2	3	5	3	2	D	Timete Dominum omnes sancti	GR 648 LU 1726 SYG 192 GB 216 GS 213	gr	1
D	-2	0	3	2	3	5	7	5	D	Interrogatus a Judaeis	WA 191	an	1
D	-2	0	3	2	5	2	3	0	D	Congregati sunt Deus	AR 197*	re	1
D	-2	0	3	2	5	3	2	3	D	Custodi me Domine ut pupillam	GR 345 LU 1021 *SYG 79 *GB 70^{v} GS 41 151	gr	1
D	-2	0	3	2	5	3	2	3	D	Repleta est spiritu sancto	PM 164	re	1
D	-2	0	3	5	-2	0	-2	0	D	Audi benigne creator	ST 18	hy	2
a	-2	0	3	5	0	-4	-2	0	D	Dulce lignum dulces clavos	WA 308 ×LA 395 462	an	1
D	-2	0	3	5	0	-2	0	-2	D	Caelorum regi psallite	ST 15	hy	2
D	-2	0	3	5	0	-2	0	-2	D	Regi polorum debitas	ST 11	hy	2
D	-2	0	3	5	0	-2	0	-2	D	Summi vatis praeconium	ST 13	hy	2
E	-2	0	3	5	0	1	0	-2	E	Alleluia: casta generatio in perpetuum	GR 100**	al	3
E	-2	0	3	5	0	1	0	-2	E	Kyrie	MEL #157		
D	-2	0	3	5	0	2	3	5		Justificati gratis per gratiam Gratificavit nos	GR 538	trv	
D	-2	0	3	5	0	3	0	-2	D	Sacerdos et pontifex ... ora pro nobis	AR 577^{15} [55] LU 262^{4} 1173 AM 656 739 *PM 336	an	1
D	-2	0	3	5	0	3	0	-2	D	Sacerdos et pontifex ... sic placuisti	AR 81* LU 1840 *PM 308 *LA 537	an	1
D	-2	0	3	5	0	3	2	-2	D	O acceptabilem Deo	WA 285	re	1
D	-2	0	3	5	0	3	2	0	D	Alleluia: positis autem genibus	SYG 22	al	1
D	-2	0	3	5	0	3	2	0	D	Alleluia: qui me invenerit	GR 26**	al	1
a	-2	0	3	5	0	3	2	0	G	Alleluia: quinque prudentes virgines	GS 231	al	7
D	-2	0	3	5	0	3	2	0	D	Alleluia: reddet Deus mercedem	GS 216	al	2
D	-2	0	3	5	0	3	2	0		Qui me invenerit inveniet	GR 26**	alv	
D	-2	0	3	5	0	3	2	0		Reddet Deus mercedem	GS 216	alv	
D	-2	0	3	5	0	3	5	7		Quoniam in me speravit Qui habitat	GR 95 LU 533 GS 35 GB 65 SYG 73	trv	
D	-2	0	3	5	0	7	5	3	D	Kyrie	MEL #201		
D	-2	0	3	5	2	3	0	-2	D	Torcular calcavi solus	AR 760 LU 1537	an	2

D	-2	0	3	5	2	3	0	3	D	Qui operatus est Petro	WA 329 LA 422	an	1
D	-2	0	3	5	3	0	-2	0	D	Laus et perennis gloria Deo	AR 518 LU 914 AM 535 *WA 158	an	2
E	-2	0	3	5	3	0	1	0	E	Agnus Dei	SCH #184		3
D	-2	0	3	5	3	0	2	0	D	Sanctissimus monachorum pater	PM 168 LR 371	re	1
D	-2	0	3	5	3	0	2	3	D	Audivi vocem de caelo venientem	PM 236 *WA 394	re	1
D	-2	0	3	5	3	0	2	3		Et ne avertas faciem Exaudi me	GR 9**	trv	
D	-2	0	3	5	3	0	2	3		Quae Gabrielis archangeli dictis Gaude Maria	GR [78] LU 1266	trv	
D	-2	0	3	5	3	0	2	3		Qui cogitaverunt malitias Eripe me	GR 208 OHS 534 LU 725 GS 99 *SYG 137 *GB 116v	trv	
D	-2	0	3	5	3	0	2	3		Remissionem peccatorum Gratificavit nos	GR 538	trv	
D	-2	0	3	5	3	0	3	-2		Adducentur in laetitia Afferentur regi ... post eam	OTT 163 *SYG 5 *GB 4v	ofv	
D	-2	0	3	5	3	0	3	-2	D	Custodi me Domine de manu	GR 189 LU 614 OHS 278 OTT 52 *SYG 126 GB 113 *GS 91	of	
D	-2	0	3	5	3	0	3	5		In caritate perpetua dilexi te Jam hiems	GR 615	trv	
D	-2	0	3	5	3	0	3	5		Jerusalem quae aedificatur Laetatus sum in his	SYG 101	trv	
D	-2	0	3	5	3	0	3	5		Quoniam ipse liberavit Qui habitat	GR 95 LU 533 GS 35 *GB 65 SYG 73	trv	
D	-2	0	3	5	3	0	5	3	D	Hic est dies verus Dei	ST 278	hy	2
E	-2	0	3	5	3	1	0	-2	E	Christe salvator pietatis auctor	ST 239	hy	4
E	-2	0	3	5	3	1	3	1	E	Oleo caput meum	WA 338	an	4
D	-2	0	3	5	3	2	-2	0	D	Spiritus Domini super me propter	GR 58**	int	2
D	-2	0	3	5	3	2	0	-3	D	Kyrie	MEL #196		
D	-2	0	3	5	3	2	0	-2	D	Alleluia: reddet Deus mercedem	SYG 191	al	1
D	-2	0	3	5	3	2	0	-2	D	Ave sancte rex Edwarde	WA 199	an	2
D	-2	0	3	5	3	2	0	-2	D	Beatorum martyrum veneranda	WA 379	an	1
D	-2	0	3	5	3	2	0	-2	D	Deum time et mandata	WA 88	re	2
D	-2	0	3	5	3	2	0	-2	D	Hic super excelsae	WA 277	an	2
D	-2	0	3	5	3	2	0	-2	D	Hujus diei gloria	ST 327	hy	2
D	-2	0	3	5	3	2	0	-2		Patruum imitans Excellenti prosapia	WA 282	rev	
a	-2	0	3	5	3	2	0	-2	D	Venite et accendite	SYG 47	an	1
D	-2	0	3	5	3	2	0	2	D	Alleluia	PM 218	an	2
D	-2	0	3	5	3	2	0	2	D	Antequam te ascenderet	WA 233	an	2

D	-2	0	3	5	3	2	0	2	D	Candida virginitas paradisi	PM 264 VP 40	re	1
D	-2	0	3	5	3	2	0	2	D	Decus praesulum Dunstanus	WA 315	an	1
D	-2	0	3	5	3	2	0	2	D	Gloriosus Dei martyr	VP 199	re	1
D	-2	0	3	5	3	2	0	2	D	O praeclara stella maris	VP 187	re	1
D	-2	0	3	5	3	2	0	2	D	O quam gloriosum ... regnant innocentes	VP 84	re	1
D	-2	0	3	5	3	2	0	2	D	Princeps sancte caelestis	WA 383	re	1
D	-2	0	3	5	3	2	0	3	D	Alleluia: Christus resurgens ex mortuis	GR 269 LU 827 *SYG 165 *GB 135^{v} GS 126	al	1
D	-2	0	3	5	3	2	0	3	D	Alleluia: potestas ejus potestas	GR 639 LU 1711	al	1
D	-2	0	3	5	3	2	0	3	D	Biduanis ac triduanis	WA 406	an	2
D	-2	0	3	5	3	2	0	3		Christus resurgens ex mortuis	GR 269 LU 827 *SYG 165 *GB 135^{v} GS 126	alv	
D	-2	0	3	5	3	2	0	3	D	In cordis laetitia	WA 285	an	2
D	-2	0	3	5	3	2	0	3	D	Sancta mater Anna	WA 339	an	1
D	-2	0	3	5	3	2	0	3	D	Sancte pater Cuthberte	WA 294	an	1
D	-2	0	3	5	3	2	0	3		Timete Dominum omnes sancti	SYG 192	alv	
D	-2	0	3	5	3	2	0	5	D	Jam lucis orto sidere	AR 13 LU 224 AM 81 ST 3 264	hy	2
D	-2	0	3	5	3	2	0	5	D	Jam lucis splendor rutilat	ST 415	hy	2
D	-2	0	3	5	3	2	0	5	D	O Christi mater caelica	ST 352	hy	2
D	-2	0	3	5	3	2	3	0	D	Iste est de prioribus theologis	VP 122 *WA 290	re	1
D	-2	0	3	5	3	2	3	0	D	Lux vera lucis radium	ST 337	hy	1
D	-2	0	3	5	3	2	3	2		Domine Domine virtus salutis Eripe me	GR 208 OHS 534 LU 725 GS 99 *GB 116^{v} SYG 137	trv	
D	-2	0	3	5	3	2	3	5	D	Da pacem Domine in diebus nostris	AR 144* LU 1867 VP 17 13* LA 300	an	2
D	-2	0	3	5	3	2	3	5		Redemptionem misit ... in populo	GR 266 LU 822 *SYG 248	alv	
D	-2	0	3	5	3	5	0	2	D	Centum quadraginta	LA 60 WA 45	re	1
D	-2	0	3	5	3	5	0	2	D	Cuthbertus puer bone	WA 292	re	1
D	-2	0	3	5	3	5	0	2	D	In omnem terram exivit sonus eorum	LA 510	re	1
D	-2	0	3	5	3	5	0	2	D	Magnus sanctus Paulus	PM 129 LA 430 WA 265	re	1
D	-2	0	3	5	3	5	0	2	D	Sanctus Benedictus plus appetiit	PM 144 LR 321 LA 368 WA 297	re	1
D	-2	0	3	5	3	5	0	2	D	Sanctus Sebastianus dixit	LA 329	re	1
D	-2	0	3	5	3	5	3	0		Quoniam angelis suis mandavit Qui habitat	GR 95 LU 533 GS 35 GB 65 SYG 73	trv	
E	-2	0	3	5	3	5	3	1	E	Christe cunctorum dominator alme	ST 44	hy	4
E	-2	0	3	5	3	5	3	1	E	Ecce jam noctis tenuatur umbra lucis	ST 212	hy	4

E	-2	0	3	5	3	5	3	1	E	Hic locus nempe vocitatur aula	ST 44	hy	4
E	-2	0	3	5	3	5	3	1	E	O nimis felix meritique celsi	ST 233	hy	4
E	-2	0	3	5	3	5	3	1	E	Ut queant laxis resonare fibris	ST 233 259 295	hy	4
a	-2	0	3	5	3	5	3	2		Nisi quod Dominus erat Anima nostra	OTT 145 *GB 27^{v} SYG 26	ofv	
a	-2	0	3	5	3	5	3	5		Aperiam in parabolis Portas caeli	OTT 60 *GB 136^{v} *SYG 158	ofv	
E	-2	0	3	5	3	5	3	5	E	Postquam surrexit Dominus a coena	GR 200 OHS 447 LU 672 *SYG 130	an	4
a	-2	0	3	5	3	5	7	3	a	Faciem meam non averti	AR 426 OHS 186 198 AM 404 *WA 114 LA 184	an	4
a	-2	0	3	5	3	5	7	3	a	Gratia Dei in me vacua	AR 609 756 LU 1348 AM 793 941 *WA 266 *LA 431	an	4
a	-2	0	3	5	3	5	7	3	a	Media nocte clamor factus	LR 224 *WA 434 LA 546	an	4
a	-2	0	3	5	3	5	7	5	a	A summo caelo egressio ejus	LR 95 *WA 147 *LA 244	an	4
D	-2	0	3	5	3	5	7	5	D	Alleluia: repletus sum consolatione	GR 547	al	1
a	-2	0	3	5	3	5	7	5	a	Angelus Domini descendebat de caelo	AR 377 LU 1084 AM 350 *WA 90 LA 135	an	4
a	-2	0	3	5	3	5	7	5	a	Annuntiate populis et dicite	AR 241 AM 216 *WA 18 *LA 24	an	4
a	-2	0	3	5	3	5	7	5	a	Ascendit Deus in jubilatione	AR 875 LR 99 LU 1675 AM 1075 *WA 147 *LA 247	an	4
D	-2	0	3	5	3	5	7	5	D	Candidato martyrum choro	PM 196	an	1
a	-2	0	3	5	3	5	7	5	a	Custodiebant testimonia	LR 140 *WA 412 LA 508	an	4
D	-2	0	3	5	3	5	7	5	D	Ecce jam noctis tenuatur umbra lucis	ST 166	hy	2
D	-2	0	3	5	3	5	7	5	D	Ecce jam noctis tenuatur umbra lux	AR 9	hy	1
a	-2	0	3	5	3	5	7	5	a	Laetentur caeli ... ante faciem	LR 60 LU 387 *WA 49 *LA 33	an	4
a	-2	0	3	5	3	5	7	5	a	Laetentur caeli ... quia venit	LR 100	an	4
D	-2	0	3	5	3	5	7	5		Lux perpetua lucebit sanctis In circuitu tuo	WA 423	rev	
a	-2	0	3	5	3	5	7	5	a	Magister dicit tempus meum	AR 418 LU 1100 AM 396 *WA 114 LA 174	an	4
D	-2	0	3	5	3	5	7	5	D	Ne magnitudo revelationum	WA 331 LA 425	an	1
D	-2	0	3	5	3	5	7	5		Non Moyses dedit vobis panem Comedetis carnes	LR 123 LU 927	rev	
a	-2	0	3	5	3	5	7	5	a	Oculi Domini respexerunt	LR 176	an	4
a	-2	0	3	5	3	5	7	5	a	Popule meus quid feci	AR 93 409 AM 102 117 389 *WA 108 *LA 171	an	4

D	-2	0	3	5	3	5	7	5		Positis autem genibus beatus	SYG 22	alv	
a	-2	0	3	5	3	5	7	5	a	Post partum virgo inviolata	LR 251 *LA 350 383 477	an	4
a	-2	0	3	5	3	5	7	5	a	Propheta magnus surrexit	AR 403 567 LU 1044 1096 AM 380 607	an	4
a	-2	0	3	5	3	5	7	5	a	Prudentes virgines aptate lampades	AR 577[21] [87] LU 2629 1215 AM 683 746	an	4
a	-2	0	3	5	3	5	7	5	a	Quaerite Dominum dum inveniri	AR 221 AM 192 *WA 9 *LA 7	an	4
a	-2	0	3	5	3	5	7	5	a	Vestitus erat veste	AR 759 LU 1537 AM 946	an	4
E	-2	0	3	5	3	5	7	8	E	Si ego Dominus et magister	GR 202 OHS 449 LU 674 *SYG 130	an	4
a	-2	0	3	5	3	5	8	5	G	Memor esto fili	LA 289 *WA 176	re	7
E	-2	0	3	5	3	5	8	5	D	Veniens a Libano	PM 235 LA 229 *WA 140	re	1
D	-2	0	3	5	7	0	-2	-5	D	Gloria Christe tuo	WA 300	re	1
D	-2	0	3	5	7	3	2	5		Aspicientes in auctorem fidei Christo igitur	GR 482	trv	
D	-2	0	3	5	7	3	2	5		At illa dixit etiam Dixit dominus mulieri	SYG 85 GS 47	trv	
D	-2	0	3	5	7	3	2	5		O quam bonus et suavis Emitte spiritum	GR [93] LU 1279	trv	
D	-2	0	3	5	7	3	2	5		Qui cogitaverunt supplantare Eripe me	GR 208 OHS 534 LU 725 GS 99 *GB 116v *SYG 137	trv	
D	-2	0	3	5	7	3	2	5		Quoniam defecit in dolore Miserere mei	GR [145]	trv	
D	-2	0	3	5	7	3	2	5		Specie tua et pulchritudine Diffusa est gratia	GS 228	trv	
D	-2	0	3	5	7	3	5	7	D	Kyrie	MEL #200		
D	-2	0	3	5	7	3	7	10	D	Agnus Dei	SCH #242		1
a	-2	0	3	5	7	5	3	0	a	Jure Petro ecclesiae	WA 278	an	2
D	-2	0	3	5	7	5	3	5	D	Angeli eorum ... qui est	AR 866 LU 1665	an	1
a	-2	0	3	5	7	5	3	5	a	Crastina die delebitur	AR 256 LU 363 AM 232 *WA 26 *LA 30	an	4
a	-2	0	3	5	7	5	3	5	a	Egredietur Dominus de loco	AR 238 AM 213 *WA 17 *LA 22	an	4
a	-2	0	3	5	7	5	3	5	a	Emitte agnum Domine	AR 239 AM 214 *WA 17 *LA 23	an	4
D	-2	0	3	5	7	5	3	5		Gloria et honore coronasti ... Domine et constituisti	GS 208	alv	
D	-2	0	3	5	7	5	3	5	D	Qui me segregavit	WA 330	an	1
a	-2	0	3	5	7	5	3	5		Qui propitiatur omnibus Benedic anima mea	OTT 110 GB 72 SYG 80	ofv	

a	-2	0	3	5	7	5	3	5	a	Rorate caeli desuper	AR 238 AM 213 *WA 17 *LA 23	an	4
a	-2	0	3	5	7	5	3	5	a	Sicut ablactatus est	LR 338	an	4
D	-2	0	3	5	7	5	3	5	D	Te lucis ante terminum	ST 78 84	hy	2
a	-2	0	3	5	7	5	3	5	a	Ut cognoscamus Domine	AR 239 AM 214 *WA 17 *LA 23	an	4
E	-2	0	3	5	7	5	3	5	a	Verbum supernum prodiens a patre	ST 171	hy	2
E	-2	0	3	5	7	5	3	5	a	Vox clara ecce intonat	ST 171 AM 184	hy	2
D	-2	0	3	5	7	5	7	3		Eripe me Domine ab homine malo Custodi me	OTT 52 GB 113 SYG 126	ofv	
D	-2	0	3	5	7	5	7	3		Martinus episcopus migravit Martinus igitur obitum	SYG 225	ofv	
D	-2	0	3	5	7	5	7	3	G	Verbum supernum prodiens a patre	ST 272	hy	8
D	-2	0	3	5	7	5	7	5	D	Alleluia: in Deo salutare meum	GR 622[4]	al	1
D	-2	0	3	5	7	5	7	5	D	Alleluia: salvabo populum meum Israel	GR [140]	al	1
D	-2	0	3	5	7	5	7	5	G	Angeli Domini Dominum	AR 857 LU 1660 AM 1059 *LA 472	an	tp 4
a	-2	0	3	5	7	5	7	5		Appropinquaverunt persequentes me Benedictus ... et non tradas	OTT 48 *GB 104 SYG 116 GS 77	ofv	
D	-2	0	3	5	7	5	7	5	G	Martyres Domini Dominum	AR [42] LU 1154 AM 648 LA 520	an	tp
D	-2	0	3	5	7	5	7	5	G	Verbum salutis omnium	ST 365	hy	8
D	-2	0	3	5	7	5	7	5	G	Verbum supernum prodiens a patre	ST 365	hy	8
D	-2	0	3	5	7	5	7	5	G	Vox clara ecce intonat	ST 365	hy	8
D	-2	0	3	5	8	5	8	3	G	Verbum supernum prodiens a patre	ST 216	hy	2
D	-2	0	3	7	5	2	0	3	D	Sanctus	THAN #188		1
a	-2	0	3	7	5	3	2	0	a	O quam admirabilis vir	WA 390	re	2
a	-2	0	3	7	5	3	5	7	a	Da mihi in disco caput	AR 830 LU 1621 AM 1027 *WA 363 LA 454	an	4
a	-2	0	3	7	5	3	5	7	a	Dignare me laudare te	LR 251 *WA 268 LA 348	an	4
E	-2	0	3	7	5	3	5	7	E	Dum sacramenta offerret	LA 483	an	4
a	-2	0	3	7	5	3	5	7	a	Exibunt aquae vivae	AR 894[7] LU 1706 AM 1093	an	4
a	-2	0	3	7	5	3	5	7	a	Gaude Maria virgo	LR 251 *WA 268 LA 350 383	an	4
E	-2	0	3	7	5	3	5	7	E	Hic est praepositus paradisi	LA 467	an	4
a	-2	0	3	7	5	3	5	7	a	Thesaurizate vobis thesauros	AR 359 AM 333 *WA 84 LA 126	an	4
G	-2	0	5	4	5	2	-2	0	G	Invocabit me et ego exaudiam	GR 93 LU 532 *SYG 72 *GB 64^v *GS 34	int	8
d	-2	0	5	7	5	0	3	2		Fiat pax in virtute tua Laetatus sum	GR 139 LU 560 GB 89^v GS 63 162 SYG 100	grv	

d	-2	0	5	7	5	0	3	2		Fiat pax in virtute tua Rogate quae	GR [135] LU 1285	grv	
G	-2	0	7	9	7	9	7	9		Quasi rosa plantata	GR 614 LU 1669	alv	
E	-2	1	-2	-4	-2	0	-2	-4	E	Laus Deo patri parilique proli	AR 519 LU 914 *AM 536 *WA 158	an	4
E	-2	1	-2	-4	-2	0	-2	0	E	Jesu Christe auctor vitae	ST 234	hy	4
E	-2	1	-2	-4	-2	0	-2	0	E	Praesul insignis Oswalde	WA 286	an	4
E	-2	1	-2	-4	-2	0	-2	0	E	Sancte Dei pretiose protomartyr	ST 219	hy	4
E	-2	1	-2	-4	-2	0	-2	0	E	Tibi Christe splendor patris	ST 237	hy	4
E	-2	1	-2	-4	-2	0	-2	0	E	Urbs beata Jerusalem	ST 240	hy	4
E	-2	1	-2	-4	-2	1	-2	0	E	Jesu Christe auctor vitae	ST 394	hy	4
E	-2	1	-2	-4	-2	1	-2	0	E	Urbs Jerusalem beata	LR 231 AM 694	hy	4
E	-2	1	-2	-4	0	1	3	5	E	Omnis expertem maculae Mariam	AR 635 LU 1382	hy	4
E	-2	1	-2	0	-2	-4	-2	0	D	Alleluia: nonne cor nostrum ... loqueretur	GB 131	al	2
E	-2	1	-2	0	-2	-4	-2	0	E	O mundi lampas et margarita	PM 170	an	4
E	-2	1	-2	0	-2	-4	0	-2	E	O gloriosa Dei genitrix	PM 272	an	4
E	-2	1	-2	0	1	0	1	3	E	O dignissima Christi sponsa	AM 1133 *PM 210	an	3
a	-2	1	0	-4	-2	-4	-2	-4	F	Intende voci orationis meae	GR 135 OTT 83 SYG 98 *GB 87^{v} *GS 60 142	of	5
a	-2	1	0	-2	-4	-2	0	-2	D	Cor Jesu sacratissimum miserere	AR 92* LU 1853		1
E	-2	1	0	-2	-4	-2	0	-2	E	Isti sunt viri sancti quos	WA 325	an	4
E	-2	1	0	-2	-4	-2	0	-2	E	Sanctum est verum lumen	WA 398 *LA 478	an	4
a	-2	1	0	-2	0	-4	-5	-4		Benedic anima mea Dominum et omnia	GR 636	alv	
a	-2	1	0	-2	0	-4	-5	-4		Benedicite Domino omnes virtutes ejus	GR 612 LU 1664	alv	
a	-2	1	0	-2	0	-4	-5	-4		Emitte spiritum tuum	GR 293 LU 879 SYG 183 GB 187^{v} *GS M 137	alv	
a	-2	1	0	-2	0	-4	-5	-4		Excita Domine potentiam tuam	GR 8 LU 336 GS 4 SYG 7 GB 5^{v}	alv	
a	-2	1	0	-2	0	-4	-5	-4		Fecisti viriliter et confortatum	GR 39**	alv	
a	-2	1	0	-2	0	-4	-5	-4		Lauda Jerusalem Dominum lauda	GR [136] LU 1285 SYG 259	alv	
a	-2	1	0	-2	0	-4	-5	-4		Laudate pueri Dominum	GR 42 260 OHS 827 LU 428 805 GS p 123 216 SYG 161 GB 142^{v}	alv	
a	-2	1	0	-2	0	-4	-5	-4		Pauper et inops laudabunt	GR 424 LU 1352^{v}	alv	
a	-2	1	0	-2	0	-4	-5	-4		Qui posuit fines tuos	GR [137] LU 1286 GS f	alv	
a	-2	1	0	-2	0	-4	0	3	F	Benedicite Deum caeli	AR 891 LU 1701	an	5
a	-2	1	0	-2	0	-4	0	3	a	Haec dies quam fecit	AR 445 OHS 730 771 LU 783	an	2

a	-2	1	0	-2	0	-4	0	3	a	Haec dies quam fecit	GR 241 LU 778 OHS 709 SYG 152 *GB 125 GS 117	gr	2
E	-2	1	0	-2	0	-4	0	3	D	Iste confessor Domini sacratus	ST 200	hy	1
a	-2	1	0	-2	0	-2	-4	-5		Pro salute et augmento gregis Fidelis namque	PM 309	rev	
a	-2	1	0	-2	0	-2	-4	-2	D	Lex Domini irreprehensibilis	GR 122 SYG 91 GB 81 GS 53	int	1
e	-2	1	0	-2	0	-2	-3	-5	a	Jam lucis orto sidere	ST 142	hy	2
a	-2	1	0	-2	0	-2	1	0		Kyrie ... pater de caelis	PM 284 VP 34		
E	-2	1	0	-2	0	-2	1	0	E	Translato ad caelestia	WA 314	an	4
E	-2	1	0	-2	0	1	0	-2		Pro omnibus mortuus est Christus	GR 480 LU 1434	alv	
E	-2	1	0	-2	0	3	5	3	E	In choro confessorum	WA 315	an	4
a	-2	1	0	1	-2	-4	-2	-4		Custodi innocentiam et vide	GR 529	alv	
a	-2	1	0	1	-2	-4	-2	-4		De excelso misit ignem	GR 501 LU 1473	alv	
E	-2	1	0	1	0	-2	-4	-2	E	Intuens in caelum	WA 51 *LA 43	an	4
E	-2	1	0	1	3	1	0	-2	E	Implevit eos Dominus	WA 375	an	4
E	-2	1	0	1	3	1	0	-2	E	Multitudo angelorum	WA 398	an	4
E	-2	1	0	1	3	5	8	5	E	Jesu quadragenariae	ST 112	hy	4
E	-2	1	3	1	0	-2	0	-2	E	Laudemus Dominum quod doctrinis	WA 291	an	4
D	-2	2	-2	2	0	2	3	5	D	Gaudete in Domino semper	GR 6 LU 334 SYG 6 GB 5 GS 4	int	1
a	-2	2	0	-4	-2	0	-2	-4	D	Ille homo qui dicitur Jesus	AR 403 LU 1095 AM 378 *LA 164 *WA 105	an	1
a	-2	2	0	-2	-5	-4	-2	-4	D	Ad laudem sanctae Mariae	ST 456	hy	2
d	-2	2	0	-2	-3	-2	-3	-5	G	Kyrie laudes pangamus	MEL #2		
d	-2	2	0	-2	-3	-2	0	-2	G	Deus magnus Dominus	LA 80	inv	7
a	-2	2	0	-2	0	-4	-5	-4		Laudate Dominum in sanctis	SYG 224	alv	
a	-2	2	0	-2	0	-4	-5	-4		Qui posuit fines tuos Lauda Jerusalem Dominum	SYG 259	alv	
a	-2	2	0	-2	0	-4	-5	-4		Vindica Domine sanguinem ... super terram	SYG 175 191 *GB 269	alv	
a	-2	2	0	-2	0	-4	0	-2	G	Exaudi Deus orationem meam et ne	GR 129 OTT 36 SYG 95 GB 84 GS 56	of	8
a	-2	2	0	-2	0	2	3	5	G	Alleluia: stetit Jesus in medio	SYG 162	al	7
a	-2	2	0	-2	0	3	2	0	G	Scapulis suis obumbrabit ... Dominus et	GR 98 OTT 32 LU 537 *SYG 74 GB 66v GS 36	of	8
a	-2	2	0	-2	0	3	2	3	G	Non enim judicavi me scire	GR 477 LU 1429	of	8
D	-2	2	0	-2	0	3	5	3	D	Ego autem cum mihi molesti	GR 604 LU 1646	of	2
a	-2	2	0	-2	2	0	-2	2		Kyrie ... pater de caelis	AR 183* LU 1876		
G	-2	2	0	2	0	-2	2	0	G	Veniens vir splendidissimus	GB 166v *SYG 174	of	8

G	-2	2	0	2	0	2	0	-2	G	Nunc sancte nobis spiritus	ST 77	hy	8
G	-2	2	0	2	0	2	0	-2	G	Rector potens verax Deus	ST 78	hy	8
G	-2	2	0	2	0	2	0	-2	G	Rerum Deus tenax vigor	ST 78 268	hy	8
G	-2	2	0	2	0	5	7	5	G	Alleluia: venite ad me omnes	GR 648 [114] LU 973 1726 *SYG 218	al	8
G	-2	2	0	2	4	0	2	5	G	Linguam refrenans temperet	ST 474	hy	8
G	-2	2	0	2	4	5	4	2	G	Christum rogemus et patrem	ST 42	hy	8
G	-2	2	0	2	4	5	4	2	G	Fallax ad patibulum	ST 44	hy	8
G	-2	2	0	2	4	5	4	2	G	Impleta gaudent viscera	ST 38	hy	8
G	-2	2	0	2	4	5	4	2	G	Jam Christus astra ascenderat	ST 38	hy	8
G	-2	2	0	2	4	5	4	2	G	Post Petrum primum principem	ST 44	hy	8
G	-2	2	0	2	4	5	4	2	G	Stabat mater dolorosa	ST 47	hy	8
D	-2	2	0	2	5	2	0	2	D	Alleluia: ipse est directus	GR 566 LU 1581	al	1
D	-2	2	0	3	0	-2	0	3	D	Miserere mei Deus miserere	GR 88 LU 526 SYG 65 GB 62 *GS 31	gr	1
D	-2	2	0	3	5	2	0	3		Beatus qui lingua sua	GR 29**	alv	
D	-2	2	0	3	5	2	0	3		Regnavit Dominus super omnes	GR 288 LU 855 GS K *GB 179^{v}	alv	
D	-2	2	0	3	5	3	2	3	D	Alleluia: isti sunt duae olivae	SYG 199 *GS n	al	1
D	-2	2	0	3	5	7	3	0	D	Clamaverunt justi et Dominus	GR 455 SYG 172 GB 167^{v} *GS 210	int	2
G	-2	2	0	5	2	4	2	0	G	Alleluia: virtutes caeli movebuntur	GS 3 SYG 4	al	8
G	-2	2	0	5	7	5	4	2	G	Kyrie	MEL #90		
D	-2	2	3	0	2	-2	2	3	D	Virginitas caelum post lapsum	AR 132* VP 203	re	1
D	-2	2	3	2	0	2	0	3	D	Contra spem in spem	GR 426 LU 1353^{v}	co	2
D	-2	2	3	2	0	2	0	3	D	Domine Dominus noster	GR 117 SYG 87 *GB 77 GS 49	co	2
D	-2	2	3	2	0	3	7	5	D	O Nazarene dux Bethleem	ST 117	hy	1
D	-2	2	3	5	2	0	3	2		Hortus conclusus est	GB 232	alv	
D	-2	2	3	5	3	0	-2	3	D	Angelus Domini nuntiavit	AR 219 AM 191 *LR 251 LA 7 380 WA 8	an	1
D	-2	2	3	5	3	0	-2	3	D	Dignus es Domine Deus	WA 139	an	1
D	-2	2	3	5	3	0	-2	3	D	Loquere Domine quia audit	AR 517 LU 907 AM 534 WA 164 *LA 273	an	1
D	-2	2	3	5	3	0	-2	3	D	Obsecro Domine aufer	AR 541 LU 987 AM 577 *LA 275	an	1
D	-2	2	3	5	3	2	3	2	D	Alleluia: suxerunt mel de petra	GB 151^{v}	al	1
D	-2	2	3	5	3	2	3	2		Suxerunt mel de petra	GB 151^{v}	alv	
D	-2	2	3	5	3	5	3	2	E	Vinea mea electa	SYG 139	an	4

D	-2	2	3	5	7	5	3	2	D	Jesu corona virginum	ST 203	hy	2
G	-2	2	4	2	0	-2	0	2		Spiritus Dei ornavit caelos	SYG 185	alv	
G	-2	2	4	2	0	5	4	2	G	Advenit ignis divinus	WA 153	re	8
G	-2	2	4	5	4	5	7	5	G	Hodie nobis de caelo pax	LU 376 *LR 57 *LA 32 *WA 28	re	8
D	-2	2	5	2	-2	0	2	5	D	Alleluia: ascendens Christus in altum	GS 135	al	1
D	-2	2	5	2	-2	0	2	5	D	Alleluia: corona aurea super caput	GR 14**	al	1
D	-2	2	5	2	-2	0	2	5	D	Alleluia: habet in vestimento	GR 641 LU 1712	al	1
D	-2	2	5	2	-2	0	2	5	D	Alleluia: judicabunt sancti nationes	SYG 188 GS 199	al	1
D	-2	2	5	2	-2	0	2	5	D	Alleluia: non dilexerunt animas suas	GR 109**	al	1
D	-2	2	5	2	-2	0	2	5	D	Alleluia: quae est ista quae progreditur	GR 75**	al	1
D	-2	2	5	3	2	-2	0	-2	D	Alleluia: Domine Deus meus in te speravi	GR 322 LU 962 GB 248 *GS f 167	al	1
D	-2	2	5	3	2	-2	0	-2	D	Alleluia: laudem Domini loquetur	GR 52 LU 448	al	1
D	-2	2	5	3	2	-2	0	-2	D	Alleluia: surgens Jesus Dominus ... stans	SYG 163	al	1
D	-2	2	5	3	2	-2	0	2	D	Alleluia: beati estis ... qui mer istis	SYG 222	al	1
D	-2	2	5	3	2	-2	0	2		Beati estis sancti ... qui meruistis	SYG 222	alv	
D	-2	2	5	3	2	0	2	3	D	Alleluia: ecce sacerdos magnus qui ... et inventus	SYG 215	al	1
D	-2	2	5	3	2	3	2	0	D	Alleluia: jubilate Deo omnis terra	GB 148	al	1
D	-2	2	5	3	2	3	2	0		Jubilate Deo omnis terra	GB 148	alv	
G	-2	2	5	4	0	-2	0	2	G	Adjutor meus et liberator	AR 164 LU 300	an	8
G	-2	2	5	4	0	[0	0	0]	G	Alleluia	WA 131	an	8
G	-2	2	5	4	0	2	0	-2	G	Vestimentum tuum candidum	AR 586 LU 1320 AM 764	an	8
G	-2	2	5	4	0	4	5	2	G	Amplius lava me Domine	WA 67 *LA 95	an	8
G	-2	2	5	4	0	4	5	2	G	Annuntiaverunt opera Dei	LR 136 WA 411 LA 506	an	8
G	-2	2	5	4	0	4	5	2	G	Avertet Dominus captivitatem	WA 65 LA 92	an	8
G	-2	2	5	4	0	4	5	2	G	Benignitatem fecit Dominus	LR 126	an	8
G	-2	2	5	4	0	4	5	2	G	Data est mihi omnis potestas	AR 452 OHS 820 LU 803 AM 465 *WA 135 LA 222	an	8
G	-2	2	5	4	0	4	5	2	G	Ecce te rogavi	AM 815	an	8
G	-2	2	5	4	0	4	5	2	G	Et nunc reges intelligite	AR 782 LU 1553	an	8
G	-2	2	5	4	0	4	5	2	G	In loco pascuae ibi	AR [161] LU 1787	an	8
G	-2	2	5	4	0	4	5	2	G	Labia mea laudabunt	AM 362	an	8

G	-2	2	5	4	0	4	5	2	G	Lapidaverunt Stephanum et ipse	AR 273 LU 414 1583[A] AM 250 *WA 37 *LA 47	an	8
G	-2	2	5	4	0	4	5	2	G	Laudate Dominum secundum multitudinem	AR 195	an	8
G	-2	2	5	4	0	4	5	2	G	Natus est nobis hodie salvator	WA 48 LA 31	an	8
G	-2	2	5	4	0	4	5	2	G	Potens in terra erit semen	WA 415 LA 421	an	8
G	-2	2	5	4	0	4	5	2	G	Quaerite Dominum et inveniet	WA 66	an	8
G	-2	2	5	4	0	4	5	2	G	Quia vidisti me Thoma	AR 466 595 LU 1326 AM 479 774 WA 138 *LA 230	an	8
G	-2	2	5	4	0	4	5	2	G	Quoniam in te confidit	WA 65 *LA 92	an	8
G	-2	2	5	4	0	4	5	2	G	Sepelierunt Stephanum	AR 278 LU 420 1583[B] AM 254 LA 43	an	8
G	-2	2	5	4	0	4	5	4	G	Alleluia	WA 127	an	8
G	-2	2	5	4	2	0	-2	0		Pretiosa in conspectu Domini	GB 164	alv	
G	-2	2	5	4	2	0	-2	0		Universae angelorum virtutes	GB 169	alv	
G	-2	2	5	4	2	0	2	4	E	Christe redemptor omnium ex patre	ST 177	hy	3
G	-2	2	5	4	2	0	2	4	G	Martyrum rector diadema splendor	ST 150	hy	8
G	-2	2	5	4	2	0	2	4		Virtutes caeli movebuntur	SYG 4 GS 3	alv	
G	-2	2	5	4	2	4	5	2	G	Quaerite Dominum et vivet	LA 95	an	8
G	-2	2	5	4	2	5	7	5	G	Crux benedicta nitet	WA 370	an	8
D	-2	2	5	7	5	3	0	2	D	Almi prophetae progenies pia	ST 53	hy	2
G	-2	2	5	7	5	4	0	-2	G	Electi sunt in Christo	WA 373	an	7
G	-2	2	5	7	5	4	2	4	G	Mea doctrina non est mea	LA 164	an	8
G	-2	2	5	7	5	4	2	5	G	Adorate Dominum in aula	LR 233 *LA 82 *WA 61	an	8
G	-2	2	5	7	5	4	2	5	G	Archangele Michael constitui te	AR 856 LU 1660 AM 1059 *WA 383 *LA 472	an	8
G	-2	2	5	7	5	4	5	7	G	Speciosa facta es et suavis	WA 139	re	8
D	-2	3	0	-2	0	2	[0	0]	E	Kyrie	MEL #193		
D	-2	3	0	2	0	-2	3	5	D	Laetentur omnes qui sperant ... in aeternum	LR 381 *WA 395 *LA 474	an	1
D	-2	3	2	0	-2	0	-2	3		Nonne cor nostrum ... dum loqueretur	SYG 155 GS 118	alv	
D	-2	3	2	0	-2	0	3	5	D	Aurora lucis rutilat	ST 118	hy	2
D	-2	3	2	0	-2	0	3	5	D	Beati estis sancti ... meruistis	AM 877	an	1
D	-2	3	2	0	-2	0	3	5	D	Beati estis sancti ... meruistis ... ideoque	WA 394	an	1
D	-2	3	2	0	2	0	-2	0	D	Fulgebunt justi et tamquam	AM 880 WA 393 *LA 520	an	1

D	-2	3	2	0	2	0	-2	0	D	Per signum crucis de inimicis	AM 1041 *SYG 142 *WA 371	an	2
D	-2	3	2	0	5	3	2	0	D	Veni spiritus alme	WA 153	an	1
D	-2	3	2	0	7	5	3	2	D	Adesto sancta trinitas	AR 180*	hy	1
a	-2	3	2	0	7	5	3	2	a	Apostolorum passio	ST 42	hy	1
D	-2	3	2	0	7	5	3	2	D	Exsultet caelum laudibus	AM 621	hy	1
D	-2	3	2	0	7	5	3	2	D	Exsultet orbis gaudiis	AR [6] LU 1116	hy	1
D	-2	3	2	0	7	5	3	2	D	Jam lucis orto sidere	ST 73	hy	1
a	-2	3	2	0	7	5	3	2	a	O praeferenda gloria	ST 39	hy	1
a	-2	3	2	0	7	5	3	2	a	Stephano primo martyri	ST 39	hy	1
a	-2	3	2	0	7	5	3	2	a	Verso crucis vestigio	ST 42	hy	1
D	-2	3	2	3	5	7	5	7	D	Exaltabor in gentibus	LR 99	an	2
E	-2	3	5	1	0	3	1	0		Expandi manus meas Eripe me ... Domine	SYG 125	ofv	
D	-2	3	5	3	0	-2	3	2	D	Regina caeli laetare alleluia	AR [131] AM 718 LA 215	an	1
E	-2	3	5	3	1	3	1	0	E	Sidus solare revehit	ST 160	hy	3
D	-2	3	5	3	2	5	7	5	D	Lauda anima mea Dominum	AR 131	an	1
a	-2	3	5	3	5	0	-4	0	G	Agnus Dei VII	GR 27* LU 36 SCH #55		8
D	-2	3	5	3	5	7	3	5	D	Beatus Gregorius a diebus	WA 289	an	1
D	-2	3	5	3	5	7	3	5	D	Caeleste beneficium introivit	WA 366	an	1
D	-2	3	5	3	5	7	5	2	D	Caritas Dei diffusa ... inhabitantem	AR 515 AM 531 *PM 90	an	1
D	-2	3	5	3	5	7	5	2	D	Exaudiat Dominus orationes	AR 551 LU 995 AM 589 LA 300	an	1
D	-2	3	5	3	5	7	5	2	D	In tuo adventu	WA 8	an	1
D	-2	3	5	3	5	7	5	2	D	Paulus et Joannes dixerunt ad Terentianum	LA 410	an	1
D	-2	3	5	3	5	7	5	3	D	Ab ipso pueritiae suae	LR 318 WA 296 LA 366	an	1
D	-2	3	5	3	5	7	5	3	D	Accepto pane Judas	LA 188	an	1
D	-2	3	5	3	5	7	5	3	D	Ad hanc vocem Christi ... Sebastiani	LA 330	an	1
D	-2	3	5	3	5	7	5	3	D	Cinctus ergo fide	WA 385	an	1
D	-2	3	5	3	5	7	5	3	D	Dum in hac terra	LR 319 WA 296 LA 367	an	1
D	-2	3	5	3	5	7	5	3	D	Erat Petrus dormiens	WA 340 LA 415	an	1
D	-2	3	5	3	5	7	5	3	D	Erat quidam regulus	AR 571 LU 1107 *AM 611 LA 318	an	1
D	-2	3	5	3	5	7	5	3	D	Exiens Petrus apostolus	WA 340 LA 416	an	1
D	-2	3	5	3	5	7	5	3	D	Hi sancti viri ... Eleutherii	WA 389	an	1
D	-2	3	5	3	5	7	5	3	D	Paradisi porta per Evam	WA 135 LA 442	an	1

D	-2	3	5	3	5	7	5	3	D	Qui vult venire ... sequatur ... dicit	LA 527	an	1
D	-2	3	5	3	5	7	5	3	D	Sanctus Dionysius qui tradente	WA 384	an	1
D	-2	3	5	3	5	7	5	3	D	Sonant ibi jugiter	LA 326	an	1
D	-2	3	5	3	5	7	5	3	D	Tali namque ad Dominum	WA 389	an	1
D	-2	3	5	3	5	7	5	3	D	Tua est potentia	AR 551 LU 995 AM 589	an	1
D	-2	3	5	3	5	7	5	7	D	Beatus Gregorius in cathedra	AM 832	an	1
D	-2	3	5	3	5	7	5	7	D	Coenantibus autem accepit Jesus	AR 437 *AM 434 *LA 195	an	1
D	-2	3	5	3	5	7	5	7	D	Cum iratus fueris	AR 172	an	1
D	-2	3	5	3	5	7	5	7	D	Deposuit Dominus potentes	AR 184	an	1
D	-2	3	5	3	5	7	5	7	D	Erat pater Jesu	LR 309	an	1
D	-2	3	5	3	5	7	5	7	D	Euntes in mundum docete ... baptizantes	LA 222 252	an	1
D	-2	3	5	3	5	7	5	7	D	Herodes videns	WA 43	an	1
D	-2	3	5	3	5	7	5	7	D	Illi autem profecti	LR 104 *WA 150 *LA 252 253	an	1
D	-2	3	5	3	5	7	5	7	D	In lege Domini Oswaldus	WA 282	an	1
D	-2	3	5	3	5	7	5	7	D	Invenit Philippus Nathanael	LR 313	an	1
D	-2	3	5	3	5	7	5	7	D	Jesus autem transiens	AR 391 LU 1089 AM 366 WA 99 LA 154	an	1
D	-2	3	5	3	5	7	5	7	D	Mirabantur omnes qui audiebant	LA 343	an	1
D	-2	3	5	3	5	7	5	7	D	Qui verbum Dei retinent	AR 350 LU 504 AM 322 325 *WA 79 *LA 119	an	1
D	-2	3	5	3	5	7	5	7	D	Sebastiani martyris	ST 20	hy	2
D	-2	3	5	3	5	7	5	8	D	Beati pacifici beati mundo	AR [4] LU 1112 AM 623 *WA 412 *LA 511	an	1
D	-2	3	5	3	5	7	5	8	D	Cum immundus spiritus exierit	AR 390 LU 557 AM 364 *WA 99 *LA 153	an	1
D	-2	3	5	3	5	7	5	8	D	Deposuit potentes sanctos	WA 67 *LA 103	an	1
D	-2	3	5	3	5	7	5	8	D	Dum esset summus pontifex	AR 577^{16} [66] LU 262^{4} 1181 *AM 663 741 826 *LA 532	an	1
D	-2	3	5	3	5	7	5	8	D	Haec est virgo sapiens et una	AR [87] LU 1210 AM 678 *WA 434 *LA 545	an	1
D	-2	3	5	3	5	7	5	8	D	Transeunte Domino clamabat	AR 356 LU 511 AM 329 *WA 83 *LA 122 125	an	1
E	-2	3	5	3	5	7	8	5	E	Pius adolescens Dunstanus	WA 312	re	3
D	-2	3	5	3	5	7	8	7	D	Ab insurgentibus in me	OHS 500 LU 706 WA 123 LA 198	an	1
D	-2	3	5	3	5	7	8	7	D	Beata Dei genitrix virgo	AM 36 130 165 749	an	1
E	-2	3	5	3	5	7	8	7	E	Congratulamini mihi omnes ... quia quem quaerebam	OHS 803 *LR 91 *WA 132	re	3

D	-2	3	5	3	5	7	8	7	D	Cum accepisset acetum	AR 440 OHS 477 (nm) AM 444 LA 188	an	1
D	-2	3	5	3	5	7	8	7	D	Cum essem parvula placui	AR 882[3] LU 1686 AM 1082	an	1
D	-2	3	5	3	5	7	8	7	D	Cum facis eleemosynam	AR 361 AM 334 WA 84 LA 126	an	1
D	-2	3	5	3	5	7	8	7	D	Dabit ei Dominus sedem	AR 669 [140] LU 1417 AM 862 WA 19 LA 24 379	an	1
D	-2	3	5	3	5	7	8	7	D	De quinque panibus	AR 399 LU 559 AM 374 WA 102 LA 162	an	1
D	-2	3	5	3	5	7	8	7	D	Dum conturbata fuerit anima	AR 439 OHS 513 LU 716 AM 441 442 WA 124 LA 201	an	1
D	-2	3	5	3	5	7	8	7	D	Joannes vocabitur nomen	AR 736 LU 1504 AM 924 WA 323 LA 408	an	1
D	-2	3	5	3	5	7	8	7	D	Nuptiae factae sunt	WA 62 *LA 106	an	1
D	-2	3	5	3	5	7	8	7	D	Qui me confessus fuerit	AR [15] LU 1125 AM 640 WA 419 LA 527	an	1
D	-2	3	5	3	5	7	8	7	D	Qui vult venire	AR 577[13] [21] LR 157 LU 262 1128 *AM 644 737	an	1
D	-2	3	5	3	5	7	8	7	D	Sancta Dei genitrix virgo	WA 353 LA 449	an	1
D	-2	3	5	3	5	7	8	7	D	Sunt de hic stantibus	AM 256 *AR 280 WA 42 LA 56	an	1
D	-2	3	5	3	5	7	8	7	D	Tradetur enim gentibus	AR 384 LU 1087 AM 358 WA 94	an	1
D	-2	3	5	3	5	7	8	7	D	Tu autem cum oraveris	AR 361 AM 335 WA 85 LA 126	an	1
E	-2	3	5	3	5	7	8	10	E	Quare detraxistis sermonibus	LA 287	an	3
D	-2	3	5	3	5	7	9	7	D	Cum esset summus pontifex	WA 426	an	1
D	-2	3	5	3	5	7	9	7	D	De sub cujus pede fons	WA 410	an	1
D	-2	3	5	3	5	7	9	7	D	Duo mihi Domine talenta	LA 532	an	1
D	-2	3	5	3	5	7	9	7	D	Ego mittam vobis	WA 152	an	1
D	-2	3	5	3	5	7	9	7	D	Hesterna die Dominus	LA 43	an	1
D	-2	3	5	3	5	7	9	7	D	Intrepidus itaque candentis	WA 261	an	1
D	-2	3	5	3	5	7	9	7	D	Invenerunt in modum	WA 410 LA 494	an	1
D	-2	3	5	3	5	7	9	7	D	Joannes apostolus ... a Christo	LA 52	an	1
D	-2	3	5	3	5	7	9	7	D	Quinque mihi Domine	WA 426	an	1
D	-2	3	5	3	5	7	9	7	D	Si male locutus sum	LA 187	an	1
D	-2	3	5	3	5	7	9	7	D	Stat a dextris ejus	WA 255 LA 335	an	1
D	-2	3	5	3	5	7	9	7	D	Stolam jucunditatis induit eum	LA 538	an	1
D	-2	3	5	3	5	7	9	7	D	Unguentum effusum nomen	WA 435 *LA 541	an	1
D	-2	3	5	3	5	7	9	7	D	Vidit supra montem	WA 410	an	1
D	-2	3	5	3	5	7	9	7	D	Vos qui secuti ... regeneratione	SYG 55	co	1

D	-2	3	5	3	5	7	9	10	D	Ecce nomen Domini venit	AR 211 LU 317 AM 186 *LA 1	an	1
D	-2	3	5	3	5	7	10	7	D	Ait autem angelus ne timeas	AR 661 LU 1408	an	1
D	-2	3	5	3	5	7	10	7	D	Dedisti Domine habitaculum	AR 929 LU 1761 AM 1148 *PM 213 WA 410 LA 496	an	1
D	-2	3	5	3	5	7	10	7	D	Dedit ei Dominus potestatem	AR 894[6] LU 1705 AM 1092	an	1
D	-2	3	5	3	5	7	10	7	D	Dominus veniet occurrite	AR 251 256 LU 357 AM 227 233 *WA 19 24 *LA 21	an	1
D	-2	3	5	3	5	7	10	7	D	Et omnes angeli stabant	AR 898 LU 1729 AM 1103 WA 397	an	1
D	-2	3	5	3	5	7	10	7	D	Et ut perfecerunt omnia	LR 310	an	1
D	-2	3	5	3	5	7	10	7	D	Hoc est testimonium	AR 249 AM 224 WA 23 *LA 16	an	1
D	-2	3	5	3	5	7	10	7	D	In tua patientia possedisti	AR 591 LU 1322 AM 769 WA 242 LA 320	an	1
D	-2	3	5	3	5	7	10	7	D	Nisi ego abiero	WA 150 LA 247	an	1
D	-2	3	5	3	5	7	10	7	D	Per arma justitiae	AR 97 PM 51 *AM 107 122 WA 89	an	1
D	-2	3	5	3	5	7	10	7	D	Perpetuum nobis Domine	WA 384	an	1
D	-2	3	5	3	5	7	10	7	D	Quid molesti estis	WA 110 LA 183	an	1
D	-2	3	5	3	5	7	10	7	D	Secundum multitudinem miserationum	AR 353 AM 326 WA 78 LA 123	an	1
D	-2	3	5	3	5	7	10	7	D	Tu es pastor ovium ... traditae	AM 792 823 933 943 988 PM 126 *AR 598 750 798 *LU 1330 1516 LA 411 *WA 281 328	an	1
D	-2	3	5	3	5	7	10	9	D	Si quis introierit	WA 156 *LA 265	an	1
E	-2	3	5	3	5	8	5	3	E	Corde natus ex parentis	ST 367	hy	3
E	-2	3	5	3	5	8	7	3	E	Ad hujus quoque spectat	WA 291	an	3
E	-2	3	5	3	5	8	7	5	E	Accedens Petrus ad Jesum	WA 100	an	3
E	-2	3	5	3	5	8	7	5	E	Qui meditabitur in lege	GR 90 LU 529 *SYG 67 *GB 63 GS 32	co	3
E	-2	3	5	3	5	8	7	8	E	Ab adolescentia pugnando	WA 289	an	3
E	-2	3	5	3	5	8	7	8	E	Annuntiaverunt inter gentes	LR 140	an	3
E	-2	3	5	3	5	8	7	8	E	Haec est generatio	WA 421	an	3
E	-2	3	5	3	5	8	7	8	E	Laudate Deum omnes angeli	AR 866 LU 1666 *AM 1068	an	3
E	-2	3	5	3	5	8	7	8		Laudate Dominum Deum nostrum	GR 41**	alv	
E	-2	3	5	3	5	8	7	8	E	Valerius igitur episcopus	WA 256	an	3
E	-2	3	5	3	5	8	10	8	E	Ascendente Jesu in naviculam	WA 71	an	3
E	-2	3	5	3	5	8	10	8	E	Quis ex vobis homo	AR 538[15] LU 1102 *AM 571 *LA 310	an	3

D	-2	3	5	3	7	3	5	7	D	Misericordia tua Domine magna	LA 100 *WA 69	re	1
D	-2	3	5	3	7	3	5	7	D	Puellae saltanti imperavit	AR 829 LU 1620 AM 1026 *WA 363 *LA 454	an	1
D	-2	3	5	3	7	3	5	7	D	Qui me sanum fecit	AR 377 LU 1084 AM 350 *WA 90	an	1
D	-2	3	5	3	7	5	2	3	D	Ego sum panis vivus qui ... et panis	AR 512 AM 528	an	1
D	-2	3	5	3	7	5	2	3	D	Joannes et Paulus dixerunt ad Gallicanum	AR 744 LU 1510 *WA 325 *LA 411	an	1
D	-2	3	5	3	7	5	2	3	D	Maternitas tua Dei genitrix	AM 1085	an	1
D	-2	3	5	3	7	5	2	3	D	Nativitas tua Dei genitrix	AR 837 LU 1627 AM 1035 *WA 364 *LA 455	an	1
D	-2	3	5	3	7	5	3	2	D	Habebitis autem hunc diem	AM 953	an	1
D	-2	3	5	3	7	5	3	5	D	Amen dico vobis quia nemo propheta	AR 391 LU 1089 AM 366 *WA 99 *LA 154	an	1
D	-2	3	5	3	7	5	3	5	D	Amen dico vobis quia non praeteribit	AR 576 LU 1080 AM 618	an	1
D	-2	3	5	3	7	5	3	5	D	Amen dico vobis quod uni	AM 829 974	an	1
D	-2	3	5	3	7	5	3	5	D	Conventione autem facta	AR 343 LU 496 AM 314 *LA 114	an	1
D	-2	3	5	3	7	5	3	5	D	Unus ex duobus qui secuti	AR 579 LU 1304 AM 754 *WA 232 *LA 502	an	1
D	-2	3	5	3	7	5	7	3	D	Corpora sanctorum in pace	AR [41] LU 1153 AM 648 *WA 423 *LA 520	an	1
D	-2	3	5	3	7	5	7	5	D	Montes et colles cantabunt	AR 225 LU 332 AM 196 *WA 12 LA 11	an	1
D	-2	3	5	3	7	5	7	5	E	Unguentum in capite	SYG 233	co	4
D	-2	3	5	3	7	5	7	5	D	Veni electa mea	AR [88] [98] LU 1211 1233 AM 679 687	an	1
D	-2	3	5	3	7	5	7	8	D	In Deo speravi non timebo	AR 137 LU 279[K]	an	1
D	-2	3	5	3	7	5	7	9	D	Amen dico vobis mundus plorabit	LA 236	an	1
D	-2	3	5	3	7	5	8	7	D	Admoniti Magi in somnis	AR 334 LU 483 *AM 300 *LA 69 *WA 57	an	1
D	-2	3	5	3	7	5	8	7	D	Antequam convenirent	AM 191 *AR 220 *WA 8 LA 6	an	1
D	-2	3	5	3	7	5	8	7	D	Ecce puer meus electus	AR 280 LU 424 AM 256 *WA 42 *LA 56	an	1
D	-2	3	5	3	7	5	8	7	D	Euge serve bone in modico fidelis	AR [74] LU 1195 *AM 670 *LA 540	an	1
D	-2	3	5	3	7	5	8	7	D	Ex utero senectutis	AR 733 LU 1496 AM 921 *WA 320	an	1
D	-2	3	5	3	7	5	8	7	D	Herodes iratus occidit	AR 283 LU 427 *AM 260 *WA 46 *LA 61	an	1
D	-2	3	5	3	7	5	8	7	D	Pater venit hora	AR 487 *AM 503	an	1
D	-2	3	5	3	7	8	7	5	D	Ancilla fidelis et sponsa	AM 1132	an	1
D	-2	3	5	3	7	8	7	5	D	Clarifica me pater	AR 420 427 OHS 192 LU 1101 AM 398 406 *WA 110 *LA 175	an	1

D	-2	3	5	3	7	8	7	5	D	Ecce veniet desideratus	AR 251 LU 357 AM 227 *WA 19 24 LA 21	an	1
D	-2	3	5	3	7	8	7	5	D	Qui mihi ministrat	AR [16] LU 1125 AM 640 *WA 419 *LA 528	an	1
D	-2	3	5	3	7	8	7	5	D	Stans a dextris ejus	AR 613 LU 1351^{v} AM 798 *PM 129	an	1
D	-2	3	5	3	7	9	7	5	D	A finibus terrae laudes	LA 23	an	1
D	-2	3	5	3	7	9	7	5	D	Qui verbum meum audit	LA 165	an	1
D	-2	3	5	3	7	9	10	9	D	Venerunt ad monumentum	AR 467 AM 480	an	1
D	-2	3	5	3	7	10	7	5	D	Currebant duo simul	AR 452 OHS 825 AM 465 *WA 136 *LA 222	an	1
D	-2	3	5	3	7	10	7	5	D	Deficiente vino jussit	AR 336 LU 488 AM 306 *WA 63 *LA 106	an	1
D	-2	3	5	3	7	10	7	5	D	Joannes et Paulus agnoscentes	AR 743 LU 1510 *WA 324	an	1
D	-2	3	5	3	7	10	7	5	D	Vidi turbam magnam	AR 898 LU 1728 AM 1102 *WA 397	an	1
D	-2	3	5	3	7	10	12	10	D	In corde Gertrudis	AM 1127	an	1
D	-2	3	5	3	8	7	8	10	D	Alleluia: laetatus sum in his	GR 5 LU 329 *SYG 3 *GB 3 GS 162	al	1
E	-2	3	5	7	3	5	7	5	E	Tertio Christum Petrus	WA 278	an	3
E	-2	3	5	7	3	5	8	5	E	Perfecto corde Maria	WA 336	re	3
E	-2	3	5	7	3	5	8	7	E	Angelus Domini descendit ... et accedens ... et dixit	SYG 147	an	3
E	-2	3	5	7	3	5	8	7	E	Dum oraret sanctus	WA 249	an	3
D	-2	3	5	7	5	3	2	3	D	Laudamus nomen tuum	AR 72 *AM 42	an	1
D	-2	3	5	7	5	3	2	5	D	Immense caeli conditor	ST 253	hy	2
E	-2	3	5	7	5	3	5	3	G	Alleluia: Christus resurgens ex mortuis	SYG 168	al	8
D	-2	3	5	7	5	3	5	3	D	Auxilium meum a Domino	AR 100 OHS 224 LU 282	an	1
D	-2	3	5	7	5	3	5	3	D	Immense caeli conditor	ST 183	hy	2
D	-2	3	5	7	5	3	5	3	D	Lucis creator optime	ST 438	hy	2
D	-2	3	5	7	5	3	5	3	F	Ne recorderis peccata	AR [166] LU 1792 LA 555 *WA 437	re	6
D	-2	3	5	7	5	3	5	7	D	Fulgebat in venerando	WA 287	re	1
D	-2	3	5	7	5	3	5	7	D	Immense caeli conditor	ST 271	hy	2
D	-2	3	5	7	5	3	5	7	D	Intravit Maria in domum Symonis	WA 338	an	1
D	-2	3	5	7	5	3	5	7	D	Posui adjutorium super potentem	PM 314 LR 199 LA 531 WA 425	re	1
D	-2	3	5	7	5	3	5	7	D	Tradent enim vos in conciliis	AR [8] LU 1112 AM 621 WA 414 LA 508	an	1
E	-2	3	5	7	5	3	5	8	G	Alleluia: hosanna filio David	SYG 2	al	8

E	-2	3	5	7	5	3	5	8	G	Alleluia: pulchra facie	SYG 42	al	8
E	-2	3	5	7	5	3	5	8	E	Beatus Vincentius applicatus	WA 258	an	3
E	-2	3	5	7	5	3	5	8	E	In excessu	WA 327	an	3
E	-2	3	5	7	5	3	5	8	E	Miles Christi gloriose	WA 391	re	3
E	-2	3	5	7	5	7	5	3	E	Egredietur Dominus de Samaria	LA 9 *WA 11	re	3
D	-2	3	5	7	5	7	5	3	E	Egredietur Dominus et proeliabitur	LA 24 *WA 14	re	3
a	-2	3	5	7	5	7	5	3	a	Peccata mea Domine sicut sagittae	LA 84 WA 62	re	1
D	-2	3	5	7	5	7	5	3	D	Tria sunt munera pretiosa	LA 72 WA 55	re	1
D	-2	3	5	7	5	7	5	7	D	Aspice Domine de sede	LA 301 WA 183	re	1
D	-2	3	5	7	5	7	5	8		Beati immaculati in via Confitebor tibi	OTT 44 *GB 98 SYG 110	ofv	
D	-2	3	5	7	5	7	5	8		Beati quorum remissae sunt Laetamini in Domino	OTT 140 GB 44 SYG 41	ofv	
E	-2	3	5	7	5	7	8	7	E	Exaudi Domine populum tuum confitentem	GB 160v	an	3
E	-2	3	5	7	5	7	8	7	E	Exaudi Domine populum tuum toto	GB 160v	an	3
a	-2	3	5	7	5	7	8	7	c	Gaude Maria virgo	PM 146 AM 1195 VP 130 *LA 354 WA 271	re	6
E	-2	3	5	7	5	7	8	7	E	Libera Domine populum	GB 154v	an	3
E	-2	3	5	7	5	7	8	10		Cum sederit filius ... tunc	SYG 157	alv	
D	-2	3	5	7	5	7	10	5	F	Gratias tibi Domine	WA 385	re	6
E	-2	3	5	7	5	8	3	5	E	Virtute magna reddebant	OHS 779 *PM 217 *LR 87 *LA 210 WA 133 305	re	3
E	-2	3	5	7	8	5	3	1	E	Audite verbum Domini gentes	LA 4 WA 4	re	3
E	-2	3	5	7	8	5	3	1	E	Virga de Jesse generata stirpe	ST 240	hy	3
E	-2	3	5	7	8	5	3	5		Quid bonum ejus est	GR 55**	alv	
E	-2	3	5	7	8	5	3	5		Quoniam confirmata est super nos	SYG 250	alv	
E	-2	3	5	7	8	5	3	5		Si enim non abiero	SYG 168	alv	
E	-2	3	5	7	8	5	8	5		Domine Deus meus clamavi Exaltabo te	GR 160 *GS 75 GB 101 SYG 113	grv	
D	-2	3	5	7	8	7	5	3	D	Caecilia famula tua	WA 407	an	1
D	-2	3	5	7	8	7	5	3	D	Cum inducerent puerum	AM 803 *AR 621 LA 347 WA 268	an	1
D	-2	3	5	7	8	7	5	3	D	Exaltata est gloriosa	PM 278	an	1
D	-2	3	5	7	8	7	5	8	D	Consilium fecerunt inimici	WA 115 LA 186	an	1
D	-2	3	5	7	8	7	8	5	D	Exaudi nos Domine qui exaudisti	PM 49 VP 120 *GB 161	an	1
D	-2	3	5	7	8	7	8	7	D	Egredietur virga ... et replebitur	AR 245 WA 17 *LA 22	an	1
E	-2	3	5	7	8	7	8	10	E	Beatus Maurus patricio	AM 778	an	3
E	-2	3	5	7	8	7	8	10	E	De luce sanctus praesul	WA 285	an	3

E	-2	3	5	7	8	7	8	10	E	Quam pulchra es Gertrudis	AM 1128	an	3
E	-2	3	5	7	8	7	10	8	E	Viderunt eam ... vernantem	AM 1073	an	3
E	-2	3	5	7	8	10	5	3		Cum transieris per aquam Ab oriente	GR (4)	grv	
E	-2	3	5	7	8	10	7	8		Quis vestrum habebit	SYG 177	alv	
E	-2	3	5	7	8	10	7	8		Quoniam non in finem Adjutor in opportunitatibus	GR 74 LU 498 *GS 24 GB 56 *SYG 58	grv	
D	-2	3	5	7	8	10	8	7	D	Pange lingua gloriosi corporis	AR 104* GR 153* VP 7* LU 950 AM 547	hy	1
E	-2	3	5	7	8	10	8	7	E	Recordare virgo mater Dei	AR 3 (sup 1)	an	3
D	-2	3	5	7	8	10	8	7	D	Tantum ergo sacramentum	AR 89* AM 1258	hy	1
D	-2	3	5	7	9	10	7	9	D	Alleluia: loquebar Domine de testimoniis	SYG 39 *GB 244	al	1
D	-2	3	5	7	9	10	9	5	D	Pange lingua gloriosi proelium	ST 385	hy	1
D	-2	3	5	7	10	12	9	10	D	Semen cecidit ... centuplum	WA 79	an	1
E	-2	3	5	8	5	3	5	7	E	Illuxerunt coruscationes	GR 571 LU 1585	int	3
E	-2	3	5	8	5	3	5	8	E	Cum esset desponsata ... Jesu	AR 649 687 LU 1437 *AM 837 885	an	3
E	-2	3	5	8	5	3	5	8		Pulchra Sion filia pro mortali Surge virgo	PM 209	rev	
E	-2	3	5	8	5	3	5	8	E	Regni caelestis per fructum	PM 268	re	3
E	-2	3	5	8	5	7	5	3	E	Patriarchae nostri Abrahae	WA 293	re	3
E	-2	3	5	8	5	7	8	7	E	Adonai Domine Deus	LR 424 LA 290 *WA 178	re	3
E	-2	3	5	8	5	7	8	10	E	Sapientia reddidit justis	LU 1440	int	3
E	-2	3	5	8	5	7	10	8	D	Lucis creator optime	ST 156	hy	1
E	-2	3	5	8	5	8	3	5	E	Iste est Odo abbas mirabilis	PM 210	re	3
E	-2	3	5	8	5	8	3	5	E	Spiritus sanctus procedens	PM 87 LR 111 LA 261 *WA 154	re	3
E	-2	3	5	8	5	8	3	5	E	Super salutem et omnem ... dilecta	PM 263 LR 377 *WA 357	re	3
E	-2	3	5	8	5	8	3	5	E	Super salutem et omnem ... dilexi	PM 111 LA 279 *WA 169	re	3
E	-2	3	5	8	5	8	5	3	E	Confessio et pulchritudo	GR 578 LU 1593 *SYG 79 *GB 70v *GS 40 194	int	3
E	-2	3	5	8	5	8	5	8		Diffusa est gratia in labiis Afferentur regi	OTT 155 *GB 30 *SYG 29	ofv	
E	-2	3	5	8	5	8	5	8	E	Hostis Herodes impie	ST 256 275	hy	3
E	-2	3	5	8	5	8	7	3	E	Caecilia me misit	LA 491	an	3
E	-2	3	5	8	7	3	7	8	E	In tribulatione lapidum	WA 33	an	3
E	-2	3	5	8	7	3	7	8	E	Quando natus es ineffabiliter	AR 294 LU 443 *AM 271 WA 50 *LA 64	an	3
E	-2	3	5	8	7	5	3	5	E	A solis ortus cardine	ST 143	hy	3

E	-2	3	5	8	7	5	3	5	E	Ad thronum majestatis	WA 358	an	3
E	-2	3	5	8	7	5	3	5	E	Adesto sancta trinitas	ST 114	hy	3
a	-2	3	5	8	7	5	3	5	c	Adversio parvulorum	WA 171	re	6
E	-2	3	5	8	7	5	3	5	E	Caecilia famula tua	AR 925 LU 1757 *AM 1140 LA 494	an	3
E	-2	3	5	8	7	5	3	5	E	Caecilia me misit	LA 491 WA 406	re	3
E	-2	3	5	8	7	5	3	5	E	Christe redemptor omnium ex patre	ST 117	hy	3
E	-2	3	5	8	7	5	3	5	E	Communione calicis quo Deus	LR 121 LU 924	an	3
E	-2	3	5	8	7	5	3	5	E	Copiosae caritatis	WA 242	an	3
E	-2	3	5	8	7	5	3	5	E	Cor arca legem continens	AR 538[8] VP 21*	hy	3
E	-2	3	5	8	7	5	3	5	E	En ut superba criminum	AR 538[3] LU 978 VP 19*	hy	3
E	-2	3	5	8	7	5	3	5	E	Jesu corona virginum	ST 405	hy	3
E	-2	3	5	8	7	5	3	5	E	Nunc sancte nobis spiritus	AR 538[10] LU 969	hy	3
E	-2	3	5	8	7	5	3	5	E	Quem parentes	WA 248	an	3
E	-2	3	5	8	7	5	3	5	E	Salvete Christi vulnera	AM 950	hy	3
E	-2	3	5	8	7	5	3	5	E	Te lucis ante terminum	AR 538[6] LU 966	hy	3
E	-2	3	5	8	7	5	7	5	E	Quinque fatuae virgines	WA 430	an	3
E	-2	3	5	8	7	5	7	8	E	Aeterna Christi munera apostolorum	ST 195	hy	3
E	-2	3	5	8	7	5	7	8	E	Alleluia: si filii et heredes	GR 480 LU 1434	al	3
E	-2	3	5	8	7	5	7	8	E	Deus tuorum militum	AR [13[2]] LU 1127	hy	3
E	-2	3	5	8	7	5	7	8	E	Gregorius praesul meritis	PM 140 VP 123	re	3
E	-2	3	5	8	7	5	7	8	E	Occasum tanti pontificis	WA 285	re	3
D	-2	3	5	8	7	5	7	10	a	In nomine Domini Dei nostri	WA 227	an	3
E	-2	3	5	8	7	5	7	10	E	Quo abiit dilectus tuus	AR 675 LU 1423	an	3
E	-2	3	5	8	7	5	7	10		Si filii et heredes	GR 480 LU 1434	alv	
E	-2	3	5	8	7	5	8	5	E	Alleluia: salvum me fac Deus	GR [139]	al	3
E	-2	3	5	8	7	5	8	7	E	Aeterna Christi munera et apostolorum	ST 60	hy	3
E	-2	3	5	8	7	5	8	7	E	Alleluia: laudate Dominum Deum nostrum	GR 41**	al	3
E	-2	3	5	8	7	5	8	7	E	De patre verbum prodiens	ST 220	hy	3
E	-2	3	5	8	7	5	8	7	E	Exaltasti Domine caput	WA 282	an	3
E	-2	3	5	8	7	5	8	7	E	Hostis Herodes impie	ST 221	hy	3
E	-2	3	5	8	7	5	8	7	E	Jesu corona virginum	ST 63	hy	3
E	-2	3	5	8	7	5	8	7	E	Jesu redemptor omnium	ST 244	hy	3
E	-2	3	5	8	7	5	8	7	E	Martyr Dei qui unicum	ST 101	hy	3

E	-2	3	5	8	7	5	8	7	E	Ortu Phoebi jam proximo	ST 241	hy	3
E	-2	3	5	8	7	5	8	7	E	Petre pontifex inclite	ST 234	hy	3
E	-2	3	5	8	7	5	8	7	E	Praecipita Domine omnes	WA 185	re	3
E	-2	3	5	8	7	5	8	7	E	Salvete flores martyrum	ST 221	hy	3
E	-2	3	5	8	7	8	5	3		Usquequo Domine oblivisceris Illumina oculos	OTT 87 *GB 81 SYG 92	ofv	
E	-2	3	5	8	7	8	5	7	E	Humiliavit semetipsum Dominus	GR [106]	int	3
E	-2	3	5	8	7	8	5	8	E	Aperite mihi portas justitiae	GR 33**	int	3
E	-2	3	5	8	7	8	5	10	E	Si diligis me Simon Petre	GR [2[1]] LU 1122[1]	int	3
E	-2	3	5	8	7	8	7	3	E	Dum steteritis ante reges	LR 138 *LA 506 *WA 412	re	3
E	-2	3	5	8	7	8	7	3	E	Ex omni corde laudaverunt	WA 375	an	3
E	-2	3	5	8	7	8	7	5	E	Ecce angelus Domini apparuit	LR 303	an	3
E	-2	3	5	8	7	8	7	5	E	Euntibus animalibus ibant	WA 374	re	3
E	-2	3	5	8	7	8	7	5	E	Favus distillans labia tua	PM 274 LR 247 375 WA 354 LA 456	an	3
E	-2	3	5	8	7	8	7	5	E	Gloria laudis resonet in ore	AR 518 LU 914 *AM 536 *WA 158	an	3
E	-2	3	5	8	7	8	7	5	E	In diademate capitis Aaron	PM 225 *LA 229 385 *WA 141	re	3
D	-2	3	5	8	7	8	7	5	D	Libera me Domine de viis inferni	AR [173] LU 1798 *PM 317 *LA 556	re	1
E	-2	3	5	8	7	8	7	5	E	Si iniquitates observaveris	GR 383 LU 1070 *SYG 259 *GB 263[v] GS d	int	3
E	-2	3	5	8	7	8	7	5	E	Trahe me post te in odorem	LR 219	an	3
E	-2	3	5	8	7	8	7	8	E	Cum pervenisset beatus Andreas ... videns	WA 232	an	3
E	-2	3	5	8	7	8	7	8	E	In nomine Domini omne genu	GR 190 OHS 320 LU 616 *SYG 126 *GB 113[v] *GS 91	int	3
E	-2	3	5	8	7	8	7	8	E	In nomine Jesu omne genu	GR 50 561 LU 446 1574	int	3
E	-2	3	5	8	7	8	7	8	E	Sancti Dei omnes qui estis	WA 398	an	3
E	-2	3	5	8	7	8	7	8	E	Sub altare Dei clamabant	WA 44	an	3
E	-2	3	5	8	7	8	10	7	E	Qui de terra est	WA 49 *LA 63	an	3
E	-2	3	5	8	7	8	10	8	E	Beatus vir qui in lege ... voluntas	LR 191 WA 424 *LA 529	an	3
E	-2	3	5	8	7	8	10	8	E	Calicem salutaris ... et sacrificabo	AR 526 LU 956 *AM 544	an	3
D	-2	3	5	8	7	8	10	8	D	Cum audisset Job nuntiorum	AR 546 LU 991 *AM 582 *WA 171 *LA 286	an	1
E	-2	3	5	8	7	8	10	8	E	Ego autem in Domino gaudebo	AR 299 LU 451 *AM 277	an	3
E	-2	3	5	8	7	8	10	8	E	In mediis flammis	WA 247	an	3
E	-2	3	5	8	7	8	10	8	E	Jesu corona celsior	AR [77]	hy	3

E	-2	3	5	8	7	8	10	8	E	Non est privatus	WA 315	an	3
E	-2	3	5	8	7	8	10	8	E	Pretiosa sunt Thebaeorum corpora	WA 377	an	3
E	-2	3	5	8	7	8	10	8	E	Pudore bono repletus	WA 239	an	3
E	-2	3	5	8	7	8	10	8	E	Rex gloriose martyrum	ST 307	hy	3
E	-2	3	5	8	7	8	10	8	E	Sanctimonia et magnificentia	LR 265	an	3
E	-2	3	5	8	7	8	10	8	E	Trahe nos virgo	AR 587 LU 1321 *AM 764	an	3
E	-2	3	5	8	7	8	10	8	E	Ut audivit salutationem	AR 771 LU 1541 *AM 954	an	3
E	-2	3	5	8	7	8	10	8	E	Vidit igitur assistere	WA 342	an	3
E	-2	3	5	8	7	10	8	7	E	Benedictum propheticis condecoremus	LR 329	an	3
E	-2	3	5	8	10	8	5	7	E	Dum complerentur dies	AR 503 LU 884 *AM 520 *WA 153 LA 261 264	an	3
E	-2	3	5	8	10	8	5	8	E	Lustra sex qui jam peracta	ST 91	hy	3
E	-2	3	5	8	10	8	5	8	E	Pange lingua gloriosi proelium	ST 90	hy	3
a	-2	3	5	8	10	8	5	8	a	Pange lingua gloriosi proelium	ST 188	hy	3
E	-2	3	5	8	10	8	7	5	E	Induxerunt puerum Jesum	LR 309	an	3
E	-2	3	5	8	10	8	7	5	E	Quando nata est virgo	WA 364	an	3
D	-2	3	7	5	7	5	8	7	D	Recordare mei Domine omni	GR 385 OTT 125 LU 1072 *GS e	of	1
D	-2	5	3	0	-2	5	3	5	E	Proba me Domine	SYG 85	gr	4
D	-2	5	3	2	0	2	5	7	[E]	Agnus Dei	SCH #241		4
c	-1	-5	-3	-7	-8	-5	-8	-12	E	Corde natus ex parentis	ST 341	hy	3
c	-1	-5	-3	-5	-8	-7	-5	-10	C	Benedicamus Domino Ib	AR 59* LR 44 LU 124		5
c	-1	-5	-3	-5	-8	-7	-5	-10	C	Ite missa est IIb	GR 11* LU 22		5
f	-1	-5	-3	-5	-8	-5	-10	-8	F	Agnus Dei	SCH #3		5
c	-1	-5	-3	-5	-3	0	2	0	F	Laetamini cum Jerusalem	AR 248 *AM 223 *WA 19 *LA 17	an	5
c	-1	-5	-3	-1	-3	-1	0	-3	G	Benediximus vobis in nomine	WA 64 LA 90	an	8
c	-1	-5	-3	-1	-3	-1	0	-3		Et tu Domine qui dicere Rogamus te Domine	LA 557	rev	
c	-1	-5	-3	-1	-3	-1	0	-3	G	Illuminatio mea et salus mea	AR 86 LU 279B LA 82	an	8
c	-1	-5	-3	-1	-3	-1	0	-3		Memento Domine animae Rogamus te Domine	LA 557	rev	
c	-1	-5	-3	-1	-3	0	-3	-5	G	De necessitatibus meis libera	LA 104	an	8
c	-1	-5	-3	-1	-3	0	2	0		Cumque illi omnia Igitur Lucianus	WA 345	rev	
F	-1	-5	-3	-1	0	-1	-3	-5	E	Et subito circumfulsit	LA 340	an	4
c	-1	-5	-3	-1	0	-1	-3	-5	G	Juste judicate filii	WA 65 *LA 92	an	8
F	-1	-5	-3	-1	0	2	0	2	E	Recessit igitur scienter	WA 297 *LA 367	an	4

c	-1	-5	-3	0	-1	-5	-3	0		Ille namque tenet Caritas est summum	SYG 132	anv	
c	-1	-5	-3	0	-1	-3	0	2		Hic erit magnus Ecce concipies	WA 302	rev	
F	-1	-5	-3	0	-1	-3	0	4	D	Templum Domini sanctum est	LR 237 *WA 318 *LA 549	an	2
F	-1	-5	-3	0	-1	2	0	-1	E	Quae est ista quae processit	PM 261 LR 253 *LA 443 WA 355	re	4
c	-1	-5	-3	0	2	0	-1	-3		Quid in me ergo displicuit Quo progrederis	WA 348 *LA 435	rev	
c	-1	-5	-3	0	2	0	-1	0	G	Contumelias et terrores ... et Dominus	AR 430 OHS 306 316 AM 410 WA 117 LA 187	an	8
c	-1	-5	-3	0	2	0	-1	0	G	Terra tremuit et quievit	OHS 392 LU 647 LR 87 WA 119 LA 192	an	8
F	-1	-5	-1	-3	-5	0	2	0	D	Unus est enim magister	AR 382 LU 1086 AM 356 *WA 94 *LA 144	an	2
c	-1	-5	-1	-3	0	-3	-5	-7	G	Deus meus in te confido	AR 114 LU 279^{E}	an	8
c	-1	-5	-1	-3	0	2	0	-3		Tum rex tum proceres Orbata pontifice	WA 284	rev	
c	-1	-5	-1	0	-3	-5	-7	-5	G	In sanctitate et justitia	AR 780	an	8
c	-1	-5	-1	0	-3	-5	-3	-5	G	Dominus in templo sancto	LR 95 WA 147 LA 244	an	8
c	-1	-5	-1	0	-3	-5	-3	-5	G	Dominus in templo sancto ... sedes	LR 232	an	8
c	-1	-5	-1	0	-3	-5	-3	-5	G	Ego vos elegi ... quia mundus	WA 413	an	8
c	-1	-5	-1	0	-3	-5	-3	-5	G	Lumen ad revelationem	AR 620 GR 428 PM 132 LU 1357 1366 AM 803 *LA 350 SYG 47 GS 180	an	8
c	-1	-5	-1	0	-3	-5	-3	-5	G	Missus sum ad oves	WA 94 *LA 143	an	8
c	-1	-5	-1	0	-3	-5	-3	-5	G	Omnes de Saba venient	AR 333 LU 482 AM 300	an	8
c	-1	-5	-1	0	-3	-5	-3	-5	E	Pastor eximius pastoralis	AM 832	an	3
c	-1	-5	-1	0	-3	-5	-3	-5	G	Sacrificabo hostiam laudis	AR 299 LU 452	an	8
F	-1	-5	-1	0	-3	-5	-3	0	D	Isti sunt sancti qui pro testamento	AR [46] LU 1156 AM 651 *WA 424 LA 520	an	2
F	-1	-5	-1	0	-3	-1	-5	-3	D	A planta pedis	AR 843 LU 1639 AM 1048	an	2
f	-1	-3	-6	-5	-3	-5	-8	-10	f	Jam lucis orto sidere	ST 74	hy	6
c	-1	-3	-5	-10	-8	-7	-5	-7	E	Deus meus misericordia	AR 139 LU 279^{M}	an	3
c	-1	-3	-5	-7	-5	-3	-7	-8	G	Stephanus autem plenus gratia	AR 276 LU 413 AM 252 LA 40	an	8
c	-1	-3	-5	-7	-5	-3	0	-1	G	Beatus venter qui te	WA 47 *LA 33	an	8
c	-1	-3	-5	-7	-3	-7	-3	0	F	Ponent Domino gloriam	WA 18 *LA 20	an	5
c	-1	-3	-5	-7	-3	0	-1	-5	G	Ite missa est VII	GR 28* LU 37		8
c	-1	-3	-5	-7	-3	0	2	0	F	Kyrie	MEL #8		
c	-1	-3	-5	-3	-8	-7	-5	-3	E	Dixi vobis jam	WA 104	an	4

c	-1	-3	-5	-3	-8	-7	-3	-1	E	Erat ei pro omnibus	WA 287	an	3
c	-1	-3	-5	-3	-7	-8	-10	-3	D	Hinc tota Teutonia	ST 312	hy	1
c	-1	-3	-5	-3	-7	-8	-3	-5	F	Agnus Dei	SCH #26		5
c	-1	-3	-5	-3	-7	-5	-3	0	G	Discerne causam meam Deus	AR 111	an	8
c	-1	-3	-5	-3	-7	-3	0	2	F	Fac Domine judicium injuriam	AR 431 OHS 309 350	an	5
c	-1	-3	-5	-3	-5	-7	-8	-7	G	Sancti estis dicit Dominus	AM 878	an	8
c	-1	-3	-5	-3	-5	-7	-5	-3	G	Deus deorum Dominus	OHS 299 (nm) WA 65 LA 90	an	8
c	-1	-3	-5	-3	-5	-7	-5	-3	G	Domus Jacob de populo	WA 64	an	8
c	-1	-3	-5	-3	-5	-7	-5	-3	G	In Israel magnum nomen	AM 66 67 *WA 69 *LA 101	an	8
c	-1	-3	-5	-3	-5	-7	-5	-3	G	Ite et vos in vineam	AR 344 LU 497 AM 314 WA 75 LA 114	an	8
c	-1	-3	-5	-3	-5	-7	-5	-3	G	Per singulos dies	AM 156 157 *LA 102	an	8
c	-1	-3	-5	-3	-5	-7	-5	-3	G	Tolle quod tuum est	AR 346 AM 317 *WA 75 *LA 115	an	8
c	-1	-3	-5	-3	-5	-7	-3	0	G	Beatus populus cujus Dominus	AR 203 OHS 42 LU 309	an	8
c	-1	-3	-5	-3	-5	-3	-7	-5	G	Bonum est confiteri Domino	AM 67 68 *WA 69 *LA 101	an	8
c	-1	-3	-5	-3	-5	-3	-7	-5	G	Credidi propter quod locutus	AM 134 135 *WA 64	an	8
c	-1	-3	-5	-3	-5	-3	-5	-7	G	Domine virtus et laetitia	WA 35	an	8
c	-1	-3	-5	-3	-5	-3	-5	-7	F	Magnificat anima mea	WA 64	an	5
c	-1	-3	-5	-3	-5	-3	-5	[0]	G	Intellige clamorem meum	WA 64 *LA 89	an	8
c	-1	-3	-5	-3	-5	-3	-1	[0]	G	Te decet hymnus	AM 53 54 *AR 126 WA 67 *LA 95	an	8
F	-1	-3	-5	-3	-5	-3	0	-1	D	Heu me quia incolatus meus	AR [143] LU 1773 AM 1151 *WA 435 *LA 560	an	2
F	-1	-3	-5	-3	-5	-3	0	2	F	Domine Deus virtutum beati	LR 386 WA 396 LA 476	an	6
F	-1	-3	-5	-3	-5	0	2	0	D	Opera manuum tuarum	AR [145] LU 1775 *AM 1153 1154 *WA 435 *LA 560	an	2
c	-1	-3	-5	-3	-1	-3	-5	-8	G	Bene fundata est domus Domini	AR [107] LU 1247 AM 698 WA 319 LA 552	an	8
c	-1	-3	-5	-3	-1	-3	-5	-8	G	Hoc est praeceptum meum	AR [2] LU 1111 AM 622 *WA 414 *LA 511	an	8
c	-1	-3	-5	-3	-1	-3	-5	-3	G	Aquam quam ego dedero	AR 394 LA 155 WA 100	an	8
c	-1	-3	-5	-3	-1	-3	-5	-3	G	Collocet eum Dominus	AR [10] LU 1114 AM 626 WA 415 LA 421 512	an	8
c	-1	-3	-5	-3	-1	-3	-5	-3	G	Dextera Domini fecit virtutem	AR 379 AM 352 WA 93 LA 141	an	8
c	-1	-3	-5	-3	-1	-3	-5	-3	G	Ecce ancilla Domini	AR 247 669 [140] LU 1417 AM 223 863 LA 379	an	8

c	-1	-3	-5	-3	-1	-3	-5	-3	G	Ecce completa sunt	AR 255 AM 220 231 WA 27 LA 31	an	8
F	-1	-3	-5	-3	-1	-3	-5	-3	E	Perseverans ulcus illud	WA 250	an	4
c	-1	-3	-5	-3	-1	-3	-5	-3	G	Propitius esto peccatis	WA 67 *LA 97	an	8
c	-1	-3	-5	-3	-1	-3	-5	-3	G	Si quis per me intraverit	LA 527	an	8
c	-1	-3	-5	-3	-1	-3	-5	-3	G	Verax est pater	WA 159	an	8
c	-1	-3	-5	-3	-1	-3	-5	-3	G	Vindica Domine sanguinem ... super terram	LR 182 LA 516	an	8
F	-1	-3	-5	-3	-1	-3	-1	0	E	Christe sanctorum decus angelorum	ST 454	hy	4
F	-1	-3	-5	-3	-1	-3	-1	0	D	Credimus Christum filium	WA 407 *LA 490	an	2
F	-1	-3	-5	-3	-1	-3	-1	0	E	Exemplum merear fieri	WA 352	an	4
F	-1	-3	-5	-3	-1	-3	-1	2	E	Exsultet caelum laudibus	ST 195	hy	4
F	-1	-3	-5	-3	-1	-3	-1	2	D	Sanctus	THAN #130		1
F	-1	-3	-5	-3	-1	-3	0	-1	E	Decantande speciosis	WA 241	an	4
F	-1	-3	-5	-3	-1	-3	0	2	D	Biduo vivens pendebat	WA 237 *LA 500	an	1
F	-1	-3	-5	-3	-1	0	-5	0	E	Saule frater Dominus misit	LA 342	an	4
f	-1	-3	-5	-3	-1	0	-1	-3	F	Agnus Dei	SCH #2		5
F	-1	-3	-5	-3	-1	0	-1	0	E	Felix per omnes festum mundi cardines	ST 297	hy	4
F	-1	-3	-5	-3	-1	0	2	0		Gavisi sunt discipuli	SYG 163	alv	
F	-1	-3	-5	-3	-1	0	2	0	E	Quodcumque vinclis	LR 432 AM 822	hy	4
c	-1	-3	-5	-3	-1	0	2	0	c	Respice Domine de sanctuario ... super	LA 549	an	6
F	-1	-3	-5	-3	-1	0	2	0	D	Tuam Deus deposcimus pietatem	WA 398	an	2
F	-1	-3	-5	-3	-1	0	2	0	E	Vindica Domine sanguinem	WA 421	an	4
F	-1	-3	-5	-3	-1	0	2	4	F	Kyrie	MEL #126		
F	-1	-3	-5	-3	-1	2	4	2	E	Exsultet caelum laudibus	ST 241 AM 624	hy	4
F	-1	-3	-5	-3	-1	2	4	6	E	Ave maris stella Dei mater alma	ST 91	hy	4
F	-1	-3	-5	-3	0	-5	-3	0	D	Consolamini consolamini popule	AM 231 *AR 254 LA 17 *WA 18	an	2
F	-1	-3	-5	-3	0	-3	-1	0	E	Adnue Christe saeculorum Domine	ST 100	hy	4
F	-1	-3	-5	-3	0	-3	-1	0	E	Andrea pie	ST 240	hy	4
F	-1	-3	-5	-3	0	-3	-1	0	E	Aurea luce et decore roseo	ST 95	hy	4
F	-1	-3	-5	-3	0	-3	-1	0	E	Aurea luce et decore roseo	ST 233	hy	4
F	-1	-3	-5	-3	0	-3	-1	0	E	Aurea luce et decore roseo	ST 432	hy	4
F	-1	-3	-5	-3	0	-3	-1	0	E	Bartholomaee	ST 241	hy	4
F	-1	-3	-5	-3	0	-3	-1	0	E	Beate pastor Petre	AR 599 752 LU 1516	hy	4
F	-1	-3	-5	-3	0	-3	-1	0	E	Beate Simon	ST 241	hy	4

F	-1	-3	-5	-3	0	-3	-1	0	E	Bina caelestis	ST 240	hy	4
F	-1	-3	-5	-3	0	-3	-1	0	E	Cum non posset levare	WA 283	re	4
F	-1	-3	-5	-3	0	-3	-1	0	E	Decora lux aeternitatis auream	AR 747 LU 1522	hy	4
F	-1	-3	-5	-3	0	-3	-1	0	E	Doctor egregie Paule	ST 234	hy	4
F	-1	-3	-5	-3	0	-3	-1	0	E	Egregie doctor Paule mores instrue	AR 607 752 LU 1349	hy	4
F	-1	-3	-5	-3	0	-3	-1	0	E	Jacobe juste	ST 241	hy	4
F	-1	-3	-5	-3	0	-3	-1	0	E	Janitor caeli doctor orbis pariter	ST 234	hy	4
F	-1	-3	-5	-3	0	-3	-1	0	E	Luca fidelis	ST 241	hy	4
F	-1	-3	-5	-3	0	-3	-1	0	E	Matthaee sancte	ST 241	hy	4
F	-1	-3	-5	-3	0	-3	-1	0	E	Matthia juste	ST 241	hy	4
F	-1	-3	-5	-3	0	-3	-1	0	E	O Thoma Christi	ST 240	hy	4
F	-1	-3	-5	-3	0	-3	-1	0	E	Proni rogamus	ST 241	hy	4
F	-1	-3	-5	-3	0	-3	-1	0	E	Salve crux sancta salve mundi gloria	ST 230	hy	4
F	-1	-3	-5	-3	0	-3	-1	2	E	Ave maris stella Dei mater alma	ST 429 AR [118] LU 1261 AM 704	hy	4
F	-1	-3	-5	-3	0	-3	0	-1	E	Adnue Christe saeculorum Domine	ST 195	hy	4
F	-1	-3	-5	-3	0	-3	0	-1	E	Aurea luce et decore roseo	ST 191	hy	4
F	-1	-3	-5	-3	0	-1	-3	0	E	Apostolorum splendido	ST 292	hy	4
F	-1	-3	-5	-3	0	-1	0	-3	E	Aurea luce et decore roseo	ST 296	hy	4
F	-1	-3	-5	-3	0	-1	0	2	E	Dele iniquitatem meam	AR 111	an	4
F	-1	-3	-5	-3	0	-1	0	2	E	Felix per omnes festum mundi cardines	ST 54 95 431	hy	4
F	-1	-3	-5	-3	0	-1	0	2	E	Miris modis repente liber	AR 797 LU 1578	hy	4
F	-1	-3	-5	-3	0	-1	0	2	E	O Roma felix quae tantorum	ST 96	hy	4
F	-1	-3	-5	-3	0	-1	0	2	E	Petrus beatus catenarum laqueos	ST 96	hy	4
F	-1	-3	-5	-3	0	-1	0	2	E	Quodcumque in orbe nexibus revinxeris	AR 597 LU 1334	hy	4
c	-1	-3	-5	-3	0	-1	2	0		Puri cordis munditiae Pius adolescens	WA 312	rev	
F	-1	-3	-5	-3	0	-1	2	4	E	Ave maris stella Dei mater alma	ST 281	hy	4
F	-1	-3	-5	-3	0	2	-3	0	D	Salvete flores martyrum	ST 447	hy	2
c	-1	-3	-5	-3	0	2	0	2	c	Descendit spiritus sanctus	LA 75	an	6
c	-1	-3	-5	-3	0	2	0	2	c	Et alias oves habeo	LA 235	an	6
F	-1	-3	-5	-3	0	2	0	4	F	Ave regina caelorum ave	AR 69[1] OHS 175 LR 47 LU 278 AM 179	an	6
F	-1	-3	-5	-3	0	2	0	4	D	Oblatus est quia ipse voluit	AR 433 OHS 404 LU 657 AM 418 419 LA 194 WA 120	an	2
c	-1	-3	-5	-1	-3	-5	-7	-3	G	Veritas de terra	LU 380 *LR 60 *WA 29 *LA 33	an	8

c	-1	-3	-5	-1	-3	-5	-3	-1	b	Ecce jam noctis tenuatur umbra lucis	ST 359	hy	4
c	-1	-3	-5	-1	-3	0	-3	-5	G	Pater si non potest	GR 184 OHS 146 LU 603 *SYG 124 GB 111 GS 89	co	8
F	-1	-3	-5	-1	-3	0	-1	-3	D	Positis autem genibus beatus	WA 35	an	1
F	-1	-3	-5	-1	-3	2	0	-3	E	Ad coenam agni providi	ST 113	hy	4
F	-1	-3	-5	-1	-3	2	0	-1	E	Ad regias agni dapes	AR 454 LU 814	hy	4
f	-1	-3	-5	-1	0	2	0	2		Et in terra	BOS #3		
F	-1	-3	-5	-1	2	4	2	0	E	Agnus Dei	SCH #162		4
c	-1	-3	-5	0	-3	-5	-7	-5	G	Ecce advenit dominator Deus	WA 47	an	8
c	-1	-3	-5	0	2	0	2	-3	G	Gloria	BOS #5		IV
F	-1	-3	-5	0	2	0	3	2	D	Spiritu principali confirma	AM 66 *WA 69 *LA 101	an	1
F	-1	-3	-5	0	2	0	4	2	D	Alleluia	AM 68	an	1
c	-1	-3	-5	0	2	4	2	0	F	Domine tu mihi lavas pedes	GR 201 OHS 448 LU 673 SYG 130	an	5
c	-1	-3	-5	0	2	4	2	0		Non est alia natio Qui manducat	LR 131	rev	
F	-1	-3	-5	0	2	4	5	4	F	Kyrie alme pater Jesu	MEL #125		
C	-1	-3	-5	0	2	4	5	4	C	Kyrie	MEL #221		
c	-1	-3	-5	0	2	4	5	7	c	Agnus Dei	SCH #25		8
c	-1	-3	-5	0	2	5	4	2		Optimam partem quae non valet Relinquens Maria	WA 336	rev	
c	-1	-3	-5	2	0	2	4	2	G	Ego sum via ... nemo	AR 695 AM 894 *LA 394	an	7
b^{b}	-1	-3	-1	-5	-6	-5	-3	-5	F	Agnus Dei ad lib II	GR 93* LU 88		6
c	-1	-3	-1	-5	-3	-5	-8	-5		Pereunt pericula cessat Si quaeris	VP 176	rev	
F	-1	-3	-1	-5	-3	-1	0	2	E	Deus tu conversus	AR 170	an	4
c	-1	-3	-1	-5	-3	0	-1	-3		Kyrie ... pater de caelis	PM 286 VP 36		
F	-1	-3	-1	-5	-3	0	-1	0	E	Vir Dei Gamaliel	WA 342	an	4
F	-1	-3	-1	-5	-3	0	2	4	D	En rex venit mansuetus	GS 81		1
F	-1	-3	-1	-3	-5	-3	-5	-3	F	O gloriosum praesulem	PM 131	re	6
F	-1	-3	-1	-3	-5	-3	-5	-3		Quid ergo miserrimus Libera me Domine de morte	WA 438	rev	
F	-1	-3	-1	-3	-5	-3	-1	-5	E	Ecce jam noctis tenuatur umbra lux	AR 8	hy	4
F	-1	-3	-1	-3	-5	-3	-1	-3	E	Ego rogavi Dominum ... in	WA 247	an	4
F	-1	-3	-1	-3	-5	-3	-1	-3	D	Inito consilio venenum	WA 300	an	2
F	-1	-3	-1	-3	-5	-3	-1	-3	D	Iste est discipulus	WA 43	an	2
c	-1	-3	-1	-3	-5	-3	-1	-3	E	Omnis interea populus	WA 234	an	3
F	-1	-3	-1	-3	-5	-3	-1	-3	D	Redemptor mundi signo crucis	SYG 130	co	2

F	-1	-3	-1	-3	-5	-3	-1	-3	E	Te invocamus te adoramus	WA 158	an	4
F	-1	-3	-1	-3	-5	-3	-1	0	E	Ecce ascendimus ... et consummabuntur	AR 355 AM 328 WA 82 LA 124	an	4
F	-1	-3	-1	-3	-5	-3	-1	0	E	Juvenes et virgines	WA 82	an	4
c	-1	-3	-1	-3	-5	-3	-1	0	G	Loquamur nunc usque mane	AM 815	an	8
F	-1	-3	-1	-3	-5	-3	-1	2	E	Beata nobis gaudia	ST 449	hy	4
F	-1	-3	-1	-3	-5	-3	-1	2	E	Conditor alme siderum	ST 70	hy	4
F	-1	-3	-1	-3	-5	-3	-1	2	E	Et ecce apparuerunt eis	AR 806 LU 1589 AM 998	an	4
F	-1	-3	-1	-3	-5	-3	-1	2	E	Fiebat interea praediorum	WA 244	an	4
c	-1	-3	-1	-3	-5	-3	-1	2	b	Kyrie XVIII Deus genitor	GR 58* LU 62		4
F	-1	-3	-1	-3	-5	-3	-1	2	E	Rex sine fine manens	PM 110	an	4
F	-1	-3	-1	-3	-5	-3	0	-3	E	Kyrie o summe rex (etc.)	MEL #124		
F	-1	-3	-1	-3	-5	-3	0	-1	D	Invocabat Scholastica Dominum	LR 294	an	2
F	-1	-3	-1	-3	-5	-3	0	-1	E	Pacem tuam da nobis Domine	AR 144* VP 30	an	4
F	-1	-3	-1	-3	-5	-3	0	-1	D	Vado ad eum ... sed quia	AR 480 LU 829 AM 495 *WA 145 *LA 241	an	1 2
F	-1	-3	-1	-3	-5	-3	0	-1	D	Virgo Dei genitrix quem totus	ST 79	hy	2
c	-1	-3	-1	-3	-5	-3	0	2	c	Dum inventum esset	WA 346	an	6
F	-1	-3	-1	-3	-5	-3	0	2	D	Virgo Dei genitrix quem totus	AR 133* VP 42 LU 1865	hy	2
c	-1	-3	-1	-3	-5	0	2	4	c	Ponens Petrus genua	WA 326	an	6
F	-1	-3	-1	-3	-5	2	4	2	[E]	Agnus Dei	SCH #153		4
F	-1	-3	-1	-3	-5	2	4	2	C	Sanctus	THAN #129		5
F	-1	-3	-1	-3	-1	-3	-5	-1	G	Gloria	BOS #41		IV
F	-1	-3	-1	-3	-1	-3	-1	-3	D	Coena facta dixit	WA 121	an	1
F	-1	-3	-1	-3	-1	0	2	4	E	O vere beatum in cujus ore	LA 482	re	4
F	-1	-3	-1	-3	0	-3	0	-3		Non adorabitis Deum alienum In die sollemnitatis	OTT 61 GB 139v *SYG 159	ofv	
F	-1	-3	-1	-3	0	-1	0	2	E	Hinc horrendo carceris	WA 261	an	4
F	-1	-3	-1	-3	0	-1	0	2	E	Ingressus angelus ad Mariam	WA 301	an	4
F	-1	-3	-1	-3	0	-1	0	2	E	Sacerdotes sancti incensum	AR 531 LU 940	an	4
c	-1	-3	-1	0	-5	-7	-3	0	G	Quare ergo rubrum est	AR 760 LU 1537 AM 946	an	8
c	-1	-3	-1	0	-5	-3	-5	-7	G	Aures ad nostras deitatis preces	ST 383	hy	7
c	-1	-3	-1	0	-5	-3	-5	-7	G	Praeco praeclarus sacer et propheta	ST 393	hy	7
F	-1	-3	-1	0	-5	-3	0	-5	D	Dominus Jesus postquam coenavit	GR 201 OHS 448 LU 672 *WA 213	an	2
F	-1	-3	-1	0	-5	-3	0	-5	D	Dominus Jesus postquam coenavit	GR 197 OHS 463 LU 679 SYG 129 GB 115v *GS 95	co	2

F	-1	-3	-1	0	-5	-3	0	2	D	Framea suscitare adversus eos	AR 426 OHS 188 203 AM 405 *WA 114 LA 184	an	2
F	-1	-3	-1	0	-5	-3	0	2	F	Gregorius respiciens	AM 834	an	6
F	-1	-3	-1	0	-5	0	-1	-3	G	Sanctus	THAN #128		8
c	-1	-3	-1	0	-3	-5	-7	-3	G	Summa ingenuitas ista est	LA 357 *WA 273	an	8
F	-1	-3	-1	0	-3	-5	-3	-1	D	Miserere mei Deus secundum	AR 154*		
F	-1	-3	-1	0	-3	-5	-3	-1	D	O Domine salvum me fac	AR 365 AM 341 *WA 88 LA 132	an	2
c	-1	-3	-1	0	-3	0	-1	-5	G	Cultor Dei memento	ST 113	hy	8
c	1	3	1	0	-1	-5	-7	-5	G	Lux de luce apparuisti	AR 332 LU 482 AM 298 *WA 54 *LA 69	an	8
c	-1	-3	-1	0	-1	-5	-3	-5	G	Deus meus eripe me	OHS 371 LU 629 *WA 118 *LA 189	an	8
b^b	-1	-3	-1	0	-1	-5	-3	[0]	F	Kyrie	MEL #14		
F	-1	-3	-1	0	-1	-5	-3	0	D	Scuto bonae voluntatis	LR 149 *WA 416 *LA 522	an	2
c	-1	-3	-1	0	-1	-5	-1	0	G	Dixit angelus ad Petrum	AR 751 799 LU 1515 1577 AM 935 989 *WA 328 *LA 415	an	8
F	-1	-3	-1	0	-1	-3	-8	-5	D	Responsum accepit Simeon ... Christum	GR 430 PM 135 LU 1359 SYG 47 *GS i	an	2
c	-1	-3	-1	0	-1	-3	-5	-7	F	Agnus Dei	SCH #24		5
c	-1	-3	-1	0	-1	-3	-5	-7	G	Aures ad nostras deitatis preces	ST 414	hy	8
F	-1	-3	-1	0	-1	-3	-5	-3	E	Agnus Dei III	GR 14* LU 25 SCH #161		4
c	-1	-3	-1	0	-1	-3	-5	-3	G	Hodie scietis quia veniet	AR 255 LU 358 AM 232 *WA 26 LA 30	an	8
F	-1	-3	-1	0	-1	-3	-5	0	E	In caelis gaudent	WA 432	an	4
F	-1	-3	-1	0	-1	-3	0	-1	D	Redime Domine de interitu	GB 157	an	1
F	-1	-3	-1	0	-1	0	-3	-1	D	Aspice Domine quia facta	LA 302 *WA 183	re	1
F	-1	-3	-1	0	-1	0	-1	-3	C	Pange lingua gloriosi proelium	ST 452	hy	6
F	-1	-3	-1	0	-1	0	-1	0	E	Te laudant angeli	WA 28	re	4
F	-1	-3	-1	0	-1	0	2	0	E	Per signum sanctae ac venerandae crucis	SYG 142	an	4
c	-1	-3	-1	0	2	-1	0	-3	E	Sanctus VI	GR 24* LU 33 THAN #17		3
F	-1	-3	-1	0	2	-1	0	-3	D	Videns Dominus flentes sorores	PM 348	an	1
F	-1	-3	-1	0	2	-1	0	-1	D	Videns Dominus flentes sorores	GR 148 GS 69	co	1
F	-1	-3	-1	0	2	-1	2	4	D	In dedicatione hujus templi	WA 319	an	1
F	-1	-3	-1	0	2	-1	2	4	E	Venite ad me omnes	AR 5387 LU 977 *AM 566	an	4
F	-1	-3	-1	0	2	0	-1	-3	E	Adeptus est sedem	WA 41 *LA 54	an	4
F	-1	-3	-1	0	2	0	-1	-3	E	Benedictus Dominus quia visitavit	WA 64	an	4
F	-1	-3	-1	0	2	0	-1	-3	E	Factum est in una	WA 157	an	4

F	-1	-3	-1	0	2	0	-1	-3	E	Quid faciam quia dominus	AR 560 LU 1016 AM 598 *LA 313	an	4
F	-1	-3	-1	0	2	0	-1	0	E	Exsultabunt sancti in gloria	WA 423	an	4
F	-1	-3	-1	0	2	0	-1	[0]	E	Kyrie	MEL #123		
F	-1	-3	-1	0	2	0	-1	2	E	Lumine vultus tui	WA 33	an	4
F	-1	-3	-1	0	2	0	-1	2	E	Norunt infantes laudare	WA 43	an	4
F	-1	-3	-1	0	2	0	-1	2	F	Nova regis praeconia	ST 139	hy	5
F	-1	-3	-1	0	2	0	2	-3	E	Ite nuntiate fratribus meis	AM 485 *AR 471 LA 233 234	an	4
c	-1	-3	-1	0	2	0	2	0	G	Genti peccatrici populo	LA 306 *WA 186	re	7 8
F	-1	-3	-1	0	2	0	2	4	E	Duo homines ascenderunt	LA 314	an	4
F	-1	-3	-1	0	2	0	2	4	E	Quomodo multiplicasti tuam	WA 288	an	4
c	-1	-3	-1	0	2	4	0	2	G	De terra plasmasti	WA 439	an	7
F	-1	-3	-1	0	2	4	2	-1	D	Saepe expugnaverunt me	AM 135	an	2
F	-1	-3	-1	0	2	4	2	-1	D	Circumdantes circumdederunt me	AR 422 OHS 66 AM 400 *WA 113 LA 181	an	1 2
F	-1	-3	-1	0	2	4	2	-1	D	Reges terrae et omnes populi	AR 397 AM 373 WA 103 LA 162	an	1
F	-1	-3	-1	0	2	4	2	0	E	Flabit spiritus ejus	WA 60	an	4
F	-1	-3	-1	0	2	4	2	0	E	Laudabo Deum meum	AR 127 AM 160 WA 60 LA 105	an	4
F	-1	-3	-1	0	2	4	2	0	E	Vide humilitatem meam	WA 64	an	4
F	-1	-3	-1	0	2	4	2	4	D	Ecce vere Israelita	LA 540	an	1
F	-1	-3	-1	0	2	4	2	4	E	Emissiones tuae paradisus	WA 354 *LA 456	an	4
F	-1	-3	-1	0	2	4	2	4	D	Reges Tharsis et insulae	LR 70 WA 53 LA 67	an	1
F	-1	-3	-1	0	2	4	2	4	E	Vidimus stellam ejus ... et venimus	AR 332 *AM 299 LA 67	an	4
F	-1	-3	-1	0	2	7	6	4		Salvum me fac Deus	GR [139]	alv	
F	-1	-3	-1	2	-1	-3	0	-1	E	Christus lux indeficiens	ST 47	hy	4
F	-1	-3	-1	2	-1	0	-1	-3	E	Consurgens Joseph accepit	LR 304	an	4
F	-1	-3	-1	2	0	-1	-3	-1	E	Absolve Domine animas eorum	SYG 237	co	4
F	-1	-3	-1	2	4	0	-1	2	E	Ad coenam agni providi	ST 35	hy	4
F	-1	-3	-1	2	4	0	-1	2	E	Anglorum jam apostolus	LR 434 AM 831	hy	4
F	-1	-3	-1	2	4	0	-1	2	E	Jesu redemptor omnium	AR [59] AM 660	hy	4
F	-1	-3	-1	2	4	0	-1	2	E	Mella cor obdulcantia	AM 833	hy	4
F	-1	-3	-1	2	4	0	-1	2	E	Rex Christe Martini decus	LR 454	hy	4
F	-1	-3	-1	2	4	2	0	-1		Miserere miserere miserere O vera ... unitas	WA 162	anv	
F	-1	-3	-1	2	4	2	0	2	E	Angelus Domini astitit	LA 415	an	4

F	-1	-3	-1	2	4	2	0	2	E	Et facta est comes	WA 389	an	4
F	-1	-3	-1	2	4	2	0	2	E	Plantaverat autem ... paradisum	WA 75	an	4
F	-1	-3	-1	2	4	2	0	2	E	Sanctissime confessor Domini	PM 332 341 AM 855 967 WA 298	an	4
F	-1	-3	-1	2	4	2	0	2	E	Sit laus sit honor Christo	WA 337	an	4
F	-1	-3	-1	2	4	2	4	7	E	Memorare o piissima virgo Maria	AR 124*		4
F	-1	-3	-1	2	4	2	4	7	E	Tota pulchra es amica	AR 124* PM 274 VP 54 *WA 360	an	4
F	-1	-3	-1	2	4	5	4	2	E	Asperges me Domine hyssopo	GR 4* LU 13	an	4
F	-1	-3	-1	2	4	6	4	2	E	Apostolus Petrus respondit	WA 327	an	4
c	-1	-3	-1	4	2	4	2	0		Et in terra	BOS #10		
c	-1	-3	0	-5	-3	-5	-7	-3	F	Hic est qui venit per aquam	PM 163	re	5
c	-1	-3	0	-3	-5	-3	-7	-5	E	Sic eum volo manere	WA 42 *LA 56	an	3
F	-1	-3	0	-3	-1	0	2	0	E	Pantata enyosa	GB 119	an	4
c	-1	-3	0	-1	-5	-7	-5	-3	G	Pax vobis nolite timere	AR 891 LU 1702	an	8
c	-1	-3	0	-1	-5	-3	-5	-7	G	Tunc sanctus Andreas	WA 234	an	8
c	-1	-3	0	-1	-5	-3	-1	0	F	Kyrie	MEL #6		
c	-1	-3	0	-1	-5	-1	2	0	G	Respondens autem infans	WA 404	an	8
c	-1	-3	0	-1	-3	-5	-7	-5	F	Pacem relinquo vobis ... dicit	GR [138] LU 1287	co	5
c	-1	-3	0	-1	-3	-5	-3	-8	E	Ego sum Raphael angelus ... alleluia	AR 893	an	3
c	-1	-3	0	-1	-3	-5	-3	-2	F	Pacem meam do vobis	GR 301 LU 895 SYG 186 GB 192 GS 139	co	5
F	-1	-3	0	-1	-3	-5	-3	-1	D	Alleluia	AM 56	an	2
F	-1	-3	0	-1	-3	-5	-3	-1	D	Caeli caelorum laudate	AM 56 WA 65 *LA 95	an	2
F	-1	-3	0	-1	-3	-5	-3	-1	D	Clamant clamant clamant	PM 36 VP 85	an	2
F	-1	-3	0	-1	-3	-5	-3	-1	D	Domine Deus in adjutorium	WA 66 LA 95	an	2
F	-1	-3	0	-1	-3	-5	-3	-1	E	Iste cognovit justitiam	WA 428 *LA 528	an	4
F	-1	-3	0	-1	-3	-5	-3	-1	E	Pange lingua gloriosae lanceae	ST 334	hy	4
c	-1	-3	0	-1	-3	-5	-3	-1	G	Quid est homo quia magnificas	LR 334	an	8
F	-1	-3	0	-1	-3	-5	-3	0	D	A timore inimici	AR 192 *AM 52 53 *WA 67 LA 95	an	2
F	-1	-3	0	-1	-3	-5	-3	0	D	Lux orta est super nos	WA 32 *LA 38	an	1
c	-1	-3	0	-1	-3	-5	-1	-3	G	O ineffabilem virum	WA 400 *LA 481	an	8
c	-1	-3	0	-1	-3	-5	0	2	F	Caeli aperti sunt	WA 54 LA 76	an	5
c	-1	-3	0	-1	-3	-1	-5	-3	G	Sancti Dei vobis apertus est	PM 205	an	7 8
F	-1	-3	0	-1	-3	-1	0	2	E	Habitabit in tabernaculo	OHS 592 LR 153 LU 752 WA 124 416 *LA 201 523	an	4

F	-1	-3	0	-1	-3	-1	0	2	E	Pater juste mundus te	AR 421 OHS 46 LU 578 *AM 399	an 4
F	-1	-3	0	-1	-3	-1	0	2	E	Pater sanctus dum intentam	LR 324 *WA 300 *LA 375	an 4
F	-1	-3	0	-1	-3	-1	0	2	E	Sciens Jesus quia venit	AR 6 (sup 2)	an 4
F	-1	-3	0	-1	0	-1	0	2	E	Date nobis de oleo	WA 431	an 4
F	-1	-3	0	-1	0	2	-5	-3	D	Benedicat nos Deus	WA 103 *LA 162	an 2
F	-1	-3	0	-1	0	2	0	-1	E	Adoremus regem saeculorum	WA 238	inv 4
F	-1	-3	0	-1	0	2	0	-1	E	Quis scit si convertatur	WA 84	an 4
F	-1	-3	0	-1	0	2	0	-1	E	Vox de caelis sonuit	WA 57 *LA 75	an 4
F	-1	-3	0	-1	0	2	0	2	E	Quae est ista quae ascendit de	WA 356	an 4
F	-1	-3	0	-1	0	2	4	2	E	Domine dilexi decorem	LA 548	re 4
F	-1	-3	0	-1	0	2	4	2	E	Metuebat Herodes Joannem	LA 451 *WA 362	re 4
F	-1	-3	0	-1	0	2	4	6	E	Cumque carnifices apostolum	WA 232	an 4
F	-1	-3	0	-1	2	4	2	0	D	Volo pater ut ubi ego sum	AR [16] LU 1126 AM 641 *WA 419 *LA 441 527	an 1
F	-1	-3	0	2	0	2	0	-3	D	Narraverunt mihi iniqui	GR 473 LU 1427	int 2
F	-1	-3	0	2	0	2	0	-1	D	Qui biberit aquam	SYG 99 *GS 61	co 1
F	-1	-3	0	2	0	2	0	[0]	F	Intende in me	WA 65	an 6
F	-1	-3	0	2	0	2	4	0	D	Data est mihi omnis potestas	GR 258 OHS 819 LU 803 *SYG 161 *GB 142 *GS 123	co 1
F	-1	-3	0	2	0	4	2	0	D	Excita Domine potentiam tuam	AR 175 LU 279[Q]	an 1
c	-1	-3	0	2	0	4	5	4	G	Date ei de fructu manuum	AR 577[22] [101] LU 1236 AM 688 747	an 7
c	-1	-3	0	2	4	0	-3	-1	G	Alleluia	AM 84	7
c	-1	-3	0	2	4	0	-1	-3	G	Loquebantur variis linguis	AR 504 LU 884 AM 521 WA 153 LA 262 265	an 7
c	-1	-3	0	2	4	2	-5	-3	G	Parcat tibi soror	AM 815	an 7
F	-1	-3	0	2	4	2	0	-1	D	Ecce sto ad ostium et pulso	GR 453 LU 1396	co 1
F	-1	-3	0	2	4	2	0	-1	E	Memor sit Dominus sacrificii	LR 121 LU 928	an 4
F	-1	-3	0	2	4	2	0	2	E	Juste et sancte vivendo	WA 242	an 4
F	-1	-3	0	2	4	2	0	2	D	Si mihi Dominus salvator	AR 348 AM 320	an 1
F	-1	-3	0	2	4	2	0	2	E	Sicut novellae olivarum	AR 526 LU 956 AM 545	an 4
c	-1	-3	0	2	4	5	7	5	[G]	Agnus Dei	SCH #35	7
F	-1	-3	2	0	-3	4	2	0	E	Deus cujus sedes est caelum	PM 241	an 4
F	-1	-3	2	0	-1	-3	-1	0	E	Agnus Dei	SCH #152	1
F	-1	-3	2	0	-1	-3	0	-1	E	Rerum salus intermina	ST 281	hy 4
F	-1	-3	2	4	2	4	6	7	E	Cum complerentur dies Pentecostes	LR 109 LU 873 LA 255 *WA 152	re 3

F	-1	-3	2	4	2	4	7	6	E	Non turbetur cor ... ego	LR 102 LA 248 *WA 147	re	3
F	-1	-3	2	4	7	6	9	7	E	Dicit mater Jesu	LR 315	re	3
F	-1	-3	4	-3	-1	0	4	2	F	Kyrie	MEL #131		
F	-1	-3	4	2	-1	0	-3	4	F	Agnus Dei	SCH #160		5
F	-1	-3	4	2	-1	0	-3	4	F	Sanctus	THAN #127		5
c	-1	0	-3	-7	-3	0	2	0	F	Laetamini omnes in Domino	LR 266	an	5
c	-1	0	-3	-5	-7	-5	-3	-5	G	Tu gloria Jerusalem ... nostri	AR 586 631 LU 1320 1381 AM 764	an	8
c	-1	0	-3	-5	-7	-5	-3	-1	C	Alleluia	AM 138 141	an	8
c	-1	0	-3	-5	-7	-5	-3	-1	G	Benedic anima mea Dominum	WA 70 LA 103	an	8
c	-1	0	-3	-5	-7	-5	-3	-1	G	De profundis clamavi ad te	AR 140 OHS 356 LU 291 AM 138 139 WA 66 LA 93	an	8
c	-1	0	-3	-5	-7	-5	-3	-1	G	Deo nostro jucunda	AR 147 AM 161 WA 60 *LA 105	an	8
c	-1	0	-3	-5	-3	-5	-7	-5	G	Data sunt ei incensa	WA 381 *LA 467	an	8
c	-1	0	-3	-5	-3	-5	-7	-5	G	Martyrum chorus laudate Dominum	AR [42] LU 1154 *AM 648 LA 520	an	8
c	-1	0	-3	-5	-3	-5	-7	-5	G	Sancti omnes intercedant	AM 166 713 1011	an	8
c	-1	0	-3	-5	-3	-5	-3	-5	G	Dextera Domini salvavit eos	LR 140	an	8
F	-1	0	-3	-5	-3	-1	-3	-1	D	Et erat ibi usque ad obitum	GR 7**	co	1
F	-1	0	-3	-5	-3	-1	-3	-1	D	Reposita est mihi corona	GR 477 LU 1430	co	1
c	-1	0	-3	-5	-3	-1	0	-1	E	Isti sunt sancti qui passi	LA 60 *WA 45	re	3
F	-1	0	-3	-5	-3	-1	0	2	D	Omnis pulchritudo Domini	PM 85 LR 97 LA 245 *WA 147	re	1 2
F	-1	0	-3	-5	-3	-1	2	4	E	Joseph vir ejus cum esset	AR 649 LU 1401 *AM 837	an	4
F	-1	0	-3	-5	-3	0	-3	-5	D	Audi Israel praecepta Domini	LA 160 WA 102	re	2
F	-1	0	-3	-5	-3	0	-3	-5	D	Sancte Michael archangelorum	LA 470	re	2
F	-1	0	-3	-5	-3	0	-3	-1	D	Ego sum resurrectio et vita	AR [181] [186] GR 111* LU 1769 1804 *AM 1166 LA 559	an	2
F	-1	0	-3	-5	-3	0	-3	-1	D	Virgo gloriosa semper evangelium	AR 926 LU 1757 AM 1143 *LA 488 WA 405	an	2
F	-1	0	-3	-5	-3	0	-3	0	E	Alma Christi quando fides	ST 301	hy	4
F	-1	0	-3	-5	-3	0	-1	-5	D	Ingrediar in locum	WA 439	an	2
F	-1	0	-3	-5	-3	0	-1	-5	D	Omnipotens sermo tuus	AR 252 LU 357 *AM 228 *WA 19 25 *LA 22	an	2
F	-1	0	-3	-5	-3	0	-1	-3	E	Dixit mater ejus ad illum	AR 653 LU 1406 AM 842	an	4
F	-1	0	-3	-5	-3	0	-1	-3	E	Dixit mater Jesu	AR 324 LU 474	an	4
c	-1	0	-3	-5	-3	0	2	0	c	Ecce exaltata est	WA 359	an	6
F	-1	0	-3	-5	-3	0	2	0	F	Tibi Domine psallam	AR 126	an	6

c	-1	0	-3	-5	-1	-5	-3	0	E	Lux perpetua lucebit sanctis	LR 168 LA 387 WA 306	re	3
c	-1	0	-3	-5	-1	-3	-1	0	G	Auribus percipite	WA 65	an	8
c	-1	0	-3	-5	-1	-3	-1	0	G	Alleluia	AM 154 157	an	8
c	-1	0	-3	-5	-1	-3	-1	0	G	Bene fac Domine bonis	LA 102	an	8
c	-1	0	-3	-5	-1	-3	-1	0	G	Domine in caelo misericordia	AR 146 AM 40 *WA 64 *LA 89	an	8
c	-1	0	-3	-5	-1	-3	-1	0	G	Portio mea Domine	AM 154 155 WA 70 LA 102	an	8
c	-1	0	-3	-5	-1	-3	-1	0	G	Visita nos Domine	WA 70 LA 104	an	8
c	-1	0	-3	-5	-1	0	-3	-5	G	Domine clamavi ad te	AR 182 LU 303 AM 151 152 *WA 68 *LA 99	an	8
c	-1	0	-3	-5	-1	0	-3	-5	G	In tua justitia	AR 91 LU 279[c] WA 61 *LA 82	an	8
c	-1	0	-3	-5	-1	0	-3	0	G	Dominus dixit ad me	LR 55 LU 371 *WA 27 *LA 31	an	8
c	-1	0	-3	-5	0	2	0	-1	G	Jacob autem genuit Joseph	GR 487 LU 1277[B]	co	8
c	-1	0	-3	-5	0	2	0	2	c	Decius dixit ad beatum	WA 352	an	6
F	-1	0	-3	-5	0	2	0	2	F	Domine qui operati sunt	LR 382 WA 395 *LA 475	an	6
F	-1	0	-3	-5	0	2	0	2	F	Ex domo orationis	AM 779	an	6
F	-1	0	-3	-5	0	2	0	2	F	Exiit sermo inter fratres	AR 283 LU 426	an	6
c	-1	0	-3	-5	0	2	0	2	c	Fortitudo mea et laus	WA 82	an	6
F	-1	0	-3	-5	0	2	0	2	F	In hac ergo fidei	WA 389	an	6
F	-1	0	-3	-5	0	2	0	7	F	Sanctus	THAN #126		5
F	-1	0	-3	-5	0	2	4	0	F	Hodie intacta virgo	VP 73 *WA 32 *LA 38	an	6
F	-1	0	-3	-5	0	2	4	2	D	Dominus secus mare Galilaeae	GR 390 SYG 231 GB 245 GS g	int	1
F	-1	0	-3	-5	0	2	4	2	F	Lutum fecit ex sputo	GR 146 GS 68	co	6
F	-1	0	-3	-5	0	2	4	2	D	Redimet Dominus animas	GB 76	co	1
c	-1	0	-3	-5	0	2	4	2	G	Salve crux quae in corpore	LA 500	an	8
F	-1	0	-3	-5	0	2	4	5	F	Dignus a dignis	WA 43	an	6
F	-1	0	-3	-5	0	2	4	7	D	Domine puer meus jacet	LR 402	re	1
F	-1	0	-3	-1	-5	-3	0	2	D	Ego sum qui sum	OHS 753 LR 83 WA 128 LA 207 *224	an	1 2
F	-1	0	-3	-1	-5	-3	0	2	F	Modicum et non videbitis me dicit	AR 473 LU 820 AM 487 WA 143 LA *231 236	an	6
c	-1	0	-3	-1	-5	0	2	4	F	Beati Stephani aperientes	WA 344	an	6
F	-1	0	-3	-1	-3	-5	-3	-5	D	Ego sum resurrectio et vita	GB 266v	co	2
F	-1	0	-3	-1	-3	-5	-3	-1		Assumpta est Maria ... angeli	GS 195	alv	
F	-1	0	-3	-1	-3	-5	-3	-1		Assumpta est Maria ... gaudent	GS 195	alv	
F	-1	0	-3	-1	-3	-5	-3	-1		Dies illa dies irae calamitatis Libera me de morte	PM 321 AR [174] GR 102* LU 1767 LA 557 *WA 438	rev	

c	-1	0	-3	-1	-3	-5	-3	-1	E	Hodie dilectus Domini	SYG 57	co	3
F	-1	0	-3	-1	-3	-5	-3	-1		Per manus autem apostolorum	GS y	alv	
c	-1	0	-3	-1	-3	-5	-3	-1	G	Redime me Deus Israel	GR 159 SYG 113 GB 100^{v} *GS 74	co	7
c	-1	0	-3	-1	-3	-5	-3	0	c	Beatus Dunstanus exilio	WA 313	re	6
F	-1	0	-3	-1	-3	-5	-3	0	F	Non turbetur cor ... neque	AR 694 LU 1465^{A} AM 892 *LA 392 WA 308	an	6
F	-1	0	-3	-1	-3	-5	-3	0		Post partum virgo inviolata	GR [77] LU 1265 *GS r *SYG 48 *GB 220^{v}	alv	
F	-1	0	-3	-1	-3	-5	-3	0	D	Tunc assumpsit eum diabolus	AR 370 LU 531 *AM 343 WA 89 LA 133	an	2
F	-1	0	-3	-1	-3	-5	-1	-3	D	Genuit puerpera regem	AR 264 LU 396 AM 240 WA 31 *LA 37	an	2
F	-1	0	-3	-1	-3	-5	0	2	F	Domine quis habitabit	GR 131 SYG 96 GS 58 GB 85	co	6
F	-1	0	-3	-1	-3	-5	0	2	F	Ecce sic benedicetur omnis	GR [125] LU 1292 SYG 234	co	6
c	-1	0	-3	-1	-3	-5	0	2	c	O Maria mater pia	WA 339	an	6
F	-1	0	-3	-1	-3	-5	0	2	F	Unde huic sapientia	LU 1444	co	6
c	-1	0	-3	-1	-3	-5	2	-1	c	Agnus Dei	SCH #23		6
c	-1	0	-3	-1	-3	-5	2	-1	c	Sanctus	THAN #16		6
F	-1	0	-3	-1	-3	-1	0	2	D	Factum est dum tolleret	LA 272 WA 167	re	1
F	-1	0	-3	-1	-3	-1	0	2		Requiem aeternam dona eis Domine Libera me Domine de morte	AR [174] PM 321 GR 102* LU 1767 *LA 557	rev	
F	-1	0	-3	-1	0	-1	-5	0	D	Dominus regit me	GR 151 LU 567 SYG 109 *GB 97 *GS 71	co	2
F	-1	0	-3	-1	0	2	4	2	E	Ascendens Christus in altum	LR 102	re	4
c	-1	0	-3	0	-5	-3	-5	-7	G	Alleluia	AM 103	an	8
c	-1	0	-3	0	-5	-3	-5	-7	G	Aspice in me et miserere	AM 101	an	8
c	-1	0	-3	0	-5	-3	-5	-3	G	Magnus sanctus Paulus	PM 163 *WA 330 *LA 423	an	8
F	-1	0	-3	0	-5	0	-1	0	D	Dominus firmamentum meum	GR 332 LU 1001 *SYG 241 GB 249 *GS 145	co	2
c	-1	0	-3	0	-3	0	-3	-5		Domine abstraxisti ab inferis Exaltabo te	OTT 96 *GB 62^{v} SYG 66	ofv	
F	-1	0	-3	0	-1	-5	-3	0	D	Quem vidistis pastores	AR 264 LU 395 AM 240 WA 31 *LA 40	an	2
F	-1	0	-3	0	-1	-3	-1	-3	D	Dominus custodit te ab omni	LA 560	an	2
F	-1	0	-3	0	-1	0	2	4	E	Adjutor et susceptor meus	LR 414 *LA 168 WA 108	re	4
F	-1	0	-3	0	2	0	-1	-3	D	Tempus est ut revertar ... vos	LA 290 *WA 177	re	2
F	-1	0	-3	0	2	0	-1	0	E	Fili noli deficere	WA 170	re	4
F	-1	0	-3	0	2	0	-1	0	E	Sic veniet quemadmodum	WA 151 *LA 244 245	an	4

F	-1	0	-3	0	2	4	7	6	D	Agnus Dei	SCH #159		1
F	-1	0	-3	2	-1	2	4	9	E	Confiteantur tibi Domine	GR 92**	int	3
F	-1	0	-3	2	4	2	4	6	E	Exaudi Domine populum tuum confitentem ... populi	WA 231	an	3
F	-1	0	-3	4	2	4	0	2	D	Kyrie	MEL #130		
c	-1	0	-1	-5	-3	0	-1	0		Quod contractum fuerat Ego pascam	GR 66**	trv	
c	-1	0	-1	-5	-1	2	0	2	G	Semen cecidit ... aliud	AR 350 LU 509 *AM 322 325 *WA 79 LA 119	an	8
c	-1	0	-1	-5	-1	2	0	2	G	Semen cecidit ... in patientia	AR 350 LU 504 *AM 321 LA 118	an	8
c	-1	0	-1	-5	0	-3	-5	-8		Hymnum dicite et superexaltate Benedictus es	GS 44	trv	
c	-1	0	-1	-5	0	-1	0	-1		Ipse fecit nos et non ipsi nos Jubilate Domino	GR 82 LU 513 *GS 28 *GB 59^{v} *SYG 62	trv	
f	-1	0	-1	-3	-5	-12	-10	-8	F	Agnus Dei	SCH #1		5
f	-1	0	-1	-3	-5	-12	-10	-8	F	Sanctus	THAN #2		5
c	-1	0	-1	-3	-5	-7	-5	-3	G	In aeternum et in saeculum	WA 70	an	8
c	-1	0	-1	-3	-5	-7	-3	0	F	Dignum namque est	PM 253	an	5
f	-1	0	-1	-3	-5	-1	2	0		Et in terra	BOS #5		
F	-1	0	-1	-3	-5	0	2	0	F	Festum colentes celebre	ST 192	hy	6
F	-1	0	-1	-3	-5	0	2	0	F	Nunc sancte nobis spiritus	ST 173	hy	6
F	-1	0	-1	-3	-5	0	2	4	D	Benedictus es in firmamento ... in saecula	AR 342 AM 312 *WA 74 LA 114	an	1
F	-1	0	-1	-3	-5	0	2	4	E	Hymnum dicite et superexaltate	AR 354 AM 327 *WA 79 LA 124	an	4
F	-1	0	-1	-3	-1	-5	-3	-5	D	Meus cibus est	WA 100	an	2
F	-1	0	-1	-3	-1	-3	-5	-3		Tremens factus sum ego Libera me Domine de morte	AR [174] PM 321 LU 1767 GR 102* LA 557	rev	
F	-1	0	-1	-3	-1	0	2	4	E	Tanto namque feliciores	WA 256	an	4
F	-1	0	-1	-3	0	-1	0	-1	D	Sana Domine animam meam	AR [168] LU 1794 *WA 64 437 *LA 88 556	an	2
F	-1	0	-1	-3	2	0	-1	-3		Misertus enim est Deus Igitur Joseph	WA 95	rev	
F	-1	0	-1	-3	2	4	0	-1	E	Alleluia: delectatio bona	WA 144	re	3
F	-1	0	-1	-3	2	6	2	4	E	Alleluia: judica judicium	WA 144	re	3
c	-1	0	-1	0	-3	0	-1	-3	b	Sanctus	THAN #15		
F	-1	0	-1	0	-1	-3	-1	0	D	Kyrie	MEL #129		
F	-1	0	-1	0	2	0	-1	-3	E	Mentem sanctam spontaneum	WA 275 *LA 361	an	4
F	-1	0	-1	0	2	4	2	-1	E	Ascendens in altum alleluia	WA 148 *LA 247	re	4
F	-1	0	-1	0	2	4	2	4		Audite itaque domus David Confortamini et iam	OTT 9 *GB 7 SYG 8	ofv	

F	-1	0	-1	0	4	2	4	6	D	Ubi sunt misericordiae tuae	GB 160	an	1
c	-1	0	2	-3	-5	-7	-3	-5	G	Venit Maria Magdalene	SYG 146	an	7
F	-1	0	2	-3	-1	0	-1	-3		Loquebar Domine de testimoniis	SYG 39 GB 244	alv	
c	-1	0	2	-1	0	2	-3	-5		Domini est terra Tollite portas	OTT 14 *GB 13 *SYG 14	ofv	
c	-1	0	2	-1	2	4	2	0	G	Domine ostende nobis patrem	AR 694 LU 1465[E] AM 893 *WA 307 LA 393	an	7
c	-1	0	2	-1	2	4	2	0	G	Et ingressae non invenerunt	WA 138	an	7
c	-1	0	2	0	-3	-5	-3	0		Intente vigilans Auditor legis	WA 282	rev	
c	-1	0	2	0	-3	-1	-3	-5	G	Ego principium qui et loquor	AR 382 LU 1085, AM 355 *WA 94 LA 144	an	8
F	-1	0	2	0	-3	-1	-3	0	E	Benedicta es virgo Maria	GS q	gr	4
F	-1	0	2	0	-3	-1	-3	0	E	Benedicta et venerabilis ... quae sine tactu	GR [76] LU 1264 GB 220 GS q	gr	4
F	-1	0	2	0	-3	-1	-3	0	E	Dolorosa et lacrimabilis	GR 595 LU 1633[V]	gr	4
F	-1	0	2	0	-3	-1	-3	0	E	Domine praevenisti eum	GR [48] LU 1207 *SYG 224 *GB 53 GS 222	gr	4
c	-1	0	2	0	-3	0	-1	-3	G	Ego gloriam meam	AR 414 LU 569 AM 391	an	8
c	-1	0	2	0	-1	-3	-5	-3	G	Quare jejunavimus	LA 126	an	8
c	-1	0	2	0	-1	-3	-1	0	G	Beatus es et bene tibi	PM 128 LA 331	an	8
c	-1	0	2	0	-1	-3	-1	0	G	Cum (Dum) venerit filius	AR 238 AM 212 LA 22 *WA 17	an	8
c	-1	0	2	0	-1	-3	-1	0	G	Ego daemonium non habeo	AR 412 LU 568 AM 391 *WA 108 LA 172	an	8
f	-1	0	2	0	-1	-3	-1	0		Requiem aeternam dona eis Domine In loco viridi	VP 242	rev	
F	-1	0	2	0	-1	-3	-1	0	E	Surrexit Christus et illuxit	WA 135	an	4
c	-1	0	2	0	-1	-3	0	-1	G	Ego qui loquor justitiam	AR 759 LU 1537 AM 945	an	8
F	-1	0	2	0	-1	-3	0	-1		Hostias et preces tibi Domine offerimus Domine Jesu Christe	SYG 235	ofv	
c	-1	0	2	0	-1	-3	0	-1	G	Pater diligit filium	WA 105	an	8
F	-1	0	2	0	-1	-3	2	-3	D	Kyrie	MEL #128		
f	-1	0	2	0	-1	0	-1	-3		Adduxerunt autem eum Jesum tradidit	OHS 507 LU 711 *LA 199	rev	
c	-1	0	2	0	-1	0	-1	-3		De profundis clamavi ad te Rogamus te Domine	LA 557	rev	
c	-1	0	2	0	-1	0	-1	-3		Dies mei sicut umbra Rogamus te Domine	LA 557	rev	
c	-1	0	2	0	-1	0	-1	-3		Felix certe et omni Beata progenies	WA 367	rev	
c	-1	0	2	0	-1	0	-1	-3		Requiem aeternam dona ei Domine Rogamus te Domine	LA 557	rev	

c	-1	0	2	0	-1	0	-1	-3		Sancti per fidem vicerunt Isti viventes	WA 413	rev	
c	-1	0	2	0	-1	0	2	0	G	Veniet fortior me	AR 221 AM 192 WA 9 LA 7	an	8
c	-1	0	2	0	2	-1	0	-1	G	Contumelias et terrores ... qui erant	OHS 241 (nm) LA 178 *WA 116	re	7
c	-1	0	2	0	2	0	-3	-1		Beati immaculati in via Benedictus ... in labiis	OTT 28 *GB 60 *SYG 62	ofv	
c	-1	0	2	0	2	0	-1	-3	G	Ego in altissimis habitavi	AR 544 LU 990 AM 580 WA 168 *LA 281	an	8
c	-1	0	2	0	2	0	-1	-3	G	Recordare mei Domine et tuere	WA 114 LA 185	an	8
F	-1	0	2	0	2	0	-1	0	E	Agnus Dei	SCH #158		4
c	-1	0	2	0	2	0	2	4	F	O salutaris hostia fulget dies	ST 314	hy	5
c	-1	0	2	0	2	4	2	0	G	Clamaverunt justi et Dominus	LR 135 *WA 411 LA 505	an	7
c	-1	0	2	0	2	4	2	0	G	Ornaverunt faciem templi	LA 296 *WA 181	re	7
c	-1	0	2	0	2	4	2	0	G	Pretiosa in conspectu Domini	LA 473 512	an	7
c	-1	0	2	0	2	4	2	4	G	Benedicta filia tu a Domino	AR 821 882^3 LU 1606 1686 AM 1014 1082 LA 448 *WA 358	an	7
c	-1	0	2	0	2	4	2	4	G	Confortatus est principatus	AR [11] LU 1115 AM 627 WA 415 LA 421 512	an	7
c	-1	0	2	0	2	4	2	4	G	Dixit Judas fratribus	LA 147 *WA 96	re	7
c	-1	0	2	0	2	4	2	4	G	Dixit Judas Simoni	LA 297 *WA 182	re	7
c	-1	0	2	0	2	4	2	4	G	Dum aurora finem ... dixit	LA 493	re	7
c	-1	0	2	0	2	4	2	4	G	Fluctus tui super me	LA 305 *WA 186	re	7
c	-1	0	2	0	2	4	2	4	G	Gloriosae virginis Mariae ortum	LA 457 *WA 365	re	7
c	-1	0	2	0	2	4	2	4	G	Puer meus noli timere	LA 434 *WA 349	re	7
c	-1	0	2	0	2	4	2	4	G	Surge pater et comede	LA 137	re	7
F	-1	0	2	0	2	4	2	7	G	Benedictus Deus patrum	SYG 136	an	8
F	-1	0	2	4	0	-1	-3	-5	D	Confundantur superbi quia injuste	GR [54] LU 1220 SYG 228 GB 244^v GS 231	co	1
F	-1	0	2	4	0	-1	-3	-5	D	Praedicabant apostoli	OHS 437 LU 664	co	1
c	-1	0	2	4	0	-1	-3	0		Misericordia et veritas obviaverunt Deus tu convertens	OTT 6 *SYG 4 *GB 3	ofv	
F	-1	0	2	4	2	-1	-3	-1	E	Jesu nostra redemptio	ST 231	hy	4
F	-1	0	2	4	2	-1	0	2	E	Mane surgens Jacob	LR 240 LA 552	re	4
F	-1	0	2	4	2	-1	0	2	E	Nocte os meum perforatur	LA 285 WA 173	re	4
F	-1	0	2	4	2	-1	0	2	E	Petre amas me	LR 361 LA 417 WA 279	re	4
F	-1	0	2	4	2	-1	0	2		Praedicator veritatis et doctor Tu es vas	GR 420 GS 178	trv	
F	-1	0	2	4	2	0	-3	-1	E	Hujus obtentu Deus alme nostris	LR 213	hy	4

F	-1	0	2	4	2	0	-3	-1	E	Jesu nostra redemptio	GR 156* AM 506	hy	4
F	-1	0	2	4	2	0	-3	-1	E	Virginis proles opifexque matris	LR 212 213	hy	4
F	-1	0	2	4	2	0	-3	0	E	Cor dulce Jesu quis tuum	AR 1 (sup 2)	hy	4
F	-1	0	2	4	2	0	-3	0	E	E corde Jesu prodiit	AR 5 (sup)	hy	4
F	-1	0	2	4	2	0	-3	0	E	Nunc sancte nobis spiritus	AR 493 LU 846	hy	4
F	-1	0	2	4	2	0	-3	0	E	O salutaris hostia quae caeli	AR 93*	hy	4
F	-1	0	2	4	2	0	-3	0	E	Quicumque Christum quaeritis	AR 803 LU 1590	hy	4
F	-1	0	2	4	2	0	-3	0	E	Salutis humanae sator	AR 488 GR 155* LU 852	hy	4
F	-1	0	2	4	2	0	-3	0	E	Te lucis ante terminum	AR 490 LU 844	hy	4
F	-1	0	2	4	2	0	-1	0	D	Sanctus	THAN #125		2
c	-1	0	2	4	2	0	2	0	G	Domine non habeo	WA 90 (inc illeg) LA 135	an	7
F	-1	0	2	4	2	0	4	6	F	Agnus Dei	SCH #157		6
F	-1	0	2	4	2	0	4	6	F	Kyrie	MEL #127		
F	-1	0	2	4	2	0	4	6	F	Sanctus	THAN #124		6
F	-1	0	2	4	2	4	2	0		Stantes erant pedes Laetatus sum	SYG 101	trv	
F	-1	0	2	4	2	4	2	4		Ait illi Jesus Dixit Dominus mulieri	SYG 85 *GS 47	trv	
F	-1	0	2	4	2	4	2	4	E	Redemit Dominus populum	LA 305 WA 184	re	3
F	-1	0	2	4	2	4	2	9	D	Lux ecce surgit aurea	ST 318	hy	1
F	-1	0	2	4	5	4	2	0	E	Erubescant et conturbentur	GR 106 SYG 81 GB 72^{v} GS 42	co	4
c	-1	0	2	4	5	4	2	0	G	Erubescant et revereantur	GR 187 OHS 214 LU 608 SYG 125 GB 112 GS 90	co	7
F	-1	0	2	4	5	4	2	0	F	Supplex sacramus canticum	ST 21	hy	5
F	-1	0	2	4	6	4	2	4	G	Agnus Dei	SCH #156		3
c	-1	0	4	0	-1	2	4	0		Ipse fecit nos et non ipsi nos Jubilate Deo	OTT 23 *GB 36^{v} *SYG 32	ofv	
F	-1	0	4	6	4	2	4	2		In te confirmatus sum Spes mea Domine	LA 115	rev	
c	-1	2	-1	0	-3	-5	0	-1		Mox illis clamantibus Quadam die tempestate	WA 240	rev	
F	-1	2	-1	0	-3	-1	-3	0	E	Si tibi gratum vis	WA 244	re	3
c	-1	2	0	-3	-5	-7	-5	-3		Magnus et metuendus Tui sunt caeli	OTT 18 *GB 19^{v} *SYG 20	ofv	
F	-1	2	0	-3	-1	-3	-1	0	D	Ista est speciosa inter filias	PM 312 LR 378 *WA 356	re	2
F	-1	2	0	-3	-1	-3	0	-3	E	Vidi conjunctos viros	PM 216 LR 141 *LA 507 *WA 412	re	4
c	-1	2	0	-3	0	-1	-3	-5		De mundi hujus Occasum tanti	WA 285	rev	

c	-1	2	0	-1	-3	-5	-3	-5		Restitui numerum gaudet Regni caelestis	PM 268	rev	
F	-1	2	0	-1	-3	-1	0	-3	D	Ave gratia plena Dei genitrix	VP 103 SYG 46 *GB 46^{v} GS 180	an	1
F	-1	2	0	-1	0	-3	5	7		Ave Maria gratia plena ... et benedictus	GB 11^{v}	alv	
c	-1	2	0	-1	0	2	0	-3		Confiteantur Domino misericordiae	GR 411	alv	
c	-1	2	0	-1	0	2	0	-3		Diffusa est gratia in labiis	GR 405 LU 1323 SYG 5 GB 4^{v} GS 228	alv	
c	-1	2	0	-1	0	2	0	-3		Domine dilexi decorem	GB 174	alv	
c	-1	2	0	-1	0	2	0	-3		Dominus dixit ad me	GR 29 LU 394 SYG 15 GB 14 *GS 14	alv	
c	-1	2	0	-1	0	2	0	-3		Dominus in Sina in sancto	GR 286 LU 848 GS 136 SYG 179 GB 178^{v}	alv	
c	-1	2	0	-1	0	2	0	-3		Dominus regnavit exsultet terra	GR 72 LU 490 GS 23 SYG 42	alv	
c	-1	2	0	-1	0	2	0	-3		Dominus salvavit manum tuam	GR 464	alv	
c	-1	2	0	-1	0	2	0	-3		Haec dies quam fecit	GR 259 OHS 827 LU 805 GS 123 SYG 161 GB 142^{v}	alv	
c	-1	2	0	-1	0	2	0	-3		In omnem terram exivit sonus	GB 267	alv	
c	-1	2	0	-1	0	2	0	-3		Inebriabuntur ab ubertate	GR 425	alv	
c	-1	2	0	-1	0	2	0	-3		Lauda anima mea Dominum	SYG 256 *GS 166	alv	
c	-1	2	0	-1	0	2	0	-3		Mittat tibi Dominus	SYG 232	alv	
c	-1	2	0	-1	0	2	0	-3		Mittat vobis Dominus	GR [123] LU 1289	alv	
c	-1	2	0	-1	0	2	0	-3		Nimis honorati sunt amici tui	GR 644 LU 1720 GB 267^{v}	alv	
c	-1	2	0	-1	0	2	0	-3		Ostende nobis Domine misericordiam	GR 2 LU 320 SYG 2 GB 1 *GS 1	alv	
c	-1	2	0	-1	0	2	0	-3		Paras mihi mensam	LU 1623^{C}	alv	
c	-1	2	0	-1	0	2	0	-3		Salve regina misericordiae	LU 1476^{E}	alv	
c	-1	2	0	-1	0	2	0	-3		Specie tua et pulchritudine	GR [70] LU 1218 GS 227 SYG 29 GB 273	alv	
c	-1	2	0	-1	0	2	0	-3		Spiritus est Deus	SYG 187	alv	
c	-1	2	0	-1	2	0	-3	0		Veni sponsa Christi accipe coronam	GB 273^{v}	alv	
c	-1	2	0	2	-3	-7	-5	-3	G	Cogitaverunt impii et locuti sunt	OHS 384 LU 639 *WA 118 *LA 190	an	8
F	-1	2	0	2	4	2	-1	-3	F	Agnus Dei	SCH #155		6
F	-1	2	3	2	0	-3	0	-1	E	Jesu nostra redemptio	PM 95	hy	4
F	-1	2	4	-1	0	-3	-5	0	F	Adorate Deum alleluia	LR 74	an	6
F	-1	2	4	-1	0	-3	-5	0	F	Adorate Dominum alleluia in aula	LR 74 *LA 69 *WA 54	an	6
F	-1	2	4	-1	0	-3	-5	0	F	Cognoverunt Dominum alleluia	AR 478 *AM 492	an	6
F	-1	2	4	-1	0	-3	-5	0	F	Dominus in caelo alleluia	LR 100 *WA 148 *LA 247	an	6

F	-1	2	4	-1	0	-3	-5	0	F	Dominus in Sion alleluia	LR 100 *WA 148 *LA 247	an	6
F	-1	2	4	-1	0	-3	-5	0	F	Lux orta est justo	LR 140 *WA 412 *LA 43 507	an	6
F	-1	2	4	-1	0	-3	-5	0	F	Nimis exaltatus est alleluia	LR 100 *WA 148 *LA 247	an	6
F	-1	2	4	-1	0	-3	-5	0	F	Pax vobis ego sum alleluia	AM 478 496 *AR 464 481 LA 230	an	6
F	-1	2	4	-1	0	-3	-5	0	F	Tristitia vestra alleluia vertetur	AR 477 *AM 491	an	6
F	-1	2	4	0	-3	-5	0	-1	F	Gavisi sunt discipuli	LA 230	an	6
F	-1	2	4	0	-3	-5	0	-1	F	Ipse invocabit me alleluia	LU 384 *LR 60 *WA 49 LA 33	an	6
F	-1	2	4	0	-3	-5	0	-1	F	Notum fecit Dominus alleluia	LU 388 *LR 61 LA 33 *WA 49	an	6
F	-1	2	4	0	-3	-5	0	-1	F	Spiritus paraclitus alleluia	LA 263	an	6
F	-1	2	4	0	-3	-5	0	-1	F	Spiritus sanctus docebit vos	LA 263	an	6
F	-1	2	4	0	-1	-3	-5	-3	D	Florete flores quasi lilium	GR 622 LU 1677	co	1
F	-1	2	4	0	-1	-3	-5	0	F	Adorate Dominum alleluia omnes	WA 54 LA 69	an	6
F	-1	2	4	0	-1	-3	-5	0	F	Verbum caro factum est alleluia	WA 29 *LA 31	an	6
F	-1	2	4	-1	0	-3	-5	0	F	Ego sum vitis vera alleluia	AR 465 *AM 479	an	6
F	-1	2	4	-1	0	-3	-5	0	F	Euntes in mundum alleluia docete	AR 469 *AM 483	an	6
F	-1	2	4	0	-3	-5	0	-1	F	Ecce ego vobiscum sum alleluia	LA 222	an	6
F	-1	2	4	0	-1	0	-3	-5	F	Surrexit Dominus vere	LA 221	an	6
F	-1	2	4	0	-1	0	-3	-5	F	Verba quae locutus sum	LA 263	an	6
F	-1	2	4	2	0	-3	0	-1	E	Quicumque Christum quaeritis	LR 445	hy	4
F	-1	2	4	2	0	-3	0	-1	E	Tristes erant apostoli	LR 163	hy	4
F	-1	2	4	2	0	-3	0	2	F	Specie tua et pulchritudine	GR [60] LU 1226 SYG 39 GB 42^v GS 226	gr	5
F	-1	2	4	2	0	2	4	2	E	Deus creator omnium	ST 144	hy	4
F	-1	2	4	2	0	2	4	2	E	Te lucis ante terminum	AR 59 LU 267	hy	4
F	-1	2	4	2	4	2	0	[0]	F	Spera in Domino	WA 63 *LA 87	an	6
c	-1	2	4	2	4	2	4	2		Pascha nostrum immolatus	GR 242 OHS 710 LU 779 GS 117 *SYG 153 GB 125^v	alv	
F	-1	2	4	7	4	2	4	2	E	Quam pulchri super montes	GR 60**	co	4
E	1	-4	-2	0	1	0	1	-2	E	Juravit Dominus et non paenitebit	SYG 33 GB 40^v *GS 221	gr	3
E	1	-4	-2	1	-2	0	1	3	E	Jerusalem cito veniet salus	LR 392 *LA 8 *WA 9	re	4
E	1	-4	-2	3	8	5	3	5		Benedicat vobis Dominus ex Sion	GR [124] LU 1290	alv	
E	1	-4	-2	3	8	5	3	5		Pretiosa in conspectu Domini	GR [19] LU 1151 *SYG 218	alv	
b	1	-2	-4	-2	-4	-6	-7	-9	E	Plaudat laetitia lux hodierna	ST 239	hy	3
b	1	-2	-4	-2	0	1	-2	-4	E	Gloria	BOS #11		II

a	1	-2	-4	-2	0	1	-2	-4		Kyrie ... pater de caelis	PM 281 283 VP 31 33		
E	1	-2	-4	-2	0	1	-2	-4	D	Te lucis ante terminum	AR 364 LU 540	hy	2
E	1	-2	-4	-2	1	0	-2	0	E	Jesu sacrator mentium	ST 164	hy	4
E	1	-2	-4	-2	1	3	1	3	F	Haec aula accipiet	WA 317	an	6
E	1	-2	-4	-2	1	3	1	3	F	In voce exsultationis	LR 122 LU 930	an	6
b	1	-2	-4	1	0	-2	-4	-2	E	Kyrie	MEL #13		
E	1	-2	-4	1	3	1	3	1	F	Mox pater suos	WA 295	an	6
E	1	-2	-4	1	3	1	3	5	F	O quam gloriosum ... gaudent	WA 45	an	6
E	1	-2	-4	1	3	1	3	5	F	Observa fili praecepta	AR 545 LU 991 *AM 582 *LA 281	an	6
b	1	-2	-4	1	3	5	3	1	c	O admirabile beati Gregorii	WA 291	an	6
E	1	-2	-4	3	5	3	5	3	E	Non conturbetur cor	WA 149	re	4
E	1	-2	0	-4	-2	0	1	3	E	Credo videre bona Domini	AR [163] OHS 605 LU 763 1789 *WA 125 437 *LA 203 555	an	4
b	1	-2	0	-4	-2	1	3	1		Respice in me et exaudi me Illumina oculos	OTT 87 GB 81 SYG 92	ofv	
E	1	-2	0	-4	-2	3	5	1	E	Jerusalem quae aedificatur	GR 141 LU 563 SYG 102 GB 91 GS 64	co	4
E	1	-2	0	-4	0	3	5	3	E	Sanctus	THAN #151		3
b	1	-2	0	-2	-4	-2	0	-2	b	Nunc sancte nobis spiritus	ST 267	hy	4
E	1	-2	0	-2	-4	-2	1	0	E	In visione sancta	WA 312	re	4
b	1	-2	0	1	-4	0	1	-2	G	Domine quinque talenta	GR 396 LU 1311 *SYG 38 *GB 42 *GS 223	co	7
E	1	-2	0	1	-4	0	1	-2	D	Ego sum pastor bonus alleluia	GR 265 LU 439 819 *SYG 165 GB 147v *GS 128	co	2
E	1	-2	0	1	-4	0	1	-2	D	Ego sum pastor bonus et cognosco	GR 48 LU 438	co	2
b	1	-2	0	1	-4	0	1	-2	G	Ego sum vitis vera	GR (19) *SYG 171 *GB 163 *GS 210	co	8
b	1	-2	0	1	-4	0	1	-2	G	Ego sum vitis vera	OHS 790 *LR 89 *WA 305	re	5 8
E	1	-2	0	1	3	1	0	-2	E	Alleluia	AM 79	an	4
E	1	-2	0	1	3	1	0	1	E	In cymbalis benesonantibus	AM 79 *WA 70 *LA 105	an	4
E	1	-2	0	1	3	5	3	8	E	Missus est Gabriel angelus	SYG 57	int	3
E	1	-2	0	3	5	3	0	1	E	Date et dabitur vobis mensuram	GR 634 LU 1696	co	3
E	1	-2	0	3	5	3	1	-2	E	Benedicite omnes angeli Domini	GR 611 LU 1657 *GB 171 GS 198	co	3
E	1	-2	1	-2	-4	-2	0	-2	E	Adesto summa suavitas	ST 233	hy	4
E	1	-2	1	-2	-4	-2	0	-2	E	Beata nobis gaudia	ST 232	hy	4
E	1	-2	1	-2	-4	-2	0	-2	E	Conscendat usque sidera	ST 234	hy	4
E	1	-2	1	-2	-4	-2	0	-2	E	Omnes superni ordines	ST 237	hy	4

E	1	-2	1	0	1	-2	1	3	E	Audiens Christi confessor	WA 240	re	4
b	1	-2	1	0	1	3	1	0		Numquid fortitudo lapidum Vir erat	OTT 122 *GB 262 SYG 256	ofv	
E	1	-2	1	0	1	3	5	3	G	Quoniam non fuit dolus	WA 288	an	8
E	1	-2	1	3	0	1	3	5	E	Christus resurgens ex mortuis	OHS 822	re	4
E	1	-2	1	3	1	0	1	0	E	Tempus est ut revertar ... dicit	LR 101 *LA 249 *WA 148	re	4
E	1	-2	3	0	3	5	3	5	E	Dum clamarem ad Dominum	GR 344 LU 1020 SYG 67 GB 63 GS 32 151	int	3
E	1	-2	3	0	3	5	3	5	E	Extuli electum de populo	LU 1623[A]	int	3
E	1	-2	3	0	3	5	3	5	E	Gaudens gaudebo in Domino	GR 400 LU 1316	int	3
E	1	-2	3	0	3	5	8	7	E	Vocem jucunditatis annuntiate	GR 270 LU 830 SYG 168 GB 151 GS 130	int	3
E	1	-2	3	0	3	5	10	8	E	Cognovi Domine quia aequitas	GR [68] LU 1239 GB 229^{v} GS 226	int	3
E	1	-2	3	0	3	5	10	8	E	Ecce oculi Domini super timentes	GR 494 SYG 176 GB 171^{v} GS 212	int	3
E	1	-2	3	0	3	5	10	8	E	Redemisti nos Domine	GR 536 LU 1532	int	3
E	1	-2	3	5	0	3	5	3	E	Alleluia: rosa vernans caritatis	VP 52	al	4
E	1	-2	3	5	0	3	5	3		Cujus partus Rosa vernans	VP 52	alv	
E	1	-2	3	5	1	0	1	-2	E	Alleluia: benedicat vobis Dominus	GR [124] LU 1290	al	4
E	1	-2	3	5	1	0	1	-2	E	Alleluia: pretiosa in conspectu Domini	GR [19] LU 1151 SYG 218	al	4
E	1	-2	3	5	1	0	1	-2	E	Alleluia: qui sanat contritos corde	SYG 258 *GS d	al	3
E	1	-2	3	5	3	5	6	5		Ego autem in innocentia Proba me Domine	SYG 85	grv	
E	1	-2	3	5	3	5	6	5		Justitiam tuam non abscondi Memor fui	GR 564 LU 1580	grv	
a	1	-2	3	5	3	5	7	8	a	Beatus servus quem cum venerit	GR [45] LU 1203 GS 223 SYG 28 GB 29	co	3
E	1	-2	3	5	3	5	7	8		Dixit Dominus Domino meo Juravit Dominus	GS 221 SYG 33 GB 40^{v}	grv	
E	1	-2	3	5	3	5	7	8		In convertendo inimicum meum Exsurge Domine	GR 123 LU 553 GS 54 GB 82 SYG 93	grv	
E	1	-2	3	5	3	5	7	8		Quia satiavit animam inanem Confiteantur Domino	GR 631 LU 1694	grv	
E	1	-2	3	5	3	5	8	7		Eructavit cor meum Afferentur regi ... proximae	OTT 155 *GB 30 *SYG 29	ofv	
E	1	-2	3	5	3	7	5	7	E	Miserere mihi Domine quoniam conculcavit	GR 156 SYG 111 GB 99 GS 73	int	3
a	1	-2	3	5	7	5	7	8	a	Exaudi Domine vocem meam ... alleluia	GR 287 LU 854 SYG 181 GB 182 *GS 136	int	1
E	1	-2	3	5	7	8	5	3		Ego autem in innocentia Lavabo	SYG 86	ofv	

E	1	-2	3	5	7	10	8	5		Qui sanat contritos corde	SYG 258 *GS d	alv	
E	1	-2	3	5	8	5	3	1	E	Dies absoluti praetereunt	ST 224	hy	3
E	1	-2	3	5	8	5	8	10		Effunde frameam et conclude Exsurge Domine	GR 185 OHS 208 LU 607 *GS 89 *GB 111^{v} *SYG 124	grv	
E	1	-2	3	5	8	7	5	3	E	O quam glorifica luce coruscas	ST 132	hy	3
E	1	-2	3	5	8	7	8	7		Non judicavi me scire Mihi autem absit	GR 481	grv	
E	1	-2	3	5	8	7	10	8		Sperent in te qui noverunt	GR 94**	alv	
E	1	-2	3	5	8	7	10	8		Spiritus Domini replevit orbem	GS a 140	alv	
E	1	-2	3	5	8	10	8	5	E	Crux fidelis inter omnes ... sustinens	ST 33	hy	3
E	1	-2	3	7	3	5	7	8	E	Alleluia: adducentur regi virgines	GR [61] LU 1217 *GS 231 GB 29^{v}	al	3
E	1	-2	3	7	3	5	7	8	E	Alleluia: beatam me dicent omnes	GR 587^{5}	al	3
E	1	-2	3	7	3	5	7	8	E	Alleluia: benedictus Dominus Deus meus	GR 465	al	3
E	1	-2	3	7	3	5	7	8	E	Alleluia: crastina erit vobis salus	GB 12^{v}	al	3
E	1	-2	3	7	3	5	7	8	[E]	Alleluia: exsultent justi Dei in conspectu	GB 269^{v}	al	3
E	1	-2	3	7	3	5	7	8	E	Alleluia: ingressa Agnes turpitudinis	GB 45	al	3
E	1	-2	3	7	3	5	7	8	E	Alleluia: paratum cor meum Deus	GR 378 LU 1064 GB 259^{v} *GS 158 SYG 253	al	3
E	1	-2	3	7	3	5	7	8	E	Alleluia: quid bonum ejus est	GR 55**	al	3
E	1	-2	3	7	3	5	7	8	E	Alleluia: quoniam confirmata est	SYG 250	al	3
E	1	-2	3	7	3	5	7	8	E	Alleluia: veni Domine et noli tardare	GR 22 LU 354 SYG 7 GB 11 *GS 12	al	3
E	1	-2	3	7	3	5	8	7		Judica Domine nocentes me Ego autem dum mihi	GR 187 OHS 258 LU 610 *GS 90 *GB 112^{v} *SYG 125	grv	
E	1	-2	3	7	5	7	8	7	E	Alleluia: jubilate Deo omnis terra	GR 65 LU 479 *SYG 32 GB 256 *GS 20	al	3
E	1	-2	3	7	5	7	8	10	E	Alleluia: si enim non abiero	SYG 168	al	4
E	1	-2	3	8	5	3	5	7	E	Ego autem sicut oliva	GR [1] *SYG 170 *GB 22^{v} *GS 202	int	3
E	1	-2	3	8	5	3	5	7	E	Minuisti eum paulo minus	GR 517 LU 1493	int	3
E	1	-2	3	8	5	3	8	5	E	Dedit illi Deus sapientiam	GR 422 LU 1352	int	3
E	1	-2	3	8	5	8	5	3	E	Repleatur os meum laude tua	GR 302 LU 897 *SYG 186 *GB 192^{v} *GS 140	int	3
E	1	-2	3	8	5	8	5	3	E	Sermo meus et praedicatio	GR 544 LU 1543	int	3
E	1	-2	3	8	10	8	10	8		Eructavit cor meum Constitues eos	OTT 131 GB 206^{v} SYG 203	ofv	
E	1	0	-4	-2	0	3	5	3	E	Agnus Dei	SCH #183		3

E	1	0	-4	-2	1	0	1	3	E	Quid vobis videtur	AR 568 LU 1051 *AM 609 *LA 317	an	4
a	1	0	-2	-4	-5	-2	0	-4	D	Aeterni patris filium	ST 306	hy	1
b	1	0	-2	-4	-2	-7	-4	-9	E	Kyrie	MEL #12		
b	1	0	-2	-4	-2	-4	-6	-7	E	Alma Dei porta David	ST 315	hy	3
b	1	0	-2	-4	-2	-4	-2	0		Et in terra	BOS #42		
a	1	0	-2	-4	-2	0	-4	-7		Kyrie ... pater de caelis	PM 77		
E	1	0	-2	-4	-2	0	1	0	E	Christe sanctorum decus angelorum	ST 316	hy	4
E	1	0	-2	-4	-2	0	1	0	E	Lux ecce surgit aurea	ST 279	hy	4
E	1	0	-2	-4	-2	1	-2	0	E	Doctor egregie Paule	AM 790 936	hy	4
E	1	0	-2	-4	-2	1	-2	0	E	Jam bone pastor Petre	AM 824 936 990	hy	4
E	1	0	-2	-4	-2	1	0	1	E	Aurea luce et decore roseo	ST 296 (var)	hy	4
E	1	0	-2	-4	-2	1	0	3	E	Ave Katherina martyr et regina	ST 297	hy	4
E	1	0	-2	-4	-2	1	0	3	E	Ave maris stella Dei mater alma	ST 281	hy	4
a	1	0	-2	-4	0	-2	-4	-5	D	Lux hodierna fulget in arva	ST 82	hy	1
a	1	0	-2	-4	0	3	5	3		Igne me examinasti In craticula	WA 346	rev	
a	1	0	-2	0	-7	-4	-2	0	D	Benedicamus Domino V	AR 61* LU 126		1
a	1	0	-2	0	-7	-4	-2	0	D	Ite missa est XI	GR 41* LU 48		1
a	1	0	-2	0	-7	-4	-2	0	D	Kyrie XI orbis factor	MEL #16 GR 38* LU 46		1
e	1	0	-2	0	-7	-4	-2	0	a	Sanctus	THAN #3		3
a	1	0	-2	0	-7	-4	0	-2	D	Kyrie ad lib X orbis factor	GR 82* LU 85		1
E	1	0	-2	0	-5	-4	-2	0		Aufer a plebe tua opprobrium Benedictus es ... in labiis	GB 60	ofv	
b	1	0	-2	0	-4	-6	-7	-4	E	Agnus Dei	SCH #42		4
b	1	0	-2	0	-4	-6	-7	-4	E	Sanctus	THAN #36		4
a	1	0	-2	0	-2	-4	-5	-7	D	O Verena sponsa Christi	ST 323	hy	1
E	1	0	-2	0	-2	-4	-2	0	E	Ecce jam noctis tenuatur umbra lucis	ST 85 AM 35	hy	4
b	1	0	-2	0	-2	-4	-2	0	b	Kyrie XV dominator Deus	GR 51* LU 56		4
E	1	0	-2	0	-2	-4	-2	0	E	Nocte surgentes vigilemus omnes	ST 85	hy	4
E	1	0	-2	0	-2	0	1	3	E	Euge serve bone et fidelis ... intra	AR 577[19] [82] LU 262[8] 1200	an	4
E	1	0	-2	0	1	-2	-4	-2	E	Agnus Dei	SCH #180		4
E	1	0	-2	0	1	-2	-4	-2	E	Kyrie	MEL #152		
E	1	0	-2	0	1	0	-2	-4	E	Kyrie Deus genitor alme	MEL #151		
E	1	0	-2	0	3	0	-4	-2	E	Agnus Dei	SCH #178		3
E	1	0	-2	0	3	0	-4	-2	E	Agnus Dei	SCH #179		3

E	1	0	-2	0	3	0	-4	-2	E	Sanctus	THAN #150		3
E	1	0	-2	0	3	1	0	-2	E	Gloria	BOS #47		II
E	1	0	-2	0	3	1	0	-2	E	Sanctus	THAN #149		4
E	1	0	-2	0	3	5	0	1	E	Kyrie genitor ingenite	MEL #150		
E	1	0	-2	0	3	5	0	3	E	Agnus Dei	SCH #177		3
E	1	0	-2	0	3	5	0	3	E	Sanctus	THAN #148		3
E	1	0	-2	0	3	5	3	1	E	Verbum supernum prodiens nec patris	ST 344	hy	3
E	1	0	-2	0	3	5	7	8	E	Agnus Dei	SCH #176		3
E	1	0	-2	0	3	5	7	8	E	Kyrie	MEL #148		
E	1	0	-2	0	3	5	7	8	E	Kyrie immense conditor	MEL #149		
E	1	0	-2	0	3	5	7	8	E	Sanctus	THAN #147		3
E	1	0	-2	0	7	8	7	5	E	Agnus Dei	SCH #175		3
E	1	0	-2	0	7	8	7	5	E	Sanctus	THAN #146		3
E	1	0	-2	1	3	5	3	1	[E]	Agnus Dei	SCH #174		4
E	1	0	-2	3	0	1	0	-2	E	Sanctus	THAN #145		3
E	1	0	-2	3	1	0	-2	0	E	Haec est dies quam fecit	PM 147	an	4
E	1	0	-2	3	1	0	3	5	E	O gloriosa domina	ST 356	hy	3
E	1	0	-2	3	5	1	3	0	E	Alleluia: dixit Dominus Domino meo	SYG 248	al	3
e	1	0	-2	3	5	3	0	1		Ait illis Pilatus Egressus Jesus	WA 123	rev	
E	1	0	-2	3	5	3	1	0	E	Kyrie	MEL #147		
E	1	0	-2	3	5	3	1	0	E	Pange lingua praeconium	ST 336	hy	3
E	1	0	-2	3	5	3	1	3		Missus est angelus Domini	GR 637	alv	
E	1	0	-2	3	5	3	5	3	E	Beatus Anselmus saeculi	AM 872	an	3
E	1	0	-2	3	5	3	5	8	E	Beatus Hugo piscator Dei	PM 149	re	3
E	1	0	-2	3	5	3	5	8	E	Corde natus ex parentis	ST 274	hy	3
E	1	0	-2	3	5	3	5	8	E	Dignus est agnus	GR 638 LU 1709	int	3
E	1	0	-2	3	5	3	5	8	E	Dum sanctificatus fuero	GR 145 (38) LU 859 *SYG 104 *GB 93 *GS 66	int	3
E	1	0	-2	3	5	3	5	8	E	Factum est cor meum	GR 505 LU 1477	int	3
E	1	0	-2	3	5	3	5	8	E	In caritate perpetua dilexit nos	AR 538[7] LU 977	an	3
E	1	0	-2	3	5	3	5	8	E	Non invenientes Jesum regressi	AR 653 LU 1406 *AM 842	an	3
E	1	0	-2	3	5	3	5	8	E	Omnis gloria ejus filiae	GR 47**	int	3
E	1	0	-2	3	5	3	5	8		Si testimonium hominum	GR 538 LU 1534	alv	
E	1	0	-2	3	5	7	8	5		Hosanna filio David	SYG 2	alv	
E	1	0	-2	3	5	7	8	5		Pulchra facie sed pulchrior	SYG 42	alv	

E	1	0	-2	3	5	7	8	7	E	Gloria	BOS #44		II
E	1	0	-2	3	5	7	8	7	E	Gloria	BOS #45		II
E	1	0	-2	3	5	7	8	7	E	Gloria	BOS #46		II
E	1	0	-2	3	5	7	8	7	E	Kyrie	MEL #146		
E	1	0	-2	3	5	7	8	7	E	Sanctus	THAN #144		3
E	1	0	-2	3	5	8	5	3	E	Dies absoluti praetereunt	ST 283	hy	4
E	1	0	-2	3	5	8	5	8		Qui timent te videbunt me	GR 73**	alv	
E	1	0	-2	3	5	8	7	5	E	Aeterna Christi munera apostolorum	LR 134	hy	3
E	1	0	-2	3	5	8	7	5	E	Aeterna Christi munera et martyrum	LR 175	hy	3
E	1	0	-2	3	5	8	7	5		Beata es virgo Maria quae sub cruce	LU 1476c	alv	
E	1	0	-2	3	5	8	7	5		Cognoverunt discipuli Dominum	GR 264 LU 817	alv	
E	1	0	-2	3	5	8	7	5		Domine Deus salutis meae	GR 351 LU 1029 GS 152 *SYG 245 *GB 254	alv	
E	1	0	-2	3	5	8	7	5	E	Quem crescentem virtutibus	WA 311	an	3
E	1	0	-2	3	5	8	7	5		Quis sicut Dominus Deus	GR 19**	alv	
E	1	0	-2	3	5	8	7	8	E	Agnus Dei	SCH #173		3
E	1	0	-2	3	5	8	7	8	E	Veni redemptor gentium	ST 177	hy	3
E	1	0	-2	3	5	8	10	8	E	Ira justa conditoris	LR 442	hy	3
E	1	0	-2	3	5	8	10	8	E	Pange lingua gloriosi corporis	AR 527 103* GR 198 152* PM 93 OHS 469 VP 9 5* LU 957	hy	3
E	1	0	-2	3	5	8	10	8	E	Tantum ergo sacramentum	AR 88* GR 158* LU 954	hy	3
E	1	0	-2	3	8	10	8	5	E	Pange lingua gloriosi proelium	ST 286	hy	3
E	1	0	-2	3	10	8	7	8	E	Sancte pater Aredi	SYG 219	int	3
E	1	0	-2	5	3	0	1	-2	E	Sanctus	THAN #143		3
e	1	0	-2	5	3	1	0	-2	[F]	Agnus Dei	SCH #5		5
E	1	0	-2	5	3	5	0	1	E	Agnus Dei	SCH #172		3
E	1	0	-2	5	3	5	0	1	E	Sanctus	THAN #142		3
E	1	0	-2	5	3	5	3	1	E	Agnus Dei	SCH #171		3
E	1	0	-2	5	3	5	3	1	E	Sanctus	THAN #141		3
E	1	0	-2	5	7	3	0	-4	E	Sanctus	THAN #140		3
b	1	0	1	-2	0	-7	-4	-2	E	Gloria	BOS #10		II
b	1	0	1	-2	1	-4	-2	0		Vidi non servantes pactum Benedictus ... non tradas	OTT 48 *GB 104 *SYG 116	ofv	
E	1	0	1	-2	3	5	8	7	E	Haec est quae nescivit	AR [88] LU 1211 *AM 679 WA 353 *LA 347	an	3
b	1	0	1	0	-4	-2	0	-2		Pro eo ut diligerent me Domine fac mecum	OTT 37 *GB 85v *SYG 96	ofv	

b	1	0	1	0	1	0	1	0		Deus laudem meam Domine fac mecum	OTT 37 GB 85^v SYG 96	ofv	
E	1	0	1	3	5	3	5	3		Et completa oratione Domine non aspicias	SYG 56	trv	
E	1	0	1	5	3	1	0	1	D	Agnus Dei	SCH #170		1
E	1	3	-2	-4	-2	0	3	5	E	Sancta Maria succurre ... festivitatem	AR [121] LU 1254	an	4
E	1	3	-2	-4	-2	0	3	5	E	Sancta Maria succurre ... maternitatem	AR 882^5 AM 1083 *WA 354	an	4
E	1	3	-2	0	-2	5	3	1	E	Simon Barjona tu vocaberis	WA 341 *LA 365	an	4
E	1	3	-2	3	1	0	-2	0	E	Solemnizet laete festa	ST 317	hy	3
e	1	3	0	-2	0	-4	-5	-7	F	Agnus Dei	SCH #4		5
E	1	3	0	1	0	-2	3	5	E	Agnus Dei	SCH #169		4
E	1	3	0	1	0	-2	3	5	E	Gloria	BOS #42		II
E	1	3	0	1	0	-2	3	5	E	Kyrie	MEL #145		
E	1	3	0	1	0	-2	3	5	E	Sanctus	THAN #139		3
E	1	3	0	3	1	0	-2	0	E	Juvenes et virgines	LU 1829	an	4
E	1	3	0	3	5	3	1	0	E	Serve bone et fidelis quia	AM 673 743	an	4
E	1	3	0	3	5	10	8	7	E	O beatum virum in cujus transitu	SYG 224	int	3
E	1	3	1	-2	-4	-2	0	3	E	O quam praeclara sunt	AM 817	an	4
b	1	3	1	-2	-4	1	0	1		Notam fecisti in populis Quis Deus ... tu es	LR 342 WA 159	rev	
E	1	3	1	-2	0	-2	0	3	[D]	Agnus Dei	SCH #168		2
E	1	3	1	-2	1	-2	1	3	E	Exsultate Deo adjutori	LA 98	an	4
E	1	3	1	-2	1	0	1	-2	E	Jubilate Deo omnis terra	AR 3 *WA 69 *LA 101	an	4
E	1	3	1	-2	1	0	1	3	E	Rex sempiterne lucis auctor unice	ST 141	hy	3
E	1	3	1	-2	3	1	0	3		Ut vitium virtus operiret Ad nutum Domini	AR 130* PM 187 *WA 365	rev	
E	1	3	1	0	-2	-5	-4	[0]	E	Kyrie	MEL #141		
E	1	3	1	0	-2	-4	-2	0	E	Jam lucis orto sidere	ST 154	hy	4
E	1	3	1	0	-2	-4	-2	0	E	Kyrie	MEL #144		
E	1	3	1	0	-2	-4	-2	1	E	Sitivit anima mea ad nomen	AR 302 LU 450 AM 279	an	4
E	1	3	1	0	-2	-4	3	5	E	Ecce tu pulcher es	WA 162	an	3
E	1	3	1	0	-2	0	-2	-4	E	Adeste sancti plurimo	AM 906	hy	3
E	1	3	1	0	-2	0	-2	-4	E	Chorus novae Jerusalem	ST 36	hy	3
E	1	3	1	0	-2	0	-2	-4	E	Claro paschali gaudio	AM 634	hy	3
E	1	3	1	0	-2	0	-2	-4	E	Deus tuorum militum	AR [24] AM 630	hy	3
E	1	3	1	0	-2	0	-2	-4	E	Dum nocte pulsa lucifer	AR 712	hy	3

E	1	3	1	0	-2	0	-2	-4	E	Fortem virili pectore	AM 685	hy	3
a	1	3	1	0	-2	0	-2	-4		Fulget ideo sicut sol Gloriosi Domine	WA 260	rev	
E	1	3	1	0	-2	0	-2	-4	E	Invicte martyr unicum	AR [31]	hy	3
E	1	3	1	0	-2	0	-2	-4	E	Jam lucis orto sidere	ST 71	hy	3
E	1	3	1	0	-2	0	-2	-4	E	Jesu corona celsior	AM 673	hy	3
E	1	3	1	0	-2	0	-2	-4	E	Jesu corona virginum	AM 677	hy	3
E	1	3	1	0	-2	0	-2	-4	E	Jesu redemptor omnium	AM 660	hy	3
E	1	3	1	0	-2	0	-2	-4	E	Jucunda patrum rediit	AM 876	hy	3
E	1	3	1	0	-2	0	-2	-4	E	Martyr Dei Venantius	AR 711 LU 1469	hy	3
E	1	3	1	0	-2	0	-2	-4	E	Paschale mundo gaudium	AR [30]	hy	3
E	1	3	1	0	-2	0	-2	-4	E	Rex gloriose martyrum	AR [26] LU 1144 AM 631 881	hy	3
E	1	3	1	0	-2	0	-2	-4	E	Sacrata nobis gaudia	AM 879	hy	3
E	1	3	1	0	-2	0	-2	-4	E	Tristes erant apostoli	AR [22] LU 1121 AM 630	hy	3
E	1	3	1	0	-2	0	-2	-4	E	Tu vincis in martyribus	AM 636	hy	3
E	1	3	1	0	-2	0	-2	3	E	Agnus Dei	SCH #167		4
E	1	3	1	0	-2	0	1	-2	E	Aeterna Christi munera et martyrum	LR 164	hy	3
E	1	3	1	0	-2	0	1	-2	E	Aeterna sapientia	ST 233	hy	3
E	1	3	1	0	-2	0	1	-2	E	Chorus novae Jerusalem	ST 230	hy	3
E	1	3	1	0	-2	0	1	-2	E	Deus tuorum militum	LR 163	hy	3
E	1	3	1	0	-2	0	1	-2	E	Rex sempiterne Domine	LR 82	hy	4
E	1	3	1	0	-2	0	1	-2	E	Tristes erant apostoli	LR 162	hy	3
E	1	3	1	0	-2	0	1	0	[E]	Agnus Dei	SCH #166		4
E	1	3	1	0	-2	0	3	5	E	Jesu Christe patris unigenite	ST 48	hy	4
E	1	3	1	0	-2	0	3	5	E	Kyrie	MEL #143		
E	1	3	1	0	-2	0	3	5	E	Kyrie III Deus sempiterne	MEL #142 GR 11* LU 22		4
E	1	3	1	0	-2	0	3	5	E	Te Deum patrem ... et ore	AR 523 LU 916 AM 541 VP 28 18* WA 158	an	4
E	1	3	1	0	-2	0	3	5		Tollite jugum meum	GR 325 [112] LU 972	alv	
E	1	3	1	0	-2	1	0	-2	E	Chorus novae Jerusalem	ST 289	hy	4
E	1	3	1	0	-2	1	0	1	E	Egredere Emmanuel	ST 273	hy	4
E	1	3	1	0	-2	3	1	0	E	Venerandae virginis	ST 309	hy	4
E	1	3	1	0	-2	3	5	3	E	Rex gloriose martyrum	ST 242	hy	4
E	1	3	1	0	-2	3	5	8	E	Adonai Domine Deus	AR 549 LU 993	an	3
b	1	3	1	0	1	-2	-4	0	G	Tu gloria Jerusalem ... tui	AR 784	an	7
E	1	3	1	0	1	-2	1	3	E	Alleluia: vindica Domine sanguinem	SYG 175 191	al	4

e	1	3	1	0	1	0	-2	-4		Dum adhuc longe esset Surgam et ibo	VP 117	rev	
E	1	3	1	0	1	0	-2	0	E	Ad tua solemnia	ST 355	hy	4
E	1	3	1	0	1	0	-2	0	E	Kyrie	MEL #140		
a	1	3	1	0	1	3	0	-2	G	Esto nobis Domine turris	LA 162	re	8
b	1	3	1	0	1	3	5	3	G	In proxima est tribulatio	LA 169 WA 106	re	7
b	1	3	1	0	1	3	5	3	G	In tribulationibus exaudi	GB 157	an	7
b	1	3	1	0	1	5	3	1	G	Circumdate Scholasticam	LR 290	an	7
b	1	3	1	0	1	5	3	1	G	Cum angelis et pueris	AR 422 GR 175 PM 58 OHS 69 98 LU 585 *AM 400 *WA 113 209 *LA 181	an	7
E	1	3	1	0	3	5	3	1	E	Sapientiam sanctorum ... pronuntiat	AM 981	an	4
b	1	3	1	3	1	-2	1	0	G	Serve bone et fidelis intra	AR [75] LU 1196 AM 671 LA 536	an	7
b	1	3	1	3	1	0	-2	-4	G	Et valde mane una sabbatorum	LA 215 232	an	7
b	1	3	1	3	1	0	-2	-4	G	Ingressus Paulus in synagogam	WA 264 LA 343	an	7
E	1	3	1	3	1	0	1	3	E	Vigilate animo in proximo	AR 248 AM 223 WA 20 LA 25	an	4
b	1	3	1	3	1	3	1	-2	G	Laudabilis populus quem Dominus	LA 304 WA 184	re	8
E	1	3	1	3	1	5	3	1	E	Alleluia: ego sum pastor bonus et cognosco	SYG 164	al	4
b	1	3	1	5	3	5	3	1	G	Tunc ad locum dilectae	LR 325 *LA 370	an	7
E	1	3	1	5	7	5	3	5		Pater cum essem cum eis	SYG 178	alv	
E	1	3	1	5	8	5	3	1	G	Alleluia: pater cum essem	SYG 178	al	8
E	1	3	5	3	0	1	-2	-4	G	Alleluia: iste est qui ante Deum	SYG 211	al	8
E	1	3	5	3	0	1	-2	-4		Iste est qui ante Deum ... et est	SYG 211	alv	
E	1	3	5	3	0	1	3	5		Domine probasti me Mihi autem	OTT 128 GB 203 SYG 201	ofv	
E	1	3	5	3	0	3	1	0	G	Alleluia: fac nos innocuam	GR 486 LU 1441	al	8
E	1	3	5	3	0	3	1	0	G	Alleluia: hodie Maria virgo caelos ascendit	SYG 216 GS 195	al	8
E	1	3	5	3	0	3	1	0	G	Alleluia: modicum et non videbitis	SYG 166 GS 128 *GB 273^{v}	al	8
b	1	3	5	3	1	-2	1	0	G	Alleluia	AR 48 463 LU 256 812 AM 127 476	an	7
b	1	3	5	3	1	-2	1	0	G	Dixit Dominus Domino meo	OHS 156 AR 45 LU 252 AM 125 *LA 86	an	7
b	1	3	5	3	1	-2	1	0	G	Quo progrederis sine filio	WA 347 LA 433	an	7
b	1	3	5	3	1	-2	1	0	G	Vivit Dominus et benedictus Deus	AM 24 OHS 181 (nm) *LA 105	an	7
b	1	3	5	3	1	-2	1	3	G	Quid me quaeritis interficere	AR 401 LU 1094 *AM 377 *WA 104	an	7

E	1	3	5	3	1	-2	3	1	E	Justus ut palma florebit	GR [41] OTT 150 LU 1193 SYG 24 GB 25^{v} GS m 17	of	4
E	1	3	5	3	1	0	-2	-4	E	Oriens sol justitiae	WA 292	an	4
E	1	3	5	3	1	0	-2	0	E	O vera summa sempiterna unitas	WA 162	an	4
b	1	3	5	3	5	1	-2	1	G	Misit Dominus angelum ... de manu	AR 751 800 PM 173 LU 1515 1577 AM 935 990 WA 328 LA 416	an	7
b	1	3	5	3	5	1	-2	1	G	Misit Dominus angelum ... de medio	AR 814 LU 1597 AM 1006 WA 350 LA 336 441	an	7
b	1	3	5	3	5	1	3	1	G	Stella ista sicut flamma	AR 313 LU 464 *AM 291 *WA 52 *LA 71	an	7
E	1	3	5	3	5	3	1	-2	E	Alleluia	AM 47	an	4
E	1	3	5	3	5	3	1	-2	E	Dele Domine iniquitatem	AM 45	an	4
b	1	3	5	3	5	3	1	0	G	Noctem illam tenebrosus	LA 287	an	7
b	1	3	5	3	5	3	1	0	G	Vide Domine et considera	AR 428 OHS 243 249 AM 407 WA 115 LA 186	an	7
b	1	3	5	3	5	3	1	3	G	Christus Dominus fabri	LU 1437	an	7
E	1	3	5	3	5	3	1	3	b	Eripe me de inimicis meis Domine ... doce	GR 186 OHS 210 OTT 51 LU 608 SYG 125 GB 111^{v} GS 89	of	3
E	1	3	5	3	5	3	1	3		Praecinxisti me virtute Factus est Dominus	OTT 42 GB 96^{v} *SYG 108	ofv	
E	1	3	5	3	5	3	1	3		Vidimus stellam ejus ... et venimus	GR 59 LU 462 SYG 32 GB 35 GS 19	co	4
b	1	3	5	3	5	6	5	3	G	Dives ille guttam aquae	AR 385 LU 1087 AM 359	an	7
E	1	3	5	6	3	5	1	0	E	Mihi autem nimis honorati	GR 394 OTT 128 LU 1306 SYG 201 GB 203 GS z 203	of	3
E	1	3	5	7	5	3	1	0		Et in terra	BOS #9 *GR 36* *LU 43		
E	1	3	5	7	5	3	5	1	E	Judica Domine nocentes me	GB 105	co	4
E	1	3	5	7	5	3	5	1		Videns Dominus flentes sorores	GB 96	co	4
E	1	3	5	7	8	10	8	7	G	Alleluia: lux perpetua lucebit	GB 163^{v}	al	8
E	1	3	5	8	5	3	1	0	E	Dies absoluti praetereunt	ST 283	hy	4
E	1	3	7	3	5	7	8	7		Ego sum pastor bonus et cognosco	SYG 164	alv	
E	1	3	7	5	3	5	3	8	D	Aeterne rerum conditor	ST 251	hy	1
a	1	3	8	7	5	7	3	0		Imperat ubi Jesus Scande thronum	WA 355	rev	
E	1	5	7	5	7	5	7	8		Emitte spiritum tuum Spiritus Domini replevit orbem	SYG 185	ofv	
E	1	5	8	10	12	10	8	10	F	Spes nostra salus	WA 158	an	5
c	2	-5	-3	-7	-5	-3	0	2	a	Venite adoremus Deum et procidamus	GR 371 LU 1052 *SYG 252 GS 170 GB 258	int	2
d	2	-5	3	2	0	-2	0	2	[D]	Agnus Dei	SCH #7		1
c	2	-3	-7	-3	-5	-3	-5	-7		Dicet Domino susceptor meus es Scapulis suis	OTT 32 GB 66^{v} SYG 74	ofv	

c	2	-3	-7	-3	0	-1	2	0	F	Floro primariisque regni	LR 280	an	5
F	2	-3	-5	-3	0	2	0	2	E	Memor sit Dominus sacrificii	SYG 232	gr	4
G	2	-3	-5	0	2	0	2	5	E	Lumen clarum rite fulget	ST 485	hy	3
G	2	-3	-2	-5	0	2	0	-2	G	Festum nunc celebre magnaque gaudia	ST 259	hy	8
G	2	-3	-2	-3	-5	0	2	0	E	Ante diem festum Paschae ... ut	WA 213 *GS 97	an	4
G	2	-3	-2	-3	-5	0	2	0	G	Sanctus	THAN #85		8
d	2	-3	-2	0	-7	-5	-3	-2		Et in terra	BOS #23 GR 32* LU 40		
G	2	-3	-2	0	2	0	-3	-2	G	Jesus refulsit omnium	ST 257	hy	8
G	2	-3	-2	0	2	0	-3	-2	G	Lucis creator optime	ST 252 268	hy	8
G	2	-3	-2	0	2	0	2	4	E	Quis Deus magnus ... praeelegit	LR 271	re	3
G	2	-3	-2	0	2	0	2	4	E	Respexit Elias ad caput	LR 124 LU 927	re	3
G	2	-3	-2	0	2	0	2	4	E	Videte miraculum matris	PM 251 *LA 353 WA 271	re	3
G	2	-3	-2	0	2	4	5	2		Ecce quam bonum et quam jucundum ... sicut	GR 568	alv	
F	2	-3	-1	-5	-3	0	2	4	F	Quis infelici fletus aquam capiti	ST 465	hy	6
F	2	-3	0	-5	-3	-1	0	2		O crux benedicta quae sola Adoramus te	GR [104]	trv	
F	2	-3	0	2	0	-1	0	-1		Dicet Domino susceptor meus es Qui habitat	GR 95 LU 533 GS 35 GB 65 SYG 73	trv	
F	2	-3	0	2	0	-1	0	-1		Dixi Domino Deus meus Eripe me	GR 208 OHS 534 LU 725 GS 99 GB 116^{v} SYG 137	trv	
F	2	-3	0	2	0	4	2	0	E	Eduxit eos Dominus in spe	GR 255 OHS 816 LU 800 SYG 160 *GB 140 *GS 122	int	4
c	2	-3	0	4	2	0	2	5	G	Mihi autem adhaerere	GR (34)	int	7
c	2	-3	0	4	2	5	4	0	G	Eduxit Dominus populum	GR 258 OHS 825 LU 804 *SYG 161 *GB 142^{v} GS 123	int	7
c	2	-3	0	4	2	5	4	0	G	Erit quasi signum in manu	GR 84**	int	7
F	2	-3	2	4	2	4	5	4		Gaudete justi in Domino	GR 406 LU 1327 *SYG 169	alv	
G	2	-2	-3	-5	-3	-2	0	-2	G	Alleluia: vere tu es rex	GR 61 LU 472	al	8
G	2	-2	-3	-5	-3	-2	0	-2		Vere tu es rex	GR 61 LU 472	alv	
G	2	-2	-3	-5	-2	-3	-2	0	G	Exivi a patre et veni	WA 146	an	8
G	2	-2	-3	-2	-5	-3	-2	0	G	Summae Deus clementiae	LR 441	hy	8
d	2	-2	-3	-2	0	2	-2	-3		Ego autem ad Deum clamavi Exaudi Deus	OTT 36 *GB 84 SYG 95	ofv	
G	2	-2	-3	-2	0	2	0	-2	G	Nocte surgentes vigilemus omnes	ST 212	hy	8
G	2	-2	-3	-2	0	2	0	2	G	Te lucis ante terminum	ST 269	hy	8
D	2	-2	-3	-2	0	2	3	2	D	Nunc sancte nobis spiritus	ST 441	hy	2
G	2	-2	-3	-2	2	0	4	2	E	Angelus Domini descendit ... et accedens	LR 83 OHS 695 (nm) *LA 208 *WA 128	re	3

G	2	-2	0	-5	-7	-5	-2	0	G	Ecce nunc tempus ... operemur	SYG 71	an	8
D	2	-2	0	-3	-2	-5	-2	0	D	Ego clamavi quoniam exaudisti	GB 264	co	2
d	2	-2	0	-3	0	-2	-3	-5	G	Ave maris stella Dei mater alma	ST 500	hy	7
G	2	-2	0	-2	-3	-5	0	2	G	Si quaeris miracula mors	VP 176	re	8
G	2	-2	0	-2	2	5	4	2	G	Alleluia: vos estis qui permansistis	GR 548 LU 1548	al	8
G	2	-2	0	-2	2	5	4	2	G	Sanctus	THAN #84		8
G	2	-2	0	-2	2	5	4	2		Vos estis qui permansistis	GR 548 LU 1548	alv	
G	2	-2	0	2	-3	-5	-7	0	G	Justorum animae in manu ... malitiae	WA 422	re	8
c	2	-2	0	2	-3	-5	-7	0	c	Quatuor animalia ibant	WA 373	re	6
G	2	-2	0	2	-2	0	-2	2		Alleluia: ad Dominum dum tribularer	GB 263^v	al	8
G	2	-2	0	2	-2	0	2	4	G	Jesus refulsit omnium	ST 413	hy	8
G	2	-2	0	2	-2	0	2	4	G	Rector potens verax Deus	AR 32 LU 240	hy	8
D	2	-2	0	2	-2	0	2	5	E	Agnus Dei	SCH #227		4
G	2	-2	0	2	0	-2	0	2	G	Lucis creator optime	ST 268	hy	8
G	2	-2	0	2	0	-2	0	2	G	Quia ego tecum sum	WA 115	an	8
G	2	-2	0	2	0	-2	0	2	G	Stetit angelus ad sepulcrum	SYG 146	an	7
G	2	-2	0	2	0	-2	2	5	G	Insidens nostris peramanter	AR 8 (sup 2)	hy	8
G	2	-2	0	2	0	-2	2	5	G	Iste confessor Domini colentes	AR [52]	hy	8
d	2	-2	0	2	0	2	0	-3		Factus sum sicut homo ... traditus Domine Deus salutis	OTT 112 GB 74 SYG 84	ofv	
G	2	-2	0	2	0	2	0	-2		Ad Dominum dum tribularer	GB 263^v	alv	
G	2	-2	0	2	0	2	0	2	G	Adduxi vos per desertum	LA 160 *WA 103	re	7
G	2	-2	0	2	0	2	0	2	G	Cantemus Domino gloriose enim honorificatus	LA 157 *WA 101	re	8
G	2	-2	0	2	0	2	0	2	G	Elegit te Dominus sibi	SYG 232	int	8
G	2	-2	0	2	0	2	0	2		Mirabilis in excelsis Dominus Deus enim firmavit	OTT 16 GB 16 SYG 16	ofv	
G	2	-2	0	2	0	2	0	2	G	Ploremus coram Domino	LA 136	inv	7
G	2	-2	0	2	0	2	0	2	G	Tenebrae factae sunt	OHS 497 LU 703	re	7
G	2	-2	0	2	0	2	0	2	G	Tenebrae factae sunt ... tunc	LA 200 WA 123	re	7
G	2	-2	0	2	0	2	0	5	G	Docebo te quae ventura	LA 307 *WA 185	re	7
G	2	-2	0	2	0	2	0	5	G	Martine confessor Dei	ST 237	hy	8
G	2	-2	0	2	0	2	4	5	G	Audivi vocem in caelo tamquam	LA 225 *WA 140	re	7 8
G	2	-2	0	2	0	2	4	5	D	Audivi voces in caelo angelorum	LA 226 *WA 140	re	1
G	2	-2	0	2	0	2	5	4		Videbant faciem ejus Elegerunt apostoli	OTT 161	ofv	

G	2	-2	0	2	0	2	5	7		Et ego ad te Domine Domine Deus salutis	OTT 112 GB 74 SYG 84	ofv	
D	2	-2	0	2	3	5	3	2	D	Alleluia: isti sunt duo viri	SYG 208	al	1
D	2	-2	0	2	3	5	3	2	D	Beatus vir Benedictus	AM 851 WA 301 (inc illeg) *LA 374	an	1
D	2	-2	0	2	3	5	3	2		Isti sunt duo viri	SYG 208	alv	
D	2	-2	0	2	3	5	3	2		Laudate pueri Dominum Resurrexit tamquam dormiens	GB 126	alv	
D	2	-2	0	2	3	5	3	5	E	Ut queant laxis resonare fibris	ST 158	hy	4
G	2	-2	0	2	4	5	4	2	G	Jam Christus astra ascenderat	ST 453	hy	8
G	2	-2	0	2	4	5	4	2	G	Kyrie Deus excelse pater	MEL #76		
G	2	-2	0	2	4	5	7	5	G	Hesterna die Dominus	LA 46 *WA 36	re	7
G	2	-2	0	2	4	5	7	9	a	O genitrix aeterni	ST 462	hy	2
G	2	-2	0	2	5	2	5	2	G	Kyrie devote canentes	MEL #77		
D	2	-2	0	2	5	3	2	0	D	Jam lucis orto sidere	ST 75	hy	2
D	2	-2	0	2	5	3	2	0	D	O quam beatus es pie	WA 392	re	2
G	2	-2	0	2	5	4	0	4	G	Sanctorum velut aquilae	AR [47] LU 1156 AM 652 *LA 520	an	8
G	2	-2	0	2	5	4	0	4	G	Venite comedite panem meum	AR 3 (sup 2)	an	8
G	2	-2	0	2	5	4	2	0	G	A solis ortus cardine	ST 410	hy	8
G	2	-2	0	2	5	4	5	2	G	Memento mei Domine Deus	AR 439 OHS 515 LU 718 AM 442 443 WA 124 LA 201	an	8
G	2	-2	0	2	5	4	5	2	G	Sanctus	THAN #83		7
D	2	-2	0	3	0	2	0	-2	D	Ambulabunt mecum in albis	LA 57 WA 45	re	2
D	2	-2	0	3	0	2	0	-2	D	Posuisti Domine super caput	LR 156 *LA 526	re	2
D	2	-2	0	3	2	0	-2	0	D	Alleluia: resurrexit tamquam dormiens	GB 126	al	2
D	2	-2	0	3	2	3	2	3	D	Jerusalem surge et sta	GR 6 LU 330 SYG 5 *GB 4 GS 3	co	2
D	2	-2	0	3	2	3	2	3	D	Laetare mater nostra	GR 16**	co	2
D	2	-2	0	3	5	0	3	5		Quia delectasti me Domine Bonum est confiteri	GR 497	trv	
D	2	-2	0	3	5	3	0	-2	D	Clara diei gaudia modulizet ecclesia	ST 108	hy	2
D	2	-2	0	3	5	3	2	0	D	Kyrie regum summe caeli	MEL #184		
D	2	-2	0	3	5	7	3	5	D	Decantaverunt Domine nomen	GR 471	co	1
D	2	-2	0	3	5	7	3	5	D	Manducaverunt et saturati sunt	GR 84 LU 515 SYG 64 GB 61 GS 29	co	1
D	2	-2	0	3	5	7	5	3	D	Gratuletur omnis caro	ST 446	hy	2
G	2	-2	0	4	0	-2	2	5	G	Induta est caro mea	LA 283 WA 172	re	8

G	2	-2	0	5	2	5	7	5	G	Alleluia: posui adjutorium super potentem	GS 224	al	7
G	2	-2	0	5	2	5	7	9	G	Alleluia: adorabo ad templum sanctum	GR [73] LU 1251 GS 175 k SYG 48 263 *GB 174^{v}	al	7
D	2	-2	0	5	7	3	2	-2	D	Ante luciferum genitus ... mundo	AR 312 LU 463 AM 290 *WA 56 *LA 73	an	2
D	2	-2	0	5	7	3	2	-2	D	Magi intrantes domum	AR 320 LU 468	an	2
D	2	-2	0	5	7	3	2	-2	D	Suscitabit Deus caeli regnum	AR 894^{6} LU 1705 AM 1092	an	2
D	2	-2	0	7	5	0	2	5		Declinabo super eum	GR 509 LU 1482	alv	
D	2	-2	0	7	5	7	8	7		In matutinis meditabor Deus Deus meus	OTT 66 GB 147^{v} SYG 165	ofv	
D	2	-2	0	7	5	7	8	7		In multitudine virtutis Benedicite gentes	OTT 71 SYG 105 GB 93^{v}	ofv	
D	2	-2	0	7	9	7	5	3	D	Habuit Gertrudis potestatem	AM 1131	an	1
D	2	-2	0	7	10	9	5	3	D	Orbis exsultans celebret hoc festum	ST 120	hy	1
G	2	-2	2	-2	0	2	0	5	[G]	Agnus Dei	SCH #93		8
G	2	-2	2	-2	2	5	0	2		In excelso throno vidi sedere	GR 64 LU 477 SYG 32 GB 36 GS 20	int	8
G	2	-2	2	0	2	-3	-2	0	G	Hoc corpus quod pro vobis	GR 155 [104] LU 573 SYG 111 GB 98^{v} GS 72	co	8
G	2	-2	2	0	2	0	2	5	G	Mirabantur omnes qui audiebant	SYG 45	co	7
G	2	-2	2	0	2	0	2	5	G	Probasti Domine cor meum	GR 586 *GB 217^{v} *SYG 217 *GS 195	int	7
G	2	-2	2	0	2	0	2	5	G	Vidi aquam egredientem	GR 2* OHS 706 LU 12 PM 10 WA 130 222 GS 116 SYG 145	an	8
G	2	-2	2	0	2	5	2	5	G	Juravit Dominus et non paenitebit	GR [100] LU 1283	int	7
G	2	-2	2	0	2	5	4	5	G	Dicite pusillanimes confortamini	GR 9 LU 337 *SYG 7 *GB 6^{v} *GS 5	co	7
G	2	-2	2	0	2	5	4	5	G	In virtute tua Domine laetabitur	GR [10] LU 1135 SYG 51 *GB 51 *GS 205	int	7
G	2	-2	2	0	2	5	4	5	G	Proficiat nobis Domine	SYG 230	co	7
G	2	-2	2	0	2	5	7	5		In Domino laudabitur anima Immittet angelus	OTT 102 GB 71 SYG 79	ofv	
G	2	-2	2	0	2	5	7	5	G	Justorum animae in manu ... malitiae	SYG 224	int	7
G	2	-2	2	0	2	5	7	5	G	Tu es Petrus	SYG 53	int	7
G	2	-2	2	0	2	5	7	9	G	Beatus Martinus obitum	GB 242	int	7
G	2	-2	2	0	2	5	7	9	G	Domine exaudi orationem meam ... perveniat	GB 104^{v}	int	7
G	2	-2	2	0	2	5	9	7	G	Da nobis Deus auxilium	GR 106**	int	7
G	2	-2	2	0	2	5	9	7	G	Signum magnum apparuit	GR 582 LU 1601	int	7

G	2	-2	2	0	5	2	0	2	G	Immittet angelus Domini	GR 359 OTT 102 LU 1039 SYG 79 GB 71 GS 41 157	of	8
D	2	-2	2	3	2	0	2	0	D	Agnus Dei II	GR 10* OHS 851 LU 21 SCH #226		1
D	2	-2	2	3	5	3	2	0	E	Exsultemus Domino regi	WA 317	inv	4
D	2	-2	2	5	0	2	0	-2		O adoranda trinitas	SYG 261	alv	
G	2	-2	2	5	2	4	2	0	G	O quam casta mater	SYG 17	an	7
G	2	-2	2	5	2	5	7	5	G	Salvum fac populum tuum	GR 119 SYG 88 GB 78 GS 43 50 171	gr	7
D	2	-2	2	5	2	5	7	9	D	Urbs beata Jerusalem	ST 59	hy	1
G	2	-2	2	5	4	2	5	7	G	Alleluia: in die resurrectionis	GR 262 LU 809 GS 121 SYG 169 GB 140	al	7
G	2	-2	2	5	4	2	5	7	G	Alleluia: levita Laurentius bonum opus	SYG 213	al	7
G	2	-2	2	5	4	2	5	7	G	Alleluia: non vos relinquam orphanos dicit	GB 182v	al	7
G	2	-2	2	5	4	2	5	7	G	Alleluia: regnabit Deus super gentes	SYG 180	al	7
G	2	-2	2	5	4	2	5	7		Quinque prudentes virgines	GS 231	alv	
G	2	-2	2	5	7	2	5	4	G	Salve crux quae in corpore	WA 235	re	7
D	2	-2	2	5	7	5	2	3	D	Agnoscat omne saeculum	ST 218	hy	1
D	2	-2	2	5	7	5	2	3	D	Jesu salvator saeculi	ST 237	hy	1
D	2	-2	2	5	7	5	2	3	D	Martyr Dei qui unicum	ST 196	hy	1
D	2	-2	2	5	7	5	2	3	D	Rector potens verax Deus	ST 174	hy	1
G	2	-2	2	5	7	5	3	2	G	Agnoscat omne saeculum	ST 255	hy	1
G	2	-2	2	5	7	5	4	5	G	Alleluia	AR 447 OHS 741 LU 784	an	8
D	2	-2	3	0	2	0	-2	0	E	Alleluia: propter veritatem ... exaltabit	SYG 232	al	4
D	2	-2	3	0	3	5	7	3	D	Ave pater Wulstane	WA 248	an	1
D	2	-2	3	2	5	7	2	0	D	Agnus Dei	SCH #225		2
F	2	-1	-5	-3	-1	0	4	6	F	Sanctus	THAN #123		5
b^b	2	-1	-5	-1	2	4	2	0	F	Sanctus sanctus sanctus ... omnipotens	WA 159	an	5
F	2	-1	-3	0	-3	-1	-5	0	D	Speciosus forma prae filiis	OHS 296 (nm) WA 27 *LA 63	an	2
F	2	-1	-3	0	-3	0	4	6	D	Alleluia: tristitia implebit cor vestrum	SYG 168	al	1
F	2	-1	-3	0	-1	-5	-3	-1		Dicant nunc Judaei Christus resurgens	AR 164* PM 66 VP 141 WA 223	rev	
c	2	-1	0	-3	-5	-3	-1	0		Corpora ipsorum in pace Electi mei	GR 444 LU 1386	grv	

c	2	-1	0	-3	-5	-3	-1	0		Ego autem mendicus sum Beatus vir cujus est	GR 20**	grv	
c	2	-1	0	-3	-5	-3	-1	0		Misit Dominus manum suam Priusquam te formarem	GR 524 LU 1500 *GS 1 *GB 198^{v} *SYG 196	grv	
F	2	-1	0	-3	-1	-3	-5	-3	E	Hodie dilectus Domini	GB 55	co	4
F	2	-1	0	-3	0	-1	-3	-5	D	Christi virgo nec terrore	WA 254 *LA 86 331	an	1
F	2	-1	0	-1	-5	-3	0	2		Benedic anima mea Dominum: Domine Emitte spiritum	OTT 77 *GB 184 *SYG 182	ofv	
c	2	-1	0	2	-3	-7	-3	0	a	Vide quia tribulor	WA 107	re	2
c	2	-1	0	2	0	-3	-1	0	G	Deus meus eripe me	LR 413 *LA 168 *WA 107	re	8
c	2	-1	0	2	0	2	4	5		Et in terra	BOS #37		
D	2	-1	0	2	3	5	3	2	D	Popule meus quid feci	SYG 139		
F	2	-1	0	2	4	5	4	2	F	Cor arca legem continens	VP 169	hy	6
F	2	-1	0	2	4	5	4	2	F	En ut superba criminum	LR 334 VP 168	hy	6
C	2	-1	2	0	2	5	7	9	D	Dirige me Domine in veritate	GB 74^{v}	int	2
F	2	-1	2	4	0	-1	-3	-1	E	Salve festa dies	ST 482 *WA 223 *GS 116 134 173	hy	4
c	2	0	-5	-3	-7	-3	-1	-3	G	Quam bonus Deus	LA 95	an	8
c	2	0	-5	-3	-5	-7	-5	-3	G	Quam bonus Israel Deus	AR 155 LU 279^{N}	an	8
c	2	0	-5	-3	-5	-3	-7	-3	F	Elevamini portae aeternales	LR 55 96 335 OHS 604 LU 762 *WA 27 125 *LA 63 203	an	5
G	2	0	-5	-3	-5	-3	-7	0		Deus judex justus	GR 328 LU 982 *SYG 239 GB 248^{v} GS 142	alv	
G	2	0	-5	-3	-5	-3	-7	0		Vos qui secuti ... sedebitis	GB 267^{v}	alv	
F	2	0	-5	-3	-5	-3	0	-3	F	Os justi meditabitur	GR [42][48] LU 1200 SYG 33 GB 40 GS 204	int	6
F	2	0	-5	-3	-5	-3	0	2	F	Vir Dei Benedictus mundi gloriam	SYG 56	int	6
G	·2	0	-5	-3	-2	0	2	0	E	Aurora lucis rutilat	ST 449	hy	4
D	2	0	-5	-2	-3	-5	-7	0	D	Ve nobis quia peccavimus	SYG 139	an	2
G	2	0	-5	-2	-3	-5	-3	-2	G	Agnus Dei	SCH #92		2
G	2	0	-5	-2	-3	-2	-5	-3	G	Admirabile est ... in universa terra	LR 260	an	8
c	2	0	-5	-1	2	0	2	0	G	Erat autem aspectus ejus	AR 444 OHS 726 767 LU 782 *AM 454 *WA 129 137 *LA 214	an	8
c	2	0	-5	0	2	0	-7	-3		Dirige in conspectu tuo Intende voci	OTT 83 GB 87^{v} SYG 98	ofv	
c	2	0	-5	0	2	4	-1	0		Excita Domine potentiam tuam Qui regis Israel	GR 19 LU 351 GS 10 GB 10 *SYG 11	trv	
c	2	0	-5	0	2	4	-1	0		Mihi vivere Christus Qui gloriatur	GR 546	trv	

c	2	0	-5	0	2	4	-1	0		Specie tua et pulchritudine Veni sponsa	GR [52] LU 1217	trv	
G	2	0	-5	0	2	5	7	5		Quam magnificata sunt Bonum est confiteri	OTT 26 *GB 57 *SYG 59	ofv	
G	2	0	-5	0	4	2	0	5	G	Simile est regnum caelorum homini negotiatori	GR [66] 115** LU 1231 SYG 29 GB 30^v GS 230	co	8
G	2	0	-3	-7	-2	-3	-5	-7	C	O virgo sole purior	ST 21	hy	5
c	2	0	-3	-5	-7	-8	-7	-5	F	Agnus Dei	SCH #21		5
c	2	0	-3	-5	-3	-5	-3	-1		Domine nomen tuum Laudate Dominum	OTT 40 *GB 90 *SYG 102	ofv	
G	2	0	-3	-5	-3	-2	-5	-3	G	Alleluia: viriliter agite	GR (36)	al	8
G	2	0	-3	-5	-3	-2	0	2	G	Lux visa per caliginem	ST 333	hy	8
F	2	0	-3	-5	-3	-1	2	4	E	Exsultet caelum laudibus	ST 402	hy	4
F	2	0	-3	-5	-3	-1	2	4	E	Martyr Dei egregie	ST 373	hy	4
F	2	0	-3	-5	-3	0	5	4	F	Dum vitam in ara Golgothae	ST 22	hy	6
c	2	0	-3	-5	-1	-3	-5	-7		Domine Deus tu cognovisti Exspectans exspectavi	OTT 104 GB 92 SYG 104	ofv	
G	2	0	-3	-5	0	2	4	5	G	Pange sanctae Katherinae	ST 15	hy	8
G	2	0	-3	-5	0	2	5	4	E	Ad quantum vero messem	WA 238	an	3
G	2	0	-3	-2	-5	-7	-3	0	G	Iste confessor Domini sacratus	ST 103	hy	8
G	2	0	-3	-2	-5	-3	-5	-7	G	Athleta Christi Antoninus martyr	ST 55	hy	8
G	2	0	-3	-2	-5	-3	-5	-7	G	Iste confessor Domini sacratus	ST 62	hy	8
G	2	0	-3	-2	-5	-3	-2	0	G	Alleluia: iste sanctus digne in memoriam	SYG 226 GS 207	al	8
c	2	0	-3	-2	-5	-3	0	2	F	Peractis centum	WA 77	re	5
G	2	0	-3	-2	-5	-3	0	2	G	Sanctus XIII	GR 46* LU 52 THAN #82		8
G	2	0	-3	-2	-5	-3	0	2	G	Virginis proles opifexque matris	ST 245	hy	8
G	2	0	-3	-2	-5	0	2	0	G	O mirae pietatis homo	WA 250	re	8
c	2	0	-3	-2	-3	-7	-5	-7	F	Sanctus	THAN #14		5
G	2	0	-3	-2	-3	-5	-3	-7	G	Fortis en praesul	AM 870	hy	8
G	2	0	-3	-2	-3	-5	-3	-7	G	Iste confessor Domini colentes	AR [51] LU 1178 AM 664	hy	8
G	2	0	-3	-2	-3	-5	-3	-5	E	Alleluia: pro omnibus mortuus	GR 480 LU 1434	al	4
G	2	0	-3	-2	-3	-5	-3	-5	E	Alleluia: vox turturis audita	GR 442 LU 1379[1]	al	4
c	2	0	-3	-2	-3	-5	-3	-5		Et constituisti eum Gloria et honore	GR [7] LU 1133 *SYG 201	grv	
G	2	0	-3	-2	-3	-5	-3	-2	G	Kyrie nesciens principium	MEL #75		
G	2	0	-3	-2	-3	-5	-3	0	G	Adesto sancta trinitas	ST 392	hy	8
G	2	0	-3	-2	-3	-5	-3	0	G	Laus trinitati resonet perennis	ST 391	hy	8
G	2	0	-3	-2	0	-2	-5	0	D	Quique cupitis ardire	ST 65	hy	2

d	2	0	-3	-2	0	-2	-3	0		Aperis tu manum tuam Oculi omnium	GR 314 [96] LU 944 GS 59 164 GB 86^{v} SYG 97	grv	
G	2	0	-3	-2	0	-2	-3	2	E	In mandatis ejus	LA 87	an	4
G	2	0	-3	-2	0	-2	2	5	G	Cum autem ducerentur	WA 378	an	8
G	2	0	-3	-2	0	2	-2	2	G	Ecce jam noctis tenuatur umbra lucis	ST 264	hy	8
G	2	0	-3	-2	0	2	-2	2	G	Iste confessor Domini colentes	AR [49] LU 1177 AM 655	hy	8
G	2	0	-3	-2	0	2	-2	2	G	Quod chorus vatum venerandus olim	ST 276	hy	8
G	2	0	-3	-2	0	2	-2	2	G	Sedibus caeli nitidis receptos	AR 776 LU 1551	hy	8
G	2	0	-3	-2	0	2	0	-3	G	Assumpta est virgo Maria	LA 446	re	8
G	2	0	-3	-2	0	2	0	-2	G	Christe sanctorum decus angelorum	ST 237	hy	8
G	2	0	-3	-2	0	2	0	-2	G	Dum caeli sphaera volvitur	ST 469	hy	8
G	2	0	-3	-2	0	2	0	-2	G	Ecce jam noctis tenuatur umbra lucis	ST 251	hy	8
G	2	0	-3	-2	0	2	0	-2	G	Iste confessor Domini sacratus	ST 243	hy	8
G	2	0	-3	-2	0	2	0	2	G	Iste confessor Domini sacratus	ST 404	hy	8
G	2	0	-3	-2	0	2	0	2	G	Jam lucis orto sidere	ST 265	hy	8
G	2	0	-3	-2	0	2	0	2	G	Jesu quadragenariae	ST 226	hy	7
G	2	0	-3	-2	0	2	0	2	G	Martyris Christi colimus triumphum	ST 396	hy	8
G	2	0	-3	-2	0	2	0	2	D	Nunc sancte nobis spiritus	ST 179	hy	1
G	2	0	-3	-2	0	2	0	2	G	Suscipe voces pariterque laudes	ST 405	hy	8
G	2	0	-3	-2	0	2	5	2	G	Jesu quadragenariae	ST 282	hy	8
G	2	0	-3	-2	0	4	0	2	G	Tibi Christe splendor patris	ST 460	hy	8
F	2	0	-3	-1	-5	-3	0	2	D	Cor meum et caro mea	GR 503 LU 1474	co	1
F	2	0	-3	-1	-5	-3	0	2	D	Descendit Jesus cum eis	GR 63 LU 473	co	1
F	2	0	-3	-1	-5	-3	0	2	D	Videbunt in quem transfixerunt	GR 17**	co	1
F	2	0	-3	-1	-5	-3	0	2	D	Viderunt omnes fines terrae	GR 35 LU 410 SYG 21 *GB 20^{v} *GS 15	co	1
F	2	0	-3	-1	-3	0	-3	0	E	Dum deambularet Dominus	LA 111 *WA 73	re	4
F	2	0	-3	-1	-3	0	-1	0	E	Ego dixi Domine miserere	LA 91 *WA 65	re	4
F	2	0	-3	-1	-3	0	-1	0	E	Postquam impleti sunt	LA 351	re	3
c	2	0	-3	-1	-3	0	-1	0	F	Vidi civitatem ... novam ... et	LR 244	re	5
F	2	0	-3	-1	0	-5	-3	-5	F	Foderunt manus meas	GR 16**	int	6
F	2	0	-3	-1	0	-1	-5	0	D	Alleluia	AR 43 LU 246 249	an	2
F	2	0	-3	-1	0	-1	-5	0	D	Ipsi soli servo fidem	LA 355 *WA 254	an	1
F	2	0	-3	-1	0	-1	-3	0	F	Ite in orbem universum	LR 114 *LA 258 *WA 148	re	6
F	2	0	-3	-1	2	4	0	-1	E	Deus qui sedes super thronum ... esto ... quia	LA 81 *WA 60	re	4

c	2	0	-3	0	-7	-3	0	2		Magnus Dominus ... et magna virtus Angelus Domini	GR 634 LU 1699	grv	
c	2	0	-3	0	-7	-3	0	2	F	Sanguinis et aquae fluenta	PM 156 LR 344	re	5
c	2	0	-3	0	-7	-3	0	2		Vide humilitatem meam Tribulationes cordis	GR 112 LU 546 GS 39 47 GB 69v SYG 77	grv	
c	2	0	-3	0	-5	-3	0	2		Fecit Salomon solemnitatem Domine Deus in simplicitate	OTT 159 *GB 175v *SYG 264	ofv	
c	2	0	-3	0	-3	-7	-3	-5		Mittat tibi auxilium Memor sit Dominus	SYG 232	grv	
C	2	0	-3	0	-3	0	-5	-3		Laudem Domini loquetur Prope est Dominus	LU 354 GR 21 GB 7 SYG 8 GS 6	grv	
G	2	0	-3	0	-2	0	2	-2	G	Tu es pastor ovium ... tradidit	PM 160 *AM 1198 LR 363 LA 416 *WA 279	re	8
F	2	0	-3	0	-1	0	2	4	E	Inclina aurem tuam accelera	GR 338 LU 1012 *SYG 244 *GB 251 GS 149	co	4
F	2	0	-3	0	-1	2	4	0	E	Panis quem ego dabo	LR 124	re	4
c	2	0	-3	0	2	-5	-7	-3		Regnabit Deus super gentes	SYG 180	alv	
F	2	0	-3	0	2	-1	0	2	F	Anima nostra sicut passer	GR [26] LU 1167 GS 17 *SYG 25 *GB 26	gr	5
F	2	0	-3	0	2	-1	0	2	F	Anima nostra sustinet Dominum	GR 111**	gr	5
F	2	0	-3	0	2	-1	0	2	F	Aquae multae non potuerunt	GR 625 (10) LU 1690	gr	5
F	2	0	-3	0	2	-1	0	2	F	Bonum est confiteri Domino	GR 360 LU 1041 *SYG 92 *GB 81 GS 53 *158	gr	5
F	2	0	-3	0	2	-1	0	2	F	Fuit homo missus a Deo	GR 522 *SYG 195 *GB 196v GS 1 188	gr	5
c	2	0	-3	0	2	0	-1	0		Surge amica mea speciosa mea Flores apparuerunt	GR 439 LU 1376	grv	
c	2	0	-3	0	2	0	-1	0		Surge et illuminare Jerusalem Omnes de Saba	GR 57 LU 459 GB 33 SYG 30 GS J 19	grv	
c	2	0	-3	0	2	0	-1	0		Suscitans a terra inopem Quis sicut Dominus	GR 369 GS 168 GB 257v SYG 251	grv	
F	2	0	-3	0	2	0	2	-3	F	Immola Deo sacrificium	SYG 233	gr	6
F	2	0	-3	0	2	0	2	4	F	Domine convertere et eripe	GR 322 OTT 84 LU 963 GS 73 142 SYG 111 GB 99v	of	6
c	2	0	-3	0	2	4	-1	0		Percipietis immarcescibilem Venite benedicti	SYG 75	trv	
c	2	0	-3	0	2	4	0	2		Domine spes mea Confiteor tibi	GR 613 LU 1668	grv	
F	2	0	-3	0	2	5	4	5		Dominus dabit verbum	GR 59**	alv	
a	2	0	-2	-5	-7	-2	0	3	E	Invicte martyr unicum	AR [18]	hy	3
G	2	0	-2	-5	-7	0	-2	0	D	Iste confessor Domini sacratus	ST 200	hy	1
G	2	0	-2	-5	-3	-2	0	2	G	O lux beata trinitas	AM 163 533	hy	8
G	2	0	-2	-5	-3	-2	0	2	G	Tu trinitatis unitas	AM 537	hy	8

G	2	0	-2	-5	-2	-5	-2	2	G	Crux benedicta nitet	ST 483	hy	8
G	2	0	-2	-5	-2	-3	0	-2	E	Quem terra pontus aethera	ST 132	hy	4
G	2	0	-2	-5	-2	0	2	0	G	O lux beata trinitas	ST 211 364	hy	8
G	2	0	-2	-5	-2	0	2	0	G	Sacri triumphale tui	ST 12	hy	8
G	2	0	-2	-5	0	2	0	-2	E	Rex noster in cruce	WA 130 223	an	3 4
a	2	0	-2	-4	-2	0	-2	-4	D	Aeterna caeli gloria	AM 72	hy	1
a	2	0	-2	-4	-2	0	-2	-4	D	Ales diei nuntius	AM 51	hy	1
a	2	0	-2	-4	-2	0	-2	-4	D	Aurora jam spargit polum	AM 80	hy	1
a	2	0	-2	-4	-2	0	-2	-4	D	Dei fide qua vivimus	ST 416	hy	1
a	2	0	-2	-4	-2	0	-2	-4	E	Dei fide qua vivimus	ST 284	hy	4
a	2	0	-2	-4	-2	0	-2	-4	D	Lux ecce surgit aurea	AM 65	hy	1
a	2	0	-2	-4	-2	0	-2	-4	D	Nox et tenebrae et nubila	AM 57	hy	1
a	2	0	-2	-4	-2	0	-2	-4	D	Splendor paternae gloriae	AM 44	hy	1
a	2	0	-2	-4	-2	0	2	0		Spiritus sanctus in te descendet ... Dei genitrix	SYG 2	alv	
a	2	0	-2	-4	0	-2	-4	0		Vidit nocte illa oculis Veniens vir	GB 166^{v}	ofv	
G	2	0	-2	-3	-5	-3	-5	0	E	Ad te Deus de luce	WA 251	an	3
G	2	0	-2	-3	-5	-3	-2	0	[E]	Agnus Dei	SCH #91		4
d	2	0	-2	-3	-5	-3	-2	0		Et hoc vobis signum Ecce annuntio vobis	LA 36	rev	
G	2	0	-2	-3	-5	-3	-2	0	G	Psallat chorus caelestium	ST 110	hy	8
G	2	0	-2	-3	-5	-2	0	2	G	Agnus Dei XIV	GR 50* LU 56 SCH #100		8
G	2	0	-2	-3	-5	-2	2	0	G	Illuminator omnium	ST 131	hy	8
G	2	0	-2	-3	-5	0	-2	-3		Et in terra	BOS #6		
G	2	0	-2	-3	-2	-5	-3	-2	G	Kyrie	MEL #74		
G	2	0	-2	-3	-2	-5	-2	-3	G	O lux beata trinitas	ST 180	hy	8
G	2	0	-2	-3	-2	-5	-2	-3	G	Primum quaerite regnum Dei	GR 359 LU 1039 SYG 245 *GB 252^{v} GS 151	co	8
G	2	0	-2	-3	-2	-3	-2	0	E	O redemptor sume carmen	ST 496	hy	3
G	2	0	-2	-3	-2	0	-3	-2	D	Te lucis ante terminum	ST 254	hy	2
G	2	0	-2	-3	-2	0	-2	0	G	Ave maris stella Dei mater alma	AR [119] LU 1262	hy	7
G	2	0	-2	-3	-2	0	-2	0		Et in terra	BOS #20 *GR 12* LU 23		
G	2	0	-2	-3	-2	0	-2	0	G	Quod chorus vatum venerandus olim	ST 426	hy	8
G	2	0	-2	-3	-2	0	2	0	G	Aeterna Christi munera et martyrum	ST 140	hy	8
G	2	0	-2	-3	-2	0	2	0	G	Hodie praeclarissimus Deo	WA 289	re	8
G	2	0	-2	-3	-2	0	2	0	D	Jam lucis orto sidere	ST 72	hy	1

G	2	0	-2	-3	-2	0	2	0	F	Sanctus	THAN #81		3
G	2	0	-2	-3	-2	0	2	5	G	Ave maris stella Dei mater alma	ST 222	hy	7
G	2	0	-2	-3	-2	0	2	5	G	Gaude mater Anna	AM 985	hy	8
G	2	0	-2	-3	-2	0	2	5	G	Sapientiam eorum narrabunt	WA 373	an	8
G	2	0	-2	-3	-2	0	2	5	G	Una igitur pater	WA 159	an	8
G	2	0	-2	-3	0	2	5	7		Nos ejus norma Gloria Christe	WA 300	rev	
G	2	0	-2	0	-5	-2	0	2	G	Ave virgo ...	WA 360 (inc illeg)	an	8
G	2	0	-2	0	-2	-5	-2	-3	G	Adonai Domine Deus	AM 586 *WA 176	an	8
G	2	0	-2	0	-2	-5	-2	0	F	Benedicite gentes Deum	WA 66 *LA 93	an	6
a	2	0	-2	0	-2	-4	-2	0		Qui confidunt in Domino	SYG 255 GS 163	alv	
a	2	0	-2	0	-2	-4	-2	0	F	Te lucis ante terminum	ST 331	hy	6
G	2	0	-2	0	-2	0	-2	-3	F	Tu solus altissimus	WA 68	an	6
a	2	0	-2	0	-2	[0	0	0]	F	Kyrie	MEL #15		
G	2	0	-2	0	-2	0	2	5	G	Ego sum via	WA 62 63 307	an	7
G	2	0	-2	0	-2	0	2	5		Tu exsurgens misereberis Domine exaudi	OTT 53 *SYG 128	ofv	
D	2	0	-2	0	-2	0	3	2		Ecce mater nostra Ecce carissimi dies	SYG 72	anv	
D	2	0	-2	0	-2	0	3	5	D	Agnus Dei	SCH #235		1
G	2	0	-2	0	-2	2	5	2		Dispersit dedit pauperibus	GR 556 LU 1480	alv	
G	2	0	-2	0	-2	2	5	4	G	Alleluia: dispersit dedit pauperibus	GR 556 LU 1480	al	8
G	2	0	-2	0	-2	2	5	4	G	Kyrie ad lib V conditor omnium	GR 79* LU 82		7
G	2	0	-2	0	-2	2	5	4	G	Kyrie suavis tu Deus (etc)	MEL #70		
G	2	0	-2	0	-2	2	5	4	G	Missus est Gabriel a Deo	WA 200	an	8
G	2	0	-2	0	-2	2	5	7	G	Illuminans altissimus	ST 372	hy	7
G	2	0	-2	0	-2	2	5	7	G	Veni redemptor gentium	ST 365	hy	7
G	2	0	-2	0	2	-2	-3	-5	G	Suscepisti me Domine	AR 117 LU 279F	an	8
G	2	0	-2	0	2	-2	0	2	G	Sanctus	THAN #80		8
G	2	0	-2	0	2	-2	2	0	G	Kyrie rex celse	MEL #82		
G	2	0	-2	0	2	-2	2	0	G	Refulsit sol in clypeos	LA 300	an	8
G	2	0	-2	0	2	-2	2	5	G	Iste confessor Domini sacratus	ST 104	hy	8
G	2	0	-2	0	2	0	-2	-3	E	Exaudivit ergo Deus	WA 287	an	4
G	2	0	-2	0	2	0	-2	0	G	Deus adjuvat me	OHS 612 AR 135 LU 521 768 *WA 126 LA 204	an	8
G	2	0	-2	0	2	0	-2	0	G	Miserere mihi Domine et exaudi	AR 58 OHS 168 LU 266	an	8

D	2	0	-2	0	2	0	-2	0		Notum fecit Dominus salutare Cantate Domino canticum	SYG 248	alv	
G	2	0	-2	0	2	0	-2	0	G	Sedit angelus ad sepulchrum	WA 222	an	8
G	2	0	-2	0	2	0	-2	2	G	Alleluia: justum deduxit ... gloriam	SYG 229	al	8
G	2	0	-2	0	2	0	-2	2	G	Et audientes discipuli	AR 809 LU 1591	an	8
G	2	0	-2	0	2	0	-2	2	G	Exaltabo te Domine quoniam suscepisti	LR 96 *WA 147 *LA 245	an	8
G	2	0	-2	0	2	0	-2	2	G	Justificeris Domine in sermonibus	AR 432 OHS 399 LU 652 *AM 413 WA 120 LA 193	an	8
G	2	0	-2	0	2	0	-2	2		Justum deduxit ... et ostendit ... gloriam	SYG 229	alv	
G	2	0	-2	0	2	0	-2	2	G	Nocte surgentes vigilemus omnes	ST 359	hy	8
G	2	0	-2	0	2	0	-2	2	E	Splendet Bethlehemiticus campus	WA 43	an	3
G	2	0	-2	0	2	0	-2	2	G	Tres pueri jussu regis	AR 4 AM 30	an	8
G	2	0	-2	0	2	0	2	0	G	Assumptus ex eculeo	WA 258	re	7
G	2	0	-2	0	2	0	2	0	G	Beati estis cum maladixerint	LR 142	re	7
G	2	0	-2	0	2	0	2	0	G	Cognovit eum Dominus	LR 197	an	8
G	2	0	-2	0	2	0	2	0	G	Domine Deus noster qui cum patribus	WA 227	an	8
G	2	0	-2	0	2	0	2	0	G	Ecce annuntio vobis	LA 36	re	8
G	2	0	-2	0	2	0	2	0	G	Herodes enim metuebat Joannem	PM 184	an	8
D	2	0	-2	0	2	0	2	0	D	Jesu quadragenariae	ST 383	hy	1
G	2	0	-2	0	2	0	2	0	G	Vir Dei Benedictus mundi gloriam	GR (27) GB 54	int	8
D	2	0	-2	0	2	0	2	3	D	Alleluia: initio cognovi de testimoniis	GR 82**	al	2
D	2	0	-2	0	2	0	2	3	D	Alleluia: repleti sunt omnes	SYG 186	al	2
D	2	0	-2	0	2	0	2	3		Repleti sunt omnes spiritu	SYG 186	alv	
G	2	0	-2	0	2	0	2	4	G	Gaude mater ecclesia	ST 123	hy	7
G	2	0	-2	0	2	0	2	4	G	O salutaris hostia quae caeli	AR 94* LU 1854	hy	7
G	2	0	-2	0	2	0	2	4	G	Qui sunt hi sermones ... respondens	LA 218	an	8
G	2	0	-2	0	2	0	2	5	G	Agnus Dei VI	GR 24* LU 33 SCH #89		8
G	2	0	-2	0	2	0	2	5	G	Ipsius quoque gloriae	WA 291	an	8
G	2	0	-2	0	2	0	2	5	G	Jam lucis orto sidere	ST 77 172	hy	8
G	2	0	-2	0	2	0	2	5	G	Jam lucis orto sidere	AM 2 ST 266	hy	8
G	2	0	-2	0	2	0	2	5	G	Nunc sancte nobis spiritus	AM 93 108	hy	8
G	2	0	-2	0	2	0	2	5	G	Oremus omnes ad Dominum Jesum	AR 926 LU 1758 AM 1144 WA 408	an	8
G	2	0	-2	0	2	0	2	5	G	Oremus omnes ad Dominum ut ostendat	WA 409	an	8

G	2	0	-2	0	2	0	2	5	G	Rector potens verax Deus	AM 98 113	hy	8
G	2	0	-2	0	2	0	2	5	G	Rerum Deus tenax vigor	AR 38 LU 245 AM 103 118	hy	8
G	2	0	-2	0	2	0	2	5	G	Timor et tremor ... in Nineven	GB 155^{v} WA 230	an	8
G	2	0	-2	0	2	0	4	2	E	Kyrie	MEL #73		
G	2	0	-2	0	2	0	4	5	G	Solemnitatem hodiernam sanctissimi	AM 1078	hy	8
G	2	0	-2	0	2	0	5	0	G	Gloria III	BOS #20 GR 12* LU 23		8
G	2	0	-2	0	2	0	5	0	G	Gloria	BOS #21		IV
G	2	0	-2	0	2	0	5	2	G	Nativitatem hodiernam perpetuae	AR 836 *AM 1034 *WA 368 LA 461	an	8
G	2	0	-2	0	2	0	5	2	G	Solemnitatem hodiernam sanctissimi	AR 877	an	8
G	2	0	-2	0	2	0	5	4	G	Alleluia: a summo caelo egressio ejus	GR 85**	al	7
G	2	0	-2	0	2	0	5	4	G	Illumina nos Domine	AR 327	an	8
G	2	0	-2	0	2	0	5	4	G	Ite missa est Ia	GR 7* LU 19		8
G	2	0	-2	0	2	0	5	7	G	Hic est dies verus Dei	ST 35	hy	8
G	2	0	-2	0	2	0	5	7	G	Mysterium mirabile	ST 35	hy	8
G	2	0	-2	0	2	0	5	7	G	Nunc sancte nobis spiritus	ST 27	hy	8
G	2	0	-2	0	2	0	5	7	G	Salvator mundi Domine	ST 83	hy	8
G	2	0	-2	0	2	0	5	7	G	Veni creator spiritus	AR 500 73* GR 150* PM 89 ST 38 94 LU 885 AM 518 1254	hy	8
D	2	0	-2	0	2	3	0	3	D	Christe qui lux es et dies	ST 176	hy	2
D	2	0	-2	0	2	3	2	0	D	Alleluia: beatus Laurentius dum in craticula	SYG 217	al	1
D	2	0	-2	0	2	3	2	0	D	Alleluia: stabunt justi in magna constantia	SYG 172	al	2
D	2	0	-2	0	2	3	2	0	D	Christe qui lux es et dies	ST 382	hy	2
D	2	0	-2	0	2	3	2	0	D	Rex gloriose martyrum	ST 60	hy	2
D	2	0	-2	0	2	3	2	3		Memento Domine et ostende Recordare mei Domine	SYG 259	ofv	
D	2	0	-2	0	2	3	5	2	D	Alleluia: tu es Simon Bar Jona	SYG 203 *GS 189	al	1
D	2	0	-2	0	2	3	5	3	D	Alleluia: cum esset Stephanus	SYG 22	al	1
D	2	0	-2	0	2	3	5	7		Ego Dominus dabo	GR 105**	alv	
G	2	0	-2	0	2	4	0	-2	G	Aurora velut fulgida	ST 398	hy	8
G	2	0	-2	0	2	4	0	-2	G	Christe redemptor omnium ex patre	ST 410	hy	8
G	2	0	-2	0	2	4	0	-2	G	Deus sacrati nominis	ST 423	hy	8
G	2	0	-2	0	2	4	0	-2	G	Devota mente socii	ST 432	hy	8
G	2	0	-2	0	2	4	0	-2	G	Fit porta Christi pervia	ST 433	hy	8
G	2	0	-2	0	2	4	0	-2	G	Fratres alacri pectore	ST 428	hy	8

G	2	0	-2	0	2	4	0	-2	G	Infantum diem martyrum	ST 413	hy	8
G	2	0	-2	0	2	4	0	-2	G	O nata lux de lumine	ST 422	hy	8
G	2	0	-2	0	2	4	0	-2	G	Optatus votis omnium	ST 419	hy	8
G	2	0	-2	0	2	4	0	-2	G	Quem terra pontus aethera	ST 398	hy	8
G	2	0	-2	0	2	4	0	-2	G	Salvete flores martyrum	ST 413	hy	8
G	2	0	-2	0	2	4	0	-2	G	Te trina Deus unitas	ST 423	hy	8
G	2	0	-2	0	2	4	2	0		Et in terra	BOS #15		
G	2	0	-2	0	2	4	2	0	G	Lapidem quem reprobaverunt	SYG 149	an	8
G	2	0	-2	0	2	4	2	0	G	Sacerdotes Dei benedicite ... sancti	WA 429	re	8
G	2	0	-2	0	2	4	2	4	G	Agnus Dei	SCH #99		8
G	2	0	-2	0	2	4	2	4	G	Te Deus omnipotens	WA 382	an	8
G	2	0	-2	0	2	4	2	4		Venite benedicti Patris ... cum gaudio	GB 267^{v}	alv	
G	2	0	-2	0	2	4	5	0	G	Dico autem vobis amicis meis	GR [28] LU 1169 SYG 214 GB 219^{v} GS q	co	8
G	2	0	-2	0	2	4	5	0	G	Gloriosa dicta sunt	GR 404 LU 1319	co	8
G	2	0	-2	0	2	4	5	0	G	Optimam partem elegit	GR (33)	co	8
G	2	0	-2	0	2	4	5	0	G	Valde mirabilis es o Maria	GR 47**	co	8
G	2	0	-2	0	2	4	5	2	G	Gloria	BOS #23		IV
G	2	0	-2	0	2	4	5	4	G	Gloria IX	GR 32* LU 40		7
G	2	0	-2	0	2	4	5	4	G	Kyrie	MEL #72		
G	2	0	-2	0	2	4	5	7	G	Servus tuus ego sum	LA 143 WA 94	re	8
G	2	0	-2	0	2	5	2	0	G	Ave praesul alme	ST 401	hy	8
G	2	0	-2	0	2	5	2	5	G	Alleluia: dilexi quoniam exaudivit	GB 262	al	8
G	2	0	-2	0	2	5	2	5	G	Alleluia: felix es sacra virgo Maria	GR 542 LU 1539	al	8
G	2	0	-2	0	2	5	2	5		Dilexi quoniam exaudivit	GB 262	alv	
G	2	0	-2	0	2	5	4	0	G	Cum autem descendisset Jesus	AR 337 LU 1108 AM 307 WA 71 LA 106	an	8
G	2	0	-2	0	2	5	4	2	G	Angeli eorum ... patris	AR 284 AM 260 LU 431 *LA 61	an	8
G	2	0	-2	0	2	5	4	2	G	Dabo sanctis meis locum	LR 177 AM 981 WA 420 *LA 513	an	8
G	2	0	-2	0	2	5	4	2	G	De manu filiorum	WA 110 LA 201	an	8
G	2	0	-2	0	2	5	4	2	G	Domine abstraxisti ab inferis	OHS 606 LU 764 WA 125 *LA 203	an	8
G	2	0	-2	0	2	5	4	2	G	In consilio justorum	WA 394	an	8
G	2	0	-2	0	2	5	4	2	G	Kyrie	MEL #69		

G	2	0	-2	0	2	5	4	2	G	Missus est angelus Gabriel ... in civitatem	PM 246	an	8
G	2	0	-2	0	2	5	4	2	G	O beata lactentium	WA 44	an	8
G	2	0	-2	0	2	5	4	2	G	Suscepimus Deus misericordiam	LR 56 70 LU 378 WA 27 53 *LA 31	an	8
G	2	0	-2	0	2	5	4	2	G	Tamquam sponsus Dominus	LU 372 *LR 55 WA 49 *LA 31	an	8
G	2	0	-2	0	2	5	4	2	G	Unxerunt Salomonem Sadoc	AR 541 LU 987 AM 577	an	8
G	2	0	-2	0	2	5	4	2	G	Vim faciebant qui quaerebant	OHS 491 LU 698 WA 122 LA 196	an	8
G	2	0	-2	0	2	5	4	5	G	Per beatum Dionysium	WA 388	re	8
G	2	0	-2	0	2	5	4	5		Potens es Domine et veritas Inveni David	OTT 147 GB 28^{v} SYG 27	ofv	
G	2	0	-2	0	2	5	4	5	G	Qui cognoscis Domine	SYG 234	int	8
D	2	0	-2	0	2	5	7	5	[E]	Agnus Dei	SCH #236		4
G	2	0	-2	0	2	5	7	5	G	Caeli laetentur sidera	ST 401	hy	8
G	2	0	-2	0	2	5	7	5	G	Hic est dies verus Dei	ST 9	hy	8
G	2	0	-2	0	2	5	7	5	G	Jam Christus astra ascenderat	ST 10	hy	8
G	2	0	-2	0	2	5	7	5	G	Post Petrum primum principem	ST 401	hy	8
G	2	0	-2	0	2	5	7	5	G	Quadraginta annis proximus	LA 166	inv	7
G	2	0	-2	0	2	5	7	5	G	Sidus Mariae inclitum	ST 399	hy	8
G	2	0	-2	0	2	5	7	5	G	Veni creator spiritus	ST 232 260 294 390 420	hy	8
D	2	0	-2	0	3	0	2	0		Vindica Domine sanguinem ... super terram	SYG 210	alv	
D	2	0	-2	0	3	0	3	0	D	Veritas mea et misericordia	GR [6][44] OTT 148 LU 1203 SYG 38 GB 41^{v} GS 223	of	2
D	2	0	-2	0	3	2	-2	0	[D]	Gratias tibi ago Domine Jesu	WA 349	an	2
D	2	0	-2	0	3	2	0	-2	D	Expetitus a fratribus	WA 298 *LA 369	an	1
D	2	0	-2	0	3	2	0	2	D	Beatus Nicholaus adhuc	WA 242	an	1
D	2	0	-2	0	3	2	0	2		Ego sum vitis vera	SYG 171	alv	
D	2	0	-2	0	3	2	0	2	D	Orbis exsultans celebret hoc festum	ST 108	hy	1
D	2	0	-2	0	3	2	0	2		Propter veritatem ... exaltabit	SYG 232	alv	
D	2	0	-2	0	3	2	0	2		Regi autem saeculorum	SYG 262	alv	
D	2	0	-2	0	3	2	0	3	D	Vos qui reliquistis omnia	SYG 219	co	1
D	2	0	-2	0	3	2	3	2		O sancte N. sidus Sancte N. confessor	WA 428	rev	
D	2	0	-2	0	3	2	3	5	D	Ad laudem sanctae Mariae	ST 432	hy	2
D	2	0	-2	0	3	2	3	5	D	Cum coetu virgineo adveniens	PM 215	an	1
G	2	0	-2	0	3	2	3	5	D	Gloria ad lib. III	BOS #22 GR 87* LU 89		2

D	2	0	-2	0	3	2	3	5	D	In laude Martini decus	ST 434	hy	2
D	2	0	-2	0	3	2	3	5	D	Kyrie kyrion o theos pater	MEL #189		
D	2	0	-2	0	3	2	3	5	D	Martine confessor Dei	ST 434	hy	2
D	2	0	-2	0	3	2	3	5	D	O beata beatissimae	WA 334	an	1
D	2	0	-2	0	3	2	3	5	D	Oramus te beatissime	WA 334	an	1
D	2	0	-2	0	3	5	3	2	D	Agnus Dei	SCH #224		1
D	2	0	-2	0	3	5	3	2	D	Deus qui sedes super thronum ... esto ... quia	WA 70	an	1
D	2	0	-2	0	3	5	3	2	D	Domine dimitte eam	WA 93 *LA 143	an	2
D	2	0	-2	0	3	5	3	2	D	Ego sum lux mundi ... dicit	WA 105	an	1
D	2	0	-2	0	3	5	3	2		Elegit te Dominus sibi	GB 28^{v} *GS 223	alv	
D	2	0	-2	0	3	5	3	2	D	O beatum praesulem	WA 295	re	1
D	2	0	-2	0	3	5	3	2	D	Sanctus	THAN #187		1
D	2	0	-2	0	3	5	3	2	D	Vir Domini Benedictus	AM 853 WA 300 *LA 375	an	1
D	2	0	-2	0	3	5	3	5	D	Germinaverunt campi	LA 26 WA 18	re	1 2
G	2	0	-2	0	5	2	4	2	G	Benedixerunt eam omnes	GR 41**	of	8
G	2	0	-2	0	5	2	4	2	G	Si ambulavero in medio	GR 376 OTT 118 LU 1061 *SYG 97 GB 86^{v} *GS 59 163	of	8
G	2	0	-2	0	5	4	2	5	G	Ista est virgo sapiens	WA 434	an	8
G	2	0	-2	0	5	4	2	5	G	Mariae Magdalenae festum	WA 338	an	8
G	2	0	-2	0	5	4	5	7	G	Viam mandatorum tuorum	GR 502 LU 1474	of	8
a	2	0	-2	2	0	-2	0	-4	F	Agnus Dei	SCH #50		5
G	2	0	-2	2	0	-2	0	-2	G	Et in terra	BOS #30 GR 22* LU 32		
G	2	0	-2	2	0	-2	0	2	G	O mulier sancta lacrimarum	WA 337	re	8
G	2	0	-2	2	0	2	4	0	G	Jam carmine mellifluo	ST 158	hy	7
D	2	0	-2	2	3	2	0	2	D	Kyrie in praesepe Christus	MEL #183		
D	2	0	-2	2	3	5	3	2	[D]	Agnus Dei	SCH #223		2
D	2	0	-2	2	3	5	3	2	D	Alleluia: qui sequitur me non ambulat	GR [13] LU 1139	al	2
D	2	0	-2	2	3	5	3	2		Christus passus est pro nobis	GR 481	alv	
D	2	0	-2	2	3	5	3	2		Qui sequitur me non ambulat	GR [13] LU 1139	alv	
D	2	0	-2	2	3	5	3	2		Tu es Simon Bar Jona	GS 189 SYG 203	alv	
D	2	0	-2	2	3	5	7	5	D	Alleluia: hortus conclusus est	GB 232	al	1
D	2	0	-2	2	3	5	7	5	E	Magni palmam certaminis	ST 13	hy	4
D	2	0	-2	2	3	5	7	5		Stabunt justi in magna constantia	SYG 172	alv	
G	2	0	-2	2	4	0	2	0	G	Amen amen dico vobis quia plorabitis	AR 474 LU 825 *AM 489	an	8

G	2	0	-2	2	4	0	2	4	G	Dixit Jesus matri suae mulier	GR 587[6] LU 1612[4]	co	8
G	2	0	-2	2	4	0	7	5	G	Felix per omnes festum mundi cardines	ST 430	hy	8
G	2	0	-2	2	4	2	0	-2	G	O virum ineffabilem	AR 917 LU 1749 AM 1115 *WA 402 LA 486	an	8
G	2	0	-2	2	4	2	0	2	G	Kyrie	MEL #71		
G	2	0	-2	2	4	5	2	0	G	Alleluia: sanctorum sicut aquilae	SYG 210	al	7
G	2	0	-2	2	4	5	2	0	G	Dixit Dominus ad Noe	AR 347 LU 503 AM 319 *LA 1	an	8
G	2	0	-2	2	4	5	4	2	[G]	Agnus Dei	SCH #90		8
G	2	0	-2	2	4	5	4	2	G	Hymnum dicamus Domino	AR 349 AM 320 *WA 62	an	8
G	2	0	-2	2	4	5	4	2	G	Martyris ecce dies Agathae	ST 376	hy	7
G	2	0	-2	2	5	0	2	0	G	Alleluia: angelus Domini descendit ... cum splendore	SYG 162	al	7
G	2	0	-2	2	5	0	2	0	G	Alleluia: miserere mei Deus	SYG 234	al	7
G	2	0	-2	2	5	0	2	0	G	Alleluia: multifarie olim Deus loquens	GR 49 LU 441 GS H SYG 19 GB 31[v]	al	7
G	2	0	-2	2	5	0	2	0	G	Alleluia: O adoranda trinitas	SYG 261	al	7
G	2	0	-2	2	5	0	2	0	G	Alleluia: sancti et justi in Domino gaudete	GS 215	al	7
G	2	0	-2	2	5	0	2	0		Angelus Domini descendit ... cum splendore	SYG 162	alv	
G	2	0	-2	2	5	0	2	0	G	Lucis creator optime	ST 182	hy	8
G	2	0	-2	2	5	0	2	0		Miserere mei Deus miserere	SYG 234	alv	
G	2	0	-2	2	5	0	2	0		Multifarie olim Deus loquens	GR 49 LU 441 GS H SYG 19 GB 31[v]	alv	
G	2	0	-2	2	5	0	2	0		Sancti et justi in Domino	GS 215	alv	
G	2	0	-2	2	5	2	0	4	G	Unus est Dominus	WA 161	re	8
G	2	0	-2	2	5	2	4	2	G	Liberasti virgam	WA 67 *LA 96	an	8
G	2	0	-2	2	5	2	5	7	G	Ego per istos tres annos	WA 244	an	8
D	2	0	-2	2	5	3	2	5	D	Alleluia: magnus Dominus ... in civitate	SYG 242	al	1
G	2	0	-2	2	5	4	0	2	G	Avete solitudinis	AM 1119	hy	8
G	2	0	-2	2	5	4	0	2	G	Christo redemptor omnium conserva	LR 380 AM 1100	hy	8
G	2	0	-2	2	5	4	0	2	G	Festiva saeclis colitur	ST 98	hy	8
G	2	0	-2	2	5	4	0	2	G	Jesu corona caelitum	LR 455	hy	8
G	2	0	-2	2	5	4	0	2	G	Jesu salvator saeculi	AM 1105	hy	8
G	2	0	-2	2	5	4	0	2	G	Martyr Dei qui unicum	ST 101	hy	8
G	2	0	-2	2	5	4	0	2	G	Placare Christe servulis	AR 895 LU 1730	hy	8
G	2	0	-2	2	5	4	0	2	G	Rex gloriose martyrum	ST 101 103	hy	8

G	2	0	-2	2	5	4	0	2	G	Salutis aeternae dator	AR 900 LU 1722	hy	8
G	2	0	-2	2	5	4	0	2	G	Salvete cedri Libani	AM 1123	hy	8
G	2	0	-2	2	5	4	2	0	G	Alleluia: Martinus Abrahae sinu	SYG 226	al	8
G	2	0	-2	2	5	4	2	0	G	Aurora lucis rutilat	ST 288	hy	7
G	2	0	-2	2	5	4	2	0	G	Benedicamus Domino IIc	AR 60* LU 126		8
G	2	0	-2	2	5	4	2	0	G	Deus qui mundum crimine jacentem	ST 428	hy	8
G	2	0	-2	2	5	4	2	0		Martinus Abrahae sinu	SYG 226	alv	
G	2	0	-2	2	5	4	2	0	G	Martyris Christi colimus triumphum	ST 432	hy	8
G	2	0	-2	2	5	4	2	0	G	Nunc tibi virgo virginum	ST 433	hy	8
G	2	0	-2	2	5	4	2	0	G	Revertenti Abraham	WA 80	re	8
G	2	0	-2	2	5	4	2	0		Sacerdos Dei Martine pastor	SYG 226	alv	
G	2	0	-2	2	5	4	2	0	G	Sacris solemniis juncta sint gaudia	ST 46	hy	8
G	2	0	-2	2	5	4	2	4	G	Christe sanctorum decus atque virtus	ST 427	hy	8
G	2	0	-2	2	5	4	2	5	G	Alleluia: quinque prudentes virgines	GR 416 LU 1339 *SYG 45 GB 273^{v}	al	7
G	2	0	-2	2	5	4	2	5	G	Alleluia: vicerunt draconem	GR 99**	al	7
G	2	0	-2	2	5	4	2	5	G	Igne me examinasti	WA 348 *LA 436	an	8
G	2	0	-2	2	5	4	2	5	G	Martyris ecce dies Agathae	ST 88 427	hy	7
G	2	0	-2	2	5	4	2	5	G	Postquam resurrexit a mortis	SYG 149	an	7
G	2	0	-2	2	5	4	2	5	G	Principes populorum congregati	LR 135 *WA 411 LA 505	an	8
G	2	0	-2	2	5	4	2	5		Quinque prudentes virgines	GR 416 LU 1339 *GS 231 *SYG 45 *GB 273^{v}	alv	
G	2	0	-2	2	5	4	2	5		Vicerunt draconem propter sanguinem	GR 99**	alv	
G	2	0	-2	2	5	4	2	7	G	Cum aspicerem animalia	WA 374	re	7
G	2	0	-2	2	5	4	2	7		Tamquam prodigium factus	GR 622^{2} LU 1681^{3}	alv	
G	2	0	-2	2	5	4	5	2	G	Ab hominibus iniquis libera me	AR 436 OHS 627 LU 776^{D} AM 431 432 WA 121 *LA 194	an	8
G	2	0	-2	2	5	4	5	2	G	Alleluia	AR 56 58 209 LU 266 285 289 294 300 307 316	an	8
G	2	0	-2	2	5	4	5	2	G	Corripies me Domine	AR 112	an	8
G	2	0	-2	2	5	4	5	7	G	Caecus sedebat secus	LR 401 *LA 123 *WA 83	re	8
G	2	0	-2	2	5	4	5	7	G	Hic praecursor directus	LA 404 *WA 323	re	7
G	2	0	-2	2	5	4	5	7	G	Veriloquus vates	WA 294	re	7
G	2	0	-2	2	5	4	7	5		Vir obediens loquetur	GR (5)	alv	
D	2	0	-2	2	5	7	5	3	D	Alleluia: beatus qui lingua sua	GR 29**	al	1
D	2	0	-2	2	5	7	5	3	D	Alleluia: regnavit Dominus super omnes	GR 288 LU 855 *GB 179^{v} *GS K	al	1

G	2	0	-2	2	5	7	5	7	G	Cogitaverunt autem principes	WA 112 GS 83	re	8
G	2	0	-2	2	5	7	9	5	G	In servis suis alleluia	WA 307	re	8
D	2	0	-2	2	5	7	9	7	D	Cum venerimus ante	WA 205 SYG 70	an	1
G	2	0	-2	2	5	9	7	0	G	Laverunt stolas suas	WA 44	re	1
D	2	0	-2	3	2	0	2	0	D	Calix benedictionis	LR 132	re	1
D	2	0	-2	3	2	0	2	0	D	Hodie Maria virgo caelos ascendit	LR 379	re	1
D	2	0	-2	3	2	0	2	0	D	Solem justitiae regem	AR 128* PM 185 VP 211 WA 366	re	1
D	2	0	-2	3	2	0	2	3	D	Facto diluvio super terram	WA 76	re	2
D	2	0	-2	3	2	0	2	5	D	Agnus Dei XIII	GR 47* LU 53		1
D	2	0	-2	3	5	2	3	0	F	Alleluia: data est mihi	SYG 160	al	6
D	2	0	-2	3	5	3	5	7	D	Auctor donorum spiritus	WA 292	an	1
D	2	0	-2	3	5	3	5	7	D	Qui autem diligit me	WA 151	an	1
D	2	0	-2	3	5	7	2	0	D	Agnetis festum martyris	ST 373	hy	2
D	2	0	-2	3	5	7	2	0	D	Verbum patris principium	ST 370	hy	2
a	2	0	-2	5	3	2	0	-2	F	Agnus Dei	SCH #49		1
c	2	0	-1	-5	-3	-1	0	-1	[G]	Agnus Dei	SCH #20		7
c	2	0	-1	-5	-3	0	-1	0	c	Ne magnitudo revelationum	LA 428	re	6
c	2	0	-1	-5	-3	0	2	0	D	Coena facta sciens Dominus	SYG 133	an	2
F	2	0	-1	-5	-3	0	2	4	G	Benedictus qui venit in nomine	GR 260 LU 806 OHS 828 OTT 64 GS 124 SYG 161 GB 144	of	8
F	2	0	-1	-5	-3	0	2	4	G	Improperium exspectavit cor meum	GR 184 326 [115] OHS 142 OTT 49 LU 602 974 *SYG 123 *GS 88 *GB 110v	of	8
F	2	0	-1	-5	-3	0	2	4	G	Spiritus Domini replevit orbem	SYG 185	of	8
F	2	0	-1	-5	-3	0	2	4	G	Tamquam lignum quod plantatum	GR (25)	of	8
c	2	0	-1	-3	-5	-7	-3	-7		Haec requies ejus in saeculum Exsulta et lauda	LR 372	rev	
F	2	0	-1	-3	-5	-3	-1	-3	E	Exaudi Domine vocem meam ... adjutor	GR 332 LU 1002 SYG 241 GS 145 *GB 249	int	4
F	2	0	-1	-3	-5	-3	-1	2	E	Exsultet caelum laudibus	ST 100	hy	4
F	2	0	-1	-3	-5	-3	-1	2	E	Exsultet orbis gaudiis	AR [5] LU 1115	hy	4
c	2	0	-1	-3	-5	-3	0	-5		Haec speciosum forma Videte miraculum	WA 268(271)	rev	
c	2	0	-1	-3	-5	-3	0	-5		Si quis manducaverit Respexit Elias	LR 124 LU 927	rev	
c	2	0	-1	-3	-5	-3	0	-3	G	Te lucis ante terminum	ST 176	hy	8
F	2	0	-1	-3	-5	-3	0	2	F	Oremus omnes ad Dominum Jesum ... dixit	LA 494	re	6

F	2	0	-1	-3	-5	0	2	4	F	Benedicamus Domino VIII	AR 62* LU 127		6
F	2	0	-1	-3	-5	0	2	4	E	Dixit Dominus Mariae	WA 336	re	4
c	2	0	-1	-3	-1	-3	0	2		Clara quippe voce Qui cum audissent	WA 240	rev	
F	2	0	-1	-3	-1	0	-1	-3	C	Te lucis ante terminum	ST 343	hy	6
F	2	0	-1	-3	-1	0	2	0	D	Virtutum pennis ad astra	SYG 220	co	1
F	2	0	-1	-3	-1	0	2	4	E	Alleluia	AM 73 75	an	4
F	2	0	-1	-3	-1	0	2	6		Et in terra	BOS #31		
F	2	0	-1	-3	-1	0	5	4	F	Agnus Dei	SCH #140		6
F	2	0	-1	-3	-1	2	4	2	E	Servi Dei benedicite	WA 286	an	4
c	2	0	-1	-3	0	-5	-3	-5	G	Magne pater Nicholae	WA 241	re	7
c	2	0	-1	-3	0	-3	0	-1	G	Dei fide qua vivimus	ST 381	hy	8
c	2	0	-1	-3	0	-3	0	-1	G	Qua Christus hora sitiit	ST 382	hy	8
c	2	0	-1	-3	0	-3	0	-1	G	Ternis ter horis numerus	ST 382	hy	8
F	2	0	-1	-3	0	-1	-5	-3		Dicant nunc Judaei Christus resurgens	WA 133 SYG 147	anv	
c	2	0	-1	-3	0	-1	-5	-3		Domine refugium factus es Convertere Domine	GR 108 LU 1007 GS 43 147 169 GB 250 SYG 81	grv	
c	2	0	-1	-3	0	-1	-3	-5	G	Aspice in me Domine	WA 64 *LA 89	an	8
F	2	0	-1	-3	0	-1	-3	-1	E	Benigne fac in bona	AM 73	an	4
F	2	0	-1	-3	0	2	0	4		Gloria sit altissimo Iste est Joannes	PM 33	rev	
F	2	0	-1	-3	0	2	0	4		Joannes hic theologus Iste est Joannes	PM 33 WA 38(41)	rev	
F	2	0	-1	-3	0	2	4	2	F	Gaudent in caelis animae	AR 577^{14} [48] LU 262^{3} 1160 *AM 653 739 1122 *WA 351 *LA 479	an	6
F	2	0	-1	-3	0	2	4	5	F	Agnus Dei	SCH #149		2
F	2	0	-1	-3	0	2	4	5	F	Sanctus	THAN #122		6
c	2	0	-1	-3	2	-1	0	2		Domine libera animam meam Ad Dominum dum tribularer	GR 321 LU 961 GS 53 142 GB 80 SYG 91	grv	
c	2	0	-1	-3	2	-1	0	2		Sitivit anima mea ad Deum fortem Quemadmodum desiderat	GR 506 LU 1478	grv	
c	2	0	-1	-3	2	0	-1	-3	G	Alleluia	WA 71	an	8
c	2	0	-1	0	-3	-7	-5	-3	G	Alleluia	AR 187	an	8
c	2	0	-1	0	-3	-7	-5	-3	G	Filii Sion exsultent	AR 186	an	8
c	2	0	-1	0	-3	-5	-1	-5	G	Omnis plebs ut vidit	WA 83	an	8
c	2	0	-1	0	-3	-5	0	2	c	Christe cunctorum dominator alme	ST 423	hy	6
c	2	0	-1	0	-3	-5	0	2	c	Christe sanctorum decus angelorum	ST 429	hy	6

c	2	0	-1	0	-3	0	-1	-5	F	Aquae multae non potuerunt	LR 215	an	5
c	2	0	-1	0	-3	0	-1	-5	G	Erat enim in sermone	LA 324	an	8
c	2	0	-1	0	-3	0	-1	-5	G	Euntes ibant et flebant	AR [11] LU 1114 *WA 394 415 LA 473 520	an	8
c	2	0	-1	0	-3	0	-1	-5	G	Justi fulgebunt sicut sol	LA 518	an	8
c	2	0	-1	0	-3	0	-1	-5	G	Omnes gentes per gyrum	AR 928 LU 1761 *AM 1146 *WA 410 LA 496	an	8
c	2	0	-1	0	-3	0	-1	-3	G	Confirma hoc Deus	AR 86* PM 328 LR 112 LU 869 1844 *WA 152 LA 257	an	8
c	2	0	-1	0	-3	0	-1	-3	G	Emitte spiritum tuum	LR 115 *WA 152 *LA 259	an	8
c	2	0	-1	0	-3	0	-1	-3	G	Factus est repente de caelo	LR 108 LU 868 *WA 152 LA 255	an	8
c	2	0	-1	0	-3	0	-1	-3	G	Illuxerunt fulgura Dei	LR 294	an	8
c	2	0	-1	0	-3	0	-1	-3	G	Per signum crucis de inimicis	AR 701 LU 1460 AM 900	an	8
c	2	0	-1	0	-3	0	2	0		Gratia Dei in me vacua Qui operatus est	GR 418 LU 1345 GB 208 *GS 178 SYG 204	grv	
F	2	0	-1	0	-3	2	4	6	E	Pater cum essem cum eis	GR 289 LU 856 *SYG 179 *GB 183 *GS L 134	co	4
c	2	0	-1	0	-1	-5	-1	0	G	Dicit Andreas Simoni	GR 392 *SYG 231 *GB 245^{v} *GS g	co	8
c	2	0	-1	0	-1	-3	-5	-3		Et in terra	BOS #36		
c	2	0	-1	0	-1	-3	-1	0	G	Reges videbunt et consurgent	LR 351 *WA 321 LA 403	an	8
c	2	0	-1	0	-1	-3	-1	0	G	Regnum ejus regnum sempiternum	AR 894^{1} OHS 831 LU 1715 AM 1088	an	8
F	2	0	-1	0	-1	-3	0	-1	E	Benigne fac Domine	AR 191	an	4
c	2	0	-1	0	-1	-3	0	-1	G	Ego dormivi et somnum	OHS 755 WA 128 LA 212 224	an	8
c	2	0	-1	0	-1	-3	0	-1	G	Post dies octo ... ingressus	AR 463 LU 815 AM 477 WA 136 *LA 230	an	8
F	2	0	-1	0	2	-3	-1	0	F	Induit me Dominus vestimento	LR 228 LA 335 *WA 253	re	6
c	2	0	-1	0	2	0	-3	0	G	Alleluia	AR 37 LU 244	an	8
c	2	0	-1	0	2	0	-3	0	G	Quid retribuam Domino	AR 538^{2} LU 965	an	8
c	2	0	-1	0	2	0	-3	0	G	Zelus domus tuae comedit me	OHS 367 LU 626 *WA 117 *LA 189	an	8
c	2	0	-1	0	2	0	-1	-3	G	Deus meus es tu et confitebor	AR 354 *WA 79 *LA 123	an	8
c	2	0	-1	0	2	0	-1	0	c	Aspiciebam in visu noctis	LA 3	re	6
c	2	0	-1	0	2	0	2	0		Utinam appenderentur peccata Vir erat	OTT 122 SYG 256 GB 262	ofv	
c	2	0	-1	0	2	0	5	0		Quae est enim ... fortitudo mea Vir erat	OTT 122 GB 262 SYG 256	ofv	
F	2	0	-1	0	2	0	6	0	E	Gloria	BOS #31		II

145

F	2	0	-1	0	2	4	-1	-3	E	Dico vobis gaudium	WA 187 *LA 85	an	4
F	2	0	-1	0	2	4	2	-1	G	Tulit ergo Dominus hominem	LA 109 *WA 72	re	8
F	2	0	-1	0	2	4	2	-1	D	Venite populi ad sacrum	AR 99* *PM 105 *VP 14 *SYG 154	an	1
c	2	0	-1	0	2	4	2	0	G	Sicut civitas Catinensium	WA 247	an	7
F	2	0	-1	0	2	4	5	2	F	Bonum est confidere in Domino	GR 358 LU 1037 SYG 107 GB 95 *GS 69 157	gr	5
F	2	0	-1	0	2	4	5	2	F	In me gratia omnis viae	GR 43**	gr	5
F	2	0	-1	0	2	5	0	2	F	Nos autem gloriari	GB 234^{v}	co	6
c	2	0	-1	0	2	5	4	2	c	Paschasius proconsularis	WA 244	an	6
F	2	0	-1	0	5	4	2	4	F	Alme pater clericorum	ST 458	hy	5
F	2	0	-1	0	5	4	2	4	F	Kyrie	MEL #117		
F	2	0	-1	2	4	-1	0	-3	F	Fluminis impetus ... alleluia	LR 69 *WA 53 *LA 66	an	6
F	2	0	-1	2	4	0	-1	-3	F	Exaltare super caelos	WA 148	an	6
F	2	0	-1	2	4	0	-1	-3	F	Noli flere Maria	WA 136	an	6
F	2	0	-1	2	4	0	-1	-3	F	Non turbetur cor ... alleluia	WA 148 *LA 253	an	6
F	2	0	-1	2	4	0	-1	-3	F	Non vos relinquam ... veniam	WA 151	an	6
F	2	0	-1	2	4	0	-1	-3	F	Pacem meam do vobis	WA 148 *LA 253	an	6
F	2	0	-1	2	4	2	0	-1	E	Rex gloriose martyrum	AR [42] ST 101 103	hy	4
F	2	0	-1	2	4	2	0	2	F	Jam lucis orto sidere	AR 78 AM 1	hy	6
c	2	0	-1	2	4	2	0	2	G	Praecursor pro nobis ingreditur	LA 25 WA 22	re	7
F	2	0	-1	2	4	5	2	0	F	Ego dixi Domine miserere	GR 311 SYG 239 GB 247 GS 141	gr	5
F	2	0	-1	2	4	5	2	0	F	Gloria et honore coronasti ... et constituisti	SYG 217	gr	6
G	2	0	[0	0	0	0	0	0]	G	Kyrie	MEL #84		
G	2	[0	0	0	0	0	0	0]	E	Kyrie	MEL #85		
G	2	0	2	-3	0	-2	-3	-5	G	Domine si tu es jube me	LR 362 *LA 414 *WA 327	re	8
F	2	0	2	-3	0	2	4	2	F	Priusquam te formarem	GR 524 LU 1500 SYG 196 GB 198^{v} *GS 1	gr	5
c	2	0	2	-2	-3	-2	-3	-5	G	Gloria	BOS #3		IV
G	2	0	2	-2	0	-2	-3	-2		Dixit Moyses et Aaron Precatus est Moyses	OTT 97 GB 79 *SYG 89	ofv	
G	2	0	2	-2	0	[0	0	0]	G	Agnus Dei	SCH #101		
G	2	0	2	-2	0	2	0	2	G	Agnus Dei ... requiem	GR 101*		8
G	2	0	2	-2	0	2	0	2	G	Agnus Dei XVIII	GR 58* OHS 213 LU 63		8
G	2	0	2	-2	0	2	0	2		Attendite popule meus in legem meam Portas caeli	OTT 60 GB 136^{v} SYG 158	ofv	

G	2	0	2	-2	0	2	0	2	G	Nihil inquinatum in eam	LR 267	re	8
G	2	0	2	-2	2	5	4	5	G	Michael et angeli ejus	PM 191	re	7
G	2	0	2	-2	2	5	7	5	F	Placentes Deo facti	WA 373	an	5
c	2	0	2	0	-5	-3	-5	-7	G	Deus Israel propter te	OHS 241 (nm) WA 114	re	8
F	2	0	2	0	-5	-3	-5	0		Vitam petiit et tribuisti Desiderium animae	OTT 153 *SYG 215	ofv	
G	2	0	2	0	-5	0	-2	0	G	Ite missa est XIV	GR 50* LU 56		8
G	2	0	2	0	-5	0	-2	0	G	Kyrie XIV Jesu redemptor	GR 47* LU 54		8
G	2	0	2	0	-5	0	-2	0	D	Kyrie o theos generis (etc)	MEL #68		
c	2	0	2	0	-3	-5	-3	-1	F	Deus in loco sancto suo	GR 347 LU 1024 SYG 245 GB 253 GS 152	int	5
g	2	0	2	0	-3	-2	-3	-5		Domine in lumine vultus Laetentur omnes	PM 122 VP 97	rev	
G	2	0	2	0	-3	-2	0	2	G	Domine secundum actum meum	AR [172] LU 1798 *LA 555 *WA 437	re	8
F	2	0	2	0	-3	-1	0	2		In capite libri scriptum Hostiam et oblationem	GR 61	trv	
F	2	0	2	0	-3	0	-1	0		Ad te clamaverunt et salvi Deus Deus meus	GR 180 OHS 109 LU 594 GS 86 GB 109 SYG 122	trv	
F	2	0	2	0	-3	0	-1	0		Eripiam eum et glorificabo Qui habitat	GR 95 LU 533 GS 35 GB 65 SYG 73	trv	
F	2	0	2	0	-3	0	-1	0		Futurum est enim ut Herodes Angelus Domini	GR 6**	trv	
F	2	0	2	0	-3	0	-1	0		Lex Dei ejus in corde Apud Dominum	GR 528	trv	
F	2	0	2	0	-3	0	2	-1		Nequando dicant gentes Adjuva nos	GR [131]	trv	
c	2	0	2	0	-3	0	2	4		Fluminis impetus ... civitatem Adjuvabit eam	GR [56] LU 1221 GS 181 *GB 50 SYG 50	grv	
F	2	0	2	0	-3	0	2	5	F	Respice in me et miserere mei	GR 327 LU 981 SYG 240 GB 248 GS 143	int	6
F	2	0	2	0	-3	2	-1	0		Speravit in Domino Deus Deus meus	GR 180 OHS 109 LU 594 *GS 86 *GB 109 *SYG 122	trv	
c	2	0	2	0	-3	2	0	2	G	Laetatus sum in his	GR 139 LU 560 SYG 100 *GB 89v *GS 63 162	gr	7
c	2	0	2	0	-3	2	0	2	G	Rogate quae ad pacem	GR [135] LU 1285	gr	7
G	2	0	2	0	-2	-5	-3	-2	G	Spiritus Domini replevit orbem	LR 118 *LA 256 *WA 155	re	8
G	2	0	2	0	-2	0	-2	-5	G	Vos qui transituri estis	LA 161 *WA 102	re	8
G	2	0	2	0	-2	0	-2	0	G	Caelestium contemplator	WA 313	re	7
G	2	0	2	0	-2	0	-2	2	G	Kyrie	MEL #81		
G	2	0	2	0	-2	0	2	-2	G	Dixit Ruben fratribus suis	LA 150 *WA 97	re	8
G	2	0	2	0	-2	0	2	-2	G	Trium puerorum cantemus	AR 379 AM 352 WA 93 LA 85	an	8

D	2	0	2	0	-2	0	2	0	[D]	Agnus Dei	SCH #222		2
G	2	0	2	0	-2	0	2	0	G	Beata es N. quae propter Deum	LR 230	re	7
G	2	0	2	0	-2	0	2	0	G	Psallite Deo qui ascendit	WA 150	re	8
D	2	0	2	0	-2	0	2	3		Magnus sanctus Paulus	GR 419 LU 1346	alv	
G	2	0	2	0	-2	0	2	5	G	Adam vetus quod polluit	ST 367	hy	8
G	2	0	2	0	-2	0	2	5	G	Agnoscat omne saeculum	ST 367	hy	8
G	2	0	2	0	-2	0	2	5	G	Audi fili mi	WA 171	re	7
G	2	0	2	0	-2	0	2	5	G	Derelinquat impius viam	LA 131	re	8
G	2	0	2	0	-2	0	2	5		Everte cor ejus in odium Recordare mei	OTT 125	ofv	
G	2	0	2	0	-2	0	2	5	G	In monte Oliveti oravit	GR 168 *OHS 375 *LU 633 LA 189 WA 118	re	8
G	2	0	2	0	-2	0	2	5	G	Labia insurgentium et cogitationes	AR 427 OHS 191 219 WA 114 LA 185 AM 406	an	8
G	2	0	2	0	-2	0	2	5	G	Nunc tibi virgo virginum	ST 399	hy	8
G	2	0	2	0	-2	0	2	5	G	O sancta mundi domina	ST 399	hy	8
G	2	0	2	0	-2	0	2	5	G	Per lignum servi facti sumus	SYG 175 *GS 186 236	co	8
G	2	0	2	0	-2	0	2	5	G	Radix Jesse floruit	ST 367	hy	8
G	2	0	2	0	-2	0	2	5	G	Statura erat rotarum	WA 374	re	8
G	2	0	2	0	-2	0	2	5	G	Unum in tribus colimus	ST 391	hy	8
G	2	0	2	0	-2	0	2	5		Ut discam mandata Servus tuus	LA 143 WA 94	rev	
D	2	0	2	0	-2	0	3	2	D	Kyrie	MEL #182		
G	2	0	2	0	-2	2	0	5	G	Gaude sacrata meritis	ST 145	hy	8
D	2	0	2	0	-2	2	3	5	D	Alleluia: beatus Petrus dum penderet	SYG 203	al	1
D	2	0	2	0	-2	2	3	5		Beatus Petrus dum penderet	SYG 203	alv	
D	2	0	2	0	-2	2	3	5		Hoc jam tertio	SYG 160	alv	
G	2	0	2	0	-2	2	4	5	G	Alleluia: exaudi Deus orationem	GB 246v *SYG 243	al	7
G	2	0	2	0	-2	2	5	2	G	O sancte N. concivis	WA 418	re	8
G	2	0	2	0	-2	2	5	4	G	Aperiens Tobias os suum	WA 177	re	8
G	2	0	2	0	-2	2	5	4	G	Deus Domini mei Abraham	LA 122 *WA 83	re	8
G	2	0	2	0	-2	2	5	4	G	Sumite psalterium jucundum	PM 192	re	7
G	2	0	2	0	-2	2	5	4	F	Vos qui aliquando eratis	VP 186	re	5
G	2	0	2	0	-2	2	5	4	F	Vos qui transituri estis	LR 412	re	5
G	2	0	2	0	-2	2	5	7	G	Adducunt beato Mauro caecum	LR 278	re	8
G	2	0	2	0	-2	2	5	7	G	Alleluia: post dies octo ... stetit	GR 262 LU 810 *GS 124 SYG 163 GB 144v	al	7

G	2	0	2	0	-2	2	5	7	G	Alleluia: sancti et justi in Domino gaudete	SYG 222	al	7
G	2	0	2	0	-2	2	5	7	G	Antequam comedam suspiro	LA 282 *WA 172	re	7
G	2	0	2	0	-2	2	5	7	G	Ave Maria gratia plena ... spiritus	PM 244 LA 3 378	re	7
G	2	0	2	0	-2	2	5	7	G	Beata progenies unde Christus	PM 262 LR 249 *LA 459 *WA 367	re	7
G	2	0	2	0	-2	2	5	7		Sancti et justi in Domino	SYG 222	alv	
D	2	0	2	0	-2	3	5	7	D	Simile est regnum caelorum sagenae	WA 430	an	1
G	2	0	2	0	-2	5	4	2	G	Kyrie	MEL #80		
c	2	0	2	0	-1	-3	-1	-5	G	Senex puerum portabat	LA 348 WA 270	re	8
c	2	0	2	0	-1	-3	-1	0	G	Avertantur retrorsum et erubescant	OHS 370 LU 628 *WA 118 *LA 189	an	8
c	2	0	2	0	-1	-3	-1	0	c	Sanctus	THAN #13		
c	2	0	2	0	-1	-3	0	-1	G	Alleluia	AM 162 473	an	7
c	2	0	2	0	-1	-3	0	-1	G	Regnum tuum Domine	AM 160 *WA 60 *LA 105	an	7 8
c	2	0	2	0	-1	0	-1	-3	c	Paucitas dierum meorum	LA 284 *WA 173	re	6
c	2	0	2	0	-1	0	2	-3	G	Quis mihi tribuat	WA 173	re	8
c	2	0	2	0	-1	0	2	-1		Me autem propter innocentiam Domine spes mea	GR 518 LU 1494	grv	
c	2	0	2	0	-1	0	2	0		Igne me examinasti Probasti Domine	GR 579 LU 1594 GS 194 GB 217^{v} SYG 213	grv	
c	2	0	2	0	2	-3	2	0		Inclina aurem tuam ad precem Domine Deus salutis	OTT 112 *GB 74 SYG 84	ofv	
G	2	0	2	0	2	-2	0	2	G	Os suum aperuit sapientiae	LR 226	re	7
D	2	0	2	0	2	-2	2	5	D	Extrahentes Joseph de lacu	LA 147	re	1
c	2	0	2	0	2	0	-1	-3		Statuit supra petram pedes meos Exspectans exspectavi	OTT 104 GB 92 SYG 104	ofv	
D	2	0	2	0	2	0	2	-2	D	Beata Agatha ingressa carcerem	PM 137 LA 362 *WA 275	re	1
G	2	0	2	0	2	0	2	0	G	Iterum autem videbo vos	LA 237	an	8
c	2	0	2	0	2	0	2	0		Verba mea auribus percipe Gloriabuntur in te	OTT 135	ofv	
c	2	0	2	0	2	0	2	0		Verba mea auribus percipe Intende voci	OTT 83 GB 87^{v} *SYG 98	ofv	
C	2	0	2	0	2	0	2	4	D	Alleluia: confessor Domini Benedicte	SYG 207	al	2
G	2	0	2	0	2	0	2	4	G	Dixit Joseph underim fratribus	LA 151 *WA 98	re	7
F	2	0	2	0	2	0	2	4	F	Esto mihi in Deum protectorem	GR 339 LU 1013 SYG 103 GB 91 GS 64 149	gr	5
G	2	0	2	0	2	0	2	4	G	Formavit igitur Dominus hominem	LA 109 *WA 72	re	8
G	2	0	2	0	2	0	2	4		Vos estis lux mundi	SYG 218 GB 235^{v}	alv	
G	2	0	2	0	2	0	2	5	G	Coepit Hippolytus tristis	WA 352	re	7

G	2	0	2	0	2	0	2	5	G	Ecce ego mitto vos	LR 136 LA 506 *WA 411	re	7
G	2	0	2	0	2	0	2	5	G	Ecce homo sine querela	WA 426	re	7
G	2	0	2	0	2	0	2	5	G	Honestum fecit illum	LR 154 206 *LA 526	re	7
G	2	0	2	0	2	0	2	5	G	Nuntiaverunt Jacob	LR 410 *LA 152 WA 98	re	7
G	2	0	2	0	2	0	2	5	G	Oremus omnes ad Dominum dixit	WA 409	re	7
G	2	0	2	0	2	0	2	5	G	Surgens ergo mane Jacob	LA 550	re	7
G	2	0	2	0	2	0	2	5	G	Videntes Joseph a longe	LR 408 *LA 146 WA 96	re	8
G	2	0	2	0	2	0	5	4	G	Noli esse mihi Domine	LA 177 *WA 111	re	8
G	2	0	2	0	2	0	7	5	G	Gloriosus es Oswaldus	WA 390	re	7
D	2	0	2	0	2	3	2	0	D	Agnus Dei	SCH #221		2
C	2	0	2	0	2	4	0	-3	C	Grata facta est a Domino	LA 321 *WA 244	re	6
F	2	0	2	0	2	4	0	-3	F	Tuam crucem adoramus ... passionem	SYG 130	co	6
c	2	0	2	0	2	4	0	-3	c	Tuam crucem adoramus ... passionem	WA 369	re	6
G	2	0	2	0	2	4	0	-2	G	Advenerunt nobis dies	AR 87 *AM 97 112 *PM 48 WA 89	an	8
G	2	0	2	0	2	4	0	-2	G	Stetit Moyses coram Pharaone	LA 156 WA 101	re	8
F	2	0	2	0	2	4	0	-1	F	Christus factus est pro nobis	AR 434 OHS 410 LU 659 AM 420	an	5
F	2	0	2	0	2	4	0	-1	F	Christus factus est pro nobis	GR 196 OHS 444 LU 669 GS v 94 235 SYG 129 GB 115	gr	5
F	2	0	2	0	2	4	0	2	F	Alleluia	WA 136 137	inv	6
G	2	0	2	0	2	4	0	2	G	Dixit angelus ad Jacob	LA 140 *WA 93	re	7
F	2	0	2	0	2	4	0	2	F	Exiit sermo inter fratres	GR 39 LU 422 SYG 24 GB 24^{v} GS 16	gr	5
c	2	0	2	0	2	4	0	2	c	Occurrit beato Joanni	WA 39 LA 49	an	6
F	2	0	2	0	2	4	0	4	F	Nesciens mater virgo virum	PM 39 *WA 32 *LA 39	an	6
F	2	0	2	0	2	4	0	4	F	Regali ex progenie	AR 834 LU 1626 AM 1032 *WA 368 *LA 461	an	6
c	2	0	2	0	2	4	2	0		Agnus Dei	SCH #19		
G	2	0	2	0	2	4	2	0	G	Agnus Dei	SCH #86		
F	2	0	2	0	2	4	2	4	F	Videns Jacob vestimenta	LA 148 WA 96	re	6
F	2	0	2	0	2	4	5	2	F	Ego sapientia habito	GR 25**	gr	5
G	2	0	2	0	2	4	5	4	G	O crux gloriosa	LA 397 *WA 369	re	7
G	2	0	2	0	2	4	5	4	G	Unus ex discipulis meis	OHS 391 LU 645 *LA 191 *WA 118	re	8
G	2	0	2	0	2	4	5	7	G	Ibat igitur Saulus	LA 344 *WA 263	re	7
G	2	0	2	0	2	4	5	7	G	Ostendit mihi angelus fontem	LA 227 *WA 141	re	7

G	2	0	2	0	2	4	5	7	G	Sepelierunt Stephanum	LA 45	re	7
F	2	0	2	0	2	4	7	4	F	Bonitas Domini Dei	LU 1444	of	5
F	2	0	2	0	2	4	7	4	F	Populum humilem salvum	GR 341 LU 1015 OTT 93 *SYG 107 GB 95^{v} *GS 69 149	of	5
c	2	0	2	0	2	5	4	2	D	Alleluia: spiritus sanctus procedens	GS M 137	al	2
G	2	0	2	0	2	5	4	2	G	Beati estis sancti ... meruistis ... ideoque	LR 389 *WA 396	re	7
G	2	0	2	0	2	5	4	2	G	Fulgebunt justi et tanquam	WA 429	re	7
G	2	0	2	0	2	5	4	5	G	Ductus est Jesus in desertum ... accedens	LA 131 WA 87	re	7
G	2	0	2	0	2	5	4	5	G	Ecce radix Jesse ascendet	LA 15 380 WA 15	re	8
G	2	0	2	0	2	5	4	5	G	Eripe me de inimicis meis Deus	GR 161 OTT 46 SYG 113 GB 101^{v} GS 75	of	7
G	2	0	2	0	2	5	4	5	G	Facta autem hac voce	LA 260 WA 155	re	7
G	2	0	2	0	2	5	4	5	G	Hic est fratrum amator	LA 298 WA 182	re	7
G	2	0	2	0	2	5	4	5	G	Hic est praepositus paradisi	WA 383	re	7
G	2	0	2	0	2	5	4	5	G	In principio erat verbum	LR 66	re	7
G	2	0	2	0	2	5	4	5	G	In principio erat verbum ... omnia	WA 30	re	7
G	2	0	2	0	2	5	4	5	G	Isti sunt agni novelli	OHS 823 LR 169 LA 212 WA 134 305	re	7
G	2	0	2	0	2	5	4	5	G	Isti sunt duae olivae	WA 329	re	7
G	2	0	2	0	2	5	4	5	c	Jussit Valerianus	WA 351	re	7
G	2	0	2	0	2	5	4	5	G	Nolite timere non separabuntur	LA 327	re	7
c	2	0	2	0	2	5	4	5		Quando certa lege Gyrum caeli	WA 168	rev	
G	2	0	2	0	2	5	4	5	G	Spiritus sanctus replevit totam	LR 116 *LA 258 WA 156	re	7
G	2	0	2	0	2	5	4	5	G	Ubi est Abel frater tuus	LA 112 WA 74	re	7
G	2	0	2	0	2	5	4	5	G	Viri Galilaei quid admiramini	LR 105 LA 250 WA 149	re	7
G	2	0	2	0	2	5	4	5	G	Zoe uxor Nicostrati	LA 327	re	7
G	2	0	2	0	2	5	7	5	G	Dixit Dominus ad Adam	WA 73	re	7
C	2	0	2	0	2	5	7	5	D	Factum est silentium ... committeret	LA 465 WA 380	re	1
G	2	0	2	0	2	5	7	5	G	Immisit Dominus soporem ... et cum	LR 343	re	7
G	2	0	2	0	2	5	7	5	G	Martyres sancti per fidem	WA 422	re	7
G	2	0	2	0	2	5	7	5	G	Missus est Gabriel angelus	PM 23 *LA 3 377	re	7
G	2	0	2	0	2	5	7	5	G	Non vos me elegistis	LR 118	re	8
G	2	0	2	0	2	5	7	5	G	Tollite hinc vobiscum	LR 409 *LA 149 *WA 97	re	7
G	2	0	2	0	2	5	7	5	G	Tollite jugum meum	LR 137 *LA 506 WA 411	re	7

G	2	0	2	0	4	2	0	4	G	Alleluia: videbitis et gaudebit	GR 510 LU 1483	al	8
F	2	0	2	0	4	2	4	2	F	Adjuva sancte tuos precibus	SYG 230	gr	6
G	2	0	2	0	4	5	2	5	G	Sanctus	THAN #79		8
C	2	0	2	0	5	4	5	7	D	Ecce Dominus veniet et omnes ... tunc	LA 19	re	1
G	2	0	2	0	5	4	5	7	G	O Cuthberte	WA 296	an	8
D	2	0	2	0	7	9	7	5	D	Ad coenam agni providi	ST 53	hy	1
D	2	0	2	3	0	-2	0	3	D	Magnum salutis gaudium	ST 118	hy	2
D	2	0	2	3	5	2	0	3	D	Alleluia: dilexisti justitiam	SYG 229	al	1
D	2	0	2	3	5	3	2	3	D	Alleluia: quia factus es susceptor	GR 470	al	2
D	2	0	2	3	5	3	2	3	D	Alleluia: sacerdos sit sanctus sicut	GR [119]	al	2
D	2	0	2	3	5	3	5	8	F	Libera nos salva nos	WA 158	an	6
c	2	0	2	4	0	-3	-5	0	c	Hodie dies illuxit	WA 153	an	6
c	2	0	2	4	0	-3	-5	0	c	Laetentur omnes qui sperant ... in aeternum	PM 122 VP 97	re	6
F	2	0	2	4	0	-3	-1	0	F	Accepit Jesus calicem	LR 128 LU 932	re	6
F	2	0	2	4	0	-3	-1	0	d	Agnus Dei	SCH #139		6
c	2	0	2	4	0	-3	-1	0	c	Igne fervoris divini	WA 294	re	6
c	2	0	2	4	0	-3	0	2	c	Principes persecuti sunt me	LA 182 *WA 113	re	6
c	2	0	2	4	0	-2	-3	-2	c	Magne Deus nostrae laudis	WA 318	re	6
c	2	0	2	4	0	-2	0	5	c	In circuitu tuo	WA 392	an	6
F	2	0	2	4	0	-1	-3	0	G	Hodie afflictus sum valde	OHS 625 LU 776^{c}	an	8
F	2	0	2	4	0	-1	-3	2	G	Spiritus et animae justorum	AR [29] LU 1121 AM 633 *WA 307	an	8
F	2	0	2	4	0	-1	2	-1	F	Genuisti qui te fecit	AR 882^{3} LU 1686	an	6
c	2	0	2	4	0	2	-3	2	a	Factus sum sicut homo	OHS 613 LU 770 *WA 126 LA 204	an	4
c	2	0	2	4	0	2	-3	2	a	O mors ero mors tua	AR 440 OHS 618 LU 773 AM 445 *WA 127 LA 206	an	4
c	2	0	2	4	0	2	-3	2	a	Sion renovaberis	AR 229 LU 1083 AM 201 *WA 13 *LA 12	an	4
F	2	0	2	4	0	2	0	-3	F	Agnus Dei VIII	GR 31* LU 39 SCH #138		6
F	2	0	2	4	0	2	0	-3		Et ex corde diligamus Ubi caritas	GR 204 OHS 451	anv	
c	2	0	2	4	0	2	0	-3	c	Numquam inquinatum corpus	WA 245	re	6
F	2	0	2	4	0	2	0	-3		Timeamus et amemus Deum Ubi caritas	GR 204 OHS 451	anv	
F	2	0	2	4	0	2	0	-1	F	Ecce sacerdos magnus qui	GR [32] LU 1183 1495^{A} SYG 27 GB 28^{v} GS 220	gr	5

F	2	0	2	4	0	2	0	-1	F	Pontifex sacerdos magnus inter fratres	GR [118]	gr	5
F	2	0	2	4	0	2	0	-1	F	Propter fratres meos	GR 527 LU 1512	gr	5
c	2	0	2	4	0	2	0	2	c	Agnus Dei	SCH #18		8
F	2	0	2	4	0	2	0	2	F	Domine Deus virtutum non discedimus	GR 111**	int	6
c	2	0	2	4	0	2	0	2	c	Honor virtus et potestas	WA 160	re	6
F	2	0	2	4	0	2	0	2	F	Justi epulentur ... delectentur	GR 412 SYG 214 GB 219^{v} GS 211	int	6
c	2	0	2	4	0	2	0	2	c	Sanctus	THAN #12		8
F	2	0	2	4	0	2	0	4	F	Beati qui custodiunt judicium	GR 91**	of	6
F	2	0	2	4	0	2	0	4	F	Gaudeamus omnes fideles	PM 37 *WA 32 *LA 38	an	6
c	2	0	2	4	0	2	0	4	c	Psallentes Christo Christum	WA 248	inv	6
F	2	0	2	4	0	2	0	5	F	Agnus Dei	SCH #148		6
F	2	0	2	4	0	2	0	5	F	Homo guidam fecit ... et misit	AR 112* PM 105 LR 419 LU 1856 AM 1189 VP 15	re	6
F	2	0	2	4	0	2	0	5	F	Virgo flagellatur crucianda	PM 214 VP 251	re	6
F	2	0	2	4	0	2	0	5	F	Virgo parens Christi benedicta	AR 131* VP 39 LU 1862	re	6
c	2	0	2	4	0	2	0	5	c	Vita verbo est Wulstanus	WA 248	an	7
F	2	0	2	4	0	2	4	2	F	Adoremus Dominum qui vos	WA 109	inv	6
c	2	0	2	4	0	2	4	2	c	Adoremus Dominum quoniam	LA 96 WA 67	inv	6
F	2	0	2	4	0	2	4	2	F	Christus apparuit nobis	WA 57	inv	6
F	2	0	2	4	0	2	4	2	F	Dominum Deum nostrum	LA 103 WA 70	inv	6
c	2	0	2	4	0	2	4	2	c	Dominum qui fecit nos	LA 100 WA 69	inv	6
c	2	0	2	4	0	2	4	2	c	Prope est jam Dominus	LA 22 WA 17	inv	6
F	2	0	2	4	0	2	4	2	F	Regem cui omnia vivunt	AR [152] LU 1779	inv	6
F	2	0	2	4	0	2	4	2	F	Regem venturum Dominum	WA 8	inv	6
F	2	0	2	4	0	2	5	4	F	Virgo potens sicut turris	AR 871 LU 1679 AM 1072	an	6
F	2	0	2	4	0	4	5	4	F	Virgo hodie fidelis	VP 73 WA 30 *LA 38	an	6
F	2	0	2	4	0	4	7	4	F	Speciosa facta es et suavis ... viderunt	PM 276	an	6
F	2	0	2	4	2	-1	0	2	D	Petrus quidem servabatur	LA 415	an	1
F	2	0	2	4	2	-1	0	5	F	Kyrie	MEL #116		
G	2	0	2	4	2	0	-3	-2	G	Kyrie Jesu redemptor (etc)	MEL #64		
c	2	0	2	4	2	0	-3	-2	c	Omnes sancti qui estis	WA 397	re	6
G	2	0	2	4	2	0	-2	2	[G]	Agnus Dei	SCH #88		8
c	2	0	2	4	2	0	-1	0	G	Dominus mecum est tamquam	LA 178 *WA 111	re	7 8
c	2	0	2	4	2	0	2	-3	a	Joseph opifex sancte	LU 1447	an	4

F	2	0	2	4	2	0	2	-3	F	Scindite corda vestra	WA 86	re	6
c	2	0	2	4	2	0	2	-3	a	Sion noli timere	AR 223 LU 1081 AM 194 WA 9 20 *LA 22	an	4
c	2	0	2	4	2	0	2	-3	a	Vade jam et noli peccare	WA 90	an	4
F	2	0	2	4	2	0	2	0	F	Domine Deus in simplicitate cordis	GR [74] OTT 159 LU 1252 SYG 264 GB 175v GS 175	of	6
F	2	0	2	4	2	0	2	0	F	Holocaustum et pro peccato	GR [115] LU 974	of	6
F	2	0	2	4	2	0	2	0	F	Non habemus hic manentem	GR 23**	of	6
F	2	0	2	4	2	0	2	0	F	O quam admirabile est nomen	WA 33	an	6
F	2	0	2	4	2	0	2	0	F	Requiem aeternam dona eis Domine	GR 94* LU 1807 SYG 235 *GB 265v GS 232	int	6
F	2	0	2	4	2	0	2	0	F	Splendor paternae gloriae	ST 441	hy	6
G	2	0	2	4	2	0	2	0	G	Venite benedicti patris ... quod	SYG 75	tr	8
c	2	0	2	4	2	0	2	0	c	Vere felicem praesulem	WA 289	re	6
F	2	0	2	4	2	0	2	4	F	Ave Maria gratia plena	WA 7	inv	6
F	2	0	2	4	2	0	2	4	D	Christe caelorum habitator alme	ST 423	hy	2
F	2	0	2	4	2	0	2	4	D	Fili praebe mihi cor tuum	AM 566	an	1
F	2	0	2	4	2	0	2	4	F	In manu tua Domine	LA 93 *WA 66	inv	6
G	2	0	2	4	2	0	2	4	b	Jesu redemptor omnium	AR [57]	hy	4
F	2	0	2	4	2	0	2	4	F	Mitte manum tuam	GR 263 407 LU 811 1328 SYG 164 GB 146 GS h 125	co	6
F	2	0	2	4	2	0	2	4	D	O pater sancte mitis atque pie	ST 423	hy	2
F	2	0	2	4	2	0	2	4	D	O veneranda trinitas laudanda	ST 422	hy	2
F	2	0	2	4	2	0	2	4	F	Venite exsultemus Domino	WA 63	inv	6
c	2	0	2	4	2	0	2	5	c	Praeditus hinc juvenis	WA 284	re	6
F	2	0	2	4	2	0	5	4	F	Kyrie	MEL #121		
F	2	0	2	4	2	4	0	2	F	Flores apparuerunt in terra	GR 439 LU 1376	gr	5
F	2	0	2	4	2	4	0	2	F	Propter veritatem ... et deducet	GR 583 620 (31) LU 1676 SYG 215 GB 222v GS s	gr	5
F	2	0	2	4	2	4	2	0	F	Angelus Domini Raphael apprehendit	GR 634 LU 1699	gr	5
F	2	0	2	4	2	4	2	0	F	Domine Dominus noster	GR 342 LU 1017 *SYG 244 GB 252 GS 150	gr	5
F	2	0	2	4	2	4	2	0	F	Domine spes mea	GR 518 LU 1494	gr	5
F	2	0	2	4	2	4	2	0	F	Ibant parentes Jesu	LR 314	re	6
F	2	0	2	4	2	4	2	0	G	Isti sunt sermones	AR 483 *AM 498 *WA 134 *LA 219	an	8
c	2	0	2	4	2	4	2	0	c	Jubilemus Deo salutari	LA 90 WA 65	inv	6
F	2	0	2	4	2	4	2	0	E	Juxta vestibulum et altare	GR 85 LU 523 WA 206 GS 30	an	4

C	2	0	2	4	2	4	2	0	E	Ne reminiscaris Domine delicta mea	AR 547 LU 992 1840 *AM 584 *WA 176	an	4
F	2	0	2	4	2	4	2	0	D	Non in justificationibus	GB 160	an	1
F	2	0	2	4	2	4	2	0	F	Quoniam respexisti humilitatem	GR (35)	gr	5
F	2	0	2	4	2	4	2	0	F	Spiritu sancto replevit	WA 156	re	5
F	2	0	2	4	2	4	2	0	F	Spiritus Domini super me propter	GR [100] LU 1283[A]	gr	5
F	2	0	2	4	2	4	2	0	F	Unam petii a Domino ... omnibus	GR 60 1** LU 471	gr	5
F	2	0	2	4	2	4	2	0	F	Unam petii a Domino ... ut videam	GR 92 *SYG 68 GB 64 GS 33	gr	5
F	2	0	2	4	2	4	2	4	G	Dicite invitatis ecce prandium	AR 570 AM 610 *WA 190 *LA 318	an	8
G	2	0	2	4	2	4	5	4		Beati estis sancti ... qui cotidie	SYG 222	alv	
F	2	0	2	4	2	4	5	4	F	Sanctificavit Moyses altare	GR 374 OTT 114 LU 1057 *SYG 254 *GB 259[v] GS 162	of	5
G	2	0	2	4	2	4	5	7	E	Ad nutum Domini nostrum	AR 130* *PM 187 *WA 365	re	3
C	2	0	2	4	2	4	5	7	D	Alleluia: verba mea auribus percipe	GR 312 *GS 141 *SYG 239 *GB 247[v]	al	2
F	2	0	2	4	2	4	6	2	G	Qui sunt hi sermones	AR 448 OHS 778 LU 788 AM 461 *LA 217 231	an	8
F	2	0	2	4	2	4	7	2	F	O veneranda martyrum gloriosa	VP 255 *WA 423	re	6
C	2	0	2	4	2	5	4	5	E	Similitudo vultus animalium	WA 372	re	3
F	2	0	2	4	2	7	4	7	G	Alleluia: spiritus omnia scrutatur	SYG 186	al	8
C	2	0	2	4	5	2	0	2	D	Ait Petrus principibus	WA 326	an	2
F	2	0	2	4	5	2	0	2	F	Caput tuum ut Carmelus	AM 971 *AR 787	an	6
C	2	0	2	4	5	2	0	2	D	Cui sol luna	WA 379	an	2
G	2	0	2	4	5	2	0	2	E	Homo quidam fecit ... et vocavit	AR 537 LU 1101 AM 557 *WA 187 *LA 310	an	3
F	2	0	2	4	5	2	0	2	F	Maria ergo unxit pedes	AM 977 *AR 793 *GS 96 SYG 132	an	6
C	2	0	2	4	5	2	0	2	D	Praesul Christi Dunstanus	WA 312	re	1
F	2	0	2	4	5	2	0	2	D	Qui sine peccato templi est oblatus	ST 486	hy	2
G	2	0	2	4	5	2	4	2	G	Ad coenam agni providi	ST 419	hy	8
C	2	0	2	4	5	2	4	2	D	Angeli archangeli ... patriarchae	AR 897 LU 1721 AM 1101 LA 479	an	2
G	2	0	2	4	5	2	4	2	E	Et ingressae non invenerunt	LA 223 *234	an	3
G	2	0	2	4	5	2	4	2	E	Gloriosae virginis Mariae ortum	WA 368	an	3
G	2	0	2	4	5	2	4	5	G	Aurora caelum purpurat	AR 458	hy	8
G	2	0	2	4	5	2	4	5	G	Aurora lucis rutilat	AM 455 470	hy	8
G	2	0	2	4	5	2	4	5	G	Nunc sancte nobis spiritus	AM 472 LU 808	hy	8
G	2	0	2	4	5	2	4	5	G	Te lucis ante terminum	AM 469	hy	8

G	2	0	2	4	5	4	0	2	E	Petrus quidem servabatur	AR 799 LU 1577 AM 989	an	3
c	2	0	2	4	5	4	2	-3	D	Gloria	BOS #2		I
F	2	0	2	4	5	4	2	0	F	Agnus Dei	SCH #142		6
c	2	0	2	4	5	4	2	0	c	Ascendente Jesu in naviculam	AR 338 LU 1108 *AM 308 LA 107	an	6
G	2	0	2	4	5	4	2	0	G	Beata nobis gaudia	ST 122	hy	7
G	2	0	2	4	5	4	2	0	E	Claudus quidam cum vidisset	LA 412	an	3
C	2	0	2	4	5	4	2	0	E	Diligebat autem eum Jesus	LA 48	an	4
G	2	0	2	4	5	4	2	0	E	Diligebat autem eum Jesus	LA 55 *WA 40	re	3
G	2	0	2	4	5	4	2	0	E	Domum istam protege Domine	LA 550 *SYG 135	an	3
F	2	0	2	4	5	4	2	0	F	Gloria	BOS #38		III
G	2	0	2	4	5	4	2	0	D	Isti sunt sancti qui pro testamento	LA 390	re	2
G	2	0	2	4	5	4	2	0	D	Lignum vitae crucem	SYG 141	an	1
F	2	0	2	4	5	4	2	0		Memoria memor ero Accepit Jesus	LR 128 LU 932	rev	
F	2	0	2	4	5	4	2	0	G	Missus est angelus Raphael	AR 890 LU 1701	an	8
F	2	0	2	4	5	4	2	0	G	Missus est Gabriel angelus	AR 247 668 [139] LU 1416 AM 222 861 *WA 18 *LA 24 376	an	8
C	2	0	2	4	5	4	2	0	D	O crux mirabile signum	SYG 141	an	1
F	2	0	2	4	5	4	2	0	F	Qui operatus est Petro	GR 418 LU 1345 SYG 204 GB 208 GS 178 h (inc)	gr	5
c	2	0	2	4	5	4	2	0	F	Sanctus	THAN #11		5
G	2	0	2	4	5	4	2	0	G	Sanctus	THAN #78		8
G	2	0	2	4	5	4	2	0	F	Verbum supernum prodiens nec patris	ST 350	hy	6
G	2	0	2	4	5	4	2	4	G	Adduxisti sanctos tuos	LA 551	re	7
c	2	0	2	4	5	4	2	4	c	Benedicta sit creatrix	AR 520 LU 908 *AM 538 *WA 162	an	6
C	2	0	2	4	5	4	2	4	D	Gloriosa es Maria Magdalena	WA 335	re	1
G	2	0	2	4	5	4	2	4	E	Gloriosi principes terrae	LA 418	an	3
C	2	0	2	4	5	4	2	4	E	Homo erat in Jerusalem	LA 352	an	4
G	2	0	2	4	5	4	2	4	G	Kyrie omnipotens pater	MEL #67		
c	2	0	2	4	5	4	2	4	c	Loquens Dominus ad Noe	WA 76	an	6
G	2	0	2	4	5	4	2	4	E	Multa quidem et alia	LA 230 234	an	3
C	2	0	2	4	5	4	2	4	E	Ne reminiscaris Domine delicta nostra	PM 328 LA 293	an	4
G	2	0	2	4	5	4	2	4	E	Quantam denique messem	WA 239	re	3
C	2	0	2	4	5	4	2	4	E	Quis ex vobis arguet	WA 108	an	4
G	2	0	2	4	5	4	2	5	G	Agnus Dei	SCH #87		8

C	2	0	2	4	5	4	2	5	E	In honore beatissimae Mariae	WA 353	inv	4
C	2	0	2	4	5	4	2	5	E	In honore beatissimae matronae	WA 339	inv	4
G	2	0	2	4	5	4	2	5	G	Mirabantur omnes de his	GR 73 LU 491 SYG 43 *GS 24	co	7
F	2	0	2	4	5	4	2	5	F	Regina caeli laetare alleluia	AR 67 OHS 743 LU 275 AM 176	an	6
F	2	0	2	4	5	4	2	5	F	Regina caeli laetare alleluia	AR 69^{1} OHS 744 LR 48 LU 278 AM 179	an	6
F	2	0	2	4	5	4	2	7	F	Gloria	BOS #27		III
G	2	0	2	4	5	4	5	2	G	Alleluia: justum deduxit ... regnum	GB 271	al	8
F	2	0	2	4	5	4	5	4	F	Introibo in domum tuam	GR 2**	of	5
F	2	0	2	4	5	4	5	4	F	Quid bonum ejus est	GR 628 LU 1691	of	5
G	2	0	2	4	5	4	5	4		Surrexit altissimus de sepulcro	SYG 158 *GS 127	alv	
G	2	0	2	4	5	4	5	7	G	Simon Petrus cum audisset	LA 220	an	8
F	2	0	2	4	5	4	7	4	F	Locus iste a Deo factus	GR [72] LU 1251 *SYG 263 GB 173^{v} GS 175	gr	5
F	2	0	2	4	5	4	7	4	F	Nova bella elegit Dominus	GR 40**	gr	5
C	2	0	2	4	5	7	4	2		Unus autem ex illis Caiphas Collegerunt pontifices	GR 166 GS 84	rev	
G	2	0	2	4	5	7	5	2	G	Alleluia: sancti tui Domine florebunt	SYG 222	al	8
G	2	0	2	4	5	7	5	4	G	Alleluia: vos estis lux	GB 235^{v} *SYG 218	al	7
G	2	0	2	4	5	7	5	4	G	Elegit Dominus virum de plebe	LA 329	re	7
G	2	0	2	4	5	7	5	4	G	Factus est mihi Dominus	LA 101 *WA 69	re	7
G	2	0	2	4	5	7	5	4	G	Impii super justum	LA 45 *WA 35	re	7
G	2	0	2	4	5	7	5	4	G	Ingressus Paulus in synagogam	LA 345 *WA 265	re	7
C	2	0	2	4	5	7	5	7	D	Alleluia: beati qui persecutionem	GB 267^{v}	al	2
C	2	0	2	4	5	7	5	7	D	Alleluia: expansis manibus beata	GB 244	al	1
G	2	0	2	4	5	7	5	9		Dixit Dominus Domino meo	SYG 248	alv	
F	2	0	2	4	6	4	2	0	F	Sanctus	THAN #121		6
F	2	0	2	4	6	7	2	0	F	Quinque prudentes virgines	GR [64] LU 1228 SYG 42 GB 45 *GS 230	co	5
F	2	0	2	4	6	7	6	7		Data est mihi omnis potestas	SYG 160	alv	
F	2	0	2	4	6	7	9	11	G	Audite vocem hymni	ST 498	hy	8
F	2	0	2	4	7	5	4	2	F	Benedicamus Domino XVIIb	GR 57*		6
F	2	0	2	4	7	5	4	2	F	Kyrie XVIIb	GR 56* LU 61		6
F	2	0	2	4	7	5	4	2	F	Kyrie	MEL #114		
F	2	0	2	4	7	6	2	4	G	Ecce de quo Joannes	WA 47	an	8

F	2	0	2	4	7	6	2	6	G	Stetit Jesus in medio	AR 449 OHS 782 *AM 462 WA 134 *LA 219 232	an	8
F	2	0	2	4	7	6	2	6	G	Videte manus meas	AR 449 OHS 787 LU 792 *AM 462 WA 139 *LA 219	an	8
G	2	0	2	5	0	2	0	-2	D	Kyrie creator	MEL #62		
G	2	0	2	5	0	2	0	2	E	Dilexisti justitiam et odisti	LR 221 *LA 543 *WA 431	re	3
G	2	0	2	5	2	0	2	0	G	Benedicam Dominum in omni tempore	GR 350 LU 1028 SYG 246 GB 253^{v} *GS 154	gr	7
C	2	0	2	5	2	0	2	0		Deus docuisti me	GR 519	alv	
G	2	0	2	5	2	0	2	0	E	Erit sanguis agni vobis	AR 767 LU 1531 *AM 951 *PM 164	an	3
C	2	0	2	5	2	0	2	0		Et esto ibi usque dum dicam Angelus Domini	GR 6**	trv	
C	2	0	2	5	2	0	2	0		Fiat pax in virtute tua Laetatus sum in his	SYG 101	trv	
C	2	0	2	5	2	0	2	0		Populo qui nascetur Deus Deus meus	GR 180 OHS 109 LU 594 *GS 86 GB 109 SYG 122	trv	
G	2	0	2	5	2	0	4	0	E	Corde et animo Christo	WA 367	re	4
C	2	0	2	5	2	0	5	7	D	Pontificalis apex	WA 277	an	1
C	2	0	2	5	2	4	0	2	D	Ingressus angelus ad Mariam	WA 301	re	1
C	2	0	2	5	2	4	2	0	D	Alme confessor Domini	WA 428	an	1
C	2	0	2	5	2	4	2	0	D	Iter faciente Jesu	AR 355 LU 510 AM 329 *WA 83 *LA 124	an	1
C	2	0	2	5	2	4	2	0	D	Simile est regnum caelorum decem ... quinque	WA 435	an	1
C	2	0	2	5	2	4	2	0	D	Simile est regnum caelorum homini negotiatori	AM 685 746	an	1
C	2	0	2	5	2	4	2	0	D	Stans beata Agatha	AR 624 LU 1372 *AM 806 WA 276 (inc illeg) LA 364	an	1
c	2	0	2	5	2	4	2	0	c	Veniat dilectus meus	WA 354 *LA 456	an	6
F	2	0	2	5	2	4	5	4	F	Ideo sunt ante thronum	AR 764 LU 1529 *AM 949	an	6
G	2	0	2	5	2	4	5	4	E	Quadam die tempestate	WA 240	re	3
G	2	0	2	5	2	4	5	4	E	Videns ergo vir beatus	WA 288	re	3
C	2	0	2	5	2	4	5	7	D	Alleluia: ego sum vitis vera	SYG 171	al	2
C	2	0	2	5	2	4	5	7	E	Christus Jesus splendor Patris	AR 804 LU 1584 *AM 997	an	4
G	2	0	2	5	2	7	5	7	G	Alleluia: fundamenta ejus	SYG 263	al	7
G	2	0	2	5	4	0	2	0	G	Miserere mei fili David	AR 358 LU 518 AM 332 *WA 83 *LA 125	an	8
G	2	0	2	5	4	0	2	0	E	O crucifer bone lucis sator	ST 479	hy	4
G	2	0	2	5	4	0	2	5	G	Alleluia: beati estis ... qui cotidie	SYG 222	al	8

G	2	0	2	5	4	2	0	2	G	Alleluia: dedit illi Dominus scientiam	GB 272	al	8
G	2	0	2	5	4	2	0	2	E	Arridebat parvulus occisori	WA 43	an	3
G	2	0	2	5	4	2	0	2	E	Continge ergo sepulchrum	WA 243	an	3
C	2	0	2	5	4	2	0	2	D	Exsultet caelum laudibus	ST 337	hy	2
F	2	0	2	5	4	2	0	2		In ecclesiis benedicite Confirma hoc	OTT 79 *GB 189v SYG 183	ofv	
G	2	0	2	5	4	2	0	2	E	Pretiosi Dei sancti	PM 200	an	3
G	2	0	2	5	4	2	0	2	E	Serve bone et fidelis intra	AR [56] LU 1177 *AM 658 *WA 427	an	3
C	2	0	2	5	4	2	0	5	D	Ego sum alpha et omega ... ego sum	PM 69	an	1
C	2	0	2	5	4	2	0	5	D	Ego sum alpha et omega ... manus	WA 136 225 *SYG 147 *GS 125	an	1
C	2	0	2	5	4	2	0	5	[D]	Tibi Christe splendor patris	ST 194	hy	[1]
G	2	0	2	5	4	2	4	2	E	Adhuc eo loquente	AR 806 LU 1589	an	3
G	2	0	2	5	4	2	4	2	E	Alabastrum unguenti	WA 335	an	3
G	2	0	2	5	4	2	4	2	G	Beata nobis gaudia	ST 294	hy	8
C	2	0	2	5	4	2	4	2	D	Clamabat autem mulier	WA 94 *LA 142	an	1
G	2	0	2	5	4	2	4	2	E	Dum jactantur puppes	WA 292	an	3
C	2	0	2	5	4	2	4	2	D	Ecce carissimi dies illa	WA 207 *SYG 72	an	2
C	2	0	2	5	4	2	4	2	E	Ego enim ex Deo	WA 90	an	4
F	2	0	2	5	4	2	4	2	F	Gloriosi principes terrae	AR 774 *AM 958 *WA 325	an	6
G	2	0	2	5	4	2	4	2	E	Hortus conclusus amica mea	WA 356	an	4
G	2	0	2	5	4	2	4	2	E	Infra annos adolescentiae	LR 274	an	3
C	2	0	2	5	4	2	4	2	E	Pretiosus martyr Christi	WA 36	an	4
G	2	0	2	5	4	2	4	5	G	Laetentur omnes qui sperant ... quoniam	LR 192 *WA 424 *LA 529	an	8
c	2	0	2	5	4	2	5	2	c	Ne perdideris me Domine	LA 94 *WA 62	re	6
G	2	0	2	5	4	2	5	2	E	Regem angelorum Dominum	LR 449	inv	3
G	2	0	2	5	4	2	5	2	E	Regem apostolorum Dominum	LR 134 *WA 411	inv	3
G	2	0	2	5	4	2	5	2	E	Regem archangelorum Dominum	LR 447 *LA 464	inv	3
G	2	0	2	5	4	2	5	2	E	Regem praecursoris Dominum	LR 345 *LA 400 *WA 320	inv	3
C	2	0	2	5	4	2	5	2	D	Summa laus dulcis melodia	PM 174 *WA 379	an	2
C	2	0	2	5	4	2	5	4	D	Alleluia: spiritus qui a Patre	GB 191v	al	2
G	2	0	2	5	4	2	5	7	G	Sanctus Benedictus dilectum	LR 277	re	7
c	2	0	2	5	4	2	7	5		Gabrielem archangelum scimus Gaude Maria	PM 146 *AM 1195 VP 130 *LA 354 *WA 271	rev	
c	2	0	2	5	4	2	7	9		Beata es quae credidisti Gaude Maria	VP 130	rev	

F	2	0	2	5	4	5	2	0	F	Alleluia: Dominus dabit verbum evangelizantibus	GR 59**	al	6
F	2	0	2	5	4	5	2	0	F	Alleluia: surrexit Christus jam	GS 131	al	6
G	2	0	2	5	4	5	2	4	E	Benedictus in dies	LR 323	an	3
F	2	0	2	5	4	5	4	2	D	Cives caelestis patriae	ST 65	hy	1
c	2	0	2	5	4	5	4	2	c	Jesum quem quaeritis	LA 216 *234	an	6
C	2	0	2	5	4	5	4	5	E	Omnipotentem semper adorent	ST 489 GS 172	hy	4
G	2	0	2	5	4	5	7	5	G	Alleluia: fundata est domus ... supra	SYG 264	al	7
G	2	0	2	5	4	5	7	5	G	Angelus ad pastores ait	LR 63 LA 32	re	7
C	2	0	2	5	4	5	7	5	D	Architectus Deus fundavit	GB 174	alv	
G	2	0	2	5	4	5	7	5	G	Beatus vir qui suffert tentationem	LR 160 *WA 418	re	7
G	2	0	2	5	4	5	7	5	G	Crux fidelis inter omnes ... sustinuit	PM 152 WA 369	re	7
G	2	0	2	5	4	5	7	5	G	Gloria et honore coronasti ... Domine et constituisti	LR 160 LA 526 WA 418	re	7
G	2	0	2	5	4	5	7	5	G	Hic est praecursor dilectus	LR 353 VP 177	re	7
G	2	0	2	5	4	5	7	5	G	Homo peregre profectus	GR 92**	co	7
G	2	0	2	5	4	5	7	5	G	Hortus conclusus soror mea	LR 270	re	7
C	2	0	2	5	4	5	7	5	E	In adventu summi regis	PM 22	an	4
G	2	0	2	5	4	5	7	5	G	Paradisi portas aperuit nobis	PM 51 LA 129 WA 86	re	8
G	2	0	2	5	4	5	7	5	E	Quasi unum ex paradisi	PM 34 WA 38 *LA 48	an	3
G	2	0	2	5	4	5	7	5	G	Qui sunt isti qui ut nubes	LA 510	re	7
G	2	0	2	5	4	5	7	5		Quoniam praevenisti eum in benedictionibus Corona aurea	GR 12**	grv	
G	2	0	2	5	4	5	7	5	G	Tibi laus tibi gloria ... in saecula	WA 160	re	7
G	2	0	2	5	4	5	7	5	G	Tolle puerum et matrem	GR 46 LU 436 SYG 30 GB 31^v GS H	co	7
G	2	0	2	5	4	5	7	9	G	Alleluia: surrexit altissimus Dominus	GB 146	al	7
F	2	0	2	5	7	4	2	0		Unus autem ex ipsis Caiphas Collegerunt pontifices	WA 210 *SYG 117 *GR 105^v	anv	
C	2	0	2	5	7	4	2	4	D	Alleluia: Christus passus est pro nobis	GR 481	al	1
C	2	0	2	5	7	5	2	5	D	Beatus Dei athleta	WA 259	re	1
G	2	0	2	5	7	5	4	2	G	Alleluia: O quam beata es virgo	GB 223	al	7
G	2	0	2	5	7	5	4	2	G	Alleluia: O quam beatus est Dei apostolus	GB 227	al	7

C	2	0	2	5	7	5	4	2	E	Lucem tuam Domine nobis concede	VP 30	an	4
C	2	0	2	5	7	5	4	2		Potestas ejus potestas aeterna	GR 639 LU 1711	alv	
G	2	0	2	5	7	5	4	5	G	Damasci praepositus gentis	WA 265	re	7
G	2	0	2	5	7	5	4	5	G	Haec est virgo sapiens quam	LR 225 *LA 544 WA 432	re	7
G	2	0	2	5	7	5	4	5	G	Hic est Martinus electus	PM 343 *LA 481 WA 399	re	7
G	2	0	2	5	7	5	4	5	G	Meruit esse hostia	WA 350	re	7
G	2	0	2	5	7	5	4	5		O quam beata es virgo	GB 223	alv	
G	2	0	2	5	7	5	4	5		O quam beatus est Dei	GB 227	alv	
G	2	0	2	5	7	5	4	5	G	Sebastianus Mediolanensium	LA 325	re	7
G	2	0	2	5	7	5	4	5	G	Tantas per illum Dominus	WA 387	re	7
E	2	0	2	5	7	5	7	5	G	Alleluia: ecce quam bonum et quam	GB 201^{v}	al	8
G	2	0	2	5	7	5	7	9	G	Protexisti me Deus a conventu	GR [15] LU 1146 SYG 169 GB 153 GS 205	int	7
G	2	0	2	5	7	5	7	10	G	Tenuisti manum dexteram	GR 462 LU 1418	int	7
F	2	0	2	6	4	2	4	2	F	Jesum quem quaeris	WA 134	an	6
D	2	0	3	0	2	0	-2	0		Nonne cor nostrum ... dum loqueretur	GB 131	alv	
D	2	0	3	0	2	0	-2	3	D	Non auferetur sceptrum	LA 18 *WA 23	re	2
D	2	0	3	5	2	0	3	2	D	Euge nunc Dunstane	WA 313	an	1
D	2	0	3	5	2	3	0	-2	D	Ambulans Jesus juxta mare	WA 232 *LA 497	an	1
D	2	0	3	5	3	2	0	-2	D	Ambiens speciosus ejus	WA 40	an	1
D	2	0	3	5	3	2	0	7	D	Sanctus	THAN #186		1
D	2	0	3	5	7	9	10	12	D	Kyrie	MEL #181		
c	2	0	4	2	0	-3	-1	-3		Gressus meos dirige secundum	GR [143]	alv	
F	2	0	4	2	0	-1	0	-3		Posui adjutorium meum super potentem Veritas mea	OTT 148 GB 41^{v} SYG 38	ofv	
F	2	0	4	2	0	-1	2	4	F	Agnus Dei	SCH #151		6
F	2	0	4	2	0	2	0	2	F	Anima nostra sicut passer	GB 210^{v} SYG 206 GS 219	co	6
F	2	0	4	2	0	2	0	2	F	Panem de caelo dedisti nobis	GR 356 LU 1035 *SYG 248 *GB 254^{v} GS 156	co	5
F	2	0	4	2	0	2	0	2	F	Veritas mea et misericordia	GR 64** GS 223	co	6
F	2	0	4	2	0	2	0	4	F	Simon Joannis diligis me	GR 531 SYG 204 GS o *GB 203^{v}	co	6
F	2	0	4	2	4	0	2	4	G	Ego sum panis vivus qui	WA 157	an	8
F	2	0	4	2	4	0	4	7	F	Justi decantaverunt Domine	GR 444 LU 1384	int	5
F	2	0	4	2	4	2	0	2	F	Gloria et divitiae	GR 572 LU 1587	of	6
C	2	0	4	2	5	4	0	2	D	Gratias tibi Deus gratias	AR 517 LU 907 AM 534	an	1
G	2	0	4	2	5	4	0	4	G	Veri adoratores adorabunt	LA 155 WA 100 (inc illeg)	an	8

G	2	0	4	2	5	4	2	0	G	Mirabantur omnes in verbis	LR 310	an	8
G	2	0	4	2	5	4	2	4	G	Confundantur omnes qui	AR 139 OHS 355 LU 290	an	8
G	2	0	4	2	5	4	2	5	G	Diviserunt sibi vestimenta mea	OHS 479 LU 688 *WA 122 LA 195	an	8
G	2	0	4	2	5	4	2	5	G	In innocentia cordis	AR 130	an	8
G	2	0	4	2	5	4	2	5	G	Longe fecisti notos meos	OHS 502 LU 707 *WA 123 LA 198	an	8
C	2	0	4	2	5	9	7	5	D	Alleluia: angelus Domini apparuit	GR 5**	al	1
C	2	0	4	2	5	9	7	5	D	Alleluia: Deus docuisti me a juventute	GR 519	al	1
C	2	0	4	2	5	9	7	5	D	Alleluia: ego Dominus inebriabo animam	GR 91**	al	1
F	2	0	4	2	7	6	7	9	G	Spiritus qui a Patre procedit	AR 513 LU 896 AM 529	an	8
F	2	0	4	2	7	6	7	9	G	Spiritus qui a Patre procedit	GR 299 LU 892 *GB 191^{v} *GS 139	co	8
C	2	0	4	5	2	5	7	9	D	Hodie sanctus Maurus	AM 782	an	1
G	2	0	4	5	4	0	2	-2	E	Sanctus	THAN #77		3
G	2	0	4	5	4	2	0	2	G	Kyrie immense conditor	MEL #61		
C	2	0	4	5	4	2	0	5	D	Tibi Christe splendor patris	ST 97	hy	2
C	2	0	4	5	4	2	4	2	D	Surgens Dominus Jesus stans	SYG 149	an	1
G	2	0	4	5	4	2	5	7	G	Insurrexerunt in me testes iniqui	OHS 481 LU 690 *WA 122 *LA 195	an	8
G	2	0	4	5	4	5	4	7		Cognoscetur Dominus judicia Sperent in te	OTT 85 *GB 100 *SYG 112	ofv	
G	2	0	4	5	4	5	7	5	E	Gloriosus confessor ... orationem	AM 964	an	3
c	2	0	4	5	7	2	0	2	G	Hic est discipulus qui testimonium	LA 50 *WA 40	re	7
G	2	0	4	5	7	5	4	0	G	Alleluia: tamquam filiis dico dilatamini	GR 547	al	8
G	2	0	4	5	7	5	4	7	G	Vadis propitiator ad immolandum	PM 188 *WA 122	re	7
F	2	0	4	6	2	0	-3	-1	F	Sanctus	THAN #120		6
F	2	0	4	6	7	2	0	2	F	Dixit Dominus Deus non est	LA 110 *WA 73	re	5
F	2	0	4	7	4	6	7	4	G	Tibi soli peccavi Domine	AR 150 *AM 58 *WA 68 *LA 98	an	8
F	2	0	4	7	4	7	9	4	F	Non pepercisti animae tuae	AR 3 (sup 1)	an	6
G	2	0	4	7	5	4	2	4	E	Fac benigne in bona voluntate	AR 387 AM 361 *WA 98 LA 152	an	3
G	2	0	4	7	5	4	2	5	G	Alleluia: tamquam prodigium factus sum	GR 622^{2} LU 1681^{3}	al	8
F	2	0	4	7	6	2	-1	0	G	Fecit mihi magna	AR 301 LU 445 AM 278	an	8
F	2	0	4	7	6	2	4	2	G	Hic est beatissimus evangelista	VP 84	an	8

F	2	0	4	7	6	4	2	0	G	Ecce nunc palam loqueris	WA 146 *LA 243	an	8
F	2	0	4	7	6	4	2	4	G	Ego sum Gamaliel	WA 343	an	8
F	2	0	4	7	6	4	6	7	G	Alleluia	AM 61	an	8
F	2	0	4	7	6	4	6	7	G	Stephanus vidit caelos	AR 274 AM 251 LU 1583[A] *WA 37 LA 43	an	8
F	2	0	4	7	6	4	7	6	G	Vidi civitatem ... ornatam	WA 135	an	8
F	2	0	4	7	6	7	4	0	G	Ecce nunc tempus ... in his	AR 372 LU 540 AM 345 *WA 85 *LA 134	an	8
F	2	0	4	7	6	7	4	2	G	Ego sum pastor ovium	AR 467 LU 816 AM 481 WA 142 LA 235	an	8
F	2	0	4	7	6	7	9	7	G	Ecce ego vobiscum sum omnibus diebus	AR 10 (sup 2)	an	8
F	2	0	4	7	9	7	4	2	G	Missus est angelus Gabriel ... in civitatem	AM 886	an	8
F	2	0	4	7	9	7	4	6	G	Collaudate regem	WA 149	an	8
F	2	0	4	7	9	7	4	6	G	Exaltate regem regum	AR 492 LU 851 AM 509 LA 251	an	8
F	2	0	4	7	9	7	6	4	F	Alleluia	AM 50	an	5
F	2	0	4	7	9	7	6	4	G	Confitebor tibi Domine quoniam	AR 342 AM 312 *WA 74 *LA 113	an	8
F	2	0	4	7	9	7	6	4	G	Rabbi quid peccavit homo	AR 402 LU 1095 AM 378	an	8
F	2	0	4	7	9	7	6	4	G	Rabbi quis peccavit hic	WA 104 LA 164	an	8
F	2	0	4	7	9	7	9	7	F	Omnes angeli ejus	AR 354 WA 79 *LA 92 124	an	5
F	2	0	4	7	9	7	9	7	F	Vox clamantis in deserto	AR 228 LU 1082 AM 200 *WA 13 *LA 12	an	5
F	2	0	4	7	9	11	12	11		Et in terra	BOS #32		
G	2	0	5	0	2	0	-3	-5		Gemma lucens Rosa vernans	VP 52	alv	
G	2	0	5	0	2	0	-3	-5		Rosa vernans castitatis	VP 52	alv	
G	2	0	5	0	2	5	7	5	G	Almi prophetae progenies pia	ST 296	hy	8
D	2	0	5	0	3	2	0	7	D	Kyrie	MEL #190		
G	2	0	5	2	0	4	0	2	G	Sanctus	THAN #76		7
C	2	0	5	2	4	2	0	5	D	Lugebat autem Judam	AR 550 LU 994 *AM 588	an	1
C	2	0	5	2	5	7	9	10	D	Nonne cor nostrum ... dum loqueretur	AR 480 AM 495 *WA 63 133 LA 218	an	1
F	2	0	5	4	0	2	0	2	F	Agnus Dei	SCH #141		5
G	2	0	5	4	2	-5	-2	-3		Salve virga florens	VP 53	alv	
G	2	0	5	4	2	0	-5	0	G	Kyrie	MEL #63		
c	2	0	5	4	2	0	-1	-3	c	Agnus Dei	SCH #22		5
G	2	0	5	4	2	0	2	0	G	Hymnizemus regi Christo	ST 310	hy	8

c	2	0	5	4	2	0	2	4		Condemnat autem justus	GR 71**	alv	
G	2	0	5	4	2	0	2	4	E	Sancta virgo Scholastica	LR 292	re	3
G	2	0	5	4	2	0	4	5	G	Kyrie	MEL #66		
C	2	0	5	4	2	0	5	7	D	Fructum salutiferum	LR 120 LU 922	an	1
C	2	0	5	4	2	0	5	7	D	Iste dilectus Joannis	ST 412	hy	2
C	2	0	5	4	2	0	5	7	D	Lacte quondam profluentes	AM 1021	hy	2
C	2	0	5	4	2	0	5	7	D	Te beata sponsa Christi	AM 813	hy	2
C	2	0	5	4	2	0	5	7	D	Tibi Christe splendor patris	ST 58 429 LR 447 AM 1056	hy	2
G	2	0	5	4	2	0	7	9		Virga Jesse floruit	GR ⌊79⌋ LU 1267	alv	
F	2	0	5	4	2	4	-3	0	F	Agnus Dei	SCH #147		1
F	2	0	5	4	2	4	0	-3	F	Kyrie	MEL #115		
F	2	0	5	4	2	4	0	2		Audi filia ... quia concupivit	GB 272^v	alv	
F	2	0	5	4	2	4	0	2		Domine in virtute tua	GR 333 LU 1003 GB 249^v GS 144 *SYG 240	alv	
F	2	0	5	4	2	4	0	2		Magnificat anima mea ... et exsultavit	GR 587^3 49** LU 1612^2	alv	
G	2	0	5	4	2	4	0	2	G	Sanctus ad lib. III	GR 91* LU 87 THAN #230		8
F	2	0	5	4	2	4	0	2		Vir Dei Benedictus omnium justorum	GR (25)	alv	
C	2	0	5	4	2	4	0	5		Surrexit quasi ignis	GR 66**	alv	
G	2	0	5	4	2	4	0	7	G	Sanctus	THAN #75		
G	2	0	5	4	2	4	2	0	G	Magne pater Augustine	ST 133	hy	7
G	2	0	5	4	2	4	2	0	G	Sanctus	THAN #74		8
G	2	0	5	4	2	4	2	4		Christus resurgens ex mortuis	SYG 168	alv	
G	2	0	5	4	2	5	2	5	E	Regem baptizatum Dominum	WA 58	inv	3
C	2	0	5	4	2	9	7	11		Surgens Dominus Jesus et stans	SYG 156	alv	
G	2	0	5	4	5	2	0	2	G	Prima autem die azymorum	SYG 120 *WA 208	an	8
F	2	0	5	4	5	2	0	4	F	Sanctus	THAN #118		5
G	2	0	5	4	5	4	2	0	D	Miserere et parce clementissime	AR 159*		1
G	2	0	5	4	5	7	[0	0]	G	Kyrie	MEL #65		
G	2	0	5	4	5	7	4	5	G	Apparuerunt apostolis dispertitae	LR 112 *LA 260 *WA 156	re	7
G	2	0	5	4	5	7	5	2	G	Circumduxit eam et docuit	GR 618 LU 1671	co	7
G	2	0	5	4	5	7	5	4	G	Alleluia: haec est vera fraternitas	GR 495 LU 1492^A 1508 *GB 231^v	al	8
c	2	0	5	4	5	7	5	4	c	Ecce jam cari noscite	WA 300	re	6
G	2	0	5	4	5	7	5	4		Haec est vera fraternitas	GR 495 LU 1492^A 1508 GB 231^v	alv	

G	2	0	5	4	5	7	5	4	G	Pectore sincero Maria	WA 337	re	7
G	2	0	5	4	5	7	5	7	G	Cum sanctus Benedictus in cella	LR 327 *LA 370 *WA 299	re	7
G	2	0	5	4	5	7	5	7	G	Laudabile miraculum	WA 289	re	7
G	2	0	5	4	5	7	5	7	G	Sanctus Benedictus post triduum	LR 298	re	7
G	2	0	5	4	5	7	9	5		Exsultate Deo adjutori	GR 348 LU 1026 GS 150 SYG 244 GB 253	alv	
G	2	0	5	4	5	7	9	5	G	Febus et Cornelius	WA 409	re	7
G	2	0	5	4	5	7	9	5		Haec est generatio	GR 114**	alv	
G	2	0	5	4	5	7	9	5	G	Lapides pretiosi omnes	PM 239 LR 242 LA 550	re	7
G	2	0	5	4	5	7	9	5		Nihil inquinatum in eam	GR 51**	alv	
G	2	0	5	4	5	7	9	5	G	Vos qui secuti ... sedebitis ... dicit	WA 413	re	8
G	2	0	5	4	5	7	9	7	G	Aurora lucis rutilat	ST 287	hy	8
G	2	0	5	4	5	7	9	7		Exsultabo et laetabor	GR [148] *LU 841B	alv	
G	2	0	5	4	5	7	9	10		Confitebuntur caeli mirabilia ... etenim	GR [16] LU 1147 1465B SYG 171 GS 216 (nm)	alv	
G	2	0	5	4	7	9	7	5	G	Alleluia: confitebuntur caeli ... etenim	GR [16] LU 1147 1465B SYG 171 GS 216 (nm)	al	7
G	2	0	5	4	7	9	7	5	G	Alleluia: de profundis clamavi ad te	GR 388 LU 1076 *SYG 255 *GB 264v GS 164	al	7
G	2	0	5	4	7	9	7	5	G	Alleluia: exsultabo et laetabor	GR [148] *LU 841B	al	7
G	2	0	5	4	7	9	7	9	G	Alleluia: Domine refugium factus es nobis	GR 355 (39) LU 1034 GS 153 SYG 245 *GB 254v	al	7
G	2	0	5	4	7	9	7	9	G	Alleluia: justum deduxit ... regnum	SYG 214	al	7
G	2	0	5	4	7	9	7	9	G	Alleluia: surrexit altissimus de sepulcro	SYG 158 GS 127	al	7
G	2	0	5	4	7	9	7	9		De profundis clamavi ad te	GR 388 LU 1076 *SYG 255 *GB 264v *GS 164	alv	
G	2	0	5	7	4	0	2	5	G	Alleluia: vir obediens loquetur	GR (5)	al	7
G	2	0	5	7	5	2	4	2		Venite ad me omnes	GR 648 [114] LU 973 1726 *SYG 218	alv	
G	2	0	5	7	5	4	0	2	C	Benedicamus Domino Id	AR 59* LU 125		5
G	2	0	5	7	5	4	0	2		In multitudine presbyterorum	GR 528 LU 1513	alv	
C	2	0	5	7	5	4	2	5	D	O quam veneranda es egregie	LA 537	an	1
G	2	0	5	7	5	7	2	0		Posui adjutorium super potentem	GS 224	alv	
C	2	0	5	7	5	7	9	7	C	Cum audisset populus quia Jesus	GR 172 PM 56 GS 80 *SYG 117	an	5
G	2	0	5	7	9	5	4	5		Gloria et honore coronasti ... Domine et constituisti	GB 23 *SYG 201	alv	
G	2	0	5	7	9	7	4	7	G	Ingressus est Raphael angelus	PM 199	an	7

C	2	0	5	7	9	7	5	4	D	In die quando venerit	SYG 71	an	1
C	2	0	5	7	9	7	9	11	D	Dum commiterent bellum	WA 383 *LA 471	an	1
G	2	0	5	7	9	7	10	7		Mane nobiscum Domine	SYG 156	alv	
G	2	0	5	7	9	7	10	7		Quoniam Deus magnus Dominus	GR 361 LU 1042 GS 156 SYG 246 GB 255^{v}	alv	
C	2	0	5	7	9	11	9	7	D	Excelsi regis filium	WA 379	an	1
F	2	0	6	4	0	2	0	4	F	Sanctus	THAN #119		5
C	2	0	7	4	5	4	2	4	D	Alleluia: hoc jam tertio	SYG 160	al	1
G	2	0	7	4	5	7	2	0	G	Egredietur virga ... et flos	GR 622^{6} LU 1684	gr	7
C	2	0	7	5	2	0	2	7	E	Tenuisti manum dexteram	GR 179 OHS 108 LU 593 *SYG 122 GB 109 *GS 86	gr	4
C	2	0	7	5	2	0	7	4	G	Dilexisti justitiam et odisti	GR [52] LU 1216 *SYG 5 *GB 4 *GS 226	gr	8
G	2	0	7	5	4	5	2	0	G	In sanctitate fulgida	WA 431	re	8
G	2	0	7	5	7	10	7	9	G	Lapides torrentes illi	WA 36	re	7
G	2	0	7	9	7	9	7	9		Quasi palma exaltata	GR 34**	alv	
a	2	3	-2	0	-2	-4	-2	0	D	Filiae Jerusalem venite	LR 169 *LA 389 *WA 304	re	1
D	2	3	-2	0	2	3	-2	0	D	Magnum salutis gaudium	ST 9	hy	1
D	2	3	-2	0	2	3	-2	0	D	Stephano primo martyri	ST 8	hy	1
D	2	3	-2	0	3	5	7	5	E	Exsulta filia Sion	GR 32 LU 406 SYG 17 *GB 16^{v} *GS F	co	4
D	2	3	-2	2	0	3	2	3	D	Ex ore infantium Deus	GR 40 LU 427 SYG 25 GB 26 GS 17	int	2
D	2	3	-2	2	0	3	5	7	E	Caro mea vere est cibus ... qui	LU 1623^{E}	co	4
a	2	3	0	-2	-4	-2	0	-2	G	Agatha sancta dixit	LA 357	an	8
D	2	3	0	-2	0	2	5	7	D	Agnus Dei XI	GR 41* LU 48 SCH #220		1
D	2	3	0	-2	0	3	0	2	D	Senex puerum portabat	AR 619 LU 1355 AM 801 LA 356 *WA 272	an	1
D	2	3	0	-2	0	3	2	-2	D	Calicem salutaris ... et nomen	AR 436 OHS 477 (nm) *AM 429 430 *WA 121 LA 194	an	2
D	2	3	0	-2	0	3	2	-2	D	Spiritus Domini super me evangelizare	AR 240 *AM 215 *WA 18 LA 24	an	2
D	2	3	0	-2	0	3	2	0	D	Gemma caelestis pretiosa regis	AM 961	hy	1
D	2	3	0	-2	0	3	2	0	D	Inter aeternas superum	AM 854	hy	1
D	2	3	0	-2	0	3	2	0	D	Iste confessor Domini colentes	AR [69] LU 1198	hy	1
D	2	3	0	-2	0	3	2	0	D	Laudibus cives resonent canoris	AM 848	hy	1
D	2	3	0	-2	3	5	3	5	D	Gloria tibi trinitas	AR 518 LU 914 AM 535 *WA 158	an	1
D	2	3	0	-2	3	5	3	7	D	Ecce Dominus meus omnia	AR 1 (sup 1)	an	1
D	2	3	0	-2	3	5	7	5	D	Alleluia: haec est virgo sapiens quam	GS 228	al	2

D	2	3	0	-2	3	5	7	5	D	Hodie egressa est virga	AR 590 LU 1321 AM 767	an	1
D	2	3	0	-2	3	5	7	5	D	Jucundis pangat mentibus	ST 125	hy	1
D	2	3	0	-2	5	7	5	3		Lux maris gaude	ST 305	hy	
D	2	3	0	2	0	-2	0	2	D	Alleluia: qui confidunt in Domino	GB 266^v	al	1
D	2	3	0	2	0	-2	0	3	D	Complaceat tibi Domine ... respice	AR [167] LU 1793	an	2
D	2	3	0	2	0	-2	0	3	D	Dominus Deus auxiliator	AR 421 OHS 65 AM 399 *WA 113 LA 181	an	2
D	2	3	0	2	0	-2	0	3	D	Dominus tamquam ovis ad victimam	AR 433 OHS 400 LU 653 *AM 414 415 *WA 120 LA 193	an	2
D	2	3	0	2	0	-2	0	3	D	Estote ergo misericordes	AR 521 LU 909 *AM 538 *WA 187 *LA 311	an	1
D	2	3	0	2	0	-2	0	3	D	Felix namque es sacra virgo et omni	LA 459	an	1
D	2	3	0	2	0	-2	0	3	D	Ignem veni mittere	AR 538^5 LU 966 AM 564	an	1
D	2	3	0	2	0	-2	3	5	D	Dabit illi Dominus Deus sedem	AR 894^5 LU 1704 AM 1091	an	1
D	2	3	0	2	0	2	0	2	D	Alleluia: beatus es Simon	GB 204^v	al	1
D	2	3	0	2	0	2	3	0	D	Deus omnium exauditor	LA 267 *WA 165	re	1
D	2	3	0	2	0	2	3	0	D	Justorum animae in manu ... mortis	LR 189	re	1
D	2	3	0	2	0	3	2	0	D	Si offers munus tuum	AR 556 LU 1005 AM 594 *WA 188 LA 312	an	1
D	2	3	0	2	3	0	3	7	D	Columna es immobilis	AR 593 AM 771 *WA 247 *LA 322	an	1
D	2	3	0	2	3	2	0	-2	D	Erat vultu placido	LA 373 *WA 333	re	1
D	2	3	0	2	3	5	7	5	E	In toto corde meo alleluia	LA 239 *WA 144	re	3 4
a	2	3	0	3	0	3	0	3	a	Rector potens verax Deus	ST 148	hy	2
D	2	3	0	3	5	7	5	7	D	Cum invocarem te exaudisti	GR 102 SYG 77 *GB 69 *GS 38	co	2
D	2	3	0	5	3	2	0	-2	D	Sanctus	THAN #185		1
D	2	3	0	5	3	2	3	0	E	Vos qui secuti ... dicit Dominus	GB 236^v	co	4
D	2	3	0	7	0	2	3	7	F	Agnus Dei	SCH #219		5
a	2	3	2	-2	0	2	3	2	[G]	Agnus Dei	SCH #48		7
D	2	3	2	-2	0	2	3	2	E	Vir iste in populo	LA 503 *WA 236	re	4
D	2	3	2	-2	2	3	0	-2		O Joachim sancte conjux	GR 585 LU 1609	alv	
D	2	3	2	-2	2	3	0	-2		O quam pulchra est casta generatio	GR 104**	alv	
D	2	3	2	-2	3	2	0	3	D	Sanctus XIV	GR 49* LU 55 THAN #184		1
d	2	3	2	0	-2	-3	-2	0		Viri usque gloria Regis iram non	WA 251	rev	
d	2	3	2	0	-2	0	-2	-5	C	Hodie summi consules	WA 329	an	6
d	2	3	2	0	-2	0	-2	-3		Quae apparuit intercessori Oswaldus bajulus	WA 284	rev	

D	2	3	2	0	-2	0	-2	0	D	Benedicta et venerabilis ... quae sine tactu	PM 249	re	2
G	2	3	2	0	-2	0	-2	0		Quam magna multitudo In te speravi	OTT 101 *GB 68^{v} *SYG 76	ofv	
D	2	3	2	0	-2	0	-2	3	D	Alleluia: in Deo speravit cor meum	GR [146]	al	1
D	2	3	2	0	-2	0	-2	3	D	Alleluia: non vos relinquam orphanos vado	GR 289 LU 856 GS K SYG 187	al	1
D	2	3	2	0	-2	0	-2	3	D	Alleluia: nonne cor nostrum ... loqueretur	GS 118 SYG 155	al	1
D	2	3	2	0	-2	0	-2	3		Non vos relinquam ... vado	GR 289 LU 856 GS K SYG 187	alv	
D	2	3	2	0	-2	0	2	0	D	O pie Deus qui primum hominem	OTT 178 *SYG 237	of	2
D	2	3	2	0	-2	0	2	0		Tota pulchra es Maria	GR 402 LU 1318	alv	
D	2	3	2	0	-2	0	2	3	D	Agnus Dei	SCH #218		2
D	2	3	2	0	-2	0	2	5	D	Agnus Dei	SCH #217		1
D	2	3	2	0	-2	0	3	2	D	Sanctus	THAN #183		1
D	2	3	2	0	-2	3	5	7	D	Ad coenam agni providi	ST 290 (var)	hy	1
a	2	3	2	0	-2	3	5	7	c	Alleluia: attendite popule meus	GB 253 *GS 149 *SYG 243	al	6
D	2	3	2	0	-2	3	5	7	D	Alleluia: benedicamus patrem	GR [85] LU 1274	al	1
D	2	3	2	0	-2	3	5	7	D	Alleluia: ego sum pastor bonus et cognosco	GR 47 264 LU 818	al	1
D	2	3	2	0	-2	3	5	7	D	Alleluia: ego sum pastor bonus qui pasco	SYG 165	al	1
D	2	3	2	0	-2	3	5	7	D	Alleluia: hic est vere martyr qui pro Christo	SYG 229	al	1
D	2	3	2	0	-2	3	5	7	D	Alleluia: iterum videbo vos	SYG 166	al	1
D	2	3	2	0	-2	3	5	7	D	Alleluia: mirabilis Dominus noster	GR 414 GS 216 SYG 176 GB 268^{v}	al	1
D	2	3	2	0	-2	3	5	7	D	Alleluia: per signum sanctae crucis	SYG 174	al	1
D	2	3	2	0	-2	3	5	7	D	Alleluia: post excessum beatissimi Martini	SYG 227	al	1
D	2	3	2	0	-2	3	5	7	D	Corde et animo Christo	LA 459	re	1
D	2	3	2	0	-2	3	5	7	D	Mirabantur omnes de his	GB 40	co	1
D	2	3	2	0	-2	3	5	7		Stabat sancta Maria	GR 596 LU 1633^{v}	alv	
D	2	3	2	0	-2	3	5	7		Stabunt justi in magna constantia	GS 185	alv	
D	2	3	2	0	-2	5	3	2	D	Egregie Christi martyr Sebastiane	LA 326	an	1
D	2	3	2	0	2	0	-2	0	D	Ego vox clamantis	LA 16	an	1
D	2	3	2	0	2	0	-2	0	D	Euge serve bone et fidelis ... dicit	AR 577^{15} [61] LU 262^{5} 1181 AM 661 740 LA 529	an	1
D	2	3	2	0	2	0	-2	0	D	Praecursor Christi magne baptista	PM 159	an	2

D	2	3	2	0	2	0	2	0	D	Ibat igitur Saulus	LA 340 WA 262 (inc illeg)	an	1
D	2	3	2	0	2	3	2	0	D	Domine ne in ira tua	LR 398 *LA 81 *WA 60	re	1
G	2	3	2	0	2	3	5	7	[G]	Agnus Dei	SCH #84		2
D	2	3	2	0	2	5	3	2		Et in terra	GR 87* LU 89		
D	2	3	2	3	0	7	3	0	D	Agnus Dei	SCH #216		1
D	2	3	2	3	0	7	3	0	D	Kyrie	MEL #180		
D	2	3	2	3	0	7	3	0	D	Sanctus	THAN #182		1
D	2	3	2	3	2	0	3	5	D	Ora pro nobis beate Martine	SYG 225	gr	2
D	2	3	2	3	5	3	2	5	E	Amen dico vobis quod uni	GR 101 GS 219 *GB 68 *SYG 193	co	4
D	2	3	2	3	5	3	2	5	D	Amen dico vobis quod vos	GR [47] LU 1206 *GS 179 SYG 45 55 *GB 209^v	co	1
D	2	3	2	3	5	3	2	5	D	Quae mihi fuerunt lucra	GR 622^5 LU 1681^6	co	1
D	2	3	2	3	5	3	5	7	C	Nemo te condemnavit mulier nemo	SYG 100	co	8
D	2	3	2	3	5	7	3	8	E	Confirma hoc Deus	GR 295 [94] LU 882 OTT 79 *GS 137 234 *GB 189^v *SYG 183	of	4
D	2	3	5	0	3	2	0	2	E	Secus decursus aquarum	LR 176 *WA 420 LA 513	an	4
D	2	3	5	2	3	0	-2	3	D	Ne tacueris Deus	AR 202 LU 279^v	an	1
a	2	3	5	2	3	0	2	3	G	Odo princeps altissime	ST 64	hy	7
D	2	3	5	2	3	2	-2	0	D	Erat pater ejus	AR 321 LU 468	an	1
D	2	3	5	2	3	2	0	-2	D	Eleemosynas illius enarrabit	AR 851	an	1
D	2	3	5	2	3	2	0	-2	D	Omnes qui habebant infirmos	AR 394 LU 1091 AM 369 *WA 157	an	1
D	2	3	5	2	3	2	0	-2	D	Qui me misit mecum est	AR 382 LU 1085 AM 356 WA 94 *LA 144	an	1
D	2	3	5	2	3	2	0	2		Et in terra	BOS #45		
D	2	3	5	2	3	2	0	2	D	Judicii signum tellus sudore madescit	ST 494	hy	1
D	2	3	5	2	3	2	0	2	E	Regrediente anima	AM 965	an	4
D	2	3	5	2	3	2	0	3	D	A bimatu et infra	AR 284 LU 427 AM 260 *WA 46	an	2
D	2	3	5	2	3	2	0	3	D	Caecus magis ac magis	AR 357 LU 516 AM 330 WA 83 *LA 125	an	1
D	2	3	5	2	3	2	0	3	D	Convertere Domine et deprecabilis	AR 150	an	1
D	2	3	5	2	3	2	0	3	D	Eruisti Domine animam	WA 438	an	1
D	2	3	5	2	3	2	0	3	D	Fulcite me floribus	AR 675 844 LU 1423 1639 AM 1048	an	1
D	2	3	5	2	3	2	0	3	D	Qui non colligit mecum	AR 389 LU 556 AM 364 *WA 97 LA 153	an	1

D	2	3	5	2	3	2	0	3	D	Vidit populus claudum	WA 340 LA 413	an	2
D	2	3	5	2	3	2	0	5	D	Agnus Dei	SCH #215		1
D	2	3	5	2	3	2	0	5	D	Gloria	BOS #53		I
D	2	3	5	2	3	2	0	5	D	Kyrie	MEL #179		
D	2	3	5	2	3	2	0	5	D	Sanctus	THAN #179		1
D	2	3	5	2	3	2	0	5	D	Sanctus	THAN #180		1
D	2	3	5	2	3	2	0	5	D	Sanctus	THAN #181		1
D	2	3	5	2	3	5	2	0	D	Alleluia: benedictus es Domine super sceptrum	SYG 261	al	1
D	2	3	5	2	3	5	2	0	D	Alleluia: per te Dei genitrix nobis est	GR 552 LU 1557 GS u	al	1
D	2	3	5	2	3	5	2	0		Benedictus es Domine super spectrum	SYG 261	alv	
D	2	3	5	2	3	5	2	3	D	Laurentius ingressus est	AR 813 LU 1596 *AM 1005 *WA 350 *LA 440	an	1
D	2	3	5	2	3	5	2	3	D	Omnis qui petit accipit	LA 243	an	1
D	2	3	5	2	3	5	3	2	D	Christus Dei filius	LU 1446	an	1
D	2	3	5	2	3	5	3	2	D	Ecce crucem Domini	AR 700 LU 1460 AM 899 1041 WA 369 *LA 463	an	1
D	2	3	5	2	5	2	0	3	E	Ambulabunt mecum in albis	LA 56	an	4
D	2	3	5	2	5	3	2	3	E	Primo dierum omnium	ST 84	hy	4
D	2	3	5	2	5	3	2	3	E	Somno refectis artubus	ST 86 182 213	hy	4
D	2	3	5	2	5	7	3	2	D	Ait dominus villico	AR 559 AM 598	an	1
D	2	3	5	2	5	7	3	2	E	Appenderunt mercedem meam	AR 426 OHS 189 215 AM 405 WA 114 LA 184	an	4
D	2	3	5	2	5	7	3	2	D	Ascendit Joseph a Galilaea	LR 302	an	1
D	2	3	5	2	5	7	3	2	D	Dederunt hostiam pro Domino	WA 269	an	1
D	2	3	5	2	5	7	3	2	D	Dixit Dominus paralytico	AR 569 AM 609 WA 190 LA 318	an	1
D	2	3	5	2	5	7	3	2	D	Dixit Dominus villico	WA 188 LA 313	an	1
D	2	3	5	2	5	7	3	2	D	Genuisti qui te fecit	AM 1082	an	1
D	2	3	5	2	5	7	3	2	D	Germinavit radix Jesse	AR 295 LU 443 *AM 272 WA 50 LA 65	an	1
D	2	3	5	2	5	7	3	2	D	In circuitu populi	AR 120 OHS 288 LU 286	an	1
D	2	3	5	2	5	7	3	2	D	Inclinavit se Jesus	AR 395 LU 1092 AM 370 WA 100 LA 155	an	1
D	2	3	5	2	5	7	3	2	E	Innuebant patri ejus	AR 736 LU 1503 AM 924 WA 323 LA 86 407	an	4
D	2	3	5	2	5	7	3	2	D	Visionem quam vidistis	AR 378 LU 550 AM 351	an	1
D	2	3	5	2	5	7	3	2	D	Visionem quam vidistis	GR 573 LU 1587	co	1

D	2	3	5	3	0	-2	0	3	E	En martyris Laurentii	ST 397	hy	4
D	2	3	5	3	0	2	3	-2	D	Laetamini in Domino et exsultate	GR 415 456 [20] OTT 140 LU 1151 1337 SYG 41 GB 44 *GS 218	of	1
D	2	3	5	3	0	2	3	2	E	Ejus quoque laudabile	WA 291	an	4
D	2	3	5	3	0	2	3	2	E	Intemerata virgo quae redemptorem	PM 270	an	4
D	2	3	5	3	0	2	3	2	E	Maternitas tua Dei genitrix	AR 882^{6} LU 1687	an	4
D	2	3	5	3	0	2	3	2	E	Rubum quem viderat	AR 295 LU 443 AM 272 WA 50 *LA 65	an	4
D	2	3	5	3	0	2	3	2		Solve jubente Deo terrarum	GR 563 LU 1576 GS 192 *SYG 203	alv	
D	2	3	5	3	0	3	2	-2	D	Fac mecum Domine signum	GR 134 SYG 98 GB 87^{v} *GS 60	int	2
D	2	3	5	3	0	3	2	-2	E	Quod dico vobis in tenebris ... dicit	GR [31] LU 1173 *GB 231 *GS t 220	co	4
D	2	3	5	3	0	3	5	3	D	Haec est virgo prudens	LR 217 LA 545	re	1
D	2	3	5	3	0	3	5	3	D	Impetum fecerunt unanimiter	LA 44 *WA 34	re	1
D	2	3	5	3	0	3	5	3	D	In conspectu gentium	LA 467 *WA 380	re	1
D	2	3	5	3	0	3	5	3	D	In dedicatione templi	LR 233 LA 548	re	1
D	2	3	5	3	0	3	5	3	D	O quam metuendus est locus	LR 239 *LA 550	re	1
D	2	3	5	3	0	3	5	3	D	Propter veritatem ... et deducet	LR 221 LA 545 *WA 431	re	1
D	2	3	5	3	0	3	5	3	D	Quam magna multitudo	LA 88 *WA 63	re	1
D	2	3	5	3	0	3	5	3	D	Seniores populi consilium	OHS 398 LU 651 LA 193 *WA 119	re	1
D	2	3	5	3	0	3	5	7	D	Frange esurienti panem	LA 131	re	1
D	2	3	5	3	0	3	5	7	D	Qui custodiebant animam	LA 170 *WA 107	re	1
D	2	3	5	3	2	0	-2	0	[D]	Agnus Dei	SCH #213		2
D	2	3	5	3	2	0	-2	3	D	At Jesus conversus	AR 574 LU 1077 AM 615 LA 320	an	1
D	2	3	5	3	2	0	-2	3	D	Nostrae matris praeconia	ST 136	hy	2
D	2	3	5	3	2	0	-2	3	D	Visitasti terram et inebriasti	GR 443 LU 1379	co	1
D	2	3	5	3	2	0	2	0	E	Alme pater Augustine doctor	ST 235	hy	3
D	2	3	5	3	2	0	2	0	D	Kyrie	MEL #178		
D	2	3	5	3	2	0	2	3		Post excessum beatissimi Martini	SYG 227	alv	
D	2	3	5	3	2	0	2	3	D	Quare detraxistis sermonibus	LA 283 *WA 172	re	1
D	2	3	5	3	2	0	3	0	D	Dixit Dominus Jesus quid est	LA 266	an	1
D	2	3	5	3	2	0	3	0	D	Exsultet caelum laudibus	ST 134	hy	2
D	2	3	5	3	2	0	3	2	[D]	Agnus Dei	SCH #214		2
a	2	3	5	3	2	0	3	2	G	Jerusalem gaude gaudio	AR 231 *LA 16 LU 338 AM 204	an	7

D	2	3	5	3	2	0	3	2	D	Tellus ac aethra jubilent	ST 326	hy	2
D	2	3	5	3	2	0	3	5	D	Cognoverunt omnes a Dan	AR 538^{14} LU 980 AM 571 WA 164 *LA 273	an	1
D	2	3	5	3	2	0	3	5	D	Jesus haec dicens	WA 79 *LA 119	an	1
D	2	3	5	3	2	0	3	7	D	Exsultabunt Domino ossa	AR [176] GR 107* LU 1764 1799 *AM 1161 *WA 438 *LA 559	an	1
D	2	3	5	3	2	0	5	0	D	Kyrie	MEL #176		
D	2	3	5	3	2	0	5	3	D	Kyrie	MEL #177		
D	2	3	5	3	2	0	7	5	E	Media vita in morte sumus	AR 152* PM 45 VP 106	re	4
D	2	3	5	3	2	3	0	-2	E	Impietatibus nostris	AR 130	an	4
D	2	3	5	3	2	3	0	2	E	Audi benigne conditor	ST 185	hy	4
D	2	3	5	3	2	3	5	7	D	Cum inducerent puerum ... dicens	LA 352	re	1
D	2	3	5	3	2	5	7	10	E	Gaude visceribus mater in intimis	ST 339	hy	3
D	2	3	5	3	5	3	0	2	E	Somno refectis artubus	ST 279	hy	4
D	2	3	5	3	5	3	2	0	D	Sacrificium Deo spiritus	WA 70	an	1
D	2	3	5	3	5	3	2	3	E	Aeterna caeli gloria	ST 214	hy	3
D	2	3	5	3	5	3	2	3	E	Ales diei nuntius	ST 213	hy	3
D	2	3	5	3	5	3	2	3	E	Aurora jam spargit polum	ST 214	hy	3
D	2	3	5	3	5	3	2	3	E	Consors paterni luminis	ST 213 253	hy	3
D	2	3	5	3	5	3	2	3	E	Lux ecce surgit aurea	ST 214	hy	3
D	2	3	5	3	5	3	2	3	E	Nox atra rerum contegit	ST 214	hy	3
D	2	3	5	3	5	3	2	3	E	Nox et tenebrae et nubila	ST 214	hy	3
D	2	3	5	3	5	3	2	3	E	Primo dierum omnium	ST 210 250 262	hy	3
D	2	3	5	3	5	3	2	3	E	Rerum creator optime	ST 213	hy	3
D	2	3	5	3	5	3	2	3	E	Somno refectis artubus	ST 252	hy	3
D	2	3	5	3	5	3	2	3	E	Splendor paternae gloriae	ST 213	hy	3
D	2	3	5	3	5	3	2	3	E	Summae Deus clementiae	ST 214	hy	3
D	2	3	5	3	5	3	2	3	E	Tu trinitatis unitas	ST 214	hy	3
D	2	3	5	3	5	7	3	2	D	In aeternum misericordia ejus	AR 2 (sup)	an	1
D	2	3	5	3	5	7	5	3	G	Deus creator omnium	ST 214	hy	8
D	2	3	5	3	5	7	5	3	G	Lucis creator optime	AR 49 LU 257	hy	8
D	2	3	5	3	5	7	5	7	E	Domine exaudi orationem meam ... perveniat	GR [142] OHS 345 OTT 53 LU 623 SYG 128 *GS 93 GB 114^{v}	of	3
D	2	3	5	3	5	7	5	7	E	Domine exaudi orationem meam ... perveniat ... ne	GR 194	of	3
D	2	3	5	3	5	7	5	7	E	Lavabo inter innocentes	SYG 86	of	3

D	2	3	5	3	5	7	10	7	G	Domine Deus salutis meae	GR 110 307 LU 544 905 OTT 112 SYG 84 *GB 74 *GS b 46 173	of	8
D	2	3	5	7	0	2	3	5	E	A solis ortus cardine	ST 31 219 275 366 AM 242	hy	3
D	2	3	5	7	0	2	3	5	E	Enixa est puerpera	ST 31	hy	3
D	2	3	5	7	0	2	3	5	E	Hostis Herodes impie	LR 69 AM 288	hy	3
D	2	3	5	7	0	2	3	5	E	Hujus diei gloria	ST 234	hy	3
D	2	3	5	7	0	2	3	5	E	Jesus refulsit omnium	VP 93	hy	3
D	2	3	5	7	0	2	3	5	E	Joannes in principio	ST 369	hy	3
D	2	3	5	7	0	2	3	5	E	O sola magnarum urbium	AM 292	hy	3
D	2	3	5	7	0	2	3	5	E	Salvete flores martyrum	ST 277	hy	3
D	2	3	5	7	0	2	3	5	E	Solemnis dies advenit	ST 256	hy	3
D	2	3	5	7	0	2	3	5	E	Stephano primo martyri	ST 220	hy	3
D	2	3	5	7	0	2	3	5	E	Votiva cunctis orbita	ST 395	hy	3
D	2	3	5	7	0	2	5	3	E	A solis ortus cardine	ST 81 178 AR 266 LU 400	hy	3
D	2	3	5	7	0	2	5	3	E	Crudelis Herodes Deum regem	AR 308 LU 464	hy	3
D	2	3	5	7	0	2	5	3	E	Hostis Herodes impie	ST 180	hy	3
D	2	3	5	7	0	2	5	3	E	O sola magnarum urbium	AR 313 LU 456	hy	3
D	2	3	5	7	0	2	5	3	E	Rex gloriose martyrum	ST 103	hy	3
D	2	3	5	7	0	2	5	3	E	Solemnis dies advenit	ST 220	hy	3
D	2	3	5	7	0	2	5	3	E	Tellus ac aethra jubilent	SYG 135	hy	4
D	2	3	5	7	0	3	5	3	E	Beata nobis gaudia	ST 146	hy	3
D	2	3	5	7	2	3	5	3	D	Alleluia: benedictio Dei in mercedem	GR 452	al	1
D	2	3	5	7	2	3	5	3	D	Alleluia: declinabo super eum	GR 509 LU 1482	al	1
D	2	3	5	7	3	0	2	0	D	Agnus Dei	SCH #234		1
D	2	3	5	7	3	2	0	-2	D	Vos qui reliquistis omnia	AR [8] *AM 624 882 1124 *WA 332 *LA 428	an	1 2
D	2	3	5	7	3	5	0	2	G	Aeterna caeli gloria	ST 363	hy	8
D	2	3	5	7	3	5	0	2	G	Ales diei nuntius	ST 363	hy	8
D	2	3	5	7	3	5	0	2	G	Aurora jam spargit polum	ST 363	hy	8
D	2	3	5	7	3	5	0	2	G	Lux ecce surgit aurea	ST 363	hy	8
D	2	3	5	7	3	5	0	2	G	Nox et tenebrae et nubila	ST 363	hy	8
D	2	3	5	7	3	5	0	2	G	Splendor paternae gloriae	ST 362	hy	8
D	2	3	5	7	5	0	2	3	E	Loquebatur Christus ad dilectam	AM 1135	an	4
D	2	3	5	7	5	2	3	2	D	Quod uni ex minimis	AR 373 AM 346 *WA 89 *LA 134	an	1

D	2	3	5	7	5	2	3	5	E	Ecce quod concupivi jam video	AR 604 AM 787 WA 255	an	4
D	2	3	5	7	5	2	3	5	E	Jam toto subitus vesper eat polo	AR 840 LU 1640 AM 1045	hy	4
D	2	3	5	7	5	2	5	7	D	Unus militum lancea	AR 538[6] LU 977 AM 565	an	1
D	2	3	5	7	5	3	0	2	E	Jesu nostra redemptio	ST 390	hy	4
D	2	3	5	7	5	3	0	2	E	Jesus refulsit omnium	ST 372	hy	4
D	2	3	5	7	5	3	2	0	E	Christe cunctorum dominator alme	ST 406	hy	4
D	2	3	5	7	5	3	2	0	E	Christo caelorum agmina	ST 301	hy	4
a	2	3	5	7	5	3	2	0	G	Ecce ascendimus ... et consumma-buntur ... prophetas	LA 124	an	7
D	2	3	5	7	5	3	2	0	D	Manifestavit se Jesus	WA 135	an	1
D	2	3	5	7	5	3	2	0	E	Primo dierum omnium	ST 181	hy	4
D	2	3	5	7	5	3	2	0	E	Summe confessor sacer et sacerdos	ST 404	hy	4
D	2	3	5	7	5	3	2	0	E	Virginis proles opifexque matris	ST 105 405	hy	4
D	2	3	5	7	5	3	2	3	D	Sanctus	THAN #178		2
D	2	3	5	7	5	3	5	3	E	Triduanas a Domino poposci	AR 925 LU 1757 AM 1141 WA 408 *LA 490	an	4
D	2	3	5	7	5	3	5	7		Et in terra	BOS #48 GR 42* LU 49		
D	2	3	5	7	5	3	5	7	G	Signum salutis pone Domine	PM 108	an	8
D	2	3	5	7	5	7	5	3	D	Medicinam carnalem corpori	AR 625 LU 1371 *AM 807 *WA 276 LA 363	an	1
D	2	3	5	7	5	7	5	3	E	Simile est regnum caelorum thesauro	GR 110**	co	4
D	2	3	5	7	5	7	5	7	E	Christus apparuit nobis	LR 68 WA 53	inv	4
D	2	3	5	7	5	7	5	7	E	Christus natus est nobis	LU 368 LR 54 LA 31 WA 27	inv	4
D	2	3	5	7	5	7	5	7		Memento nostri Domine Patres nostri in Aegypto	GB 75[v]	ofv	
D	2	3	5	7	5	7	5	7	G	Mirabilis Deus in sanctis	GR [24] OTT 141 LU 1165 SYG 175 GB 171 *GS 217	of	8
D	2	3	5	7	5	7	5	9	G	Virginis proles opifexque matris	ST 105	hy	8
D	2	3	5	7	5	7	5	10	E	Gaude visceribus mater in intimis	ST 299 (var)	hy	4
D	2	3	5	7	5	7	10	7		Crucifixus surgens a mortuis	SYG 164	alv	
D	2	3	5	7	5	7	10	7		Ingressa Agnes turpitudinis	GB 45	alv	
D	2	3	5	7	5	7	10	9	G	Stabunt justi in magna constantia	LR 164	an	8
D	2	3	5	7	5	7	10	12	E	Claris conjubila Gallia laudibus	PM 338 LR 427	hy	3
D	2	3	5	7	5	7	10	12	E	Custodes hominum psallimus angelos	AR 863 LR 449 LU 1666	hy	3
D	2	3	5	7	5	7	10	12		In salicibus in medio ejus Super flumina	OTT 119 GB 102[v] *SYG 115	ofv	
D	2	3	5	7	5	7	10	12	E	Qui te posthabitis	AM 776	hy	3
D	2	3	5	7	5	7	10	12	E	Sanctorum meritis inclyta gaudia	AR [38] LU 1159 ST 102	hy	3

D	2	3	5	7	5	10	7	5		Tantam gratiam et virtus Intempestae noctis	SYG 57	ofv	
D	2	3	5	7	5	10	12	10	E	Gaude visceribus mater in intimis	ST 299 397	hy	4
A	2	3	5	7	8	10	7	12	E	Patres nostri in Aegypto	GB 75v	of	4
D	2	3	5	7	10	7	5	10	G	Oratio mea munda est	GR 577 OTT 164 SYG 212 GB 216v *GS 193	of	8
D	2	3	5	7	10	12	10	9	E	Sanctorum meritis inclyta gaudia	ST 403	hy	3
D	2	3	5	10	7	5	3	2		Mittat tibi auxilium Memor sit Dominus	SYG 232	ofv	
Γ	2	3	7	5	2	3	0	7	[D]	Agnus Dei	SCH #212		1
D	2	3	7	5	8	7	5	3		Specie tua et pulchritudine Diffusa est	OTT 156 *GB 49 *SYG 46	ofv	
F	2	4	-3	-1	0	2	4	6	F	Agnus Dei	SCH #135		6
F	2	4	0	-5	-3	-5	0	-5	[F]	Agnus Dei	SCH #134		6
F	2	4	0	-5	-3	-5	0	-5	G	Sanctus	THAN #117		6
F	2	4	0	-5	-3	0	2	0	F	Populi autem non credentibus	WA 404	an	6
c	2	4	0	-3	-5	0	-1	0	c	Alleluia: condemnat autem justus	GR 71**	al	6
F	2	4	0	-3	-5	0	2	5	F	Ex altari tuo Domine	LR 126 LU 936	an	6
G	2	4	0	-3	-2	-3	-5	-7	E	Caelum terra pontus aethra	ST 465	hy	4
c	2	4	0	-3	-2	0	2	0	c	Erexit nobis Dominus ... sicut	WA 65	an	6
G	2	4	0	-3	2	0	7	4	G	Sanctus	THAN #73		7
c	2	4	0	-2	-3	-2	0	2	c	Gloriam mundi	WA 240	an	6
G	2	4	0	-2	0	2	5	4	G	Cum appropinquaret Dominus Jerosolymam	GR 171 *PM 54 WA 208 *GS 79 *SYG 118 GB 105	an	7
G	2	4	0	-2	0	2	5	4	G	Cum audisset populus quia Jesus	GB 107	an	7
F	2	4	0	-1	-3	-5	-3	0	F	Adhuc eo loquente	AM 999	an	6
F	2	4	0	-1	-3	-5	0	2	F	Hic accipiet benedictionem	LU 1827	an	6
c	2	4	0	-1	-3	-5	0	2	c	Infunde precamur Domine	LA 538	an	6
F	2	4	0	-1	-3	-5	0	2	F	Tuam ipsius animam	AR 673 LU 1422 AM 867	an	6
F	2	4	0	-1	-3	-1	-5	-3	F	Accepit Joseph puerum	LR 304	an	6
F	2	4	0	-1	-3	-1	-3	-5	F	Vobis datum est nosse	AR 351 LU 510 AM 323 WA 77 *LA 119	an	6
F	2	4	0	2	-3	0	-1	2	F	Mementote mirabilium ejus	GR 85**	gr	5
F	2	4	0	2	-3	0	-1	2	F	Respice Domine in testamentum	GR 354 LU 1033 *SYG 106 *GB 94v GS 68 156	gr	5
F	2	4	0	2	-1	0	2	0	[F]	Agnus Dei	SCH #150		6
c	2	4	0	2	0	-3	-5	0	c	Dixit autem Dominus ad Abraham	WA 80	re	5
F	2	4	0	2	0	-3	-5	0	F	O Christi pietas omni prosequenda	PM 119 WA 242	an	6
c	2	4	0	2	0	-3	-1	0	c	Adest frater curiosus	WA 292	an	6

F	2	4	0	2	0	-3	-1	0	F	Alleluia	AM 90	an	6
F	2	4	0	2	0	-3	0	2	F	Domine refugium factus est	AR 145 *AM 60 61 *WA 68 LA 98	an	6
F	2	4	0	2	0	-1	-3	-5	D	Nunc sancte nobis spiritus	ST 346	hy	2
F	2	4	0	2	0	-1	-3	-5	F	O quam suavis est Domine	AR 529 97* LU 917 *AM 548 VP 8 4*	an	6
F	2	4	0	2	0	-1	-3	-5	F	Sanctus VIII	GR 30* LU 38 THAN #116		6
F	2	4	0	2	-1	0	-3	0	G	Ego clamavi quoniam exaudisti	GR 386 LU 1073 SYG 240 GS 144	co	8
F	2	4	0	2	-1	0	-3	0	G	Ego sum pauper et dolens	GR 605 LU 1647	co	8
F	2	4	0	2	-1	0	7	9	F	Concordi laetitia propulsa	AR 136*		6
F	2	4	0	2	0	-1	-3	-1	F	Benedictus Dominus susceptor	AR 203 OHS 41 LU 308	an	6
F	2	4	0	2	0	-1	-3	0	F	Alleluia	AR 205 452 LU 312 AM 39 41	an	6
F	2	4	0	2	0	-1	-3	0	F	Benedictus Dominus Deus meus	AM 155 156 WA 70 *LA 102	an	6
F	2	4	0	2	0	-1	-3	0	F	Date magnitudinem Deo	AM 75 78	an	6
F	2	4	0	2	0	-1	-3	2	F	Ascendit autem Joseph a Galilaea	AR 688	an	6
F	2	4	0	2	0	-1	-3	2	F	Misit Dominus verbum suum	GR 68 LU 485 SYG 35 GB 37^{v} GS 21	gr	5
F	2	4	0	2	0	-1	0	-3	F	Dilectae animam e carcere	AM 1136	an	6
F	2	4	0	2	0	-1	2	0	D	Caeli Deus sanctissime	ST 363 AM 148	hy	1
F	2	4	0	2	0	-1	2	0	D	Immense caeli conditor	ST 362 AM 137	hy	1
F	2	4	0	2	0	-1	2	0	D	Magnae Deus potentiae	AM 153 ST 363	hy	1
F	2	4	0	2	0	-1	2	0	D	Plasmator hominis Deus	AM 158 ST 363	hy	1
F	2	4	0	2	0	-1	2	0	D	Telluris ingens conditor	ST 363 AM 142	hy	1
G	2	4	0	2	0	[0	0	0]	G	Kyrie Jesu rex caeli	MEL #53		
F	2	4	0	2	0	2	-1	2	D	Domine descende ut sanes	WA 191	an	1
F	2	4	0	2	0	2	0	-3	F	Benedictus Deus Israel	AM 45 LA 89	an	6
F	2	4	0	2	0	2	0	-1	F	Exsultate Deo adjutori	WA 68	an	6
F	2	4	0	2	0	2	0	-1	D	Mel et lac ex ejus ore	LA 332	an	1
F	2	4	0	2	0	2	0	2	[D]	Agnus Dei	SCH #133		2
c	2	4	0	2	0	2	0	2	[c]	Alleluia: benedictus es Dei filius	GB 148	al	6
c	2	4	0	2	0	2	0	2	c	Alleluia: justi fulgebunt sicut sol	GB 268^{v}	al	6
C	2	4	0	2	0	2	0	5	c	Alleluia: in resurrectione tua Christe	GB 146^{v}	al	6
G	2	4	0	2	0	2	5	4	G	Alleluia: benedictus es Domine Deus patrum ... saecula	GR 306 309 LU 904 911 *GS c *SYG 260 *GB 213	al	8
G	2	4	0	2	0	2	5	4	G	Alleluia: crastina die delebitur	GR 25 LU 361	al	8

G	2	4	0	2	0	2	5	4	G	Alleluia: tanto tempore vobiscum sum	GR 489 LU 1465[C]	al	8
c	2	4	0	2	0	4	7	5	c	Sanctus	THAN #10		5
F	2	4	0	2	0	5	4	2	F	Ave verum corpus natum	AR 100* LU 1856		6
F	2	4	0	2	4	0	-3	0	a	Ostende nobis Domine misericordiam	GR 11 SYG 9 GB 8 *GS 7	gr	2
C	2	4	0	2	4	[0	0	0]	D E	Kyrie genitor eleison	MEL #217		
F	2	4	0	2	4	0	2	4	F	Ascendit Christus super caelos	PM 179 *WA 358	an	6
G	2	4	0	2	4	0	5	4	G	Rex Christe Martini decus	ST 461	hy	7
F	2	4	0	2	4	2	-1	0	G	Parvulus filius hodie	AR 265 LR 64 LU 399 *AM 242 *WA 32 *LA 35	an	8
F	2	4	0	2	4	2	0	-3	F	Alleluia	GR 237 OHS 688 LU 776[KK] AM 450	an	6
F	2	4	0	2	4	2	0	-1	F	Exaltabuntur cornua justi	LR 139 WA 412 LA 507	an	6
F	2	4	0	2	4	2	0	-1	D	Kyrie	MEL #106		
F	2	4	0	2	4	2	0	-1	F	Salutare vultus mei	AR 107 AM 46 *WA 65 *LA 92	an	6
F	2	4	0	2	4	2	0	[0]	F	Miserere mei Deus	AM 38 LA 89 *WA 64	an	6
F	2	4	0	2	4	2	0	2	D	Domine salva nos	AR 338 LU 492 AM 308	an	1
F	2	4	0	2	4	2	0	2	D	Gloria	BOS #29		I
F	2	4	0	2	4	2	0	4	G	Alleluia: candor est lucis aeternae	GR 572 LU 1586	al	7
F	2	4	0	2	4	2	0	4	G	Alleluia: caro mea vere est cibus	GR 314 [96] LU 1045	al	7
F	2	4	0	2	4	2	0	4	G	Alleluia: concussum est mare	GR 609 LU 1655 GS 198	al	7
F	2	4	0	2	4	2	0	4	G	Alleluia: diffusa est gratia	SYG 5	al	8
F	2	4	0	2	4	2	0	4	E	Alleluia: iterum autem videbo vos	GS 129 *SYG 166	al	3
F	2	4	0	2	4	2	0	4	G	Alleluia: laetabitur justus in Domino	SYG 209 GS 207	al	8
F	2	4	0	2	4	2	0	4	G	Alleluia: levita Laurentius bonum opus	GR 579 LU 1595 GS 194	al	7
F	2	4	0	2	4	2	0	4	G	Alleluia: minuisti eum Domine paulo	GR 451	al	7
F	2	4	0	2	4	2	0	4	G	Alleluia: nativitas gloriosae virginis	GS u	al	8
F	2	4	0	2	4	2	0	4	G	Alleluia: optimam partem elegit	GS 191	al	8
F	2	4	0	2	4	2	0	4	G	Alleluia: solemnitas gloriosae virginis	GR 620 LU 1676[A]	al	7
F	2	4	0	2	4	2	4	0	D	Mihi vivere Christus	WA 330 *LA 422	an	1
F	2	4	0	2	4	2	4	2	G	Nato Domino angelorum	LR 61 WA 47 LA 37	an	8
G	2	4	0	2	4	5	4	2	G	Alleluia: venite benedicti Patris	GB 267[V]	al	8
G	2	4	0	2	4	5	4	2	G	Ave maris stella Dei mater alma	ST 124 AR [127]	hy	7

C	2	4	0	2	4	5	4	2	D	Clamant clamant clamant	WA 44	an	2
F	2	4	0	2	4	5	4	2	F	Divinis donis Aurea	ST 470	hy	6
G	2	4	0	2	4	5	4	2	G	Marcellinum atque Petrum	ST 17	hy	7
C	2	4	0	2	4	5	4	2	D	Nunc sancte nobis spiritus	AM 185	hy	2
G	2	4	0	2	4	5	4	2	G	Sanctus	THAN #66		8
G	2	4	0	2	4	5	4	2	G	Sanctus	THAN #63		8
G	2	4	0	2	4	5	4	5	G	Kyrie auctor caelorum (etc)	MEL #52		
c	2	4	0	2	4	5	4	5	c	Sanctus	THAN #9		8
C	2	4	0	2	4	5	7	4		Nuptiae factae sunt	SYG 35	alv	
F	2	4	0	2	4	6	4	2		Cumque in sopore Veniens vir	SYG 174	ofv	
F	2	4	0	2	4	6	4	2	G	Gloria VI	BOS #30 GR 22* LU 32		8
G	2	4	0	2	4	7	4	5	E	Kyrie XVI	GR 54* LU 59		3
F	2	4	0	2	4	7	4	7	a	Deriventur fontes tui	GR 555 LU 1562	gr	2
C	2	4	0	2	4	7	5	4		Misericordias Domini in aeternum	SYG 245	alv	
F	2	4	0	2	4	7	6	4	G	Michael Gabriel cherubim et seraphim	PM 154 *WA 381 *LA 468	an	8
F	2	4	0	2	4	7	6	7	G	Alleluia: laetamini in Domino et exsultate	GB 269 GS 217 (nm)	al	8
F	2	4	0	2	4	7	6	7	G	Alleluia: Laurentius bonum opus	GB 218	al	8
F	2	4	0	2	4	7	6	7		Laetamini in Domino et exsultate	GB 269 GS 217 (nm)	alv	
F	2	4	0	2	4	7	6	7		Laurentius bonum opus	GB 218	alv	
F	2	4	0	2	4	7	6	7	G	Potens es Domine eripere	AR 397 AM 372 *WA 103 LA 162	an	8
G	2	4	0	2	5	4	2	0	G	Alleluia: benedictus sit Dei filius	SYG 261	al	8
G	2	4	0	2	5	4	2	0	G	Alleluia: oculis ac manibus in caelum	SYG 225	al	8
c	2	4	0	2	5	4	2	0	c	Crux fidelis inter omnes ... dulcia	WA 370	an	6
G	2	4	0	2	5	4	2	0	a	Laudes magnificas altithrono Deo	ST 55	hy	2
G	2	4	0	2	5	4	2	0	a	Sanctorum meritis inclyta gaudia	ST 61	hy	2
G	2	4	0	2	5	4	2	4	G	Clarum decus jejunii	ST 187	hy	7
C	2	4	0	2	5	4	2	4	D	Deus creator omnium	VP 28	hy	1
G	2	4	0	2	5	4	2	4	G	Jam lucis orto sidere	AR 14 LU 224	hy	8
G	2	4	0	2	5	4	2	4	G	Nunc sancte nobis spiritus	AR 26 LU 235	hy	8
C	2	4	0	2	5	4	2	4	C	Pie colamus annua	ST 114	hy	5
G	2	4	0	2	5	4	2	4	G	Rector potens verax Deus	AR 32 LU 241	hy	8
G	2	4	0	2	5	4	2	4	G	Rerum Deus tenax vigor	AR 38 LU 245	hy	8

G	2	4	0	2	5	4	2	4	a	Summe largitur praemii	ST 32 89 186	hy	2
C	2	4	0	2	5	4	2	5	D	Lauda mater ecclesia	ST 123	hy	2
G	2	4	0	2	5	4	5	7	G	Fidelis servus et prudens ... ut det	GR 570 [34][41][50] LU 1185 GB 52^v *SYG 56 *GS 224	co	7
C	2	4	0	2	5	4	5	7	E	Sint lumbi vestri ... et vos	GB 234	co	3
C	2	4	0	2	5	7	2	4	D	Sanctus ad lib. I	GR 90* LU 86 THAN #229		1
G	2	4	0	2	5	7	5	4	a	Urbis cives Andegavae	ST 149	hy	2
F	2	4	0	4	6	7	6	4	F	Gloria	BOS #37		III
G	2	4	0	4	7	5	4	2	G	Alleluia: ego dilecto meo et ad me	GR 626 LU 1691	al	8
c	2	4	0	4	7	5	7	4	c	Hodie veri solis	WA 323	an	6
F	2	4	0	4	7	6	7	9	G	Tristis est anima mea	OHS 378 LU 635 *LA 189 *WA 118	re	8
G	2	4	0	5	2	0	-2	0	G	O quam glorifica luce coruscas	ST 207	hy	8
F	2	4	0	5	4	2	0	-1	F	Kyrie	MEL #110		
F	2	4	0	5	4	2	4	0	F	Agnus Dei	SCH #132		5
F	2	4	0	5	4	2	4	0	F	Caeli cives applaudite	ST 325	hy	6
F	2	4	0	5	4	2	4	0	F	Gloria	BOS #36		III
F	2	4	0	5	4	2	4	0	F	Kyrie clementissime (etc)	MEL #111		
F	2	4	0	5	4	2	4	0	F	Sanctus	THAN #113		5
F	2	4	0	5	4	2	4	0	F	Sanctus	THAN #114		5
F	2	4	0	5	4	2	4	2	F	Agnus Dei	SCH #131		6
F	2	4	0	6	4	2	0	-1	F	Sanctus	THAN #115		6
F	2	4	0	6	4	6	4	6	F	Sacrae parentes virginis	ST 344	hy	5
G	2	4	0	7	5	4	0	2	G	Agnus Dei	SCH #85		8
G	2	4	0	7	5	4	0	2	G	Sanctus	THAN #72		8
G	2	4	0	7	5	4	2	0	G	Ite missa est XII	GR 44* LU 51		8
G	2	4	0	7	5	4	2	0	G	Kyrie XII pater cuncta (etc)	GR 42* LU 48 MEL #58		8
G	2	4	2	-5	-2	-3	-5	-3	G	Kyrie	MEL #79		
F	2	4	2	-3	0	-1	-3	-1	D	Kyrie	MEL #109		
G	2	4	2	-2	0	4	5	7	G	Dixit Jerus discipulis suis ego mittam	WA 151	an	8
F	2	4	2	-1	-3	0	3	2		Sub pennis eorum Quatuor facies	WA 372		
F	2	4	2	-1	0	-3	0	4	G	Gressus meos dirige Domine	GR 137 OTT 39 *SYB 99 *GB 88^v *GS 62	of	8
F	2	4	2	-1	0	2	0	-1	D	Domine bonum est	AR 380 LU 545 AM 354 *WA 90 (inc illeg) *LA 136	an	1
F	2	4	2	-1	0	2	0	-1	D	Petite et accipietis quaerite	GR 284 [412] LU 843 SYG 178 GB 162^v *GS 133	co	1

F	2	4	2	-1	0	2	0	2		De utero senectutis	GB 198^{v}	alv	
F	2	4	2	-1	0	2	0	2		Gloriosae virginis Mariae nativitatem	GB 231^{v}	alv	
F	2	4	2	-1	0	2	0	2	F	Justus cum ceciderit	GR [13] LU 1139	gr	5
F	2	4	2	-1	0	2	0	2	F	Justus non conturbabitur	GB 162^{v} GS 206	gr	5
F	2	4	2	-1	0	2	0	2		Repleti sunt apostoli	GB 192	alv	
F	2	4	2	-1	0	2	4	0	G	Bonum est sperare in Domino	AR 396 AM 372 WA 103 *LA 161	an	8
F	2	4	2	-1	0	2	4	0	G	Dominus mihi adjutor est	AR 387 AM 362 WA 98 *LA 152	an	8
F	2	4	2	0	-3	-5	-3	0	F	Fecit Joas rectum	AR 5'12 LU 988 AM 579	an	6
G	2	4	2	0	-3	-2	0	2	G	Rex Christe clementissime	ST 126	hy	8
F	2	4	2	0	-3	-1	0	2	F	Gloria	BOS #39		III
G	2	4	2	0	-3	0	-3	-2	D	Sanctus	THAN #71		1
F	2	4	2	0	-3	0	2	0	F	In excelsis laudate Deum	AR 349 *WA 64	an	6
F	2	4	2	0	-3	0	2	0	F	In sanctis ejus	AM 64 *WA 68 *LA 99	an	6
G	2	4	2	0	-2	0	-3	0	E	Sanctus	THAN #70		4
G	2	4	2	0	-2	0	2	0	G	Haec est vera fraternitas	LA 517	re	8
G	2	4	2	0	-2	0	2	0	G	Lux mundi beatissima	ST 378	hy	8
G	2	4	2	0	-2	0	4	7	E	Agnus Dei	SCH #79		3
G	2	4	2	0	-2	2	0	2	G	Aeterne rex altissime	ST 93 390	hy	8
G	2	4	2	0	-2	2	0	2	G	Amorem sensus erige	ST 384	hy	8
G	2	4	2	0	-2	2	0	2	G	Rex confessorum gloria	ST 402	hy	8
G	2	4	2	0	-2	2	0	2	G	Silvestri almi praesulis	ST 370	hy	8
G	2	4	2	0	-2	2	0	2	G	Tu Christe nostrum gaudium	ST 94	hy	8
G	2	4	2	0	-2	2	0	2	G	Verbum supernum prodiens nec patris	AM 552	hy	8
G	2	4	2	0	-2	2	0	4	G	Sanctus	THAN #69		8
F	2	4	2	0	-1	0	-3	-1	G	Scriptum est enim quia domus	AR 374 561 LU 1019 AM 347 600 *WA 188 LA 314	an	8
F	2	4	2	0	-1	0	2	-3	F	Mirabilia opera tua	AR 180 LU 301	an	6
F	2	4	2	0	-1	0	2	0	F	Laetabitur justus in Domino ... laudabuntur	GR [18] LU 1149 SYG 170 GB 53^{v} GS 210	co	5
F	2	4	2	0	-1	0	2	0	F	Laetabitur justus in Domino ... laudabuntur	LR 171 *WA 304	re	5
F	2	4	2	0	-1	0	2	4	F	Agnus Dei IV	GR 17* OHS 421 LU 27 SCH #136		6
F	2	4	2	0	-1	2	-1	0	D	Caeli Deus sanctissime	AR 142	hy	1
F	2	4	2	0	-1	2	-1	0	D	Hominis superne conditor	AR 183	hy	1

F	2	4	2	0	-1	2	-1	0	D	Immense caeli conditor	AR 101 LU 517	hy	1
F	2	4	2	0	-1	2	-1	0	D	Magnae Deus potentiae	AR 161	hy	1
F	2	4	2	0	-1	2	-1	0	D	Telluris alme conditor	AR 122 LU 518	hy	1
F	2	4	2	0	-1	2	0	-1	D	Immense caeli conditor	ST 86	hy	2
F	2	4	2	0	2	-5	-3	0	G	Cumque perfusis lacrimis	LR 295	re	8
c	2	4	2	0	2	-3	-5	-3	F	Alleluia: lapis revolutus est	PM 67 *WA 138	an	5
c	2	4	2	0	2	-3	-5	-3	F	Alleluia: noli flere Maria	PM 67 *WA 138 LA 222	an	5
c	2	4	2	0	2	-3	-5	-3	F	Alleluia: quem quaeris mulier	PM 67 LA 221 *WA 138	an	5
F	2	4	2	0	2	-3	-5	-3	F	Decantemus Domino canticum	WA 250	an	6
c	2	4	2	0	2	-3	-5	-3		Et in terra	BOS #1 GR 25* LU 34		
c	2	4	2	0	2	-3	2	0	a	Domine magnus es tu	AR 127 *AM 55 56	an	4
F	2	4	2	0	2	-3	2	0	G	Innova signa et immuta mirabilia	GR 87**	co	8
G	2	4	2	0	2	-2	0	[0]	G	Agnus Dei	SCH #98		8
c	2	4	2	0	2	0	-3	-2	c	Pro te Jesu Christe morte	WA 249	re	6
F	2	4	2	0	2	0	-3	-1		Custodi me Domine de manu Eripe me	GR 208 LU 725 OHS 534 GS 99 GB 116^{v} SYG 137	trv	
F	2	4	2	0	2	0	-3	-1		Disposui testamentum	SYG 34 GS 222 *GB 272	alv	
F	2	4	2	0	2	0	-3	-1		Dixit Moyses ad populum Erit vobis	OTT 63 *GB 141^{v} SYG 160	ofv	
F	2	4	2	0	2	0	-3	-1		In manibus portabunt te Angelis suis	GR [144]	trv	
F	2	4	2	0	2	0	-3	-1		In manibus portabunt te Qui habitat	GR 95 LU 533 GS 35 GB 65 SYG 73	trv	
F	2	4	2	0	2	0	-3	-1		Lapidem quem reprobaverunt	SYG 161	alv	
F	2	4	2	0	2	0	-3	-1		Memoriam abundantiae suavitatis Magnificentiam	GR 99**	trv	
F	2	4	2	0	2	0	-3	-1		Nunc cum eo regnas	LU 1476^{D}	alv	
F	2	4	2	0	2	0	-3	-1		Operuit caelos majestas Domine audivi	GR 206 OHS 529 LU 721 GS 98 GB 116 SYG 136	trv	
F	2	4	2	0	2	0	-3	-1		Percussus sum sicut foenum Domine exaudi	GR 191 OHS 324 LU 619 GS 92 GB 114 SYG 127	trv	
F	2	4	2	0	2	0	-3	-1		Tu es Petrus	GR 409 534 LU 1122^{3} 1520 SYG 203	alv	
F	2	4	2	0	2	0	-3	0	F	Cantate Domino canticum	WA 67	an	6
F	2	4	2	0	2	0	-3	0	F	Eructavit cor meum	WA 64 *LA 88	an	6
G	2	4	2	0	2	0	-2	0	G	Cor meum et caro mea	GR 626	tr	8
G	2	4	2	0	2	0	-2	0	G	De profundis clamavi ad te	GR 75 LU 499 SYG 59 GB 56^{v} GS 25	tr	8

G	2	4	2	0	2	0	-2	0	G	Deus judex justus	AM 14	an	8
G	2	4	2	0	2	0	-2	0	G	Inveni quem diligit anima	GR (11)	tr	8
G	2	4	2	0	2	0	-2	0	G	Kyrie	MEL #51		
G	2	4	2	0	2	0	-2	0	G	Meum est consilium et aequitas	GR 26**	tr	8
G	2	4	2	0	2	0	-2	0	G	Nolite diligere mundum	GR 22**	tr	8
G	2	4	2	0	2	0	-2	0	G	Notus in Judaea Deus	GR [136] LU 1286	tr	8
G	2	4	2	0	2	0	-2	0	G	Qui confidunt in Domino	GR 139(40) LU 561 SYG 101 GB 90 GS 63	tr	8
G	2	4	2	0	2	0	-2	0	G	Qui gloriatur in Domino	GR 546	tr	8
G	2	4	2	0	2	0	-2	0	G	Sicut cervus desiderat	GR 232 OHS 673 LU 776[BB] SYG 151 GB 120 GS 112	tr	8
G	2	4	2	0	2	0	-2	2	G	Surgite sancti de mansionibus	WA 226	an	8
F	2	4	2	0	2	0	-1	-3	F	Alleluia	WA 68	an	6
c	2	4	2	0	2	0	-1	-3	F	Alleluia: resurrexit Dominus	WA 138	an	5
F	2	4	2	0	2	0	-1	-3	F	Benedictus Dominus in aeternum	WA 69 *LA 100	an	6
F	2	4	2	0	2	0	-1	-3	F	Benedixisti Domine terram tuam	WA 68 *LA 98	an	6
F	2	4	2	0	2	0	-1	0	D	Adjutorium nostrum in nomine	AR 120 OHS 287 LU 285 *LA 99	an	1
F	2	4	2	0	2	0	-1	[0]	F	Kyrie	MEL #120		
F	2	4	2	0	2	0	[0	0]	F	Kyrie	MEL #103		
F	2	4	2	0	2	0	2	-3	G	Domine memorabor justitiae tuae	GR 365 LU 1046 SYG 107 GB 95 GS 69 160	co	8
F	2	4	2	0	2	0	2	-3	F	Illuminare illuminare Jerusalem	AM 1185 *LR 75 *LA 72 *WA 53	re	5
G	2	4	2	0	2	0	2	-3	G	Kyrie	MEL #57		
G	2	4	2	0	2	0	2	0	G	Beatus vir cujus est auxilium	GR 450 LU 1394	tr	8
G	2	4	2	0	2	0	2	0	G	Deus docuisti me	GR 72**	tr	8
G	2	4	2	0	2	0	2	0	G	Ego diligentes me diligo	GR 61**	tr	8
G	2	4	2	0	2	0	2	0	G	Qui regis Israel intende	GR 19 LU 351 SYG 11 GB 10 GS 10	tr	8
C	2	4	2	0	2	0	2	0	D	Verbum iniquum et dolosum	LA 278 WA 169	re	1
F	2	4	2	0	2	0	2	4	F	In universa terra nomen	WA 282	an	6
F	2	4	2	0	2	0	2	4	F	Jam lucis orto sidere	ST 67 167	hy	6
F	2	4	2	0	2	0	2	4	F	Jam tibi fili	WA 256	an	6
c	2	4	2	0	2	0	2	4	c	Nunc ergo nomen Domini	WA 287	an	6
G	2	4	2	0	2	0	2	4	G	Sanctus	THAN #68		8
F	2	4	2	0	2	0	2	4	D	Vade Satana non temptabis	WA 88 LA 133	an	1
C	2	4	2	0	2	0	4	2	D	Jam lucis orto sidere	ST 73	hy	2

F	2	4	2	0	2	0	4	2	G	Ponam in Sion salutem	AR 254 *AM 230 *LA 17	an	8
G	2	4	2	0	2	0	4	5	G	Kyrie omnipotens genitor lumenque	MEL #56		
F	2	4	2	0	2	0	4	6	G	Longo contritus carcere	SYG 148	an	8
F	2	4	2	0	2	0	4	7	F	Sanctus	THAN #112		5
G	2	4	2	0	2	0	5	4	G	Jesu nostra redemptio	ST 190	hy	8
G	2	4	2	0	2	0	5	7	G	Absolve Domine animas omnium	GR 95* LU 1809	tr	8
G	2	4	2	0	2	0	5	7	G	Attende caelum et loquar	GR 231 LU 776U OHS 656 GS 112 *SYG 151 GB 119v	tr	8
G	2	4	2	0	2	0	5	7	G	Beatus vir qui timet	GR [8] LU 1442 GS 203 SYG 55 *GB 52v	tr	8
G	2	4	2	0	2	0	5	7	G	Benedicamus patrem et filium cum	GB 214v	tr	8
G	2	4	2	0	2	0	5	7	G	Benedictus Dominus Deus Israel	GR 64 LU 478 SYG 32 GB 36 GS 20	gr	7
G	2	4	2	0	2	0	5	7	G	Cantemus Domino gloriose enim honorificatus	GR 229 LU 776R OHS 652 SYG 150 GB 119 GS 111	tr	8
G	2	4	2	0	2	0	5	7	G	Ego autem cum mihi molesti	GR 566	tr	8
G	2	4	2	0	2	0	5	7	G	Factus es spes mea Domine	GR 424 LU 1353	tr	8
G	2	4	2	0	2	0	5	7	G	In columbae specie vidit	SYG 56	tr	8
G	2	4	2	0	2	0	5	7	G	Jubilate Domino omnis terra	GR 82 LU 513 SYG 62 GB 59v GS 28	tr	8
G	2	4	2	0	2	0	5	7	G	Laudate Dominum omnes angeli	GR 636 SYG 83 GS 46	tr	8
G	2	4	2	0	2	0	5	7	G	Laudate Dominum omnes gentes	GR 110 237 OHS 683 LU 776II SYG 83 GB 74 GS 46 115 173	tr	8
G	2	4	2	0	2	0	5	7	G	Nunc dimittis servum tuum	GB 49	tr	8
G	2	4	2	0	2	0	5	7	G	Nunc ergo filii audite me	GR 587[3] LU 1612[3]	tr	8
G	2	4	2	0	2	0	5	7	G	Posuisti Domine super caput	GB 46	tr	8
G	2	4	2	0	2	0	5	7	G	Probasti nos Deus igne	GR 108**	tr	8
G	2	4	2	0	2	0	5	7	G	Sacerdotes ejus induam salutari	LU 1623C	tr	8
G	2	4	2	0	2	0	5	7	G	Vinea facta est dilecto	GR 230 OHS 654 LU 776S SYG 150 GB 120 GS 111	tr	8
G	2	4	2	0	2	0	7	5	G	Beatus ille servus quem cum venerit	AR [74] LU 1196 AM 671 *WA 427 *LA 540	an	7 8
F	2	4	2	0	2	4	0	-3	D	Immense caeli conditor	ST 271	hy	2
F	2	4	2	0	2	4	0	2	G	Omnes sunt administratorii	AM 1066 *AR 865	an	8
F	2	4	2	0	2	4	0	2	F	Surrexit Christus de sepulcro	AM 31 474	an	6
F	2	4	2	0	2	4	0	4	G	Lauda Deum tuum Sion	AR 172	an	8
F	2	4	2	0	2	4	2	-1	D	Ex more docti mystico	ST 186 225 415	hy	1
F	2	4	2	0	2	4	2	-1	D	Nunc sancte nobis spiritus	AM 339	hy	1
F	2	4	2	0	2	4	2	0	F	Aedificavit Moyses altare	LR 233 WA 318 LA 549	an	6

F	2	4	2	0	2	4	2	0	G	Animam meam dilectam	OHS 499 LU 704 LA 197	re	6 8
F	2	4	2	0	2	4	2	0	G	Aperi nobis festinanter	WA 345	re	7
G	2	4	2	0	2	4	2	0	D	Constitutus a Deo	WA 33	an	2
G	2	4	2	0	2	4	2	0		Dedit illi Dominus scientiam	GB 272	alv	
G	2	4	2	0	2	4	2	0	G	Egregie Christi martyr Sebastiane	PM 127	re	7
F	2	4	2	0	2	4	2	0		Et in terra	BOS #29		
F	2	4	2	0	2	4	2	0	D	Ex more docti mystico	ST 282	hy	1
F	2	4	2	0	2	4	2	0	D	Inclinate aurem vestram	WA 67 LA 97	an	1
C	2	4	2	0	2	4	2	0	D	Mittens Dominus et alios	WA 371	an	2
F	2	4	2	0	2	4	2	0	G	Pater Abraham miserere	WA 187 *LA 145	an	8
F	2	4	2	0	2	4	2	0	F	Sanctificavit Dominus tabernaculum	LA 547	an	6
F	2	4	2	0	2	4	2	0	G	Sanctus	THAN #111		8
F	2	4	2	0	2	4	2	0	D	Secundum magnam misericordiam	AR 348 AM 319 *WA 65 LA 92	an	1
G	2	4	2	0	2	4	2	0	G	Talis est dilectus meus	LA 458	an	8
F	2	4	2	0	2	4	2	0	D	Tu solus altissimus	LA 98	an	1
F	2	4	2	0	2	4	2	0	D	Vexilla regis prodeunt fulget	ST 227 257 286	hy	1
F	2	4	2	0	2	4	2	4		Audi filia ... et obliviscere Diffusa est gratia	SYG 49	trv	
F	2	4	2	0	2	4	2	4	D	Aufer a me opprobrium	GR 370 GS 170 SYG 252 *GB 258	co	2
F	2	4	2	0	2	4	2	4	G	Domine si conversus fuerit	LA 271 WA 167	re	8
F	2	4	2	0	2	4	2	4	G	Dominus qui eripuit me	LA 268 WA 165	re	8
F	2	4	2	0	2	4	2	4		Dum virgo Deum et hominem Gaude Maria	GR [78] LU 1266	trv	
F	2	4	2	0	2	4	2	4	G	Fili quid fecisti ... ego	WA 58	an	8
F	2	4	2	0	2	4	2	4	D	Gloria	BOS #28		I
F	2	4	2	0	2	4	2	4	G	Gloria in excelsis Deo ... alleluia	AR 267 LU 402 AM 243 *WA 32 LA 38	an	8
F	2	4	2	0	2	4	2	4		Intercede pro nobis ad Deum Tu es vas	GR 420 LU 1346 *GS 178 SYG 44	trv	
G	2	4	2	0	2	4	2	4	G	Justi autem in perpetuum vivent	LA 478	re	8
F	2	4	2	0	2	4	2	4	G	Modicum et non videbitis me alleluia	GR 268 LU 24 *SYG 167 GB 149v GS 129	co	8
F	2	4	2	0	2	4	2	4		O vos omnes ... sicut Stabat sancta Maria	GR 471 LU 1634	trv	
F	2	4	2	0	2	4	2	4	G	Petrus et Paulus duo sunt	WA 332	an	8
F	2	4	2	0	2	4	2	4		Roga quae ad pacem Laetatus sum in his	SYG 101	trv	

C	2	4	2	0	2	4	2	4	D	Sanctus	THAN #227		2
C	2	4	2	0	2	4	2	4	D	Sanctus	THAN #228		2
F	2	4	2	0	2	4	2	4	G	Solemnitatem Magdalenae	WA 336	an	8
F	2	4	2	0	2	4	2	4		Spiritus sanctus superveniet Ave Maria	GR 459 LU 1412 GS 183 SYG 57	trv	
F	2	4	2	0	2	4	2	4	F	Tollite hostias et introite	GR 162 *SYG 114 *GB 102 GS 76	gr	5
F	2	4	2	0	2	4	2	4	G	Veste sancta utetur pontifex	GR [121]	co	8
F	2	4	2	0	2	4	2	7	G	Et dicebant ad invicem	WA 131	an	8
C	2	4	2	0	2	4	5	2	D	Tua sunt haec Christe	WA 376	an	1
c	2	4	2	0	2	4	5	4	c	Aeterna Christi munera apostolorum	ST 402	hy	6
c	2	4	2	0	2	4	5	4	c	Aeterna Christi munera et martyrum	ST 403	hy	6
G	2	4	2	0	2	4	5	4	E	Alleluia: defecit caro mea et cor meum	GR 506 LU 1479	al	3
G	2	4	2	0	2	4	5	4	E	Alleluia: obtulerunt discipuli	SYG 156	al	3
G	2	4	2	0	2	4	5	4	E	Alleluia: sacerdotes tui Domine Deus	GR 89** SYG 211	al	3
F	2	4	2	0	2	4	5	4	F	Apostolorum passio	ST 431	hy	6
C	2	4	2	0	2	4	5	4	D	Christi fortis hic athleta	WA 295	an	2
G	2	4	2	0	2	4	5	4		Defecit caro mea et cor	GR 506 LU 1479	alv	
C	2	4	2	0	2	4	5	4		Evangelizare pauperibus misit	GR 67**	alv	
G	2	4	2	0	2	4	5	4	G	Jam lucis orto sidere	AM 2 82	hy	8
G	2	4	2	0	2	4	5	4	E	Magna enim sunt judicia	LA 279 *WA 170	re	3
C	2	4	2	0	2	4	5	4	D	Non vos relinquam ... venio	LA 255	an	2
G	2	4	2	0	2	4	5	4	G	Nunc sancte nobis spiritus	AM 85 94 109	hy	8
G	2	4	2	0	2	4	5	4		Obtulerunt discipuli Domino	SYG 156	alv	
G	2	4	2	0	2	4	5	4	G	Rector potens verax Deus	AM 88 99 114	hy	8
G	2	4	2	0	2	4	5	4	G	Rerum Deus tenax vigor	AM 91 104 119	hy	8
c	2	4	2	0	2	4	5	4	c	Rex angelorum praepotens	ST 386	hy	6
C	2	4	2	0	2	4	5	4	D	Rogamus te Domine Deus quia	GB 156	an	1
G	2	4	2	0	2	4	5	4		Sacerdotes tui Domine Deus	GR 89**	alv	
G	2	4	2	0	2	4	5	4		Sacerdotes tui Domine induantur	SYG 211 GB 272	alv	
c	2	4	2	0	2	4	5	4	c	Sacri Christe pontificis	ST 395	hy	6
G	2	4	2	0	2	4	5	4	G	Sanctus	THAN #67		8
c	2	4	2	0	2	4	5	4	c	Silvester pastor inclite	ST 371	hy	6
c	2	4	2	0	2	4	5	7	c	Alleluia: sacerdotes tui Domine induantur	GB 272 *SYG 211	al	6

C	2	4	2	0	2	4	5	7	D	Alleluia: surrexit Dominus et occurrens	SYG 163 *GS 120	al	1
F	2	4	2	0	2	4	6	4	F	Aeterna Christi munera	ST 100 103	hy	5
F	2	4	2	0	2	4	6	4	G	Egregio beatitudinis tuae	WA 287	an	8
F	2	4	2	0	2	4	6	4	F	Hostis Herodes impie	ST 72	hy	5
F	2	4	2	0	2	4	6	4	F	Jam lucis orto sidere	ST 72	hy	5
F	2	4	2	0	2	4	7	4		Affluens ergo misericordiae Servus Dei Nicholaus	WA 241	rev	
F	2	4	2	0	2	4	7	4		Et in terra	BOS #28		
F	2	4	2	0	2	4	7	4	G	Species firmamenti super caput	WA 375	re	8
F	2	4	2	0	2	4	7	5	F	Aeterna sapientia	ST 127	hy	5
C	2	4	2	0	2	4	7	5	C	Tantum ergo sacramentum	AR 89* LU 1851	hy	5
F	2	4	2	0	2	4	7	6	G	Dilecti Deo et hominibus	WA 375	an	8
F	2	4	2	0	2	4	7	6	G	Petite et accipietis quaerite	AR 485 AM 501 *WA 146 *LA 242	an	8
F	2	4	2	0	2	4	7	6	G	Respexit Dominus humilitatem	AR 143 AM 149	an	8
F	2	4	2	0	2	4	7	9	F	O Dei sapientia	ST 343	hy	5
G	2	4	2	0	2	5	2	0	a	Inventor rutili dux bone luminis	GS 104	hy	2
G	2	4	2	0	2	5	2	0	a	O vos unanimes Christiadum chori	AM 908 *LR 452	hy	2
G	2	4	2	0	2	5	2	0	a	Sanctorum meritis inclyta gaudia	AM 646	hy	2
C	2	4	2	0	2	5	2	4	D	Ornaverunt faciem templi	LA 301	an	1
G	2	4	2	0	2	5	4	2	G	Obduxere polum nubila caeli	ST 493	hy	8
C	2	4	2	0	2	5	4	5	D	Adest praeclara festivitas	WA 335	an	1
G	2	4	2	0	2	5	4	5	D	Kyrie	MEL #50		
C	2	4	2	0	2	5	7	5	D	Domine si adhuc populo ... subire	LA 481 WA 400	re	2
C	2	4	2	0	2	5	7	5	D	Vovete et reddite Domino	GR 368 LU 1050 SYG 251 GB 257 GS 161	co	2
F	2	4	2	0	2	7	9	7		Magna est gloria ejus In virtute	OTT 152 *GB 51v *SYG 52	ofv	
F	2	4	2	0	4	2	[0	0]	G	Kyrie	MEL #112		
F	2	4	2	0	4	2	0	2	D	Firmamentum meum et refugium	LA 82	re	1
F	2	4	2	0	4	2	0	2		Pro hac orabit ad te Laetamini in Domino	OTT 140 *GB 44 SYG 41	ofv	
F	2	4	2	0	4	2	0	4	G	Mulier quae erat ... attulit	AR 793 LU 1568 AM 978 *SYG 132	an	8
F	2	4	2	0	4	2	4	6	G	Magnus Dominus ... valde	LA 90	an	8
C	2	4	2	0	4	2	5	4	D	Kyrie o theos yschyros	MEL #219		
C	2	4	2	0	4	2	5	7	D	Alleluia: solve jubente Deo terrarum	GR 563 LU 1576 GS 192 *SYG 203	al	1

F	2	4	2	0	4	2	7	6	G	Alleluia: audivi quasi vocem	WA 142	an	8
F	2	4	2	0	4	2	7	9	G	Agathes ingressa carcerem	WA 274	an	8
G	2	4	2	0	4	5	2	0	E	Alleluia	AM 92	an	3
G	2	4	2	0	4	5	7	9	G	Alleluia: tibi gloria hosanna	GR [109]	al	7
F	2	4	2	0	4	6	2	0	D	Surrexit Dominus de sepulcro	WA 131	an	1
F	2	4	2	0	4	6	4	2	G	Exsultavit spiritus meus	LA 93	an	8
F	2	4	2	0	4	6	7	2	G	Hodie gloriosa caeli regina	AR 637 LU 1383	an	8
F	2	4	2	0	4	6	7	4	G	Exaltare qui judicas	LA 100	an	8
F	2	4	2	0	4	6	7	4	G	Miserere nostri Domine	LA 96	an	8
F	2	4	2	0	4	6	7	6	G	Domine Deus meus in te speravi	LA 92	an	8
F	2	4	2	0	4	6	7	6		Ecce quam bonum et quam jucundum	GB 201^{v}	alv	
F	2	4	2	0	4	6	7	6		Ecce vir Dei Benedictus	GB 55	alv	
F	2	4	2	0	4	6	7	6	G	Vinea mea electa	OHS 490 LU 697 *LA 196 *WA 122	re	8
F	2	4	2	0	4	6	7	9	G	Ardens est cor meum	AR 466 AM 479 *WA 139	an	8
F	2	4	2	0	4	7	4	2	G	Nuptiae factae sunt	AR 336 AM 306	an	8
F	2	4	2	0	4	7	4	6	G	Exaltate qui judicas	WA 69	an	8
F	2	4	2	0	4	7	6	2	G	Dixit Caesar ad Hippolytum	WA 352	an	8
F	2	4	2	0	4	7	6	2	G	Habitat Deus Oswaldus	WA 283	an	8
F	2	4	2	0	4	7	6	2	G	Oportebat pati Christum	AR 486 *AM 503 WA 139 *LA 219 232	an	8
F	2	4	2	0	4	7	6	4	G	Alleluia: ecce mitto vos	GB 268	al	8
F	2	4	2	0	4	7	6	4	G	Domine in virtute tua	OHS 182 (nm) WA 60 *LA 80	an	8
F	2	4	2	0	4	7	6	4	G	Jesu redemptor omnium	ST 119	hy	8
F	2	4	2	0	4	7	6	4	G	Omnes de Saba venient ... laudem	WA 57	an	8
F	2	4	2	0	4	7	6	7	G	Isti sunt qui viventes	LR 145	re	8
F	2	4	2	0	4	7	6	7	G	Joseph autem mercatus sindonem	GR 18**	co	8
F	2	4	2	0	4	7	6	9	E	Isti viventes in carne	WA 413 *LA 508	re	4
C	2	4	2	0	4	7	9	7	E	Alleluia	AR 172* VP 153	an	4
F	2	4	2	0	4	7	9	7	G	Astiterunt justi ante Dominum	WA 324	an	8
G	2	4	2	0	5	0	2	4	E	Christe caelorum habitator alme	ST 406	hy	3
G	2	4	2	0	5	0	2	4	E	Christe qui virtus sator et vocaris	ST 369	hy	3
G	2	4	2	0	5	0	2	4	E	Christe sanctorum decus angelorum	ST 399	hy	3
G	2	4	2	0	5	0	2	4	E	Christe sanctorum decus atque virtus	ST 369	hy	3

C	2	4	2	0	5	4	2	0	D	Non vos relinquam ... vado	AM 519 *AR 502 *LU 862 WA 151 *LA 255	an	1
C	2	4	2	0	5	7	9	7	C	Festum nunc celebre magnaque gaudia	ST 453	hy	6
C	2	4	2	0	5	7	9	10	E	Alleluia: o quam pulchra est	GR [58] LU 1223 GB 223^{v}	al	4
C	2	4	2	0	5	7	9	10		O quam pulchra est casta generatio	GR [58] LU 1223 GB 223^{v}	alv	
F	2	4	2	0	6	4	2	0	F	Sanctus	THAN #110		6
F	2	4	2	0	7	4	9	7	[F]	Agnus Dei	SCH #130		6
F	2	4	2	4	-1	0	2	0	D	De Sion veniet Dominus	AR 241 AM 216 *WA 19 LA 25	an	1
F	2	4	2	4	0	2	0	-3		Quomodo in me fiet hoc Ave Maria	OTT 13 GB 12	ofv	
F	2	4	2	4	0	2	0	-1	D	Mulier quid ploras	LA 221	an	1
F	2	4	2	4	0	2	0	2	F	Agnus Dei	SCH #129		6
F	2	4	2	4	0	2	4	0	D	Sebastianus Dei cultor	LA 330	an	1
F	2	4	2	4	0	2	4	2	F	Alleluia	LA 206	an	6
F	2	4	2	4	0	2	4	2	F	Crucifixus surrexit a mortuis	AR 54 577^{24} LU 261 *AM 37 167 471 750 WA*136 138 LA 216	an	6
F	2	4	2	4	0	2	4	2	G	Sanctus	THAN #109		8
F	2	4	2	4	0	2	4	2	F	Similitudo aspectus animalium	WA 373	re	5
F	2	4	2	4	0	4	0	2	G	Ave Maria gratia plena ... benedicta	GR 23 [79] OTT 13 LU 355 1268 GS 6 GB 12	of	8
F	2	4	2	4	0	4	0	2	G	Dignas promamus Domino	GB 228^{v}	of	8
F	2	4	2	4	0	4	2	-1	D	Factus est adjutor	AR 379 *AM 352 *WA 93 *LA 142	an	1
G	2	4	2	4	0	5	7	9		Euntes in mundum universum	SYG 181	alv	
F	2	4	2	4	2	-3	0	2	G	Ave Maria Dei genitrix intacta	PM 247	an	8
F	2	4	2	4	2	-1	0	2	D	Alleluia	AR 99 LU 280 283 AM 132 136	an	1
F	2	4	2	4	2	-1	0	2	D	De Sion veniet qui regnaturus	AR 241 AM 216 *WA 19 LA 25	an	1
F	2	4	2	4	2	-1	0	2	D	Dicite pusillanimes confortamini	AR 229 AM 202 WA 13 *LA 12	an	1
F	2	4	2	4	2	-1	0	2	D	Dominus judicabit fines	AM 54 55 *WA 67 LA 95	an	1
F	2	4	2	4	2	-1	0	2	D	In viam pacis dirige	LA 105	an	1
F	2	4	2	4	2	-1	0	2	D	Inclinavit Dominus aurem	AR 98 OHS 222 LU 280 AM 133 134 *WA 64 LA 90	an	1
F	2	4	2	4	2	-1	0	2	D	Lazarus amicus noster dormit	AR 404 LU 1096 AM 380 WA 105 LA 165	an	1

F	2	4	2	4	2	-1	0	2	G	Magna et mirabilia	WA 143	an	8
F	2	4	2	4	2	-1	0	2	G	Omnis sapientia a Domino	AR 544 LU 990 AM 581 WA 168 *LA 280	an	8
F	2	4	2	4	2	-1	0	2	D	Sol et luna laudate Deum	AR 388 AM 362 WA 99 LA 153	an	1
F	2	4	2	4	2	-1	0	2	D	Super nivem dealbabuntur	AM 877	an	1
F	2	4	2	4	2	-1	2	0	G	Domine Jesu Christe pastor	LA 492 *WA 407	re	8
F	2	4	2	4	2	0	-3	0	F	Alleluia	AM 64	an	6
G	2	4	2	4	2	0	-2	0	G	Sanctus	THAN #65		8
F	2	4	2	4	2	0	-1	0	G	Domine Jesu Christe seminator	PM 212 336 *WA 407 LA 488	an	8
F	2	4	2	4	2	0	-1	0	D	Domine non est exaltatum	AR 140 OHS 356 LU 291	an	1
F	2	4	2	4	2	0	-1	0	D	Dominus defensor vitae	WA 61	an	1
F	2	4	2	4	2	0	-1	0	F	Dum ergo sint apud Deum	WA 342	an	6
c	2	4	2	4	2	0	-1	0	a	Veniet dies Domini	WA 9	an	1
F	2	4	2	4	2	0	[0	0]	E	Kyrie	MEL #104		
c	2	4	2	4	2	0	2	-3	c	Mel et lac ex ejus ore	LA 337 WA 254	re	6
F	2	4	2	4	2	0	2	0		Beati qui custodiunt judicium Confitemini Domino	GR 113 LU 547 GB 75	trv	
F	2	4	2	4	2	0	2	0		Cadent a latere tuo mille Qui habitat	GR 95 LU 533 GS 35 GB 65 SYG 73	trv	
C	2	4	2	4	2	0	2	0		Cantantibus organis Caecilia virgo	SYG 228	alv	
F	2	4	2	4	2	0	2	0		Caput circuitus eorum Eripe me	GR 208 LU 725 OHS 534 GS 99 GB 116v SYG 137	trv	
F	2	4	2	4	2	0	2	0	F	De fructu operum tuorum	GR 353 LU 1031 SYG 247 *GB 254 *GS 155	co	6
F	2	4	2	4	2	0	2	0	F	Deduc me in justitia	AR 75	an	6
F	2	4	2	4	2	0	2	0		Ecce concipies et paries Ave Maria	GR 459 LU 1412 *SYG 57	trv	
F	2	4	2	4	2	0	2	0		Et funes extenderunt Eripe me	GR 208 OHS 534 LU 725 GS 99 GB 116v *SYG 137	trv	
F	2	4	2	4	2	0	2	0		Et nos putavimus eum Vere languores	GR [108]	trv	
F	2	4	2	4	2	0	2	0		Notas fecisti mihi vias Benedicam Dominum	OTT 88 *GB 76v SYG 87	ofv	
F	2	4	2	4	2	0	2	0	G	Omnes gentes quascumque fecisti	GR 55 LU 449	co	8
F	2	4	2	4	2	0	2	0		Propter veritatem ... et deducet Diffusa est gratia	GS 228	trv	
F	2	4	2	4	2	0	2	0	D	Tollite jugum meum	WA 412	an	1
F	2	4	2	4	2	0	2	0		Tu exsurgens Domine misereberis Domine exaudi	GR 191 OHS 324 LU 619 GS 92 GB 114 *SYG 127	trv	

F	2	4	2	4	2	0	2	0	D	Venit lumen tuum	AR 312 LU 463 *AM 290 WA 56 *LA 73	an	1
F	2	4	2	4	2	0	2	4	F	Adaperiat Dominus cor ... Dominus	LA 299	an	6
F	2	4	2	4	2	0	2	4	F	Alleluia	AR 1 5 458 AM 32 475	an	6
F	2	4	2	4	2	0	2	4	G	Annuntiavi justitiam tuam	GR [2^2] LU 1122^4	tr	8
F	2	4	2	4	2	0	2	4	D	Audi Domine hymnum	LA 272 WA 167	re	1
F	2	4	2	4	2	0	2	4		Benedicat nos sancta trinitas Benedicat nos Deus	SYG 263	trv	
F	2	4	2	4	2	0	2	4	G	Desiderium animae ejus	GR [5] LU 1131 SYG 52 *GB 51^v GS 208	tr	8
F	2	4	2	4	2	0	2	4	G	Dominum Deum tuum	AR 371 LU 538 AM 344 WA 88 LA 134	an	8
F	2	4	2	4	2	0	2	4	D	Dum exiret Jacob de terra	LA 138 WA 91	re	1
F	2	4	2	4	2	0	2	4	G	Effuderunt sanguinem sanctorum	GR 42 LU 429 SYG 26 *GB 26^v	tr	8
F	2	4	2	4	2	0	2	4		Haec dies quam fecit Benedictus qui venit	OTT 64 GB 144 SYG 161	ofv	
F	2	4	2	4	2	0	2	4	F	Kyrie	MEL #105		
F	2	4	2	4	2	0	2	4		Libera me de ore leonis Deus Deus meus	GR 180 OHS 109 LU 594 GS 86 GB 109 SYG 122	trv	
F	2	4	2	4	2	0	2	4	G	Magi videntes stellam dixerunt	AR 311 LU 455 AM 289 WA 52 *LA 66	an	8
F	2	4	2	4	2	0	2	4	D	Misereris omnium Domine	GR 87 LU 525 *SYG 65 GB 62 GS 30	int	1
F	2	4	2	4	2	0	2	4	D	Ponam arcum meum in nubibus	LA 118 *WA 78	re	1
F	2	4	2	4	2	0	2	4	D	Posuerunt mortalia servorum	GR 644 LU 1492^B *SYG 191 *GB 195^v *GS 219	co	1
F	2	4	2	4	2	0	2	4	G	Scriptum est enim percutiam	AR 425 OHS 163 LU 605 AM 404 *LA 185	an	8
F	2	4	2	4	2	0	2	4	G	Spiritus ubi vult spirat	GR 307 LU 906 *SYG 187 GB 193 GS a 140	co	8
C	2	4	2	4	2	0	2	5	D	Alleluia: constitues eos principes	SYG 221	al	1
F	2	4	2	4	2	0	2	5	D	In principio Deus antequam terram	LR 421 *LA 276 *WA 168	re	1
C	2	4	2	4	2	0	2	5	D	Via recto Oriente	LR 332 *LA 374	re	2
F	2	4	2	4	2	0	4	2	G	Alleluia: sancti tui Domine florebunt	GR [19] LU 1150 GS 215 GB 239	al	8
F	2	4	2	4	2	0	4	2	G	Aperiens Petrus os suum	WA 326	an	8
F	2	4	2	4	2	0	4	2	G	Omnes terrarum incolae	ST 166	hy	8
F	2	4	2	4	2	0	4	2		Sancti tui Domine florebunt	GR [19] LU 1150 GS 215 GB 239	alv	
C	2	4	2	4	2	0	4	5	D	Alleluia: sapientia hujus mundi stultitia	GR 473 LU 1428	al	1

C	2	4	2	4	2	0	4	5	D	Kyrie	MEL #216		
C	2	4	2	4	2	0	4	5		Sapientia hujus mundi	GR 473 LU 1428	alv	
F	2	4	2	4	2	0	4	6	G	Alleluia: ecce vir Dei Benedictus reliquit	GB 55	al	8
F	2	4	2	4	2	0	4	7	G	Alleluia: ecce quam bonum et quam	GB 201v	al	8
C	2	4	2	4	2	0	4	7	D	Alleluia: valde honorandus	SYG 24	al	1
F	2	4	2	4	2	0	4	7	G	Caelestium minister donorum	WA 294	re	8
F	2	4	2	4	2	0	4	7	G	Dominus custodit te ab omni	AR [144] LU 1773 AM 1152 *WA 435	an	8
F	2	4	2	4	2	0	4	7	G	Egregius Dei martyr Vincentius	WA 261	an	8
F	2	4	2	4	2	0	4	7	F	Hic est dies verus Dei	ST 418	hy	6
F	2	4	2	4	2	0	4	7	F	Invicte martyr unicum	AR [17]	hy	6
F	2	4	2	4	2	0	4	7	G	Ista est speciosa inter filias	AR [98] LU 1233	an	8
F	2	4	2	4	2	0	4	7	G	Licuit sanguine loqui	WA 44	an	8
F	2	4	2	4	2	0	4	7	F	Martyr Dei qui unicum	ST 61 100 AM 642	hy	6
F	2	4	2	4	2	0	4	7	G	Mitte manum tuam	AR 465 AM 478 WA 137 LA 230 233	an	8
F	2	4	2	4	2	0	4	7	G	Omnes collaudunt nomen	WA 113	an	8
C	2	4	2	4	2	0	4	7		Valde honorandus est	SYG 24	alv	
C	2	4	2	4	2	0	5	7	C	Agnus Dei	SCH #264		4
C	2	4	2	4	2	0	5	7	E	Alleluia: haec est virgo sapiens et una	GR [57] LU 1222	al	4
C	2	4	2	4	2	0	7	9		Haec est virgo sapiens et una	GR [57] LU 1222	alv	
c	2	4	2	4	2	4	0	-1		Da mihi intellectum ut discam Domine vivifica	OTT 31 GB 64 *SYG 68	ofv	
F	2	4	2	4	2	4	0	2	E	Memento verbi tui servo tuo	GR 379 LU 1065 SYG 116 GB 103v GS 76 165	co	4
c	2	4	2	4	2	4	0	2	c	Super muros tuos Jerusalem	LA 302 *WA 184	re	6
F	2	4	2	4	2	4	2	-1	D	Domine non sum dignus	AR 360 *AM 334 *WA 84	an	1
F	2	4	2	4	2	4	2	-1	D	Domine puer meus jacet	AR 360 *AM 333 *WA 84 *LA 107	an	1
F	2	4	2	4	2	4	2	0	D	Alleluia: audivimus eam in Ephrata	LA 238 WA 144	re	1
F	2	4	2	4	2	4	2	0	F	Domine inminuti sumus	WA 228	an	6
C	2	4	2	4	2	4	2	0	D	Dunstanus praesul inclytus	WA 311	an	1
F	2	4	2	4	2	4	2	0	G	Hodie sanctus Joannes	WA 346	an	8
F	2	4	2	4	2	4	2	0	G	Ipse enim pater amat vos	AR 486 *AM 502	an	8
F	2	4	2	4	2	4	2	0	G	Maiolus caritate redundans	AM 875	an	8
F	2	4	2	4	2	4	2	0	G	Misit denique aquam	SYG 133	an	8

F	2	4	2	4	2	4	2	0	G	Nonne decem mundati	WA 189	an	8
F	2	4	2	4	2	4	2	0	G	Sinite parvulos venire	GR 590 LU 1616	co	8
F	2	4	2	4	2	4	2	0	G	Spiritus sanctus docebit vos	SYG 185	co	8
F	2	4	2	4	2	4	2	0	G	Video caelos apertos	GR 38 LU 418 *SYG 23 *GB 22^{v} GS 16	co	8
F	2	4	2	4	2	4	2	4	G	Agatha laetissime et glorianter	LA 357	re	8
F	2	4	2	4	2	4	2	4	G	Doceam iniquos vias	WA 106	re	8
F	2	4	2	4	2	4	2	4	G	Domine iste sanctus habitabit	LR 196 *WA 425	an	8
F	2	4	2	4	2	4	2	4	G	Erat Joseph et Maria	LA 62	an	8
F	2	4	2	4	2	4	2	4	G	Facite vobis amicos	WA 188	an	8
F	2	4	2	4	2	4	2	4	G	Ipse praeibit ante illum	LR 357 *LA 404 WA 321	re	8
F	2	4	2	4	2	4	2	4	G	Iterum autem videbo vos et gaudebit	AM 492 LA 237	an	8
F	2	4	2	4	2	4	2	4	G	Nubes lucida	WA 90	an	8
F	2	4	2	4	2	4	2	4	G	Venit lumen tuum	LR 80	re	8
F	2	4	2	4	2	4	2	4	G	Venit Michael archangelus	LA 468 *WA 381	re	8
F	2	4	2	4	2	4	5	2		Defende nos Domine / Per signum crucis	SYG 129	trv	
F	2	4	2	4	2	4	5	2		Deus a Libano veniet / Domine audivi	GR 206 OHS 529 LU 721 *GS 98 GB 116 SYG 136	trv	
F	2	4	2	4	2	4	5	2		Et quodcumque solveris / Tu es Petrus	GR 409 LU 1332 GS 182 *SYG 53	trv	
F	2	4	2	4	2	4	5	2		Memento nostri Domine / Confitemini Domino	GR 113 LU 547 GB 75 SYG 86	trv	
F	2	4	2	4	2	4	5	2		Ne tradas me a desiderio / Eripe me	GR 208 OHS 534 LU 725 GS 99 GB 116^{v} *SYG 137	trv	
F	2	4	2	4	2	4	5	4		Age nunc virgo Christi / Gaudens perenniter	SYG 238	trv	
F	2	4	2	4	2	4	6	2	G	Ipse me coronavit	LA 360 WA 274	re	8
F	2	4	2	4	2	4	6	2	G	Ipsi sum desponsata	LA 335 WA 255	re	8
F	2	4	2	4	2	4	6	2	G	Jam corpus ejus corpori meo	LA 336 WA 254	re	8
F	2	4	2	4	2	4	6	2	G	Michael archangelus venit	LA 470	re	8
F	2	4	2	4	2	4	6	2	G	Quis es tu qui venisti	LA 359 WA 273	re	8
F	2	4	2	4	2	4	6	2	G	Stephanus autem plenus gratia	WA 34	re	8
F	2	4	2	4	2	4	6	2	G	Virgo gloriosa semper evangelium	LA 490 *WA 406	re	8
F	2	4	2	4	2	4	6	4	G	Da mihi in disco caput	LA 453	re	8
F	2	4	2	4	2	4	6	4	G	Ecce constitui te	LA 406 *WA 322	re	8
F	2	4	2	4	2	4	6	4	G	Fuit vir vitae venerabilis	LR 320	re	8
F	2	4	2	4	2	4	6	4	G	Hic est dies praeclarus in quo salvator	LR 81 LA 68 *WA 55	re	8

F	2	4	2	4	2	4	6	4	G	Hic est Michael archangelus	PM 153 LA 468 *WA 382	re	8
F	2	4	2	4	2	4	6	4	G	Jam non dicam vos	PM 330 LR 110 LU 1847 VP 275 LA 257 *WA 154	re	8
F	2	4	2	4	2	4	6	4	G	Magi veniunt ab Oriente	LR 76 LA 68 *WA 53	re	8
F	2	4	2	4	2	4	6	4	G	Muro tuo inexpugnabili	LA 303 *WA 184	re	8
F	2	4	2	4	2	4	6	4	G	Notas mihi fecisti Domine	LA 82 *WA 60	re	8
F	2	4	2	4	2	4	6	4	G	Obviam sacratissimis	LR 370	re	8
F	2	4	2	4	2	4	6	4	G	Sancti et justi in Domino	LA 389	re	8
F	2	4	2	4	2	4	6	4	G	Servite Domino in timore ... et exsultate	LA 83	re	8
F	2	4	2	4	2	4	6	4	G	Vidi angelum ascendentem	LR 390	re	8
F	2	4	2	4	2	4	7	2	G	Continet in gremio	WA 50	re	8
F	2	4	2	4	2	4	7	2	G	Sexto die portari se	LR 331 *LA 373	re	8
F	2	4	2	4	2	5	2	0		Audi filia ... et obliviscere Diffusa est gratia	GS 228	trv	
C	2	4	2	4	2	7	4	5	E	Kyrie Christe caelorum	MEL #215		
G	2	4	2	4	2	7	5	4		Crucifixum in carne Sedit angelus ad	WA 222 *SYG 146	anv	
F	2	4	2	4	5	0	2	0	F	O salutaris hostia quae caeli	ST 459	hy	6
C	2	4	2	4	5	2	0	2	D	Ecce ego Joannes vidi	WA 371	an	1
F	2	4	2	4	5	2	0	4		Veni sancte spiritus reple Emitte spiritum	GR [93] LU 1279	trv	
G	2	4	2	4	5	4	0	2	G	Agnus Dei	SCH #81		8
G	2	4	2	4	5	4	0	2		Agnus Dei	SCH #83		
G	2	4	2	4	5	4	2	0	G	Agnus Dei	SCH #80		8
F	2	4	2	4	5	4	2	0	F	Agnus Dei	SCH #128		6
F	2	4	2	4	5	4	2	0	F	Alleluia alleluia: Christus hodie	WA 128	inv	6
c	2	4	2	4	5	4	2	0	c	Alleluia: quasi cedrus exaltata es	GB 224	al	6
F	2	4	2	4	5	4	2	0	F	Benedicta et venerabilis ... cujus viscera	PM 261 LR 257	re	5
F	2	4	2	4	5	4	2	0	F	Bernardus doctor inclytus	ST 45	hy	5
F	2	4	2	4	5	4	2	0	F	Bonum doctrinae gratia nomine	ST 311	hy	5
G	2	4	2	4	5	4	2	0	G	Festa celebria militans hodie	ST 308	hy	7
G	2	4	2	4	5	4	2	0	b	Gaudium mundi nova stella caeli	ST 467	hy	4
F	2	4	2	4	5	4	2	0	D	Hodie Christus natus est	AR 272 LU 413 AM 249 *WA 42 LA 39	an	1
G	2	4	2	4	5	4	2	0	G	Iste confessor Domini sacratus	ST 135	hy	8
F	2	4	2	4	5	4	2	0	F	Kyrie	MEL #107		
F	2	4	2	4	5	4	2	0	F	Kyrie	MEL #108		

G	2	4	2	4	5	4	2	0	G	Kyrie adest reducta	MEL #49		
c	2	4	2	4	5	4	2	0		Quasi cedrus exaltata es	GB 224	alv	
G	2	4	2	4	5	4	2	0	G	Qui Christe natus virgini	ST 179	hy	8
G	2	4	2	4	5	4	2	0	G	Silvestri almi praesulis	ST 445	hy	8
G	2	4	2	4	5	4	2	0	G	Templum tuum nos effice	ST 179	hy	8
G	2	4	2	4	5	4	2	0	G	Wulstane praesul inclite fulget dies	ST 178	hy	8
G	2	4	2	4	5	4	2	4		Agnus Dei	SCH #82		
G	2	4	2	4	5	4	2	4	G	Agnus Dei	SCH #97		8
C	2	4	2	4	5	4	2	4	E	Alleluia: timebunt gentes nomen tuum	SYG 249	al	4
C	2	4	2	4	5	4	2	4		Beatus Laurentius dum in craticula	SYG 217	alv	
F	2	4	2	4	5	4	2	4		Congregavit nos in unum Ubi caritas	GR 204 OHS 451 LU 675	anv	
F	2	4	2	4	5	4	2	4		Exsultemus et in ipso Ubi caritas	GR 204 OHS 451 LU 675	anv	
G	2	4	2	4	5	4	2	4	G	Kyrie caelum terramque	MEL #54		
C	2	4	2	4	5	4	2	4	E	Kyrie qui dignasti	MEL #218		
G	2	4	2	4	5	4	2	4	E	Oportet te fili gaudere	SYG 92	co	3
G	2	4	2	4	5	4	2	4	G	Sanctus	THAN #64		8
F	2	4	2	4	5	4	2	4	F	Ubi caritas et amor	GR 204 OHS 451 LU 675	an	6
C	2	4	2	4	5	4	2	5		In exitu Israel ex Aegypto	GR 381 LU 1068 GB 261	alv	
F	2	4	2	4	5	4	5	4	F	Agnus Dei	SCH #126		6
C	2	4	2	4	5	4	5	4	D	Nemo te condemnavit mulier quae	SYG 100	co	2
C	2	4	2	4	5	4	5	4		Omnis terra adoret te	SYG 35 GB 37^{v}	alv	
C	2	4	2	4	5	4	5	4		Timebunt gentes nomen tuum	SYG 249	alv	
C	2	4	2	4	5	4	5	4		Venit autem ad Simonem Coena facta sciens	SYG 133	anv	
G	2	4	2	4	5	7	4	0	E	Alleluia: cum sederit filius	SYG 157	al	3
C	2	4	2	4	5	7	4	2	D	Alleluia: beati quorum remissae sunt	SYG 241	al	1
C	2	4	2	4	5	7	4	2	E	Alleluia: cum venerit paraclitus spiritus	SYG 181	al	4
C	2	4	2	4	5	7	4	5	E	Alleluia: omnis terra adoret te	GB 37^{v} SYG 35	al	4
C	2	4	2	4	5	7	5	4	[D]	Alleluia: bonum certamen certavi	SYG 205	al	1
C	2	4	2	4	5	7	5	4	D	Alleluia: crastina die delebitur	SYG 13	al	2
C	2	4	2	4	5	7	5	4	[D]	Alleluia: de utero senectutis	GB 198^{v}	al	1
C	2	4	2	4	5	7	5	4	D	Alleluia: factus est repente	SYG 183 *GS 140	al	1
C	2	4	2	4	5	7	5	4	D	Alleluia: gloriosae virginis Mariae	GB 231^{v}	al	1

C	2	4	2	4	5	7	5	4	D	Alleluia: Martinus hic pauper	SYG 227	al	1
C	2	4	2	4	5	7	5	4	[D]	Alleluia: repleti sunt apostoli	GB 192	al	1
C	2	4	2	4	5	7	5	4	D	Alleluia: tuam crucem adoramus	SYG 173	al	1
C	2	4	2	4	5	7	5	4		Crastina die delebitur	SYG 13	alv	
G	2	4	2	4	5	7	5	4	G	Signifer invictissime	ST 468	hy	8
C	2	4	2	4	5	7	9	12	E	Salve virginale Christi	PM 265 VP 41	re	4
F	2	4	2	4	6	2	0	4	G	Fratres mei elongaverunt	LA 176 WA 110	re	8
F	2	4	2	4	6	4	2	0	F	Agnus Dei	SCH #127		6
F	2	4	2	4	6	4	2	4	G	Damasci praepositus gentis	LA 424	re	8
F	2	4	2	4	6	4	2	4	G	Domine exaudi orationem meam ... perveniat	LA 103	re	8
F	2	4	2	4	6	4	2	4	G	Domine praevenisti eum	PM 219 LR 159 205 LA 523 *WA 416	re	8
F	2	4	2	4	6	4	2	4	G	Domini est terra	LA 83 *WA 61	re	8
F	2	4	2	4	6	4	2	4	G	Ecce sacerdos magnus qui ... ideo	AR 82* PM 308 LR 194 LU 1841 LA 530 *WA 425	re	8
F	2	4	2	4	6	4	2	4	G	Hic est beatissimus evangelista	LA 50 WA 40	re	8
F	2	4	2	4	6	4	2	4	G	Iste est qui ante Deum ... et de omni	LR 208	re	8
F	2	4	2	4	6	4	2	4	G	Iste est qui ante Deum ... et omnis	LR 199 *LA 535 *WA 426	re	8
F	2	4	2	4	6	4	2	4	G	Isti sunt viri sancti quos	LR 145 LA 509 *WA 413	re	8
F	2	4	2	4	6	4	2	4	G	Kyrie	MEL #113		
F	2	4	2	4	6	4	2	4	G	Leva Jerusalem oculos	LA 9	re	8
F	2	4	2	4	6	4	2	4	G	Merito haec patimur	LA 151 *WA 97	re	8
F	2	4	2	4	6	4	2	4	G	Nihil inquinatum in eam	AM 1191	re	8
F	2	4	2	4	6	4	2	4	G	Stella quam viderant Magi	LR 78 LA 71 *WA 54	re	8
F	2	4	2	4	6	4	2	4	G	Stephanus servus Dei	PM 30 LA 44 *WA 36	re	8
F	2	4	2	4	6	4	2	4	G	Veniet nobis salus a Domino	LA 27	re	8
F	2	4	2	4	6	4	2	4	G	Vidi civitatem ... ornatam	LA 388	re	8
F	2	4	2	4	6	4	2	6	G	Alleluia: multae tribulationes	SYG 200	al	8
F	2	4	2	4	6	4	2	7	E	Alleluia: in te Domine speravi	GR 335 LU 1008 *GS 146 *GB 250 *SYG 241	al	3
F	2	4	2	4	6	4	6	4		Ego autem dixi in mea Exaltabo te	OTT 96 *GB 62^v *SYG 66	ofv	
F	2	4	2	4	6	4	6	4	F	Sanctus	THAN #108		6
F	2	4	2	4	6	4	7	2		In factis manuum tuarum Eripe me de inimicis	GB 111^v	ofv	
F	2	4	2	4	6	7	6	4	G	Alleluia: confiteantur Domino misericordiae	GR 411	al	8

F	2	4	2	4	6	7	6	4	G	Alleluia: diffusa est gratia	GR 405 LU 1323 *SYG 5 *GB 4v GS 228	al	8
F	2	4	2	4	6	7	6	4	G	Alleluia: Dominus dixit ad me	GR 29 LU 394 SYG 15 *GB 14 GS 14	al	8
F	2	4	2	4	6	7	6	4	G	Alleluia: Dominus in Sina in sancto	GR 286 LU 848 GS 136 SYG 179 *GB 178v	al	8
F	2	4	2	4	6	7	6	4	G	Alleluia: Dominus regnavit exsultet terra	GR 72 LU 490 GS 23 SYG 42	al	8
F	2	4	2	4	6	7	6	4	G	Alleluia: Dominus salvavit manum tuam	GR 464	al	8
F	2	4	2	4	6	7	6	4	G	Alleluia: haec dies quam fecit	GR 259 LU 805 OHS 827 GS 123 SYG 161 *GB 142v	al	8
F	2	4	2	4	6	7	6	4	G	Alleluia: inebriabuntur ab ubertate	GR 425	al	8
F	2	4	2	4	6	7	6	4	[G]	Alleluia: lauda anima mea	SYG 256 GS 166	al	8
F	2	4	2	4	6	7	6	4	[G]	Alleluia: mittat tibi Dominus	SYG 232	al	8
F	2	4	2	4	6	7	6	4	G	Alleluia: mittat vobis Dominus	GR [123] LU 1289	al	8
F	2	4	2	4	6	7	6	4	G	Alleluia: nimis honorati sunt	GR 644 LU 1720 *GB 267v	al	8
F	2	4	2	4	6	7	6	4	G	Alleluia: ostende nobis Domine	GR 2 LU 320 GS 1 SYG 2 *GB 1	al	8
F	2	4	2	4	6	7	6	4	G	Alleluia: paras mihi mensam	LU 1623c	al	8
F	2	4	2	4	6	7	6	4	G	Alleluia: salve regina misericordiae	LU 1476E	al	8
F	2	4	2	4	6	7	6	4	G	Alleluia: specie tua et pulchritudine	GR [70] LU 1218 GS 227 SYG 29 *GB 273	al	8
F	2	4	2	4	6	7	6	4	G	Alleluia: spiritus est Deus	SYG 187	al	8
F	2	4	2	4	7	4	2	7	E	Alleluia: ostende mihi faciem tuam	GR 440 LU 1377	al	3
F	2	4	2	4	7	5	4	2	F	Sancta mater istud agas	AR 676	hy	6
F	2	4	2	4	7	5	4	2	F	Stabat mater dolorosa	AR 672 162* VP 136 LU 1424	hy	6
F	2	4	2	4	7	5	4	2	F	Virgo virginum praeclara	AR 675 LU 1424	hy	6
F	2	4	2	4	7	6	4	7	G	Brachia peccatorum conterentur	GR 467 LU 1421	co	8
C	2	4	2	4	7	9	4	5	E	Casta generatio in perpetuum	GR 100**	alv	
F	2	4	2	4	7	9	6	7	F	Dominabitur a mari	GR 639 LU 1710	gr	5
F	2	4	2	4	7	9	6	7	F	Omnes de Saba venient ... laudem	GR 57 LU 459 *SYG 30 *GB 33 GS J 19	gr	5
F	2	4	2	4	9	7	4	6		Exsurgat Deus et dissipentur Mirabilis Deus	OTT 141 GB 171 *SYG 175	ofv	
C	2	4	2	5	0	2	0	2	D	Christe sanctorum decus angelorum	ST 160	hy	2
G	2	4	2	5	2	0	2	5	E	Immittet angelus Domini	AR 144 OHS 362 LU 293	an	3
G	2	4	2	5	2	0	4	5	D	Vidi Jerusalem descendentem	LA 228 *WA 141	re	1

F	2	4	2	5	2	4	2	-1	D	Domine si tu vis	AR 337 LU 491 AM 307	an	1
F	2	4	2	5	2	4	2	4	D	Domine si hic fuisses	AR 404 LU 1096 AM 380 WA 105 (inc illeg) *LA 165	an	1
F	2	4	2	5	4	0	2	0	F	Benedicamus Domino Ic	AR 59* LU 125		6
G	2	4	2	5	4	0	2	0	G	Ite missa est VI	GR 25* LU 34		8
G	2	4	2	5	4	0	2	0	G D	Kyrie archangeli laetantur (etc)	MEL #55		
G	2	4	2	5	4	0	2	0	G	Kyrie VI rex genitor	GR 21* LU 31		7
G	2	4	2	5	4	2	0	-2	G	Cum plebe clerus monachi	ST 153	hy	8
G	2	4	2	5	4	2	0	-2	G	Jam lucis orto sidere fulget dies	ST 116	hy	8
c	2	4	2	5	4	2	0	-2	c	Requievit arca mense septimo	WA 77	re	6
c	2	4	2	5	4	2	0	2	c	Aeterne rerum conditor	ST 358	hy	6
c	2	4	2	5	4	2	0	2	c	Amicus Dei Nicholaus	WA 242	an	6
c	2	4	2	5	4	2	0	2	c	Andreas apostolus	WA 232	an	6
c	2	4	2	5	4	2	0	2	c	Benedicamus patrem et filium in	WA 82	an	6
C	2	4	2	5	4	2	0	2	E	Christum Dei filium qui suo nos	LR 441	inv	4
C	2	4	2	5	4	2	0	2	E	Christum regem adoremus	AR 102* LR 119 LU 918 VP 6	inv	4
G	2	4	2	5	4	2	0	2	E	Ite missa est IIa	GR 11* LU 22		3
G	2	4	2	5	4	2	0	2	E	Jesu nostra redemptio	ST 37	hy	3
G	2	4	2	5	4	2	0	2	E	Kyrie II fons bonitatis (etc)	MEL #48 GR 8* LU 19 VP 165		3
G	2	4	2	5	4	2	0	2	E	Pater superni luminis	AR 789 LU 1565	hy	3
c	2	4	2	5	4	2	0	2	c	Sancti infantes martyres	ST 370	hy	6
F	2	4	2	5	4	2	0	2	F	Scio quem quaeritis	WA 135	an	6
G	2	4	2	5	4	2	0	2	E	Summi parentis unice	AR 791	hy	3
F	2	4	2	5	4	2	0	4		Corpus in cibum Transiturus	LR 132	rev	
G	2	4	2	5	4	2	0	4	G	Stabat mater dolorosa	ST 334	hy	7
C	2	4	2	5	4	2	0	5	D	Dum ingrederetur Jesus	WA 189	an	1
c	2	4	2	5	4	2	4	0	c	Hodie caelistis porta	WA 319	an	6
G	2	4	2	5	4	2	4	0	G	Kyrie theoricam practicamque (etc)	MEL #47		
C	2	4	2	5	4	2	4	2	E	Kyrie	MEL #214		
C	2	4	2	5	4	2	4	5	D	Agatha laetissime et glorianter	WA 273	re	2
C	2	4	2	5	4	2	5	4	D	Agnus Dei	SCH #263		2
C	2	4	2	5	4	2	5	9	D	Christus resurgens ex mortuis	AR 164* PM 66 VP 141 *WA 223	re	2
C	2	4	2	5	4	2	9	7	D	Alleluia: justi confitebuntur nomini	SYG 190	al	1

C	2	4	2	5	4	2	9	7	D	Christus resurgens ex mortuis	WA 133 *SYG 147	an	1 2
C	2	4	2	5	4	5	2	4	F	Domine rex omnipotens creator	GB 160^{v}	an	6
C	2	4	2	5	4	5	2	4	D	Erue a framea Deus	LA 171 *WA 108	re	2
C	2	4	2	5	4	5	2	4	D	Judas mercator pessimus	OHS 389 LU 644	re	2
C	2	4	2	5	4	5	2	4	D	Meruit esse hostia	LA 439	re	2
C	2	4	2	5	4	5	2	4	D	Misit rex incredulus	LA 453	re	2
C	2	4	2	5	4	5	2	4	D	Tua est potentia	AM 1203 *VP 262 LA 295 *WA 180	re	2
C	2	4	2	5	4	5	4	2	D	Aperi caelos tuos	WA 182	re	2
C	2	4	2	5	4	5	7	2	D	Domine Deus qui conteris	LA 292 *WA 178	re	2
C	2	4	2	5	4	5	7	2	D	Igitur dissimulata	WA 342	re	2
C	2	4	2	5	4	5	7	2	D	Posuit coronam capiti meo	LR 152 LA 525 *WA 418	re	2
C	2	4	2	5	4	5	7	2	D	Versa est in luctum	LA 286 *WA 174	re	2
C	2	4	2	5	4	5	7	2	D	Viderunt te aquae Deus	LA 237 *WA 144	re	2
C	2	4	2	5	4	5	7	5	D	Agnus Dei Christus	WA 126	re	2
C	2	4	2	5	4	5	7	5		Miserere miserere miserere O beata benedicta	WA 161	anv	
C	2	4	2	5	4	5	7	5	D	Simile est regnum caelorum decem	WA 432	re	2
C	2	4	2	5	7	5	4	2	D	Alleluia: verumtamen existimo omnia	GR 474 LU 1428	al	1
GG	2	4	2	5	7	5	4	2	D	Kyrie	MEL #226		
C	2	4	2	5	7	5	4	2		Verumtamen existimo omnia	GR 474 LU 1428	alv	
GG	2	4	2	5	7	9	7	5	D	Kyrie	MEL #225		
C	2	4	2	5	7	9	7	5	E	Sanctus	THAN #226		4
C	2	4	2	5	7	9	7	9	E	Ego pro te rogavi	LR 365 LA 417 *WA 278	re	4
F	2	4	2	6	4	2	4	6	D	Salve crux sancta salve mundi gloria	ST 454	hy	1
F	2	4	2	6	7	4	2	4	F	Tantum ergo sacramentum	AR 90* LU 1852 AM 1259	hy	5
F	2	4	2	7	6	2	4	7	G	Almi prophetae progenies pia	ST 433	hy	8
F	2	4	2	7	6	4	2	9		A summo caelo egressio ejus	GR 85**	alv	
F	2	4	2	7	6	4	6	2	G	Petite et accipietis ut gaudium	AR 485 AM 501	an	8
F	2	4	2	7	6	4	7	4	G	Beata nobis gaudia	ST 258	hy	7
F	2	4	2	7	6	4	7	4	G	Beata nobis gaudia	ST 294	hy	7
F	2	4	2	7	6	4	7	6	G	Tu es qui venturus es an alium	AR 227 LU 333 AM 199 *WA 16 *LA 11	an	8
F	2	4	2	7	6	4	7	6	G	Vitam petiit a te	LR 196 *WA 425 LA 531	an	8
F	2	4	2	7	6	7	4	2	G	Prima autem azymorum	GS 78	an	8
F	2	4	2	7	9	11	9	7	G	Alleluia: spiritus sanctus docebit vos	GR 299 LU 891 GB 191	al	8

C	2	4	2	9	10	9	7	4	E	Alleluia: qui facit angelos suos	GR 461 GB 168^{v}	al	4
C	2	4	2	9	10	9	7	4		Qui facit angelos suos	GR 461 GB 168^{v}	alv	
C	2	4	2	9	10	9	7	5	D	Benedictus es in templo sancto	LR 243	re	1
C	2	4	2	9	10	9	7	5	D	Non abscondas me Domine	PM 112	re	1
C	2	4	2	9	10	9	7	9	D	Alleluia: leva in circuitu oculos tuos	GR 45**	al	1
C	2	4	2	9	10	9	7	9	D	Alleluia: sapientiam ipsorum narrent	GR 445 LU 1386	al	1
C	2	4	2	9	10	9	7	9	D	Alleluia: surrexit Dominus de sepulcro	GR 248 LU 790 OHS 785 *GB 137^{v}	al	1
C	2	4	2	9	10	9	7	9	D	Alleluia: veni electa mea	GS 227	al	1
C	2	4	2	9	10	9	7	9	D	Alleluia: virgo Dei genitrix	GR 623 LU 1684	al	1
C	2	4	2	9	10	9	7	9	D	Expurgate vetus fermentum	OHS 814 LR 93 LA 212 WA 134	re	1
C	2	4	2	9	10	9	7	9	D	Tradiderunt corpora sua propter ... et	LR 179 LA 515 WA 421	re	1
C	2	4	2	9	10	9	12	9	D	Confirmatum est cor virginis	PM 166 *WA 49	re	1
C	2	4	2	9	11	9	7	5	D	Benedixit te Dominus in virtute	LA 291 WA 178	re	1
C	2	4	2	9	11	9	7	5	D	Confortate manus fatigatas	LA 4	re	1
C	2	4	2	9	11	9	7	5	D	Ne abscondas me Domine	LA 284 WA 173	re	1
C	2	4	2	9	11	9	7	9	D	Accedentes discipuli	LA 453 *WA 363	re	1
C	2	4	2	9	11	9	7	9	D	Alleluia: in omnem terram exivit sonus eorum	GB 267	al	1
C	2	4	2	9	11	9	7	9	D	Congregati sunt inimici	LA 297 WA 181	re	1
C	2	4	2	9	11	9	7	9	D	Exaltata est virgo Maria	LA 445	re	1
C	2	4	2	9	11	9	7	9	D	Praeparate corda vestra Domino	PM 110 LR 420 LA 268 *WA 166	re	1
C	2	4	5	0	2	5	4	2	D	Summe largitor praemii	ST 284	hy	2
C	2	4	5	0	4	2	5	2	D	Felix namque es sacra virgo Maria	AR 127* *PM 242 *LR 255 LA 447 *WA 357	re	1
G	2	4	5	2	0	-2	0	2	G	Noli me derelinquere pater	LA 433	an	8
G	2	4	5	2	0	-2	0	2	G	Tunc Valerianus perrexit	LA 490 *WA 407	an	8
G	2	4	5	2	0	-2	2	0	G	Fili a juventute tua	LA 281	an	8
G	2	4	5	2	0	2	0	-3	G	Kyrie	MEL #44		
G	2	4	5	2	0	2	0	-2	G	Dixit autem discipulis	LA 220	an	8
C	2	4	5	2	0	2	0	2	D	Immaculatam conceptionem virginis	LR 259	inv	2
G	2	4	5	2	0	2	0	2	E	Mulier quae erat ... stans	AM 585	an	3
F	2	4	5	2	0	2	4	0	F	Respondens autem Petrus	AR 806 LU 1589	an	6
G	2	4	5	2	0	2	4	2	[G]	Agnus Dei	SCH #77		8

G	2	4	5	2	0	2	4	2	E	Ostende nobis Domine lucem	AM 78 79 *AR 189	an	3
C	2	4	5	2	0	2	4	2	D	Solemnitatem rosarii virginis	LR 448	inv	2
G	2	4	5	2	0	2	4	5	[G]	Agnus Dei	SCH #76		8
C	2	4	5	2	0	2	4	5	D	Scio cui credidi	LA 424 WA 330 (inc illeg)	re	1
F	2	4	5	2	0	2	4	5		Venite comedite panem meum Homo quidam	AR 112* PM 105 LR 419 VP 15 AM 1189	rev	
G	2	4	5	2	0	2	4	7	G	Dixit Simon Petrus Domine	LA 365	an	8
C	2	4	5	2	0	2	5	4	D	Laudemus Deum nostrum ... beatae N.	LR 211	inv	2
C	2	4	5	2	0	2	5	4	D	Laudemus Deum nostrum ... Benedicti	LR 443	inv	2
C	2	4	5	2	0	2	5	4	D	Laudemus Deum nostrum ... doctoris	LR 432	inv	2
C	2	4	5	2	0	2	5	4	D	Laudemus Deum nostrum ... Joseph	LR 435	inv	2
C	2	4	5	2	0	2	5	4	D	Laudemus Deum nostrum ... Martini	LR 454	inv	2
C	2	4	5	2	0	2	5	4	D	Nativitatem virginis Mariae	LR 446	inv	2
C	2	4	5	2	0	2	5	4	D	Regem regum Dominum	LR 380 *LA 474 WA 395	inv	2
C	2	4	5	2	0	2	5	4	D	Summe largitor praemii	ST 284	hy	2
C	2	4	5	2	0	2	5	4	D	Tu es pastor ovium ... tradidit	LR 431 LA 412 WA 325	inv	2
C	2	4	5	2	0	2	5	4	D	Visitationem virginis Mariae	LR 442	inv	2
C	2	4	5	2	0	2	5	7	D	Inclyta stirps Jesse	AM 985	an	1
C	2	4	5	2	0	2	5	7	D	Kyrie	MEL #213		
C	2	4	5	2	0	2	5	7	D	Translate ad caelestia	WA 315	re	1
C	2	4	5	2	0	2	7	5	D	Sanctus	THAN #225		1
C	2	4	5	2	0	2	9	7	D	Misericors et miserator Dominus escam	AR 538[1] LU 965 AM 561	an	2
F	2	4	5	2	0	4	2	0	F	Ad coenam agni providi	ST 290	hy	6
F	2	4	5	2	0	4	2	0	F	Aurora lucis rutilat	ST 230	hy	6
C	2	4	5	2	0	4	2	0	D	Non recedet laus tua	AR 638 LU 1384 *AM 821	an	1
C	2	4	5	2	0	4	2	5	D	Alleluia: propitius esto Domine peccatis	GR [148] LU 841 *SYG 234	al	1
C	2	4	5	2	0	4	5	7	D	Alleluia: cives apostolorum et domestici	GB 268	al	2
C	2	4	5	2	0	4	5	7		Cives apostolorum et domestici	GB 268	alv	
C	2	4	5	2	0	4	5	7		Propitius esto Domine peccatis	GR [148] LU 841 SYG 234	alv	
C	2	4	5	2	0	5	7	5		Eructavit cor meum Afferentur regi ... post	GB 4^v	ofv	

C	2	4	5	2	0	5	7	9	D	Hodie illuxit nobis laetus dies	PM 161 WA 329	an	1
C	2	4	5	2	0	5	7	9	D	Martyr Dei qui unicum	ST 243	hy	2
C	2	4	5	2	0	7	5	4		Positis genibus beatus Stephanus	SYG 22	alv	
C	2	4	5	2	0	7	5	4		Vado ad eum ... sed quia	GS 130 *SYG 167	alv	
C	2	4	5	2	4	0	2	0	D	Celebremus solemniter	WA 282	re	1
C	2	4	5	2	4	0	2	0		Surrexit pastor bonus ... ovibus	SYG 164	alv	
C	2	4	5	2	4	0	2	4		Ave Maria gratia plena ... benedicta	GR [77] LU 1265 GS 184	alv	
C	2	4	5	2	4	0	2	4		Eripe me de inimicis meis Deus	GR 343 LU 1018 *SYG 242 *GB 251 GS 147	alv	
C	2	4	5	2	4	0	2	4		Loquebar de testimoniis tuis	GS 228	alv	
C	2	4	5	2	4	0	2	4		Verbo Domini caeli firmati	SYG 240	alv	
C	2	4	5	2	4	2	0	2		Apparuerunt apostolis dispertitae	SYG 186	alv	
G	2	4	5	2	4	2	0	2	E	Ecce Dominus noster	AR 225 LU 333 AM 197 *WA 12 *LA 11	an	3
C	2	4	5	2	4	2	0	2	E	Exsulta et lauda Jerusalem	WA 360	an	4
G	2	4	5	2	4	2	0	2	a	Illuminans altissimus	ST 31	hy	2
G	2	4	5	2	4	2	0	2	G	Kyrie summe sophie	MEL #43		
G	2	4	5	2	4	2	0	2	G	Sanctus	THAN #62		8
C	2	4	5	2	4	2	0	2	D	Surgite vigilemus venite	LA 8 WA 9	inv	2
C	2	4	5	2	4	2	0	2	D	Trinitati altissimae	ST 14	hy	2
C	2	4	5	2	4	2	0	4	D	Confessorum regem adoremus	LA 366 WA 296	inv	2
C	2	4	5	2	4	2	0	5	D	Alleluia: flores apparuerunt in terra	GR 442	al	1
C	2	4	5	2	4	2	0	5	C	Kyrie	MEL #211		
C	2	4	5	2	4	2	0	5	D	Pro fidei meritis vocitatur	PM 109	an	1
C	2	4	5	2	4	5	4	2	D	Alleluia: corpora sanctorum in pace	GR [23] LU 1164	al	2
G	2	4	5	2	4	5	4	2	E	Ego rogabo patrem	LR 104	re	3
C	2	4	5	2	4	5	4	2	D	Sanctus	THAN #224		1
G	2	4	5	2	4	5	4	2	E	Si enim non abiero	LR 106 LA 246	re	3
C	2	4	5	2	4	5	4	5		Corpora sanctorum in pace	GR [23] LU 1164	alv	
F	2	4	5	2	4	5	7	4	F	Stabat mater dolorosa	ST 444	hy	6
C	2	4	5	2	4	5	7	5	E	Summum venerantes bonum	WA 341	inv	4
C	2	4	5	2	4	7	4	5	D	Sanctus XV	GR 53* LU 58 THAN #223		2
C	2	4	5	2	5	2	0	2	C	Qui venturus est veniet	LA 13 *WA 14	re	6
C	2	4	5	2	5	2	5	7	D	In die qua invocavi te	OHS 62 (nm) LR 339 *LA 175 *WA 110	re	1

G	2	4	5	2	5	4	0	2	E	Dominus judex noster	AR 894[2] LU 1716	an	3
G	2	4	5	2	5	4	0	2	E	Dominus legifer noster	AR 242 *AM 217	an	3
G	2	4	5	2	5	4	0	2	E	Ego Dominus prope feci	AR 244	an	3
G	2	4	5	2	5	4	0	2	F	Kyrie	MEL #42		
C	2	4	5	2	5	4	2	0	E	Cunctis diebus vitae	WA 65 *LA 92	an	4
C	2	4	5	2	5	4	2	0	a	Cunctis diebus vitae	AM 47 48	an	ir
G	2	4	5	2	5	4	2	0	G	Quam pulchra es et quam	WA 361	an	8
G	2	4	5	2	5	4	2	4	G	A dextris est mihi Dominus	LA 81 *WA 60	re	8
G	2	4	5	2	5	4	5	2	G	Sanctus	THAN #61		7
G	2	4	5	2	5	4	5	7	E	Domine ut video propheta	AR 395 LU 1092	an	3
G	2	4	5	2	5	4	5	7	E	Domine vim patior responde	AR 429 OHS 246 *AM 408 *WA 115 *LA 186	an	3
C	2	4	5	2	5	4	5	7	D	Hi sunt ecclesiarum	WA 325	an	1
G	2	4	5	4	0	-2	2	0	G	Kyrie	MEL #60		
G	2	4	5	4	0	2	0	-2	G	Lutum fecit ex sputo	GB 94	co	8
G	2	4	5	4	0	2	0	2		Ab omni via mala prohibui Deus docuisti	GR 72**	trv	
G	2	4	5	4	0	2	0	2		Dominus quasi vir pugnator Fortitudo mea	GR 468	trv	
G	2	4	5	4	0	2	0	2		Intrate in conspectu ejus Jubilate Domino omnis terra	GR 82 LU 513 GS 28 *GB 59v *SYG 62	trv	
G	2	4	5	4	0	2	0	5	G	Alleluia: lingua pravorum peribit	GR 29**	al	7
G	2	4	5	4	0	2	0	5		Lingua pravorum peribit	GR 29**	alv	
F	2	4	5	4	0	2	4	2	D	Vexilla regis prodeunt fulget	ST 417	hy	2
G	2	4	5	4	0	2	4	5	G	Sanctus	THAN #60		8
C	2	4	5	4	0	2	5	4	D	Ad te Domine levavi animam ... Deus	LA 84 *WA 61	re	2
C	2	4	5	4	0	4	5	7	D	Alleluia: o Joachim sancte conjux	GR 585 LU 1609	al	1
C	2	4	5	4	0	4	5	7	D	Alleluia: o quam pulchra ... immortalis	GR 104**	al	1
G	2	4	5	4	2	-2	0	2	E	Nunc facta est salus	LA 469	re	3
c	2	4	5	4	2	-1	0	-3	c	Sacris solemniis juncta sint gaudia	ST 348	hy	6 8
G	2	4	5	4	2	0	-3	-2	G	Sanctus	THAN #59		8
G	2	4	5	4	2	0	-2	0	G	Sanctus	THAN #58		8
G	2	4	5	4	2	0	-2	5		Et in terra	BOS #47		
F	2	4	5	4	2	0	-1	0	F	Agnus Dei	SCH #123		6
F	2	4	5	4	2	0	-1	0	F	Sanctus	THAN #107		6
G	2	4	5	4	2	0	[0	0]	G	Kyrie summe pater summum	MEL #59		

G	2	4	5	4	2	0	2	-2	G	Ad coenam agni providi	ST 189	hy	8
G	2	4	5	4	2	0	2	-2	G	Aeterne patris unice	AM 976	hy	8
G	2	4	5	4	2	0	2	-2	G	Caelestis agni nuptias	AR 729 LU 1491	hy	8
G	2	4	5	4	2	0	2	-2	G	Gertrudis arca numinis	AM 1129	hy	8
G	2	4	5	4	2	0	2	-2	G	Haec est dies qua candidae	AR 884 AM 1086	hy	8
G	2	4	5	4	2	0	2	-2	G	Jam noctis umbrae concidunt	AM 816	hy	8
G	2	4	5	4	2	0	2	-2	G	Jesu corona virginum	AR [89] LU 1211 AM 677 771	hy	8
G	2	4	5	4	2	0	2	-2	G	Kyrie	MEL #41		
G	2	4	5	4	2	0	2	-2	G	Pater superni luminis	AM 975	hy	8
G	2	4	5	4	2	0	2	-2	G	Regis superni nuntia	AR 883 LU 1688 AM 1086	hy	8
C	2	4	5	4	2	0	2	0	C	Agnus Dei	SCH #262		4
G	2	4	5	4	2	0	2	0		Caritas Dei diffusa ... spiritum	GB 194	alv	
c	2	4	5	4	2	0	2	0	c	Hymnos dulces personemus	ST 50	hy	8
C	2	4	5	4	2	0	2	0		In Deo speravit cor meum	GR [146]	alv	
G	2	4	5	4	2	0	2	0	G	Malos male perdet ... agricolis	AM 359 WA 95 (inc illeg)	an	8
F	2	4	5	4	2	0	2	0	F	O praeclara Constantia	ST 321	hy	5
C	2	4	5	4	2	0	2	0	C	Sanctus	THAN #222		6
C	2	4	5	4	2	0	2	4	E	Agnus Dei V	GR 20* LU 30		4
C	2	4	5	4	2	0	2	4	D	Alleluia: jubilemus Christo	WA 311	inv	2
C	2	4	5	4	2	0	2	4	E	Beatus Laurentius Christi martyr	LR 446 *WA 347	inv	4
C	2	4	5	4	2	0	2	4	E	Erat vir domini Benedictus	WA 334 *LA 374	an	4
G	2	4	5	4	2	0	2	4	G	In vesperi dictamine	ST 379	hy	8
F	2	4	5	4	2	0	2	4	F	Invocabimus nomen tuum	AR 157 LU 279°	an	6
G	2	4	5	4	2	0	2	4	G	Ite missa est V	GR 21* LU 31		8
C	2	4	5	4	2	0	2	4	D	Jam lucis orto sidere	OHS 76 198 (nm)	hy	2
F	2	4	5	4	2	0	2	4	D	Jam lucis orto sidere	ST 76	hy	1
F	2	4	5	4	2	0	2	4	F	Kyrie	MEL #99		
G	2	4	5	4	2	0	2	4	G	Kyrie V magnae Deus	MEL #78 GR 18* LU 28		8
G	2	4	5	4	2	0	2	4	G	Maneant in vobis fides	GR 203 OHS 450 LU 674 *WA 214 SYG 131	an	7
c	2	4	5	4	2	0	2	4	c	Martine par apostolis	ST 401	hy	6
C	2	4	5	4	2	0	2	4	D	Nunc sancte nobis spiritus	AR 413 OHS 85 203 LU 569 AM 387	hy	2
F	2	4	5	4	2	0	2	4	D	O crux ave spes unica	LU 1461	hy	1
C	2	4	5	4	2	0	2	4	D	Popule meus quid feci	GR 211 *WA 214 GB 118 *GS 101		

C	2	4	5	4	2	0	2	4	D	Rector potens verax Deus	OHS 147 215 (nm)	hy	2
C	2	4	5	4	2	0	2	4	D	Rerum Deus tenax vigor	OHS 151 218 (nm)	hy	2
c	2	4	5	4	2	0	2	4	c	Rex Christe Martini decus	ST 400	hy	6
G	2	4	5	4	2	0	2	4	G	Sanctus	THAN #57		8
C	2	4	5	4	2	0	2	4	D	Summae Deus clementiae	AR 844 AM 1049	hy	2
C	2	4	5	4	2	0	2	4	D	Te lucis ante terminum	AR 407 LU 577	hy	2
c	2	4	5	4	2	0	2	4		Umbra futurorum praesens Magne Deus	WA 318	rev	
C	2	4	5	4	2	0	2	4		Veni sancte spiritus reple	GR 293 [92] LU 880 GB 187 *GS 138 234	alv	
F	2	4	5	4	2	0	2	4	D	Vexilla regis prodeunt fulget	AR 405 697 GR 225 227 OHS 161 ST 34 90 188 384 LU 575 AM 383 897 1038	hy	1
C	2	4	5	4	2	0	2	4		Vidi speciosam sicut columbam	SYG 177	alv	
C	2	4	5	4	2	0	2	5	E	Qui Christiano nomini	ST 291	hy	4
C	2	4	5	4	2	0	2	5	E	Sanctus	THAN #221		4
C	2	4	5	4	2	0	2	5	E	Squalent arva soli pulvere multo	ST 494	hy	4
C	2	4	5	4	2	0	2	7	D	Alleluia: veni sancte spiritus	GR 293 [92] LU 880 GB 187 GS 138 234	al	2
C	2	4	5	4	2	0	2	9	D	Sanctus	THAN #220		1
F	2	4	5	4	2	0	4	2	F	Pange lingua gloriosi proelium	ST 342	hy	6
C	2	4	5	4	2	0	4	5	D	Cumque ascendisset	WA 309 *LA 398	an	2
C	2	4	5	4	2	0	4	5		Fulgebunt justi et tamquam	GR 575 SYG 193 GB 268^{v} *GS 225	alv	
C	2	4	5	4	2	0	4	5		Iste cognovit justitiam	SYG 189	alv	
C	2	4	5	4	2	0	4	5	E	Sanctus	THAN #219		4
C	2	4	5	4	2	0	4	5		Surrexit Christus et illuxit	GR 271 LU 831 GS 127 SYG 165	alv	
C	2	4	5	4	2	0	4	5		Vox exsultationis et salutis	GB 269 *SYG 176 *GS 215	alv	
F	2	4	5	4	2	0	4	7	F	Agnus Dei	SCH #124		5
C	2	4	5	4	2	0	4	7	[E]	Agnus Dei	SCH #261		3
F	2	4	5	4	2	0	4	7	E	Confessio et pulchritudo	GR 580 LU 1595 OTT 166 *GB 219 *GS 194 q SYG 213	of	4
F	2	4	5	4	2	0	4	7	F	Sanctus	THAN #106		5
C	2	4	5	4	2	0	5	4	D	Celebremus diem istum	WA 248	re	1
C	2	4	5	4	2	0	5	7	D	Alleluia: vidi speciosam	SYG 177	al	1
G	2	4	5	4	2	0	5	7	G	Beata Dei genitrix nitor	ST 398	hy	7
G	2	4	5	4	2	0	5	7	G	Beata nobis gaudia anni	ST 391	hy	7

G	2	4	5	4	2	0	5	7	G	Deus creator omnium	ST 364	hy	7
G	2	4	5	4	2	0	5	7	G	Diem sacrati nominis	ST 401	hy	7
G	2	4	5	4	2	0	5	7	G	Hujus diei gratia	ST 396	hy	7
G	2	4	5	4	2	0	5	7	G	Lucis creator optime	ST 361	hy	7
G	2	4	5	4	2	0	5	7	G	Maria decus hominum	ST 398	hy	7
G	2	4	5	4	2	0	5	7	G	Maria templum Domini	ST 398	hy	7
G	2	4	5	4	2	0	5	7	G	Maria virgo regia	ST 399	hy	7
G	2	4	5	4	2	0	5	7	G	O singularis femina	ST 398	hy	7
C	2	4	5	4	2	0	5	7	D	Super mira potentia	WA 340	an	2
G	2	4	5	4	2	0	7	5	G	Kyrie rex Deus immense	MEL #83		
F	2	4	5	4	2	0	7	9	F	Jam lucis orto sidere	ST 74	hy	5
F	2	4	5	4	2	0	7	9	F	Sanctus	THAN #105		5
F	2	4	5	4	2	4	0	-3		Adjuva nos Deus salutaris noster Domine non secundum	GR 89 LU 527 OHS 209 *GS 31 *SYG 66	trv	
F	2	4	5	4	2	4	0	-3	D	Kyrie ad lib I clemens rector	MEL #102 GR 75* LU 79		1
F	2	4	5	4	2	4	0	-3		Vindica sanguinem servorum Adjuva nos	GR [131]	trv	
F	2	4	5	4	2	4	0	-1	D	Benedicamus Domino IIIa	AR 61*		1
G	2	4	5	4	2	4	0	2	G	Ego rogabo patrem	LA 248	re	7
G	2	4	5	4	2	4	0	2	G	Mihi vivere Christus	LA 425 *WA 331	re	7
F	2	4	5	4	2	4	0	2	F	Nunc sancte nobis spiritus	ST 319	hy	6
G	2	4	5	4	2	4	0	2	G	Regali ex progenie	LA 458 *WA 367	re	7
C	2	4	5	4	2	4	0	2	D	Saulus adhuc spirans	LA 341 *WA 263	re	1
G	2	4	5	4	2	4	0	2	G	Stetit angelus juxta aram	LA 466 *WA 380	re	7
F	2	4	5	4	2	4	0	2	D	Super flumina Babylonis	GR 379 OTT 119 LU 1065 *SYG 115 *GB 102^v GS 76 165	of	1
C	2	4	5	4	2	4	0	4	E	Agnus Dei	SCH #260		4
C	2	4	5	4	2	4	0	4	E	Sanctus	THAN #218		4
G	2	4	5	4	2	4	2	0	G	Advenit ignis divinus	LR 116 *LA 259	re	7
G	2	4	5	4	2	4	2	0	[G]	Agnus Dei	SCH #78		8
F	2	4	5	4	2	4	2	0	F	Carminibus hymnidicis	ST 149	hy	6
G	2	4	5	4	2	4	2	0	G	Ecce puer meus quem elegi	LA 54 *WA 39	re	7
C	2	4	5	4	2	4	2	0		Ecce sacerdos magnus qui ... et inventus	SYG 215	alv	
G	2	4	5	4	2	4	2	0	G	Ecce vicit leo	OHS 789 *PM 68 LR 89 LA 209 *WA 134	re	7
G	2	4	5	4	2	4	2	0		Ego dilecto meo et ad me	GR 626 LU 1691	alv	

G	2	4	5	4	2	4	2	0	G	Eram quasi agnus	OHS 396 LU 649 *LA 192 *WA 119	re	7
C	2	4	5	4	2	4	2	0	D	Hei mihi Domine quia peccavi	AR [165] LU 1791 *WA 436 *LA 555	re	2
C	2	4	5	4	2	4	2	0	D	Hodie completi sunt dies	AR 509 LU 886 *AM 524 *WA 154 (inc illeg) *LA 263	an	1
C	2	4	5	4	2	4	2	0	D	Hodie Simon Petrus ascendit	AR 754 LU 1525 AM 939 LA 421	an	1
F	2	4	5	4	2	4	2	0	F	Hora consurgit aurea	ST 327	hy	6
F	2	4	5	4	2	4	2	0	F	In mari via tua	GR (3)	int	5
F	2	4	5	4	2	4	2	0	F	Kyrie	GR 94* LU 1807		6
F	2	4	5	4	2	4	2	0	F	Kyrie	MEL #101		
G	2	4	5	4	2	4	2	0	G	Kyrie omnipotens stelligeri	MEL #46		
C	2	4	5	4	2	4	2	0	D	Magnum salutis gaudium	ST 448	hy	2
C	2	4	5	4	2	4	2	0	E	Parce Domine parce ... quem redemisti	GB 154	an	4
G	2	4	5	4	2	4	2	0	G	Simeon justus et timoratus	LA 349 *WA 269	re	7
G	2	4	5	4	2	4	2	0	G	Stola jucunditatis induit eum	LR 156 *LA 524 *WA 417	re	7
G	2	4	5	4	2	4	2	0	G	Tuam crucem adoramus ... passionem	SYG 142	an	8
C	2	4	5	4	2	4	2	4	D	Adoremus Christum regem confessorum	WA 287	inv	2
C	2	4	5	4	2	4	2	4	D	Nos autem gloriari ... in quo	WA 309	re	1
C	2	4	5	4	2	4	2	4	E	Sanctus	THAN #217		4
C	2	4	5	4	2	4	2	4	E	Tulit ergo paralyticus	AR 569 LU 1059 AM 610 *LA 318	an	4
C	2	4	5	4	2	4	2	5	D	Adoremus conditorem cunctorum	WA 335	inv	2
F	2	4	5	4	2	4	2	7	D	Aeterne rerum conditor	AR 6 AM 34 ST 84 181	hy	1
C	2	4	5	4	2	4	2	9	D	O crux admirabile ... adorandus	SYG 142	an	1
c	2	4	5	4	2	4	5	4	c	Agnus Dei	SCH #17		8
C	2	4	5	4	2	4	5	4	E	Ecce venit rex occuramus	LA 1 *WA 13	inv	4
F	2	4	5	4	2	4	5	4	F	Kyrie	MEL #100		
G	2	4	5	4	2	4	5	4	G	Kyrie ad lib VI te Christe rex	GR 80* LU 83		8
c	2	4	5	4	2	4	5	4	G	Lucis creator optime	ST 471	hy	7
G	2	4	5	4	2	4	5	4	E	Non sunt loquelae	LR 147	re	3
G	2	4	5	4	2	4	5	4		Quae nec oculus vidit Venite benedicti	SYG 75	trv	
G	2	4	5	4	2	4	5	4	E	Salvatorem exspectamus Dominum	LA 4 *WA 4	re	3
G	2	4	5	4	2	4	5	4	G	Sancti mei qui in carne	LR 187 LA 517 *WA 429	re	8

G	2	4	5	4	2	4	5	4	E	Sancti per fidem vicerunt	LR 180	re	3
G	2	4	5	4	2	4	5	4		Tamquam filiis dico	GR 547	alv	
C	2	4	5	4	2	4	5	7	D	Alleluia: aemulor enim vos Dei	GS 227	al	1
C	2	4	5	4	2	4	5	7	D	Alleluia: quam magna multitudo	GR 628	al	1
C	2	4	5	4	2	4	5	7	E	Alleluia: usque modo non petistis	SYG 168 *GS 130	al	4
G	2	4	5	4	2	4	5	7	G	Almi prophetae progenies pia	ST 12	hy	8
c	2	4	5	4	2	4	5	7	c	Christe redemptor omnium ex patre	ST 366	hy	6
C	2	4	5	4	2	4	5	7	E	Dominum qui fecit mare	WA 80	inv	4
C	2	4	5	4	2	4	5	7	D	Sanctus	THAN #216		2
C	2	4	5	4	2	4	5	7		Spiritus qui a Patre procedit	SYG 185	alv	
G	2	4	5	4	2	4	5	7		Stetit Jesus in medio	SYG 162	alv	
C	2	4	5	4	2	4	5	7	E	Venite adoremus regem regum	LR 373 LA 442 *WA 354	inv	4
C	2	4	5	4	2	4	7	4	D	Alleluia: iste cognovit justitiam	SYG 189	al	1
C	2	4	5	4	2	4	7	4	D	Crucem sanctam subiit	AR 704 LU 1461 AM 131 166 468 750 903 *WA 132 *LA 399	an	2
G	2	4	5	4	2	4	7	5	G	Caritas est summum bonum	SYG 132	an	7
C	2	4	5	4	2	4	7	5	D	Virginis alme Deus soboles	ST 126	hy	2
C	2	4	5	4	2	4	7	9	E	Signatus est beatus Oswaldus	WA 282	an	4
G	2	4	5	4	2	5	2	0		Benedicta tu inter mulieres Ave Maria	GB 55^{v}	trv	
G	2	4	5	4	2	5	2	0		Et factus est in pace Notus in Judaea	GR [136] LU 1286	trv	
G	2	4	5	4	2	5	2	0		Laetetur mons Sion Suscepimus Deus	GR 113**	trv	
G	2	4	5	4	2	5	2	0	E	Prope est ut veniat tempus	LA 14 *WA 15	re	3
G	2	4	5	4	2	5	2	0		Transivimus per ignem Probasti nos	GR 108**	trv	
G	2	4	5	4	2	5	2	4	G	Absterget Deus omnem lacrimam	LR 178 LA 514 *WA 420	re	8
F	2	4	5	4	2	5	2	4	D	Domine quinque talenta	AR [74] LU 1195 AM 670 *WA 425 LA 532	an	1
C	2	4	5	4	2	5	2	5		Justi confitebuntur ... et habitabunt	SYG 190	alv	
F	2	4	5	4	2	5	4	0	D	Dominus legifer noster	WA 19	an	1
C	2	4	5	4	2	5	4	2	E	Christum in cujus pace	LR 451	inv	4
C	2	4	5	4	2	5	4	2	E	Christum pro nobis passum	LR 333	inv	4
C	2	4	5	4	2	5	4	2	E	Christum regem crucifixum	LR 437	inv	4
C	2	4	5	4	2	5	4	2	E	Deum verum unum in trinitate	LR 440 WA 158	inv	4
C	2	4	5	4	2	5	4	2	E	Deum vivum in quem cor	LR 451	inv	4

G	2	4	5	4	2	5	4	2		Ecce sicut oculi servorum Ad te levavi	GR 124 LU 554 GS 55 GB 82^{v} *SYG 93	trv	
G	2	4	5	4	2	5	4	2		Miserere nobis Domine Ad te levavi	GR 124 LU 554 *GS 55 *GB 82^{v} *SYG 93	trv	
G	2	4	5	4	2	5	4	2		Tibi derelictus est pauper Exsurge Domine	GR [101] LU 1283[B]	trv	
G	2	4	5	4	2	5	4	5	[G]	Agnus Dei	SCH #75		8
G	2	4	5	4	2	5	7	0		Elegi abjectus esse Beatus vir	GR 450 LU 1394	trv	
G	2	4	5	4	2	5	7	0		Fiant aures tuae intendentes De profundis clamavi ad te	GR 75 LU 499 GS 25 *GB 56^{v} *SYG 59	trv	
G	2	4	5	4	2	5	7	0		Lumen ad revelationem Nunc dimittis	GB 49	trv	
G	2	4	5	4	2	5	7	4	G	Te lucis ante terminum	ST 440	hy	8
G	2	4	5	4	2	5	7	5	G	Kyrie incarnatum quoque	MEL #45		
F	2	4	5	4	2	5	7	9	G	Alleluia: ego sum pastor bonus et cognosco	GS 127	al	8
C	2	4	5	4	2	7	4	5	D	Alleluia: fulgebunt justi et tamquam	GR 575 *SYG 193 GB 268^{v} GS 225	al	1
C	2	4	5	4	2	7	4	5	D	Alleluia: surrexit Christus et illuxit	GR 271 LU 831 *GS 127 SYG 165	al	1
C	2	4	5	4	2	7	5	4	E	Alleluia: evangelizare pauperibus	GR 67**	al	3
C	2	4	5	4	2	7	5	4	E	Alleluia: tollite jugum meum	GR 325 [112] LU 972	al	3
C	2	4	5	4	2	7	5	4		Et in terra	BOS #51 GR 39* LU 46		
c	2	4	5	4	2	7	5	4	a	Surgam et ibo ad patrem	VP 117	re	1
C	2	4	5	4	2	7	5	7	E	Agnus Dei	SCH #258		4
C	2	4	5	4	2	7	5	7	E	Agnus Dei	SCH #259		4
C	2	4	5	4	2	7	5	7	E	Aurora rubens fugat noctis stellas	ST 332	hy	3
C	2	4	5	4	2	7	5	7	E	Kyrie	MEL #212		
C	2	4	5	4	2	7	5	7	E	Sanctus	THAN #215		4
C	2	4	5	4	2	9	7	5	E	Sanctus	THAN #214		4
G	2	4	5	4	5	2	0	2	G	Custodivit anima mea testimonia	GR 70**	int	8
G	2	4	5	4	5	2	0	2	G	Miserere mihi Domine secundum magnam	GR 118 OTT 35 SYG 88 GB 77^{v} *GS 50	of	8
C	2	4	5	4	5	2	0	5	D	Alleluia: mirabantur omnes de his	SYG 42	al	1
G	2	4	5	4	5	4	0	2		Audite disciplinam et estote sapientes Nunc ergo filii	GR 587[3]	trv	
G	2	4	5	4	5	4	0	2		Benedicite Dominum omnes virtutes Laudate Dominum	GR 636	trv	
G	2	4	5	4	5	4	0	2		Melior est enim fructus Ego diligentes me	GR 61**	trv	

G	2	4	5	4	5	4	2	0		Domine refugium factus es	GR 355(39) LU 1034 GS 153 SYG 245 GB 254^{V}	alv	
F	2	4	5	4	5	4	2	0		Intercede pia pro nobis Virgo parens Christi	AR 131* VP 39 LU 1862	rev	
G	2	4	5	4	5	4	2	0	E	Intuemini quantus sit	LA 20 381 *WA 24	re	3
G	2	4	5	4	5	4	2	0		Justum deduxit ... et ostendit ... regnum	SYG 214	alv	
G	2	4	5	4	5	4	2	0		Scitote quoniam Dominus	GR [129] LU 1296	alv	
F	2	4	5	4	5	4	2	0	F	Sicut in holocausto arietum	GR 338(42) LU 1012 OTT 92 *SYG 243 GB 250^{V} GS 148	of	5
G	2	4	5	4	5	4	2	0		Surrexit altissimus Dominus	GB 146	alv	
G	2	4	5	4	5	4	2	4	G	Convertimini omnes simul	SYG 65	an	8
G	2	4	5	4	5	4	2	4	G	Martyr Dei egregie	ST 425	hy	8
C	2	4	5	4	5	4	2	4	E	Mater Christi gloriosa	PM 279	an	4
G	2	4	5	4	5	4	2	4	E	O magnum mysterium et admirabile	LU 382 *LR 61 *LA 35 *WA 28	re	3
C	2	4	5	4	5	4	2	4	D	Qualem caritatem corde	AM 875	an	1
F	2	4	5	4	5	4	2	4	F	Salus populi ego sum	GR 79**	of	5
F	2	4	5	4	5	4	2	4		Sponsus amat sponsam Virgo flagellatur	PM 214 VP 251	rev	
G	2	4	5	4	5	4	2	4	E	Vota mea Domino ... coram	AR 99 OHS 222 LU 281	an	3
G	2	4	5	4	5	4	5	0		Benedicta sit sancta trinitas Benedicamus patrem	GB 214^{V}	trv	
G	2	4	5	4	5	4	5	2	G	Populus acquisitionis annuntiate	GR 255 OHS 810 LU 799 *SYG 159 *GB 139^{V} *GS 122	co	7
C	2	4	5	4	5	4	5	4	E	Benedicat Dominus corda	SYG 134	an	4
G	2	4	5	4	5	4	5	4		Laudemus et superexaltemus Benedicamus patrem	GB 214^{V}	trv	
G	2	4	5	4	5	4	5	4		Tres sunt qui testimonium dant Hic est qui venit	GR 537 LU 1533	grv	
G	2	4	5	4	5	4	5	7		Eructavit cor meum Speciosus forma	GR 45 LU 434 GB 31 SYG 30	grv	
G	2	4	5	4	5	4	5	7		Filiae regum in honore tuo Speciosus forma	GR 103**	grv	
G	2	4	5	4	5	4	5	7		Hic Deus meus et honorabo eum Cantemus Domino	GR 229 OHS 652 LU 776^{R} *GS 111 *GB 119 *SYG 150	trv	
G	2	4	5	4	5	4	5	7		Inhabitabo in tabernaculo tuo Factus es spes	GR 424 LU 1353	trv	
C	2	4	5	4	5	4	5	7		Qui pro mundi salute Protege Domine	OTT 168	ofv	
G	2	4	5	4	5	4	5	7		Timete Dominum omnes sancti Gustate et videte	GR 95**	trv	

F	2	4	5	4	5	4	7	6	D	Gloria et honore coronasti ... et constituisti	GR [2] OTT 133 LU 1137 SYG 34 GB 23^v *GS W 202	of	1
G	2	4	5	4	5	4	7	9		Homo natus est in ea Fundamenta ejus	GR 402	trv	
C	2	4	5	4	5	7	4	5	E	Omnes autem vos fratres	AR 383 LA 144	an	4
C	2	4	5	4	5	7	4	5	E	Prope est jam Dominus	LA 18	inv	4
C	2	4	5	4	5	7	4	5	E	Regem apostolorum Dominum	LA 505	inv	4
G	2	4	5	4	5	7	5	0		Altaria tua Domine Cor meum	GR 626	trv	
G	2	4	5	4	5	7	5	0		Date magnitudinem Deo Attende caelum	GR 231 OHS 656 LU 776^U *GS 112 *GB 119^v *SYG 151	trv	
G	2	4	5	4	5	7	5	0		Deus fidelis in quo Attende caelum	GR 231 LU 776^U OHS 656 *GB 119^v GS 112 *SYG 151	trv	
G	2	4	5	4	5	7	5	0		Et in omni loco Ab ortu solis	GR [97] LU 1282	trv	
G	2	4	5	4	5	7	5	0		Et maceriam circumdedit Vinea facta	GR 230 OHS 654 LU 776^S *GS 111 *GB 120 *SYG 150	trv	
G	2	4	5	4	5	7	5	0		Et spiritus et sponsa Ego sum radix	GR 45**	trv	
G	2	4	5	4	5	7	5	0		Exspectetur sicut pluvia Attende caelum	GR 231 OHS 656 LU 776^U *GS 112 *GB 119^v *SYG 151	trv	
G	2	4	5	4	5	7	5	0		Fuerunt mihi lacrimae meae Sicut cervus	GR 232 OHS 673 LU 776^{BB} *GS 112 *GB 120 *SYG 151	trv	
G	2	4	5	4	5	7	5	0		Gloria et divitiae Beatus vir qui timet	GR [8] LU 1134 *GS 203 *GB 52^v *SYG 55	trv	
G	2	4	5	4	5	7	5	0		Justitiam tuam non abscondi Annuntiavi	GR [2^2] LU 1122^4	trv	
G	2	4	5	4	5	7	5	0		Mecum sunt divitiae et gloria Ego diligentes me	GR 61**	trv	
G	2	4	5	4	5	7	5	0		Oleum effusum nomen tuum Inveni quem diligit	GR (11)	trv	
G	2	4	5	4	5	7	5	0		Opes et divitiae in domo Beatus vir qui timet	LU 1442	trv	
G	2	4	5	4	5	7	5	0		Parasti in conspectu meo mensam Ego autem cum mihi	GR 566	trv	
G	2	4	5	4	5	7	5	0		Potens in terra erit semen Beatus vir qui timet	GR [8] LU 1442 *GS 203 *GB 52^v *SYG 55	trv	
G	2	4	5	4	5	7	5	0		Qui me invenerit inveniet Nunc ergo filii	GR 587^3	trv	
G	2	4	5	4	5	7	5	0		Qui sedes super cherubim Qui regis Israel	GR 19 LU 351 *GS 10 *GB 10 *SYG 11	trv	
G	2	4	5	4	5	7	5	0		Quia viderunt oculi mei Nunc dimittis	GR 434 LU 1363 *GS k *GB 49 *SYG 50	trv	

G	2	4	5	4	5	7	5	0		Vox enim tua dulcis Domine Deus virtutum	GR 53	trv	
G	2	4	5	4	5	7	5	2		Illic David suscitabo cornu Sacerdotes	LU 1623[C]	trv	
G	2	4	5	4	5	7	5	4	E	Cum in die magni sabbati	AM 875	an	3
G	2	4	5	4	5	7	5	4	E	Ego sum Deus patrum	AM 982	an	3
C	2	4	5	4	5	7	5	4	E	Manum suam aperuit inopi	AM 690 747	an	4
C	2	4	5	4	5	7	5	4	E	Omnipotentem semper adorent	SYG 252	hy	4
G	2	4	5	4	5	7	5	4	E	Pinguis est panis Christi	AR 530 LU 940 *AM 550	an	3
GG	2	4	5	4	5	7	5	9	C	Per memetipsum juravi	LA 118 *WA 78	re	6
C	2	4	5	4	5	7	9	7	E	Hodie vas electionis	WA 291	an	4
G	2	4	5	4	5	7	9	7	E	Pastor bonus animam suam	AR 470 AM 483 *LA 235	an	3
F	2	4	5	4	7	4	2	0	D	Principes persecuti sunt me	GR [68] LU 1238 *GB 229[v] *GS t 230	co	1
C	2	4	5	4	7	5	4	0	C	Agnus Dei	SCH #257		5
G	2	4	5	7	2	0	4	7		Timete Dominum omnes sancti	SYG 212	alv	
C	2	4	5	7	2	7	5	4	E	Ingressus Paulus in synagogam	SYG 45	of	4
G	2	4	5	7	4	2	5	2	G	Alleluia: os justi meditabitur	GB 40[v]	al	7
C	2	4	5	7	4	2	5	2		Ecce miles Christi	SYG 214	alv	
C	2	4	5	7	4	2	5	2		O inclyte atque sublimis Immaculatas hostiarum preces	SYG 220	ofv	
C	2	4	5	7	4	2	5	4	D	Alleluia: ecce miles Christi	SYG 214	al	1
C	2	4	5	7	4	2	5	4	D	Alleluia: magnus sanctus Paulus	GB 208	al	1
C	2	4	5	7	4	2	9	11	E	Exaudi Deus orationem meam et clamor	SYG 129	of	4
C	2	4	5	7	4	5	2	0	D	Alleluia: in exitu Israel ex Aegypto	GR 381 LU 1068 *GB 261	al	2
C	2	4	5	7	4	5	2	0	D	Alleluia: posui vos ut eatis	GR 568	al	1
G	2	4	5	7	4	5	2	0		Os justi meditabitur	GB 40[v]	alv	
G	2	4	5	7	4	5	4	2		Ecce mitto vos	GB 268	alv	
C	2	4	5	7	4	5	7	5	D	Haec est regina virginum	PM 271 *WA 354	an	1
G	2	4	5	7	5	0	2	0		Dominus conterens bella Cantemus Domino	GR 229 OHS 652 *GB 119 *SYG 150 *GS 111	trv	
G	2	4	5	7	5	0	2	0		Gloriosa dicta sunt Fundamenta ejus	GR 402	trv	
G	2	4	5	7	5	0	2	0		Induxisti nos in laqueum Probasti nos	GR 108**	trv	
G	2	4	5	7	5	0	2	0		Sitivit anima mea ad Deum vivum Sicut cervus	GR 232 OHS 673 LU 776[BB] *GS 112 *GB 120 *SYG 151	trv	

C	2	4	5	7	5	2	4	5	D	Festum nunc celebre magnaque gaudia	ST 420	hy	2
C	2	4	5	7	5	2	4	5		Illi enim conjuncta es Gaudens perenniter	SYG 238	trv	
C	2	4	5	7	5	2	4	5		Per ipsum nobis Per signum crucis	SYG 129	trv	
C	2	4	5	7	5	2	5	4	D	Festum nunc celebre magnaque gaudia	ST 293	hy	2
C	2	4	5	7	5	2	5	7		Beati qui custodiunt judicium Confitemini Domino	SYG 86	trv	
C	2	4	5	7	5	4	2	0	E	Adoremus regem apostolorum	LA 48 *WA 38	inv	4
C	2	4	5	7	5	4	2	0	E	Alleluia: constitues eos principes	GR [2^{3}] LU 1122^{5} *SYG 194	al	4
C	2	4	5	7	5	4	2	0	D	Alleluia: gavisi sunt discipuli	SYG 163	al	2
C	2	4	5	7	5	4	2	0	D	Clarum decus jejunii	ST 226 278	hy	2
C	2	4	5	7	5	4	2	0	D	Illi homines cum signum	WA 104	an	1
G	2	4	5	7	5	4	2	0	G	Oculi omnium in te sperant	GR 314 [96] LU 944 SYG 97 GB 86^{v} *GS 59 164	gr	7
C	2	4	5	7	5	4	2	0	D	Salvete Christi vulnera	AR 765 LU 1529	hy	2
C	2	4	5	7	5	4	2	0		Surge virgo regia Veni electa	LA 446	rev	
C	2	4	5	7	5	4	2	4	D	Alleluia: timete Dominum omnes sancti	SYG 192	al	1
C	2	4	5	7	5	4	2	4	E	Apollinaris martyris	ST 15	hy	4
C	2	4	5	7	5	4	2	4	E	Sacri pontificis annuis emicat	ST 469	hy	4
C	2	4	5	7	5	4	2	5	D	Alleluia: Christo confixus sum cruci	GR 427 LU 1354^{v}	al	1
C	2	4	5	7	5	4	2	5	D	Alleluia: eduxit Dominus populum	SYG 161	al	1
C	2	4	5	7	5	4	2	5		Christo confixus sum cruci	GR 427 LU 1354^{v}	alv	
G	2	4	5	7	5	4	2	5		Et in terra	BOS #11		
G	2	4	5	7	5	4	2	5		Et in terra	BOS #12 GR 48* LU 54		
C	2	4	5	7	5	4	2	5		Loquebantur variis linguis	GR 297 LU 888 *GS 139 *GB 193 SYG 184	alv	
C	2	4	5	7	5	4	2	5		Mirabantur omnes de his	SYG 42	alv	
C	2	4	5	7	5	4	5	7		Angelus Domini descendit ... et accedens	GR 245 OHS 775 LU 786 GS 125 GB 131 SYG 159	alv	
G	2	4	5	7	5	4	5	7	G	Beata viscera Mariae	LU 389 *LR 65 LA 33 *WA 29	re	7
G	2	4	5	7	5	4	5	7		Dixi Domino Deus meus Custodi me	OTT 52 *SYG 126	ofv	
C	2	4	5	7	5	4	5	7	E	Partem beatae resurrectionis	SYG 238	co	4

C	2	4	5	7	5	4	5	7		Verbo Domini caeli firmati	GR 300 LU 893	alv	
G	2	4	5	7	5	7	5	2		Et non erat qui sepeliret Effuderunt sanguinem sanctorum	GR 42 LU 429 *GB 26^{v} *SYG 26	trv	
C	2	4	5	7	5	7	9	7		Cumque intuerentur in caelum Viri Galilaei	OTT 172 *SYG 180 *GB 180^{v}	ofv	
G	2	4	5	7	5	7	9	7		Et in terra	BOS #13 *GR 85* *LU 88		
C	2	4	5	7	5	7	9	7	D	Sanctus	THAN #213		1
C	2	4	5	7	5	7	9	7		Virgo Dei genitrix virga est Stirps Jesse	AR 129* *PM 186 *WA 303	rev	
C	2	4	5	7	5	7	9	10		Beatam me dicent ... quia ancillam	GR 587^{5} LU 1612^{4}	alv	
C	2	4	5	7	5	7	9	10		Paratum cor meum Deus	GR 378 LU 1064 *GB 259^{v} *SYG 253 *GS 158	alv	
C	2	4	5	7	5	7	9	10		Veni Domine et noli	GR 22 LU 354 *SYG 7 *GB 11 *GS 12	alv	
C	2	4	5	7	5	7	10	7		Adducentur regi virgines	GR [61] LU 1217 *GS 231 GB 29^{v}	alv	
C	2	4	5	7	5	7	11	7		Exsultent justi Dei in conspectu	GB 269^{v}	alv	
C	2	4	5	7	5	7	12	7		Crastina erit vobis salus	GB 12^{v}	alv	
C	2	4	5	7	5	9	7	5		Respondens autem angelus ... quem Angelus Domini descendit	GS 125	alv	
C	2	4	5	7	9	5	4	2	D	Abraham pater vester	AR 415 LU 577 *AM 393 *LA 172	an	2
G	2	4	5	7	9	5	7	5	c	Intempestae noctis hora	GB 55	of	6
C	2	4	5	7	9	7	4	5	D	Usque modo non petistis	AR 483 LU 830 *AM 499 *WA 146 *LA 231 242	an	2
C	2	4	5	7	9	7	5	4	D	Alleluia: dilectus meus mihi	GR (10)	al	1
C	2	4	5	7	9	7	5	4	D	Alleluia: manum suam aperuit inopi	GR 632 LU 1695	al	1
C	2	4	5	7	9	7	5	4	D	Alleluia: os justi meditabitur	SYG 199	al	1
C	2	4	5	7	9	7	5	4	D	Alleluia: qui docti fuerint fulgebunt	GR 496 LU 1466	al	1
C	2	4	5	7	9	7	5	4		Auditui meo dabis gaudium	GR [142]	alv	
C	2	4	5	7	9	7	5	4	D	Felix per omnes festum mundi cardines	ST 54	hy	1
C	2	4	5	7	9	7	5	4	D	Te Christe patris verbum virtus inclyta	ST 57	hy	1
C	2	4	5	7	9	7	5	7	G	Alleluia: confitebor tibi Domini in toto	GB 169	al	8
C	2	4	5	7	9	7	5	7	G	Alleluia: isti sunt qui venerunt	SYG 194	al	8
C	2	4	5	7	9	7	5	7	G	Alleluia: sacerdos Dei Martine	SYG 226	al	8
C	2	4	5	7	9	7	5	7		Benedictus Dominus Deus meus	GR 465	alv	

G	2	4	5	7	9	7	5	7	G	Crux alma fulget	PM 153 *SYG 142	an	7
C	2	4	5	7	9	7	5	7		Isti sunt qui venerunt	SYG 194	alv	
G	2	4	5	7	9	7	5	7	G	Occurrit piissimae genetrici	WA 359	an	7
G	2	4	5	7	9	7	5	7		Tolle puerum et matrem	SYG 30	alv	
G	2	4	5	7	9	7	5	7		Tu gloria Jerusalem ... nostri	GR 403	alv	
C	2	4	5	7	9	7	5	12	G	Gratuletur omnis caro	ST 221	hy	8
C	2	4	5	7	9	7	9	5		Et si coram hominibus ... spes Justorum animae	OTT 144 SYG 223	ofv	
C	2	4	5	7	9	7	9	5		In conspectu angelorum ... et adorabo Stetit angelus	OTT 170 GB 170^{v}	ofv	
C	2	4	5	7	9	7	9	5		Tuam Deus deposcimus pietatem Erue Domine	OTT 177 SYG 236	ofv	
C	2	4	5	7	9	7	9	12	C	Jam fulget oriens	PM 26	an	5
G	2	4	5	7	9	7	10	12	G	Alleluia: inter natos mulierum	SYG 196	al	7
G	2	4	5	7	9	7	10	12	G	Alleluia: tu Domine pater noster	GB 151^{v}	al	7
C	2	4	5	7	9	7	11	9		Exclamantes autem turbae Elegerunt apostoli	SYG 23	ofv	
C	2	4	5	7	9	7	11	12	C	Alleluia: assumpta est Maria ... exercitus	GR 584 (32) LU 1603	al	5
C	2	4	5	7	9	7	11	12	C	Alleluia: bene fundata est domus	GR [73] LU 1252 *GB 174	al	5 7
C	2	4	5	7	9	7	11	12	C	Alleluia: non derelinquet Dominus sanctos	GR 446	al	5
C	2	4	5	7	9	7	11	12	C	Alleluia: salve mater misericordiae	GR 44**	al	5
C	2	4	5	7	9	7	11	12	C	Alleluia: te gloriosus apostolorum	GR 588 LU 1613	al	5
C	2	4	5	7	9	7	11	12	C	Alleluia: te martyrum candidatus	GR [30] LU 1171 GS 18 217 SYG 192 GB 268^{v}	al	5
C	2	4	5	7	9	7	11	12		Confitebor tibi Domine in toto corde	GB 169	alv	
C	2	4	5	7	9	7	12	11	G	Alleluia: ecce jam venit plenitudo temporis	GB 31	al	8
C	2	4	5	7	9	7	12	11		Ecce jam venit plenitudo	GB 31	alv	
C	2	4	5	7	9	7	12	11		Venerunt de tribulatione	GR 108**	alv	
F	2	4	6	2	4	2	0	4	G	Cumque intuerentur in caelum	AR 491 LU 851 *AM 509 *WA 149 LA 250	an	8
F	2	4	6	4	2	-1	2	4	D	Nisi tu Domine conserves	LA 96	an	1
F	2	4	6	4	2	0	-3	-5	F	Agnus Dei	SCH #125		6
F	2	4	6	4	2	0	4	2	G	Christus est vita veniens in orbem	ST 411	hy	8
F	2	4	6	4	2	4	0	2	D	Domine ut video propheta	AM 370 WA 100 (inc illeg)	an	1

F	2	4	6	4	2	4	2	0	G	Cumque in specu	WA 300	an	8
F	2	4	6	4	2	4	7	6		Et in terra	BOS #22		
F	2	4	6	4	2	7	9	7		Ego sum pastor bonus et cognosco	GS 127	alv	
F	2	4	6	7	2	0	2	0	F	Prudentes virgines acceperunt oleum	GR 101**	co	5
F	2	4	6	7	2	4	2	0	G	Alleluia: sancte Paule apostole intercede	GB 208^{v}	al	8
F	2	4	6	7	2	4	2	0		Sancte Paule apostole intercede	GB 208^{v}	alv	
F	2	4	6	7	2	4	2	6	G	Hodie caelesti sponso	AR 315 LU 457 AM 293 *WA 56 *LA 74	an	8
F	2	4	6	7	4	0	2	0	F	Agnus Dei	SCH #146		5
F	2	4	6	7	4	2	6	2		Tu es sacerdos in aeternum	GR [4] [33] LU 1183 1495^{B} *SYG 38 *GB 272^{v}	alv	
F	2	4	6	7	4	6	2	-1	[E]	Agnus Dei	SCH #122		3
F	2	4	6	7	4	6	7	4	G	Facta est Judaea	LA 90	an	8
F	2	4	6	7	6	4	2	0	G	Deus caritas est	SYG 131	an	8
F	2	4	6	7	6	4	2	4	G	Christe redemptor omnium conserva	ST 400	hy	7
F	2	4	6	7	6	4	2	4	G	Hodie Maria virgo caelos ascendit	AR 824 LU 1607 AM 1018 *WA 360 LA 449	an	8
F	2	4	6	7	6	4	2	4	G	Jesu rex regum omnium	ST 392	hy	7
F	2	4	6	7	6	4	2	4	G	Jesu salvator saeculi	ST 400	hy	7
F	2	4	6	7	6	4	2	6	G	Hodie nata est beata ... cujus vita inclyta	LA 462	an	8
F	2	4	6	7	6	4	6	7	G	Hodie huic domui salus	LA 551	an	8
F	2	4	6	7	6	7	9	7	G	Factum est silentium ... draco	AR 859 AM 1062 *WA 384 *LA 472	an	8
F	2	4	6	7	9	7	6	2		Ecce quam bonum et quam jucundum	GB 201^{v}	alv	
F	2	4	7	2	0	2	4	2	G	Hic est vir qui non est derelictus	WA 418	re	8
F	2	4	7	2	4	0	2	4	G	Spiritus carnem et ossa	AR 481 AM 497 *LA 219	an	8
F	2	4	7	2	4	0	2	7	G	Crudelis Herodes Deum regem	AR 309 LU 465	hy	8
F	2	4	7	2	4	0	2	7	G	Gloria tibi Domine	AM 997	hy	8
F	2	4	7	2	4	0	2	7	G	Hostis Herodes impie	ST 413	hy	8
F	2	4	7	2	4	0	2	7	G	Nunc sancte nobis spiritus	AR 316 LU 458 AM 294	hy	8
F	2	4	7	2	4	0	2	7	G	Te lucis ante terminum	AR 311 LU 455 AM 290	hy	8
F	2	4	7	2	4	2	0	2	G	Alleluia: pretiosa in conspectu Domini	GB 164	al	8
F	2	4	7	2	4	2	0	2	G	Alleluia: spiritus Dei ornavit caelos	SYG 185	al	8
F	2	4	7	2	4	2	0	2	G	Alleluia: universae angelorum virtutes	GB 169	al	8

F	2	4	7	2	4	2	0	2		Spiritus ejus ornavit caelos	GR 305 LU 902	alv	
F	2	4	7	2	4	2	0	2		Surrexit Dominus vere	GR 251 OHS 797 LU 794 GS 130 SYG 155 *GB 135^{v}	alv	
F	2	4	7	2	4	2	0	4	G	Alleluia: spiritus ejus ornavit caelos	GR 305 LU 902	al	8
F	2	4	7	2	4	2	0	4	G	Alleluia: surrexit Dominus vere	GR 251 OHS 797 LU 794 GS 130 *SYG 155 GB 135^{v}	al	8
F	2	4	7	4	2	0	2	4	G	Angelus Domini descendit ... et dixit	GR 246 OHS 776 OTT 57 LU 787 GS 118 SYG 155 GB 132	of	8
F	2	4	7	4	2	0	2	4	G	Assumpta est Maria ... angeli	GR (32) OTT 167 GB 226	of	8
F	2	4	7	4	2	0	2	4	G	Beata es virgo Maria quae omnium	GR [83] LU 1272 GB 220^{v}	of	8
F	2	4	7	4	2	0	2	4		Beata et venerabilis es virgo Felix namque	OTT 188	ofv	
C	2	4	7	4	2	0	2	4		Beatus es Simon Petre Tu es Petrus	OTT 187 SYG 53	ofv	
F	2	4	7	4	2	0	2	4	G	Felix namque es sacra virgo Maria	OTT 188	of	8
F	2	4	7	4	2	0	2	4	G	Fili quid fecisti ... quid	AR 330 LU 477 *LA 106	an	8
F	2	4	7	4	2	0	2	4		Jesus stetit in medio Angelus Domini	OTT 57 SYG 155 *GB 132	ofv	
F	2	4	7	4	2	0	2	4		Magna est gloria ejus Posuisti Domine	OTT 136 GB 233^{v}	ofv	
F	2	4	7	4	2	0	2	4	G	Misit rex spiculatorem	OTT 176	of	7
F	2	4	7	4	2	0	2	4	G	Post partum virgo inviolata	GR 76**	of	8
F	2	4	7	4	2	0	2	4	G	Posuisti Domine in capite ejus	GR 48 [14] OTT 136 LU 438 1140 GS 204 GB 233^{v}	of	8
C	2	4	7	4	2	0	2	4	D	Salvum fac servum tuum	GR 105 GS 41 SYG 80 GB 72	gr	1
F	2	4	7	4	2	0	2	4		Surrexit Dominus de sepulcro Angelus Domini	GB 132	ofv	
F	2	4	7	4	2	4	2	4	G	Omnipotens Deus maestorum	GB 159	an	7
F	2	4	7	4	2	4	2	4	G	Omnipotens Deus supplices	WA 230	an	8
C	2	4	7	4	2	5	4	2	D	Ad coenam agni providi	ST 92	hy	1
F	2	4	7	4	2	5	4	2	G	Ave Maria gratia plena ... benedicta	GR 404 LU 1318	of	8
C	2	4	7	4	2	5	4	2	D	Christe redemptor omnium ex patre	AM 238	hy	1
C	2	4	7	4	2	5	4	2	D	Jesus refulsit omnium	ST 63	hy	1
F	2	4	7	4	2	5	4	5	D	Ego autem cum justitia	GR 121 SYG 91 GB 80 GS 52	int	1
F	2	4	7	4	2	5	4	5	D	Ego autem in Domino gaudebo	GR 467	int	1
F	2	4	7	4	2	5	4	5	D	Ego autem in Domino speravi	GR 132 GB 85 *GS 58 *SYG 96	int	1

F	2	4	7	4	2	6	4	2	G	Portas caeli aperuit Dominus	GR 251 OHS 798 OTT 60 LU 795 SYG 158 GB 136^{v} GS 121 139	of	8
F	2	4	7	4	2	6	4	2	G	Veni redemptor gentium	ST 409	hy	7
C	2	4	7	4	5	2	0	2		Constitues eos principes	GR [2^{3}] LU 1122^{5} SYG 194	alv	
C	2	4	7	4	5	2	0	4	D	Alleluia: interrogabat magos Herodes	GB 33^{v} *SYG 31	al	1
C	2	4	7	4	5	4	2	0		Cum esset Stephanus	SYG 22	alv	
C	2	4	7	4	5	4	2	4	D	Alleluia: juravit Dominus et non paenitebit	GR [37] LU 1187 SYG 189 *GB 41^{v}	al	1
C	2	4	7	4	5	4	2	4	D	Alleluia: rogavi pro te Petre	GR 543 LU 1543	al	1
C	2	4	7	4	5	4	2	4	D	Alleluia: spiritus Domini super me	GR [102] LU 1283^{C}	al	1
F	2	4	7	4	6	4	2	0	G	Hodie beata virgo Maria	AR 622 LU 1367 AM 805 *LA 356	an	8
F	2	4	7	4	6	4	2	4	G	Factum est in die	WA 332	an	8
F	2	4	7	4	6	7	2	0	G	Exsultavit spiritus meus	GR 587^{5} LU 1612^{3}	of	8
F	2	4	7	4	6	7	9	7		Multae tribulationes justorum	SYG 200	alv	
F	2	4	7	4	6	7	9	7		Videbitis et gaudebit cor vestrum	GR 510 LU 1483	alv	
F	2	4	7	5	2	5	4	2	G	Christe redemptor omnium ex patre	ST 274	hy	7
F	2	4	7	5	4	2	0	2	F	Agnus Dei	SCH #121		5
C	2	4	7	5	4	2	0	4	D	Salvete flores martyrum	ST 369	hy	1
C	2	4	7	5	4	2	4	5	D	Aeterna Christi munera apostolorum	LR 429	hy	1
C	2	4	7	5	4	2	4	5	D	Audit tyrannus anxius	LR 430	hy	1
C	2	4	7	5	4	2	4	5	D	Christe redemptor omnium ex patre	LR 54	hy	1
C	2	4	7	5	4	2	4	5	D	Deus tuorum militum	AR 277 LR 428 LU 419	hy	1
C	2	4	7	5	4	2	4	5	D	Exsultet orbis gaudiis	AR 280 LU 425	hy	1
C	2	4	7	5	4	2	4	5	D	Invicte martyr unicum	AR 274	hy	1
C	2	4	7	5	4	2	4	5	D	Jesu redemptor omnium	AR 260 291 LU 365	hy	1
C	2	4	7	5	4	2	4	5	D	Jesu rex admirabilis	LR 431	hy	1
C	2	4	7	5	4	2	4	5	D	Salvete flores martyrum	AR 285 LU 431	hy	1
C	2	4	7	5	4	2	5	4	D	Bellator armis inclytus	ST 43	hy	1
C	2	4	7	5	4	2	5	4	D	Jesu corona celsior	ST 44	hy	1
C	2	4	7	5	4	2	5	4	D	Profana dum succenderet	ST 43	hy	1
C	2	4	7	5	4	2	5	4	D	Te Christe rex piissime	ST 44	hy	1
C	2	4	7	5	4	5	2	0	D	Christe redemptor omnium conserva	ST 237	hy	1
C	2	4	7	5	4	5	2	0	D	Christe redemptor omnium ex patre	ST 218	hy	1
C	2	4	7	5	4	5	2	4	D	Alleluia: misericordias Domini	SYG 245	al	1

F	2	4	7	6	2	4	0	2		Benedicta tu inter mulieres	SYG 217	alv	
F	2	4	7	6	2	4	0	2	G	Ego dilecto meo et dilectus meus	GR 74**	co	8
F	2	4	7	6	2	4	2	4	G	Animae impiorum fremebant	WA 109 *LA 166	an	8
F	2	4	7	6	4	2	0	2	G	Petrus ad se reversus	WA 340	an	8
F	2	4	7	6	4	2	0	4	G	Jesu redemptor omnium	ST 104	hy	7
F	2	4	7	6	4	2	4	2	G	Abraham et semen ejus	WA 69	an	8
F	2	4	7	6	4	2	4	2	G	Fratres existimo	WA 71	an	8
F	2	4	7	6	4	2	4	2	G	Hodie Maria virgo puerum	WA 272	an	8
F	2	4	7	6	4	2	4	2	G	Impii super justum	WA 37 *LA 41	an	8
F	2	4	7	6	4	2	4	2	G	Ipse est Dominus meus	WA 343	an	8
F	2	4	7	6	4	2	4	6	G	Iste est qui contempsit	WA 426	an	8
F	2	4	7	6	4	2	7	9	G	Et si ingenua es	LA 357	an	8
F	2	4	7	6	4	6	2	4	G	Alleluia: benedicta tu inter mulieres	SYG 217	al	7
F	2	4	7	6	4	9	7	6	G	Kyrie ad laudem summae	MEL #98		
F	2	4	7	6	7	4	2	0	G	Deus misereatur et benedicat	WA 98 *LA 152	an	8
F	2	4	7	6	7	4	2	0	G	Hodie sacra virgo	AM 819	an	8
F	2	4	7	6	7	4	2	0	G	Veni et libera nos	WA 8	an	8
F	2	4	7	6	7	4	2	4	G	Ideo jurejurando fecit	AR [56] LU 1176 AM 658 *LA 536	an	8
F	2	4	7	6	7	4	2	4	G	Misi digitum meum in fixuras	AR 466 AM 480	an	8
F	2	4	7	6	7	4	2	4	G	Quoniam in te confidit	AM 46	an	8
F	2	4	7	6	7	4	6	7	G	Kyrie hagie atque benigne	MEL #119		
F	2	4	7	6	7	4	7	2	G	Nonne sic oportuit pati	AR 472 *AM 486 *WA 138 *LA 218 232	an	8
F	2	4	7	6	7	4	7	6	G	Deus misereatur nostri ... nos	AR 111	an	8
F	2	4	7	6	7	9	4	2	G	Jesus respondens mulieri	WA 94	an	8
C	2	4	7	9	5	4	7	5	D	Alleluia: Deus a Libano	SYG 4	al	2
C	2	4	7	9	5	4	7	5		Deus a Libano veniet	SYG 4	alv	
F	2	4	7	9	6	7	4	2	G	Alleluia: confitemini Domino quoniam bonus	PM 80 GR 282 GS 132 *GB 161^{v}	al	8
C	2	4	7	9	7	2	7	5	E	Ut queant laxis resonare fibris	ST 352	hy	4
F	2	4	7	9	7	5	7	9	F	Gaude mater ecclesia	ST 138	hy	5
F	2	4	7	9	7	6	2	4		Spiritus sanctus docebit vos	GR 299 LU 891 GB 191	alv	
F	2	4	7	9	7	6	7	9	G	Velociter exaudi me ... quia	LA 104	re	8
C	2	4	7	9	7	9	11	12	C	Agnus Dei	SCH #256		5
C	2	4	7	9	7	9	11	12	C	Sanctus	THAN #212		5

F	2	4	7	9	7	9	12	11	F	Kyrie	MEL #97		
F	2	4	7	9	7	9	12	11	F	Sanctus	THAN #104		5
F	2	4	9	7	5	4	2	4	D	Rorate caeli desuper ... ne irascaris	AR 145* VP 59 LU 1868		1
G	2	5	0	-2	0	2	0	2	G	Precatus est Moyses in conspectu	GR 352 OTT 97 LU 1030 *SYG 89 *GB 79 *GS 52 155	of	7 8
G	2	5	0	-2	0	2	4	5	G	Dilexisti justitiam et odisti	GR [60] LU 1225 *SYG 5 *GB 4 *GS 225	int	8
G	2	5	0	-2	0	2	5	0	G	Jubilate Deo omnis terra	GR 265 LU 821 *SYG 165 *GB 148 *GS 128	int	8
G	2	5	0	2	-3	-2	0	2	G	Kyrie princeps astrigeram	MEL #36		
G	2	5	0	2	-2	0	-2	-3	G	Vox tonitrui tui	WA 41	re	8
F	2	5	0	2	0	-3	-1	-3	F	Agnus Dei	SCH #120		5
G	2	5	0	2	0	-2	0	7	G	In vasta solitudine	ST 128	hy	7
F	2	5	0	2	0	-1	-3	-5	F	Kyrie rex Deus aeterne (etc)	MEL #96		
G	2	5	0	2	0	2	0	5	D	Rector potens verax Deus	ST 246	hy	1
G	2	5	0	2	0	2	0	5	D	Rerum Deus tenax vigor	ST 246	hy	1
G	2	5	0	2	5	2	0	5	E	Alleluia: spiritus Domini replevit orbem	GS a 140	al	4
C	2	5	0	2	5	4	2	4	D	Te lucis ante terminum	AR 212 LU 326	hy	2
C	2	5	0	4	2	0	2	4	D	Alleluia: apparuerunt apostolis	SYG 186	al	2
C	2	5	0	4	2	5	2	4	D	Agmina sacra angelorum	WA 391	re	1
C	2	5	0	4	2	5	2	4	D	Venite post me faciam vos fieri	WA 233	re	1
G	2	5	0	5	2	0	2	5	E	Auditor legis non surdus	WA 282	re	3
G	2	5	2	-2	0	2	0	-2	G	Fuit homo missus a Deo	LR 348 LA 401 *WA 320	re	7 8
G	2	5	2	-2	0	4	0	2	G	Fuit vir vitae venerabilis ... qui ab ipso	LA 367 WA 297	re	7
F	2	5	2	0	-3	-5	-3	0		Desiderium animae ejus Posuisti Domine	OTT 136 *GB 233^{V}	ofv	
F	2	5	2	0	-3	-5	-3	0		Euntes dicite discipulis ejus Angelus Domini	OTT 57 GB 132 *SYG 155	ofv	
F	2	5	2	0	-3	-5	-3	0		Paradisi porta per Evam Assumpta est	OTT 167 *GB 226	ofv	
G	2	5	2	0	-2	-3	-5	-3	G	Kyrie	MEL #40		
G	2	5	2	0	-2	-3	-5	-2	G	Christe redemptor omnium conserva	ST 98	hy	8
G	2	5	2	0	-2	-3	-5	-2	G	Christe redemptor omnium ex patre	ST 81	hy	8
G	2	5	2	0	-2	-3	-5	-2	G	Veni redemptor gentium	ST 80	hy	8
G	2	5	2	0	-2	0	-3	0	E	Sanctus III	GR 14* LU 24 THAN #56		4
G	2	5	2	0	-2	0	2	0	G	Vivo autem ego	AM 1128	an	8
G	2	5	2	0	-2	2	0	2	G	Aeterne rex altissime	ST 37	hy	8

G	2	5	2	0	2	0	-3	-2	E	Tollite jugum meum	LA 507	an	3
G	2	5	2	0	2	0	-2	-3	G	Conspicit in caelis	WA 376	an	8
G	2	5	2	0	2	0	2	-2	E	Magna est gloria ejus	GR [2] LU 1649 SYG 171 *GB 24 *GS w 202	co	4
C	2	5	2	0	2	0	2	0		Dei genitrix intercede pro nobis Gaude Maria	GR [78] LU 1266	trv	
C	2	5	2	0	2	0	2	0	D	Dilectus Deo et angelis	WA 316	an	1
C	2	5	2	0	2	0	2	4		Angelus Domini apparuit in somnis Joseph	GR 5**	alv	
C	2	5	2	0	2	0	2	4	D	Ductus est Jesus in desertum ... cum	AM 342 *AR 369 WA 88 LA 133	an	1
C	2	5	2	0	2	0	2	4		Ego Dominus inebriabo	GR 91**	alv	
C	2	5	2	0	2	0	2	5	D	Coeperunt omnes turbae	OHS 98 LU 585 LA 184 *SYG 118 GB 106^v	an	1
C	2	5	2	0	2	0	2	5	D	Cum esset sero die illa	AR 456 LU 807 AM 475 *LA 223	an	1
C	2	5	2	0	2	0	5	7	D	Mortuus sum et vita mea	AR 848 LU 1644	an	1
G	2	5	2	0	2	0	7	5	G	Sol ille verus qui Deus omnia	ST 324	hy	8
G	2	5	2	0	2	4	0	2	E	Spes mea Domine	LA 115 WA 75	re	4
G	2	5	2	0	2	4	2	-2	G	Viri sancti gloriosum sanguinem	PM 221 LR 178 *LA 514 *WA 420	re	8
C	2	5	2	0	2	4	2	0	D	Beata es Maria mater Domini	PM 277	an	1
c	2	5	2	0	2	4	2	0	c	In paradiso ecclesiae	WA 311	an	6
G	2	5	2	0	2	4	2	0		Quia factus es adjutor Eripe me	OTT 46 GB 101^v SYG 113	ofv	
C	2	5	2	0	2	4	2	4	D	Pulchra es o virgo Maria	PM 263	re	1
C	2	5	2	0	2	4	5	2	D	Inventor rutili dux bone luminis	ST 478	hy	2
C	2	5	2	0	2	4	5	4	D	Alleluia: veni sponsa Christi accipe palmam	SYG 208	al	1
C	2	5	2	0	2	4	5	4	D	Deus Deus meus ad te	GR 265 OTT 66 LU 818 *SYG 165 *GB 147^v *GS 128	of	2
C	2	5	2	0	2	4	5	7	D	Alleluia: mane nobiscum Domine	GS 126	al	1
C	2	5	2	0	2	4	5	7		Judicabunt sancti nationes	SYG 188 *GS 199	alv	
G	2	5	2	0	2	5	0	4	E	O vere beatum o ineffabilem pietate	PM 206 *WA 405	an	3
C	2	5	2	0	2	5	2	4	D	Ibat Jesus in civitatem	AR 403 566 LU 1095 *AM 379 606 *LA 164	an	1
C	2	5	2	0	2	5	2	5	D	Dum transiret Jesus	LA 315	an	1
C	2	5	2	0	2	5	4	2	D	Benedicta sit sancta trinitas	GR 203	an	2
C	2	5	2	0	2	5	4	2	D	Sicut malum inter ligna	WA 353	an	1
C	2	5	2	0	2	5	4	5	D	Candidi facti sunt Nazaraei	PM 220 LR 172 *LA 387 WA 306	re	2

C	2	5	2	0	2	5	4	5	D	Facies unctionis	OHS 413 LU 661	int	2
C	2	5	2	0	2	5	4	5	D	Invocantem exaudivit Dominus	LR 192 *WA 424 LA 529	an	2
C	2	5	2	0	2	5	4	7	D	Tu es vas electionis	PM 162 *LA 429 *WA 263	re	1
C	2	5	2	0	2	5	7	4	D	Non potest arbor bona	AR 559 LU 1013 *AM 597	an	1
C	2	5	2	0	2	5	7	5	D	Bonum certamen certavi	LA 427 WA 330	re	2
G	2	5	2	0	2	5	7	5		Dominus erigit elisos Lauda anima	OTT 67 *GB 149 *SYG 166	ofv	
G	2	5	2	0	2	5	7	5	a	Sitientes venite ad aquas	GR 149 LU 565 SYG 108 GS 70 GB 96	int	2
C	2	5	2	0	2	7	5	4	D	Felix es dilecte Deo	WA 316	an	1
C	2	5	2	0	2	7	9	7	G	Aeterni regis immensam ... Annae	WA 339	an	8
C	2	5	2	0	2	7	9	7	D	Aeterni regis immensam ... Magdalenae	WA 335	an	1
F	2	5	2	0	4	0	2	5		Caritas Dei diffusa ... inhabitantem	SYG 187	alv	
C	2	5	2	0	4	2	4	5	D	Alleluia: erit autem sanguis vobis	GR 540	al	1
C	2	5	2	0	4	2	4	5	D	Alleluia: venite comedite panem meum	GR 627	al	1
C	2	5	2	0	4	2	9	12		Erit autem sanguis vobis	GR 540	alv	
C	2	5	2	0	4	5	7	4	D	Alleluia: speciosum fecit rex angelorum	SYG 219	al	1
C	2	5	2	0	4	5	7	4		Ascendens Christus in altum	GS 135	alv	
C	2	5	2	0	4	5	7	4		Corona aurea super caput	GR 14**	alv	
C	2	5	2	0	4	5	7	5	D	Ascendens ergo Deus	WA 81	re	2
G	2	5	2	0	4	7	5	2	E	Cum esset desponsata ... ejus	GR 624 LU 1685	of	3
G	2	5	2	0	5	4	5	7	E	Introeuntem te Domine	SYG 120	an	3
C	2	5	2	0	5	7	5	4	F	Exsultavit ut gigas	GR 20 LU 352 SYG 12 GB 10v GS 11	co	6
C	2	5	2	0	5	7	5	7		Joannes est nomen ejus	GB 198v	alv	
C	2	5	2	0	5	7	9	7	D	Egressus Jesus secessit	AR 376 *AM 349 *WA 93 *LA 142	an	1
C	2	5	2	0	5	7	9	7	D	Lutum ex sputo Dominus	SYG 106	co	1
C	2	5	2	0	5	7	9	7	D	O crux splendidior cunctis	AR 699 LU 1453 AM 898 1039 *WA 309 *LA 399 *SYG 140	an	1
C	2	5	2	0	5	7	9	7	F	Praevenisti eam Domine	GR 37**	co	6
C	2	5	2	0	5	7	9	7	F	Sedebit Dominus rex	GR 642 LU 1714	co	6
C	2	5	2	0	5	7	9	7	D	Vade Anania et quaere	LA 344 *WA 264	re	1
C	2	5	2	0	5	7	9	10	D	Habebitis autem hunc diem	AR 769 LU 1538v	an	1
C	2	5	2	0	5	7	9	12	D	Kyrie	MEL #220		

C	2	5	2	0	5	7	10	7	D	Alto ex Olympi vertice	AR [108] LU 1242	hy	1
C	2	5	2	0	5	7	10	7	D	Caelestis urbs Jerusalem	AR [104] LU 1248	hy	1
G	2	5	2	4	0	2	4	0	G	Kyrie	MEL #35		
C	2	5	2	4	0	2	4	5		In conspectu tuo Domine Protege Domine plebem	SYG 174	ofv	
C	2	5	2	4	0	2	4	5	D	Osculetur me osculo	WA 162	an	1
G	2	5	2	4	0	2	5	2	E	Quis Deus magnus ... tu es	LR 342 WA 159	re	3
C	2	5	2	4	0	2	5	4		In conspectu angelorum ... adorabo	GR 635 LU 1700	alv	
C	2	5	2	4	0	2	5	4		In conspectu angelorum ... Domine	GR [87] LU 1276 GS 197	alv	
C	2	5	2	4	0	2	5	4	D	Regressus Lucianus presbyter	WA 345	an	2
C	2	5	2	4	0	2	7	4	E	Alleluia: in conspectu angelorum ... adorabo	GR 635 LU 1700	al	4
C	2	5	2	4	0	2	7	4	E	Alleluia: in conspectu angelorum ... Domine	GR [87] LU 1276 GS 197	al	4
C	2	5	2	4	0	2	7	4	E	Alleluia: inter natos mulierum	GS m	al	4
C	2	5	2	4	0	2	7	4		Inter natos mulierum	GS m	alv	
G	2	5	2	4	0	5	2	0	E	Exsultabo in Jerusalem	GR 507 LU 1481	int	3
C	2	5	2	4	0	5	7	9	D	Consummatus in brevi	GR 81**	int	1
G	2	5	2	4	2	0	2	0	[G]	Agnus Dei	SCH #96		8
G	2	5	2	4	2	0	2	0	G	Gyrum caeli circuivi	LA 277 *WA 168	re	6
C	2	5	2	4	2	0	2	0	D	O quantus luctus hominum	LA 487 *WA 402	an	1
C	2	5	2	4	2	0	2	0	D	Sancta Maria succurre ... assumptionem	WA 353	re	1
C	2	5	2	4	2	0	2	0	D	Sancta Maria succurre ... festivitatem	AM 705	an	1
G	2	5	2	4	2	0	2	0	G	Vidi portam civitatis	LR 170 LA 227 *WA 140 306	re	7 8
C	2	5	2	4	2	0	2	4	D	Antra deserti teneris sub annis	AM 928[A] *LR 345	hy	2
C	2	5	2	4	2	0	2	4		Cum inducerent puerum Responsum accepit	PM 135	anv	
C	2	5	2	4	2	0	2	4	D	O nimis felix meritique celsi	AR 737	hy	2
C	2	5	2	4	2	0	2	4	D	Ut queant laxis resonare fibris	AR 733 LU 1504 AM 922	hy	2
C	2	5	2	4	2	0	2	5	D	Accedentes carnifices	WA 234	an	2
C	2	5	2	4	2	0	2	5	[D]	Agnus Dei	SCH #255		2
C	2	5	2	4	2	0	2	5	D	Alleluia: quasi modo geniti infantes	GB 144v	al	1
G	2	5	2	4	2	0	2	5	G	Beata Dei genitrix Maria cujus	LR 62 LU 383 *LA 34 *WA 29	re	7
C	2	5	2	4	2	0	2	5	D	Hodie martyrum flores	WA 46	re	1
C	2	5	2	4	2	0	4	2	D	Dormivit Abraham cum patribus	WA 82	re	1

C	2	5	2	4	2	0	4	2	D	Pastorum summo jubilemus	WA 277	inv	2
G	2	5	2	4	2	0	5	4	G	Ecce odor filii mei	LA 137 *WA 91	re	7
G	2	5	2	4	2	0	5	4	G	In sudore vultus tui	LA 111 *WA 74	re	7
G	2	5	2	4	2	0	5	7	D	Alleluia: Christus mortuus est propter delicta	GS 127	al	2
C	2	5	2	4	2	0	5	7	D	Alleluia: salva nos Christe	SYG 173	al	1
C	2	5	2	4	2	0	5	7	D	Nolite me considerare	AM 1046	an	1
G	2	5	2	4	2	0	5	7		Omnibus omnia factus sum	GR 68**	alv	
C	2	5	2	4	2	0	5	7	D	Omnipotentem semper adorent	ST 489	hy	2
C	2	5	2	4	2	0	5	7		Salva nos Christe	SYG 173	alv	
C	2	5	2	4	2	0	5	7	D	Stans autem Jesus jussit	AR 357 LU 516 AM 331 *WA 83 LA 125	an	1
G	2	5	2	4	2	0	7	5	G	Simile est regnum caelorum homini negotiatori	AR [92][97] *577^{21} LU 262^{9} 1231 *AM 680 745 *WA 339 434 *LA 546	an	7 8
G	2	5	2	4	2	4	0	2	G	Amen amen dico vobis qui non	WA 156	an	8
C	2	5	2	4	2	5	4	2	D	Alleluia: vindica Domine sanguinem	SYG 210	al	1
C	2	5	2	4	2	5	4	5	D	Domine mi rex omnipotens	LR 425 *LA 293 *WA 179	re	2
C	2	5	2	4	2	5	7	5	D	Afferentur regi virgines post	GR 437 LU 1370 OTT 163 *SYG 5 GS 229 GB 4^{v}	of	1
C	2	5	2	4	5	2	0	2	D	Alleluia: surrexit pastor bonus ... ovibus	SYG 164	al	1
C	2	5	2	4	5	2	0	2	D	Alleluia: verbo Domini caeli firmati	SYG 240	al	2
C	2	5	2	4	5	2	0	2		Etenim universi qui te De necessitatibus	GR 102 LU 841^{A} *GS 39 *GB 69^{v} *SYG 78	trv	
C	2	5	2	4	5	2	4	0	D	Alleluia: non vos me elegistis	SYG 172 GS y	al	1
C	2	5	2	4	5	2	4	0	D	Alleluia: sancte Benedicte qui in caelis	SYG 207	al	1
C	2	5	2	4	5	2	4	2	D	Dum iret Jacob	LR 406	re	1
C	2	5	2	4	5	2	4	2		Non vos me elegistis	SYG 172 GS y	alv	
C	2	5	2	4	5	2	4	2		Sancte Benedicte qui in caelis	SYG 207	alv	
G	2	5	2	4	5	2	5	2	G	Dum iret Jacob	WA 91	re	7
C	2	5	2	4	5	4	0	2	D	Alleluia: ave Maria gratia plena	GR [77] LU 1265 GS 184	al	2
C	2	5	2	4	5	4	0	2	D	Alleluia: eripe me de inimicis	GR 343 LU 1018 *SYG 242 *GB 251 GS 147	al	2
G	2	5	2	4	5	4	0	2	a	Alleluia: loquebar de testimoniis	GS 228	al	2
C	2	5	2	4	5	4	0	2	D	Alleluia: surgens Jesus Dominus ... stetit	GS 119	al	2
C	2	5	2	4	5	4	0	2		Surgens Jesus Dominus ... stetit	GS 119	alv	
C	2	5	2	4	5	4	0	5	D	Arguebat Herodem Joannes	AR 829 LU 1620 AM 1027 *WA 361 *LA 450	an	1

C	2	5	2	4	5	4	0	5	D	Similabo eum viro sapienti	AR 577^{18}_{7} [73] LU 262^{7} 1193 AM 669 743 *WA 427 *LA 536	an	1
C	2	5	2	4	5	4	2	0	E	In occursum salvatoris	WA 22	inv	4
C	2	5	2	4	5	4	2	0	E	Venite adoremus regem confessorum	WA 424	inv	4
C	2	5	2	4	5	4	2	4		Amavit eum Dominus et ornavit	GR [39] LU 1191 GS 222 *GB 271^{v} *SYG 214	alv	
C	2	5	2	4	5	4	2	5	E	Haec tua sunt Christe	WA 316	re	4
G	2	5	2	4	5	4	5	4	E	Laetabor super populo meo	AR 4 (sup 2)	an	3
G	2	5	2	4	5	4	5	7	E	Deus in te speravi	LA 97	re	3
C	2	5	2	4	5	4	5	7	E	Oculis ac manibus in caelum	LA 483 WA 400	re	4
G	2	5	2	4	5	4	5	7		Ostende mihi faciem tuam	GR 440 LU 1377	alv	
C	2	5	2	4	5	7	2	4	E	Rex noster adveniet	LA 13	inv	4
C	2	5	2	4	5	7	4	5	E	Alleluia: amavit eum Dominus	GR [39] LU 1191 *GS 222 *GB 271^{v} *SYG 214	al	4
C	2	5	2	4	5	7	5	2	D	Ecce vir prudens	VP 257 LA 533 WA 390 (inc illeg)	re	1
C	2	5	2	4	5	7	5	2	D	Et valde mane una sabbatorum	LA 211	re	1
c	2	5	2	4	5	7	5	4	F	Jam lucis orto sidere	ST 451	hy	5
C	2	5	2	4	5	7	5	4	D	Sanctus	THAN #211		2
C	2	5	2	4	7	9	7	9	E	Sancte sacerdos Domini	WA 251	an	4
G	2	5	2	5	0	2	-2	-3	E	Liberator meus de gentibus	GR 159 *SYG 113 *GB 100^{v} GS 74	int	3
G	2	5	2	5	0	2	0	-2	E	Gustate et videte quoniam	GR 341 LU 1015 GS 150 *SYG 244 *GB 251^{v}	co	3
G	2	5	2	5	0	2	0	-2	E	Vigilate et orate	GR 11**	co	3
G	2	5	2	5	0	2	4	5	E	Benedicite Dominum omnes angeli	LA 476	an	3
G	2	5	2	5	2	0	-2	0	E	Laudate Dominum omnes gentes	LA 90	an	4
C	2	5	2	5	2	0	2	4	D	Ut queant laxis resonare fibris	ST 474	hy	2
C	2	5	2	5	2	5	4	5	E	Virgo concepit et virgo peperit	WA 269	an	4
C	2	5	2	5	2	5	7	9		Recordare quod steterim Recordare mei	OTT 125 *SYG 259	ofv	
G	2	5	2	5	2	5	9	5	G	Alleluia: Deus qui sedes ... esto	GR 331 LU 999	al	7
G	2	5	2	5	2	5	9	5		Deus qui sedes ... esto	GR 331 LU 999	alv	
G	2	5	2	5	4	0	2	0	G	Kyrie Christe redemptor (etc)	MEL #39		
G	2	5	2	5	4	0	2	0	G	Kyrie I lux et origo	GR 4* LU 16		8
G	2	5	2	5	4	0	2	4	E	Confessio et pulchritudo	LR 293	an	3
G	2	5	2	5	4	0	2	4	F	Dominus legifer noster	LA 25 *WA 19	an	6
G	2	5	2	5	4	0	2	4	E	Educ de custodia	AR 182 LU 304	an	3

G	2	5	2	5	4	0	2	4	E	Ego sum pastor bonus qui pasco	AR 469 LU 820 *AM 483 *WA 142 LA 231 235	an	3
G	2	5	2	5	4	0	2	4	E	Elisabeth Zachariae magnum virum	AR 735 LU 1503 *AM 924 WA 323 LA 407	an	3
G	2	5	2	5	4	0	2	4	E	Fidelis servus et prudens	AR [74] LU 1196 1446 *AM 671 *WA 427 LA 540	an	3
G	2	5	2	5	4	0	2	4	E	Hic est discipulus meus	AR 279 LU 424 *AM 256 *WA 42 *LA 55	an	3
G	2	5	2	5	4	0	2	4	E	Quaerentes eum tenere	AR 385 LU 1088 *AM 360 LA 145	an	3
G	2	5	2	5	4	0	2	4	E	Salva nos Christe	AR 700 LU 1460 *AM 899 1040 *WA 371 LA 462	an	3
G	2	5	2	5	4	0	2	5	E	Herodes enim tenuit	AR 829 LU 1620 AM 1026 *LA 454	an	3
G	2	5	2	5	4	0	2	5	G	In omnem terram exivit sonus eorum	GR [90]	co	8
G	2	5	2	5	4	0	2	5	E	Ista est speciosa inter filias	AR [88] LU 1211 *AM 679 688	an	3
G	2	5	2	5	4	0	4	5	G	Panem caeli dedit eis	GR 520 LU 1495	co	8
F	2	5	2	5	4	0	4	7	F	Non vos me elegistis	WA 307	an	5
G	2	5	2	5	4	0	7	5	G	Gregem tuum Domine	VP 30	an	8
G	2	5	2	5	4	2	0	2	E	Aperite illi portas	WA 439	an	3
G	2	5	2	5	4	2	0	2	E	Hic est discipulus ille qui testimonium	AR 279 LU 421 *AM 255 WA 42 LA 55	an	3
G	2	5	2	5	4	2	0	2	E	Mandatum novum do vobis	GR 200 OHS 446 LU 671 WA 214 *GS 96 SYG 130	an	3
C	2	5	2	5	4	2	0	2	D	Missus est angelus Gabriel ... in civitatem	AR 688	an	1
G	2	5	2	5	4	2	0	2	E	Non dico tibi septies	WA 100	an	3
c	2	5	2	5	4	2	0	2	a	Responsum accepit Simeon ... Dominum	WA 272	an	3
G	2	5	2	5	4	2	0	2	E	Scitote quia Dominus	AR 301 LU 445 *AM 279	an	3
G	2	5	2	5	4	2	0	4	G	Reliquit eum temptator	WA 88	an	8
C	2	5	2	5	4	5	2	4	D	Domine non aspicias peccata	LR 322 *LA 369 *WA 298	re	2
C	2	5	2	5	4	5	2	4	D	Inito consilio venenum	LR 321 *LA 368	re	2
C	2	5	2	5	4	5	2	4	D	Sepulto Domino signatum est	OHS 618 LU 773 *LA 202 *WA 125	re	2
C	2	5	2	5	4	5	2	5		Vultum tuum deprecabuntur Audi filia	GR [62] LU 1227	trv	
C	2	5	2	5	4	5	7	4		Et nunc sequimur Sicut in holocausto	OTT 92 *GB 250v *SYG 243	ofv	
C	2	5	2	5	4	5	7	4	D	Veni redemptor gentium	ST 328	hy	2
C	2	5	2	5	4	5	7	5	D	Alleluia: dilexit Andream Dominus	GR 393 LU 1305 *SYG 231 *GB 246 GS g	al	1

C	2	5	2	5	4	5	7	5	D	Alleluia: dum complerentur dies	GR 305 LU 903 *GB 187 *SYG 183	al	1
C	2	5	2	5	4	5	7	5	D	Alleluia: justus ut palma florebit	GR [49](41) LU 1207 GS 207 *SYG 198 *GB 230	al	1
C	2	5	2	5	4	5	7	5	D	Alleluia: misso Herodes spiculatore	GS 196	al	1
C	2	5	2	5	4	5	7	5	D	Alleluia: O quam bonus et suavis est	GR 303 LU 898	al	1
C	2	5	2	5	4	5	7	5	D	Alleluia: senex puerum portabat	GR 434 LU 1363 GB 47^v	al	1
F	2	5	2	5	4	5	7	5	a	Cantabo Domino qui bona tribuit	GR 323 LU 963 GS 143 *SYG 240 *GB 248	co	2
C	2	5	2	5	4	5	7	5	E	Ipsi vero non cognoverunt	LA 175 *WA 110	inv	4
G	2	5	2	5	4	5	7	9	E	Domine spes sanctorum	LR 386 *WA 395 *LA 475	an	3
G	2	5	2	5	7	5	0	2		Ibi confregit potentias Notus in Judaea	GR [136] LU 1286	trv	
F	2	5	2	5	7	5	4	0	F	Dixit Dominus ad Noe	LR 399 *LA 116 *WA 76	re	6
G	2	5	2	5	7	5	4	0		Ego autem cum justitia Perfice gressus	OTT 90 *GB 58^v SYG 61	ofv	
G	2	5	2	5	7	5	4	0		Etenim non potuerunt mihi Saepe expugnaverunt	GR 153 LU 571 GS 72 *GB 97^v *SYG 110	trv	
G	2	5	2	5	7	5	4	0		Etenim passer invenit Cor meum	GR 626	trv	
G	2	5	2	5	7	5	4	0		Quod parasti ante faciem Nunc dimittis	GR 434 LU 1363 GS k *GB 49 *SYG 50	trv	
C	2	5	2	5	7	5	4	2	E	Aedificavit Noe altare	LA 117 *WA 78	re	3
C	2	5	2	5	7	5	4	5	E	Sub throno Dei	LA 60 *WA 44	re	4
G	2	5	2	5	7	5	7	9	a	Alleluia: confitemini Domino et invocate	GR 376 LU 1060 SYG 250 *GB 162 GS 157	al	2
G	2	5	2	5	7	5	7	9	a	Alleluia: ego autem cantabo	GR 469	al	2
G	2	5	2	5	7	5	7	9	a	Alleluia: gressus meos dirige	GR [143]	al	2
G	2	5	2	5	7	9	5	4	G	Ecce ego mitto angelum	PM 194	an	8
G	2	5	2	5	9	5	7	2		Deus qui sedes super thronum	GB 36^v	alv	
G	2	5	2	5	9	5	7	5	G	Alleluia: Deus qui sedes super thronum	GB 36^v	al	7
G	2	5	2	7	4	7	4	7	G	Alleluia: pascha nostrum immolatus	GR 242 LU 779 OHS 710 GS 117 *SYG 153 *GB 125^v	al	7
G	2	5	2	7	5	7	5	7	[G]	Alleluia: euntes in mundum	SYG 181	al	7
G	2	5	2	7	5	7	5	7	[G]	Alleluia: psallite Domino	SYG 180	al	7
D	2	5	3	2	0	2	-2	3	E	Cum esset sero die illa	WA 136	an	4
D	2	5	3	2	5	3	0	2	D	Jesu corona virginum	ST 442	hy	2
D	2	5	3	5	7	5	7	5	G	Cum rex gloriae Christus	SYG 148	an	8
c	2	5	4	0	2	0	-2	-5		Et in terra	BOS #4		

c	2	5	4	0	2	0	-2	0	c	Exsultet in hac die	WA 316	an	6
G	2	5	4	0	2	0	2	0	E	Vado parare vobis locum	PM 86 WA 150 307	an	3
C	2	5	4	0	2	4	2	7	E	Regi ... jubilemus	WA 329	inv	4
C	2	5	4	0	2	4	5	0	D	Sanctorum meritis inclyta gaudia	ST 198	hy	2
G	2	5	4	0	2	4	5	2	a	Nunc ad Sicelidem mittitur insulam	LR 450	hy	2
C	2	5	4	0	2	4	5	4	D	Deus tuorum militum	ST 457	hy	2
G	2	5	4	0	2	4	5	4	E	Tu Bethlehem terra Juda	AR 246 *AM 221 *WA 17 *LA 23	an	3
G	2	5	4	0	2	4	5	7	E	Ista est columba mea	AR 630 LU 1375	an	3
G	2	5	4	0	2	5	0	2	a	Sanctorum meritis inclyta gaudia	AR [36] LU 1157	hy	2
C	2	5	4	0	2	5	4	0	D	Inventor rutili dux bone luminis	WA 217	hy	2
G	2	5	4	0	2	5	4	0	G	Iterum videbo vos alleluia	WA 143	an	8
G	2	5	4	0	2	5	4	0	a	Sanctorum meritis inclyta gaudia	ST 102	hy	2
C	2	5	4	0	2	5	4	2	D	Revelabunt caeli iniquitatem	WA 120	re	1
C	2	5	4	0	4	2	0	2	D	Virgo verbo concepit	PM 148 *WA 47 *LA 39	an	2
C	2	5	4	0	4	2	0	5	D	Unus autem ex illis ut vidit	AR 565 LU 1036 AM 604 *WA 189 *LA 316	an	1
C	2	5	4	0	4	2	0	5	D	Virgo Dei genitrix quem totus	PM 272 *WA 47 *LA 39	an	1
c	2	5	4	2	-3	2	0	-3	a	Vexilla regis prodeunt fulget	ST 18	hy	1
C	2	5	4	2	-1	0	5	4	C	Herodis insanus furor	ST 20	hy	6
C	2	5	4	2	0	-3	0	2	D	Sicut lilium inter spinas	WA 354 *LA 456	an	2
G	2	5	4	2	0	-2	0	-2	E	Domine libera animam meam	WA 66	an	3
G	2	5	4	2	0	-2	0	2	E	Quadam die cum ex more	LR 295	re	3
G	2	5	4	2	0	-2	2	0	G	Aeterne rex altissime	GR 156* PM 96 LR 94 LU 957 ST 470	hy	8
G	2	5	4	2	0	-2	2	0	G	Lux alma Jesu mentium	AR 806	hy	8
G	2	5	4	2	0	-2	2	0	G	O salutaris hostia quae caeli	AR 93*	hy	8
G	2	5	4	2	0	-2	2	0	G	Verbum supernum prodiens nec patris	AR 531 111* PM 95 VP 12 11* LU 940 AM 552	hy	8
G	2	5	4	2	0	-2	2	5	G	Kyrie rex pie	MEL #38		
G	2	5	4	2	0	2	-3	-2	E	Alleluia	AR 180 LU 301 304	an	3
G	2	5	4	2	0	2	0	-3	E	Domine probasti me	AR 179 LU 301 *AM 149 150 WA 68 *LA 99	an	3
G	2	5	4	2	0	2	0	-3	E	Malos male perdet ... aliis	AR 385 LU 1088 WA 95 *LA 145	an	3
G	2	5	4	2	0	2	0	-3	G	Martine par apostolis	ST 462	hy	8
G	2	5	4	2	0	2	0	-3	E	Quoniam in aeternum	AM 144 145 *LR 338 *WA 67 *LA 96	an	3

G	2	5	4	2	0	2	0	-2	E	Alleluia	AR 125 AM 143 147 149 152	an	3
G	2	5	4	2	0	2	0	-2	E	Dominus regnavit exsultet terra	AR 125	an	3
G	2	5	4	2	0	2	0	-2	E	Omnia quaecumque voluit	AM 143 WA 67 *LA 96	an	3
c	2	5	4	2	0	2	0	2	c	Aula Maria Dei casta	WA 367	an	6
G	2	5	4	2	0	2	0	2	G	Certamen magnum habuerunt	LR 185 *LA 518	re	8
G	2	5	4	2	0	2	0	2	E	Condescende nobis pietatis	WA 336	an	3
C	2	5	4	2	0	2	0	2	D	Convertimini ad me	WA 84	an	1
G	2	5	4	2	0	2	0	4	E	Te semper idem esse	WA 158	an	3
C	2	5	4	2	0	2	0	5	D	Stans a longe publicanus	AR 562 LU 1105 AM 601 WA 189 LA 314	an	1
F	2	5	4	2	0	2	4	-3	F	Tempore laetitiae juste	WA 336	an	6
c	2	5	4	2	0	2	4	2	c	Ave o theotocos virgo	WA 366	an	6
C	2	5	4	2	0	2	4	2	D	Digna Deo Cilinia	ST 143	hy	1
c	2	5	4	2	0	2	4	2	c	Dum autem irent emere	WA 431	an	6
G	2	5	4	2	0	2	4	2	F	Nunc sancte nobis spiritus	ST 136	hy	6
G	2	5	4	2	0	2	4	2	E	Princeps ecclesiae pastor	SYG 265		3
G	2	5	4	2	0	2	4	5	[G]	Agnus Dei	SCH #74		7
C	2	5	4	2	0	2	4	5	E	Ardua spes mundi	ST 490	hy	4
G	2	5	4	2	0	2	4	5	E	Clementissime Domine qui pro nostra	LA 559	an	3
C	2	5	4	2	0	2	4	5	C	Jesu corona virginum	ST 313	hy	6
G	2	5	4	2	0	2	4	5	G	Martine par apostolis	ST 99	hy	8
G	2	5	4	2	0	2	4	5	E	Nemo te condemnavit mulier nemo	AR 396 LU 558 *AM 371 *WA 100	an	3
G	2	5	4	2	0	2	4	5	G	Rex Christe Martini decus	ST 99 435	hy	8
G	2	5	4	2	0	2	4	5	E	Semen est verbum Dei	AR 352 *AM 324 *WA 79 *LA 120	an	3
C	2	5	4	2	0	2	4	7	E	Exsultet caelum laudibus	ST 59	hy	4
C	2	5	4	2	0	2	5	2	D	Benedicamus Domino XVIIa	GR 57*		1
C	2	5	4	2	0	2	5	2	D	Illi ergo homines	AR 399 LU 564 AM 375	an	1
C	2	5	4	2	0	2	5	2	D	In spiritu humilitatis	AR 365 AM 342 WA 88 LA 132	an	2
C	2	5	4	2	0	2	5	2	D	Kyrie	MEL #210		
C	2	5	4	2	0	2	5	2	D	Kyrie XVIIa	GR 55* LU 60		1
F	2	5	4	2	0	2	5	2	F	O quam admirabile nomen	LR 289	an	6
C	2	5	4	2	0	2	5	2	D	Triumphant sancti martyres	WA 376	an	2
C	2	5	4	2	0	2	5	4	D	Amavit eum Dominus et ornavit	AR 577^{16}[65] LU 262^{4} 1181 AM 663 740 WA 428 *LA 537	an	1

C	2	5	4	2	0	2	5	4	D	Celebremus ... apostoli quia	WA 267 (inc illeg)	an	1
C	2	5	4	2	0	2	5	4	D	Dum esset gens congregata	SYG 173	int	2
G	2	5	4	2	0	2	5	4	G	Ego sum qui testimonium	WA 105	an	8
C	2	5	4	2	0	2	5	4	D	Exsultet caelum laudibus	ST 144	hy	2
C	2	5	4	2	0	2	5	4		Hostias et preces tibi Domine laudis Domine Jesu Christe	GR 100* LU 1813 GS 232 *GB 266	ofv	
C	2	5	4	2	0	2	5	4	D	Kyrie ad lib XI salve	GR 83* LU 86		1
C	2	5	4	2	0	2	5	4	D	Non auferetur sceptrum	WA 13	an	1
C	2	5	4	2	0	2	5	4	D	Qui caelorum contines	AR 553 LU 997 AM 592 WA 183 *LA 309	an	1
G	2	5	4	2	0	2	5	4	G	Sanctus	THAN #55		8
G	2	5	4	2	0	2	5	7	G	Jesu redemptor omnium	ST 201	hy	7
C	2	5	4	2	0	2	9	7	D	Laudemus Christum regem	WA 256	inv	2
G	2	5	4	2	0	4	2	0	G	Claudus quidam cum vidisset	WA 340	an	8
G	2	5	4	2	0	4	2	0	E	Confitemini Domino quoniam in aeternum	AR 158 LU 295	an	3
G	2	5	4	2	0	4	2	0	G	Verbum salutis omnium	ST 409	hy	8
C	2	5	4	2	0	4	5	2	D	Congregavit Christus	WA 214 SYG 132	an	1
G	2	5	4	2	0	4	5	2	E	Ecce virgo concipiet ... admirabilis	LA 5 380 *WA 5	re	3
G	2	5	4	2	0	4	5	2	E	Misericordiam et justitiam	LA 103	re	3
C	2	5	4	2	0	4	5	4	D	Decus morum dux minorum	ST 444	hy	2
G	2	5	4	2	0	4	5	4	E	Ecce virgo concipiet ... Emmanuel	GR 622[6] LU 1683	int	3
C	2	5	4	2	0	4	9	7	G	Agnus Dei	SCH #265		4
G	2	5	4	2	0	5	4	5	G	Ad regias agni dapes	AR 453 LU 812	hy	8
G	2	5	4	2	0	5	7	4	G	Lucis creator optime	AR 48 LU 256 *AM 128	hy	8
C	2	5	4	2	0	5	7	5	D	Paschalis festi gaudium	ST 463	hy	2
C	2	5	4	2	0	5	7	9	D	Alleluia dulce carmen	ST 378	hy	2
C	2	5	4	2	0	5	7	9	D	O admirabile nomen Jesu	VP 98	an	1
C	2	5	4	2	0	5	7	9	D	O gente felix hospita	AR 325	hy	2
C	2	5	4	2	0	5	7	9	D	O lux beata caelitum	AR 321 LU 475	hy	2
C	2	5	4	2	0	5	9	7	D	Filii hominum scitote	LR 149 WA 416 *LA 522	an	1 2
C	2	5	4	2	0	7	9	7	C	Nunc sancte nobis spiritus	ST 246	hy	5
G	2	5	4	2	3	2	0	-2	G	Hymnum novae laetitiae	ST 139	hy	2
C	2	5	4	2	4	0	-2	3	D	Non pro his rogo tantum	GB 177[v]	co	1
C	2	5	4	2	4	[0	0	0]	E	Ite missa est XV	GR 53* LU 59		4
G	2	5	4	2	4	0	2	0	G	Cives apostolorum et domestici	WA 414	re	7

G	2	5	4	2	4	0	2	0	G	Maria ut audivit	WA 302	re	7
G	2	5	4	2	4	0	2	0	G	O Juda qui dereliquisti	WA 120	re	7
G	2	5	4	2	4	0	2	0	G	Vere Dominus est in loco	WA 91	re	7
C	2	5	4	2	4	0	2	4	D	Felix Vedastus pontifex	ST 146	hy	2
G	2	5	4	2	4	0	2	5	E	Vade Luciane et dic	WA 342	re	3
C	2	5	4	2	4	0	4	2	D	Jam decus lactentium	WA 238	an	2
G	2	5	4	2	4	0	4	7	b	Rex sanctorum angelorum	ST 491 GS 114	hy	4
C	2	5	4	2	4	0	4	7	D	Sanctus	THAN #210		1
G	2	5	4	2	4	2	0	-5	E	Apparuit iterum sanctus Gamaliel	WA 346	an	3
G	2	5	4	2	4	2	0	-3	b	Corde et voce simul	WA 364	inv	4
C	2	5	4	2	4	2	0	-1	E	Stephanus servus Dei	WA 35 *LA 43	an	4
C	2	5	4	2	4	2	0	2	[D]	Agnus Dei	SCH #253		2
C	2	5	4	2	4	2	0	2	D	Archangelus Gabriel ait ad Mariam	AR 666 LU 1413	an	1
C	2	5	4	2	4	2	0	2	D	Beata Dei genitrix virgo	AR 52 577^{23} LU 260	an	2
G	2	5	4	2	4	2	0	2	G	Collaudabunt multi ... sanctorum	WA 373	an	8
C	2	5	4	2	4	2	0	2	D	Cum videritis abominationem	AR 575 LU 1110 AM 617	an	1
C	2	5	4	2	4	2	0	2	E	Evigila super nos	PM 108	an	4
C	2	5	4	2	4	2	0	2	E	Gaude Dei genitrix virgo	AR 125* PM 167 VP 48	an	4
G	2	5	4	2	4	2	0	2	E	Hodie nata est beata ... cujus vita gloriosa	LA 456 WA 365	re	3
C	2	5	4	2	4	2	0	2	D	In virtute tua Domine Deus	WA 283	an	1
G	2	5	4	2	4	2	0	2		Lux perpetua lucebit sanctis	GB 163^{v}	alv	
G	2	5	4	2	4	2	0	2	E	Mihi osculum non dedisti	WA 338	an	3
C	2	5	4	2	4	2	0	2	D	O beatum pontificem	AR 919 LU 1750 AM 1118 LA 487	an	1
G	2	5	4	2	4	2	0	2	E	O vera summa sempiterna trinitas	WA 162	an	3
C	2	5	4	2	4	2	0	2	E	Personet aula Dei	WA 281	inv	4
G	2	5	4	2	4	2	0	2	E	Qui odit animam suam	AR 577^{13}[19] LU 262 1129 *AM 642 737 WA 419 *LA 525	an	3
C	2	5	4	2	4	2	0	2	E	Sancte Cuthberte confessor	WA 294	an	4
C	2	5	4	2	4	2	0	2	E	Solve jubente Deo terrarum	AR 801 LU 1579 WA 278	an	4
C	2	5	4	2	4	2	0	2	D	Tu Domine universorum	LA 300	an	1
G	2	5	4	2	4	2	0	2	G	Tuam crucem adoramus ... exaltationem	LA 463	an	8
C	2	5	4	2	4	2	0	5	D	Beati eritis cum vos	AM 1121 WA 415 *LA 478	an	1
C	2	5	4	2	4	2	0	5	D	Bernardus doctor mellifluus	AM 1022	an	1
G	2	5	4	2	4	2	0	5	G	De ventre matris meae	LR 350	re	7

G	2	5	4	2	4	2	0	5	G	Ecce agnus Dei	LR 64 *LA 36	re	7
C	2	5	4	2	4	2	0	5	D	Euntes in mundum universum	WA 146 *LA 253	an	1
C	2	5	4	2	4	2	0	5		Martinus signipotens	SYG 227	alv	
C	2	5	4	2	4	2	0	5	D	Sint lumbi vestri ... et vos	WA 393 430	an	1
G	2	5	4	2	4	2	0	7	G	Descendit angelus Domini	LR 352 *LA 402 *WA 321	re	7
C	2	5	4	2	4	2	4	5	D	Illuminans altissimus	ST 414	hy	2
C	2	5	4	2	4	2	4	5	D	Illuminavit hunc diem rerum	ST 434	hy	2
C	2	5	4	2	4	2	4	5	D	Sanctus	THAN #209		2
C	2	5	4	2	4	5	2	4	D	Super omnia ligna cedrorum	AR 701 AM 901 1042 *WA 371 LA 463 SYG 144	an	1
F	2	5	4	2	4	5	2	7	D	Aeterne rerum conditor	ST 262	hy	1
G	2	5	4	2	4	5	4	[0]	G	Kyrie	MEL #33		
G	2	5	4	2	4	5	4	0	E	Tanto tempore vobiscum sum ... meum	AR 695 LU 1465^{E} *AM 893 *LA 394	an	3
c	2	5	4	2	4	5	4	2	[G]	Agnus Dei	SCH #16		7
C	2	5	4	2	4	5	4	2	D	Christe redemptor omnium ex patre	ST 318	hy	2
G	2	5	4	2	4	5	4	2		Transitoriam felicitatem Quantam denique	WA 239	rev	
G	2	5	4	2	4	5	7	4	G	Lucis creator optime	ST 212	hy	7
C	2	5	4	2	4	5	7	4	E	Tanto tempore vobiscum eram	LA 188	an	4
C	2	5	4	2	4	5	7	5	E	Bonum est Domine tibi confiteri	WA 283	an	4
G	2	5	4	2	4	5	7	5	E	In patre manet	WA 159	an	3
G	2	5	4	2	4	5	7	9	G	Adoremus crucis signaculum	SYG 139	an	7
G	2	5	4	2	4	5	7	9	G	Asperges me Domine hyssopo	GR 1* PM 9 LU 11 *WA 7	an	7
C	2	5	4	2	4	7	5	2	E	Alleluia: ne timeas Zacharia ... deprecatio	SYG 198	al	4
C	2	5	4	2	4	7	9	7	E	Claves pater possedisti	WA 313	an	4
G	2	5	4	2	5	0	2	0	G	Justum deduxit ... et dedit	LR 200 *LA 525 *WA 427	re	7
G	2	5	4	2	5	0	2	0	G	Tolle arma tua	LR 405 *LA 136 *WA 91	re	7
G	2	5	4	2	5	2	0	2		Beatus homo qui audit me Nunc ergo filii	GR 587^{3} LU 1612^{3}	trv	
G	2	5	4	2	5	2	0	2		Corona tribulationis effloruit Induit eum	GR 13**	trv	
G	2	5	4	2	5	2	0	2		Et mundus transit Nolite diligere	GR 22**	trv	
G	2	5	4	2	5	2	0	2		Euntes ibant et flebant Qui seminant	GR [24] LU 1164 GS 217 *GB 50 *SYG 51	trv	
G	2	5	4	2	5	2	0	2		Inimicos eos induam confusione Sacerdotes	LU 1623^{C}	trv	

G	2	5	4	2	5	2	0	2		Posuisti super caput ejus Desiderium animae	GR [5] LU 1131 GS 208 *GB 51^{v} *SYG 52	trv	
C	2	5	4	2	5	2	0	2	D	Super muros tuos Jerusalem	AR 554 LU 997 *AM 592 *LA 308	an	1
G	2	5	4	2	5	2	0	2		Venientes autem venient Qui seminant	GR [24] LU 1164 GS 217 *GB 50 *SYG 51	trv	
C	2	5	4	2	5	2	0	5		Dilexisti justitiam et odisti	SYG 229	alv	
C	2	5	4	2	5	2	4	2	E	Te Deum patrem ... et ore	WA 161	re	4
G	2	5	4	2	5	4	0	2	E	Hodie in Jordane baptizato	LR 71 *LA 67 WA 53	re	3
G	2	5	4	2	5	4	0	2	E	Sint lumbi vestri	LR 201 *LA 534	an	3
G	2	5	4	2	5	4	0	2	E	Tollite portas principes	LR 232 WA 317 *LA 547	an	3
G	2	5	4	2	5	4	0	4	E	Tolle puerum et matrem	WA 52 *LA 350	an	3
G	2	5	4	2	5	4	2	0	E	Ego gloriam meam	WA 108 *LA 169	an	3
G	2	5	4	2	5	4	2	0		Et sicut oculi ancillae Ad te levavi	GR 124 LU 554 *GS 55 *GB 82^{v} *SYG 93	trv	
G	2	5	4	2	5	4	2	0	b	Martyris ecce dies Agathae	ST 426	hy	4
C	2	5	4	2	5	4	2	0	E	Pretiosus vir Domini	WA 312	re	4
C	2	5	4	2	5	4	2	0	E	Sapientia Domini evangelii	WA 372	an	4
G	2	5	4	2	5	4	2	5	E	Sapientiam antiquorum	WA 374	an	3
F	2	5	4	2	5	4	5	2	D	Aeterne rerum conditor	ST 262	hy	1
G	2	5	4	2	5	4	5	2	G	Gratia Dei sum id quod sum	LA 429	re	8
C	2	5	4	2	5	4	5	2	E	Nocte surgentes vigilemus omnes	ST 155	hy	4
G	2	5	4	2	5	4	5	4	E	Qui de rupe promisit	WA 295	an	3
C	2	5	4	2	5	4	5	7	E	Domine suscipe me	WA 40 *LA 51	an	4
G	2	5	4	2	5	4	5	7	E	Petrus apostolus dixit paralytico	WA 326	an	3
G	2	5	4	2	5	4	5	7	E	Praepositus paradisi januae	WA 379	an	3
C	2	5	4	2	5	4	5	7	D	Quatuor facies uni	WA 372	re	2
G	2	5	4	2	5	4	5	7		Tibi laus tibi gloria O vera ... trinitas	WA 162	anv	
G	2	5	4	2	5	7	4	2	G	Kyrie	MEL #34		
F	2	5	4	2	5	7	4	5	a	Minor sum cunctis	WA 92	re	4
C	2	5	4	2	5	7	4	5	D	Quidam autem Judaei	WA 109	an	1
G	2	5	4	2	5	7	5	0	G	Alleluia: dicite in gentibus quia Dominus	GR 256 491 LU 801 1455 OHS 817 *SYG 173 *GS 122	al	8
G	2	5	4	2	5	7	5	0	G	Alleluia: spiritus est qui vivificat	GR 304 LU 901	al	8
C	2	5	4	2	5	7	5	7	D	In craticula te Deum	AR 815 AM 1007 *WA 350 LA 441	an	1
C	2	5	4	2	5	7	5	7	F	Ne in ira tua arguas	WA 63	an	6

G	2	5	4	2	5	7	5	7	G	Nemo tollet a me	WA 115 *LA 175	an	8
G	2	5	4	2	5	7	9	7	G	Agnus Dei	SCH #73		8
C	2	5	4	2	7	5	7	4	E	Sanctus ad lib II	GR 91* LU 86 THAN #208		4
C	2	5	4	2	7	5	7	5	E	Angelus Domini astitit	WA 328	an	4
C	2	5	4	2	7	5	7	5	E	Bethlehem non est minima	WA 9	an	4
G	2	5	4	5	2	0	2	0	E	Adaperiat Dominus cor ... in diebus	LR 425 LA 295 WA 180	re	3
G	2	5	4	5	2	0	2	0	D	Benedicite Deum caeli	PM 113 LA 289 WA 177	re	1
C	2	5	4	5	2	0	2	5	D	Isti sunt sancti martyres	LA 521	an	2
C	2	5	4	5	2	0	2	5	E	Justitia indutus sum	GR 633 LU 1696	of	4
C	2	5	4	5	2	0	2	5	E	Perfice gressus meos	GR 79 LU 508 OTT 90 SYG 61 GB 58^{v} GS 27 147	of	4
G	2	5	4	5	2	0	4	5	G	Haec accepit benedictionem	LR 289	an	8
G	2	5	4	5	2	0	5	7	G	Ne tradideris me Domine in animas	GR 165 *SYG 117 GB 104 GS 77	co	7
G	2	5	4	5	2	0	5	7	G	Si manseritis in me	GR (15)	co	7
G	2	5	4	5	2	0	7	9	G	Sanctus VII	GR 27* LU 36 THAN #54		8
G	2	5	4	5	2	0	7	9	G	Sanctus	THAN #53		7
F	2	5	4	5	2	4	2	0	G	Agnus Dei	SCH #119		8
C	2	5	4	5	2	4	2	0	D	Audi benigne conditor	ST 185	hy	2
C	2	5	4	5	2	4	2	0	E	Odor nominis tui o Maria	PM 188	an	4
G	2	5	4	5	2	4	5	7	E	Corona aurea super caput	GR 12**	gr	3
G	2	5	4	5	2	4	5	7	E	Exsurge Domine fer opem	GR 143 SYG 103 GB 91^{v} *GS 65	gr	3
G	2	5	4	5	2	4	5	7	E	Hic est qui venit per aquam	GR 537 LU 1533	gr	3
G	2	5	4	5	2	4	5	7	E	Speciosus forma prae filiis	GR 45 103** LU 434 SYG 30 GB 31	gr	3
G	2	5	4	5	2	5	2	0	E	In Deo laudabo verbum	GR 127 GS 56 SYG 94 *GB 83^{v}	int	3
G	2	5	4	5	2	5	2	0		In te Domine speravi non confundar	GR 335 LU 1008 GS 146 *GB 250 *SYG 241	alv	
G	2	5	4	5	2	5	2	0		Quoniam omnes dii gentium Annuntiate inter gentes	GR [128] LU 1295	trv	
C	2	5	4	5	2	5	2	4		In te speraverunt patres Deus Deus meus	GR 180 OHS 109 LU 594 GS 86 *GB 109 SYG 122	trv	
C	2	5	4	5	2	5	2	4		Propterea confitebor tibi Persequar inimicos	GR 463	trv	
C	2	5	4	5	2	5	2	5	E	Hodie scietis quia veniet	LA 29 *WA 25	inv	4
C	2	5	4	5	2	5	2	5	E	Hodie si vocem Domini	LA 156 *WA 105	inv	4
G	2	5	4	5	2	5	7	5	E	Ego sum Deus patrum	WA 227 *GB 153^{v}	an	3

C	2	5	4	5	2	5	7	5	E	Fidelis namque et prudens dispensator	PM 309	re	4
C	2	5	4	5	2	5	7	5	D	Si quis fecerit voluntatem	WA 89	an	1
G	2	5	4	5	2	7	5	4		Ego autem cantabo fortitudinem	GR 469	alv	
G	2	5	4	5	2	7	5	7	E	Benedicite Dominum omnes angeli	GR 607 LU 1653 *GS v *GB 168	int	3
G	2	5	4	5	2	7	5	7	E	Ego sicut vitis fructificavi	PM 256 LA 225 WA 139 305	re	3
C	2	5	4	5	4	2	0	2	D	Agnus Dei	SCH #254		1
C	2	5	4	5	4	2	0	2	E	Beatus Stephanus Christi martyr	WA 33	inv	4
G	2	5	4	5	4	2	0	2	E	Gaude virgo Maria	WA 359	an	3
C	2	5	4	5	4	2	0	2	D	Sanctus	THAN #207		1
c	2	5	4	5	4	2	4	2		A Domino sanctum est Pro te Jesu	WA 249	rev	
c	2	5	4	5	4	2	4	2		Accepit ergo centuplum Ecce jam cari	WA 300	rev	
C	2	5	4	5	4	2	4	2	D	Alleluia	WA 136	an	2
C	2	5	4	5	4	2	4	2		Astiterunt reges terrae Tradiderunt me	WA 123	rev	
F	2	5	4	5	4	2	4	2		Ave Maria gratia plena Beata es virgo ... Dei	LR 258 VP 200 LA 445	rev	
F	2	5	4	5	4	2	4	2		Bonus est Dominus omnibus Desiderium cordis	LR 296	rev	
c	2	5	4	5	4	2	4	2		Ecce vere Israelita Consecrandus	WA 250	rev	
c	2	5	4	5	4	2	4	2		Hoc erit signum Benedicens ergo Deus	WA 78	rev	
G	2	5	4	5	4	2	4	2	E	Hostis Herodes impie	ST 156	hy	3
c	2	5	4	5	4	2	4	2		O viri ad vos clamito Adversio parvulorum	WA 171	rev	
c	2	5	4	5	4	2	4	2		Ostendit mihi thesauros Mel et lac	LA 337	rev	
F	2	5	4	5	4	2	4	2		Qui pascit me ab adolescentia Jam laetus	PM 142	rev	
c	2	5	4	5	4	2	4	2		Quo virtute precum Festa dies mundo	WA 350	rev	
F	2	5	4	5	4	2	4	2		Requiem aeternam dona eis Domine Ne recorderis	AR [166] LU 1792	rev	
G	2	5	4	5	4	2	4	2	E	Scapulis suis obumbrabit ... et	GR 99 LU 537 SYG 75 GB 67 *GS 37	co	3
G	2	5	4	5	4	2	4	2	c	Tradiderunt me in manus	LU 710 OHS 505 *LA 197 *WA 123	re	6
c	2	5	4	5	4	2	4	2		Ut apud Christum Beatus Nicholaus	WA 241	rev	

C	2	5	4	5	4	2	4	5	E	Alleluia: assumpta est Maria ... angeli	GS 195 *SYG 216	al	4
C	2	5	4	5	4	2	4	5	E	Alleluia: per manus autem apostolorum	GS y	al	4
C	2	5	4	5	4	2	4	5	E	Alleluia: post partum virgo inviolata permanisti	GR [77] LU 1265 GS r *SYG 48 *GB 220^{v}	al	4
C	2	5	4	5	4	2	5	4	E	Mirabilem Deum in sanctis	WA 429	inv	4
G	2	5	4	5	4	2	5	4	G	Novit Dominus viam justorum	LR 381 *WA 395 *LA 474	an	8
G	2	5	4	5	4	2	5	4	E	O beata Caecilia quae duos fratres	PM 212 *LA 489 WA 408	re	3
G	2	5	4	5	4	2	5	7	G	Audiam Domine vocem laudis	LA 84 WA 61	re	7
G	2	5	4	5	4	2	5	7	G	Populus Domini et oves	LA 146 *WA 100	inv	7
C	2	5	4	5	4	5	2	0	E	Dabit illi Dominus Deus sedem	WA 302	re	4
G	2	5	4	5	4	5	2	4		In via testimoniorum Benedictus ... in labiis	OTT 28 *GB 60 *SYG 63	ofv	
C	2	5	4	5	4	5	2	5	E	Memor fui judiciorum	GR 564 LU 1580	gr	4
C	2	5	4	5	4	5	2	5	E	Mihi autem absit gloriari	GR 481	gr	4
G	2	5	4	5	4	5	2	7	G	Populus Sion convertimini	GB 154 *WA 227	an	8
C	2	5	4	5	4	5	4	5	E	Ecce quomodo moritur	OHS 611 LU 766 *LA 198 *WA 126	re	4
C	2	5	4	5	4	5	4	5	E	Ego autem dum mihi molesti	GR 187 OHS 258 LU 610 *SYG 125 *GB 112^{v} *GS 90	gr	3
G	2	5	4	5	4	5	4	7	E	Sperent in te omnes qui noverunt	GR 329 OTT 85 LU 983 *SYG 112 GB 100 *GS 74 144	of	3
G	2	5	4	5	4	5	7	5	E	Mihi autem adhaerere	GR 498 LU 1467	of	3
G	2	5	4	5	4	5	7	5	G	Popule meus quid feci	WA 103	re	7
C	2	5	4	5	4	5	7	5	E	Postula a me et dabo tibi	GR 642 LU 1713	of	4
C	2	5	4	5	4	5	7	5	E	Recordare Domine testamenti	LA 271 WA 166	re	4
C	2	5	4	5	4	5	7	5	E	Vir Domini Cuthbertus	WA 293	re	4
G	2	5	4	5	4	7	5	2	E	Tuam coronam adoramus	GR 15**	of	3
G	2	5	4	5	4	7	5	4	E	Christus unam pro peccatis	GR [103] LU 1283^{D}	of	3
G	2	5	4	5	4	7	5	4	E	Ecce dedi verba mea	GR [2^{4}] LU 1122^{6}	of	3
C	2	5	4	5	4	7	5	7	D	In die solemnitatis vestrae	GR 254 OHS 809 OTT 61 LU 798 SYG 159 GB 139^{v} GS 122	of	1
G	2	5	4	5	7	2	5	4		Liberator meus Domine Eripe me Domine	GR 152 LU 570 GS 71 *GB 97^{v} *SYG 109	grv	
C	2	5	4	5	7	2	7	5	E	Laetentur caeli ... ante faciem	GR 29 OTT 15 LU 394 *SYG 15 *GB 15 GS 14	of	4
C	2	5	4	5	7	2	7	5	E	Tulerunt Jesum parentes ejus	GR 63 LU 472	of	4
C	2	5	4	5	7	2	7	5	E	Venite filii audite me	GR 425 LU 1353^{v} 1623^{E}	of	4

C	2	5	4	5	7	4	2	5	D	Alleluia: ave Maria gratia plena	GB 11^{v}	al	1
C	2	5	4	5	7	4	2	5		Misit in eos Dominus Operarii	LR 282	rev	
C	2	5	4	5	7	4	5	2	E	Regem confessorum Dominum	LR 190	inv	4
C	2	5	4	5	7	4	5	2	E	Regem martyrum Dominum	LR 148 175 *LA 513	inv	4
G	2	5	4	5	7	4	5	4		Ut quid Domine recessisti Tibi Domine derelictus	GR 149 LU 566 *GS 70 *GB 96 SYG 108	grv	
C	2	5	4	5	7	4	7	5	E	Gloria IV	BOS #56 GR 15* LU 26		4
C	2	5	4	5	7	4	7	9	D	Vos ascendite ad diem	AR 417 LU 1099 AM 394 WA 109 *LA 174	an	1
G	2	5	4	5	7	5	2	4	E	Ego veritatem dico vobis	WA 145	an	3
C	2	5	4	5	7	5	2	5	E	In episcopatu suo	WA 295	an	4
G	2	5	4	5	7	5	2	5		Inter natos mulierum	SYG 196	alv	
G	2	5	4	5	7	5	2	5		Tu Domine pater noster	GB 151^{v}	alv	
C	2	5	4	5	7	5	2	5		Verba mea auribus percipe	GR 312 *SYG 239 *GS 141 *GB 247^{v}	alv	
G	2	5	4	5	7	5	4	0	E	Confitemini Domino quia	AR 159 LU 296	an	3
C	2	5	4	5	7	5	4	2		Assumpta est Maria ... gaudet	GR 584(32) LU 1603	alv	
C	2	5	4	5	7	5	4	2		Bene fundata est domus Domini	GR [73] LU 1252 *GB 174	alv	
G	2	5	4	5	7	5	4	2	E	Exsultet jam angelica ... caelorum	WA 218 GS 105	hy	3
C	2	5	4	5	7	5	4	2	E	Homo quidam erat dives qui ... factum	WA 187	an	4
C	2	5	4	5	7	5	4	2	D	Lucia martyr invictissima	WA 246	re	1
C	2	5	4	5	7	5	4	2		Non derelinquet Dominus sanctos	GR 446	alv	
C	2	5	4	5	7	5	4	2	D	Salus nostra in manu ... respiciat	WA 98	re	2
C	2	5	4	5	7	5	4	2		Salve mater misericordiae mater spei	GR 44**	alv	
G	2	5	4	5	7	5	4	2	G	Sanctus	THAN #52		8
C	2	5	4	5	7	5	4	2		Te gloriosus apostolorum	GR 588 LU 1613	alv	
C	2	5	4	5	7	5	4	2		Te martyrum candidatus	GR [30] LU 1171 *GS 18 217 *SYG 192 *GB 268^{v}	alv	
C	2	5	4	5	7	5	4	2	E	Tu decus virgineum virgo Dei	PM 271	an	4
C	2	5	4	5	7	5	4	5	D	Alleluia: ave rex noster tu solus	GR [108]	al	1
C	2	5	4	5	7	5	4	5	E	Confortamini et jam nolite	GR 10 OTT 9 *SYG 8 *GB 7 GS 12	of	4
G	2	5	4	5	7	5	4	7		Confessionem et decorem induisti Emitte spiritum	OTT 77 GB 184 *SYG 182	ofv	
G	2	5	4	5	7	5	4	7	G	Quinque prudentes virgines	WA 434	an	7
C	2	5	4	5	7	5	7	2		Omnis enim natura Si quis putat	GR 31**	trv	

G	2	5	4	5	7	5	7	9	G	Jerusalem respice	WA 8 *LA 22	an	7
G	2	5	4	5	7	5	7	10	d	Nocte surgentes vigilemus omnes	ST 165	hy	2
C	2	5	4	5	7	5	9	7	G	Cum venerit paraclitus quem ego	AR 496 LU 854 AM 513 WA 151 *LA 254	an	8
C	2	5	4	5	7	9	4	0	G	Elegerunt apostoli Stephanum	GR 37 LU 417 OTT 161 *SYG 23 *GB 22 GS 16	of	8
C	2	5	4	5	7	9	5	4	G	Deus autem noster in caelo	OHS 159 AR 48 LU 256	an	tp
G	2	5	4	5	7	9	7	5	G	Ad coenam agni providi	ST 190	hy	7
G	2	5	4	5	7	9	7	5	G	Concede nobis hominem	AR 581 *AM 757 WA 236 LA 504	an	7
G	2	5	4	5	7	9	7	5	G	Cornelius centurio vir religiosus	WA 326	an	7
G	2	5	4	5	7	9	7	5	G	Cum factus esset Jesus	LA 106	an	7
C	2	5	4	5	7	9	7	5	G	Jesu salvator saeculi	ST 194	hy	8
G	2	5	4	5	7	9	7	5	G	Kyrie	MEL #37		
C	2	5	4	5	7	9	7	5	D	Nolite me considerare	AR 842 LU 1631	an	1
G	2	5	4	5	7	9	7	5	G	Quam salubre invocatum	WA 249	an	7
c	2	5	4	5	7	9	7	5		Trinitati lux Honor virtus	WA 160	rev	
C	2	5	4	5	7	9	7	9	G	Da pacem Domine in diebus nostris	WA 180	an	8
C	2	5	4	5	7	9	7	9	E	Exsurge Domine et intende	GR 185 OHS 208 LU 607 SYG 124 GB 111^v GS 89	gr	3
G	2	5	4	5	7	9	7	9	G	Suscepit Deus Israel	AR 206 LU 313 AM 163	an	7
G	2	5	4	5	7	9	7	9	G	Te gloriosus apostolorum ... te	AR 901 LU 1724 AM 1105 WA 397 LA 478	an	7
G	2	5	4	5	7	9	10	9	G	Asperges me Domine hyssopo	GR 3* LU 13	an	7
G	2	5	4	5	7	9	10	9		Post dies octo ... stetit	GR 262 LU 810 GS 124 GB 144^v	alv	
C	2	5	4	5	7	9	12	11	G	Virginis proles opifexque matris	ST 202	hy	8
G	2	5	4	7	5	2	-2	2		Sedes super thronum Sperent in te	OTT 85 *GB 100 *SYG 112	ofv	
G	2	5	4	7	5	4	5	4		Quia ecce venio Exsulta satis	OTT 11 *GB 10 *SYG 12	ofv	
C	2	5	4	7	5	7	5	2	D	In Deo raptus	LR 281	re	1
C	2	5	4	7	9	5	7	5	D	Et Jesus proficiebat	AR 325 LU 474	an	2
C	2	5	4	7	9	5	7	5	F	Posuisti Domine in capite ejus	GR [10] LU 1135 SYG 34 GB 41 GS 209	co	6
C	2	5	7	2	0	2	4	5		In quacumque die invocavero Domine exaudi	GR 191 OHS 324 LU 619 *GS 92 GB 114 SYG 127	trv	
C	2	5	7	2	0	2	5	7		Adducentur in laetitia Audi filia	GR [62] LU 1227	trv	
C	2	5	7	2	0	2	5	7		Adducentur in laetitia Omnis gloria	GR 104**	trv	

C	2	5	7	2	0	2	5	7		Et ego primogenitum Ipse invocabit	GR 640 LU 1711	trv	
C	2	5	7	2	0	2	5	7		Os justi meditabitur Apud Dominum	GR 528	trv	
F	2	5	7	2	0	7	5	7		Omnes gentes plaudite manibus	GR 337 LU 1011 *SYG 241 *GS 133 *GB 177	alv	
C	2	5	7	2	5	2	4	0		Jubilate Deo omnis terra Benedicite gentes	OTT 71 *GB 93v *SYG 105	ofv	
C	2	5	7	2	5	4	5	4		Quem proposuit Deus Gratificavit nos	GR 538	trv	
C	2	5	7	2	5	7	5	4		Benedicite Domino omnes virtutes ejus Benedicite Dominum	GR [87] LU 1276	trv	
C	2	5	7	2	5	7	5	4		Qui timetis Dominum laudate Deus Deus meus	GR 180 OHS 109 LU 594 GS 86 GB 109 SYG 122	trv	
C	2	5	7	2	5	7	5	4		Verumtamen justi confitebuntur Eripe me	GR 208 OHS 534 LU 725 GS 99 GB 116v SYG 137	trv	
C	2	5	7	2	5	7	9	7		Disciplina pacis nostrae Vere languores	GR [108]	trv	
C	2	5	7	2	7	5	4	5		Benedicta tu in mulieribus Ave Maria	GR 459 LU 1412 *GS 183 *SYG 57	trv	
D	2	5	7	3	2	5	2	3		Veni sponsa Christi accipe coronam	SYG 208	alv	
D	2	5	7	3	2	5	3	2	E	Alleluia: veni sponsa Christi accipe coronam	SYG 208	al	3
C	2	5	7	4	2	5	4	5	D	Alleluia: dedisti mihi protectionem	GR 465	al	1
C	2	5	7	4	2	5	4	5	D	Alleluia: ecce concipiet et pariet	GR 3**	al	1
C	2	5	7	4	2	5	4	5	D	Alleluia: Franciscus pauper et humilis	GR 602 LU 1643	al	1
C	2	5	7	4	2	5	4	5	D	Alleluia: hic Martinus pauper	SYG 227 GS 200	al	1
C	2	5	7	4	2	5	4	5	D	Alleluia: posuisti Domine super caput	GR [17] LU 1148 GS 206 GB 270	al	1
C	2	5	7	4	2	5	4	5	D	Alleluia: puer meus dicit Dominus	SYG 213	al	1
C	2	5	7	4	2	5	4	5	D	Alleluia: repleti fructu justitiae	GR 545 LU 1545	al	1
D	2	5	7	4	2	5	4	5	D	Alleluia: spiritus paraclitus docebit vos	GB 192	al	2
C	2	5	7	4	2	5	4	5		Dedisti mihi protectionem	GR 465	alv	
C	2	5	7	4	2	5	4	5	D	Ecce jam coram te protomartyr	PM 31 VP 79	re	1
C	2	5	7	4	2	5	4	5		Franciscus pauper et humilis	GR 602 LU 1643	alv	
C	2	5	7	4	2	5	4	5		Hic Martinus pauper	SYG 227 GS 200	alv	
C	2	5	7	4	2	5	4	5		Posuisti Domine super caput	GR [17] LU 1148 GS 206 *GB 270	alv	
C	2	5	7	4	2	5	4	5		Puer meus dicit Dominus	SYG 213	alv	

C	2	5	7	4	5	2	0	2	D	Innocentes pro Christo	AR 287 LU 432 AM 264 *WA 44 *LA 62	an	2
C	2	5	7	4	5	2	0	2	D	Laetentur omne saeculum	ST 440	hy	2
G	2	5	7	5	0	2	5	2		Torrentem pertransivit anima nostra Anima nostra	OTT 145 GB 27^v SYG 26	ofv	
C	2	5	7	5	0	5	7	4	F	Quasi modo geniti infantes	GR 261 LU 809 *SYG 162 GB 144^v	int	6
C	2	5	7	5	2	0	2	0	D	Filiae Jerusalem venite	AR 577^{11}_{1} [33] LU 262^1 1145 AM 636 735 WA 304 LA 385	an	1
C	2	5	7	5	2	0	2	0	D	O quam glorifica luce coruscas	ST 192	hy	1
C	2	5	7	5	2	4	0	-3	D	Universi qui te exspectant	GR 2 LU 320 SYG 1 GB 1 GS B 1	gr	1
G	2	5	7	5	2	4	2	0	G	Agnus Dei	SCH #72		8
C	2	5	7	5	2	4	5	4	C	Aurora lucis rutilat	ST 316	hy	6
C	2	5	7	5	2	4	5	4		Benedicat nos sancta majestas Benedicat nos Deus	SYG 263	trv	
C	2	5	7	5	2	4	5	4		Et portae inferi non praevalebunt Tu es Petrus	GR 409 LU 1332 GS 182 SYG 53	trv	
C	2	5	7	5	2	4	5	4		Et redde in hoc Domine non aspicias	SYG 56	trv	
C	2	5	7	5	2	4	5	4		Holocaustum et pro peccato Hostiam et oblationem	GR 61	trv	
C	2	5	7	5	2	4	5	4		In medio duorum animalium Domine audivi	GR 206 OHS 529 LU 721 GS 98 GB 116 SYG 136	trv	
C	2	5	7	5	2	4	5	4		Ne avertas faciem tuam a me Domine exaudi	GR 191 OHS 324 LU 619 GS 92 GB 114 SYG 127	trv	
C	2	5	7	5	2	4	5	4		Quis loquetur potentias Confitemini Domino	GR 113 LU 547 GB 75 *SYG 86	trv	
C	2	5	7	5	2	4	5	4		Specie tua et pulchritudine Diffusa est	SYG 49	trv	
C	2	5	7	5	2	4	5	7	F	Quia fecisti viriliter	GR 52**	of	6
C	2	5	7	5	2	5	2	0		In eo dum conturbata Domine audivi	GR 206 OHS 529 LU 721 *GS 98 GB 116 SYG 136	trv	
C	2	5	7	5	2	5	2	4	D	Audivi voces occisorum	WA 44	an	1
F	2	5	7	5	2	5	4	2	D	Gesta sanctorum martyrum	ST 10	hy	1
C	2	5	7	5	2	5	7	5	E	Cum transisset sabbatum	OHS 696 (nm) LR 84 LA 213 WA 129	re	4
C	2	5	7	5	2	5	7	5	E	Ecce vidi agnum stantem	LA 59	re	4
G	2	5	7	5	2	5	7	5		Qui statis in domo Domini Laudate Dominum	OTT 40 *GB 90 *SYG 102	ofv	
C	2	5	7	5	2	5	7	9		Confringam illos nec poterunt Persequar inimicos	GR 463 LU 1420	trv	

C	2	5	7	5	2	5	7	9		Ego autem ad Deum clamavi Contristatus	GR 622[3]	trv	
C	2	5	7	5	2	5	7	9		Ego autem sum vermis Deus Deus meus	GR 180 OHS 109 LU 594 GS 86 GB 109 SYG 122	trv	
C	2	5	7	5	2	5	7	9		Et ponam in saeculum saeculi semen Ipse invocabit	GR 640 LU 1711	trv	
C	2	5	7	5	2	5	7	9		Ideoque quod nascetur ex te Ave Maria	GR 459 LU 1412 GS 183 *SYG 57	trv	
C	2	5	7	5	2	5	7	9		Quam nemo principum Non judicavi	GR 476	trv	
C	2	5	7	5	2	5	7	9		Quia illic sederunt Laetatus sum in his	SYG 101	trv	
C	2	5	7	5	2	5	7	9		Quodcumque ligaveris Tu es Petrus	GR 409 LU 1332 GS 182 *SYG 53	trv	
C	2	5	7	5	2	5	7	9		Tu autem in sancto habitas Deus Deus meus	GR 180 OHS 109 LU 592 GS 86 GB 109 SYG 122	trv	
G	2	5	7	5	3	0	3	0	c	In virtute tua Domine laetabitur	GR [46] OTT 152 LU 1205 *SYG 52 GB 51^{v} *GS 209	of	6
C	2	5	7	5	4	0	2	0	D	Fidelis sermo et omni	LA 471 *WA 381	re	1
C	2	5	7	5	4	0	2	5	D	Dixit Jesus ut sciatis	AR 514 AM 530	an	1
C	2	5	7	5	4	2	0	2	D	Agnus Dei	SCH #252		2
C	2	5	7	5	4	2	0	2	D	Alleluia: erat lucerna ardens	SYG 197	al	1
C	2	5	7	5	4	2	0	2	D	Clarum decus jejunii	ST 380	hy	2
C	2	5	7	5	4	2	0	2	D	Domine rex omnipotens in ditione	AR 549 LU 993 AM 587 *WA 176 *LA 294	an	1 2
C	2	5	7	5	4	2	0	2		Erat lucerna ardens	SYG 197	alv	
G	2	5	7	5	4	2	0	2	G	Kyrie	MEL #32		
C	2	5	7	5	4	2	0	2	D	Veni desiderator bone	PM 175 *WA 351	an	1
C	2	5	7	5	4	2	0	4	E	Christe caelorum habitator alme	ST 277	hy	4
C	2	5	7	5	4	2	0	4	E	Christe supreme dominator alme	ST 300	hy	4
C	2	5	7	5	4	2	0	4	D	Gloriosae virginis Mariae ortum	AR 833 LU 1623^{F} AM 1031	an	1
C	2	5	7	5	4	2	0	5	D	Hodie nata est beata	WA 364	an	1
C	2	5	7	5	4	2	0	5	D	O beata et benedicta	WA 161	an	1
C	2	5	7	5	4	2	0	5	D	Pange lingua gloriosi proelium	ST 52	hy	1
C	2	5	7	5	4	2	4	2	D	Adhuc loquente Petro	WA 327	an	1
C	2	5	7	5	4	2	4	2	D	O martyr egregie Victor	PM 345	re	1
G	2	5	7	5	4	2	4	2	E	Salva nos Domine vigilantes	AR 64 OHS 172 LU 271	an	3
C	2	5	7	5	4	2	4	2	D	Sanctus	THAN #206		2
C	2	5	7	5	4	2	4	5		Adducentur in laetitia Diffusa est gratia	SYG 49	trv	
C	2	5	7	5	4	2	5	2	D	Abraham pater vester	WA 108	an	2

C	2	5	7	5	4	2	5	2	D	Exsultet spiritus noster	WA 281	an	1
C	2	5	7	5	4	2	5	2	D	Sanctus Joannes episcopus	WA 345	re	1
C	2	5	7	5	4	2	5	4	D	Alleluia: benedicamus patrem ... laudemus	SYG 261	al	1
C	2	5	7	5	4	2	5	4		Benedicamus patrem et filium cum ... laudemus	SYG 261	alv	
C	2	5	7	5	4	2	5	4	D	Princeps gloriosissime Michael	AR 862 LU 1662 AM 1063 LA 473	an	1
C	2	5	7	5	4	2	5	4	D	Princeps gloriosissime Raphael	AR 894 LU 1703	an	1
G	2	5	7	5	4	5	2	4	E	Deus tu convertens vivificabis	GR 6 OTT 6 LU 330 *SYG 4 *GS 3 7 *GB 3	of	3
G	2	5	7	5	4	5	4	0		Liberator meus de gentibus Intonuit de caelo	OTT 58 GB 134^v *SYG 156	ofv	
C	2	5	7	5	4	5	4	2	D	In psalterio et cithara	WA 69	an	1
C	2	5	7	5	4	5	7	4		Non calor hunc coxit Sanctas primitias	PM 267	rev	
G	2	5	7	5	4	5	7	5	a	Ante torum hujus virginis	LR 213 246 *WA 353 *LA 541	an	4
G	2	5	7	5	4	5	7	9	G	Absolve Domine animas eorum	LA 558 *WA 438	re	7
C	2	5	7	5	4	5	7	9	D	Alleluia: Dominus regnavit decorem ... fortitudinem	GR 31 LU 405 SYG 16 GB 15^v *GS E	al	2
C	2	5	7	5	4	5	7	9	D	Alleluia: propter veritatem ... deducet	GR [67] LU 1237	al	2
C	2	5	7	5	4	5	7	9	E	Tu es Deus, qui facis	GR 81 LU 512 *SYG 62 GB 59^v GS 28	gr	3
G	2	5	7	5	4	7	9	5		Et ponam in saeculum saeculi sedem Inveni David	OTT 147 *GB 28^v *SYG 27	ofv	
C	2	5	7	5	4	7	9	5		Miserere mihi Domine quoniam infirmus Domine convertere	OTT 84 GB 99^v SYG 111	ofv	
G	2	5	7	5	4	7	9	7		Benedixisti Domine terram tuam Deus tu convertens	OTT 6 GB 3 SYG 4	ofv	
G	2	5	7	5	7	0	2	0	G	O virgo super virgines benedicta	PM 255	an	7
C	2	5	7	5	7	4	2	5	D	Alleluia: dies sanctificatus illuxit nobis	GR 34 LU 409 GB 17^v GS G *SYG 19	al	2
C	2	5	7	5	7	4	2	5	D	Alleluia: Domine diligo habitaculum	LU 1623^D	al	2
C	2	5	7	5	7	4	2	5	D	Alleluia: ego Dominus dabo eis	GR 105**	al	2
C	2	5	7	5	7	4	2	5	D	Alleluia: gloria et honore coronasti ... Domine et constituisti	GS 208	al	2
C	2	5	7	5	7	4	2	5	D	Alleluia: gustate et videte quoniam	GR 616	al	2
C	2	5	7	5	7	4	2	5	D	Alleluia: hic est discipulus ille	GR 39 LU 422 GS 17 *GB 24^v *SYG 24	al	2

C	2	5	7	5	7	4	2	5	D	Alleluia: hic est sacerdos quem coronavit	GR [8][34] LU 1184	al	2
C	2	5	7	5	7	4	2	5	D	Alleluia: inveni David servum meum	GR 514 LU 1489 GS 222 SYG 38	al	2
C	2	5	7	5	7	4	2	5	D	Alleluia: justus non conturbabitur	GR 573 GS 208 *SYG 34 *GB 270	al	2
C	2	5	7	5	7	4	2	5	D	Alleluia: magnus sanctus Paulus	GR 419 LU 1346 GS 178 189	al	2
C	2	5	7	5	7	4	2	5	D	Alleluia: nunc cum eo regnas	LU 1476^{D}	al	2
G	2	5	7	5	7	4	2	5	a	Alleluia: potens in terra erit semen	GR 585	al	2
C	2	5	7	5	7	4	2	5	D	Alleluia: redemptionem misit Dominus	GR 266 LU 822 *SYG 248	al	2
C	2	5	7	5	7	4	2	5	D	Alleluia: sancti tui Domine benedicent	GR 415 LU 1336 GS 215 *GB 269^{v} *SYG 40	al	2
C	2	5	7	5	7	4	2	5	D	Alleluia: tu es Petrus et super hanc petram	GR 409 534 LU 1122^{3} 1520 *SYG 203 *GB 202^{v}	al	2
C	2	5	7	5	7	4	2	5	D	Alleluia: tu puer propheta altissimi	GR 524 LU 1501 GS 1 188 *SYG 196 *GB 197^{v}	al	2
C	2	5	7	5	7	4	2	5	D	Alleluia: video caelos apertos	GR 37 LU 416 GS 15 *GB 21^{v} *SYG 22	al	2
C	2	5	7	5	7	4	2	5	D	Alleluia: vidimus stellam ejus	GR 58 LU 460 GS 19 *GB 33^{v} *SYG 31	al	2
C	2	5	7	5	7	5	2	4		Benedicite Domino omnia opera ejus Benedicite Dominum	GR [87] LU 1276	trv	
C	2	5	7	5	7	5	2	5		Ad annuntiandum mane Bonum est confiteri	GR 497	trv	
C	2	5	7	5	7	5	2	7		Et virtutem terribilium tuorum Magnificentiam	GR 99**	trv	
C	2	5	7	5	7	5	2	7		Pars mea Domine dixi custodire Meditabor in mandatis	OTT 109 *GB 70 SYG 78	ofv	
C	2	5	7	5	7	5	4	5		Miserere mei secundum eloquium Meditabor in mandatis	OTT 109 *GB 70 SYG 78	ofv	
C	2	5	7	5	7	5	7	2	D	Mihi autem absit gloriari	GR 426 602 LU 1354 1643	int	2
C	2	5	7	5	7	5	7	2	D	Mihi autem nimis honorati	GR 392 LU 1304 SYG 54 GB 235 GS w	int	2
C	2	5	7	5	7	5	7	9	F	Cum inducerent puerum	LR 312	re	6
G	2	5	7	5	7	5	7	9	a	Intuemini quantus sit	WA 26 LA 26	an	4
G	2	5	7	5	7	5	7	9		Lapidem quem reprobaverunt Benedictus qui venit	OTT 64 GB 144 SYG 161	ofv	
G	2	5	7	5	7	9	5	7	a	Alleluia	AM 93	an	4
D	2	5	7	5	7	9	5	7	E	Infirmata est virtus	LA 185	an	4

G	2	5	7	5	7	9	5	7	a	O mulier magna est fides	AR 377 LU 1084 AM 350 *WA 92 *LA 135 140	an	4
G	2	5	7	5	7	9	5	7	a	Propter Sion non tacebo	AR 240 AM 215 *WA 18 *LA 24	an	4
G	2	5	7	5	7	9	7	5	a	A saeculo non est auditum	WA 105	an	4
C	2	5	7	5	7	9	7	5		Ad te Domine levavi animam ... Deus ... neque De necessitatibus	GR 102 LU 841[A] GS 39 *GB 69[v] SYG 78	trv	
G	2	5	7	5	7	9	7	5	a	Alieni insurrexerunt in me	OHS 494 LU 701 WA 122 *LA 197	an	4
C	2	5	7	5	7	9	7	5	F	Ambulate in dilectione	GR 483 LU 1435	of	6
G	2	5	7	5	7	9	7	5	a	Apud Dominum misericordia	AR 271 LU 412 AM 246 WA 33 *LA 39	an	4
G	2	5	7	5	7	9	7	5	a	Apud Dominum propitiatio	AR 538[3] LU 966 AM 561	an	4
G	2	5	7	5	7	9	7	5	a	Benedicam te in vita mea	AR 3 (sup 1)	an	4
G	2	5	7	5	7	9	7	5	a	Benedicta tu in mulieribus	AR 221 AM 193 LR 246 375 WA 9 268 *LA 7 444	an	4
G	2	5	7	5	7	9	7	5	a	Confundantur et revereantur	OHS 492 LU 699 WA 122 *LA 197	an	4
G	2	5	7	5	7	9	7	5	a	Confundantur qui me persequuntur	AR 422 OHS 70 AM 400 WA 113 *LA 182	an	4
G	2	5	7	5	7	9	7	5	a	Desiderio desideravi hoc Pascha	AR 419 LU 1100 AM 396 WA 110 *LA 174	an	4
G	2	5	7	5	7	9	7	5	a	Ecce veniet propheta	AR 214 LU 324 AM 188 WA 7 20 *LA 6	an	4
G	2	5	7	5	7	9	7	5	a	Ecce video caelos apertos	AR 274 LU 418 1583[B] AM 251 WA 37 *LA 47	an	4
G	2	5	7	5	7	9	7	5	a	Ego autem ad Dominum	AR 243 AM 218 WA 20 *LA 26	an	4
G	2	5	7	5	7	9	7	5	a	Elevata est magnificentia	LR 95 WA 147 LA 244	an	4
G	2	5	7	5	7	9	7	5	a	Erit mihi Dominus in Deum	LR 233 WA 318 *LA 547	an	4
G	2	5	7	5	7	9	7	5	a	Exaltata est sancta Dei genitrix	LR 374 *LA 442	an	4
G	2	5	7	5	7	9	7	5	a	Exhortatus es in virtute	AR 433 OHS 403 LU 655 AM 417 418 WA 120 *LA 194	an	4
G	2	5	7	5	7	9	7	5	a	Faciamus hic tria tabernacula	AR 381 LU 549 AM 354	an	4
G	2	5	7	5	7	9	7	5	a	Gloriosus apparuisti in conspectu	WA 380 *LA 465	an	4
G	2	5	7	5	7	9	7	5	a	In odorem unguentorum	AR 821 [98] LU 1233 1606 AM 687 1014 WA 358 LA 448	an	4
G	2	5	7	5	7	9	7	5	a	Introibo ad altare Dei ad Dominum	WA 318	an	4
G	2	5	7	5	7	9	7	5	a	Introibo in domum tuam	LR 232	an	4
G	2	5	7	5	7	9	7	5	a	Intuemini quam sit	AR 243	an	4

G	2	5	7	5	7	9	7	5	a	Invocabo nomen tuum Domine	AR 425 OHS 152 LU 604 AM 403 *LA 185	an	4
G	2	5	7	5	7	9	7	5	a	Jam enim hiems	WA 434 *LA 543	an	4
G	2	5	7	5	7	9	7	5	a	Laeva ejus sub capite meo	AR [114] LR 214 LU 1258 AM 707 *LA 541 WA 434	an	4
G	2	5	7	5	7	9	7	5	a	Non est ei species	AR 843 LU 1639 *AM 1047	an	4
G	2	5	7	5	7	9	7	5	a	Non haberes in me potestatem	AR 428 OHS 226 AM 407 WA 114 *LA 185	an	4
C	2	5	7	5	7	9	7	5		Non in perpetuum irascetur Misericors	GR [113] LU 972	trv	
G	2	5	7	5	7	9	7	5	a	Numquid redditur pro bono	AR 98 409 AM 107 122 389 *LA 171 WA 108	an	4
G	2	5	7	5	7	9	7	5	a	Oves meae vocem meam	AR 418 LU 1099 AM 395 WA 109 *LA 174	an	4
G	2	5	7	5	7	9	7	5	a	Petre amas me	WA 281 *LA 420	an	4
G	2	5	7	5	7	9	7	5	a	Plangent eum quasi unigenitum	AR 440 OHS 620 LU 775 AM 445 446 WA 127 *LA 206	an	4
C	2	5	7	5	7	9	7	5	F	Quasi modo geniti alleluia	GS 124	int	6
G	2	5	7	5	7	9	7	5	a	Si quis sitit veniat et bibat	AR 416 LU 1098 AM 394 WA 109 *LA 173	an	4
G	2	5	7	5	7	9	7	5	a	Sicut pater suscitat	WA 105	an	4
G	2	5	7	5	7	9	7	5	a	Stetit angelus juxta aram	AR 856 LU 1659 AM 1058 WA 379 *LA 465	an	4
G	2	5	7	5	7	9	7	5	a	Tempus meum nondum advenit	AR 417 LU 1098 AM 394 *LA 173	an	4
G	2	5	7	5	7	9	7	5	a	Tuam Domine excita potentiam	WA 8	an	4
G	2	5	7	5	7	9	7	5	a	Unum opus feci	WA 104	an	4
G	2	5	7	5	7	9	7	5	a	Veni Domine et noli ... Israel	AR 243 AM 218 WA 20 *LA 26	an	4
C	2	5	7	5	7	9	7	5		Voce quippe de caelo Operibus sanctis	WA 239	rev	
G	2	5	7	5	7	9	7	9	b	Effuderunt sanguinem sanctorum	LA 58 *WA 44	re	4
G	2	5	7	5	7	9	10	7	G	Ipsi vero in vanum	LA 187	an	7
G	2	5	7	5	7	9	10	7	G	Sapientia aedificavit ... excidit ... subdidit	AR 543 LU 989 AM 580 *LA 280 *WA 168 317	an	7
GG	2	5	7	5	7	9	10	9	D	Educ de carcere animam	LA 163 *WA 103	re	2
C	2	5	7	5	7	9	10	9	F	Quo abiit dilectus tuus	AR 843 LU 1639	an	6
G	2	5	7	5	7	9	10	12	G	Benedicta gloria Domini	LR 238 LA 549 *WA 318	an	7
G	2	5	7	5	7	9	10	12	G	Hi accipient benedictionem	PM 329 LU 1846 VP 274	an	7
G	2	5	7	5	7	9	10	12	G	Hic accipiet benedictionem	PM 329 LR 153 197 WA 416 425 LA 523	an	7
G	2	5	7	5	7	9	10	12	G	Puer Samuel ministrabat	AR 536 LU 960 AM 556	an	7

G	2	5	7	5	7	9	10	12		Sanctorum sicut aquilae	SYG 210	alv	
G	2	5	7	5	7	9	10	12		Veni Domine visitare	AR 223 LU 327 AM 195 WA 9 LA 7	an	7
C	2	5	7	5	7	9	11	7	D	Ipsi vero in vanum	AM 410 WA 117	an	2
D	2	5	7	5	7	10	5	3	G	Factus est repente de caelo	GB 192	of	8
D	2	5	7	5	7	10	9	7	D	Crux fidelis inter omnes ... sustinet	GR 218 222 VP 269 22*	hy	1
D	2	5	7	5	7	10	9	7	D	Lustra sex qui jam peregit	AR 410 OHS 71 192	hy	1
D	2	5	7	5	7	10	9	7	D	Lustris sex qui jam peractis	AM 386	hy	1
D	2	5	7	5	7	10	9	7	D	Pange lingua gloriosi lauream	GR 218 222 OHS 56 (nm) 578 LU 742	hy	1
D	2	5	7	5	7	10	9	7	D	Pange lingua gloriosi proelium	LR 437	hy	1
G	2	5	7	5	7	10	9	10	G	Exaltate Dominum Deum ... tabernaculum	LR 266	an	7
G	2	5	7	5	7	10	12	9	G	Alleluia: ne timeas Zacharia ... oratio	GB 196v *SYG 196	al	7
D	2	5	7	5	9	5	7	2	E	Ave caeli janua	ST 56	hy	4
C	2	5	7	5	9	7	5	7	F	Qui manducat carnem meam	GR 344 LU 1019 SYG 90 *GB 80 GS 52 159	co	6
C	2	5	7	9	4	7	5	4		Qui custodit veritatem Lauda anima	OTT 67 GB 149 *SYG 166	ofv	
G	2	5	7	9	5	2	0	5		In Domino laudabitur anima Benedicam Dominum	GR 350 LU 1028 GS 154 GB 253v SYG 246	grv	
G	2	5	7	9	5	4	2	5	G	Ecce mitto angelum ... praeparabit	AR 228 LU 1083 AM 201 WA 13 *LA 12	an	8
C	2	5	7	9	5	4	7	5		Afferentur regi virgines post Diffusa est gratia	SYG 49	trv	
C	2	5	7	9	5	4	7	5		Dilexisti justitiam Diffusa est gratia	SYG 49	trv	
G	2	5	7	9	5	7	4	7	G	Exaltate regem saeculorum	AR 107 *AM 49	an	7
G	2	5	7	9	5	7	9	5	G	Erit enim magnus	LR 352	an	7
G	2	5	7	9	5	7	9	7	a	Iste puer magnus coram Domino	AR 733 LU 1496	an	4
G	2	5	7	9	5	7	9	7	G	Iste puer magnus coram Domino	AM 921	an	7
D	2	5	7	9	5	9	7	5	E	Erit enim magnus	LA 403	an	4
C	2	5	7	9	7	4	2	0	D	Gaude visceribus mater in intimis	ST 96	hy	2
C	2	5	7	9	7	4	2	5	D	Sanctus	THAN #205		1
C	2	5	7	9	7	4	5	2	D	Afferentur regi virgines post	LR 223	re	1
C	2	5	7	9	7	4	5	2	D	In medio ecclesiae	PM 226 227 LR 203 LA 55	re	1
C	2	5	7	9	7	4	5	2	D	Montes Israel ramos vestros	LA 5 *WA 23	re	1
C	2	5	7	9	7	4	5	2	D	Nativitatem hodiernam perpetuae	LA 460 WA 366	re	1

C	2	5	7	9	7	4	5	2	D	O crux benedicta quae sola	AR 839 LU 1631 *AM 1046 *WA 370 *LA 395 *SYG 141	an	1
C	2	5	7	9	7	4	5	2	D	Sanctissime confessor Christi Benedicte	PM 145 LR 330 AM 1194 LA 372 WA 299	re	1
C	2	5	7	9	7	4	5	2	D	Surrexit Dominus de sepulcro	LA 213	re	1
C	2	5	7	9	7	4	5	4	D	Vox in Rama audita ... ploratus	WA 46	re	1
G	2	5	7	9	7	4	7	5	G	Domum tuam Domine decet	AR [106] LU 1246 AM 697 WA 319 *LA 552	an	7
C	2	5	7	9	7	5	2	5	D	Celebremus conversionem beati Pauli	LA 345 *WA 266	re	1
G	2	5	7	9	7	5	2	5	G	Dirupisti Domine vincula mea	AR [10] LU 1114 AM 626 *WA 419 *LA 527	an	7
C	2	5	7	9	7	5	7	2	D	Inflammatum est cor meum	GR 622[1] LU 1681[2]	gr	1
C	2	5	7	9	7	5	7	5		Aestimatus sum cum descendentibus Repleta est malis	GR 9**	grv	
D	2	5	7	9	7	5	7	5	D	Alleluia: nos autem gloriari	GB 165 *GS v	al	1
C	2	5	7	9	7	5	7	5		Confundantur et revereantur Adjutor meus	GR 115 GS 48 GB 76v SYG 87	grv	
C	2	5	7	9	7	5	7	5		Dederunt in escam meam fel Improperium	GR [107]	grv	
G	2	5	7	9	7	5	7	9	a	Absque tuo imperio non movebit	AR 5 (sup 1)	an	4
G	2	5	7	9	7	5	7	9	G	Alleluia: mane nobiscum Domine	SYG 156	al	7
G	2	5	7	9	7	5	7	9	G	Alleluia: quoniam Deus magnus	GR 361 LU 1042 GS 156 SYG 246 GB 255v	al	7
G	2	5	7	9	7	5	7	9	a	Commendemus nosmetipsos	AR 92 AM 100 102 115 117 WA 89	an	4
G	2	5	7	9	7	5	7	9	a	Da mercedem Domine	AR 239 AM 214 WA 17 *LA 23	an	4
C	2	5	7	9	7	5	7	9	D	Domus mea domus orationis	AR [107] LU 1247 AM 697 *WA 89 317 LA 134 552	an	1
G	2	5	7	9	7	5	7	9	a	Ecce rex veniet	AR 228 LU 1082 AM 200 WA 12 19 *LA 12	an	4
G	2	5	7	9	7	5	7	9	a	Ecce veniet Dominus princeps	AR 237 AM 212 WA 17 *LA 22	an	4
G	2	5	7	9	7	5	7	9	a	Ecce veniet Dominus ut sedeat	AR 240 AM 215 WA 18 *LA 24	an	4
G	2	5	7	9	7	5	7	9	a	Elevatis Jesus manibus	WA 149	an	4
G	2	5	7	9	7	5	7	9	a	Elevatis manibus benedixit eis	AR 492 LU 851 AM 509	an	4
G	2	5	7	9	7	5	7	9	a	Exaltare Domine in virtute	LR 96 WA 147 *LA 244	an	4
G	2	5	7	9	7	5	7	9	a	Exspectabo Dominum salvatorem	AR 222 LU 1080 AM 193 WA 4 20 LA 7	an	4
G	2	5	7	9	7	5	7	9	a	Exspectetur sicut pluvia	AR 244 AM 218 WA 20 *LA 27	an	4

C	2	5	7	9	7	5	7	9	D	Iste puer magnus coram Domino	WA 323	an	1
G	2	5	7	9	7	5	7	9	a	Judicasti Domine causam	AR 88 409 AM 97 112 389 *WA 108 *LA 171	an	4
G	2	5	7	9	7	5	7	9	a	Multa bona opera operatus	AR 418 LU 1099 AM 395 WA 109 *LA 174	an	4
G	2	5	7	9	7	5	7	9		O quam gloriosum ... regnant omnes	SYG 222	alv	
G	2	5	7	9	7	5	7	9	a	Paradisi januae per te	WA 353	an	4
D	2	5	7	9	7	5	7	9	E	Petiit puella caput Joannis	LA 453	an	4
C	2	5	7	9	7	5	7	9	D	Postulavi patrem meum alleluia	OHS 754 WA 128 *LA 210 224	an	1
G	2	5	7	9	7	5	7	9	a	Posuisti Domine super caput	LR 153 WA 416 *LA 523	an	4
G	2	5	7	9	7	5	7	9	a	Potestatem habeo ponendi animam	AR 430 OHS 226 AM 409 WA 115 *LA 187	an	4
G	2	5	7	9	7	5	7	9	a	Satiavit Dominus quinque millia	AR 399 LU 563 AM 374 WA 104 *LA 159	an	4
G	2	5	7	9	7	5	7	9	a	Sicut fuit Jonas in ventre	AR 375 AM 348 *LA 135 *WA 89	an	4
G	2	5	7	9	7	5	7	9	a	Speciosa facta es et suavis	AR [116] LU 1259 AM 708 WA 268 *LA 347	an	4
G	2	5	7	9	7	5	7	9	a	Stella quam viderant Magi	WA 57	an	4
G	2	5	7	9	7	5	7	9	a	Super te Jerusalem orietur	AR 228 LU 1082 AM 200 WA 13 *LA 12	an	4
C	2	5	7	9	7	5	9	2	[D]	Agnus Dei	SCH #251		2
C	2	5	7	9	7	5	9	12		Positis autem genibus Stephanus Elegerunt apostoli	OTT 161 GB 22	ofv	
C	2	5	7	9	7	9	5	7	D	In principio creavit Deus	LR 398 LA 108 WA 72	re	1
C	2	5	7	9	7	9	5	7	D	In principio fecit Deus	LA 108 WA 72	re	1
C	2	5	7	9	7	9	7	4	D	Ubi est thesaurus tuus	WA 84	an	1
C	2	5	7	9	7	9	7	5	G	Sancti Domini Dominum	AM 1122	an	tp
G	2	5	7	9	7	9	10	9		Exaudi Deus orationem meam et ne	GB 246v *SYG 243	alv	
G	2	5	7	9	7	9	10	12	G	Alleluia: o quam gloriosum est	SYG 222	al	7
G	2	5	7	9	7	9	10	12	G	Alleluia: vota mea Domino reddam	GR 36**	al	7
G	2	5	7	9	7	9	10	12		Vota mea Domino ... in conspectu	GR 36**	alv	
C	2	5	7	9	7	9	12	7	G	Sapientia clamitat in plateis	AR 545 LU 990 AM 581 *WA 168 LA 281	an	8
C	2	5	7	9	10	9	7	5	G	Benedictum nomen gloriae	AR 302	an	tp
C	2	5	7	9	10	9	7	5	G	Nos qui vivimus benedicimus	AM 132 133	an	tp
C	2	5	7	9	10	9	7	9		Surrexerunt autem quidam ex Judaeis Elegerunt apostoli	OTT 161 *SYG 23	ofv	
G	2	5	7	9	10	12	9	5		Ne timeas Zacharia ... oratio	SYG 196 *GB 196v	alv	

D	2	5	7	10	7	5	7	10	[D]	Agnus Dei	SCH #211		1
D	2	5	7	10	12	10	7	10	D	Homo quidem erat dives valde	ST 487	hy	1
C	2	5	9	0	4	5	2	0	F	Ex more docti mystico	ST 338	hy	6
G	2	5	9	7	5	7	9	5	a	Qui post me venit	AR 229 LU 1083 AM 202 *WA 13 LA 12 15	an	4
G	2	5	9	7	5	7	9	5	a	Sicut myrrha electa	LR 246 *WA 268 LA 347 383	an	4
D	2	5	9	7	5	7	9	5	E	Valde honorandus est	LA 52	an	4
D	2	5	9	7	5	7	9	7	E	Elevatis manibus ferebatur	LA 251	an	4
G	2	5	9	7	5	7	9	7	a	Fasciculus myrrhae dilectus	AR 675 LU 1423	an	4
G	2	5	9	7	5	7	9	7	a	Paradisi portae per te	LR 374 VP 201 LA 442	an	4
G	2	5	9	7	5	7	9	7	a	Tibi revelavi causam meam	AR 424 OHS 147 LU 604 AM 402 *LA 183	an	4
G	2	5	9	7	5	7	9	7	a	Ubi duo vel tres congregati	AR 392 LU 1090 AM 367 *WA 99 *LA 155	an	4
G	2	5	9	7	5	7	9	7	G	Ubi fratres in unum	SYG 131	an	7
G	2	5	9	7	5	7	10	9	G	Adorate eum omnes angeli	LR 338	an	7
G	2	5	9	7	5	7	10	9	G	Ipse praeibit ante illum	LR 352	an	7
C	2	5	9	7	9	5	2	5	F	Benedictio perituri super me	GR 60**	of	6
C	2	5	9	7	9	5	2	5	F	Desiderium animae ejus ... Domine	GR [50] OTT 153 LU 1208 SYG 215 GB 53^{v} GS 224	of	6
C	2	5	9	11	12	9	5	7	C	Nunc sancte nobis spiritus	ST 207	hy	5
F	2	6	0	2	0	-1	0	-1	F	Sanctus	THAN #103		5
F	2	6	2	4	2	0	4	7	F	Agnus Dei	SCH #137		6
F	2	6	7	9	6	9	7	6		Et in terra	BOS #25		
F	2	6	9	6	7	4	2	4		Misericordias tuas Domine in aeternum Confitebuntur caeli	OTT 138 *GB 153 *SYG 170	ofv	
F	2	7	2	7	4	6	7	4		Scholasticae mox nuntiat In columbae specie	GB 54^{v}	trv	
F	2	7	4	7	6	4	7	9		Declaratio sermonum tuorum Gressus meos	OTT 39 *GB 88^{v} SYG 99	ofv	
D	2	7	5	2	0	3	2	0	E	Gloriosa festivitas	ST 458	hy	4
C	2	7	5	4	2	0	2	0		Quasi modo geniti infantes	GB 144^{v}	alv	
c	2	7	5	7	9	5	2	0		Elevatio manuum mearum Dirigatur oratio	GR 109 LU 1060 GS 38 163 171 *GB 68^{v} *SYG 76	grv	
C	2	7	5	7	9	7	10	9	G	Dum medium silentium ... iter	GR 44 LU 433 SYG 29 GB 30^{v} GS 18	int	8
C	2	7	5	7	9	11	9	7	G	Noe vir justus	LA 116	re	8

F	2	7	6	4	6	7	4	2	G	Fuit vir vitae venerabilis ... qui ab ipso	AM 851	an	8
F	2	7	6	7	2	0	2	4		Et quod pingue et forte Ego pascam	GR 66**	trv	
G	2	7	9	7	9	5	4	5	G	Memento mei dum bene	LA 149 *WA 96	re	7
F	2	7	9	7	9	6	7	4		Benedicam Dominum in omni tempore Immittet angelus	OTT 102 *GB 71 *SYG 79	ofv	
F	2	7	9	11	7	2	7	9		Et exsultavit spiritus meus Magnificat anima	GR 50**	trv	
F	2	7	9	11	7	2	7	9		Et videas filios Ecce sic benedicetur	GR [123] LU 1290	trv	
F	2	7	9	11	7	2	7	9		Quam dulcia faucibus Deus docuisti	GR 72**	trv	
F	2	7	9	11	7	2	7	9		Ut fugiant a facie arcus Commovisti	GR 78 LU 507 GS 27 GB 58 SYG 60	trv	
C	2	9	[0	0	0	0	0	0]		Agnus Dei	SCH #266		
C	2	9	7	2	4	7	9	4		Benedictio Dei in mercedem	GR 452	alv	
F	2	9	7	4	7	9	2	0		Non vos relinquam ... dicit	GB 182v	alv	
C	2	9	7	5	7	5	4	2		Corona tribulationis effloruit	GR 15**	alv	
C	2	9	7	5	7	9	5	4	D	Quinquaginta annos	WA 108 *LA 172	an	1
C	2	9	7	5	7	11	9	7	D	Intempesta nocte cuncta	WA 299	an	1
C	2	9	7	9	7	5	4	7	D	O crux admirabilis evacuatio	WA 370	an	1
C	2	9	7	9	7	5	7	11	D	In principio Deus creavit	LA 108 *WA 72	re	1
C	2	9	7	9	10	9	7	9		Spiritus Domini super me propter	GR [102] LU 1283C	alv	
C	2	9	7	9	11	9	7	5	[D]	In plateis ponebantur	WA 325	an	1
C	2	9	7	10	9	10	7	5		Cantate Domino canticum ... quia	GR 364 LU 1045 *SYG 247	alv	
C	2	9	7	10	9	10	7	5		Qui timent Dominum sperent	GR 385 LU 1072 GS 160 *SYG 249	alv	
C	2	9	10	9	7	4	5	7	D	Alleluia: beatus homo qui audit me	GR 62	al	1
C	2	9	10	9	7	4	7	9	D	Vocabis nomen ejus	AR 306 LU 453 AM 283	an	1
C	2	9	10	9	7	5	7	5	D	Reversus est angelus	AR 868 *AM 1069	an	1
C	2	9	10	9	7	5	7	5	D	Rogamus te Domine Deus noster ut	VP 241	re	1
C	2	9	10	9	7	5	7	9	D	Admirabile est ... quia gloria	LR 382 *WA 395 *LA 475	an	1
C	2	9	10	9	7	5	7	9	D	Desiderium cordis ejus	GR 82**	gr	1
C	2	9	10	9	7	5	7	9	D	Dum aurora finem ... exclamavit	AR 925 AM 1142	an	1
C	2	9	10	9	7	5	7	9	D	Obtulerunt discipuli Domino	AR 482 AM 497 WA 134 LA 219	an	1
C	2	9	10	9	7	5	9	7	D	Consummatus in brevi	GR 70**	gr	1
C	2	9	10	9	7	5	9	7	D	Sapientia aedificavit ... excidit	GR 398	gr	1

C	2	9	10	9	7	9	5	4		Beatus homo qui audit me	GR 62	alv	
C	2	9	10	9	7	9	5	4		Dilectus meus mihi	GR (10)	alv	
C	2	9	10	9	7	9	5	4		Manum suam aperuit inopi	GR 632 LU 1695	alv	
C	2	9	10	9	7	9	5	4		Qui docti fuerint fulgebunt	GR 496 LU 1466	alv	
C	2	9	10	9	7	9	5	7	D	Cor mundum crea in me	AR 365 AM 341 *WA 88 206 211 LA 132	an	1
C	2	9	10	9	7	9	7	4	D	Alleluia: laudate Dominum de caelis	AR 5	an	1
C	2	9	10	9	7	9	7	5	D	Amice non facio tibi	LA 116	an	1
C	2	9	10	9	7	9	7	5	D	Beata nobis gaudia	AR 505 LU 876 AM 522 ST 38 94	hy	1
C	2	9	10	9	7	9	7	5	D	Exsultavit cor ... et exaltatum	AR 826[1] LU 1612	an	1
C	2	9	10	9	7	9	7	5	D	Flagrabat in beatissimis	WA 377	an	1
C	2	9	10	9	7	9	7	5	D	Gaudeamus omnes in ... Agathae	GR 436 LU 1368 *SYG 50 GB 49^{v}	int	1
C	2	9	10	9	7	9	7	5	D	Gaudeamus omnes in ... Annae	GR 559 LU 1571	int	1
C	2	9	10	9	7	9	7	5	D	Gaudeamus omnes in ... assumptione	GR (30) *SYG 215 GB s	int	1
C	2	9	10	9	7	9	7	5	D	Gaudeamus omnes in ... Benedicti	GR (16)	int	1
C	2	9	10	9	7	9	7	5	D	Gaudeamus omnes in ... boni consilii	GR 24**	int	1
C	2	9	10	9	7	9	7	5	D	Gaudeamus omnes in ... Joachim	GR (28)	int	1
C	2	9	10	9	7	9	7	5	D	Gaudeamus omnes in ... Josaphat	GR 653 LU 1751	int	1
C	2	9	10	9	7	9	7	5	D	Gaudeamus omnes in ... monachorum	GR (33)	int	1
C	2	9	10	9	7	9	7	5	D	Gaudeamus omnes in ... reginae	LU 1476[B]	int	1
C	2	9	10	9	7	9	7	5	D	Gaudeamus omnes in ... sanctorum	GR 647 LU 1724 GB 237	int	1
C	2	9	10	9	7	9	7	5	D	Gaudeamus omnes in ... solemnitate	GR 619 LU 1556 1675	int	1
C	2	9	10	9	7	9	7	5	D	Gaudeamus omnes in ... Thomae	GR 46 LU 437	int	1
C	2	9	10	9	7	9	7	5	D	Jam lucis orto sidere	ST 76	hy	1
G	2	9	10	9	7	9	7	5	a	Jesu salvator saeculi	ST 42	hy	1
C	2	9	10	9	7	9	7	5	D	O salutaris hostia quae caeli	AR 94*	hy	1
C	2	9	10	9	7	9	7	5	D	Omnes terrarum incolae	ST 94	hy	1
C	2	9	10	9	7	9	7	5	D	Qui diligitis Dominum	LR 387	an	1
C	2	9	10	9	7	9	7	5	D	Te saeculorum principem	AR 894[2] LU 1716	hy	1
C	2	9	10	9	7	9	7	5	D	Tu solus peregrinus es et non	AR 471 AM 485 WA 132	an	1
C	2	9	10	9	7	9	7	9	D	Beatus iste sanctus qui confisus	LR 191 WA 424 LA 529	an	1
C	2	9	10	9	7	9	7	9		De vultu tuo judicium Custodi me	GR 345 LU 1021 GS 41 151 GB 70^{v} SYG 79	grv	
C	2	9	10	9	7	9	7	9	D	Erunt prava in directa	AR 251 LU 357 AM 227 WA 24 LA 21	an	1

C	2	9	10	9	7	9	7	9	D	Quae est ista quae ascendit sicut	AR 821 LU 1600^{4} AM 1017 WA 358 LA 449	an	1
C	2	9	10	9	7	9	7	9	D	Quid hic statis tota die	AR 344 LU 502 AM 314 *WA 75 *LA 114	an	1
C	2	9	10	9	7	9	7	9		Regina adstat ad dexteram Ipse habet	LU 1476^{D}	grv	
C	2	9	10	9	7	9	10	9	D	Adoramus te Christe et benedicimus	OHS 584 SYG 141 LU 746 WA 370	an	1
C	2	9	10	9	7	9	10	9	D	Ante diem festum Paschae ... cum	AR 429 OHS 193 AM 408 LA 186	an	1
C	2	9	10	9	7	9	10	9	D	Astiterunt justi ante Dominum	AR 742 LU 1506 AM 929 LA 411	an	1
C	2	9	10	9	7	9	10	9	D	Effusum est in terra	GR 554 LU 1561	int	1
C	2	9	10	9	7	9	10	9	D	Mulieres sedentes ad monumentum	AR 441 OHS 410 625 LU 776^{B} AM 449 WA 127 LA 206	an	1
C	2	9	10	9	7	9	10	9	D	Posuerunt super caput ejus	AR 439 OHS 409 516 LU 718 AM 443 WA 124 LA 201	an	1
C	2	9	10	9	7	9	10	9	D	Praeceptor per totam noctem	AR 555 AM 593 LU 1001 WA 187 LA 311	an	1
C	2	9	10	9	7	9	10	9	D	Quod autem cecidit	AR 352 AM 324	an	1
C	2	9	10	9	7	9	12	9	D	Benedicam Dominum qui mihi tribuit	GR 116 511 LU 1004 1484 OTT 88 *SYG 87 *GB 76^{v} GS 49 146	of	1
C	2	9	10	9	7	9	12	11	a	Deprecamur te Domine	WA 227	an	1
C	2	9	10	9	7	9	12	14	D	Surrexit pastor bonus ... grege	OHS 759 *LA 86 415 *LA 212 WA 133	re	1
C	2	9	10	9	7	12	11	12	D	Amen dico vobis quidquid orantes	GR 389 LU 1077 SYG 259 GB 265 GS f 167	co	1
C	2	9	10	9	10	9	7	9		Conserva me Domine Benedicam Dominum	OTT 88 GB 76^{v} SYG 87	ofv	
C	2	9	10	9	10	9	7	9	D	Ipse habet in vestimento	LU 1476^{D}	gr	1
C	2	9	10	9	10	9	7	9	D	Posuisti Domine in capite ejus	GR (6) *SYG 43 GS 206	gr	1
C	2	9	10	9	10	9	7	9	D	Posuisti Domine super caput	GR (6) GB 45^{v} GS 206 SYG 43	gr	1
C	2	9	10	9	10	9	7	9	D	Qui timetis Dominum laudate	GR 467	gr	1
C	2	9	10	9	10	9	7	9	D	Sacerdotes ejus induam salutari	GR [36] LU 1187 SYG 209 GB 212 GS 225	gr	1
C	2	9	10	9	10	9	12	9	F	Confitebor Domino nimis in ore	GR 283 LU 842 OTT 74 *SYG 178 GB 162 *GS 132	of	6
C	2	9	10	9	10	9	12	9	F	Invocavit altissimum potentem	GR 470	of	6
C	2	9	10	9	11	12	9	7	D	In omnibus his non peccavit	AR 546 LU 992 AM 583 *WA 171 *LA 287	an	1
C	2	9	10	9	11	12	9	11	D	Et incipiens a Moyse et omnibus	AR 475 AM 489	an	1

C	2	9	10	9	12	9	7	5	D	Inclina Domine aurem ... et exaudi me salvum	GR 360 LU 1040 *SYG 249 GB 255^v GS 158	int	1
C	2	9	10	9	12	9	7	5	D	Sapientia hujus mundi	GR 475	gr	1
C	2	9	10	9	12	9	7	5		Venite et videte opera Benedicite gentes	OTT 71 GB 93^v *SYG 105	ofv	
C	2	9	10	9	12	9	7	9	D	Benedicite Dominum omnes angeli	GR 612 LU 1664	of	1
C	2	9	10	9	12	9	7	9	D	Colligite primum zizania	AR 339 LU 494 AM 309 LA 107	an	1
C	2	9	10	9	12	9	7	9	D	Confitebor tibi Domine Deus	GR 54 LU 448 OTT 44	of	1
C	2	9	10	9	12	9	7	9	D	Eutychius tulit filium	LR 274	an	1
C	2	9	10	9	12	9	7	9	D	In conspectu angelorum ... adorabo	GR 548 LU 1546	of	1
C	2	9	10	9	12	9	7	9	D	Intravit Jesus in templum	AR 374 AM 347 LA 135	an	1
C	2	9	10	9	12	9	7	9	D	Jacob autem genuit Joseph	AR 319 648 688 LU 467 1400 AM 836 886	an	1
C	2	9	10	9	12	9	7	9	D	Jubilate Deo universa terra	GR 69 OTT 69 LU 486 SYG 36 GB 38 GS 22	of	1
C	2	9	10	9	12	9	7	9		Locuti sunt adversum me Domine fac mecum	OTT 37 GB 85^v *SYG 96	ofv	
C	2	9	10	9	12	9	7	9		Locutum est os meum Jubilate Deo	OTT 69 GB 38 SYG 36	ofv	
C	2	9	10	9	12	9	7	9	D	Magnificat anima mea ... et exsultavit	GR 617 LU 1670	of	1
C	2	9	10	9	12	9	7	9	D	Recedite a me amare	AR 843 LU 1639 *AM 1047	an	1
C	2	9	10	9	12	9	7	9	D	Rorate caeli desuper	GR 21 [81] LU 353 1269 SYG 8 GB 6^v GS 5	int	1
C	2	9	10	9	12	9	7	9	D	Si duo ex vobis consenserint	AR 392 LU 1090 AM 366 LA 154	an	1
C	2	9	10	9	12	9	7	9	D	Suavi jugo tuo dominare	AR 538[1] LU 965 AM 560	an	1
C	2	9	10	9	12	9	7	9	D	Suscepimus Deus misericordiam	GR 339 432 LU 1361 SYG 48 GB 47 GS j 149	int	1
C	2	9	10	9	12	9	7	9	D	Tradiderunt corpora sua in mortem	LR 181	an	1
C	2	9	10	9	12	9	10	12	D	Confitebor tibi Domine in toto corde	GR 155 LU 573 OTT 44 SYG 110 GB 98 GS 72	of	1
C	2	9	10	9	12	11	9	7		Impulsus versatus sum Dextera Domini	OTT 25 GB 39^v SYG 43	ofv	
F	2	9	11	6	9	7	9	12		Ideoque quod nascetur ex te Ave Maria	OTT 13 *SYG 12	ofv	
F	2	9	11	9	6	9	7	9	G	Recessit pastor noster ... nam	OHS 608 LU 766 *LA 203 *WA 125	re	7 8
F	2	9	11	9	6	9	7	9	G	Recessit pastor noster ... portas	LR 341	re	7
C	2	9	11	9	7	4	5	7	D	Egressi duodecim apostoli	WA 157	an	1
C	2	9	11	9	7	5	4	2		Tu es altissimus	GB 178^v	alv	
C	2	9	11	9	7	5	4	5	D	Petrus autem servabatur	WA 340	an	1

C	2	9	11	9	7	5	7	5	D	Alleluia: ego sum vitis vera ... veri	WA 306	an	1
C	2	9	11	9	7	5	7	9	D	Cantabant sancti canticum	LA 58 WA 45	re	1
C	2	9	11	9	7	5	7	9	D	Deprecatus enim sum	WA 345	re	1
C	2	9	11	9	7	5	7	9	D	O viri misericordiae	AM 973	an	1
C	2	9	11	9	7	5	7	9	D	Subvenite sancti Dei	WA 8	an	1
C	2	9	11	9	7	5	7	9	D	Tradiderunt corpora sua ad supplicia	LA 516	an	1
C	2	9	11	9	7	9	5	4		Os justi meditabitur	SYG 199	alv	
C	2	9	11	9	7	9	7	4	D	Alleluia: ego sum vitis vera ... estis	LA 389 392	an	1
C	2	9	11	9	7	9	7	4	D	Dies Domini sicut fur	WA 25 LA 17	an	1
C	2	9	11	9	7	9	7	4	D	Lux perpetua lucebit sanctis	WA 305	an	1
C	2	9	11	9	7	9	7	5	D	Gregorius monachorum	AM 833	an	1
C	2	9	11	9	7	9	7	5	D	Luciano venerabili	WA 341	an	1
C	2	9	11	9	7	9	7	5	D	Magdalenam sua crimina	WA 336	an	1
C	2	9	11	9	7	9	7	5	D	Sapientia aedificavit ... miscuit	AM 550 *AR 530 *LU 939	an	1
C	2	9	11	9	7	9	7	5	D	Saule Saule quid me persequeris	WA 262 LA 341	an	1
C	2	9	11	9	7	9	7	5	D	Tu solus peregrinus in Jerusalem	LA 217	an	1
C	2	9	11	9	7	9	11	9	D	Adest namque beati Dionysii	WA 389	an	1
C	2	9	11	9	7	9	11	9	D	Adolescens tibi dico	WA 190	an	1
C	2	9	11	9	7	9	11	9	D	Adoramus te Christe et hymnum	GB 115v	an	1
C	2	9	11	9	7	9	11	9	D	Amen amen dico vobis antequam	WA 109	an	1
C	2	9	11	9	7	9	11	9	D	Assumpsit Jesus Petrum	AM 998	an	1
C	2	9	11	9	7	9	11	9	D	Deduc me in semitam	LA 240 *WA 145	re	1
C	2	9	11	9	7	9	11	9	D	Ecce virgo concipiet ... Emmanuel	LA 17 379	an	1
C	2	9	11	9	7	9	11	9	D	Illi homines cum vidissent	LA 163	an	1
C	2	9	11	9	7	9	11	9	D	Illo quoque negante	WA 404	an	1
C	2	9	11	9	7	9	11	9	D	Muro tuo inexpugnabili	AM 591 *AR 553 *LU 996 LA 308 *WA 183 317	an	1
C	2	9	11	9	7	9	11	9	D	Post excessum beatissimi Martini	WA 403	an	1
C	2	9	11	9	7	9	11	9	D	Quis enim in omnibus	WA 164 LA 273	an	1
C	2	9	11	9	7	9	12	9		Deprecatus sum vultum tuum Confitebor tibi	SYG 110 GB 98	ofv	
D	2	9	11	9	7	9	12	11		Non sunt loquelae In omnem terram	SYG 54	ofv	
F	2	9	11	9	11	7	6	7		Puellae saltanti imperavit Misit rex	OTT 176	ofv	
F	2	9	11	9	11	7	6	7	G	Qui regni claves	LR 367 LA 418 *WA 328	re	7

F	2	9	11	9	11	12	14	12		Replebimur in bonis domus Te decet hymnus Deus	SYG 242	alv	
C	2	9	11	9	12	9	7	5	D	Et accipiens Jesus	WA 188	an	1
C	2	9	11	9	12	9	7	9	D	Attendite a falsis prophetis	WA 188 LA 313	an	1
C	2	9	11	9	12	9	7	9	D	Compassus nutrici suae	WA 298 LA 369	an	1
C	2	9	11	9	12	9	7	9	D	Cum vidisset beatus Andreas	LA 498	re	1
D	2	9	11	9	12	9	7	9	D	Egredimini et videte ... Gertrudem	AM 1130	an	1
C	2	9	11	9	12	9	7	9	D	Exaudiat Dominus orationes	WA 180	an	1
C	2	9	11	9	12	9	7	9	D	Profitemur enim Christianae	WA 258	an	1
C	2	9	11	9	12	9	7	9	D	Simile est regnum caelorum decem	WA 430	an	1
F	2	9	11	9	12	9	7	11		In quacumque die invocavero Si ambulavero	OTT 118 GB 86^v *SYG 97	ofv	
C	2	9	11	9	12	9	11	9	D	Laetemur hodie cum ingenti	SYG 227	int	1
C	2	9	11	9	12	9	11	12	D	Invocantem Dominum exclamemus	WA 227	an	1
C	2	9	11	9	12	9	11	12	D	Miserere Domine plebi tuae	WA 229	an	1
C	2	9	12	9	7	9	4	5		Dirupisti vincula mea Dominus mihi adjutor	GR 35**	grv	
C	2	9	12	9	7	9	7	4		Desiderium animae ejus Posuisti Domine	GR (6) GB 45^v SYG 43 GS 206	grv	
C	2	9	12	9	7	9	7	4		Sapientiam ipsorum narrent	GR 445 LU 1386	alv	
a	3	-2	0	-2	-4	-2	0	3	D	Civitas Jerusalem noli flere	PM 24 *LA 8 WA 10	re	1
D	3	-2	0	2	3	5	3	2	E	Laudes omnipotens ferimus tibi	ST 490	hy	4
D	3	-2	0	3	2	3	5	3	D	Torquebatur animo Pascasius	WA 247	an	2
D	3	-2	0	3	5	3	2	0	D	Kyrie	MEL #175		
D	3	-2	0	3	5	3	5	3	D	Festa praesentis celebret diei	ST 151	hy	1
D	3	-2	0	7	8	7	5	3	D	Cum appropinquaret Dominus Jerosolymam	AR 560 LU 1104 AM 599 *WA 188 *LA 314	an	1
D	3	-2	0	7	8	7	5	8	D	Et cum ejecisset Jesus daemonium	AR 389 LU 551 *AM 363 *LA 153	an	1
E	3	-2	3	1	0	3	5	7	E	Sanctus	THAN #138		4
E	3	-2	3	1	0	8	5	3	E	Agnus Dei	SCH #182		4
E	3	-2	3	1	0	8	5	3	E	Kyrie	MEL #153		
E	3	-2	3	1	0	8	5	3	E	Kyrie	MEL #154		
E	3	-2	3	1	0	8	5	3	E	Sanctus	THAN #138		4
D	3	-2	3	5	7	5	3	2	D	Ostende mihi faciem tuam	WA 356	an	1
E	3	-2	5	8	7	5	3	5	E	Martyr fuisti studio	WA 313	an	3
a	3	0	-4	-2	-4	-9	-7	-4	F	Agnus Dei	SCH #47		6

d	3	0	-2	-5	-7	-2	-7	-2		Epulemur in azymis Pascha nostrum	SYG 153 *GB 125^{v} GS 117	alv	
d	3	0	-2	-5	-7	-2	-7	-2		Pascha nostrum immolatus Epulemur in azymis	GS 117	alv	
d	3	0	-2	-5	-7	-2	-7	-2		Psallite Domino qui ascendit	SYG 180	alv	
a	3	0	-2	-4	-2	0	-5	-7	D	Ad coenam agni providi	ST 91 (#65)	hy	1
a	3	0	-2	-4	-2	0	-5	-7	D	Impleta gaudent viscera	ST 94	hy	1
a	3	0	-2	-4	-2	0	-5	-7	D	Jam Christus astra ascenderat	ST 94	hy	1
a	3	0	-2	-4	-2	0	-5	-7	D	Jam lucis orto sidere	ST 75	hy	1
a	3	0	-2	-4	0	2	-2	5	G	Rogo te pater ut mittas	WA 187 *LA 310	an	8
a	3	0	-2	0	-5	-4	-2	-5		Virgo Dei genitrix quem totus Benedicta es virgo	GS q	grv	
a	3	0	-2	0	-5	-4	-2	-5		Virgo Dei genitrix quem totus Benedicta et venerabilis	GR [76] LU 1264 *GB 220	grv	
a	3	0	-2	0	-5	-4	-2	-5		Virgo Dei genitrix quem totus Dolorosa	GR 595 LU 1633^{v}	grv	
a	3	0	-2	0	-5	-4	-2	-5		Vitam petiit et tribuisti Domine praevenisti	GR [48] LU 1207 GS 222 GB 53 *SYG 224	grv	
a	3	0	-2	0	-4	-5	-2	-4		Israel si me audieris Ecce mitto angelum	LA 157 *WA 102	rev	
a	3	0	-2	0	-4	-5	-2	-4		Israel si me audieris Jerusalem cito veniet	LA 8 *WA 9	rev	
a	3	0	-2	0	-4	-5	-2	0		Ego enim sum Dominus Deus tuus Jerusalem cito	LR 392	rev	
a	3	0	-2	0	-4	-2	0	3	F	Miserere mihi Domine quoniam tribulor	GR 163 SYG 116 *GB 103^{v} *GS 76	int	5
a	3	0	-2	0	-2	-4	-5	-2		Quo mereamur tuo fulti O martyr egregie	PM 346	rev	
a	3	0	-2	0	-2	0	-2	-4	a	Complaceat tibi Domine ... respice	WA 437	an	2
D	3	0	-2	0	-2	0	3	2	D	Beata et venerabilis virgo	LA 35 *WA 48	re	2
D	3	0	-2	0	-2	0	3	2	D	Beata mater et innupta virgo	WA 302 LA 215 449	an	2
D	3	0	-2	0	-2	0	3	2	D	Beata mater et intacta virgo ... intercede	AR [129] AM 713 PM 243	an	2
D	3	0	-2	0	-2	3	5	7	D	Ecce sacerdos magnus Martinus	SYG 226	int	1
D	3	0	-2	0	-2	3	5	7	D	Electus a Deo pontifex	WA 285	an	1
a	3	0	-2	0	1	-2	-4	-2		Misit Dominus manum suam In medio ecclesiae	PM 227	rev	
a	3	0	-2	0	2	-2	-4	-2		Tamquam sponsus Dominus Descendit de caelis Deus	LA 32	rev	
a	3	0	-2	0	2	-2	-4	-2		Tamquam sponsus Dominus Descendit de caelis missus	PM 27 WA 31	rev	
a	3	0	-2	0	2	-2	-4	0	F	Exsultabunt omnia ligna	WA 29 *LA 64	an	5
D	3	0	-2	0	2	-2	0	2	D	Beata vere mater ecclesiae	LR 388	re	1

D	3	0	-2	0	2	-2	0	3	D	Sancta et immaculata virginitas	LR 62 247 PM 38 AR 130* LU 384 AM 1184 VP 39 *LA 34 *WA 29	re	2
G	3	0	-2	0	2	0	-2	0	G	Astiterunt reges terrae	OHS 478 LU 688 *WA 121 *LA 195	an	8
D	3	0	-2	0	2	0	-2	0	D	Beata mater et intacta virgo Maria ... intercede	LU 1476H	an	2
D	3	0	-2	0	2	0	2	0	E	Sanctus terrarum illustret petimus	ST 488	hy	4
D	3	0	-2	0	2	0	5	7	D	Lux perpetua lucebit sanctis	AR 577[11][28] LU 262[1] 1118 AM 632 735 907 WA 306	an	1
D	3	0	-2	0	2	0	5	7	E	Lux perpetua lucebit sanctis	LR 172	an	4
D	3	0	-2	0	2	0	7	8	D	Ego ex ore altissimi	LR 266	re	1
D	3	0	-2	0	2	0	7	8		Inquirentes autem Dominum Timete Dominum	GR 648 LU 1726 *GS 213 *GB 216 *SYG 192	grv	
D	3	0	-2	0	2	3	0	-2	D	Christe qui lux es et dies	VP 29	hy	2
D	3	0	-2	0	2	3	0	3	D	Christe qui lux es et dies	ST 29 89	hy	2
D	3	0	-2	0	2	3	2	0	D	Christe qui lux es et dies	ST 210 254 270	hy	2
D	3	0	-2	0	2	3	5	3	D	Justi epulentur ... et delectentur	GR 96**	of	1
D	3	0	-2	0	2	5	7	5	E	Agnus Dei	SCH #207		4
D	3	0	-2	0	3	2	-2	0	D	Via justorum recta	WA 420	an	2
D	3	0	-2	0	3	2	0	2	D	Adest dies praeclara	WA 358	an	1
D	3	0	-2	0	3	2	3	5	D	O beata infantia	PM 37 VP 88 WA *31 200 *SYG 18	an	2
D	3	0	-2	0	3	2	3	5		O sancte Dei pretiose Sancte Christi	VP 258	rev	
D	3	0	-2	0	3	2	3	5	D	Placare Christe servulis	AR 663 892	hy	2
D	3	0	-2	0	3	2	3	5	D	Te lucis ante terminum	ST 247 269	hy	2
D	3	0	-2	0	3	2	3	5	D	Te lucis auctor personant	ST 289	hy	2
D	3	0	-2	0	3	2	3	5	D	Te splendor et virtus patris	AR 854 LU 1661	hy	2
D	3	0	-2	0	3	5	3	2	D	Beata es virgo Maria quae Dominum	PM 252	an	1
D	3	0	-2	0	3	5	3	2	D	O constantia martyrum laudabilis	PM 195	re	1
D	3	0	-2	0	3	5	3	2	D	O redemptor sume carmen	OHS 425	hy	2
D	3	0	-2	0	3	5	3	2	D	Surge ergo et vade	WA 343	an	1
D	3	0	-2	0	3	5	3	7	F	Alleluia: cantate Domino canticum novum	GB 150	al	6
D	3	0	-2	0	3	5	3	7	F	Alleluia: cernentibus discipulis elevatus	GB 178v	al	6
D	3	0	-2	0	3	5	3	7	[F]	Alleluia: confitebuntur caeli ... etenim	GB 163v	al	6
D	3	0	-2	0	3	5	3	7		Cantate Domino canticum ... quia	GB 150	alv	

D	3	0	-2	0	3	5	3	7		Cernentibus discipulis elevatus	GB 178v	alv	
D	3	0	-2	0	3	5	7	9	D	Agnus Dei	SCH #210		2
D	3	0	-2	0	3	7	5	7	D	Justorum animae in manu Dei ... mortis	GR 649 [30] OTT 144 LU 1172 SYG 223	of	1
D	3	0	-2	0	7	5	3	5	D	Egredietur virga ... et flos	LR 395 LA 15	re	1
a	3	0	-2	2	0	2	3	0	D	Ego vos elegi ... ut eatis	GR 513 LU 1388 SYG 190 GB 195 GS 219	co	1
D	3	0	-2	2	0	5	7	5	D	Agnus Dei XV	GR 53* LU 58 SCH #209		1
D	3	0	-2	2	3	5	3	0	D	Peccata mea Domine sicut sagittae	PM 50 *WA 60	an	1
D	3	0	-2	2	5	7	5	10	D	Alleluia: vita nostra est abscondita	GR 63	al	1
D	3	0	-2	2	5	7	5	10		Vita nostra est abscondita	GR 63	alv	
D	3	0	-2	2	5	7	9	5	[D]	Agnus Dei	SCH #208		1
a	3	0	-2	3	2	3	5	3	G	Ad coenam agni providi	ST 91 AM 459 467	hy	8
a	3	0	-2	3	2	3	5	3	G	Deus tuorum militum corona	ST 100	hy	8
D	3	0	-2	3	5	3	5	7	D	Ad hoc tantum sub clamide	LA 324	an	1
E	3	0	-2	3	5	3	5	7	E	Alleluia: caeli enarrant gloriam Dei	GB 267	al	3
D	3	0	-2	3	5	3	5	7	F	Alleluia: posuisti Domine super caput	SYG 217	al	6
D	3	0	-2	3	5	3	5	7	D	Alleluia: timebunt gentes nomen tuum	GR 373 LU 1056 GB 39v *GS 167	al	1
D	3	0	-2	3	5	3	5	7	D	Amen amen dico vobis quia plorabitis	LA 236	an	1
D	3	0	-2	-3	5	3	5	7	D	Archangeli Michaelis interventione	WA 381 LA 473	an	1
D	3	0	-2	3	5	3	5	7	D	Caeleste beneficium introivit	PM 171	an	1
D	3	0	-2	3	5	3	5	7	D	Dum aurora finem ... exclamavit	LA 494	an	1
D	3	0	-2	3	5	3	5	7	D	Dum staret Abraham	LA 121 WA 81	re	1
D	3	0	-2	3	5	3	5	7	D	Ego enim jam delibor	LA 431	an	1
D	3	0	-2	3	5	3	5	7	D	Gloriam concinunt Deo	WA 359	an	1
D	3	0	-2	3	5	3	5	7	D	Haec est vera fraternitas	LA 521	an	1
D	3	0	-2	3	5	3	5	7		Hic martyr Domini pro Lege	SYG 223	alv	
D	3	0	-2	3	5	3	5	7	D	Huic dum eremum	LR 324	an	1
D	3	0	-2	3	5	3	5	7	D	Martinus Abrahae sinu	PM 206 LA 485 WA 401	re	1
a	3	0	-2	3	5	3	5	7	a	Nativitas gloriosae virginis	LA 459 *WA 365	re	1
D	3	0	-2	3	5	3	5	7	D	Nunc sancte nobis spiritus	ST 115	hy	2
D	3	0	-2	3	5	3	5	7	D	Nuptiae quidem paratae sunt	WA 190 LA 318	an	1
D	3	0	-2	3	5	3	5	7	D	O Petre pastor summe	WA 325	an	1
D	3	0	-2	3	5	3	5	7	D	Orabat sanctus Benedictus	WA 298	an	1

D	3	0	-2	3	5	3	5	7		Posuisti Domine super caput	SYG 217	alv	
D	3	0	-2	3	5	3	5	7	D	Pueri Hebraeorum tollentes	WA 113 207 LA 182 GS 78	an	1
D	3	0	-2	3	5	3	5	7	D	Qui dum eremum	WA 300	an	1
D	3	0	-2	3	5	3	5	7	D	Saulus adhuc spirans	WA 262 LA 340	an	1
D	3	0	-2	3	5	3	5	7	D	Si quis mihi ministraverit	AR [16] LU 1126 AM 641 WA 419 LA 437 527	an	1
D	3	0	-2	3	5	3	5	7	D	Thomas qui dicitur Didymus	WA 137	an	1
D	3	0	-2	3	5	3	5	7		Timebunt gentes nomen tuum	GR 373 LU 1056 GS 167 GB 39^{v}	alv	
D	3	0	-2	3	5	3	7	3		Confitebuntur caeli mirabilia ... et	CB 163^{v}	alv	
D	3	0	-2	3	5	3	7	3	D	Cum sol autem occidisset	LA 155	an	I
D	3	0	-2	3	5	3	7	5	D	Accepit ergo Jesus panes et cum	AR 398 LU 559 AM 374	an	1
D	3	0	-2	3	5	3	7	5	D	Amen amen dico vobis iterum videbo	AR 477 *AM 391	an	1
a	3	0	-2	3	5	3	7	5		Attendite popule meus in legem vestram	GB 253 *SYG 243 GS 149	alv	
D	3	0	-2	3	5	3	7	5	D	Jesus autem cum jejunasset	AR 369 LU 530 AM 343 *WA 88 *LA 133	an	1
D	3	0	-2	3	5	3	7	5	D	Joannes autem cum audisset	AR 226 LU 1081 AM 197 *WA 16 LA 11	an	1
D	3	0	-2	3	5	3	7	5		Laetatus sum in his	GR 5 LU 329 SYG 3 GB 3 GS 162	alv	
E	3	0	-2	3	5	3	7	8	E	Alleluia: felix namque es nimium beate Stephane	SYG 211	al	3
E	3	0	-2	3	5	3	7	8		Felix namque es nimium beate Stephane	SYG 211	alv	
D	3	0	-2	3	5	3	7	10	D	Ad Jesum autem cum venissent	AR 538[13] LU 979 AM 570	an	1
D	3	0	-2	3	5	3	7	10	D	Ait latro ad latronem	AR 438 OHS 511 LU 715 AM 439 440 *WA 120 LA 200	an	1
D	3	0	-2	3	5	3	7	10	D	Amen amen dico vobis si quis sermonem	AR 414 LU 574	an	1
D	3	0	-2	3	5	3	7	10	D	Cum iter maris cepisset	AR 928 AM 1146 LA 496	an	1
D	3	0	-2	3	5	3	7	10	D	Ille me clarificabit	LA 242	an	1
E	3	0	-2	3	5	3	7	10	E	Multa turba Judaeorum	SYG 120	an	3
D	3	0	-2	3	5	3	7	10	D	Pueri Hebraeorum portantes	GR 170 AR 423 OHS 77 93 LU 581 AM 402 *PM 53	an	1
D	3	0	-2	3	5	3	7	10	D	Pueri Hebraeorum vestimenta	AR 424 GR 170 OHS 85 94 LU 582 AM 402 *PM 53 *WA 113 207 *LA 182 *GS 78	an	1
D	3	0	-2	3	5	3	7	10	D	Sacerdos in aeternum Christus	AR 525 LU 956 AM 543	an	1
D	3	0	-2	3	5	7	0	3	D	Gloria	BOS #54		I

D	3	0	-2	3	5	7	3	5	D	Stans beata Agnes	AR 606 LU 1341 AM 789 *WA 267 *LA 339	an	1
D	3	0	-2	3	5	7	5	2	D	N. praeesse dignus	PM 231	re	1
D	3	0	-2	3	5	7	5	2	D	Virgo prudentissima	AR 819 LU 1600 AM 1012B	an	1
D	3	0	-2	3	5	7	5	3	D	Beata es Maria quae Dominum	LA 353 *WA 270	re	1
D	3	0	-2	3	5	7	5	3	D	Beati mundo corde quoniam ipsi	SYG 223	co	1
D	3	0	-2	3	5	7	5	3	D	Beatus vir qui inventus est	PM 229 LR 209	re	1
D	3	0	-2	3	5	7	5	3	D	Caeleste beneficium introivit	WA 366	re	1
E	3	0	-2	3	5	7	5	3		Caeli enarrant gloriam Dei	GB 267	alv	
D	3	0	-2	3	5	7	5	3	D	Cum audisset Jacob quod Esau	LA 141	re	1
D	3	0	-2	3	5	7	5	3	D	Descendit de caelis Deus	LR 59 LA 32	re	1
D	3	0	-2	3	5	7	5	3	D	Descendit de caelis missus	PM 27 WA 31	re	1
D	3	0	-2	3	5	7	5	3	D	Electus et dilectus	WA 290	re	1
D	3	0	-2	3	5	7	5	3	D	Herodes enim tenuit	WA 362	re	1
D	3	0	-2	3	5	7	5	3	D	Igitur perfecti sunt caeli	LA 112	re	1
D	3	0	-2	3	5	7	5	3	D	Iste sanctus digne in memoriam	LR 203 WA 391 (inc illeg)	re	1
D	3	0	-2	3	5	7	5	3		Justorum animae in manu ... malitiae	GR 561 GB 268	alv	
D	3	0	-2	3	5	7	5	3	D	[Laudemus Dominum]	WA 391	re	1
D	3	0	-2	3	5	7	5	3	D	Medicinam carnalem corpori	WA 275	re	1
E	3	0	-2	3	5	7	5	3		Nonne cor nostrum ... dum nobiscum	SYG 164	alv	
D	3	0	-2	3	5	7	5	3	D	O caelestis norma vitae	AM 968 *PM 145 *VP 129	an	1
D	3	0	-2	3	5	7	5	3	D	Sancta legio Agaunensium	PM 190	re	1
D	3	0	-2	3	5	7	5	3	D	Sancte Benedicte confessor	WA 301	re	1
D	3	0	-2	3	5	7	5	3	D	Vidi civitatem ... novam ... et	LA 551	re	1
E	3	0	-2	3	5	7	5	7	G	Alleluia: nonne cor nostrum ... nobiscum loqueretur	SYG 164	al	8
D	3	0	-2	3	5	7	5	7	D	Beata es virgo Maria quae Dominum	AR 126* *LR 249 *PM 260	re	1
D	3	0	-2	3	5	7	5	7	D	O redemptor sume carmen	ST 495	hy	2
D	3	0	-2	3	5	7	5	7	D	Praeclara festivitas	WA 248	an	1
D	3	0	-2	3	5	7	5	7	D	Quis igitur ille est	LA 138	re	1
D	3	0	-2	3	5	7	5	7	D	Si Dominus Deus meus fuerit	LA 139 WA 92	re	1
D	3	0	-2	3	5	7	5	7	D	Timete Dominum omnes sancti	LR 385 WA 395 LA 475	an	1
D	3	0	-2	3	5	7	5	10	D	Ad coenam agni providi	ST 290	hy	1
D	3	0	-2	3	5	7	5	10	D	Beata nobis gaudia	ST 421	hy	1
D	3	0	-2	3	5	7	5	10	D	Conditor alme siderum	ST 70	hy	1

D	3	0	-2	3	5	7	5	10	D	Deus tuorum militum	ST 196	hy	1
D	3	0	-2	3	5	7	5	10	D	Jam Christus astra ascenderat	LR 107 ST 391	hy	1
D	3	0	-2	3	5	7	5	10	D	Jam lucis orte sidere	ST 3 26 75 360	hy	1
D	3	0	-2	3	5	7	5	10	D	Nunc sancte nobis spiritus	AR 894^{10} LU 1708	hy	1
D	3	0	-2	3	5	7	5	10	D	Post matutinis laudibus	ST 381	hy	1
D	3	0	-2	3	5	7	5	10	D	Te lucis ante terminum	AR 502 894^{5} LU 862 1704 AM 520	hy	1
D	3	0	-2	3	5	7	5	10	D	Vexilla Christus inclyta	AR 894^{8} LU 1706	hy	1
D	3	0	-2	3	5	7	8	7	D	Ave regina caelorum mater regis	PM 270 LU 1864	an	1
D	3	0	-2	3	5	7	8	7	D	Ave rex gentis Anglorum	WA 405	an	2
D	3	0	-2	3	5	7	8	7	D	Christe cunctorum dominator alme	ST 159	hy	1
D	3	0	-2	3	5	7	8	7	D	Maria virgo semper laetare	PM 258	an	1
D	3	0	-2	3	5	7	9	7	D	Amator tuus semper	WA 233	an	1
D	3	0	-2	3	5	7	9	7	D	Gaude et laetare filia Sion	LA 18	an	1
D	3	0	-2	3	5	7	9	7	D	Muneribus datis	WA 240	an	1
D	3	0	-2	3	5	7	9	7	D	O pastor aeterne	WA 238	an	1
D	3	0	-2	3	5	7	9	7	D	Tu principum leges attendis	WA 245	an	1
D	3	0	-2	3	5	7	9	10	D	Alleluia: benedicamus patrem ... in saecula	SYG 261	al	1
D	3	0	-2	3	5	7	9	10	E	Alleluia: dextera Dei fecit virtutem	GR 269 LU 827 SYG 254 GB 234^{v} *GS 161	al	4
D	3	0	-2	3	5	7	9	10	D	Alleluia: hic martyr Domini	SYG 223	al	1
D	3	0	-2	3	5	7	9	10	D	Alleluia: justorum animae in manu Dei	GR 561 GB 268	al	1
D	3	0	-2	3	5	7	9	10	D	Arbor decora fulgida	SYG 143	an	1
D	3	0	-2	3	5	7	10	5	D	Nobilissimus siquidem natalibus	WA 238	an	1
D	3	0	-2	3	5	7	10	7	D	Arca ferebatur super aquas	WA 77	re	1
D	3	0	-2	3	5	7	10	7	D	Quod autem cecidit	LA 120	an	1
E	3	0	-2	3	5	8	7	5	E	O crux gloriosa	VP 151	re	3
D	3	0	-2	5	3	2	-2	0	D	Nemini dixeritis visionem	WA 90	an	1
D	3	0	-2	5	3	2	0	7		Qui oravit Dominum Dormivit Abraham	WA 82	rev	
b	3	0	1	-2	-4	-2	0	-2	G	Alleluia: memento Domine David	SYG 181	al	7
b	3	0	1	-2	-4	-2	0	-2		Memento Domine David	SYG 181	alv	
E	3	0	1	-2	-4	-2	1	-2	E	Sanctus X	GR 37* LU 45		4
E	3	0	1	-2	0	1	0	3	E	Fidelis servus et prudens ... amen	AM 1193 *LR 316	re	4
E	3	0	1	0	-4	-2	0	3	E	Sanctus	THAN #136		3
E	3	0	1	0	-2	0	3	5	E	Sanctus	THAN #135		3
E	3	0	1	3	5	3	5	3	E	Si enim credimus	SYG 236	int	4

D	3	0	2	-2	3	5	7	5	D	De ventre matris meae	GR 523 LU 1499 SYG 196 GB 198 GS 1	int	1
D	3	0	2	-2	3	5	7	5	D	Reliqui domum meam	GR 18**	int	1
D	3	0	2	0	-2	0	-2	3	D	O redundans flos caelestis	VP 192	an	1
D	3	0	2	0	-2	0	3	5	D	Audi benigne conditor	ST 416	hy	2
D	3	0	2	0	-2	3	5	3	D	Accepit autem omnes	WA 190 *LA 165	an	1
D	3	0	2	0	-2	3	5	3	D	Accepit ergo Jesus panes benedixit	WA 104	an	1
D	3	0	2	0	-2	3	5	3	D	Accepit ergo Jesus panes et cum	WA 104	an	1
D	3	0	2	0	-2	3	5	7	D	Accessit Jesus et tetigit	WA 190	an	1
D	3	0	2	0	-2	3	5	7	D	Ecce tu pulchra es	WA 354 *LA 455	an	1
D	3	0	2	0	-2	3	5	7	D	Fulgebunt justi sicut sol in conspectu	LR 167 AR [30] AM 633 800 811 LU 1121	an	2
D	3	0	2	0	-2	3	5	7	D	Fulgebunt justi sicut sol in regno	AM 1121	an	2
D	3	0	2	0	-2	3	5	7	D	Sanctus Vincentius Christi	WA 257	re	1
d	3	0	2	0	2	0	2	0	G	Nunc autem manent	WA 214	an	7
D	3	0	2	3	0	-2	0	2	E	Ecce mitto angelum ... praecedat	LA 157 *WA 102	re	4
D	3	0	2	3	0	-2	0	3	E	Vitone laudabilis Hydulphe mirabilis	PM 204	re	4
D	3	0	2	3	0	3	2	3	E	Reminiscere miserationum tuarum	GR 111 LU 545 *SYG 77 *GB 69 GS 39 47	int	4
D	3	0	2	3	0	5	3	0	E	Doctrinam quasi antelucanum	GR 530 LU 1513	of	4
D	3	0	2	3	0	5	3	0	E	Honora Dominum de tua substantia	GR 569 LU 1582	of	4
D	3	0	2	3	0	5	3	0	E	Oravi Deum meum ego Daniel	GR 367 OTT 107 LU 1050 *SYG 250 *GB 256^{v} *GS 161	of	4
D	3	0	2	3	2	-2	3	7	D	In lege Domini fuit	LR 149 *WA 416 *LA 521	an	1
a	3	0	2	3	2	-2	5	3	c	Si ego verus Christi	LA 330	an	6
D	3	0	2	3	2	0	-2	0	D	In sanctis gloriosus	PM 208	an	1
a	3	0	2	3	2	0	-2	5	c	Benedicta et venerabilis sancta	WA 364	an	6
D	3	0	2	3	2	0	3	2	E	Recordare Domine testamenti	GR [139]	int	4
D	3	0	2	3	2	3	2	3	E	Confitebor tibi Domine Deus	LA 100 *LA 69	re	4
D	3	0	2	3	2	3	2	3	E	Gaudeamus omnes in ... Bartholomaei	GB 226^{v}	int	4
D	3	0	2	3	2	3	2	3	E	Patefactae sunt januae	LA 46 *WA 36	re	4
D	3	0	2	3	2	5	3	2	E	Subvenite sancti Dei	AR [183] GR 107* LU 1765 *AM 1168	re	4
D	3	0	2	3	5	2	3	5	E	Benigne fac Domine	LA 104	an	4
D	3	0	2	3	5	3	5	10	D	Memento nostri Domine	GB 11 *GS 11	int	1
D	3	0	2	5	3	2	3	2	E	Quem vidistis pastores	LU 377 *LR 58 *LA 36 *WA 30	re	4

D	3	0	3	0	-2	2	-2	0	D	Exaltent eum in ecclesia	GB 244v *SYG 53	gr	2
D	3	0	3	0	-2	3	5	7	D	Hic est verus christicola	ST 340	hy	1
a	3	0	3	0	2	-2	0	3	E	Alleluia: quis vestrum habebit	SYG 177	al	3
D	3	0	3	0	2	-2	2	5	D	Nuntium vobis fero de supernis	ST 372	hy	1
D	3	0	3	0	2	-2	2	5	D	Vita sanctorum Deus angelorum	ST 387	hy	1
G	3	0	3	0	2	0	2	3	D	Recordare mei Domine omni	PM 114	re	1
D	3	0	3	0	2	0	3	2	E	Resurrexi et adhuc tecum sum	GR 240 OHS 708 LU 777 *SYG 152 *GB 123 GS K	int	4
a	3	0	3	0	2	3	-4	-2		Majestas Domini aedificavit Domine Deus in simplicitate	OTT 159 *SYG 264 *GB 175v	ofv	
D	3	0	3	0	2	3	7	10		Notum fecit Dominus salutare Cantate Domino canticum	SYG 247	alv	
a	3	0	3	0	3	-2	0	-2	F	Dum sacrum mysterium sanctus Dionysius	PM 197 *WA 386	re	5
D	3	0	3	0	3	-2	3	5	D	Vita sanctorum Deus angelorum	ST 291(var)	hy	2
D	3	0	3	0	3	0	-2	3	D	Vita sanctorum Deus angelorum	ST 291	hy	2
e	3	0	3	0	3	5	3	0	c	Jesum tradidit impius	OHS 507 LU 711 *LA 199	re	6 8
D	3	0	3	0	3	5	7	5	D	Quem dicunt homines	LR 366 *LA 419 *WA 279	re	1
D	3	0	3	0	3	7	5	3	D	Omnes gentes quascumque fecisti	GR 78**	gr	1
D	3	0	3	0	3	7	5	3		Sciant gentes quoniam nomen	GR 78 LU 506 SYG 60 GB 58 GS 26	gr	1
D	3	0	3	0	5	7	5	3		Quoniam Dominus summus terribilis Ascendit Deus	OTT 75 GB 177 SYG 179	ofv	
a	3	0	3	2	-2	0	-2	0		Et pascam illas in judicio Ego pascam	GR 66**	trv	
D	3	0	3	2	0	-2	0	-2	D	Justus non conturbabitur	GB 229 GS 205	int	1
D	3	0	3	2	0	-2	0	-2	D	Justus ut palma florebit	GR [45] LU 1204 SYG 195 GB 197v GS 205	int	1
D	3	0	3	2	0	-2	0	-2	D	O decus virginitatis	WA 356	re	1
D	3	0	3	2	0	-2	0	-2	D	Perpetuis nos Domine	WA 363	an	1
D	3	0	3	2	0	-2	0	5	D	Exaudi Domine deprecationem servorum	WA 227	an	2
D	3	0	3	2	0	-2	3	5	D	Domine Deus meus in te speravi salvum	OTT 173	of	1
D	3	0	3	2	0	-2	3	5		Domine Deus meus si feci istud Domine Deus meus in te	OTT 173	ofv	
D	3	0	3	2	0	-2	3	5	D	Regi saeculorum immortali	WA 71	an	1
D	3	0	3	2	0	2	-2	2	D	Iste confessor Domini colentes	AR [71]	hy	1
D	3	0	3	2	0	3	-2	2	D	Vita sanctorum Deus angelorum	ST 228 258	hy	1
a	3	0	3	2	3	0	3	2	G	Jesu redemptor saeculi	ST 93	hy	8

D	3	0	3	2	3	2	3	2	E	In voluntate tua Domine	GR 380 LU 1066 *SYG 256 *GB 261[V] *GS 165	int	4
D	3	0	3	2	3	2	3	5	E	Ecce nunc tempus ... commendemus	LR 403 LA 127 *WA 85	re	3
D	3	0	3	2	3	5	0	5	E	Jesum de Maria	LR 444	inv	4
D	3	0	3	2	3	5	3	0	E	Christum natum qui beatum	LR 428 *LA 40	inv	4
D	3	0	3	2	3	5	3	0	E	Ecce venit ad templum sanctum	LR 433 LA 347 *WA 268	inv	4
D	3	0	3	2	3	5	3	0	E	Justus florebit in domo	WA 415	inv	4
D	3	0	3	2	3	5	3	0	E	Tanto tempore vobiscum sum ... creditis	PM 151 *WA 307	re	4
D	3	0	3	2	3	5	3	0	E	Tota die contristatus	LA 168 *WA 106	re	4
D	3	0	3	2	3	5	3	2	E	Ecce ego vobiscum sum omnibus diebus	GR 58**	co	3
D	3	0	3	2	3	5	3	2	E	Ego autem adjuvata	LA 361 *WA 274	re	4
D	3	0	3	2	3	5	3	2	E	Intuens in caelum	LA 43 *WA 34	re	4
D	3	0	3	2	3	5	3	2	E	Tanto tempore vobiscum sum ... credis	GR 489 LU 1465[D] *SYG 172 *GB 165 *GS 185	co	4
D	3	0	3	2	3	5	7	2	E	Afferentur regi virgines proximae	GR [54] LU 1219 OTT 155 *SYG 29 *GB 30 GS 229	of	4
D	3	0	3	2	3	5	7	2	E	Exsultabunt sancti in gloria	GR [28] OTT 143 LU 1169 *SYG 191 *GB 195 GS 218	of	4
D	3	0	3	2	3	5	7	5	E	Introibo ad altare Dei ad Deum	GR 83**	of	4
D	3	0	3	2	5	3	0	2	E	Desiderium animae ejus	LR 155 207 *WA 416	re	4
E	3	0	3	5	1	0	-2	0	E	Salve festa dies	AR 166* PM 62	hy	4
a	3	0	3	5	3	0	2	0	b	Amo Christum in cujus thalamum	LA 333	re	4
D	3	0	3	5	3	0	2	0	E	Benedicta et venerabilis ... cujus viscera	LA 447 *WA 271	re	4
b	3	0	3	5	3	0	3	5	G	Attendite universi populi	AR 440 OHS 621 LU 776 *AM 446 447 *WA 127 *LA 206	an	7
E	3	0	3	5	3	1	-2	0		Benedic anima mea Dominum et omnia Benedicite Dominum	GR 608 LU 1654 GS 197 GB 168	grv	
E	3	0	3	5	3	1	-2	1	E	Benedixisti Domine terram tuam	GR 8 LU 337 OTT 8 GS 5 *SYG 7 *GB 6	of	4
E	3	0	3	5	3	1	-2	1	E	Regali ex progenie	LU 1476[F]	of	4
E	3	0	3	5	3	1	0	-2	E	Rex gloriose martyrum	AM 649	hy	4
b	3	0	3	5	3	1	3	1	G	Clamavi et Dominus	AR 100 OHS 223 LU 281	an	7
b	3	0	3	5	3	1	3	6	G	Fundatur exsultatione universae	LR 261	an	7
E	3	0	3	5	3	2	-2	0		Tu Domine pater noster Salvos fac nos	GR 51 LU 447	grv	
D	3	0	3	5	3	2	0	3		Regna terrae cantate Deo Confirma hoc	OTT 79 *GB 189[V] *SYG 183	ofv	

a	3	0	3	5	3	2	3	2	b	Numquid Dominus supplantat	LA 285 *WA 173	re	4
b	3	0	3	5	3	5	3	1	G	Exortum est in tenebris ... corde	AR 271 LU 412 *AM 246 *WA 32 LA 38	an	7
b	3	0	3	5	3	5	3	1	G	Misereor super turbam	AR 558 LU 1009 *AM 596 *WA 188 *LA 312	an	7
b	3	0	3	5	3	5	6	5	G	Discerne causam meam Domine	AR 428 OHS 244 254 *AM 407 *WA 115 *LA 186	an	7
b	3	0	3	5	3	5	6	5	G	Tulerunt Dominum meum	AR 451 OHS 811 LU 800 *AM 464 *WA 135 LA 221	an	7
E	3	0	3	5	3	5	7	5	E	Alleluia: ardens est cor meum	SYG 167	al	3
E	3	0	3	5	3	5	7	5		Ardens est cor meum	SYG 167	alv	
D	3	0	3	5	7	5	3	5	D	Et si coram hominibus ... Deus	GR [25] LU 1166 *SYG 200 GB 202 GS 219	co	1
D	3	0	3	5	7	9	7	5	D	Agnus Dei	SCH #206		1
a	3	0	3	5	7	10	7	8	c	Surrexit Dominus et apparuit	GR 246 OHS 777 LU 788 SYG 156 GB 132v GS 118	co	6
D	3	0	3	5	7	10	7	9	F	Pes enim meus stetit	SYG 86	co	6
D	3	0	3	5	8	7	5	3	F	Venite audite et narrabo	GR 398	int	6
D	3	0	3	5	8	7	8	10	E	Alleluia: crastina die delebitur	GS 13	al	4
D	3	0	3	7	3	5	3	5		Benedicat tibi Dominus ex Sion Ecce sic benedicetur	GR [123] LU 1290	trv	
D	3	0	3	7	3	5	3	5		Dicat nunc Israel Saepe expugnaverunt	GR 153 LU 571 GS 72 GB 97v SYG 110	trv	
D	3	0	3	7	3	5	3	5		Felix es sacra virgo Maria Tu gloria	GR 441 LU 1378	trv	
D	3	0	3	7	3	5	3	5		Ita oculi nostri ad Dominum Ad te levavi	GR 124 LU 554 GS 55 GB 82v SYG 93	trv	
D	3	0	3	7	3	5	3	5		Lumen ad revelationem Nunc dimittis	GR 434 LU 1363 GS k SYG 50	trv	
D	3	0	3	7	3	5	3	5		Venite comedite panem meum Ab ortu solis	GR [97] LU 1282	trv	
D	3	0	3	7	10	7	5	9		Tu es vas electionis	SYG 205	alv	
E	3	1	-2	0	-2	0	1	3	E	Vidi speciosam sicut columbam	AM 1200 *PM 178 *LR 376 *LA 443 *WA 355	re	3
b	3	1	-2	0	-2	1	0	1	F	Ecce vidimus eum	OHS 381 LU 637 *LR 336 *LA 190 *WA 118	re	5
b	3	1	-2	0	-2	1	0	1	F	Plange quasi virgo	OHS 603 LU 761 *LA 202 *WA 125	re	5
E	3	1	-2	0	-2	1	3	1	E	Sicut dilexit me pater	AM 1189	re	4
E	3	1	-2	3	5	3	5	6	E	Deus in nomine tuo salvum	GR 141 *SYG 103 *GS 64 *GB 91	int	4
E	3	1	0	-4	-2	0	-2	0	D	Agnus Dei XVI	GR 54* LU 60 SCH #164		1
E	3	1	0	-2	-4	-2	-4	-2	E	Candor est lucis aeternae et	AR 630 LU 1380	an	4

E	3	1	0	1	0	-2	-4	-2	D	Agnus Dei	SCH #165		2
E	3	1	0	1	0	-2	0	-2	E	Alleluia: beata es virgo Maria	LU 1476[c]	al	3
E	3	1	0	1	0	-2	0	-2	E	Alleluia: cognoverunt discipuli Dominum	GR 264 LU 817	al	3
E	3	1	0	1	0	-2	0	-2	E	Alleluia: Domine Deus salutis meae	GR 351 LU 1029 GS 152 *SYG 245 *GB 254	al	3
E	3	1	0	1	0	-2	0	-2	E	Alleluia: qui timent te videbunt me	GR 73**	al	3
E	3	1	0	1	0	-2	0	-2	E	Alleluia: quis sicut Dominus Deus	GR 19**	al	3
E	3	1	0	1	0	-2	0	-2	E	Alleluia: si testimonium hominum	GR 538 LU 1534	al	3
E	3	1	0	1	0	-2	0	-2	E	Ante diem festum Paschae ... ut	SYG 134	an	3
E	3	1	0	1	0	-2	1	0	E	Sanctus	THAN #134		3
E	3	1	0	1	3	5	3	5	E	Dicit Dominus Petro	GR 530 *SYG 201 *GB 202 GS o	int	4
E	3	1	0	1	3	5	3	5	E	Sicut oculi servorum in manibus	GR 99 *SYG 75 *GB 67 *GS 37	int	4
E	3	1	0	1	3	6	5	3	E	Judica me Deus et discerne	GR 151 LU 569 *SYG 109 *GS 71 *GB 97	int	4
E	3	1	0	3	0	-2	3	5		Cum venerit paraclitus spiritus	SYG 181	alv	
E	3	1	0	3	1	0	3	1		Kyrie ... pater de caelis	VP 171		
E	3	1	0	3	5	1	3	1	E	Qui biberit aquam	GR 136 *GB 88	co	3
E	3	1	5	3	1	0	-2	0	E	Approprinquante Jesu	SYG 120	an	3
a	3	2	-2	-4	-2	0	-7	-4		Inter choros confessorum O laudanda	LR 326	rev	
a	3	2	-2	-4	-2	0	-2	0		Benedictus es Domine in firmamento Benedictio et claritas	WA 160	rev	
D	3	2	-2	0	-2	0	-2	0	D	Consummatus in gloria	WA 313	an	2
D	3	2	-2	0	-2	0	3	5	D	Agnus Dei	SCH #237		1
a	3	2	-2	0	2	-2	3	5		Te martyr inclyte O sancte N. concivis	WA 418	rev	
a	3	2	-2	0	2	0	-2	0		Deferens autem signum Volens scire	WA 77	rev	
a	3	2	-2	0	2	0	3	5		Cumque exitum suum Transiens ex hoc mundo	WA 314	rev	
a	3	2	-2	0	2	0	3	5		Sancti spiritus psallebant Dunstanus archiepiscopus	WA 314	rev	
a	3	2	-2	0	3	2	0	3		Benedictus Abraham Revertenti Abraham	WA 80	rev	
D	3	2	-2	0	3	2	3	5	D	Praeclara dies ortus est	PM 344	an	2
D	3	2	-2	0	3	5	3	2	D	O redemptor sume carmen	WA 212	hy	2
a	3	2	-2	2	0	2	3	0		Offenditur ultro condonat O mirae pietatis	WA 250	rev	

D	3	2	-2	2	5	2	3	2	F	In Niniven civitate	WA 229	an	6
a	3	2	0	-2	-4	-2	0	-2	G	Nefarium tamen apud Christianorum	WA 258	an	8
a	3	2	0	-2	0	-2	-4	-2	D	Beata nobis gaudia	ST 339	hy	1
D	3	2	0	-2	0	-2	0	3	D	Christus infans non despexit	WA 43	an	2
D	3	2	0	-2	0	-2	0	3	D	Veni creator spiritus	ST 349	hy	1
D	3	2	0	-2	0	-2	3	2	D	Kyrie	MEL #188		
D	3	2	0	-2	0	-2	3	5	D	Beatus Dionysius Rusticus	WA 388	re	1
D	3	2	0	-2	0	2	0	3	D	O Martine o pie	WA 402	an	1
D	3	2	0	-2	0	2	3	5	E	Agnus Dei	SCH #201		4
a	3	2	0	-2	0	3	2	0	G	Dominus possedit me	WA 167 *LA 281	an	8
D	3	2	0	-2	0	3	2	0	D	O quam speciosa est Maria	PM 180	an	1
D	3	2	0	-2	0	3	2	3	D	Benedictio et claritas	WA 160	re	1
D	3	2	0	-2	0	3	2	3	D	Christo caelorum agmina	ST 151	hy	2
D	3	2	0	-2	0	3	5	3	F	Alleluia	WA 130	an	6
D	3	2	0	-2	0	3	5	3	D	Exsurge quare obdormis	GR 77 LU 504 SYG 60 GB 57^{v} *GS 26	int	1
D	3	2	0	-2	0	3	5	3	D	Reddit muto consonantis	WA 249	an	1
D	3	2	0	-2	0	3	5	7	D	Aemula prosequitur	WA 284	re	1
a	3	2	0	-2	0	3	5	7	a	Agnus Dei	SCH #46		2
D	3	2	0	-2	0	3	5	7	D	Agnus Dei	SCH #233		1
D	3	2	0	-2	0	3	5	7	D	Puer trimus amne	WA 250	re	1
D	3	2	0	-2	0	3	7	5	D	Kyrie	MEL #173		
D	3	2	0	-2	0	3	7	8	D	Agnus Dei	SCH #205		2
D	3	2	0	-2	0	3	7	8	D	Sanctus XII	GR 43* LU 50 THAN #177		2
D	3	2	0	-2	0	5	7	10		Et in terra	BOS #55		
D	3	2	0	-2	0	7	5	3	D	Adnue Christe saeculorum Domine	ST 130	hy	1
D	3	2	0	-2	2	3	0	7		Mane nobiscum Domine	GS 126	alv	
D	3	2	0	-2	3	-2	0	[0]		Et in terra	BOS #54		
D	3	2	0	-2	3	2	0	5	D	Alleluia: stabat sancta Maria	GR 596 LU 1633^{v}	al	2
D	3	2	0	-2	3	2	0	5	D	Alleluia: stabunt justi in magna constantia	GS 185	al	2
D	3	2	0	-2	3	5	3	5	F	Kyrie	MEL #172		
D	3	2	0	-2	3	5	7	5	D	Ad coenam agni providi	ST 229	hy	1
D	3	2	0	-2	3	5	7	5	D	Alleluia	AM 71	an	1
D	3	2	0	-2	3	5	7	5	D	In consilio justorum	LA 473	an	2
D	3	2	0	-2	3	5	7	5	D	In tympano et choro	AM 71 320 *LA 102	an	1

D	3	2	0	-2	3	5	7	5	D	O rex benigne Domine	ST 245	hy	1
D	3	2	0	-2	3	5	7	8	D	Deus Deus meus ad te	AR 342 AM 312 *WA 74 LA 113	an	1
D	3	2	0	-2	3	7	5	7	D	Haec est domus Domini	AR [107] LU 1247 AM 697 *WA 319 *LA 552	an	1
D	3	2	0	-2	3	7	5	7	D	Haec est virgo sapiens quam	AR [87] LU 1210 AM 678 *WA 434 *LA 546	an	1
D	3	2	[0	0	0	0	0	0]	E	Dei fide qua vivimus	ST 157	hy	4
D	3	2	0	2	-2	-3	-2	0	D	Agnus Dei	SCH #204		1
D	3	2	0	2	-2	-3	-2	0	D	Sanctus	THAN #176		1
a	3	2	0	2	-2	0	-2	-4		Biduo vivens pendebat	SYG 231	alv	
a	3	2	0	2	-2	0	-2	-4		Diffusa est gratia in labiis	SYG 5	alv	
a	3	2	0	2	-2	0	-2	-4		Laetabitur justus in Domino ... laudabuntur	SYG 209 *GS 207	alv	
D	3	2	0	2	-2	0	-2	0	D	Alleluia	AM 123 LU 290 292	an	2
D	3	2	0	2	0	-2	0	2	D	Scimus quidem te pater	WA 403	an	1
D	3	2	0	2	0	-2	0	2	E	Succurre nobis genitrix Christi	PM 280	an	4
D	3	2	0	2	0	-2	0	3	D	Cum venit paraclitus spiritus	WA 145	an	2
D	3	2	0	2	0	-2	2	3		Hodie beata virgo Maria Responsum accepit Simeon	SYG 47 *GS i	anv	
D	3	2	0	2	0	-2	3	5	D	Benedictus sit Dominus	WA 251	an	1
D	3	2	0	2	0	-2	3	5	D	Dixit Jesus ad legisperitos	WA 190	an	1
D	3	2	0	2	0	-2	3	5	D	Joannes apostolus ... virgo	WA 38 *LA 48	an	1
D	3	2	0	2	3	0	-2	0	D	Exsurge Domine non praevaleat	LA 95	an	1
D	3	2	0	2	3	2	0	-2	D	Alleluia	AR 139	an	2
D	3	2	0	2	3	2	0	-2	D	Beati omnes qui timent	AR 139 OHS 354 LU 290 *AM 121 *LA 102	an	2
D	3	2	0	2	3	2	5	3	E	Qui Lazarum resuscitasti	AR [159] LU 1786 *LA 554 *WA 436	re	4
D	3	2	0	2	3	5	3	2	E	Mihi autem adhaerere	WA 68	re	4
D	3	2	0	2	5	2	3	2	E	Nunc sancte nobis spiritus	AM 568 1095	hy	4
D	3	2	0	2	5	2	3	2	E	O quam beata femina	ST 152	hy	4
D	3	2	0	2	5	2	3	2	E	Te lucis ante terminum	AM 564 1091	hy	4
D	3	2	0	2	5	3	0	3	E	Hodie nata est virgo	WA 364	an	4
D	3	2	0	2	5	3	2	0	D	Kyrie Deus pater auctor	MEL #174		
a	3	2	0	3	-2	0	-2	-4		Nativitas gloriosae virginis	GS u	alv	
a	3	2	0	3	-2	0	-2	-4		Optimam partem elegit	GS p 191	alv	
D	3	2	0	3	0	-2	0	3	D	Felix Maria unxit	WA 337	re	1
D	3	2	0	3	0	-2	3	5	[D]	Agnus Dei	SCH #203		1

D	3	2	0	3	0	-2	3	5		Beati quorum remissae sunt	SYG 241	alv	
D	3	2	0	3	0	-2	3	5	D	Kyrie	MEL #187		
D	3	2	0	3	0	-2	3	5	D	Sanctus	THAN #175		1
a	3	2	0	3	2	0	-4	0	F	In sole posuit tabernaculum	WA 27 *LA 63	an	5
D	3	2	0	3	2	0	-2	0	D	Da nobis Domine auxilium	WA 66 LA 93	an	2
D	3	2	0	3	2	0	-2	0	D	Inclina Domine aurem ... et exaudi me	WA 69 LA 100	an	2
a	3	2	0	3	2	0	2	-2	E	Alleluia: missus est angelus Domini	GR 637	al	3
D	3	2	0	3	2	3	5	3	E	Adoremus Deum qui in sanctis	WA 43	inv	4
D	3	2	0	3	2	3	5	3	D	Amen amen dico vobis qui credit	WA 157	an	1
G	3	2	0	3	2	3	5	3	G	Amo Christum in cujus thalamun	WA 254	re	7
a	3	2	0	3	5	3	0	-2		Mole peccatorum gravati O mulier sancta	WA 337	rev	
D	3	2	0	5	3	5	7	5	E	O virgo Maria quae genuisti	PM 273	an	4
a	3	2	3	0	-4	-2	0	-2	F	Laudate Dominum omnes gentes	GR [130] LU 1297	co	5
a	3	2	3	0	-4	0	-2	-4	F	Servite Domino in timore et exsultate	GR 93(43) *SYG 68 *GB 64^{v} *GS 34	co	5
D	3	2	3	0	-2	0	-2	3		Christus mortuus est propter delicta	GS 127	alv	
D	3	2	3	0	-2	0	2	3	D	Locutus est ad me unus	LA 225 *WA 140	re	2
a	3	2	3	0	-2	0	3	-2	F	Non vos relinquam ... veniam	GR 303 LU 899 *SYG 188 *GB 194 GS b	co	5
D	3	2	3	0	-2	3	5	3	D	Illumina faciem tuam super servum	GR 76 LU 501 SYG 60 GB 57^{v} GS 25	co	1
D	3	2	3	0	-2	3	5	7		Confitebor tibi Domine in toto corde Domine Deus meus in te	OTT 173	ofv	
a	3	2	3	0	1	0	-4	0	G	Dum venerit paraclitus spiritus	GR 270 LU 828 *SYG 168 *GB 151 GS 130	co	8
D	3	2	3	0	3	2	0	-2	D	Alleluia	AR 106	an	2
a	3	2	3	0	3	2	3	0	a	Locutus est Dominus ad Abraham	LR 402 LA 120 WA 80	re	2
D	3	2	3	0	3	2	3	2	E	De necessitatibus meis eripe	GR 104 *SYG 80 *GB 72 GS 41	int	4
D	3	2	3	0	3	2	3	5	E	Terra tremuit et quievit	GR 243 OHS 712 OTT 55 LU 781 *SYG 153 *GB 128 GS 117	of	4
D	3	2	3	0	3	5	7	5	E	Judica Domine nocentes me	GR 185 OHS 206 LU 606 SYG 124 *GB 111 *GS 89	int	4
D	3	2	3	2	-2	0	3	2	D	Vos qui in turribus	WA 178	re	2
D	3	2	3	2	0	2	0	-2	E	Exsultemus et laetemur in Domino	WA 314	re	4
D	3	2	3	2	0	3	2	0	D	Cantabo Domino qui bona tribuit	AM 18 *LA 99	an	2

D	3	2	3	2	0	3	2	3	D	Cantate Domino et benedicite	AR 106 *WA 69 *LA 101	an	2
D	3	2	3	2	3	2	3	5	E	Misericordia Domini plena	GR 263 LU 816 *SYG 164 *GB 146 *GS 127	int	4
D	3	2	3	2	3	5	7	5	E	Miseratio hominis circa proximum	GR 631 LU 1693	int	4
D	3	2	3	2	3	5	7	5	E	Prope es tu Domine	GR 11 *SYG 9 *GB 8 GS 6	int	4
D	3	2	3	5	0	-2	2	5	D	Ecce virgo concipiet ... Emmanuel	GR 23 462 LU 356 *SYG 9 *GB 7v GS 6	co	1
D	3	2	3	5	0	-2	2	5	D	Sacerdos magnus qui in vita	GR 570 LU 1583	co	1
D	3	2	3	5	0	3	2	3	D	Audivi vocem de caelo dicentem	WA 435	an	2
D	3	2	3	5	0	3	2	3	D	In omnem terram exivit sonus eorum	LR 135 *WA 411 LA 505	an	2
D	3	2	3	5	0	3	5	3	D	Ad monumentum Lazari	WA 105	an	1
D	3	2	3	5	2	0	3	0	D	Alleluia: ego dilecto meo et dilectus	GR 52**	al	1
D	3	2	3	5	2	0	3	0	D	Alleluia: ego vos elegi de mundo	GR 630 LU 1487	al	1
D	3	2	3	5	2	0	3	0	D	Alleluia: iste est qui pro lege Dei	SYG 210	al	1
D	3	2	3	5	2	0	3	0	D	Alleluia: justi epulentur et exsultent ... delectentur	GR [27] LU 1168 SYG 190 *GB 269v GS 216	al	1
D	3	2	3	5	2	0	3	0	D	Alleluia: justi epulentur et exsultent ... parasti	GR 56**	al	1
D	3	2	3	5	2	0	3	0	D	Alleluia: magnus sanctus Paulus	GS 178 189	al	1
D	3	2	3	5	2	0	3	0	D	Alleluia: paraclitus spiritus sanctus	GS 138	al	1
D	3	2	3	5	2	0	3	0	D	Alleluia: plantatus in domo	SYG 189	al	1
D	3	2	3	5	2	0	3	0	D	Alleluia: post dies octo ... stetit	SYG 163	al	1
D	3	2	3	5	2	0	3	2	D	Alleluia: surgens Dominus Jesus	SYG 156	al	1
D	3	2	3	5	2	0	3	2	D	Dormiunt in terrae pulvere	GR (22)	co	1
D	3	2	3	5	2	0	3	2	D	In conceptione sua	LR 261	an	1
D	3	2	3	5	2	0	3	2	D	O beata virgo Maria	AR 826[2] LU 1612	an	1
D	3	2	3	5	2	3	0	3	D	Ancilla Christi sum	WA 273 LA 357	an	2
D	3	2	3	5	2	3	2	0	D	Beata viscera Mariae	GR [80] LU 1268 *GB 220v GS 195	co	1
D	3	2	3	5	2	3	2	0	D	Felices sensus beatae Mariae	GR 601 LU 1637	co	1
D	3	2	3	5	2	3	2	0	D	Quicumque fecerit voluntatem	GR 456 SYG 206 GB 211v GS p	co	1
D	3	2	3	5	2	3	2	3	D	Beatum canimus Dei Apostolum	GB 229	co	1
D	3	2	3	5	2	3	2	3	D	In salutari tuo anima mea	GR 383 LU 1069 *SYG 258 GB 263 *GS d 166	co	1
D	3	2	3	5	2	5	3	2		Ne discesseris a me Exaudi me	GR 9**	trv	

D	3	2	3	5	3	0	-2	0	E	Sacerdotes sancti incensum	AM 551	an	4
D	3	2	3	5	3	0	2	0	E	Doctor bonus et amicus	LA 499 *WA 234	re	3
D	3	2	3	5	3	0	2	3	G	Gloria	BOS #52		IV
D	3	2	3	5	3	0	3	2	E	Christus pro nobis humiliavit	SYG 128	int	4
D	3	2	3	5	3	0	3	2	E	Nos autem gloriari ... in quo	GR 195 490 OHS 257 439 LU 667 1454 *SYG 125 GB 112^{v} GS 90 235	int	4
D	3	2	3	5	3	2	0	2	D	Cantantibus organis Caecilia Domino	AR 924 LU 1756 AM 1140 *WA 408 LA 493	an	1
D	3	2	3	5	3	2	0	2	E	Sancti spiritus dono	WA 290	an	4
a	3	2	3	5	3	2	0	3	G	Dum veniet filius	WA 17	an	8
D	3	2	3	5	3	2	0	3	D	Puer natus in Bethlehem alleluia	AR 149*		1
D	3	2	3	5	3	2	3	0	D	Communicantes Christi passionibus	GR 484 LU 1436	co	1
a	3	2	3	5	3	2	3	2	a	Cantate Domino alleluia	GR 273 LU 833 SYG 169 GB 152^{v} GS 131	co	2
a	3	2	3	5	3	2	3	2		Deus auribus nostris / Exsurge Domine	GR 143 *GS 65 *GB 91^{v} SYG 103	grv	
a	3	2	3	5	3	2	3	2		Ne quaeso Domine irascaris / Ait autem Abraham	WA 81	rev	
D	3	2	3	5	3	5	3	2	D	Redime me Domine et miserere	GR 115 SYG 87 GB 76 GS 48	int	2
D	3	2	3	5	3	5	3	7	F	Cantate Domino canticum ... alleluia	GR 268 LU 826 *SYG 167 *GB 149^{v} GS 129	int	6
D	3	2	3	5	3	5	7	5	E	Alleluia: imperatrix reginarum	VP 51	al	4
D	3	2	3	5	3	5	7	5		Flores apparuerunt in terra / Jam hiems	GR 615	trv	
D	3	2	3	5	3	5	7	5		Resurrexit tamquam dormiens	GB 126	alv	
D	3	2	3	5	3	7	5	7	D	Cantate Deo alleluia	LA 240 *WA 143	re	2
D	3	2	3	5	3	7	5	7	D	In servis suis alleluia	LR 168	re	1
D	3	2	3	5	7	0	-2	3	D	Hymnis angelicis ora resolvimus	LR 288	hy	2
D	3	2	3	5	7	0	-2	3	D	Te Joseph celebrent agmina	AR 650 LR 436 LU 1447 AM 839 884	hy	1
D	3	2	3	5	7	3	8	7	G	Servus Dei Nicholaus	WA 241	re	8
D	3	2	3	5	7	5	3	2	D	Salve crux sancta salve mundi gloria	AR 163* ST 120	hy	1
D	3	2	3	5	7	5	3	5	E	Alleluia: gaudete justi in Domino	GR 406 LU 1327 SYG 169	al	4
D	3	2	3	5	7	5	3	5	E	Alleluia: laudate pueri Dominum	GR 42 260 OHS 827 LU 428 805 GS p 123 216 SYG 161 *GB 142^{v}	al	4
D	3	2	3	5	7	5	3	5	E	Alleluia: nunc ergo ora pro nobis	GR 39**	al	4
D	3	2	3	5	7	5	3	5	E	Alleluia: pauper et inops laudabunt	GR 424 LU 1352^{v}	al	4

D	3	2	3	5	7	5	3	5	E	Alleluia: suscitans a terra inopem	GR 20**	al	4
D	3	2	3	5	7	5	3	5	F	Confiteantur tibi populi Deus	GR [126] LU 1294	gr	5
D	3	2	3	5	7	5	3	5		Domine, ne memineris Domine non secundum	GR 89 OHS 209 LU 527 *SYG 66 GS 31	trv	
D	3	2	3	5	7	5	3	5		Et in terra	BOS #52		
D	3	2	3	5	7	5	3	5	F	Imitatores mei estote	GR 548 LU 1546	co	6
D	3	2	3	5	7	5	3	5		Infirmata est in paupertate Miserere mei	GR [145]	trv	
D	3	2	3	5	7	5	3	5		Invocabit me et ego exaudiam Qui habitat	GR 95 LU 533 GS 35 *GB 65 *SYG 73	trv	
D	3	2	3	5	7	5	3	5		Si quis in verbo non offendit Si quis putat	GR 31**	trv	
D	3	2	3	5	7	5	3	5		Super aspidem et basiliscum Angelis suis	GR [144]	trv	
D	3	2	3	5	7	5	3	5		Super aspidem et basiliscum Qui habitat	GR 95 LU 533 *GS 35 *GB 65 *SYG 73	trv	
D	3	2	3	5	7	5	7	5		A sagitta volante Qui habitat	GR 95 LU 533 *GS 35 *GB 65 *SYG 73	trv	
D	3	2	3	5	7	5	7	5		Acuerunt linguas suas Eripe me	GR 208 OHS 534 LU 725 *GS 99 *GB 116V *SYG 137	trv	
D	3	2	3	5	7	5	7	5		Adducentur regi virgines Audi filia	GR [62] LU 1227	trv	
D	3	2	3	5	7	5	7	5		Adducentur regi virgines Omnis gloria	GR 104**	trv	
D	3	2	3	5	7	5	7	5		Deus meus clamabo per diem Deus Deus meus	GR 180 OHS 109 LU 594 GS 86 *GB 109 *SYG 122	trv	
D	3	2	3	5	7	5	7	5	G	Diffusa est gratia in labiis	GR [58] OTT 156 LU 1223 *SYG 46 *GB 49 *GS 181	of	8
D	3	2	3	5	7	5	7	5	G	Diligis justitiam et odisti	OHS 418 LU 663	of	8
D	3	2	3	5	7	5	7	5	G	In cujus nomine	WA 258	an	8
D	3	2	3	5	7	5	7	5		Quomodo inquit fiet istud Ave Maria	GR 459 LU 1412	trv	
D	3	2	3	5	7	5	7	5		Tuam crucem adoramus ... passionem Adoramus te	GR [104]	trv	
D	3	2	3	5	7	5	7	8	D	Beati pauperes spiritu quoniam ipsorum	GR 24**	co	1
D	3	2	3	5	7	5	7	9	G	Memor esto fili	WA 175	an	8
D	3	2	3	5	7	5	7	10	G	In me gratia omnis viae	GR 621 LU 1676B	of	8
D	3	2	3	5	7	8	5	3		Quia factus es susceptor	GR 470	alv	
D	3	2	3	5	7	8	5	3		Sacerdos sit sanctus	GR [119]	alv	
D	3	2	3	5	7	9	5	3		Eduxit Dominus populum	SYG 161	alv	
D	3	2	3	7	2	5	3	2	D	Kyrie	MEL #186		

D	3	2	3	7	5	3	2	3	D	Revelabitur gloria Domini	GR 26 LU 362 *SYG 14 *GB 13^{v} *GS 13	co	1
D	3	2	3	7	5	3	2	3	D	Volavit ad me	GR 32**	co	1
D	3	2	3	7	5	3	5	3	D	Cibavit illum Dominus pane	GR 83**	co	1
D	3	2	3	7	5	7	3	5	D	O quantum in cruce spirant amorem	PM 157 VP 169	an	1
D	3	2	3	7	5	7	8	7	F	Benedictionem omnium gentium	GR (26)	co	6
D	3	2	5	2	-2	0	2	5	D	Agnus Dei	SCH #202		1
D	3	2	5	2	-2	0	2	5	D	Sanctus	THAN #174		1
D	3	2	5	3	0	2	0	2	E	Pater sanctus dum intentam	LA 371 *WA 298	re	4
D	3	2	5	3	0	2	0	3	E	Sicut cedrus exaltata sum	PM 260 LR 252 *LA 443 *WA 355	re	4
D	3	2	5	3	0	2	5	3	D	Fortem virili pectore	AR [99] LU 1234 AM 684	hy	2
D	3	2	5	3	0	2	5	3	D	Jesu corona virginum	AR [90]	hy	2
D	3	2	5	3	2	3	0	-2		Iste est qui pro lege Dei	SYG 210	alv	
D	3	2	5	3	2	3	0	-2		Paraclitus spiritus sanctus	GS 138	alv	
D	3	2	5	3	2	3	0	2		Leva in circuitu	GR 45**	alv	
D	3	2	5	3	2	3	0	2		Post dies octo ... stetit	SYG 163	alv	
D	3	2	5	3	2	3	0	2		Virgo Dei genitrix quem totus	GR 623 LU 1684	alv	
D	3	2	5	3	2	3	0	3		Hic est vere martyr qui pro Christo	SYG 229	alv	
D	3	2	5	3	2	3	0	3		Veni electa mea ... quia	GS 227	alv	
D	3	2	5	3	2	3	0	7		Ego dilecto meo et dilectus meus	GR 52**	alv	
D	3	2	5	3	2	3	0	7		Ego vos elegi ... ut eatis	GR 630 LU 1487	alv	
D	3	2	5	3	2	3	0	7		Justi epulentur ... delectentur	GR [27] *GB 269^{v} GS 216 SYG 190	alv	
D	3	2	5	3	2	3	0	7		Justi epulentur ... parasti	GR 56**	alv	
D	3	2	5	3	2	3	0	7		Magnus sanctus Paulus	GS 178 189	alv	
D	3	2	5	3	2	3	0	7		Plantatus in domo Domini	SYG 189	alv	
D	3	2	5	3	2	5	0	2	D	Deus creator omnium	ST 5	hy	2
D	3	2	5	3	5	2	3	5	E	Intempestae noctis hora	SYG 57	of	3
D	3	2	5	3	5	2	3	5	E	Memor sit Dominus omni	SYG 233	of	4
D	3	2	5	7	3	5	3	2	D	Alleluia: beatus vir qui suffert	GR [43] LU 1202 *GS 207 *SYG 218	al	1
D	3	2	5	7	8	7	3	5	D	Qui vult venire ... sequatur	GR [12] LU 1138 *SYG 44 GB 46 217 GS 209	co	1
D	3	2	7	9	7	9	7	10		Inter apostolos vocatione / A Christo de caelo	SYG 44	grv	
E	3	5	-2	0	3	5	8	7		Dies diei eructat / In omnem terram	SYG 54	ofv	
a	3	5	0	-4	-2	0	-2	0		Ut tuo nos interventu / Sancta Maria clemens	WA 357	rev	

D	3	5	0	2	3	2	0	-2	D	Temptavit Deus Abraham	LA 121 *WA 81	re	1 2
D	3	5	2	3	0	-2	0	3	D	Clamor inquit Dominus	WA 81	re	1
D	3	5	2	3	0	5	2	3	F	Beatus vir cujus est nomen	GR 20**	gr	5
D	3	5	2	3	0	5	2	3	F	Beatus vir qui timet	GR [11] LU 1136 *GS 206 SYG 51 GB 51	gr	5
D	3	5	2	3	2	5	3	5		Memor multitudinis misericordiae Patres nostri in Aegypto	GB 75v	ofv	
D	3	5	2	3	5	0	-2	0	G	Ab ortu solis usque ad occasum	GR [97] LU 1282	tr	8
D	3	5	2	3	5	0	-2	0	G	Ad te levavi oculos ... qui	GR 124 LU 554 *SYG 93 *GB 82v GS 55	tr	8
A	3	5	2	3	5	0	-2	0	D	Emitte spiritum tuum	GR [93] LU 1279	tr	2
D	3	5	2	3	5	0	-2	0	G	Filii hominum in tegmine	GR 55**	tr	8
D	3	5	2	3	5	0	-2	0	G	Fortitudo mea et laus ... iste	GR 468	tr	8
D	3	5	2	3	5	0	-2	0	G	Fundamenta ejus in montibus	GR 402	tr	8
D	3	5	2	3	5	0	-2	0	G	Induit eum Dominus vestimentis	GR 13**	tr	8
D	3	5	2	3	5	0	-2	0	G	Qui seminant in lacrimis	GR [24] LU 1164 *SYG 51 *GB 50 GS 217	tr	8
A	3	5	2	3	5	0	-2	0	D	Si quis putat se religiosum esse	GR 31**	tr	2
D	3	5	2	3	5	0	-2	0	G	Suscepimus Deus misericordiam	GR 113**	tr	8
D	3	5	2	3	5	0	-2	0	G	Te Deum patrem	GR [84] LU 1273	tr	8
A	3	5	2	3	5	0	-2	0	D	Tu es vas electionis	GR 420 LU 1346 *SYG 44 *GS 178	tr	2
D	3	5	2	3	5	0	-2	0	G	Tu gloria Jerusalem ... nostri	GR 441 LU 1378	tr	8
D	3	5	3	0	-2	0	-2	3	E	Calix benedictionis	GR 541 LU 1535	of	4
D	3	5	3	0	-2	0	-2	3	E	Factus est Dominus firmamentum	GR 150 OTT 42 LU 567 SYG 108 GB 96v GS 70	of	4
D	3	5	3	0	-2	0	2	0	D	Confessor Dei Nicholaus	WA 239	re	1
a	3	5	3	0	-2	0	2	3		Et in terra	BOS #19 GR 8* LU 19		
D	3	5	3	0	-2	0	3	2		Exspectans exspectavi Dominum Domine ad adjuvandum	GB 104v	ofv	
a	3	5	3	0	-2	3	5	2		Dixit Dominus ad Moysen Precatus est Moyses	OTT 97 *GB 79 *SYG 89	ofv	
D	3	5	3	0	-2	3	5	7	D	Felix namque es sacra virgo Maria	GR [82] LU 1271 *GB 233 *GS r	of	1
D	3	5	3	0	-2	3	5	7	D	Levita Vincentius dixit	WA 257	re	1
E	3	5	3	0	-2	3	5	8	E	Felix namque es beata virgo	WA 366	an	4
D	3	5	3	0	-2	3	7	5	D	Ave gratia plena Dominus tecum	GR 443 LU 1379	of	1
D	3	5	3	0	2	-2	0	3	G	Gustate et videte quoniam	GR 95**	tr	8
D	3	5	3	0	2	3	2	0	D	Gloriosus Dei amicus	VP 254 *WA 260	re	1
D	3	5	3	0	2	3	2	0	D	Iniquitates nostrae Domine	GB 156v *WA 228	an	1

D	3	5	3	0	2	3	2	0	D	Inundaverunt aquae Domine	GB 159^{v}	an	1
D	3	5	3	0	2	3	2	0		Longe a salute mea Deus Deus meus	GR 180 OHS 109 LU 594 GS 86 GB 109 SYG 122	trv	
D	3	5	3	0	2	3	5	3	F	Exsulta et lauda habitatio	GR 54**	gr	5
D	3	5	3	0	3	0	-2	0		Illumina faciem tuam super servum In te speravi	OTT 101 *GB 68^{v} SYG 76	ofv	
D	3	5	3	0	3	0	3	-2	D	Dominus dixit ad me	GR 27 LU 392 SYG 14 GB 13^{v} GS 13	int	2
D	3	5	3	0	3	2	0	-2	D	Benedicat nos Deus ... et metuant	WA 158	re	1
D	3	5	3	0	3	5	2	3	F	Ad Dominum dum tribularer	GR 321 LU 961 *SYG 91 *GB 80 GS 53 142	gr	5
D	3	5	3	0	3	5	2	3	F	Protector noster aspice Deus	GR 108 LU 1003 *SYG 75 *GB 67^{v} GS 37 43 144 171	gr	5
D	3	5	3	0	3	5	3	-2	F	Aedificabuntur in te deserta	GR (5)	of	6
D	3	5	3	0	3	5	3	-2	F	Gloriabuntur in te omnes	GR 526 LU 1508 OTT 135 SYG 200 GB 201^{v} GS 218	of	6
a	3	5	3	0	3	5	3	2		Quoniam ad te orabo Domine Gloriabuntur in te	OTT 135 GB 201^{v} SYG 200	ofv	
D	3	5	3	0	3	5	3	5	D	Corpora sanctorum in pace	PM 200 LR 188 *LA 519	re	1
D	3	5	3	0	3	5	3	5	D	Cum inducerent puerum ... dixit	WA 270	re	1
D	3	5	3	0	3	5	3	5	D	Post passionem Domini	WA 385	re	1
D	3	5	3	0	3	5	3	5	D	Propter testamentum Domini	PM 207 LR 186 *LA 517 WA 422	re	1
D	3	5	3	0	3	5	3	5	D	Qui consolabatur me	WA 175	re	1
a	3	5	3	0	3	7	8	5	c	Repletus sancto spiritu	GB 54	gr	6
D	3	5	3	0	5	10	7	3		Dominus regnavit decorem induit Deus enim firmavit	OTT 16 *GB 16 *SYG 16	ofv	
E	3	5	3	1	0	-2	0	3	E	Si ignoras te	WA 162	an	4
E	3	5	3	1	0	1	3	1	E	Fidelia omnia mandata	AM 125 WA 63 *LA 87	an	4
E	3	5	3	1	3	1	-2	1	E	Beatus vir qui timet	WA 63	an	4
E	3	5	3	1	3	1	3	5		Et in terra	BOS #21		
E	3	5	3	1	3	5	3	0	D	Ex more docti mystico	ST 379	hy	1
E	3	5	3	1	3	5	3	0	D	Jam lucis orto sidere	ST 206	hy	1
E	3	5	3	1	3	5	3	0	D	Nunc sancte nobis spiritus	AR 370 LU 531	hy	1
D	3	5	3	2	-2	0	3	0		Diligam te Domine virtus mea Intonuit de caelo	OTT 58 *GB 134^{v} *SYG 156	ofv	
a	3	5	3	2	0	-2	0	-4	D	Sanctorum meritis inclyta gaudia	ST 199	hy	1
a	3	5	3	2	0	-2	0	2	G	Te lucis ante terminum	ST 79 84	hy	8
D	3	5	3	2	0	-2	0	3	D	Dum staret Abraham	WA 80	an	1
D	3	5	3	2	0	2	-2	-3	D	Agnus Dei	SCH #200		1

a	3	5	3	2	0	2	0	-2	G	Te lucis ante terminum	AR 58 AM 170	hy	8
D	3	5	3	2	0	2	3	2		Beatus es Simon Bar-jona	GB 204v	alv	
D	3	5	3	2	0	3	-2	0	F	Iste confessor Domini sacratus	ST 153	hy	6
D	3	5	3	2	0	3	0	2		Tristitia implebit cor	SYG 168	alv	
D	3	5	3	2	0	3	0	7		Per signum sanctae crucis	SYG 174	alv	
D	3	5	3	2	0	3	2	0	D	Sanctus	THAN #173		1
D	3	5	3	2	0	3	5	7	D	Alleluia: tota pulchra es Maria	GR 402 LU 1318	al	1
D	3	5	3	2	3	-2	0	3		Cantate Domino psalmum dicite Confirma hoc	OTT 79 *GB 189v SYG 183	ofv	
D	3	5	3	2	3	0	3	5	E	Alleluia: custodi innocentiam	GR 529	al	4
D	3	5	3	2	3	0	3	5	E	Alleluia: de excelso misit ignem	GR 501 LU 1473	al	4
D	3	5	3	2	3	0	3	5	E	Alleluia: laetamini cum Jerusalem	GR 510 LU 1483	al	4
a	3	5	3	2	3	2	-2	0		Adhuc me loquente et orante Oravi Deum	OTT 107 *GB 256v *SYG 250	ofv	
D	3	5	3	2	3	2	0	2	D	Si ambulem in medio umbrae	GR 137 SYG 99 GB 88v GS 61	gr	1
D	3	5	3	2	3	5	3	5	D	Invenerunt in modum	WA 409	re	1
D	3	5	3	2	3	5	7	5	D	Sacris solemniis juncta sint gaudia	ST 304	hy	1
D	3	5	3	2	3	7	5	3	D	Beata gens cujus est	GR 366 [91] LU 1048 *SYG 105 *GB 93 GS 67 160 234	gr	1
D	3	5	3	2	5	7	3	5	F	Sacerdos Dei Martine pastor	GB 243v	co	6
D	3	5	3	5	0	-2	3	5		Beati qui persecutionem	GB 267v	alv	
D	3	5	3	5	0	-2	3	5		Expansis manibus beata	GB 244	alv	
D	3	5	3	5	0	-2	3	5		Repletus sum consolatione	GR 547	alv	
a	3	5	3	5	0	3	2	0	G	Qui sedes Domine super Cherubim	GR 7 LU 335 SYG 6 GB 5v GS 4	gr	7
D	3	5	3	5	0	3	5	7	G	Dunstanus archiepiscopus	WA 314	re	8
D	3	5	3	5	0	3	5	7	G	Participem me fac	LA 132 *WA 88	re	8
D	3	5	3	5	2	0	2	3	D	Alleluia: obtulerunt discipuli	GB 133v	al	2
D	3	5	3	5	2	0	3	5	D	Alleluia: disposui testamentum	GB 272 *SYG 34 *GS 222	al	2
D	3	5	3	5	2	0	3	5	D	Alleluia: elegit te Dominus sibi	GB 28v *GS 223	al	2
D	3	5	3	5	2	0	3	5	[D]	Alleluia: hic est vere martyr quem coronavit	SYG 226	al	2
D	3	5	3	5	2	0	3	5	D	Alleluia: justum deduxit ... regnum	GB 271	al	2
D	3	5	3	5	2	0	3	5	D	Alleluia: lapidem quem reprobaverunt	SYG 161	al	2
D	3	5	3	5	2	0	3	5	[D]	Alleluia: Martialis magnus	SYG 208	al	2
D	3	5	3	5	2	0	3	5	D	Alleluia: oculis ac manibus in caelum	GB 242v	al	2

D	3	5	3	5	2	0	3	5	[D]	Alleluia: ora pro nobis beate Clemens	GB 245	al	2
D	3	5	3	5	2	0	3	5	D	Alleluia: posui adjutorium super potentem	GB 272	al	2
D	3	5	3	5	2	0	3	5	D	Alleluia: Saturninus pontifex magnus	SYG 230	al	1
a	3	5	3	5	2	3	2	-2	G	De ore prudentis procedit mel	OHS 780 *PM 230 *LR 88 *LA 384 *WA 306	re	7 8
D	3	5	3	5	2	3	2	0	D	Alleluia: in exitu Israel ex Aegypto	SYG 248	al	2
D	3	5	3	5	3	-2	0	3	F	In medio ecclesiae	GR [38] LU 1190 *SYG 24 GS 16 *GB 24	int	6
E	3	5	3	5	3	0	1	3	E	Fidelis Dominus in omnibus	AR 205 OHS 44 LU 312	an	4
D	3	5	3	5	3	0	2	-2	G	Annuntiate inter gentes gloriam	GR [128] LU 1295	tr	8
D	3	5	3	5	3	0	2	-2	G	Nunc dimittis servum tuum	GR 434 LU 1363 *SYG 50 *GS k	tr	8
E	3	5	3	5	3	0	3	5	E	Gloria XV	BOS #43 GR 51* LU 57		4
D	3	5	3	5	3	2	3	5	F	Exsultent in Domino sancti	LR 162 WA 304	inv	6
D	3	5	3	5	3	2	3	5	F	Sanctificavit tabernaculum ... venite	WA 319	inv	6
D	3	5	3	5	3	2	3	5	F	Surrexit Dominus vere	OHS 746 LR 82 LU 765 *LA 217 *WA 131	inv	6
D	3	5	3	5	3	2	3	5	F	Suscipiens Jesum in ulnas	VP 102 *LA 350 *WA 270	re	6
a	3	5	3	5	3	2	5	8	G	Bonum est confiteri Domino alleluia	LA 240 *WA 144	re	7
a	3	5	3	5	3	2	5	8	G	Dicant nunc qui redempti	LR 418 LA 241	re	7
a	3	5	3	5	3	2	5	8	G	Exaltare Domine alleluia in virtute	LR 98 *LA 246 *WA 147	re	7
A	3	5	3	5	3	5	3	2		Salvator mundi salva ... et cuncta Protege Domine	OTT 168 *GB 167 *SYG 174	ofv	
a	3	5	3	5	3	5	3	5		Adjuva me Domine Deus Confitebor Domino	OTT 74 *GB 162 *SYG 178	ofv	
A	3	5	3	5	3	5	3	5	D	Alleluia: ecce virgo concipiet	SYG 2	al	2
A	3	5	3	5	3	5	3	5	D	Alleluia: laudate Dominum omnes gentes	SYG 256 GS b *GB 263^{v}	al	2
A	3	5	3	5	3	5	3	5	D	Alleluia: nativitas tua Dei genitrix	GB 232	al	2
A	3	5	3	5	3	5	3	5	D	Alleluia: surrexit Christus qui creavit	GR 254 OHS 808 LU 798 SYG 159 GB 150 GS 129	al	2
a	3	5	3	5	3	5	3	5		In mente habete diem Erit vobis	OTT 63 GB 141^{v} SYG 160	ofv	
a	3	5	3	5	3	5	3	5		Quia ecce captaverunt Eripe me	OTT 46 *GB 101^{v} SYG 113	ofv	
D	3	5	3	5	3	5	3	5	F	Repleti sunt omnes spiritu	LA 264 *WA 154	inv	6
D	3	5	3	5	3	5	7	5	D	Ante me non est formatus	AR 230 LU 334 *AM 203 *WA 13 *LA 12	an	1

a	3	5	3	5	3	5	7	5	c	Ascendens Christus in altum	LA 252 *WA 150	inv	6
D	3	5	3	5	3	5	7	5	F	Beata es virgo Maria Dei genitrix	LR 258 VP 200 LA 445 WA 357	re	6
D	3	5	3	5	3	5	7	5	F	Beatus es Simon Bar-Jona	LR 367 *LA 418 WA 328	re	6
D	3	5	3	5	3	5	7	5	F	Confiteor tibi pater	GR 613 LU 1668	gr	5
D	3	5	3	5	3	5	7	5	F	In Deo confisum est	OHS 416 LU 662	gr	5
D	3	5	3	5	3	5	7	5	F	In Deo speravit cor meum	GR 348 LU 1025 *SYG 98 GB 87^v GS 60 152	gr	5
a	3	5	3	5	3	5	8	5	F	Exspectans exspectavi Dominum	GR 362 OTT 104 LU 1043 SYG 104 GB 92 *GS 66 159	of	5
A	3	5	3	5	3	5	8	7	D	Ad te Domine levavi animam ... Deus ... neque	GR 3 LU 321 OTT 5 SYG 2 GB 1^v GS 2 33 51 152	of	2
A	3	5	3	5	3	5	8	7	D	Alleluia: initium sapientiae timor	GR 112**	al	2
A	3	5	3	5	3	5	8	7	D	Alleluia: oculus Dei respexit illum	GR 604 LU 1646	al	2
A	3	5	3	5	3	5	8	7	D	Alleluia: sicut cinnamomum	GR 34**	al	2
a	3	5	3	5	7	3	2	3	G	Liberasti nos Domine ex affligentibus	GR 387 LU 1075 GS e *SYG 258 GB 264^v	gr	7
a	3	5	3	5	7	3	2	3	G	Salvasti enim nos Deus	GR 98**	gr	7
D	3	5	3	5	7	3	2	5	D	Recordare quod steterim	GS 78	of	1
D	3	5	3	5	7	3	2	5	D	Recordare virgo mater in conspectu	GR 600 47** LU 1557 1637	of	1
D	3	5	3	5	7	3	5	3	F	Discerne causam meam Domine	GR 158 SYG 112 GB 100 GS 74	gr	5
A	3	5	3	5	7	3	5	3	D	Kyrie virginis odas	MEL #224		
D	3	5	3	5	7	3	5	3	F	Pacifice loquebantur mihi	GR 164 SYG 116 GB 103^v GS 77	gr	5
a	3	5	3	5	7	3	5	7	a	Ad te Domine levavi animam ... veni	AR 242 AM 217 *WA 20 *LA 27	an	4
a	3	5	3	5	7	3	5	7	a	Ex Aegypto vocavi	AR 222 LU 1083 AM 194 *WA 16 *LA 7	an	4
D	3	5	3	5	7	3	5	7	D	Ex quo facta est vox	AR 248 772 LU 1541 AM 224 955 *WA 19 *LA 26	an	1
D	3	5	3	5	7	5	-2	0	G	Dixit Dominus mulieri	WA 94 *LA 143	an	8
D	3	5	3	5	7	5	0	3	G	Jesu corona celsior	ST 371	hy	8
D	3	5	3	5	7	5	0	3	E	Te Deum laudamus	WA 5		3
D	3	5	3	5	7	5	0	5		Adversum me exercebantur Improperium exspectavit	OTT 49 GB 110^v SYG 123	of	
D	3	5	3	5	7	5	3	5	F	Christum regem crucifixum	LR 437	inv	6
E	3	5	3	5	7	5	3	5		Et in terra	BOS #43 GR 51* LU 57		
D	3	5	3	5	7	5	3	5	D	Nativitas tua Dei genitrix	WA 366	re	1

D	3	5	3	5	7	5	3	5	D	Qui me dignatus est	WA 274	re	1
D	3	5	3	5	7	5	3	5	F	Regem apostolorum Dominum	LR 162	inv	6
D	3	5	3	5	7	5	3	5	F	Regem confessorum Dominum	LR 190	inv	6
D	3	5	3	5	7	5	3	5	F	Regem virginum Dominum	LR 211	inv	6
D	3	5	3	5	7	5	7	3	D	Alleluia: justus germinabit sicut lilium	GR [40](42) LU 1192 *SYG 207 *GB 270^{v} GS 222	al	1
a	3	5	3	5	7	5	7	5	c	Abscondi tamquam aurum	LA 85 WA 61	re	6
D	3	5	3	5	7	5	7	5	F	Annuntiavi justitiam in coetu	LU 1623^{B}	gr	5
D	3	5	3	5	7	5	7	5	F	Da nobis Deus auxilium	GR 107**	gr	5
D	3	5	3	5	7	5	7	5	F	Diffusa est gratia in labiis	GR 559 LU 1572 *SYG 6 GB 5 GS 230	co	6
D	3	5	3	5	7	5	7	5	F	Dixerunt discipuli ad beatum Martinum	GB 242	gr	5
D	3	5	3	5	7	5	7	5	F	Electi mei non laborabunt	GR 444 LU 1386	gr	5
D	3	5	3	5	7	5	7	5	F	Honora Dominum de tua substantia	GR 349 LU 1026 *SYG 246 GB 253^{v} GS 153	co	6
D	3	5	3	5	7	5	7	5	G	In die resurrectionis ... congregabo	SYG 146	an	8
D	3	5	3	5	7	5	7	5	F	Propitius esto Domine peccatis	GR 107 LU 999 *SYG 81 GB 78^{v} GS 42 51 145 170	gr	5
D	3	5	3	5	7	5	7	5	F	Quemadmodum desiderat cervus	GR 506 LU 1478	gr	5
D	3	5	3	5	7	5	7	5	F	Suscepimus Deus misericordiam	GR 433 LU 1362 *SYG 48 *GB 47^{v} GS j	gr	5
E	3	5	3	5	7	8	5	0	E	Crucem tuam adoramus	GR 217 OHS 577 LU 741 *VP 273 *LA 463 *GS 102 SYG 141	an	4
A	3	5	3	5	7	8	5	3	D	Miserator Dominus escam	AR 525 LU 956 AM 544	an	2
A	3	5	3	5	7	8	5	8	D	Kyrie o pater immense	MEL #223		
a	3	5	3	5	7	8	7	3		Confitemini Domino quoniam bonus Haec dies	GR 241 LU 778 OHS 709 GS 117 *GB 125 *SYG 152	grv	
a	3	5	3	5	7	8	7	3		Dicant nunc qui redempti Haec dies	GR 247(241) OHS 784(709) LU 790(778) *GS 119(117) SYG 156(152) *GB 133(125)	grv	
a	3	5	3	5	7	8	7	3		Dicat nunc Israel Haec dies	GR 245(241) OHS 774(709) LU 786(778) *GS 118(117) *SYG 155(152) *GB 131(125)	grv	
a	3	5	3	5	7	8	7	3		Jucundus homo qui miseretur Deriventur fontes	GR 555 LU 1562	grv	
a	3	5	3	5	7	8	7	3		Quis ascendet in montem Tollite portas	GR 9 LU 1269 *GS 5 *GB 6^{v} *SYG 8	grv	
E	3	5	3	5	7	8	7	5	E	Aurora caelum purpurat	AR 459	hy	3
A	3	5	3	5	7	8	7	5	D	Igitur Joseph ductus	WA 95	re	2
E	3	5	3	5	7	8	7	5	E	Te Deum laudamus	GR 147*		3

E	3	5	3	5	7	8	7	5	E	Te Deum laudamus	AR 69* GR 144* LR 37 LU 1834 OHS 791 VP 25		3
E	3	5	3	5	7	8	7	5	E	Te Deum laudamus	AR 66* GR 141* LU 1832 *AM 1250 LR 34 OHS 761 PM 96 VP 22 15*		3
A	3	5	3	5	8	5	0	3	D	Puer fletum subsecute	WA 299	re	1
A	3	5	3	5	8	5	3	5	D	Cibavit eos ex adipe frumenti	GR [95] SYG 184 LU 1282 GB 191	int	2
A	3	5	3	5	8	5	3	5	D	Cibavit eos ex adipe frumenti ... alleluia	GR 297 313 LU 887 943 GS 138	int	2
A	3	5	3	5	8	5	3	8	D	Laudate Dominum Deum nostrum	WA 178	re	2
A	3	5	3	5	8	5	7	5		Nativitas tua Dei genitrix	GB 232	alv	
A	3	5	3	5	8	5	7	5		Surrexit Christus qui creavit	GR 254 OHS 808 LU 798 *SYG 159 GB 150 GS 129	alv	
A	3	5	3	5	8	5	8	3	D	Jesu corona virginum	ST 244	hy	2
E	3	5	3	5	8	7	3	5		Oravit Moyses Dominum Sanctificavit Moyses	OTT 114 GB 259v SYG 254	ofv	
E	3	5	3	5	8	7	5	7	E	In caelesti collegio	VP 226	hy	4
E	3	5	3	5	8	7	5	8	E	Proles de caelo prodiit	ST 442	hy	3
E	3	5	3	5	8	7	8	10	G	Maria quae mortalium	AR 4 (sup 1)	hy	8
a	3	5	3	5	8	10	8	7		Si oblitus fuero tui Super flumina	OTT 119 GB 102v SYG 115	ofv	
D	3	5	3	7	3	7	10	5	F	Adesto dolori meo Deus	LA 286	re	6
D	3	5	3	7	5	0	3	5	G	Bellator armis inclytus	ST 6	hy	8
D	3	5	3	7	5	0	3	5	G	Caeli Deus sanctissime	AM 148	hy	8
D	3	5	3	7	5	0	3	5	G	Immense caeli conditor	AM 136	hy	8
D	3	5	3	7	5	0	3	5	G	Jesu corona celsior	ST 16	hy	8
D	3	5	3	7	5	0	3	5	G	Magnae Deus potentiae	AM 153	hy	8
D	3	5	3	7	5	0	3	5	G	Miraculum laudabile	ST 7	hy	8
D	3	5	3	7	5	0	3	5	G	Plasmator hominis Deus	AM 157	hy	8
D	3	5	3	7	5	0	3	5	G	Telluris ingens conditor	AM 141	hy	8
a	3	5	3	7	5	3	0	2		Confitemini Domino et invocate	GR 376 LU 1060 *SYG 250 GB 162 GS 157	alv	
D	3	5	3	7	5	3	5	3	F	Beatam me dicent ... quia fecit	GR 584 LU 1604	co	6
D	3	5	3	7	5	7	3	7	D	Alleluia: ego rogabo patrem	SYG 185	al	1
D	3	5	3	7	5	7	3	7	D	Alleluia: ego veritatem dico	SYG 167	al	1
D	3	5	3	7	5	7	3	7	D	Alleluia: vir Domini Benedictus	SYG 207	al	1
E	3	5	3	7	5	7	5	[0]	[E]	Agnus Dei	SCH #181		4
a	3	5	3	7	5	7	5	3	F	Euntes praedicate evangelium	SYG 233	co	5
D	3	5	3	7	5	7	5	3	F	Repletus sancto spiritu	SYG 56	gr	6

D	3	5	3	7	5	7	10	7	D	Alleluia: cantate Domino canticum novum	GR 364 LU 1045 SYG 247	al	1
D	3	5	3	7	5	7	10	7	D	Alleluia: omnes gentes plaudite manibus	GR 337 LU 1011 SYG 241 *GS 133 GB 177	al	1
D	3	5	3	7	5	7	10	7	D	Alleluia: qui timent Dominum sperent	GR 385 LU 1072 *GS 160 SYG 249	al	1
D	3	5	3	7	5	7	10	7	D	Alleluia: timete Dominum omnes sancti	SYG 212	al	1
A	3	5	3	7	8	7	5	7		Pulcher virtutibus Immaculatas hostiarum	SYG 220	ofv	
a	3	5	3	7	8	10	5	3	c	Responsum acceperat Simeon	LA 349 *WA 269	re	6
D	3	5	3	7	9	10	7	5	G	Introduxit vos Dominus	GR 244 OHS 773 LU 785 SYG 154 GB 129 *GS 118	int	8
E	3	5	3	8	7	3	5	1	C	Ave maris stella Dei mater alma	ST 115	hy	5
D	3	5	3	8	7	5	3	2	F	Languentibus in purgatorio	AR 198*	hy	6
E	3	5	3	8	7	5	3	5		Dulce lignum dulces clavos	GR 491 LU 1456 GS 185 235 SYG 174 *GB 165	alv	
D	3	5	3	8	7	5	3	5	F	Transiturus de mundo	LR 132	re	6
E	3	5	3	8	7	5	3	8	G	Alleluia: dulce lignum dulces clavos	GR 491 LU 1456 GS 185 235 SYG 174 *GB 165	al	8
D	3	5	3	8	7	5	7	3	F	Alleluia: audi filia ... quia concupivit	GB 272^v	al	6
D	3	5	3	8	7	5	7	3	F	Alleluia: Domine in virtute tua	GR 333 LU 1003 GB 249^v GS 144 *SYG 240	al	6
D	3	5	3	8	7	5	7	3	F	Alleluia: in omnem terram exivit sonus eorum	GS x	al	6
D	3	5	3	8	7	5	7	3	F	Alleluia: magnificat anima mea Dominum	GR 587^3 49** LU 1612^2	al	6
D	3	5	3	8	7	5	7	3	F	Alleluia: vir Dei Benedictus	GR (25)	al	6
E	3	5	3	8	7	5	7	3	G	Alleluia: virga Jesse floruit	GR [79] LU 1267	al	8
D	3	5	3	8	7	5	7	3		In omnem terram exivit sonus eorum	GS x	alv	
A	3	5	3	8	7	8	10	8	D	Excellenti prosapia	WA 282	re	2
A	3	5	7	0	3	5	7	8	D	Adjutor meus et liberator	GR 115 SYG 87 GB 76^v GS 48	gr	2
E	3	5	7	3	0	1	3	1	E	Laetatus sum in his	AR 100 OHS 225 LU 282	an	4
A	3	5	7	3	0	3	0	3	D	Benedicite gentes Dominum	GR 272 OTT 71 LU 832 GS 67 131 SYG 105 GB 93^v	of	2
A	3	5	7	3	0	3	2	3	D	Desiderium pauperum exaudivit	GR 589 LU 1616	of	2
A	3	5	7	3	0	5	3	5	D	Angelus Domini apparuit Joseph	LR 310	re	2
A	3	5	7	3	0	5	3	5	D	Angelus Domini vocavit	LA 121 WA 82	re	2
D	3	5	7	3	2	0	3	0	G	Ante sex dies passionis	GS 81	an	8

A	3	5	7	3	2	0	3	7	D	Exsurge Domine adjuva nos	GR 274 429 PM 133 LU 835 1358 *WA 226	an	2
D	3	5	7	3	2	0	5	7	G	Insigne praeconium alme	WA 384	an	8
D	3	5	7	3	5	3	2	0	F	Exaltent eum in ecclesia	GR 408 $[2^1]$ LU 1122^2 *GB 244^v GS 182	gr	5
D	3	5	7	3	5	3	2	0	F	Quis sicut Dominus Deus	GR 369 GS 168 SYG 251 GB 257^v	gr	5
D	3	5	7	3	5	3	2	0	F	Timebunt gentes nomen tuum	GR 71 LU 489 *SYG 42 GB 39 GS 23 159	gr	5
D	3	5	7	3	5	3	5	2	D	Caeli Deus sanctissime	ST 214	hy	2
D	3	5	7	3	5	3	5	2	D	Immense caeli conditor	ST 213	hy	2
D	3	5	7	3	5	3	5	2	D	Magnae Deus potentiae	ST 214	hy	2
D	3	5	7	3	5	3	5	2	D	Plasmator hominis Deus	ST 214	hy	2
D	3	5	7	3	5	3	5	2	D	Telluris ingens conditor	ST 213	hy	2
E	3	5	7	3	5	3	5	7	G	Alleluia: confitemini Domino quoniam bonus	GR 236 LU 776^{II} OHS 682 SYG 152 *GB 122 *GS 115	al	8
D	3	5	7	3	5	7	10	7		Persequar inimicos meos Factus est Dominus	OTT 42 GB 96^v SYG 108	ofv	
D	3	5	7	3	5	8	7	5	F	O quam praeclara sunt	VP 106	an	6
D	3	5	7	3	7	10	9	7	G	Lex veritatis fuit in ore ejus	GR 526 LU 1511	int	8
D	3	5	7	3	7	10	9	7	G	Lux fulgebit hodie super nos	GR 30 LU 403 SYG 15 GB 15 GS E	int	8
D	3	5	7	3	7	10	9	7	G	Vidi civitatem ... novam ... sicut	GR 439 LU 1376	int	8
D	3	5	7	5	-2	0	3	5	G	Domine dilexi decorem	SYG 85	int	8
D	3	5	7	5	-2	0	3	5	G	Domine ne longe facias	GR 178 OHS 106 LU 592 SYG 121 GB 108^v *GS 86	int	8
D	3	5	7	5	0	3	2	3	G	In hymnis et confessionibus	PM 115 LA 296 *WA 181	re	8
A	3	5	7	5	0	3	5	7	D	Repleta est malis	GR 9**	gr	2
D	3	5	7	5	0	3	5	7	G	Sanctus	THAN #172		8
E	3	5	7	5	1	3	8	3	G	Alleluia: scitote quoniam Dominus ipse est	GR [129] LU 1296	al	8
D	3	5	7	5	2	0	3	7	D	Plaudat chorus fidelium	ST 130	hy	1
D	3	5	7	5	2	3	0	2	G	Elegit Deus beatum Hilarium	PM 342	re	8
D	3	5	7	5	2	3	5	2	D	Vos qui secuti ... sedebitis	GR 448 LU 1392	co	1
D	3	5	7	5	2	3	5	3	F	Beatus quicumque times	LU 1442	gr	5
E	3	5	7	5	3	1	3	5	E	A viro iniquo	AM 150 *WA 68 *LA 99	an	4
D	3	5	7	5	3	2	0	-2		Animae eorum in bonis Requiem aeternam	GB 265^v *GS 232	grv	
D	3	5	7	5	3	2	0	3	D	Benedicamus Domino IV	AR 61* LR 44 LU 126		1
a	3	5	7	5	3	2	0	3		Famulos respice Christe Beatam Aredii animam	SYG 219	grv	

D	3	5	7	5	3	2	0	3	D	Ite missa est IX	GR 35* LU 43		1
D	3	5	7	5	3	2	0	3	D	Kyrie alme pater fili (etc)	MEL #171		
D	3	5	7	5	3	2	0	3	D	Kyrie IX cum jubilo	GR 32* LU 40		1
D	3	5	7	5	3	2	0	3	E	Nocte surgentes vigilemus omnes	ST 263	hy	4
a	3	5	7	5	3	2	3	0		A summo caelo egressio In sole posuit tabernaculum	GR 14 LU 344 GS 8 *SYG 10 GB 8^{v}	grv	
a	3	5	7	5	3	2	3	0		Ad annuntiandum mane Justus ut palma	GR [42] LU 1201 GS 202 GB 23 SYG 195	grv	
a	3	5	7	5	3	2	3	0		Benedictus qui venit in nomine Haec dies	GR 256(241) OHS 817(709) LU 801(778) GS 122(117) SYG 160(152) GB 140(125)	grv	
a	3	5	7	5	3	2	3	0		Benedixisti Domine terram tuam Ostende nobis Domine	GR 11 GS 7 GB 8 SYG 9	grv	
a	3	5	7	5	3	2	3	0		Caeli enarrant gloriam Dei A summo caelo	GR 13 LU 343 GS 8 SYG 10 *GB 8^{v}	grv	
a	3	5	7	5	3	2	3	0		Caeli enarrant gloriam Dei In omnem terram	GR 629 LU 1486 GS x GB 202^{v}	grv	
a	3	5	7	5	3	2	3	0		Cantate Domino canticum ... laus Exsultabunt sancti	GR 646 GS 214 GB 210 SYG 205	grv	
D	3	5	7	5	3	2	3	0		Confiteantur Domino misericordiae Exaltent eum	GB 244^{v} SYG 53	grv	
a	3	5	7	5	3	2	3	0		Dextera Domini fecit virtutem Haec dies	GR 250(241) OHS 796(709) LU 793(778) GS 120(117) SYG 157(152) GB 135^{v}(125)	grv	
a	3	5	7	5	3	2	3	0		Dinumerabo eos et super arenam Nimis honorati	GR 391 LU 1326 GS w GB 235 SYG 54	grv	
a	3	5	7	5	3	2	3	0		Dixit Dominus Domino meo Tecum principium	GR 28 LU 393 GS 13 GB 13^{v} SYG 14	grv	
a	3	5	7	5	3	2	3	0		Domine quis habitabit Qui ambulat fraudulenter	GR 30**	grv	
a	3	5	7	5	3	2	3	0		Et exaltent eum in ecclesia Sacrificent Domino	GR 89**	grv	
a	3	5	7	5	3	2	3	0		Excita Domine potentiam tuam Domine Deus virtutum	GR 15 LU 345 GS 8 GB 8 SYG 10	grv	
a	3	5	7	5	3	2	3	0		Filii tui sicut novellae Uxor tua	GR [122] LU 1289	grv	
a	3	5	7	5	3	2	3	0		In manibus portabunt te Angelis suis	GR 94 LU 533 GS 34 GB 65 SYG 72	grv	
a	3	5	7	5	3	2	3	0		In memoria aeterna Requiem aeternam	GR 95* LU 1808 SYG 235	grv	
a	3	5	7	5	3	2	3	0		Memores erunt nominis tui Exsultabit cor meum	GR 587^{1} LU 1612^{1}	grv	
a	3	5	7	5	3	2	3	0		Potens in terra erit semen Dispersit dedit pauperibus	GR 576 LU 1608 GS 193 GB 216^{v} SYG 212	grv	
a	3	5	7	5	3	2	3	0		Priusquam montes fierent Domine refugium	GR 381 LU 1067 GB 262 SYG 256 GS 34 165	grv	

a	3	5	7	5	3	2	3	0		Qui regis Israel intende Excita Domine	GR 15 LU 347 GS 9 GB 9 SYG 10	grv	
a	3	5	7	5	3	2	3	0		Qui regis Israel intende Hodie scietis	GR 24 LU 360 SYG 13 GB 12^{v} GS 12	grv	
D	3	5	7	5	3	2	3	0		Quia eripuit animam Convertere animam	GB 265^{v}	grv	
a	3	5	7	5	3	2	3	0		Salvum me fac Deus Ne avertas faciem	GR 190 OHS 322 LU 617 GS 91 GB 113^{v} SYG 127	grv	
a	3	5	7	5	3	2	3	0		Si mei non fuerint Ab occultis meis	GR 130 GS 57 SYG 81 *GB 84^{v}	grv	
a	3	5	7	5	3	2	3	0		Tu autem Domine in aeternum Dies mei sicut umbra	GB 104^{v}	grv	
D	3	5	7	5	3	2	3	2	G	Ante sex dies solemnis Paschae	PM 57 GR 174 *WA 207 *SYG 119 *GB 106^{v}	an	8
D	3	5	7	5	3	2	3	5	G	Agnus Dei	SCH #232		2
D	3	5	7	5	3	2	3	5	G	Dixit Dominus ad Adam	AR 341 LU 496 AM 311 LA 1	an	8
D	3	5	7	5	3	5	3	0		Obtulerunt discipuli Domino	GB 133^{v}	alv	
D	3	5	7	5	3	5	3	2		Quae meruit Dominum progenerare Candida virginitas	PM 264 VP 40	rev	
D	3	5	7	5	3	5	3	2	D	Sanctus	THAN #171		1
A	3	5	7	5	3	5	3	7	D	Jam Christus sol justitiae	AM 338	hy	2
E	3	5	7	5	3	5	3	7	E	Nunc sancte nobis spiritus	ST 154	hy	3
A	3	5	7	5	3	5	3	8	D	Dominus fortitudo plebis suae	GR 334 LU 1006 SYG 242 GB 249^{v} GS 146	int	2
D	3	5	7	5	3	5	7	5	F	Alleluia: tu es vas electionis	SYG 205	al	6
D	3	5	7	5	3	5	7	5	E	Cum rex gloriae Christus	WA 225	an	3
E	3	5	7	5	3	5	7	5	a	Det vobis Deus idipsum	GR [133]	of	2
E	3	5	7	5	3	5	7	5	a	Dextera Domini fecit virtutem	GR 72 196 492 OHS 455 LU 677 1457 OTT 25 *SYG 43 GB 39^{v} GS 23 57 95	of	2
a	3	5	7	5	3	5	7	5		Et in terra	BOS #2		
D	3	5	7	5	3	5	7	5		Et in terra	BOS #39		
E	3	5	7	5	3	5	7	5	a	In omnem terram exivit sonus eorum	GR 406 LU 1327 OTT 130 SYG 54 GB 236 GS z 203	of	2
A	3	5	7	5	3	5	7	5	D	O virum ineffabilem	GB 243^{v}	of	2
A	3	5	7	5	3	5	7	8	D	Ecce advenit dominator Dominus	GR 57 LU 459 SYG 30 GB 32 GS J	int	2
A	3	5	7	5	3	5	7	8	D	Salve sancta parens	GR [75] LU 1263 GS q *GB 220	int	2
A	3	5	7	5	3	5	7	8	D	Signum salutis pone Domine	GB 157^{v}	an	2
A	3	5	7	5	3	5	7	8	D	Veni et ostende nobis	GR 13 LU 343 *SYG 10 *GB 8^{v} *GS 7	int	2

A	3	5	7	5	3	5	8	5	D	Dominus illuminatio mea	GR 330 LU 998 *SYG 241 GB 248^v GS 144	int	2
A	3	5	7	5	3	5	8	5	D	In sanctis crescens	WA 293	re	2
A	3	5	7	5	3	5	8	5	D	Per ipsam te deprecor	WA 243	re	2
E	3	5	7	5	3	5	8	5	a	Vir erat in terra nomine Job	GR 382 OTT 122 LU 1069 SYG 256 GB 262 GS 166	of	2
A	3	5	7	5	3	5	8	7	D	Accinxit fortitudine	LR 228	re	2
A	3	5	7	5	3	7	5	7	D	A facie furoris tui	LA 305 WA 186	re	2
D	3	5	7	5	3	7	5	7	G	Adesto dolori meo Deus	WA 174	re	8
a	3	5	7	5	3	7	5	7	D	Gloria ad lib. II	BOS #13 GR 85* LU 88		2
D	3	5	7	5	3	7	9	10	G	Praecursor Domini venit	LR 356 384 AM 1197 *LA 405 *WA 322	re	8
A	3	5	7	5	3	8	10	8	D	Loquebantur variis linguis ... prout	LA 259	re	2
D	3	5	7	5	7	3	0	2	G	Sustinuimus pacem et non venit	LA 303 *WA 184	re	8
D	3	5	7	5	7	3	0	3	G	Auditu auris audivi	WA 175	re	8
D	3	5	7	5	7	3	0	3	G	Beatissimus Christi martyr	WA 351	re	8
D	3	5	7	5	7	3	0	3	G	Beatus vir qui metuit	LR 165 LA 384 WA 304	re	8
D	3	5	7	5	7	3	0	3	G	Multiplicati sunt qui tribulant	LR 415 LA 166 WA 105	re	8
D	3	5	7	5	7	3	0	3	D	Tu puer propheta ... praeibis ... faciem	GR 525 LU 1502 *SYG 199 *GB 200^v GS m	co	2
D	3	5	7	5	7	3	0	3	D	Tu puer propheta ... praeibis ... faciem	LR 358	re	1
D	3	5	7	5	7	3	5	3	F	Diffusa est gratia in labiis	GR [69] LU 1240 SYG 28 *GB 29^v *GS 227	gr	5
D	3	5	7	5	7	3	5	3	F	Venite filii audite me	GR 336(39) LU 1010 *SYG 105 GB 93 GS 67 *148 168	gr	5
D	3	5	7	5	7	3	5	7	G	Iste homo ab adolescentia	LA 534 WA 426	re	8
D	3	5	7	5	7	5	2	3	E	Deus meus impolluta via	GR 97**	int	4
D	3	5	7	5	7	5	2	3	G	Diem festum sacratissimae	LA 332 WA 253	re	8
D	3	5	7	5	7	5	3	5	G	Adducam eos in montem	GR 446 LU 1387	of	8
D	3	5	7	5	7	5	3	5	D	Adesto Deus unus	WA 158	an	1
D	3	5	7	5	7	5	3	5	G	Cantantibus organis Caecilia virgo	LA 489 WA 406	re	8
D	3	5	7	5	7	5	3	5	G	Capillus de capite vestro	GR (22)	of	8
D	3	5	7	5	7	5	3	5	D	Emitte spiritum sanctum	SYG 21	an	1
D	3	5	7	5	7	5	3	5		Facta est Judaea In exitu Israel	SYG 248	alv	
D	3	5	7	5	7	5	3	5	E	Justitiae Domini rectae	GR 126 OTT 94 LU 555 SYG 93 GB 82^v GS 55 151	of	4

D	3	5	7	5	7	5	3	5		Legem pone mihi Domine et viam Levabo oculos	OTT 34 GB 67v SYG 76	ofv	
D	3	5	7	5	7	5	3	5	G	Levabo oculos meos et considerabo	GR 100 OTT 34 *SYG 76 GB 67v GS 38	of	8
D	3	5	7	5	7	5	3	5	F	Qui me dignatus est	GR 437 LU 1370 *SYG 51 GB 50v GS 181	co	6
D	3	5	7	5	7	5	3	5	G	Tamquam aurum in fornace	LR 184 LA 519	re	8
A	3	5	7	5	7	5	3	5	D	Te decet laus te decet hymnus	AM 1261 *AR 209 *LR 42	hy	2
D	3	5	7	5	7	5	3	5	G	Tribularer si nescirem	PM 48 LR 404 VP 119 LA 130 WA 87	re	8
D	3	5	7	5	7	5	3	7	G	Si oblitus fuero tui	LR 417 LA 237 WA 143	re	8
D	3	5	7	5	7	5	7	3		In exitu Israel ex Aegypto	SYG 248	alv	
D	3	5	7	5	7	5	7	3	G	Juravit Dominus et non paenitebit	LR 195 *LA 531 WA 425	re	8
a	3	5	7	5	7	5	7	3		Pereant peccatores a facie Mirabilis Deus	OTT 141 GB 171 SYG 175	ofv	
D	3	5	7	5	7	5	7	5	G	Abscondite eleemosynam in sinu	LA 129 *WA 86	re	8
D	3	5	7	5	7	5	7	5		Beatus es Simon Petre Tu es Petrus	SYG 203	alv	
D	3	5	7	5	7	5	7	5	G	Cilicio Caecilia membra	LA 491 WA 406	re	8
D	3	5	7	5	7	5	7	5	G	Congregatae sunt gentes	LA 298 WA 181	re	8
D	3	5	7	5	7	5	7	5	G	Dedisti Domine habitaculum	LA 495 WA 409	re	8
D	3	5	7	5	7	5	7	5	G	Disrumpam vincula populi	WA 182	re	8
D	3	5	7	5	7	5	7	5	E	Exaudivit de templo sancto	GR 282 LU 840 SYG 177 GB 161v GS 132	int	4
D	3	5	7	5	7	5	7	5	G	Exclamantes autem Judaei	WA 35	re	8
D	3	5	7	5	7	5	7	5	G	Exemplo vitae venerabilis	LR 291	re	8
D	3	5	7	5	7	5	7	5	G	Medicinam carnalem corpori	LA 362	re	8
A	3	5	7	5	7	5	7	5	D	Narrabo nomen tuum	LA 238 *WA 143	re	2
D	3	5	7	5	7	5	7	5	G	Non eris inter virgines	WA 432	re	8
D	3	5	7	5	7	5	7	5	G	Orante sancto Clemente apparuit	PM 213 LA 495 *WA 409	re	8
D	3	5	7	5	7	5	7	5	G	Orietur stella ex Jacob	LA 23 WA 5	re	8
D	3	5	7	5	7	5	7	5	G	Sanctificamini filii Israel	LA 29 WA 26	re	8
D	3	5	7	5	7	5	7	5	G	Sic eum volo manere	LA 53 WA 41	re	8
D	3	5	7	5	7	5	7	5	G	Sicut mater consolatur	LA 8 *WA 10	re	8
D	3	5	7	5	7	5	7	5	G	Tulerunt Dominum meum	OHS 802 LR 90 LA 211 WA 131	re	8
D	3	5	7	5	7	5	7	5	G	Vocavit angelus Domini	LA 122	re	8
D	3	5	7	5	7	5	7	9	G	Adest namque beati Dionysii	WA 387	re	8
D	3	5	7	5	7	5	7	9	G	Ait autem Abraham	WA 81	re	8

D	3	5	7	5	7	5	7	9	G	Alieni non transibunt	WA 10 LA 4	re	8
D	3	5	7	5	7	5	7	9	G	Angustiae mihi undique	LA 304 *WA 185	re	8
D	3	5	7	5	7	5	7	9	G	Attendite popule meus legem	LA 159 WA 102	re	8
D	3	5	7	5	7	5	7	9	G	Beata Caecilia dixit Tiburtio	LA 492 *WA 407	re	8
D	3	5	7	5	7	5	7	9	G	Beatus Andreas de cruce	WA 235	re	8
D	3	5	7	5	7	5	7	9	G	Benedic Domine domum istam	LR 235 LA 548	re	8
D	3	5	7	5	7	5	7	9	G	Constantes estote videbitis	LA 29 WA 25	re	8
D	3	5	7	5	7	5	7	9	G	Contristatus est rex	WA 362	re	8
D	3	5	7	5	7	5	7	9	G	Deus canticum novum	LA 239 WA 145	re	8
D	3	5	7	5	7	5	7	9	G	Dum aurora finem ... dixit	WA 408	re	8
D	3	5	7	5	7	5	7	9	G	Erat namque in sermone	LA 325	re	8
D	3	5	7	5	7	5	7	9	G	Erumpant montes	LA 10	re	8
D	3	5	7	5	7	5	7	9	G	In conspectu angelorum ... et adorabo	AM 1202 *LR 384 *VP 216 LA 466 WA 381	re	8
D	3	5	7	5	7	5	7	9	G	In hoc ergo loco	WA 388	re	8
D	3	5	7	5	7	5	7	9	G	In isto loco promissio	LA 330	re	8
D	3	5	7	5	7	5	7	9	G	In tempore illo consurget	LA 469 WA 382	re	8
D	3	5	7	5	7	5	7	9	G	Maria Magdalene et altera	OHS 758 LA 209 WA 131	re	8
D	3	5	7	5	7	5	7	9	G	Non discedimus a te	LR 19 WA 24	re	8
D	3	5	7	5	7	5	7	9	G	O Hippolyte si credideris	WA 351	re	8
D	3	5	7	5	7	5	7	9	G	Pacifice loquebantur mihi	LA 170 WA 107	re	8
D	3	5	7	5	7	5	7	9	G	Sebastianus Dei cultor	LA 324	re	8
D	3	5	7	5	7	5	7	10	G	Disciplinam et sapientiam	LR 114 *LA 257 *WA 154	re	8
D	3	5	7	5	7	5	7	10	G	Elegit eum Dominus et excelsum	PM 311	re	8
D	3	5	7	5	7	5	7	10	G	Iste homo perfecit omnia	LR 207 WA 426	re	8
D	3	5	7	5	7	5	7	10	G	Ornatam monilibus	PM 259 LR 253 VP 220 *LA 445 WA 356	re	8
D	3	5	7	5	7	5	7	10	G	Ostendit mihi Dominus civitatem	LR 272	re	8
A	3	5	7	5	7	5	8	7	D	Barrabas latro dimittitur	WA 122	re	2
A	3	5	7	5	7	5	8	7	D	In patre manet	WA 50	re	2
D	3	5	7	5	7	5	8	7	E	Intonuit de caelo Dominus	GR 249 OTT 58 LU 791 OHS 786 SYG 156 GB 134^{v} GS 119 138	of	4
D	3	5	7	5	7	5	8	7	E	Intonuit Dominus de caelo	GR (14)	of	4
A	3	5	7	5	7	5	8	7	D	Surrexerunt quidem de Synagoga	LA 42	re	2
D	3	5	7	5	7	5	8	7	D	Synagoga populorum circumdederunt	OHS 242 (nm) WA 111	re	2
D	3	5	7	5	7	5	10	12	E	Gaude visceribus mater in intimis	ST 236	hy	3

D	3	5	7	5	7	5	10	12	E	Sanctorum meritis inclyta gaudia	ST 242	hy	3
E	3	5	7	5	7	8	7	5	E	Alleluia: spiritus Domini replevit orbem	SYG 183	al	3
E	3	5	7	5	7	8	7	5	[E]	Alleluia: spiritus ubi vult spirat	SYG 186	al	3
A	3	5	7	5	7	8	7	8	D	Deprecamur te Domine	GB 157	an	2
A	3	5	7	5	7	8	7	8	D	Non nos demergat Domine	GB 159^v	an	2
A	3	5	7	5	7	8	10	7	D	Accedite ad Dominum et	GR 106**	of	2
E	3	5	7	5	7	8	10	7	a	Tollite portas principes	GR 26 OTT 14 LU 362 *SYG 14 *GB 13 *GS 13	of	2
D	3	5	7	5	7	9	7	3	G	Numquid scis quare	WA 185	re	8
D	3	5	7	5	7	9	7	5	G	Afflicti pro peccatis nostris	VP 262 LA 84 *WA 62	re	8
D	3	5	7	5	7	9	7	5	G	Astiterunt reges terrae	OHS 616 LU 771 *LA 205	re	8
D	3	5	7	5	7	9	7	5	G	Beatam me dicent ... quia fecit	PM 258 LR 257 LA 444 *WA 356	re	8
D	3	5	7	5	7	9	7	5	G	In illo tempore exauditae	PM 198	re	8
D	3	5	7	5	7	9	7	5	D	Kyrie	MEL #170		
D	3	5	7	5	7	9	7	5	G	Omni tempore benedic Deum	LA 288 *WA 176	re	8
D	3	5	7	5	7	9	7	5	G	Orantibus in loco isto	LR 238	re	8
D	3	5	7	5	7	9	7	5	G	Percussit Saul mille	LA 268	re	8
D	3	5	7	5	7	9	7	5	G	Repleatur os meum laude ut hymnum	LA 97 *WA 67	re	8
E	3	5	7	5	8	5	3	5	G	Inveni David servum meum	GR [9][34] OTT 147 LU 1185 *SYG 27 GB 28^V *GS 223	of	8
A	3	5	7	5	8	5	3	5	D	Praevaluit David in Philisthaeum	LA 269 WA 165	re	2
A	3	5	7	5	8	5	7	5	D	Sicut fui cum Moyse	LA 160 WA 102	re	2
D	3	5	7	5	8	5	7	5	G	Transite ad me omnes	LR 263	re	8
A	3	5	7	5	8	5	7	8	D	In te speravi Domine	GR 356 [125] LU 1035 OTT 101 SYG 76 *GB 68^V *GS 38 156	of	2
E	3	5	7	5	8	5	7	8	a	Ne avertas faciem tuam a puero	GR 190 OHS 322 LU 617 SYG 127 *GB 113^V *GS 91	gr	2
A	3	5	7	5	8	7	8	5	D	Beatus Laurentius clamavit	LA 438 *WA 349	re	2
A	3	5	7	5	8	7	8	5	D	Beatus Laurentius oravit et dixit	LA 440	re	2
A	3	5	7	5	8	7	8	5	D	Constitues eos principes	LR 143 *WA 413	re	2
E	3	5	7	5	8	7	8	5	a	Dixerunt discipuli ad beatum Martinum	LA 484 *WA 399	re	2
A	3	5	7	5	8	7	8	5	D	Docebit nos Dominus vias	LA 15 *WA 10	re	2
A	3	5	7	5	8	7	8	5	D	Emitte agnum Domine	LR 395 LA 26 382 *WA 18	re	2
A	3	5	7	5	8	7	8	5	D	Exaudiat Dominus orationes	LA 299 *WA 180	re	2

A	3	5	7	5	8	7	8	5	D	Fundata est domus Domini	PM 239 LR 234 AM 1190 LA 549	re	2
A	3	5	7	5	8	7	8	5	D	Initium sapientiae timor	LA 278 *WA 170	re	2
A	3	5	7	5	8	7	8	5	D	Levita Laurentius bonum opus	PM 174 LA 434 *WA 347	re	2
A	3	5	7	5	8	7	8	5	D	Ne perdas cum impiis	LA 168 *WA 109	re	2
A	3	5	7	5	8	7	8	5	D	Nos alium Deum nescimus	LA 291 *WA 177	re	2
A	3	5	7	5	8	7	8	5	D	Obtulerunt pro eo Domino	GR 431 PM 136 LU 1360 LA 351	re	2
A	3	5	7	5	8	7	8	5	D	Refulsit sol in clypeos	LA 295 WA 182	re	2
A	3	5	7	5	8	7	8	5	D	Rorate caeli desuper	LA 26 *WA 19	re	2
A	3	5	7	5	8	7	8	5	D	Si bona suscepimus	LR 422 LA 282 *WA 171	re	2
A	3	5	7	5	8	7	8	5	D	Substrato cilicio in ecclesia	LR 287	re	2
A	3	5	7	5	8	7	8	7	D	Spem in alio numquam habui	WA 179	re	2
A	3	5	7	5	8	7	8	10	D	Beatus Andreas de cruce	LA 502	re	2
A	3	5	7	5	8	7	8	10	D	Conforta me rex sanctorum	WA 179	re	2
A	3	5	7	5	8	7	8	10	D	De ore leonis libera me	LA 172	re	2
A	3	5	7	5	8	7	8	10	D	In mari via tua	LA 157 WA 101	re	2
A	3	5	7	5	8	7	8	10	D	Inclinans faciem meam	WA 175	re	2
A	3	5	7	5	8	7	8	10	D	Joannes baptista arguebat	WA 362	re	2
A	3	5	7	5	8	7	8	10	D	Ne avertas faciem tuam a puero	WA 107	re	2
A	3	5	7	5	8	7	8	10	D	Opprobrium factus sum nimis	OHS 185 (nm) LA 180	re	2
A	3	5	7	5	8	7	8	10	D	Peccavimus Domine et tu iratus	WA 229 *GB 157	an	2
A	3	5	7	5	8	7	8	10	D	Puellae saltanti imperavit	LA 452 *WA 362	re	2
A	3	5	7	5	8	7	8	10	D	Qui caelorum contines	LA 306 WA 185	re	2
A	3	5	7	5	8	7	8	10	D	Qui vicerit faciem illum	LA 51 WA 39	re	2
A	3	5	7	5	8	7	8	10	D	Reposita est mihi corona	LA 427 WA 331	re	2
A	3	5	7	5	8	7	8	10	D	Strinxerunt corporis membra	LA 437 WA 348	re	2
A	3	5	7	5	8	7	8	10	D	Tu Domine universorum	VP 246 LA 299 WA 182	re	2
A	3	5	7	5	8	10	8	7	D	Ascendit Joseph a Galilaea	LR 311	re	2
A	3	5	7	5	8	10	8	7	D	Repleti sunt omnes spiritu	AM 1187 LU 875 *PM 90 *LR 110 LA 256 WA 152	re	2
D	3	5	7	5	10	7	5	3		Salvum me fac Deus Improperium exspectavit	OTT 49 *GB 110^v *SYG 123	ofv	
D	3	5	7	8	5	3	5	3	F	Convertere Domine aliquantulum et deprecare	GR 108 LU 1007 SYG 81 GB 250 GS 43 147 169	gr	5
a	3	5	7	8	5	3	5	8		Illusionem regis cognoscens Repletus sancto spiritus	GB 54	grv	
E	3	5	7	8	7	5	3	1	E	Agnes beatae virginis	ST 329	hy	3

A	3	5	7	8	7	8	10	5	D	Civitatem istam tu circumda	LA 307 *WA 186	re	2
A	3	5	7	8	7	8	10	5	D	Laetentur caeli ... jubilate	LA 5 *WA 5	re	2
D	3	5	7	9	7	5	7	0	D	O quanta qualia sunt illa sabbata	ST 324	hy	1
D	3	5	7	9	7	5	7	5	D	Agnus Dei	SCH #199		1
D	3	5	7	9	7	5	7	5	F	Beati omnes qui timent	SYG 234	gr	6
D	3	5	7	9	10	12	10	9	G	Alleluia: caritas Dei diffusa est	GB 194	al	8
E	3	5	7	10	8	5	8	5		Spiritus Domini replevit orbem	SYG 183	alv	
E	3	5	7	10	8	5	8	5		Spiritus ubi vult spirat	SYG 186	alv	
D	3	5	7	10	9	10	7	3	G	Moyses famulus Domini	LA 158 WA 101	re	8
D	3	5	7	12	10	9	7	10	D	Dies absoluti praetereunt	ST 333	hy	1
E	3	5	8	3	5	3	1	3	E	Venit ad Petrum	SYG 134 *GS 97	an	3
E	3	5	8	3	5	8	7	5	E	Aeterne rerum conditor	ST 323	hy	3
E	3	5	8	3	7	5	3	5	a	Meditabor in mandatis tuis	GR 114 301 LU 548 894 OTT 109 SYG 78 *GB 70 *GS 40 48 139 168	of	2
A	3	5	8	5	3	5	3	5	D	Kyrie	MEL #222		
A	3	5	8	5	3	5	3	5	D	Veniente Domino Jesu	SYG 119	an	2
A	3	5	8	5	3	5	3	7	D	O sol salutis intimis	AR 367	hy	2
A	3	5	8	5	3	5	8	3	D	Veni electa mea ... quia	PM 237 LR 216 *LA 446 *WA 355	re	2
A	3	5	8	5	3	5	8	7	D	Festina ne tardaveris	LA 10 WA 15	re	2
A	3	5	8	5	3	5	8	7	D	Laetetur cor quaerentium	GR 146 SYG 106 GB 94^{v} GS 68 169	int	2
A	3	5	8	5	3	5	8	10	D	Salvos nos fac Domine	GR [133]	int	2
E	3	5	8	5	3	7	3	5	G	Alleluia: caritas Dei diffusa est	SYG 187	al	8
A	3	5	8	5	3	7	8	10		Ecce virgo concipiet ... Jesum	SYG 2	alv	
A	3	5	8	5	7	5	3	5		Laudate Dominum omnes gentes	SYG 256 *GB 263^{v} *GS b	alv	
A	3	5	8	5	7	5	3	7	D	Exsultemus cuncti in Deo	GB 227	gr	2
A	3	5	8	5	7	5	3	7	D	Gloriosus Deus in sanctis	GR [22] LU 1163 *SYG 40 GB 43^{v} *GS 212	gr	1
E	3	5	8	5	7	8	5	3	a	A summo caelo egressio	GR 13 LU 343 *SYG 10 *GS 8 *GB 8	gr	2
E	3	5	8	5	7	8	5	3	a	Ab occultis meis munda me Domine	GR 130 *SYG 81 *GS 57 *GB 84^{v}	gr	2
E	3	5	8	5	7	8	5	3	a	Dispersit dedit pauperibus	GR 576 LU 1608 SYG 212 GB 216^{v} *GS 193	gr	2
E	3	5	8	5	7	8	5	3	a	In omnem terram exivit sonus eorum	GR 629 LU 1486 *GS x *GB 202^{v}	gr	2
E	3	5	8	5	7	8	5	3	a	In sole posuit tabernaculum	GR 14 LU 344 SYG 10 *GB 8^{v} *GS 8	gr	2

E	3	5	8	5	7	8	5	3	a	Qui ambulat fraudulenter	GR 30**	gr	2
E	3	5	8	5	7	8	5	3	a	Sacrificent Domino sacrificium laudis	GR 89**	gr	2
A	3	5	8	5	7	8	7	5	D	Improperium exspectavit cor meum	GR [107]	gr	2
E	3	5	8	5	7	8	10	8	G	Commovisti Domine terram	GR 78 LU 507 SYG 60 GB 58 *GS 27	tr	8
E	3	5	8	5	7	8	10	8	G	Exsurge Domine Deus exaltetur	GR [101] LU 1283^{B}	tr	8
E	3	5	8	5	7	8	10	8	G	In columbae specie vidit	GB 54^{v}	tr	8
E	3	5	8	5	7	8	10	8	G	Magnificat anima mea	GR 50**	tr	8
A	3	5	8	5	8	5	3	5	D	De profundis clamavi ad te	GR 388 LU 1076 OTT 126 SYG 258 *GB 265 *GS f 167	of	2
A	3	5	8	5	8	5	3	7		Convertere animam meam	GB 265^{v}	gr	2
E	3	5	8	5	8	7	5	7	a	Omnipotens adorande colende	PM 128 *LA 337 *WA 255	re	2
A	3	5	8	5	8	7	8	5	D	Emendemus in melius	PM 47 GR 86 LU 524 *LA 128 *WA 85	re	2
A	3	5	8	5	8	12	10	8	D	Anima nostra sicut passer	GR 43 OTT 145 LU 430 SYG 26 GB 27^{v} GS 18	of	2
a	3	5	8	7	5	3	0	-2	[D]	Agnus Dei	SCH #45		1
D	3	5	8	7	5	3	0	3	F	Hodie scietis quia veniet ... salvabit	GR 24 LU 359 SYG 13 GB 12^{v} *GS 12	int	6
A	3	5	8	7	5	3	5	3	D	Jam lucis orto sidere	ST 172	hy	2
E	3	5	8	7	5	3	5	3	E	Jesu redemptor omnium	ST 62	hy	3
a	3	5	8	7	5	7	3	5	c	In loco viridi Domine	VP 242	re	6
A	3	5	8	7	5	7	5	3	D	Ecce virum a virtute	WA 249	re	2
A	3	5	8	7	5	7	5	3	C	Martyr Dei qui unicum	ST 457	hy	6
D	3	5	8	7	8	5	3	7		Surrexit Christus jam non moritur	GS 131	alv	
A	3	5	8	7	8	5	7	5	D	Dominator Domine caelorum	PM 113 LA 292 *WA 178	re	2
A	3	5	8	7	8	5	7	5	D	In te jactatus sum	LA 169 *WA 106	re	2
E	3	5	8	7	8	7	5	3	a	Sanctus	THAN #133		2
A	3	5	8	7	8	7	5	7	D	Agnus Dei XII	GR 44* LU 50 SCH #267		2
E	3	5	8	7	8	7	5	7	a	Miserere Domine populo tuo	WA 179	re	2
A	3	5	8	7	8	10	8	5	D	Domine non est alius	WA 228	an	2
A	3	5	8	7	8	10	8	7	D	Cibavit illum pane vitae	WA 41 426	re	2
A	3	5	8	10	5	7	5	3		Confessor Domini Benedicte	SYG 207	alv	
A	3	5	8	10	8	7	5	12	D	De sublime praeceps	WA 249	an	2
E	3	5	8	10	8	7	8	5	E	Exsultemus Deo caeli	ST 235	hy	3
E	3	5	8	10	8	7	8	5	E	Festa patris Augustini	ST 235	hy	3
d	3	5	9	7	5	3	0	-2	[G]	Agnus Dei	SCH #6		7

D	3	7	5	0	5	7	10	7	G	Laudamini in nomine sancto	GR 114**	of	8
D	3	7	5	3	0	2	0	-2	E	Per lignum crucis de inimicis	GB 246^{v}	co	4
D	3	7	5	3	0	2	0	2	D	Agnus Dei	SCH #231		1
D	3	7	5	3	0	2	0	2	D	Sanctus	THAN #170		1
D	3	7	5	3	0	2	0	7	D	Agnus Dei	SCH #230		1
D	3	7	5	3	2	0	-2	0	D	Sancta Maria virginum piissima	PM 278	an	1
D	3	7	5	3	2	0	2	0	D	Kyrie X alme pater	GR 35* LU 43		1
A	3	7	5	3	5	8	5	8	D	Majorem caritatem nemo habet	GR 654 LU 1752	of	2
E	3	7	5	3	5	8	7	5	a	Homo Dei ducebatur	PM 117 *LA 500 WA 233	re	2
A	3	7	5	3	5	8	7	8	D	Fuerunt sine querela	LR 138 *LA 509 *WA 413	re	2
D	3	7	5	3	5	12	10	9	G	Hodie devicta morte	WA 130	an	8
E	3	7	5	7	3	0	1	3	E	In domum Domini laetantes	LA 102	an	4
A	3	7	5	7	3	2	0	3	D	Narrabo omnia mirabilia	GR 118 SYG 88 *GB 77^{v} GS 50 142	co	2
D	3	7	5	7	3	5	3	5	F	Sederunt principes	GR 36 LU 416 *SYG 22 *GB 21 *GS 15	gr	5
D	3	7	5	7	5	3	2	0	G	Spiritus Domini replevit orbem	AR 504 875 LU 884 1677 AM 520 1076 *WA 153 *LA 261	an	8
D	3	7	5	7	5	3	5	3	F	A Christo de caelo vocatus	SYG 44	gr	6
E	3	7	5	7	5	3	5	3		Caeli enarrant gloriam Dei In omnem terram	OTT 130 SYG 54 GB 236	ofv	
A	3	7	5	7	5	3	5	3		Dies diei eructat In omnem terram	GB 236	ofv	
A	3	7	5	7	5	3	5	3		In tribulatione invocavi Dominum Dextera Domini	OTT 25 SYG 43	ofv	
A	3	7	5	7	5	3	5	3		O beatum virum Martinum O virum ineffabilem	GB 243^{v}	ofv	
D	3	7	5	7	5	3	7	8	F	Benedicta es tu virgo Maria	GR 401 LU 1317	gr	5
D	3	7	5	7	5	3	7	8	F	Benedictus es Domine qui intueris	GR 308 LU 910 SYG 260 GB 213 *GS c	gr	5
D	3	7	5	7	5	3	7	8	F	Constitues eos principes	GR 393 533 LU 1519 SYG 202 GB 204 *GS x	gr	5
D	3	7	5	7	5	7	5	3	G	Comedite pinguia et bibite	GR 370 *SYG 251 GB 258 GS 169	co	8
D	3	7	5	7	5	7	5	3	G	Lavabo inter innocentes	GR 162 *SYG 114 *GB 102 GS 75	co	8
D	3	7	5	7	5	7	5	3	G	Responsum accepit Simeon ... Christum	GR 435 LU 1365 *SYG 50 *GB 49^{v} GS 181	co	8
D	3	7	5	7	5	7	5	3	G	Spiritus Domini replevit orbem	GR [91] LU 1279 GS M 234 SYG 183	int	8
D	3	7	5	7	5	7	5	3	G	Spiritus Domini replevit orbem ... alleluia	GR 292 LU 878 GB 185 SYG 183 GS M 234	int	8

D	3	7	5	7	5	7	5	7	G	Oravit sanctus Andreas	LA 501 *WA 235	re	8
D	3	7	5	7	5	7	5	7	G	Videte quoniam non soli mihi	GR 530 LU 1514	co	8
D	3	7	5	7	8	7	5	7		Et factus est in pace Terra tremuit	OTT 55 GB 128 SYG 153	ofv	
E	3	7	5	8	5	3	5	3	a	Exaltabo te Domine quoniam ... Domine clamavi	GR 90 LU 528 OTT 96 SYG 66 GB 62ᵛ *GS 31 153	of	2
E	3	7	5	8	5	7	8	5	a	Exsultabit cor meum in salutari	GR 587[1] LU 1612[1]	gr	2
E	3	7	5	8	5	7	8	5	a	Exsultabunt sancti in gloria	GR 646 SYG 205 *GB 210 *GS 214	gr	2
A	3	7	5	8	7	8	5	7	D	Amavit eum Dominus et ornavit	PM 223 LR 201 LA 532 *WA 427	re	2
A	3	7	5	8	10	8	7	5	D	Innuebant patri ejus	LR 354 *LA 406 WA 322	re	2
D	3	7	8	7	5	3	5	3	D	Gens fidelis jucundetur	ST 315	hy	1
D	3	7	8	7	5	7	5	3	F	Justorum animae in manu ... malitiae	GR 413 LU 1547 SYG 194 GB 171 GS 213	gr	5
D	3	7	8	7	5	7	5	3	F	Probasti Domine cor meum	GR 579 LU 1594 SYG 213 GB 217ᵛ GS 194	gr	5
D	3	7	10	7	5	7	5	8		Notus in Judaea Deus Terra tremuit	OTT 55 *GB 128 SYG 153	ofv	
F	4	0	2	0	-1	-3	0	4	F	A solis ortus cardine	ST 337	hy	5
F	4	0	2	4	2	-1	0	2		Domine ne in ira tua Domine convertere	OTT 84 GB 99ᵛ *SYG 111	ofv	
c	4	0	2	4	2	0	-3	0		Vitam petiit et tribuisti In virtute	OTT 152 GB 51ᵛ SYG 52	ofv	
G	4	0	2	4	5	7	5	4	G	Servi Domini benedicite	AM 832	an	7
F	4	0	4	2	5	4	2	0	G	Nardi Maria pistici	ST 443	hy	2
F	4	0	4	7	9	11	7	9		Ad annuntiandum mane Bonum est confiteri	GR 360 LU 1041 *GS 53 158 *GB 81 *SYG 92	grv	
F	4	2	-3	0	-1	0	-3	-1	G	O Domine quia ego servus	GR 453 74** LU 1395	of	8
F	4	2	-3	2	4	7	4	2	G	Bonum est confiteri Domino	GR 76 LU 501 OTT 26 *SYG 59 *GB 57 *GS 25	of	8
F	4	2	-1	0	-3	-5	-3	0		Kyrie ... pater de caelis	PM 284 VP 34		
F	4	2	-1	0	2	-1	0	-3	E	In prole mater	PM 251 *WA 268 *LA 348	an	4
F	4	2	-1	0	2	0	2	-3		Bonum certamen certavi	SYG 205	alv	
F	4	2	-1	0	2	0	2	-3		Factus est repente de caelo	SYG 183 *GS 140	alv	
F	4	2	-1	0	2	0	2	-3		Justus ut palma florebit	GR [49](41) LU 1207 *GS 207 SYG 198 *GB 230	alv	
F	4	2	-1	0	2	0	2	-3		Martinus hic pauper	SYG 227	alv	
F	4	2	-1	0	2	0	2	-3		Senex puerum portabat	GR 434 LU 1363 *GB 47ᵛ	alv	
F	4	2	-1	0	2	0	2	-3		Tuam crucem adoramus ... passionem	SYG 173	alv	
G	4	2	0	-2	0	-2	-3	-2	E	Sanctus	THAN #51		4

F	4	2	0	-1	-3	2	0	-5	D	Sanctorum meritis inclyta gaudia	ST 135	hy	1
F	4	2	0	-1	0	-5	-1	2		Misericordia et veritas praeibunt Tui sunt caeli	OTT 18 *GB 19^{v}	ofv	
Γ	4	2	0	2	0	-3	0	2	F	Domine in tua misericordia	GR 310 *SYG 238 GB 247 GS 141	int	5
c	4	2	0	2	0	-1	-3	-1	[a]	Agnus Dei	SCH #15		2
C	4	2	0	2	0	2	4	7	E	Ut queant laxis resonare fibris	ST 475	hy	4
F	4	2	0	2	0	2	5	4	F	Voce mea ad Dominum	SYG 76 *GS 38	co	6
F	4	2	0	2	0	4	2	4	D	Dominus Jesus postquam locutus	WA 150	an	1
F	4	2	0	2	0	4	7	4	F	Cor meum conturbatum est	GR 8**	int	5
F	4	2	0	2	0	4	7	4	F	Lignum habet spem	GR 466 LU 1421	of	6
C	4	2	0	2	4	5	7	5	E	Sanctus	THAN #204		4
C	4	2	0	2	5	4	5	7	E	Dignus es Domine Deus	GS 82	an	4
F	4	2	0	4	-1	0	-1	-3		Iterum autem videbo vos	GS 129 *SYG 166	alv	
G	4	2	0	4	2	0	2	4	a	Recordare mei Domine omni	GB 263^{v} *SYG 259	of	2
G	4	2	0	4	2	0	4	2		Kyrie ... pater de caelis	AR 185* LU 1878 AM 1256		
F	4	2	0	4	2	0	4	7		Avertantur retrorsum et erubescant Domine in auxilium	OTT 106 GB 80^{v} SYG 91	ofv	
F	4	2	0	4	2	0	4	7		Praeceptum Domini lucidum Justitiae Domini	OTT 94 GB 82^{v} SYG 93	ofv	
F	4	2	0	4	2	4	5	4	D	Numquid est in idolis	WA 231	an	1
G	4	2	0	4	5	7	4	5	G	Agnus Dei	SCH #71		8
F	4	2	0	4	7	6	4	7	F	Agnus Dei	SCH #117		5
F	4	2	0	4	7	9	7	4	F	Agnus Dei	SCH #118		6
F	4	2	4	-1	0	2	-1	2	D	Diffusa est gratia in labiis	LR 56 LU 373 *WA 49 *LA 31	an	1
C	4	2	4	-1	0	2	0	-1		Mira res hanc speculationem Intempesta noctis hora	GB 55	ofv	
F	4	2	4	-1	0	2	6	4	G	Christus semel oblatus est	GR 541 LU 1535	co	8
F	4	2	4	0	-3	-1	0	-1	E	Illumina oculos meos ne unquam	GR [147]	int	4
F	4	2	4	0	-3	2	0	-1	E	Illumina oculos meos nequando	GR 331 OTT 87 LU 1000 SYG 92 GB 81 GS 54 145	of	4
F	4	2	4	0	-3	2	0	-1	E	Non participentur sancta	GR [120]	of	4
c	4	2	4	0	-1	-3	-5	-3	E	Dominus virtutum ipse est rex	GR 157 *SYG 112 *GB 99^{v} *GS 73	co	3
c	4	2	4	0	-1	-3	-5	-3	E	Quam magna multitudo	GR 507 LU 1480	co	3
F	4	2	4	0	-1	-3	-1	0	F	Pascha nostrum immolatus	GR 243 OHS 716 LU 781 SYG 154 *GB 128^{v} *GS 117	co	6
F	4	2	4	0	-1	-3	0	2	D	Alleluia: O vos omnes ... sicut	GR 597 LU 1634^{v}	al	2
F	4	2	4	0	-1	-3	0	2		O vos omnes ... sicut	GR 597 LU 1634^{v}	alv	

F	4	2	4	0	-1	0	-1	-3	D	Dominus dabit benignitatem	GR 3 LU 322 SYG 3 GB 2 GS 2	co	1
F	4	2	4	0	-1	0	-1	-3	D	Ignem veni mittere	GR 562 LU 1575	co	1
F	4	2	4	0	2	-3	0	-1	D	De manu omnium	AR 129 AM 58	an	1
F	4	2	4	0	2	-3	0	-1	D	Exsurge Domine et judica	OHS 386 LU 641 *WA 118 *LA 191	an	1
F	4	2	4	0	2	0	2	-1	D	Exsurge Domine non praevaleat	AM 17 OHS 59 (nm) *WA 67	an	1
F	4	2	4	0	2	4	5	4	D	Peccantem me quotidie	AR [171] LU 1797 LA 556 *WA 437	re	1
F	4	2	4	0	2	5	2	4	D	Iterum videbo vos alleluia	LA 236 *231	an	1
F	4	2	4	0	4	7	4	7	F	Cantemus Domino gloriose enim magnificatus	GR 38**	int	5
F	4	2	4	0	4	7	4	7	F	Circumdederunt me gemitus mortis	GR 73 LU 497 SYG 58 *GB 56 *GS 24	int	5
F	4	2	4	2	-1	0	2	0	D	Mandavit Dominus benedictionem	LR 338	an	1
F	4	2	4	2	0	2	-3	4	D	Apertis thesauris suis	AR 313 LU 463 AM 291 WA 56 LA 74	an	1
F	4	2	4	2	0	2	0	-3	D	Estote fortes in bello	AR [13] LU 1118 AM 628 *WA 410 LA 512	an	1
F	4	2	4	2	0	2	0	-3	D	Exsurgens Joseph a somno	AR 652 LU 1402 AM 840	an	1
F	4	2	4	2	0	2	0	-1	D	Domine Deus meus in te speravi	WA 66	an	1
F	4	2	4	2	0	2	0	4	D	Dominus quidem Jesus	LA 253	an	1
G	4	2	4	2	0	5	4	5	E	Paratus esto Israel	PM 25 *LA 18 *WA 14	re	3
F	4	2	4	2	4	0	2	4	G	Confitebuntur caeli mirabilia ... etenim	SYG 190	gr	8
F	4	2	4	2	4	0	2	4	G	Deus exaudi orationem meam	GR 156 SYG 111 GB 99 GS 73	gr	8
F	4	2	4	2	4	0	2	4	G	Deus vitam meam nuntiavi	GR 128 SYG 94 GB 83v GS 56	gr	8
F	4	2	4	2	4	2	4	2	G	Multi enim sunt vocati	WA 76 *LA 116	an	8
G	4	2	4	5	2	4	2	0	E	Ille nempe Daciani	ST 466	hy	4
G	4	2	4	5	4	0	2	0	G	Ecce quam bonum et quam jucundum	AR 640 AM 821	an	8
G	4	2	4	5	4	0	2	0	G	Sub throno Dei	AR 284 LU 431 AM 261 *WA 46 LA 61	an	8
G	4	2	4	5	4	2	0	2		Gaudete justi in Domino Vox exsultationis	LA 390	rev	
F	4	2	4	5	4	2	0	4	F	Magnificat anima mea ... quia fecit	LR 270	re	5
G	4	2	4	5	4	2	4	2		Jubilate Deo omnis terra	GR 65 LU 479 SYG 32 GB 256 GS 20	alv	
G	4	2	4	5	4	5	4	2	E	Oportet te fili gaudere	GB 81v	co	3

C	4	2	4	5	4	5	7	4		In spiritu humilitatis Sicut in holocaustum	SYG 243	ofv	
G	4	2	4	5	7	5	4	0		Benjamin et Manasse Qui regis	SYG 11	trv	
F	4	2	4	7	6	4	2	4	G	Zachaee festinans descende	AR [110] LU 1244 AM 700 *WA 319 *LA 546	an	8
F	4	2	4	7	6	4	7	6	G	Alleluia: Domine dilexi decorem	GB 174	al	8
F	4	2	4	7	6	4	7	6	[G]	Alleluia: in omnem terram exivit sonus eorum	GB 267	al	8
F	4	2	4	7	6	4	7	6	[G]	Alleluia: veni sponsa Christi accipe coronam	GB 273^{v}	al	8
C	4	2	4	9	7	5	4	2	D	Kyrie ad monumentum (etc)	MEL #209		
C	4	2	5	2	0	5	7	5	F	Nocte surgentes vigilemus omnes	ST 263	hy	6
G	4	2	5	2	4	5	2	0	a	Angelis suis mandavit	GR 94 LU 533 *GS 34 *SYG 72 *GB 65	gr	2
G	4	2	5	2	4	5	2	0	a	Domine Deus virtutum converte	GR 15 LU 345 *SYG 10 *GS 8 *GB 9	gr	2
G	4	2	5	2	4	5	2	0	a	Domine refugium factus es	GR 381 LU 1067 SYG 256 *GS 34 165 *GB 262	gr	2
G	4	2	5	2	4	5	2	0	a	Excita Domine potentiam tuam	GR 15 LU 347 *SYG 10 *GS 9 *GB 9	gr	2
G	4	2	5	2	4	5	2	0	a	Hodie scietis quia veniet ... salvabit	GR 24 LU 360 SYG 13 *GB 12^{v} *GS 12	gr	2
G	4	2	5	2	4	5	2	0	a	Justus ut palma florebit	GR [42] LU 1201 SYG 195 GB 23 *GS 202	gr	2
G	4	2	5	2	4	5	2	0	a	Nimis honorati sunt amici tui	GR 391 LU 1326 *SYG 54 *GB 235 *GS w	gr	2
G	4	2	5	2	4	5	2	0	a	Requiem aeternam dona eis Domine	GR 95* LU 1808 *SYG 235 *GB 265^{v} *GS 232	gr	2
G	4	2	5	2	4	5	2	0	a	Tollite portas principes	GR 9 LU 1269 *SYG 8 *GB 6^{v} *GS 5	gr	2
G	4	2	5	2	4	5	2	0	a	Uxor tua sicut vitis	GR [122] LU 1289	gr	2
G	4	2	5	2	5	2	0	4	a	Dies mei sicut umbra	GB 104^{v}	gr	2
G	4	2	5	4	0	2	-2	2	G	Maria autem conservabat	AR 329 LU 476 WA 47	an	8
F	4	2	5	4	0	2	0	2	F	Ingressus Aaron tabernaculum	GR 17**	of	6
C	4	2	5	4	0	2	5	4	D	Remansit puer Jesus	AR 323 LU 469 AM 301	an	2
G	4	2	5	4	0	5	4	5	G	Vidit Jacob scalam summitas	PM 240 LR 241 WA 318 LA 547	an	7
G	4	2	5	4	2	-2	2	4	a	Assumpsit Jesus discipulos	AR 380 LU 1085 AM 353 *WA 90 *LA 136	an	2
G	4	2	5	4	2	0	2	0	E	Elegit Dominus Sion	AR 141 OHS 357 LU 292	an	3
G	4	2	5	4	2	0	2	5	G	Jesu redemptor omnium	ST 404	hy	8
G	4	2	5	4	2	0	2	5	G	Jesu redemptor saeculi	ST 382	hy	8
G	4	2	5	4	2	0	5	2	E	Frumentum Christi sum	GR 427 LU 1354^{v}	co	3

G	4	2	5	4	2	0	5	2	E	Justorum animae in manu ... malitiae	GR 505 LU 1549 *SYG 173 *GB 167v *GS 219	co	3
G	4	2	5	4	2	0	5	2	E	Religio munda et immaculata	GR 557 LU 1564	co	3
F	4	2	5	4	2	4	0	-1	D	Congregavit nos in unum	SYG 132	an	1
F	4	2	5	4	2	4	0	2	F	Electa mea candida sicut nix	LR 263	re	6
c	4	2	5	4	2	4	0	2	c	Scio Domine quia morti	WA 174	re	6
G	4	2	5	4	2	5	0	2	G	Deus creator omnium	ST 28	hy	8
G	4	2	5	4	2	5	0	2	G	Te lucis ante terminum	AR 59 LU 266	hy	8
G	4	2	5	4	2	5	4	0	G	Te lucis ante terminum	AM 170	hy	8
G	4	2	5	4	2	5	4	2	G	Christe redemptor omnium ex patre	ST 177	hy	8
G	4	2	5	7	5	4	0	4	G	Sanctorum corpora sacer	WA 377	an	7
C	4	2	5	7	5	4	2	5	D	Agnus Dei	SCH #250		1
G	4	2	5	7	5	4	7	5	G	Alleluia: exsultabunt sancti in gloria	SYG 169 GS 216 (nm)	al	7
G	4	2	5	7	5	4	7	5		Exsultabunt sancti in gloria	SYG 169 GS 216 (nm)	alv	
F	4	2	7	4	2	7	9	7	F	Relinquens Maria activam	WA 336	re	5
F	4	2	7	4	2	9	7	9	F	Exemplum veniae Mariam	WA 335	an	5
F	4	2	7	5	4	2	7	9	F	Relinquens Wulstanus	WA 248	an	5
C	4	2	7	5	4	5	2	0	[D]	Agnus Dei	SCH #249		1
C	4	2	7	5	4	5	2	9	D	Sanctus II	GR 10* LU 21 OHS 850 THAN #203		1
F	4	2	7	6	4	2	7	9		Da gaudiorum praemia / Gloria patri	WA 160	rev	
F	4	2	7	9	7	2	7	9		Non est inventus similis / Ecce sacerdos	GR [32] LU 1183 1495A GS 220 GB 28v *SYG 27	grv	
F	4	2	7	9	7	2	7	9		Propter quod et Deus / Christus factus est	GR 196 AR 434 LU 669 OHS 444 GS v, 94 235 GB 115 *SYG 129	grv	
F	4	2	7	9	7	2	7	9		Sed sic eum volo manere / Exiit sermo	GR 39 LU 422 GS 16 GB 24v *SYG 24	grv	
F	4	2	7	9	7	4	2	7	F	Qui cum audissent	WA 240	re	5
F	4	2	7	9	7	4	7	0		Defecit caro mea et cor / Aquae multae	GR 625 LU 1690	grv	
F	4	2	7	9	7	4	7	4		Dilectus meus mihi / Sicut lilium	GR 75**	grv	
F	4	2	7	9	7	4	7	4		Quia in eo laetabitur / Anima nostra sustinet	GR 111**	grv	
F	4	2	7	9	7	4	7	4		Quoniam aedificavit Dominus / Timebunt gentes nomen	GR 71 LU 489 GS 23 159 GB 39 SYG 42	grv	
F	4	2	7	9	7	4	7	9		Benedictus Dominus quoniam mirificavit / Quoniam respexisti	GR (35)	grv	

F	4	2	7	9	7	4	7	9		Domine Deus virtutum exaudi Protector noster	GR 108 LU 1003 GS 37 43 144 171 GB 67^v SYG 75	grv	
F	4	2	7	9	7	4	7	9		Et adorabunt eum omnes Dominabitur a mari	GR 639 LU 1710	grv	
F	4	2	7	9	7	4	7	9		Evangelizare pauperibus misit Spiritus Domini	GR [100] LU 1283^A	grv	
F	4	2	7	9	7	4	7	9		Notam facite in populis Exsulta et lauda	GR 54**	grv	
F	4	2	7	9	7	4	7	9		Notam fecit Dominus salutare Viderunt omnes	GR 33 LU 409 GS G GB 17^v SYG 19	grv	
F	4	2	7	9	7	4	7	9		Perfecisti eis qui sperant Quam magna multitudo	GR 449 LU 1393	grv	
F	4	2	7	9	7	4	7	9		Revelabit Dominus condensa Tollite hostias	GR 162 *GS 76 GB 102 SYG 114	grv	
F	4	2	7	9	7	4	7	9		Si exprobramini in nomine Communicantes	GR 508 LU 1482	grv	
F	4	2	7	9	7	6	4	2	F	Coenantibus illis accepit Jesus	AR 115* LR 127 LU 931	re	5
F	4	2	7	9	7	6	7	6	F	Cum scirem ego Gamaliel	WA 343	re	5
F	4	2	7	9	7	9	7	4		Ut valeant famuli Adjuva sancte tuos	SYG 230	grv	
F	4	2	7	9	7	9	7	6		Exsurge Domine et judica Respice Domine	GR 354 LU 1033 GS 68 156 GB 94^v SYG 106	grv	
F	4	2	7	9	7	9	7	11		Benedicat nos Deus ... et metuant Confiteantur tibi	GR [126] LU 1294	grv	
F	4	2	7	9	7	9	7	11		Custodi innocentiam et vide Propter fratres	GR 527 LU 1512	grv	
F	4	2	7	9	7	9	7	11		Emitte lucem tuam Discerne causam	GR 158 GS 74 GB 100 SYG 112	grv	
F	4	2	7	9	7	9	7	11		Illusionem regis cognoscens Repletus sancto spiritu	SYG 56	grv	
F	4	2	7	9	7	9	7	11		Invadent enim gregem Dixerunt discipuli	GB 242	grv	
F	4	2	7	9	7	9	7	11		Labores manuum tuarum Beati omnes qui timent	SYG 234	grv	
F	4	2	7	9	7	9	7	11		Quoniam elevata est magnificentia Domine Dominus	GR 342 LU 1017 GS 150 GB 252 SYG 244	grv	
F	4	2	7	9	7	9	7	11		Sicut audivimus ita et vidimus Suscepimus Deus	GR 433 LU 1362 SYG 48 GB 47^v GS j	grv	
F	4	2	7	9	7	9	7	11		Ut misericors fieret Pontifex sacerdos	GR [118]	grv	
F	4	2	7	9	7	9	7	11		Ut testimonium perhiberet Fuit homo	GR 522 GS 188 l GB 196^v SYG 195	grv	
F	4	2	7	9	7	9	7	11		Vidisti Domine ne sileas Pacifice loquebantur	GR 164 GS 77 GB 103^v SYG 116	grv	
C	4	2	7	9	7	9	7	12	E	Alleluia: beatus quem elegisti	GR 519 LU 1479	al	3

F	4	2	7	9	7	12	11	9	F	Praesul Christi Wulstanus	WA 250	re	5
F	4	2	7	9	7	12	11	9	F	Te lucis ante terminum	ST 330	hy	5
G	4	5	0	4	5	2	0	4	E	Orietur in diebus	LU 379 *LR 56 *WA 27 LA 33	an	3
G	4	5	2	0	-2	0	2	0	G	Benedictus Dei famulus	WA 300	an	8
G	4	5	2	0	2	0	-3	-2	E	Laudate Dominum quia benignus	AR 112	an	3
F	4	5	2	0	2	4	[0	0]	a	Cantemus Domino gloriose	AM 61 63	an	ir
F	4	5	2	0	2	4	2	4		Exspectans exspectavi Dominum Domine ad adjuvandum	OTT 42 *SYG 106	ofv	
F	4	5	2	0	2	4	2	4	F	Majorem hac dilectionem	GR 553 LU 1559	int	5
F	4	5	2	0	4	0	2	0	D	Tota pulchra es Maria	AR 586 LU 1320 AM 763	an	1
G	4	5	2	0	4	2	0	-3	G	Agnus Dei ad lib I	GR 92* LU 87 SCH #95		8
F	4	5	2	0	4	2	4	2	D	Pulchra et decora filia	WA 358	an	1
G	4	5	2	0	4	2	5	4	E	Diffusa est gratia in conceptione	LR 261	an	3
G	4	5	2	0	4	5	2	5	G	Adhaesit anima mea ... cremata	AR 814 LU 1597 AM 1006	an	8
G	4	5	2	0	4	5	2	5	G	Adhaesit anima mea ... lapidata	AR 274 LU 418 1583[A] AM 250 *LA 47 *WA 37	an	8
F	4	5	2	4	0	4	2	4	D	Pulchra es et decora	AR 821 LU 1606 AM 1015 *LR 220 *LA 448 *WA 358	an	1
G	4	5	2	4	2	0	2	0	E	Placebo Domino in regione	AR [142] LU 1772 *AM 1150 *WA 435	an	3
F	4	5	2	4	2	0	2	5	a	Laudate Dominum omnes gentes	AR 72	an	1
G	4	5	2	4	2	4	2	0	G	Agnus Dei	SCH #70		8
G	4	5	2	4	2	4	2	0		Ostende nobis Domine misericordiam Benedixisti Domine	OTT 8 *GB 6 *SYG 7	ofv	
G	4	5	2	4	5	4	2	0	E	Omnes amici mei derelinquerunt	OHS 485 LU 693 *LA 195 *WA 122	re	3
G	4	5	2	5	2	5	2	0		Loquetur pacem gentibus Exsulta satis	OTT 11 GB 10 SYG 12	ofv	
G	4	5	2	5	4	0	2	0	E	Bonorum meorum non indiges	AM 21	an	3
G	4	5	2	5	4	0	2	4	E	Accipiens Simeon puerum	AR 620 LU 1366 AM 802 WA 272 *LA 355	an	3
G	4	5	2	5	4	0	2	4	E	Hoc jam tertio	WA 135	an	3
G	4	5	2	5	4	0	2	4	E	Nigra sum sed formosa	AR [115] LR 219 LU 1784 AM 707 *WA 353 LA 543	an	3
G	4	5	2	5	4	2	0	2	E	Simeon justus et timoratus	AR 620 LU 1366 AM 802 *LA 355	an	3
F	4	5	2	5	4	2	0	2	D	Simeon justus et timoratus	WA 272	an	1
G	4	5	2	5	4	2	0	4	G	Sanctorum precibus istorum	AM 829	an	8
G	4	5	2	5	4	7	4	5	G	Jerusalem Jerusalem quae occidis	LA 45	an	7
G	4	5	2	7	5	7	5	4	E	Benedicite Dominum omnis anima	GB 168	int	3

G	4	5	4	0	2	4	2	0		Dicite in gentibus quia Dominus	GR 256 491 LU 801 1455 OHS 817 SYG 173 *GS 122	alv	
G	4	5	4	0	2	4	2	0		Spiritus est qui vivificat	GR 304 LU 901	alv	
G	4	5	4	2	0	2	4	0	G	Alleluia: sancte Vincenti levita	GB 46	al	8
C	4	5	4	2	0	2	4	0		Assumpta est Maria ... angeli	SYG 216	alv	
C	4	5	4	2	0	2	4	0		Usque modo non petistis	SYG 168 *GB 130	alv	
G	4	5	4	2	0	2	4	2	G	Alleluia: laudanda tremenda	GB 213^{v}	al	8
c	4	5	4	2	0	2	4	2		Benedictus es Dei filius	GB 148	alv	
c	4	5	4	2	0	2	4	2		Benedictus es Domine Deus	GB 213	alv	
G	4	5	4	2	0	2	4	2		Benedictus sit Dei filius	SYG 261	alv	
c	4	5	4	2	0	2	4	2		In resurrectione tua Christe	GB 146^{v}	alv	
c	4	5	4	2	0	2	4	2		Justi fulgebunt sicut sol	GB 268^{v}	alv	
G	4	5	4	2	0	2	4	2		Laudanda tremenda	GB 213^{v}	alv	
G	4	5	4	2	0	2	4	2		Oculis ac manibus in caelum	SYG 225	alv	
G	4	5	4	2	0	2	4	2		Sancte Vincenti levita	GB 46	alv	
G	4	5	4	2	0	2	4	5	G	Jam lucis orto sidere	ST 265	hy	7
F	4	5	4	2	4	2	-1	0	[F]	Agnus Dei	SCH #116		5
F	4	5	4	2	4	2	-1	0	F	Sanctus	THAN #102		6
F	4	5	4	2	4	2	0	2	D	Alliga Domine in vinculis	AM 411 WA 117 LA 188	an	1
F	4	5	4	2	4	2	0	2	F	Dicit Dominus implete hydrias aqua	GR 70 LU 487 SYG 37 GB 39 GS 22	co	6
F	4	5	4	2	4	2	0	2	F	Gloria et honore coronasti	GR [7] LU 1133 SYG 201	gr	5
F	4	5	4	2	4	2	0	2	F	Sicut lilium inter spinas	GR 75**	gr	5
F	4	5	4	2	4	2	0	4	F	Domine ad adjuvandum me	GR 147 OTT 42 SYG 106 GS 68	of	6
F	4	5	4	2	4	5	2	0		Et in terra	BOS #27		
F	4	5	4	2	4	5	4	0		Bonum est confiteri Domino Justus ut palma	OTT 150 GB 25^{v}	ofv	
C	4	5	4	2	4	5	4	2	E	In tribulatione clamamus	GB 156^{v}	an	4
C	4	5	7	2	4	2	4	2		Et in terra	BOS #41		
C	4	5	7	4	2	0	4	7	D	Exsurge Domine adjuva nos	PM 69	an	2
c	4	5	7	4	2	4	7	5	c	Sanctus	THAN #8		7
C	4	5	7	4	5	4	2	0	D	Alleluia: spiritus qui a patre	SYG 185	al	1
G	4	5	7	4	5	7	5	2	G	Helena sancta dixit	WA 309 *LA 398	an	7
F	4	5	7	4	5	7	5	4	F	Qui mihi ministrat	GR [15] LU 1141 SYG 213 GB 219 GS q 210	co	5
G	4	5	7	4	5	7	9	7	G	Benedicta tu inter mulieres	AR 772 LU 1541	an	7

G	4	5	7	4	5	7	9	7	G	Cum vocatus fueris	AR 568 LU 1047 AM 608 *WA 190 *LA 317	an	7
G	4	5	7	4	5	7	9	7	G	Ex ipsi vicerunt draconem	AR 764 LU 1529	an	7
G	4	5	7	4	5	7	9	7	G	Exsultate justi et gloriamini	AR 96 LU 279[E]	an	7
G	4	5	7	4	5	7	9	7	G	Lapides torrentes illi	AR 273 LU 414 1583[A] *AM 250 *WA 37 LA 47	an	7
G	4	5	7	4	5	7	9	7	G	Magnificavit Dominus facere	AR 121 OHS 289 LU 286	an	7
G	4	5	7	4	5	7	9	7	G	Prae timore autem ejus	AR 444 OHS 727 768 LU 782 *AM 454 LA 214 233 *WA 129 137	an	7
G	4	5	7	4	5	7	9	7	G	Sub tuum praesidium confugimus	AR [134] 123* PM 207 VP 37 18* LU 1861 AM 1258	an	7
G	4	5	7	4	7	5	4	2		Et in terra	GR 18* LU 28		
G	4	5	7	4	7	9	7	4	G	Sanctae trinitatis fidem Martinus	WA 398 *LA 480	an	7
G	4	5	7	4	7	9	7	5	G	Induere vestimentis	WA 269	an	7
G	4	5	7	4	7	9	7	5	G	Perambulabant in innocentia	LR 141	an	7
G	4	5	7	4	7	9	7	5	G	Philippe qui videt me	AR 694 LU 1465[E] AM 893 *LA 394	an	7
G	4	5	7	4	7	9	7	9	G	Qui persequebantur justum	AR 580 LU 1308 *AM 756 *LA 504	an	7
C	4	5	7	5	2	4	5	7	E	Hostis Herodes impie	ST 276	hy	4
G	4	5	7	5	2	4	5	7	G	Oswaldus bajulus crucis	WA 284	re	7
G	4	5	7	5	2	5	0	4	G	Quomodo fiet istud angele	AR 249 669 LU 1415 AM 225 864 *LA 22 377	an	7
G	4	5	7	5	2	5	4	0	G	Magnificatus est rex pacificus	AR 259 LU 364 AM 236 *WA 26 LA 31	an	7
G	4	5	7	5	2	5	4	0	G	Martine misit nos Dominus	WA 399 *LA 483	an	7
G	4	5	7	5	2	5	4	0	G	Martinus adhuc catechumenus	WA 398 *LA 480	an	7
G	4	5	7	5	2	5	4	2	G	Alleluia	AM 54	an	7
G	4	5	7	5	2	5	4	5	G	Amplius lava me Domine	AR 130 AM 52	an	7
G	4	5	7	5	2	5	4	5	G	Magnificabitur usque ad terminos	AR 894[7] LU 1706 AM 1093	an	7
G	4	5	7	5	2	5	4	7	G	Erexit Jacob lapidem	LR 238 *WA 318	an	7
C	4	5	7	5	4	2	0	2	C	Jam lucis orto sidere	ST 245	hy	6
G	4	5	7	5	4	2	4	0	G	Ego veritatem dico vobis	AR 480 *AM 496 *LA 241	an	7
G	4	5	7	5	4	2	4	2		Et in terra	GR 5* LU 16		
C	4	5	7	5	4	2	4	5		Dic mihi fili mi Vae nobis quia peccavimus	SYG 139	anv	
F	4	5	7	5	4	5	2	4	F	Jerusalem gaude gaudio	WA 16	an	5
G	4	5	7	5	4	5	7	9	G	Beatae Gertrudis verba	AM 1135	an	7
G	4	5	7	5	4	5	7	9	G	Erexit nobis Dominus	AR 110 AM 51 LA 92	an	7

G	4	5	7	5	4	5	7	9	G	In civitate Domini clare sonant	PM 203	an	7
G	4	5	7	5	4	5	7	9	G	Laetare virgo mater alleluia	AM 1075	an	7
G	4	5	7	5	4	5	7	9	G	Misericordia et veritas obviaverunt	LR 265	an	7
G	4	5	7	5	4	5	7	9	G	Obedientiae pennis elatus	AM 778	an	7
G	4	5	7	5	4	5	7	9	G	Obedientiae speculum Maurus	LR 279	an	7
G	4	5	7	5	4	5	7	9	G	Sicut laetantium omnium habitatio ... Scholastica	LR 293	an	7
G	4	5	7	5	4	5	7	9	G	Viderunt eam ... et beatam	AR 882[3] LU 1687 AM 1082	an	7
F	4	5	7	5	7	4	2	7	F	Veni dilecte mi	WA 163	an	5
G	4	5	7	5	7	5	2	5	G	Egregie Dei antistes	WA 311	an	7
G	4	5	7	5	7	5	4	2	G	Benedixisti Domine terram tuam	AR 166	an	7
G	4	5	7	5	7	5	4	2	G	Dum tribularer clamavi	AR 429 OHS 245 280 AM 408 *WA 115 LA 186	an	7
G	4	5	7	5	7	5	4	5	G	Quis tibi videtur	WA 189	an	7
G	4	5	7	5	7	9	7	4	G	Benedicamus Domino	LU 127		7
G	4	5	7	5	7	9	7	4	G	Caecilia me misit	WA 406	an	7
G	4	5	7	5	7	9	7	4	G	Ite missa est Ib	GR 7* LU 19		7
G	4	5	7	5	7	9	7	5	G	Agatha ingressa carcerem	LA 360	an	7
G	4	5	7	5	7	9	7	5	G	Dum praeliaretur Michael	AR 856 LU 1659 AM 1058 WA 383 *LA 471	an	7
G	4	5	7	5	7	9	7	5	G	Venite omnes exsultemus	WA 200	an	7
G	4	5	7	5	7	9	7	9	G	Ecce apparebit Dominus et non mentietur	AR 224 LU 332 AM 196 WA 12 *LA 11	an	7
G	4	5	7	5	9	7	4	7	G	Baptizatur Christus	WA 59 *LA 77	an	7
G	4	5	7	5	9	7	4	7	G	Cum orasset Judas	WA 309 *LA 398	an	7
G	4	5	7	5	9	7	4	7	G	Dixit Romanus ad beatum	WA 347 *LA 433	an	7
G	4	5	7	5	9	7	4	7	G	Interrogatus te Dominum	WA 348 *LA 436	an	7
G	4	5	7	5	9	7	4	7	G	Miroque modo inermi	WA 386	an	7
G	4	5	7	5	9	7	4	7	G	Oculi tui sancta Dei genitrix	WA 353	an	7
G	4	5	7	5	9	7	4	7	G	Tunc acceptabis sacrificium	AR 396 AM 371 WA 103 *LA 161	an	7
G	4	5	7	5	9	7	4	7	G	Tunc invocabis et Dominus	AR 363 LU 530 AM 340 *WA 84	an	7
G	4	5	7	5	9	7	4	7	G	Viri Galilaei quid aspicitis	AR 491 LU 850 AM 508 *LA 250 WA 149	an	7
G	4	5	7	5	9	7	5	4	G	Sanctus	THAN #50		7
G	4	5	7	5	9	7	5	7	[G]	Agnus Dei	SCH #69		8
G	4	5	7	5	9	7	5	7	G	Et qui praeibant increpabant	AR 356 LU 515 *AM 329 331 LA 125	an	7

G	4	5	7	5	9	7	5	7	G	Sancti mei qui in isto saeculo	AM 878	an	7
G	4	5	7	5	9	7	5	7	G	Sebastianus dixit ad Nicostratum	LA 331	an	7
G	4	5	7	5	9	7	5	7	G	Sebastianus vir Christianissimus	LA 324	an	7
G	4	5	7	5	9	7	5	9	G	Artem fabri fideliter	LU 1446	an	7
G	4	5	7	5	9	7	9	5		Benedicite Anania Azaria Benedictus es in firmamento	GS 44	trv	
G	4	5	7	5	9	7	9	5	G	Omnes nationes venient	AR 333 AM 299 WA 57	an	7
G	4	5	7	5	9	7	9	5	G	Valerianus in cubiculo	AR 924 LU 1756 AM 1140 WA 408 LA 493	an	7
G	4	5	7	5	9	7	9	7		Benedicite aquae quae super Benedictus es in firmamento	GS 44	trv	
G	4	5	7	5	9	7	9	7	G	Caecus sedebat secus	WA 81 *LA 125	an	7
G	4	5	7	5	9	7	9	7	G	Laetabitur justus in Domino ... laudabuntur	LA 524	an	7
G	4	5	7	5	9	7	9	7		Laudate eum omnes angeli ejus Laudate Dominum	GR [86] LU 1275	grv	
G	4	5	7	5	9	7	9	7	G	Sebastianus Mediolanensium	LA 323	an	7
G	4	5	7	5	9	7	9	7	G	Vade Anania et quaere	AR 608 LU 1343 AM 791 WA 263	an	7
G	4	5	7	5	9	7	10	9	G	Joseph fili David noli timere	AR 691 AM 889 WA 25 *LA 30	an	7
G	4	5	7	9	4	5	7	5	G	Cum intraret Jesus in domum	AR 567 AM 607 *LA 316	an	7
G	4	5	7	9	5	2	5	4	G	Maria stabat ad monumentum	AR 450 OHS 804 AM 463 WA 135 *LA 220	an	7
G	4	5	7	9	5	7	4	5	G	Assumpta est Maria ... angeli	AR 820 875 AM 1013 1076 LU 1605 LA 448 *WA 358	an	7
G	4	5	7	9	5	7	4	5	G	Jugum enim meum	WA 412 *LA 507	an	7
G	4	5	7	9	5	7	4	5	G	Sedere autem mecum	LA 144	an	7
G	4	5	7	9	5	7	4	5	G	Statuit ea in aeternum	AR 379 AM 353 *WA 93 LA 142	an	7
G	4	5	7	9	5	7	5	4	G	Cum evigilasset Jacob	WA 318 *LA 547	an	7
G	4	5	7	9	5	7	5	4	G	In Galilaea Jesum	WA 138 *LA 222	an	7
G	4	5	7	9	5	7	5	4	G	In sanctitate serviamus	AR 149 AM 65 LA 99	an	7
G	4	5	7	9	5	7	5	4	G	Venit Maria nuntians	WA 135 *LA 221 233	an	7
G	4	5	7	9	5	7	5	7	G	Dum flerem ad monumentum	WA 139	an	7
G	4	5	7	9	5	9	10	9	G	Et ecce vox de nube	AR 807 LU 1000	an	7
c	4	5	7	9	7	2	5	4	c	Jesu amor unice	ST 48	hy	6
G	4	5	7	9	7	2	5	4	G	Semen cecidit ... centuplum	LA 119	an	7
F	4	5	7	9	7	2	7	9		Adjuva nos Deus salutaris noster Propitius esto	GR 107 LU 999 GS 42 51 145 170 GB 78^{v} *SYG 81	grv	

F	4	5	7	9	7	4	0	4	F	Te gestientem gaudiis	ST 22	hy	6
G	4	5	7	9	7	4	5	7	G	Aurora lucis rutilat	ST 287	hy	8
G	4	5	7	9	7	4	5	7	G	Salutem ex inimicis	LA 95	an	7
G	4	5	7	9	7	4	5	7	G	Salvator mundi salva ... qui per crucem	OHS 584 LU 747 *LA 463 *SYG 141	an	7
G	4	5	7	9	7	4	7	5	G	Lucia virgo quid a me	AR 592 LU 1324 *AM 770 *WA 243 *LA 322	an	7
F	4	5	7	9	7	4	7	9		Adjuva me Domine Deus Sederunt principes	GR 36 LU 416 *SYG 22 GB 21 GS 15	grv	
G	4	5	7	9	7	5	2	4	G	Benedictionem omnium gentium	AR 2 (sup 1) AM 979	an	7
G	4	5	7	9	7	5	2	4	G	Dixit autem dominus servo	WA 191	an	7
C	4	5	7	9	7	5	2	4	E	Jesu nostra redemptio	ST 293	hy	4
G	4	5	7	9	7	5	2	4	G	Jubilate Deo in voce	AR 70	an	7
G	4	5	7	9	7	5	2	4	G	Omnis spiritus laudet Dominum	AR 189 [180] LU 1803 AM 1165 1166 WA 438 *LA 559	an	7
G	4	5	7	9	7	5	2	5	G	Nomen sempiternum dabo	AM 980	an	7
G	4	5	7	9	7	5	2	7	G	Cito euntes dicite	WA 129 *137 *LA 216	an	7
G	4	5	7	9	7	5	4	0	G	Multiplicasti Deus misericordiam	AR 150	an	7
G	4	5	7	9	7	5	4	2	G	Alleluia	AR 70	an	7
G	4	5	7	9	7	5	4	2	G	Dixerunt discipuli ad beatum Martinum	AR 917 LU 1748 AM 1115 WA 402 *LA 486	an	7
G	4	5	7	9	7	5	4	2	G	Ecce ascendimus ... et filius	AR 383 LU 1086 AM 357 WA 94 *LA 144	an	7
G	4	5	7	9	7	5	4	2	G	Imitator Domini Oswaldus	WA 286	an	7
G	4	5	7	9	7	5	4	2	G	In pace factus est locus	OHS 612 LU 769 WA 126 *LA 204	an	7
G	4	5	7	9	7	5	4	2	G	Non lotis manibus	AR 393 LU 1091 AM 368	an	7
G	4	5	7	9	7	5	4	2	b	O sator rerum reparator aevi	ST 422	hy	4
G	4	5	7	9	7	5	4	2	G	Oculi tui Deus respexerunt	WA 283	an	7
G	4	5	7	9	7	5	4	2	G	Sanctificavit tabernaculum ... altissimus	LR 335	an	7
G	4	5	7	9	7	5	4	2	b	Ut queant laxis resonare fibris	ST 429	hy	4
G	4	5	7	9	7	5	4	5	G	Ad te de luce	AR 354 GR 297 AM 327 WA 79 *LA 124	an	7
c	4	5	7	9	7	5	4	5	c	Agnus Dei	SCH #14		
G	4	5	7	9	7	5	4	5	G	Angelus Gabriel apparuit Danieli	AR 660 LU 1410	an	7
G	4	5	7	9	7	5	4	5	G	Deus tuorum militum	ST 44	hy	7
G	4	5	7	9	7	5	4	5	G	In paradisum deducant	WA 439	an	8
G	4	5	7	9	7	5	4	5	G	In paradisum deducant ... chorus	AR [185] GR 109* LU 1768	an	7

C	4	5	7	9	7	5	4	5	E	Jesu nostra redemptio	ST 293	hy	4
G	4	5	7	9	7	5	4	5	G	Jesu redemptor omnium	AR [58]	hy	7
G	4	5	7	9	7	5	4	5	G	Lux o decora patriae	AR 778	hy	7
G	4	5	7	9	7	5	4	5	G	Magnum salutis gaudium	ST 34 42	hy	7
G	4	5	7	9	7	5	4	5	G	Maria virgo semper laetare	WA 353 366	an	7
G	4	5	7	9	7	5	4	5	G	Poenas cucurrit fortiter	ST 44	hy	7
G	4	5	7	9	7	5	4	5	G	Ramos virentes sumpserat	ST 35	hy	7
G	4	5	7	9	7	5	7	0	G	Custodes hominum psallimus angelos	AM 1065	hy	7
G	4	5	7	9	7	5	7	0	G	Martinae celebri plaudite nomini	AR 614	hy	7
G	4	5	7	9	7	5	7	0	G	Non illam crucians ungula	AR 617	hy	7
G	4	5	7	9	7	5	7	0	G	Panis angelicus fit panis hominum	AR 96*		7
C	4	5	7	9	7	5	7	0	C	Sanctorum meritis inclyta gaudia	ST 197	hy	5
G	4	5	7	9	7	5	7	0	G	Tu natale solum protege	AR 615	hy	7
G	4	5	7	9	7	5	7	4	G	Erumpant montes	WA 18 *LA 7	an	7
G	4	5	7	9	7	5	7	4	G	Viderunt omnes termini terrae	LR 338	an	7
G	4	5	7	9	7	5	7	5	G	Cum jejunatis nolite fieri	AR 359 AM 332 *WA 84 *LA 126	an	7
G	4	5	7	9	7	5	7	5	G	De caelo veniet dominator	AR 227 LU 1082 *AM 199 *WA 12 *LA 11 381	an	7
G	4	5	7	9	7	5	7	9		Ascendo ad patrem meum	SYG 180	alv	
G	4	5	7	9	7	5	7	9	G	Ego sum panis vitae	LR 128	re	7
G	4	5	7	9	7	5	7	9	G	Mel et lac ex ejus ore	WA 254	an	7
G	4	5	7	9	7	5	7	9	G	Non sum missus nisi ad oves	LA 135	an	7
G	4	5	7	9	7	5	7	9	G	Nunc dimittis Domine	WA 272 *LA 350	an	7
G	4	5	7	9	7	5	7	9	G	Regis iram non formidans	WA 251	re	7
F	4	5	7	9	7	5	7	12	F	Ite missa est VIII	GR 31* LU 39		5
F	4	5	7	9	7	5	7	12	F	Kyrie VIII de angelis	MEL #95 GR 28* LU 37		5
G	4	5	7	9	7	5	9	7	G	Exsultavit cor ... qui humiliat	AR 131	an	7
G	4	5	7	9	7	5	9	7	G	In viam pacis et prosperitatis	PM 308	an	7
G	4	5	7	9	7	5	9	10	G	Mulier cum parit tristitiam	LA 236	an	7
G	4	5	7	9	7	5	9	10	G	Oculis ac manibus in caelum	AR 918 LU 1749 AM 1116 *WA 402 LA 487	an	7
G	4	5	7	9	7	5	9	10	G	Omnes inimici mei audierunt	AR 431 OHS 308 AM 410 *WA 117 LA 187	an	7
G	4	5	7	9	7	5	9	12	G	Si manseritis in me	AR 696 LU 1465[F] AM 895 LA 394	an	7
G	4	5	7	9	7	5	10	9	G	Videntes stellam Magi	AR 331 LU 481 *AM 298 WA 55 *LA 74	an	7

G	4	5	7	9	7	9	5	2	G	Afferte Domino filii Dei	LR 69 *LA 66 *WA 53	an	7
G	4	5	7	9	7	9	5	2	G	Cantate Domino canticum ... laus	AR 230 AM 202 WA 13 *LA 5	an	7
G	4	5	7	9	7	9	5	2	G	Cantate Domino canticum ... quia	LR 294	an	7
G	4	5	7	9	7	9	5	2	G	Ecce vir Oriens nomen ejus	AR 894[1] LU 1715 AM 1089	an	7
G	4	5	7	9	7	9	5	2	G	Tulerunt lapides ut jacerent	WA 107	an	7
G	4	5	7	9	7	9	5	4	G	In loco pascuae ibi Dominus	AR 153 LU 279[M] *LA 555	an	7
G	4	5	7	9	7	9	5	7	G	Gabriel angelus descendit ad Zachariam	AR 664	an	7
F	4	5	7	9	7	9	5	9		Et in terra	BOS #26		
G	4	5	7	9	7	9	7	5	G	Alleluia	PM 232	an	7
G	4	5	7	9	7	9	7	5	G	Apparuit caro suo	WA 39 *LA 51	an	7
G	4	5	7	9	7	9	7	5	G	Beata Caecilia dixit ad Tiburtium	WA 407 *LA 489	an	7
G	4	5	7	9	7	9	7	5	G	In fide et lenitate ipsius	PM 232 LR 197 *WA 429	an	7
G	4	5	7	9	7	9	7	5	G	Laudate Dominum qui sanat	AR 152	an	7
G	4	5	7	9	7	9	7	5	G	Qui me dignatus est	AR 626 LU 1371 AM 808 WA 276 *LA 363	an	7
G	4	5	7	9	7	9	10	9	G	Magnificemus Christum regem	LA 90	an	7
G	4	5	7	9	7	9	10	9	G	Mane nobiscum quoniam	AR 476 AM 491 *WA 138 *LA 218 234	an	7
G	4	5	7	9	7	9	10	9	G	Ubi est caritas et dilectio	WA 214 SYG 131	an	7
G	4	5	7	9	7	9	10	12	G	Si diligeretis me gauderetis	LA 394	an	7
G	4	5	7	9	7	9	10	12	G	Videns praeses beatorum	WA 378	an	7
C	4	5	7	9	7	9	11	12	C	Alleluia: beatus vir sanctus Martinus	GR 652 LU 1747 *GB 242[v]	al	5 7
C	4	5	7	9	7	9	11	12	C	Alma redemptoris mater	AR 69 LR 46 LU 277 AM 178	an	5
C	4	5	7	9	7	9	11	12		Beatus vir sanctus Martinus	GR 652 LU 1747 *GB 242[v]	alv	
C	4	5	7	9	7	9	11	12	C	Dignum canentes angeli	ST 19	hy	5
C	4	5	7	9	7	9	11	12	C	Quodcumque in orbe nexibus revinxeris	ST 19	hy	5
C	4	5	7	9	7	9	12	14	G	Sanctorum meritis inclyta gaudia	ST 198	hy	8
G	4	5	7	9	7	10	9	5	G	Mecum est maxima merces	WA 387	re	7
G	4	5	7	9	7	10	9	10	G	Sancti Dei omnes intercedere	AR [132] *WA 398	an	7
G	4	5	7	9	10	7	9	10	G	Anima mea liquefacta est	PM 275 *WA 361	an	7
G	4	5	7	9	10	9	5	7	G	Nesciens mater virgo virum	PM 250 *LA 35 *WA 48	re	7
G	4	5	7	9	10	9	5	9	G	Ut videam voluntatem Domini	WA 318	an	7
G	4	5	7	9	10	9	7	9	G	Virgo Maria non est tibi similis	PM 186	an	7
G	4	5	7	9	10	12	10	9	G	Ave stella matutina peccatorum medicina	PM 277	an	7

F	4	5	7	9	11	7	5	4	F	Introduxit me rex	WA 360	an	5
F	4	5	7	9	11	9	7	4	F	In craticula te Deum ... affatus	WA 346	re	5
G	4	5	7	9	12	7	9	7	G	Ascendo ad patrem meum	AR 492 LU 845 AM 510 WA 150 LA 251	an	7
G	4	5	7	9	12	7	9	7	G	Descendi in hortum nucum ... alleluia	LR 252	an	7
G	4	5	7	9	12	7	9	7	G	Descendi in hortum nucum ... revertere	PM 243 WA 356 LA 458	an	7
G	4	5	7	9	12	7	9	7	G	Exortum est in tenebris	AR 538^2 LU 965 *AM 561	an	7
F	4	5	7	9	12	7	9	7	F	Gloria	BOS #26		III
G	4	5	7	9	12	7	9	7	G	Introibo ad altare Dei summam	LR 125 LU 934	an	7
F	4	5	7	9	12	11	9	7	F	Agnus Dei	SCH #115		5
F	4	5	7	9	12	11	9	7	F	Alma redemptoris mater	AR 65 LU 273 *AM 173 *WA 303	an	5
F	4	5	7	9	12	11	9	7	F	Sanctus	THAN #100		5
G	4	5	7	10	9	5	9	7	G	Egressi de ergastulo	WA 378	an	7
G	4	5	7	10	9	10	9	5	G	In die tribulationis meae Deum	OHS 393 LU 647 *WA 119 *LA 192	an	7
F	4	6	7	4	2	7	9	7	F	Sanctus	THAN #101		5
F	4	6	7	4	7	9	7	4	F	Austriae decus princeps et patrone	ST 331	hy	5
F	4	6	7	6	4	2	4	2	G	Alleluia: beatus Laurentius oravit	GB 217^v	al	8
F	4	6	7	9	7	2	5	4		Beatus vir qui timet	GR [46] LU 1205 *GS 208 *SYG 44 GB 270	alv	
F	4	6	7	9	7	2	6	4		Ecce adest dies	SYG 216	alv	
F	4	6	7	9	7	2	6	4		Primus ad Sion dicet	SYG 170 *GS 204 v	alv	
F	4	6	7	9	7	4	0	2	F	Agnus Dei	SCH #144		5
F	4	6	7	9	7	6	4	2		Beatus Laurentius oravit et dixit	GB 217^v	alv	
F	4	6	7	9	7	6	7	9	G	Jucundare filia Sion	AR 213 LU 323 AM 187 *WA 6 *LA 6	an	8
F	4	6	7	9	7	9	7	9	F	Intellige clamorem meum	GR 114 LU 549 SYG 78 GB 70^v *GS 40 48	co	5
F	4	6	7	9	11	12	11	9	F	Gloria	BOS #32		III
F	4	7	4	2	4	5	2	0	F	Jubilate Deo omnis terra	GR 66 OTT 23 LU 480 SYG 32 GB 36^v *GS 20 65	of	5
F	4	7	4	2	4	5	2	0	F	Videbam coram me vitem	GR 37**	of	5
C	4	7	4	2	4	5	4	2	G	Alleluia: surrexit quasi ignis	GR 66**	al	8
F	4	7	4	2	4	7	[0	0]		Et in terra	BOS #7		
F	4	7	4	2	7	9	7	9	F	Agnus Dei IX	GR 34* OHS 462 LU 42 SCH #114		5
F	4	7	4	2	7	9	7	9	F	Benedictus Deus qui misit	AR 866 LU 1665 AM 1068	an	5

F	4	7	4	2	7	9	7	9		Eructavit cor meum Regnum mundi	LR 227 PM 234 VP 260 *WA 432	rev	
F	4	7	4	2	7	9	7	9	F	Hic summista vatidicus	WA 311	an	5
F	4	7	4	2	7	9	7	9	F	Isti etenim maximo	WA 342	an	5
F	4	7	4	2	7	9	7	9	F	Regnum mundi et omnem	LR 227 PM 234 VP 260 *WA 432	re	5
F	4	7	4	2	7	9	7	9	F	Sanctus	THAN #99		5
F	4	7	4	2	7	9	7	9	F	Tandem ad sponsi	WA 244	an	5
F	4	7	4	2	7	9	7	12		Cumque intraveritis terram Vos qui transituri	LR 412 *LA 161 *WA 102	rev	
G	4	7	4	5	7	2	4	0		Ibi confregit cornu arcum Terra tremuit	OTT 55 *GB 128 *SYG 153	ofv	
F	4	7	4	6	4	2	0	[0]		Et in terra	BOS #35		
F	4	7	4	6	4	2	0	4	F	Gloria	BOS #35		III
F	4	7	4	6	4	2	4	2	G	Pro pace regum et principum	GB 155	an	8
F	4	7	4	6	7	2	4	2	F	Dixit Jesus discipulo ecce mater	GR 86**	of	6
F	4	7	4	6	7	2	4	6		Tu humiliasti sicut vulneratum Tui sunt caeli	OTT 18 GB 19^{v} *SYG 20	ofv	
F	4	7	4	7	4	6	7	2	F	Sub umbra illius	GR 625 LU 1689	int	5
F	4	7	4	7	4	6	7	2	F	Verba mea auribus percipe	GR 136 SYG 99 GB 88^{v} GS 61	int	5
F	4	7	4	7	4	7	4	7		Confiteantur Domino misericordiae Exaltent eum	GR 408 [2^{1}] LU 1122^{2} GS 182	grv	
F	4	7	4	7	4	7	4	7		Confiteantur Domino misericordiae Misit Dominus verbum suum	GR 68 LU 485 GS 21 GB 37^{v} SYG 35	grv	
F	4	7	4	7	4	7	4	7		Congregate illi sanctos ejus Ex Sion species	GR 4 LU 328 GB 2^{v} SYG 3 GS 3	grv	
F	4	7	4	7	6	2	4	7	F	Ex Sion species decoris	GR 4 LU 328 SYG 3 GB 2^{v} GS 3	gr	5
F	4	7	4	7	6	7	4	7	F	Eructavit cor meum	GR 65**	gr	5
F	4	7	4	7	6	7	6	4	F	Adjuvabit eam Deus vultu suo	GR [56] LU 1221 *SYG 50 *GB 50 GS 181	gr	5
F	4	7	4	7	6	7	9	7	F	Benedictus qui venit in nomine	GR 31 SYG 15 *GB 15^{v} GS E	gr	5
F	4	7	4	7	6	7	9	7	F	Benedictus qui venit in nomine	LA 37 WA 48	re	5
F	4	7	4	7	6	7	9	7	F	Quam magna multitudo	GR 449 LU 1393	gr	5
F	4	7	4	7	9	4	7	9		Suscipiant montes pacem Reges Tharsis	OTT 21 GB 34 SYG 31	ofv	
G	4	7	4	7	9	5	4	5	G	Revertere in terram Juda	WA 52 *LA 355	an	7
C	4	7	4	7	9	7	4	7	C	Dum duceretur Petrus	AR 194* VP 183 *GB 207	an	5
F	4	7	4	7	9	7	5	4	F	Ecce jam venit plenitudo	AR 238 AM 213 WA 17 *LA 22	an	5

C	4	7	4	7	9	7	5	4	E	Lauda anima mea Dominum	GR 267 OTT 67 LU 823 899 SYG 166 *GB 149 GS K a 129	of	4
F	4	7	4	7	9	7	6	7	F	Quadraginta dies et noctes	LA 117 WA 76	re	5
F	4	7	4	7	9	7	9	5	F	Benedicam Dominum in omni tempore	LA 88 WA 63	re	5
F	4	7	4	7	9	7	9	6	F	Immisit Dominus soporem ... et tulit	LA 110 WA 73	re	5
F	4	7	4	7	9	7	9	7	F	Alleluia: beatus vir qui timet Dominum	GR [46] LU 1205 GS 208 SYG 44 GB 270	al	5
F	4	7	4	7	9	7	9	7	F	Alleluia: ecce adest dies	SYG 216	al	5
F	4	7	4	7	9	7	9	7	F	Alleluia: primus ad Sion dicet	SYG 170 GS v 204	al	5
F	4	7	4	7	9	7	9	7	F	Ecce veniet Dominus princeps	LA 15	re	5
F	4	7	4	7	9	7	9	7		Locutus est Dominus ad Moysen Sanctificavit Moyses	OTT 114 GB 259^{v} SYG 254	ofv	
F	4	7	4	7	9	7	9	7	F	Misit Dominus angelum ... conclusit	LA 303 *WA 184	re	5
F	4	7	4	7	9	7	9	12	F	Paratur nobis mensa	LR 122	an	5
F	4	7	4	7	9	7	9	12	F	Qui pacem ponit fines	AR 526 LU 957 AM 545	an	5
F	4	7	4	7	9	7	11	9	F	Alleluia: regem martyrum	LA 386	inv	5
F	4	7	4	7	9	7	11	9	F	Kyrie	MEL #94		
F	4	7	4	7	9	7	11	9	F	Kyrie ad lib. IV altissime	GR 78* LU 81		5
F	4	7	4	7	9	7	12	9	F	Lingua pangat et cor tangat	ST 322	hy	5
C	4	7	4	12	11	7	4	0	C	Agnus Dei	SCH #248		3
F	4	7	4	12	11	7	4	0	F	Sanctus	THAN #98		5
G	4	7	5	2	0	5	4	7	E	Benedictus es in firmamento ... gloriosus	SYG 82 GB 9^{v} 73 193^{v} 258^{v}	hy	3
G	4	7	5	2	0	5	4	7	G	Benedictus es in firmamento ... gloriosus	GS 44	tr	8
G	4	7	5	2	0	5	4	7	E	Laudate Dominum de caelis	GR [86] LU 1275	gr	3
G	4	7	5	2	4	5	4	7	G	Benedictus es Domine doce me ... et non tradas	GR 165 OTT 48 *SYG 116 GB 104 *GS 77	of	8
G	4	7	5	2	4	5	4	7	E	Benedictus es Domine doce me ... in labiis	GR 83 OTT 28 LU 514 *SYG 62 GB 60 *GS 29	of	3
G	4	7	5	2	4	5	4	7	E	Cognoscetur Dominus ab Aegypto	GR 7**	of	3
G	4	7	5	2	4	5	7	4	G	Considerabam ad dexteram	AR 437 OHS 630 LU 776^{F} AM 433 *WA 121 *LA 194	an	7
G	4	7	5	2	5	0	4	2	G	Victricem manum tuam	GR 252 OHS 805 LU 796 SYG 158 GB 137 *GS 121	int	8
G	4	7	5	2	5	4	2	0	G	Quam magnificata sunt	AR 187	an	7
G	4	7	5	2	5	4	2	0	G	Redemptionem misit ... populo	AR 271 LU 412 AM 246 WA 32 LA 38	an	7
G	4	7	5	2	5	4	2	5	G	Mirificavit Dominus sanctos	LR 381 *WA 395 *LA 474	an	7

G	4	7	5	2	5	4	2	5	G	Sacerdos Dei Martine aperti	WA 400 LA 483	an	7
C	4	7	5	2	5	4	5	2	E	Adoremus Dominum qui fecit	LA 80 *WA 60 165	inv	4
G	4	7	5	2	5	4	5	2	G	Responsum accepit Simeon ... Dominum	AR 620 LU 1366 *AM 802 *LA 355	an	7
G	4	7	5	2	5	4	5	7	G	Constitues eos principes	LR 135 LA 505 *WA 411	an	7
G	4	7	5	4	0	2	0	-2	b	Dilexisti justitiam et odisti	GR [71] LU 1241 SYG 217 *GB 219^v	co	4
G	4	7	5	4	0	2	0	-2	b	Sub umbra illius	GR 53**	co	4
G	4	7	5	4	0	2	0	2	b	Ab occultis meis munda me Domine	GR 142 SYG 103 GB 91^v GS 65	co	4
G	4	7	5	4	0	2	0	2	b	Per signum crucis de inimicis	GR 492 LU 1457	co	4
G	4	7	5	4	2	0	2	5	G	Quis est iste qui venit	AR 759 LU 1536 AM 945	an	7
F	4	7	5	4	2	7	9	7	F	Cum sancto sancte	WA 283	re	5
F	4	7	5	4	2	7	9	7	F	Nisi granum frumenti	WA 419 LA 439	an	5
C	4	7	5	4	5	2	5	7	E	Alleluia: vindica Domine sanguinem	GB 269	al	4
G	4	7	5	4	5	7	5	4	G	Alleluia: quasi palma exaltata	GR 34**	al	7
G	4	7	5	4	5	7	5	4	G	Alleluia: quasi rosa plantata	GR 614 LU 1669	al	7
G	4	7	5	4	5	7	5	4	G	Alleluia: qui ad justitiam erudiunt	GR 497 LU 1467	al	7
G	4	7	5	4	5	7	5	4	G	Alleluia: te decet hymnus Deus	GR 346 LU 1022 GS 148 *SYG 242 *GB 252	al	7
F	4	7	5	4	5	7	9	7	F	Dum transiret Dominus	AR 563 LU 1105 AM 602 LA 315	an	5
F	4	7	5	4	5	7	9	7	F	Nazaraeus vocabitur puer	AR 733 LU 1497 LR 352 *WA 322	an	5
C	4	7	5	4	5	7	9	7	E	Tibi Domine derelictus est	GR 149 LU 566 *SYG 108 *GB 96 *GS 70	gr	3
G	4	7	5	4	5	9	7	0	G	Nazaraeus vocabitur puer	LA 403	an	7
F	4	7	5	4	7	9	7	9	F	Ideoque dico tibi	WA 338	an	5
F	4	7	5	4	7	9	7	9	F	Innocenter puerilia	WA 240	an	5
G	4	7	5	4	7	9	7	9		Probavit me Dominus sicut aurum Oratio mea	OTT 164 *GB 216^v *SYG 212	ofv	
G	4	7	5	7	5	4	2	5	G	Custodi me a laqueo	AR 437 OHS 629 LU 776^E AM 432 *WA 121 LA 194	an	7
G	4	7	5	7	5	4	2	5	G	Juravit Dominus et non paenitebit	AR [10] LU 1114 *AM 626 *WA 415 LA 421	an	8
F	4	7	5	7	5	4	2	5	F	Levita Vincentius dixit	WA 256	an	5
c	4	7	5	7	5	4	7	9		Optans suorum Maria Maria Magdalene ut cognovit	WA 336	rev	
G	4	7	5	7	5	7	9	7	G	Confitebuntur caeli mirabilia ... et	GR [17] LU 1148 OTT 138 SYG 170 *GB 153 GS 209	of	7

G	4	7	5	7	9	7	10	12	G	Non duplices sermonem	GR 32**	of	7
F	4	7	5	7	9	7	11	9	F	Alleluia: ascendens Christus in altum	WA 146	inv	5
G	4	7	5	9	7	5	4	5		Fac cum servo tuo Domine Domine vivifica	OTT 31 *GB 64 *SYG 68	ofv	
F	4	7	6	2	4	2	0	2		Et aedificavit turrim Vinea facta est	SYG 150	trv	
F	4	7	6	2	4	2	0	2		Et benedictus fructus ventri Ave Maria	GB 55^{v}	trv	
F	4	7	6	2	4	2	0	2		Scitote quod Dominus Jubilate Domino omnis terra	GR 82 LU 513 GS 28 GB 59^{v} SYG 62	trv	
F	4	7	6	2	4	2	0	2		Vinea enim Domini Vinea facta est	SYG 150	trv	
F	4	7	6	2	6	7	4	2	G	Obtulerunt pro eo Domino	AR 621 LU 1366 AM 803 WA 270 LA 355	an	8
F	4	7	6	4	2	4	2	0	F	Omnis vallis implebitur	WA 20 *LA 27	an	5
F	4	7	6	4	2	7	9	7	F	Alleluia	PM 228	an	5
F	4	7	6	4	2	7	9	7	F	Bene omnia fecit	AR 563 LU 1027 AM 602 WA 189 LA 315	an	5
F	4	7	6	4	2	7	9	7	F	Ego crucis Christi	WA 232	an	5
F	4	7	6	4	2	7	9	7	F	Intellexit Deus clamorem	WA 282	an	5
F	4	7	6	4	2	7	9	7	F	Responderunt prudentes virgines	WA 431	an	5
F	4	7	6	4	2	7	9	7	F	Sanctus	THAN #97		5
F	4	7	6	4	2	7	9	7	F	Sicut novit me pater	AR 471 AM 485 WA 142 LA 235	an	5
F	4	7	6	4	2	7	9	7	F	Videntibus cunctis splendor	WA 234	an	5
F	4	7	6	4	6	4	2	7	F	Hic tanguntur	WA 295	an	5
F	4	7	6	4	6	7	9	4	F	Ne in ira tua arguas	LA 87	an	5
F	4	7	6	4	7	6	2	4		Accedite ad eum et illuminamini Venite filii	GR 336(39) LU 1010 GS 67 148 168 GB 93 SYG 105	grv	
F	4	7	6	4	7	6	2	4		Benedicite Deum caeli Benedictus es Dominus qui	SYG 260 GS c *GB 213	grv	
F	4	7	6	4	7	6	2	4		Benedictus es Domine in firmamento Benedictus ... qui intueris	GR 308 LU 910 GB 213 SYG 260	grv	
F	4	7	6	4	7	6	2	4		Dum sacramenta offerret Ora pro nobis beate Martine	SYG 225	grv	
F	4	7	6	4	7	6	2	4		Pro patribus tuis nati sunt Constitues eos	GR 393 533 LU 1519 GS x GB 204 SYG 202	grv	
F	4	7	6	4	7	6	2	4		Tu gloria Jerusalem ... nostri Benedicta es	GR 401 LU 1317	grv	
F	4	7	6	4	7	6	4	2	F	Ecce factus est sacer ille	PM 190 *WA 377	an	5
F	4	7	6	4	7	6	4	6	F	Alleluia: diligam te Domine	GB 249 *SYG 239 *GS 143	al	5

F	4	7	6	4	7	9	7	4	F	Haurietis aquas	AR 238 *AM 213 WA 17 LA 22	an	5
F	4	7	6	4	7	9	7	6	F	Delectare in Domino et dabit	LA 88 WA 64	re	5
F	4	7	6	4	7	9	7	6	F	Sacerdotes Dei benedicite ... aeternum	WA 393	an	5
F	4	7	6	4	7	9	7	9	F	Fili praebe mihi cor tuum	AR 538^{7} LU 977	an	5
F	4	7	6	4	9	7	6	7	F	Laudem dicite Deo nostro	LR 388 *WA 397 *LA 476	an	5
F	4	7	6	7	6	4	2	7	F	Alleluia: exaltabo te Deus	GR 54	al	5
F	4	7	6	7	6	4	7	0	F	Paganorum multitudo fugiens	AR 626 AM 809 WA 276 *LA 364	an	5
F	4	7	6	7	6	4	7	9	F	Anima Scholasticae ex arca	LR 300	re	5
F	4	7	6	9	7	6	7	12	F	Agnus Dei	SCH #113		5
F	4	7	6	9	7	9	7	4	F	Communicantes Christi passionibus	GR 508 LU 1482	gr	5
F	4	7	6	9	7	9	7	4	F	Tribulationes cordis mei dilatatae	GR 112 LU 546 SYG 77 GB 69^{v} GS 39 47	gr	5
F	4	7	9	4	7	9	7	9	F	Dominum qui fecit nos	LA 80 *WA 95	inv	5
F	4	7	9	6	7	4	7	4	F	Gloria	BOS #34		III
F	4	7	9	6	7	9	11	7	F	Aeterne rector siderum	AR 867	hy	5
F	4	7	9	6	7	9	11	7	F	Orbis patrator optime	AM 1069	hy	5
F	4	7	9	6	7	9	11	7	F	Proles de caelo prodiit	ST 443	hy	5
F	4	7	9	7	4	5	4	2	F	Agnus Dei	SCH #112		5
C	4	7	9	7	4	5	4	2		Beatus vir qui suffert tentationem	GR [43] LU 1202 *GS 207 SYG 218	alv	
F	4	7	9	7	4	5	4	2	F	Sanctus	THAN #96		5
F	4	7	9	7	4	7	0	4		Concaluit cor meum intra me Eructavit cor meum	GR 65**	grv	
F	4	7	9	7	4	7	0	4		Propter veritatem ... et deducet Diffusa est gratia	GR [69] LU 1240 GS 227 GB 29^{v} SYG 28	grv	
F	4	7	9	7	4	7	0	4		Propter veritatem ... et deducet Specie tua	GR [60] LU 1226 GS 226 SYG 39	grv	
F	4	7	9	7	4	7	0	4		Si dederit homo omnem Aquae multae	GR (10)	grv	
F	4	7	9	7	4	7	2	4	F	Orante beatissimo ad Dominum	WA 289	re	5
F	4	7	9	7	4	7	4	2		Potens in terra erit semen Beatus vir qui timet	GR [11] LU 1136 GS 206 GB 51 SYG 51	grv	
F	4	7	9	7	4	7	4	7		Liberator meus de gentibus Populum humilem	OTT 93 GB 95^{v} SYG 107	ofv	
F	4	7	9	7	4	7	5	4	F	Nunc sancte nobis spiritus	ST 320	hy	5
F	4	7	9	7	4	7	6	4	F	Sanctus	THAN #95		5
F	4	7	9	7	4	7	9	11		A Domino factum est Benedictus qui venit	GR 31 LU 404 GS E GB 15^{v} SYG 15	grv	

F	4	7	9	7	4	7	9	11	F	In circuitu tuo ... ubi constituisti	VP 256 *LA 518 *WA 429	re	5
F	4	7	9	7	4	7	11	9	F	Viderunt omnes fines terrae	GR 33 LU 409 SYG 19 GB 17^v GS G	gr	5
F	4	7	9	7	5	4	2	0	F	Adoro te devote latens Deitas	AR 100* LU 1855 VP 13	hy	5
C	4	7	9	7	5	4	2	4	C	Rector potens verax Deus	ST 137	hy	5
F	4	7	9	7	5	4	5	7	F	Eduxit Dominus Abram	WA 80	re	5
G	4	7	9	7	5	4	7	9		Promittentes tecum in carcerem Vadis propitiator	PM 188	rev	
F	4	7	9	7	5	7	4	2	F	Stans in aede	WA 251	re	5
F	4	7	9	7	5	7	4	5	F	Rex virtutum assis nobis	WA 252	an	5
F	4	7	9	7	5	7	9	7	F	Ecce jam venit plenitudo	WA 23	re	5
F	4	7	9	7	5	7	9	7	F	Exsultat in gloria	WA 286	an	5
F	4	7	9	7	6	4	7	6		Ubi collisi sunt currus Nova bella elegit	GR 40**	grv	
F	4	7	9	7	6	4	7	9	F	Desiderium meum omnipotens	WA 175	re	5
F	4	7	9	7	6	4	7	9	F	In jejunio et fletu orabunt	PM 49 LA 128 *WA 86	re	5
F	4	7	9	7	6	4	7	9	F	Indicabo tibi homo	LA 306 WA 186 (inc illeg)	re	5
F	4	7	9	7	6	7	4	0	[F]	Agnus Dei	SCH #145		5
F	4	7	9	7	6	7	4	7		Et in terra	BOS #33		
F	4	7	9	7	6	7	4	7	F	Sancte Paule apostole praedicator ... ad Deum	VP 185	re	5
F	4	7	9	7	6	7	6	4		Qui insurgunt in me confundantur Confitebor Domino	OTT 74 *GB 162 SYG 178	ofv	
F	4	7	9	7	6	7	9	11	F	Divine ductor Raphael	VP 233	hy	6
F	4	7	9	7	6	7	9	11	F	Gaude mater ecclesia	VP 206	hy	5
F	4	7	9	7	6	9	11	7	G	Ab omni via mala prohibui	LA 134 WA 89	re	8
F	4	7	9	7	6	9	11	7	F	Adhuc multa habeo	AR 482 AM 497 *LA 242	an	5
F	4	7	9	7	9	4	2	4	F	Benedic anima mea Domino et noli	GR 105 OTT 110 *GS 42 169 SYG 80 *GB 72	of	5
F	4	7	9	7	9	4	2	4	F	Domine in lumine vultus	GR 101**	of	5
c	4	7	9	7	9	7	2	4	c	Cum audisset populus quia Jesus	WA 208	an	5
F	4	7	9	7	9	7	4	2	F	Adeamus cum fiducia	GR 587^1 43** LU 1612^1	int	5
F	4	7	9	7	9	7	4	6	F	Loquebar de testimoniis tuis	GR 395 591 [51] LU 1215 1309 1618 SYG 39 GB 42^v *GS 225	int	5
F	4	7	9	7	9	7	6	2	F	Cogitationes cordis ejus	GR 324 [111] LU 970	int	5
F	4	7	9	7	9	7	6	2	F	Domine refugium factus es	GR 101 SYG 76 *GB 68 *GS 38	int	5

F	4	7	9	7	9	7	6	2	F	Virgines laudent nomen	GR 102**	int	5
F	4	7	9	7	9	7	6	4	c	Adorna thalamum ... amplectere	GR 430 PM 134 LU 1359 GS i 180 *SYG 46 *GB 46^{v}	an	6
F	4	7	9	7	9	7	6	4	F	Dexteram meam et collum	LA 333 WA 253	re	5
F	4	7	9	7	9	7	6	7	G	Adorna thalamum ... quem	LA 348 *WA 268	re	8
F	4	7	9	7	9	7	9	4		Audi filia ... quia concupivit Propter veritatem	GR 620 (31) LU 1676 GS s GB 222^{v} SYG 215	grv	
F	4	7	9	7	9	7	9	4		Audi filia ... quia concupivit Specie tua	GB 42^{v}	grv	
F	4	7	9	7	9	7	9	4		Bonum est sperare in Domino Bonum est confidere	GR 358 LU 1037 GS 69 157 GB 95 SYG 107	grv	
F	4	7	9	7	9	7	9	4		Dominus robur est In Deo confisum	OHS 416 LU 662	grv	
F	4	7	9	7	9	7	9	4	F	In te Domine sperent	WA 86	re	5
F	4	7	9	7	9	7	9	4		Laqueus contritus est Anima nostra	GR 41 [26] LU 1167 GS 17 GB 26 SYG 25	grv	
F	4	7	9	7	9	7	9	4		Posuit in ea verba signorum Mementote mirabilium	GR 85**	grv	
F	4	7	9	7	9	7	9	4		Ut videam voluptatem Domini et protegar Unam petii	GR 92 GS 33	grv	
F	4	7	9	7	9	7	9	4		Ut videam voluptatem Domini et visitem Unam petii	GR 1** GB 64 SYG 68 GS 33	grv	
F	4	7	9	7	9	7	9	4		Visi sunt oculis Justorum animae	GR 413 LU 1547 GS 213 GB 171 SYG 194	grv	
F	4	7	9	7	9	7	9	7	c	Confitemini Domino filii	WA 228	an	5
F	4	7	9	7	9	7	9	7	c	Decantabat populus in Israel	LA 226 WA 141	re	6
F	4	7	9	7	9	7	9	7		Diligam te Domine virtus mea	SYG 239 GB 249 *GS 143	alv	
F	4	7	9	7	9	7	9	7		Orietur in diebus ejus Reges Tharsis	OTT 21 *GB 34 *SYG 31	ofv	
F	4	7	9	7	9	7	9	11		Tota die miseretur Justus non conturbabitur	GB 162^{v} *GS 206	grv	
F	4	7	9	7	9	11	7	4	F	Elegit Mariam Deus	LR 264	re	5
F	4	7	9	7	9	11	7	4	F	Pulchra facie sed pulchrior	LR 218 *LA 336 *WA 255	re	5
F	4	7	9	7	9	11	7	9		Ad te Domine clamavi In Deo speravit	GR 348 LU 1025 *GS 60 152 *GB 87^{v} SYG 98	grv	
F	4	7	9	7	9	11	7	9		Deus in te speravi Esto mihi in Deum	GR 339 LU 1013 GS 64 149 GB 91 SYG 103	grv	
F	4	7	9	7	9	11	7	9		Posuerunt mortalia servorum Vindica Domine	GR 643 GS 214 *GB 195 SYG 190	grv	
F	4	7	9	7	9	11	7	9		Tota die miseretur Justus cum ceciderit	GR [13] LU 1139	grv	

C	4	7	9	7	9	11	9	7	[E]	Agnus Dei	SCH #247		4
F	4	7	9	7	9	11	9	11	c	Sacerdos Dei Lucianus	WA 344	re	6
F	4	7	9	7	9	12	11	7	F	Sanctus sanctus sanctus ... omnipotens	PM 92	an	5
C	4	7	9	7	9	12	11	9	D	Crux fidelis inter omnes ... sustinens	ST 481 WA 216 GS 102	hy	1
F	4	7	9	7	9	12	11	9	F	Obsecro Domine memento	AR 543 LU 989 *AM 579	an	5
C	4	7	9	7	9	12	11	9	C	Salve regina mater	AR 69[1] LR 48 LU 279 AM 180	an	5
F	4	7	9	7	11	9	7	4	F	Admirabile nomen Jesu	LR 430	inv	5
F	4	7	9	7	11	9	7	6	F	Alleluia: Christum Dominum ascendentem	LR 94	inv	5
F	4	7	9	7	11	9	7	6	F	Alleluia: spiritus Domini replevit orbem	LR 107 LU 863 *LA 255 *WA 152	inv	5
F	4	7	9	7	11	9	7	6		Laudate nomen ejus / Jubilate Deo	OTT 23 *GB 36v *SYG 32	ofv	
F	4	7	9	7	11	9	7	12	F	Jucundantur et laetantur	ST 464	hy	5
G	4	7	9	10	9	5	2	5	G	Revertere revertere Sunamitis	LR 214	an	7
F	4	7	9	11	7	4	7	9	F	Joseph cum intraret	LA 148 *WA 96	re	5
F	4	7	9	11	7	6	9	11		Beatus qui intelligit super egenum / Ego dixi Domine miserere mei	GR 311 GS 141 GB 247 SYG 239	grv	
F	4	7	9	11	7	6	9	11		Justitiam tuam non abscondi / Annuntiavi	LU 1623[B]	grv	
F	4	7	9	11	7	9	7	2		Deus cui adstat angelorum / Locus iste	GR [72] LU 1251 GS 175 GB 173v *SYG 263	grv	
F	4	7	9	11	7	9	7	6		Beati qui habitant in domo ... in saecula / Unam petii a Domino	GR 60 LU 471	grv	
F	4	7	9	11	7	9	7	6		Beatus homo qui audit me / Ego sapientia	GR 25**	grv	
F	4	7	9	11	7	9	7	6		In Deo faciemus virtutem / Da nobis Deus	GR 107**	grv	
F	4	7	9	11	7	9	7	6		Laborem manuum tuarum / Beatus quicumque	LU 1442	grv	
F	4	7	9	11	7	9	7	9		Quoniam elevata est magnificentia / Gloria et honore	SYG 217	grv	
F	4	7	9	11	7	9	7	9		Transite ad me omnes / In me gratia	GR 43**	grv	
F	4	7	9	11	7	11	12	9		Tibi laus tibi gloria / Te jure laudant	WA 162	anv	
F	4	7	9	11	9	7	9	7	F	Agnus Dei	SCH #111		5
C	4	7	9	11	9	7	9	7	D	Alleluia: de quacumque tribulatione	GR 486 LU 1441	al	1
F	4	7	9	11	12	11	9	7	F	Kyrie	MEL #93		

G	4	7	10	7	5	9	7	5		Juxta est Dominus his Clamaverunt justi	GR [29] LU 1170 *GS 213 GB 194 SYG 188	grv	
F	4	7	11	9	11	9	7	9		Et erunt ut complaceant Justitiae Domini	OTT 94 GB 82^v SYG 93	ofv	
C	4	7	12	11	7	9	7	12	C	Attende Domine et miserere	AR 158* LU 1871		5
G	5	0	2	5	2	0	2	5	E	Adjutor in opportunitatibus	GR 74 LU 498 *GB 56 GS 24 *SYG 58	gr	3
D	5	0	5	7	5	3	5	0		Cognovi Domine quia aequitas Gressus meos	OTT 39 *GB 88^v *SYG 99	ofv	
G	5	2	-2	0	2	0	-2	2	G	Facta sunt enim haec	AR 538^9 LU 969 *AM 567	an	8
G	5	2	-2	0	2	0	4	5	G	Simon dormis non potuisti	AR 431 OHS 193 *AM 411 *WA 117 *LA 188	an	8
G	5	2	-2	0	2	0	5	2	G	Laetabitur justus in Domino ... laudabuntur	GR [12] LU 1138 SYG 43 GB 45^v GS z 205	int	8
G	5	2	-2	0	4	5	7	5	G	Cantabant sancti canticum	WA 46 *LA 61	an	8
G	5	2	-2	0	4	7	5	4	G	Generatio haec prava	AR 375 AM 348 *WA 89 *LA 135	an	8
G	5	2	-2	0	5	4	2	5	G	Discede a me pabulum	WA 252 *LA 332	an	8
G	5	2	0	-5	0	2	0	2	G	Dies sanctificatus illuxit nobis	LR 73 LA 70 WA 55	re	8
G	5	2	0	-3	-2	0	4	5	G	Agnus Dei	SCH #68		8
G	5	2	0	-3	-2	0	4	5	G	Sanctus IV	GR 17* LU 27 OHS 421 THAN #49		8
G	5	2	0	-2	0	2	-2	-3	G	Iste est Gregorius qui simoniacam	PM 156	an	8
G	5	2	0	-2	0	2	0	-2	G	Adaperiat Dominus cor ... in diebus	AR 550 LU 993 AM 587	an	8
G	5	2	0	-2	0	2	0	-2	G	Angelis suis Deus mandavit	AR 865 LU 1665 *AM 1067	an	8
G	5	2	0	-2	0	2	0	-2	G	Angelus autem Domini descendit	AR 443 OHS 723 765 LU 782 *AM 453 WA 129 *136 *LA 214 229	an	8
G	5	2	0	-2	0	2	0	-2 q	G	Beatus Dionysius caelestis	PM 198	an	8
G	5	2	0	-2	0	2	0	-2	G	Beatus Laurentius dum in craticula	AR 816 LU 1598 AM 1009 *WA 347 LA 441	an	8
G	5	2	0	-2	0	2	0	-2	G	Benedicite Dominum omnes electi	AR 899 LU 1729 AM 1103 *WA 397	an	8
G	5	2	0	-2	0	2	0	-2	G	Complaceat tibi Domine ... festina	LA 556	an	8
G	5	2	0	-2	0	2	0	-2	G	Confido in Domino	WA 399 LA 480	an	8
G	5	2	0	-2	0	2	0	-2	G	Convertere Domine aliquantulum et ne	AR 241 AM 216 *WA 19 LA 25	an	8
G	5	2	0	-2	0	2	0	-2	G	Convertimini ad Dominum	WA 84	an	8
G	5	2	0	-2	0	2	0	-2	G	Descendit angelus Domini	LR 355	an	8
G	5	2	0	-2	0	2	0	-2	G	Ego sum ostium dicit Dominus	AR 511 AM 527 *LA 265	an	8
G	5	2	0	-2	0	2	0	-2	G	Illumina Domine his	WA 70	an	8

G	5	2	0	-2	0	2	0	-2	G	Illumina Domine sedentes	AR 191	an	8
G	5	2	0	-2	0	2	0	-2	G	Illuminare Domine his	AM 81 586	an	8
G	5	2	0	-2	0	2	0	-2	G	Levita Laurentius bonum opus	AR 813 LU 1593 AM 1005 WA 346 LA 437	an	8
G	5	2	0	-2	0	2	0	-2	G	Multitudo languentium veniebant	LA 328	an	8
G	5	2	0	-2	0	2	0	-2	G	Opera quae ego facio	WA 95	an	8
G	5	2	0	-2	0	2	0	-2	G	Respondens autem angelus ... nolite	AR 444 OHS 728 770 LU 783 AM 454 WA 129 137 LA 216	an	8
G	5	2	0	-2	0	2	0	-2	G	Respondens autem Dominus	WA 432	an	8
G	5	2	0	-2	0	2	0	-2	G	Sancte Michael archangele	WA 381	an	8
G	5	2	0	-2	0	2	0	-2	G	Tantas per illum Dominus	WA 385	an	8
G	5	2	0	-2	0	2	0	-2	G	Tu es Domine qui restitues	PM 329 VP 274 LU 1845	an	8
G	5	2	0	-2	0	2	0	2	G	Beata Agnes in medio flammarum	AM 785 *AR 602 *LU 1338 LA 338 WA 252	an	8
G	5	2	0	-2	0	2	0	2	G	Benedicite Domino in opere	LR 269	an	8
G	5	2	0	-2	0	2	0	2	G	Ego non ab homine	WA 95	an	8
G	5	2	0	-2	0	2	0	2	G	Ego pro te rogavi	WA 280 *LA 419	an	8
G	5	2	0	-2	0	2	0	2	G	Exivi a patre et veni	AR 487 AM 503 *LA 243	an	8
G	5	2	0	-2	0	2	0	2	G	Extollens quaedam mulier	AR 390 LU 557 AM 365 WA 99 *LA 154	an	8
G	5	2	0	-2	0	2	0	2	G	Gloria Libani data	AR 787 LU 1558	an	8
G	5	2	0	-2	0	2	0	2	G	Illuxit nobis dies	LA 39	an	8
G	5	2	0	-2	0	2	0	2	G	In caritate perpetua dilexit nos	AM 565	an	8
G	5	2	0	-2	0	2	0	2	G	Nonne iste est David	WA 164 *LA 273	an	8
G	5	2	0	-2	0	2	0	2	G	Quanto eis praecibiebat	WA 189	an	8
G	5	2	0	-2	0	2	0	2	G	Repleti sunt omnes spiritu	AR 504 LU 884 *AM 521 WA 63 153 LA *254 261	an	8
G	5	2	0	-2	0	2	0	4	G	Agathes sancta dixit	WA 273	an	8
G	5	2	0	-2	0	2	0	4	G	Alleluia	AM 29 474	an	8
G	5	2	0	-2	0	2	0	4	G	Andreas Christi famulus	AR 580 LU 1308 AM 755 WA 234 LA 504	an	8
G	5	2	0	-2	0	2	0	4	G	Beata quae credidisti	LU 1476[A]	an	8
G	5	2	0	-2	0	2	0	4	G	Beati qui habitant in domo ... in saecula	LR 236 *WA 429	an	8
G	5	2	0	-2	0	2	0	4	G	Beatus Martinus dixit Juliano	LA 483	an	8
G	5	2	0	-2	0	2	0	4	G	Chorus angelorum	WA 8	an	8
G	5	2	0	-2	0	2	0	4	G	Christus me misit	WA 235 *LA 498	an	8
G	5	2	0	-2	0	2	0	4	G	Concussum est mare	WA 381 LA 467	an	8

G	5	2	0	-2	0	2	0	4	G	Cosmas et Damianus	WA 377	an	8
G	5	2	0	-2	0	2	0	4	G	Cum his qui oderunt pacem	AR 436 OHS 626 LU 776[D] AM 430 431 WA 121 *LA194	an	8
G	5	2	0	-2	0	2	0	4	G	Damasci praepositus gentis	AR 610 757 LU 1349 *AM 793 942 WA 266 *LA 431	an	8
G	5	2	0	-2	0	2	0	4	G	Dansque illi sancta	WA 386	an	8
G	5	2	0	-2	0	2	0	4	G	Descendit Jesus cum Maria	LU 1439	an	8
G	5	2	0	-2	0	2	0	4	G	Dominus Jesus Christus	WA 400 *LA 482	an	8
G	5	2	0	-2	0	2	0	4	G	Ego sum lux mundi	LA 165	an	8
G	5	2	0	-2	0	2	0	4	G	Ego sum panis vivus dicit Dominus	AR 512 LU 895 AM 528 LA 266	an	8
G	5	2	0	-2	0	2	0	4	G	Exiliit claudus	WA 340 LA 412	an	8
G	5	2	0	-2	0	2	0	4	G	Expansis manibus orabat	WA 405 LA 488	an	8
G	5	2	0	-2	0	2	0	4	G	Fili recordare quia recepisti	AR 384 LU 1087 *AM 358 WA 187 *LA 145	an	8
G	5	2	0	-2	0	2	0	4	G	Hic vir despiciens mundum	AR 577[19] [85] LU 262[7] 1199 AM 675 744 WA 417 LA 528	an	8
G	5	2	0	-2	0	2	0	4	G	Hortus conclusus es ... hortus	WA 353	an	8
G	5	2	0	-2	0	2	0	4	G	Hymnus omnibus sanctis ejus	AR 899 LU 1729 *AM 1104 *WA 397	an	8
G	5	2	0	-2	0	2	0	4	G	In caelesti regno	WA 393	an	8
G	5	2	0	-2	0	2	0	4	G	In caelestibus regnis	AR [48] LU 1157 AM 799 811 LA 390 391	an	8
G	5	2	0	-2	0	2	0	4	G	Jam hiems transiit ... surge	AR [98][116] LU 1233 1259 *AM 687 707	an	8
G	5	2	0	-2	0	2	0	4	G	Joannes et Paulus cognoscentes	LA 411	an	8
G	5	2	0	-2	0	2	0	4	G	Libenter gloriabor	AR 609 756 LU 1348 AM 793 941 WA 266 LA 430	an	8
G	5	2	0	-2	0	2	0	4	G	Martinus episcopus migravit	WA 401	an	8
G	5	2	0	-2	0	2	0	4	G	Maximilla Christo amabilis	AR 580 LU 1308 AM 756 LA 504	an	8
G	5	2	0	-2	0	2	0	4	G	Misit rex incredulus	AR 830 LU 1621 *AM 1029 WA 363	an	8
G	5	2	0	-2	0	2	0	4	G	Nolite expavescere	LR 90 *WA 133 LA 216	an	8
G	5	2	0	-2	0	2	0	4	G	Nolite judicare ut non judicemini	AR 523 LU 916 AM 542 WA 187 LA 311	an	8
G	5	2	0	-2	0	2	0	4	G	Nolite timere eos qui corpus	LA 520	an	8
G	5	2	0	-2	0	2	0	4	G	Nolite timere non separabuntur	LA 326	an	8
G	5	2	0	-2	0	2	0	4	G	Ora pro nobis beata Anna	WA 340	an	8
G	5	2	0	-2	0	2	0	4	G	Ora pro nobis beate Martine	WA 402	an	8

G	5	2	0	-2	0	2	0	4	G	Paulus et Joannes dixerunt Juliano	AR 742 LU 1509 WA 324 LA 410	an	8
G	5	2	0	-2	0	2	0	4	G	Per te Lucia virgo	AR 592 LU 1324 AM 770 WA 243 LA 322	an	8
G	5	2	0	-2	0	2	0	4	G	Petrus apostolus et Paulus doctor	AR 775 LU 1547 *AM 959 WA 332 *LA 426	an	8
G	5	2	0	-2	0	2	0	4	G	Petrus et Joannes ascendebant	AR 751 LU 1515 *AM 934 WA 328 *LA 412	an	8
G	5	2	0	-2	0	2	0	4	G	Reposita est mihi corona	LA 426 WA 331	an	8
G	5	2	0	-2	0	2	0	4	G	Saulus qui et Paulus	WA 331 *LA 425	an	8
G	5	2	0	-2	0	2	0	4	G	Si ignem adhibeas	WA 274 *LA 357	an	8
G	5	2	0	-2	0	2	0	4	G	Simon Joannis diligis me	WA 281 *LA 420	an	8
G	5	2	0	-2	0	2	0	4	G	Surgens Jesus mane	AR 464 *AM 477 *LA 232	an	8
G	5	2	0	-2	0	2	0	4	G	Ter virgis caesus sum	AR 610 757 LU 1349 *AM 794 942 WA 265 331 *LA 426	an	8
G	5	2	0	-2	0	2	0	4	G	Tristitia vestra vertetur ... et	AR 475 *AM 490	an	8
G	5	2	0	-2	0	2	0	4	G	Veni sponsa Christi accipe coronam	AR 577[20][86] LU 262[8] 1209 *AM 678 744 LA 545	an	8
G	5	2	0	-2	0	2	0	4	G	Venite post me dicit Dominus	LA 497	an	8
G	5	2	0	-2	0	2	0	4	G	Vespere autem sabbati	AR 442 GR 239 *AM 450 *WA 127 *LA 207 234	an	8
G	5	2	0	-2	0	2	0	4	G	Voca operarios et redde	AR 344 LU 502 *AM 315 WA 73 *LA 114	an	8
G	5	2	0	-2	0	2	0	4	G	Vos estis cives sanctorum	PM 310	an	8
G	5	2	0	-2	0	2	0	5	G	Ad dandam scientiam	WA 67	an	8
G	5	2	0	-2	0	2	0	5	G	Beatus Petrus apostolus	WA 332 *LA 421	an	8
G	5	2	0	-2	0	2	0	5	G	In Franciam missus	LR 279	an	8
G	5	2	0	-2	0	2	0	5	G	Nec illud silendum est	WA 388	an	8
G	5	2	0	-2	0	2	0	5	G	Surgens Jesu mane	WA 130	an	8
G	5	2	0	-2	0	2	0	7	G	In die magno festivitatis	AR 416 LU 1098 AM 393 *WA 109 *LA 173	an	8
G	5	2	0	-2	0	2	0	7	G	Inventa bona margarita	LR 225 *LA 545	an	8
G	5	2	0	-2	0	2	0	7	G	Nolite timere quinta enim die	AR 245 AM 219 WA 20 LA 24	an	8
G	5	2	0	-2	0	2	0	7	G	Nunc facies fortiter	WA 386	an	8
G	5	2	0	-2	0	2	4	2	G	Beati quos elegisti ... clamabunt	LA 476	an	8
G	5	2	0	-2	0	2	4	2	G	Beati quos elegisti ... etenim	WA 395	an	8
G	5	2	0	-2	0	2	4	2	G	Dixit autem dominus servo	AR 572 LU 1107 *AM 612 *LA 319	an	8
G	5	2	0	-2	0	2	4	5	G	Priusquam te formarem	LR 346 *WA 320 *LA 400	an	8

G	5	2	0	-2	0	2	5	4	G	In principio et ante saecula	LR 60 WA 29 *LA 64	an	8
G	5	2	0	-2	2	0	4	5	G	Iratus rex Saul	WA 164 LA 273	an	8
G	5	2	0	-2	2	0	5	4	G	Et dicebant ad invicem	LA 215	an	8
G	5	2	0	-2	2	5	4	0	G	Mauri laudes propheticis	LR 284	an	8
G	5	2	0	2	-2	0	2	0	G	Beata es Maria quae credidisti	AR 233 769 [123] LU 339 1538^{v} AM 207 709 953 *WA 12 *LA 379	an	8
G	5	2	0	2	-2	0	2	0	G	Faciam te in gentem magnam	GR (24)	int	8
G	5	2	0	2	-2	0	2	0	G	Ne timeas Maria invenisti	AR 218 668 [139] LU 1417 AM 190 862 *WA 8 *LA 6 379	an	8
c	5	2	0	2	-2	0	2	5	G	Deus in adjutorium meum	GR 350 LU 1027 SYG 89 GB 78^{v} GS 51 154	int	7
G	5	2	0	2	-2	0	2	5	G	Miserere mihi Domine quoniam ad te	GR 363 LU 1044 SYG 249 GB 256 *GS 159	int	8
G	5	2	0	2	-2	2	0	2	G	Oportet te fili gaudere	GR 122 *GS 54	co	8
G	5	2	0	2	0	-2	0	-2	G	Cum vidissent turbae	LA 163	an	8
G	5	2	0	2	0	-2	0	2	G	A Christo de caelo vocatus	WA 264 LA 345	an	8
G	5	2	0	2	0	-2	0	2	G	Adonai Domine Deus	LA 294	an	8
G	5	2	0	2	0	-2	0	2	G	Alleluia	AM 6 87	an	8
G	5	2	0	2	0	-2	0	2	G	Alleluia: tuus sum ego	AR 35 LU 241 243	an	8
G	5	2	0	2	0	-2	0	2	G	Audistis quia dictum est	AR 556 LU 1103 AM 594 *LA 311	an	8
G	5	2	0	2	0	-2	0	2	G	Beatam me dicent ... quia ancillam	AR 246 773 [125] AM 221 711 957 LU 1263 1542 WA 16 LA 17 *383	an	8
G	5	2	0	2	0	-2	0	2	G	Beatam me dicent ... quia fecit	AR 585 LU 1313 AM 763	an	8
G	5	2	0	2	0	-2	0	2	G	Beati qui habitant in domo	AR 177 LU 279^{Q}	an	8
G	5	2	0	2	0	-2	0	2	G	Beatus Andreas orabat	AR 579 LU 1307 AM 755 *LA 504 WA 237	an	8
G	5	2	0	2	0	-2	0	2	G	Cilicio Caecilia membra	WA 406 *LA 488	an	8
G	5	2	0	2	0	-2	0	2	G	Clamavit populus ad regem	PM 143	an	8
G	5	2	0	2	0	-2	0	2	G	Cum venerit paraclitus spiritus	AR 481 AM 496	an	8
G	5	2	0	2	0	-2	0	2	G	Cum videris nudum	LA 126	an	8
G	5	2	0	2	0	-2	0	2	G	Descendit hic justificatus	AR 562 LU 1023 AM 601	an	8
G	5	2	0	2	0	-2	0	2	G	Deus qui praecinxit me virtute	GR 463 LU 1419	gr	7
G	5	2	0	2	0	-2	0	2	G	Dilexit Andream Dominus	LA 497	an	8
G	5	2	0	2	0	-2	0	2	G	Dispersit dedit pauperibus	AR 851 LU 1649	an	8
G	5	2	0	2	0	-2	0	2	G	Dixit autem pater ad servos	AR 386 LU 551 *AM 361 WA 95 (inc illeg) *LA 146	an	8

G	5	2	0	2	0	-2	0	2	G	Dixit autem paterfamilias	AR 346 *AM 317 WA 75 *LA 115	an	8
G	5	2	0	2	0	-2	0	2	G	Dixit Jesus discipulis suis afferte	AR 450 OHS 800 *AM 463 LA 220	an	8
G	5	2	0	2	0	-2	0	2	G	Ecclesia illisque necdum	WA 385	an	8
G	5	2	0	2	0	-2	0	2	G	Ego plantavi Apollo rigavit	AR 609 756 LU 1348 AM 792 941 *WA 266 *LA 430	an	8
G	5	2	0	2	0	-2	0	2	G	Et valde mane una sabbatorum	AR 445 OHS 692 LU 776^{KK} AM 456 WA 129	an	8
G	5	2	0	2	0	-2	0	2	G	Exaltata est virgo Maria	AR 876 LU 1678 AM 1076	an	8
G	5	2	0	2	0	-2	0	2	G	Exibant autem daemonia	AR 393 LU 1091 AM 368 LA 267	an	8
G	5	2	0	2	0	-2	0	2	G	Ingresso Zacharia templum	AR 661 735 LU 1408 1497 AM 923 WA 320 *LA 400	an	8
G	5	2	0	2	0	-2	0	2	G	Istarum est enim regnum	AR 645 LU 262^{11} 1237 AM 691 748	an	8
G	5	2	0	2	0	-2	0	2	G	Istorum est enim regnum	AR 577^{14} [40] LR 181 LU 262^{2} 1154 AM 647 738 WA 422 *LA 516	an	8
G	5	2	0	2	0	-2	0	2	G	Jacta cogitatum tuum	GR 328 LU 982 SYG 67 GB 63^{v} *GS 32 49 143	gr	7
G	5	2	0	2	0	-2	0	2	G	Laetamini in Domino et exsultate	WA 421	an	8
G	5	2	0	2	0	-2	0	2	G	Ne timeas a facie	LR 347 *LA 400	an	8
G	5	2	0	2	0	-2	0	2	G	Non ego te desero	WA 347 *LA 433	an	8
G	5	2	0	2	0	-2	0	2	G	Non enim loquetur a semetipso	AR 482 AM 498	an	8
G	5	2	0	2	0	-2	0	2	G	Non licet mihi facere	AR 347 AM 318 WA 75	an	8
G	5	2	0	2	0	-2	0	2	G	Oleum effusum nomen tuum	AR 301 LU 445 *AM 279	an	8
G	5	2	0	2	0	-2	0	2	G	Per viscera misericordiae	AR 170 AM 73 LA 102	an	8
G	5	2	0	2	0	-2	0	2	G	Praeclara salutis aurora	AR 633	an	8
G	5	2	0	2	0	-2	0	2	G	Quo amplius gentilitatis	WA 384	an	8
G	5	2	0	2	0	-2	0	2	G	Sine macula sanctus Stephanus	WA 34	an	8
G	5	2	0	2	0	-2	0	2	G	Suavis Dominus universis	AR 204 OHS 44 LU 311	an	8
G	5	2	0	2	0	-2	0	3	G	Non omnis qui dicit mihi	WA 188 *LA 313	an	8
G	5	2	0	2	0	-2	2	0	G	Beatus Laurentius dixit Domine	WA 347	an	8
G	5	2	0	2	0	-2	2	0	G	Beatus Laurentius dixit mea	WA 347 *LA 434	an	8
G	5	2	0	2	0	-2	2	0	G	Ego rogavi Dominum ... mihi	LA 323	an	8
G	5	2	0	2	0	-2	2	0	G	Sub manu continuo	LA 342 *WA 264	an	8
G	5	2	0	2	0	-2	2	0	G	Zoe uxor Nicostrati	LA 331	an	8
G	5	2	0	2	0	-2	2	5	E	Salvum me fac Deus	GR 10**	of	3
G	5	2	0	2	0	2	0	-2	G	Beatus Laurentius orabat ... Domine	LA 432	an	8

G	5	2	0	2	0	2	0	-2	G	Beatus Laurentius orabat ... gratias	AR 814 LU 1597 AM 1006 WA 350 LA 437	an	8
G	5	2	0	2	0	2	0	-2	G	Clamabat Eliseus ad Eliam	LA 275	an	8
G	5	2	0	2	0	2	0	-2	G	Clarissimis cotidie viris	LA 324	an	8
G	5	2	0	2	0	2	0	-2	G	Convocatis Jesus duodecim ... misit ... et sanare	LA 266	an	8
G	5	2	0	2	0	2	0	-2	G	Dedit se ut liberaret	AR 304 *AM 281	an	8
G	5	2	0	2	0	2	0	-2	G	Liberiori generi	LR 319 WA 296 LA 367	an	8
G	5	2	0	2	0	2	0	-2	G	Magnificat anima mea ... quia respexit	AR 103 AM 137 *PM 165	an	8
G	5	2	0	2	0	2	0	-2	G	Non potest filius a se	LA 165	an	8
G	5	2	0	2	0	2	0	-2	G	Oportet nos mundum	GB 158	an	8
G	5	2	0	2	0	2	0	-2	G	Praevaluit David in Philisthaeum	AR 539 LU 986 AM 575 WA 164 LA 273	an	8
G	5	2	0	2	0	2	0	-2	G	Respexit me et exaudivit	AR 115 LU 279[F]	an	8
G	5	2	0	2	0	2	0	-2	G	Resplenduit facies ejus	AR 805 LU 1589	an	8
G	5	2	0	2	0	2	0	2	G	Beata nimium et Deo	WA 389	an	8
G	5	2	0	2	0	2	0	2	G	Herodes rex apposuit	AR 799 LU 1577 *AM 989	an	8
G	5	2	0	2	0	2	0	2	G	Maurus junior cum bonis	LR 274	an	8
G	5	2	0	2	0	2	0	2	G	Non veritus incredulae	WA 385	an	8
G	5	2	0	2	0	2	0	2	G	Tristitia vestra alleluia convertetur	LR 165 *LA 386 *WA 305	re	8
G	5	2	0	2	0	2	4	2	G	Benedicite Dominum omnes angeli	WA 396	an	8
G	5	2	0	2	0	2	4	2	G	Cum turba plurima convenirent	AR 349 AM 321 WA 79 LA 119	an	8
G	5	2	0	2	0	2	5	4	E	Accessistis ad Sion montem	AR 763 LU 1528 *AM 948[B]	an	3
G	5	2	0	2	0	2	5	4	E	Dominus in Sion magnus	LR 127	an	3
G	5	2	0	2	0	4	5	7	G	Defuncto Herode angelus	LR 304	an	8
G	5	2	0	2	0	7	5	4	G	Beata mater et intacta virgo ... sentiant	AR 881 LU 1681 *AM 1080	an	8
G	5	2	0	2	4	2	0	2	G	Nolite soliciti esse dicentes	AR 565 810 AM 605 1003 *WA 189 *LA 316	an	8
G	5	2	0	2	4	2	0	5	G	Alleluia: veni sponsa Christi accipe coronam	GB 272[V]	al	7
G	5	2	0	2	4	2	0	5		Veni sponsa Christi accipe coronam	GB 272[V]	alv	
G	5	2	0	2	4	5	2	4	E	Inseparabilis fides passioque	LA 427	an	3
G	5	2	0	2	4	5	4	2	E	Laetamini in Domino et exsultate	LR 385 *WA 395 *LA 475	an	3
G	5	2	0	2	4	5	7	4	E	Et venerunt festinantes	AM 887	an	3
G	5	2	0	2	4	7	5	7	G	Priusquam te formarem	LR 349 *LA 402 *WA 322	re	7

G	5	2	0	2	5	0	2	0	G	Sanctissima membra	LR 369	an	8
G	5	2	0	2	5	2	4	5	E	Cognovit autem pater quia illa hora	AR 571 LU 1066 *AM 612 WA 191 LA 319	an	3
G	5	2	0	2	5	2	4	5	E	Dicebat Jesus turbis ... propterea	AR 412 LU 1097 *AM 390	an	3
G	5	2	0	2	5	2	4	5	G	Dicebat Jesus turbis ... responderunt	LA 173	an	7
G	5	2	0	2	5	2	4	5	E	Dum fortis armatus custodit	AR 388 LU 1089 *AM 363 *LA 153 *WA 99	an	3
G	5	2	0	2	5	2	4	5	E	Et intravit cum illis	AR 477 *AM 492 *WA 138	an	3
G	5	2	0	2	5	2	4	5	E	Et respicientes viderunt	AR 446 OHS 730 LU 783 *AM 460 *WA 130 *LA 214	an	3
G	5	2	0	2	5	2	4	5	E	Intravit autem rex	AR 570 LU 1062 *AM 611	an	3
G	5	2	0	2	5	2	4	5	E	Si in digito Dei ejicio	AR 389 LU 552 *AM 363 *WA 99 LA 150	an	3
G	5	2	0	2	5	2	4	5	E	Viderunt eam ... vernantem	AR 872 LU 1680	an	3
G	5	2	0	2	5	2	5	4	E	Auferte ista hinc	AR 400 LU 1093 *AM 376 LA 163	an	3
G	5	2	0	2	5	2	5	4	E	Beatissimus Stephanus projectus	WA 343	an	3
G	5	2	0	2	5	2	5	4	E	Collaudabunt multi ... ejus	WA 428 *LA 539	an	3
G	5	2	0	2	5	2	5	4	E	Dum esset rex in accubitu suo	AR [97][114] LU 1232 1258 *AM 686 706 *WA 434 *LA 543	an	3
G	5	2	0	2	5	2	5	4	E	Qui sequitur me non ambulat ... dicit	AR 405 [16] LU 1097 1125 *AM 381 640 WA 419 LA 527	an	3
G	5	2	0	2	5	4	5	2	E	Dixit autem Maria ad angelum ... quomodo	AR 662 LU 1409	an	3
G	5	2	0	2	5	4	5	4	E	Ait Dominus Deus ad serpentem	AR 587 LU 1315 *AM 765	an	3
G	5	2	0	2	5	4	5	7	E	Adhaereat lingua mea	AR 160 LU 297	an	3
F	5	2	0	2	5	4	7	5	F	Jam laetus moriar quia vidi	PM 142	re	6
G	5	2	0	4	0	2	5	4		Benedicite spiritus et animae Benedictus es in firmamento	GS 44	trv	
G	5	2	0	4	0	2	5	4		Confitemini Domino quoniam bonus	GR 236 282 LU 776[II] OHS 682 *PM 80 *SYG 152 *GB 122 161[v] GS *115 132	alv	
F	5	2	0	4	0	2	5	7	F	Si diligis me Simon Petre	LR 360 LA 413 WA 277	re	6
G	5	2	0	4	2	0	2	0	G	Cum vidisset turba	WA 191	an	8
G	5	2	0	4	5	2	4	5	E	Dominus Deus Israel	SYG 233	int	3
G	5	2	0	4	5	4	2	5	E	Benedictus Dominus die cotidie	SYG 238	int	3
G	5	2	0	4	5	4	5	7	[D]	Dixit autem Jesus ad mulierem	SYG 132	an	1
G	5	2	0	4	5	7	5	4	E	Si diligitis me mandata	AR 695 LU 1465[F] AM 894 *WA 151	an	3

G	5	2	0	4	5	7	5	4	E	Si quis diligit me sermonem	AR 510 LU 889 AM 526 *WA 153 *LA 262	an	3
G	5	2	0	4	5	7	9	7	E	Mercenarius est cujus non sunt	AR 470 AM 484 *LA 235	an	3
G	5	2	0	4	5	7	9	7	G	Prostratus est saevissimus	LA 343	an	7
G	5	2	0	4	7	5	4	2	G	Laudemus virum gloriosum	AR 824 LU 1610	an	8
G	5	2	0	5	2	0	2	5	E	Dispersit dedit pauperibus	GR 576 LU 1607 *SYG 212 *GB 216 GS 193	int	3
G	5	2	0	5	2	5	4	7	G	Adhaesit anima mea ... cremata	WA 350 LA 440	an	8
G	5	2	0	5	4	2	5	4	E	Loquetur Dominus pacem	GR 516 LU 1492 *SYG 193 *GB 196 *GS 212	int	3
G	5	2	0	5	4	2	5	4	E	Timete Dominum omnes sancti	GR 574 *SYG 192 *GB 215^{v} *GS 211	int	3
G	5	2	0	5	4	5	2	4		Benedictus es qui intueris abyssos Benedictus sit	OTT 81 GB 215 *SYG 262	ofv	
G	5	2	0	5	4	5	2	4		Lingua mea calamus scribae Constitues eos	OTT 131 GB 206^{v} SYG 203	ofv	
G	5	2	0	5	4	5	7	5	G	Deus tuorum militum	ST 197	hy	8
G	5	2	0	5	4	5	7	5	E	Fecit me Dominus quasi patrem	LR 306	re	3
G	5	2	0	5	4	5	7	5	G	Si consurrexistis cum Christo	GR 249 OHS 787 LU 791 SYG 157 GB 135 GS 120	co	7
G	5	2	0	5	4	5	7	9	G	Martinus Abrahae sinu	SYG 225	co	7
C	5	2	0	5	7	2	5	7	F	Kyrie	MEL #208		
G	5	2	0	5	7	5	4	2	E	Caeciliam intra cubiculum	LA 491 *WA 407	re	3
G	5	2	0	5	7	5	4	2	G	Deus tuorum militum	ST 388 400	hy	8
G	5	2	0	5	7	5	4	2	G	Martyr Dei qui unicum	ST 404	hy	8
G	5	2	0	5	7	9	7	5	G	Kyrie pater excelse	MEL #27		
D	5	2	3	0	2	0	5	7	E	Ora pro nobis beate Martine	WA 401	re	4
G	5	2	4	0	2	4	0	2		Benedicite frigus Benedictus es in firmamento	GS 44	trv	
G	5	2	4	0	2	4	0	2		Benedicite ignis et aestus Benedictus es in firmamento	GS 44	trv	
G	5	2	4	0	2	4	0	2		Benedicite maria et flumina Benedictus es in firmamento	GS 44	trv	
G	5	2	4	0	2	4	0	2		Benedicite omnia opera Benedictus es in firmamento	GS 44	trv	
G	5	2	4	0	2	4	0	2		Benedicite stellae caeli Benedictus es in firmamento	GS 44	trv	
G	5	2	4	0	2	4	0	2		Benedicite volucres caeli Benedictus es in firmamento	GS 44	trv	
F	5	2	4	2	0	-3	0	2	F	Clama in fortitudine	LR 394 LA 23 *WA 17	re	6
G	5	2	4	2	0	-2	0	2	G	Servite Domino in timore	WA 64 *LA 89	an	8
G	5	2	4	2	0	2	4	2	G	Almi prophetae progenies pia	ST 430	hy	8

G	5	2	4	2	0	2	4	2	E	Caritas Dei diffusa ... inhabitantem	GR 304 501 LU 900 1472 *SYG 187 *GS a *GB 193	int	3
G	5	2	4	2	0	2	4	2	G	Quis possit amplo famine praepotens	ST 432	hy	8
G	5	2	4	2	0	2	4	5	E	Cognovimus Domine quia peccavimus	SYG 65	an	3
F	5	2	4	2	0	2	4	7	F	Laetare Jerusalem et conventum	GR 138 LU 559 *SYG 100 GB 89^{v} *GS 63	int	5
G	5	2	4	2	0	2	5	4	E	Agnosce o Vincenti	WA 261	an	3
G	5	2	4	2	0	4	5	7	G	Pater peccavi in caelum	LR 407 LA 145 *WA 87	re	7
C	5	2	4	5	2	5	7	5	D	Alleluia	WA 71	an	2
G	5	2	4	5	4	2	0	2	E	Veni sponsa Christi accipe coronam	PM 233 LR 215 *LA 542	re	3
G	5	2	4	5	4	7	9	7	E	Quis ascendet in montem	GR 520 LU 1495 GS 57	of	3
G	5	2	4	5	7	5	4	0	E	Deus Israel conjungat vos	GR [121] LU 1288	int	3
G	5	2	4	5	7	5	4	5		Gloria creatori omnipotenti Ecce Adam quasi unus	LA 112	rev	
G	5	2	4	5	7	5	7	9	G	Venite benedicti patris ... quod	AR 373 *AM 346 *WA 89 *LA 134	an	7
C	5	2	4	7	4	5	4	5	a	Passer invenit sibi domum	GR 126 LU 556 *GS 55 *GB 83	co	1
G	5	2	5	0	5	2	7	5	E	Omnia quae fecisti nobis	GR 377 LU 1063 *SYG 114 *GB 102 *GS 76 164	int	3
G	5	2	5	2	0	2	4	5	E	Me oportet minui	LA 18 *WA 11	re	3
C	5	2	5	2	0	5	7	9	D	Quod chorus vatum venerandus olim	ST 374	hy	1
a	5	2	5	3	5	7	3	2	G	Maxima pars fratrum	LR 285	re	7
G	5	2	5	4	0	2	5	4	G	Introibo ad altare Dei ad Deum	GR 80 LU 508 *GS 27 *SYG 61 *GB 59	co	8
G	5	2	5	4	0	7	5	2	G	Sancti tui Domine florebunt	AR [29] LU 1120 *AM 632 *WA 132	an	8
G	5	2	5	4	2	0	2	-2	E	Tibi dixit cor meum	GR 117 *GB 77 *SYG 88 GS 49	int	3
G	5	2	5	4	2	0	5	2	E	Veni de Libano sponsa mea	GR 613 LU 1668	int	3
G	5	2	5	4	2	5	4	2	G	Jesu redemptor saeculi	ST 215	hy	8
G	5	2	5	4	5	2	0	2	E	Docetefilios vestros	LA 387 *WA 142	re	3
G	5	2	5	4	5	2	0	2	E	Exsulta satis filia Sion	GR 20 OTT 11 LU 352 SYG 12 *GB 10 GS 11	of	3
G	5	2	5	4	5	7	5	4	G	Credo quod redemptor meus	PM 320 AR [158] LU 1785 LA 554 WA 436	re	8
G	5	2	5	7	5	4	0	2	G	Non recedet memoria	WA 373	an	7
G	5	2	5	7	5	7	5	7	G	Almi prophetae progenies pia	ST 393	hy	7
G	5	2	5	7	5	7	5	7	G	Assertor aequi non ope regia	ST 399	hy	7
D	5	3	-2	0	2	3	5	3	D	Jam Christus astra ascenderat	ST 421	hy	1

E	5	3	1	0	1	3	5	3	E	Aurora lucis rutilat	ST 452	hy	4
D	5	3	2	-2	0	-2	0	3	D	In universa terra gloria	LR 150 *WA 416 *LA 522	an	2
D	5	3	2	-2	0	2	0	3	D	Consurge consurge induere	AR 254 AM 230 WA 18 *LA 17	an	2
D	5	3	2	-2	0	3	0	3	D	Paratus esto Israel	AR 244 *WA 8 *LA 26	an	2
D	5	3	2	-2	0	3	2	-2	D	Constantes estote videbitis	AR 242 *AM 217 *WA 20 *LA 26	an	2
D	5	3	2	-2	0	3	2	-2	D	De Sion exibit lex	AR 221 AM 192 *WA 9 61 LA 7	an	2
D	5	3	2	-2	0	3	2	-2	D	Rectus Dominus Deus	AR 192	an	2
D	5	3	2	-2	0	3	2	0	D	Michael archangele veni	WA 380 *LA 465	an	2
D	5	3	2	0	2	0	-2	0	D	Spiritu intelligentiae replevit	WA 373	an	1
D	5	3	2	0	5	7	5	7	G	Kyrie	MEL #169		
D	5	3	2	3	0	-2	0	3	D	Afferentur in laetitia	LR 335	an	2
D	5	3	2	3	5	3	2	0	D	Gloria XI	BOS #51 GR 39* LU 46		2
D	5	3	2	3	5	7	5	3	G	Alleluia	WA 70	an	8
D	5	3	2	3	5	7	5	3	G	Confitebor Domino nimis in ore	WA 70	an	8
E	5	3	5	1	-2	0	1	0	G	Vespere sabbati quae lucescit	SYG 146	an	7
a	5	3	5	3	0	2	0	5		Quoniam ... non revertetur oculus Vir erat	OTT 122 *SYG 256 *GB 262	ofv	
D	5	3	5	3	2	3	5	2	G	Quo progrederis sine filio	LA 435 *WA 348	re	8
b	5	3	5	6	5	3	5	3		Quoniam praevenisti eum in benedictionibus Desiderium animae	LA 525	rev	
D	5	3	5	7	5	3	2	-2	G	In medio et in circuitu	WA 376	an	8
A	5	3	5	7	5	3	8	5	D	O crux benedicta quae sola	LA 396 *WA 308	re	2
D	5	3	5	7	5	7	5	3	G	Tamquam ad latronem existis	OHS 496 LU 702 *LA 196	re	8
D	5	3	5	7	5	7	5	7	G	Dulce lignum dulces clavos	LA 396 WA 308	re	8
G	5	3	5	7	5	7	5	7	G	Gaudeo plane quia hostia	LA 439 WA 349	re	8
D	5	3	5	7	5	7	5	7	G	Misit Herodes rex manus	PM 183 *LA 450 *WA 362	re	8
D	5	3	5	7	5	7	5	7	G	Misso Herodes spiculatore	LA 452	re	8
D	5	3	5	7	5	7	5	7	G	Noli me derelinquere pater	LA 435 WA 348	re	8
D	5	3	5	7	5	7	5	7	G	O beatum virum Martinum	LA 482 *WA 400	re	8
D	5	3	5	7	5	7	5	7	G	Postquam sexaginta annos	LR 286	re	8
D	5	3	5	7	5	7	5	7	G	Splendida facta est facies	LA 159 WA 101	re	8
A	5	3	5	7	5	7	5	7	D	Valde honorandus est	LA 49 WA 39	re	2
D	5	3	5	7	5	7	5	7	G	Vides o frater Luciane	WA 344	re	8
D	5	3	5	7	5	7	5	7	G	Vidi sub altare Dei	LA 60	re	8

D	5	3	5	7	5	7	9	5	F	Erit vobis hic dies	GR 257 OTT 63 LU 802 OHS 818 SYG 160 *GB 141v GS 123	of	6
D	5	3	5	7	5	7	9	7	G	Misit me vivens pater	AR 116* LR 131 LU 938	re	8
D	5	3	5	7	5	7	9	7	G	O beatum virum in cujus transitu	VP 243 *LA 485 *WA 401	re	8
D	5	3	5	7	5	7	9	7	G	Verbum caro factum est ... cujus	WA 30	re	8
D	5	3	5	7	5	7	9	7	G	Verbum caro factum est ... et vidimus	LR 67 LU 390 LA 34	re	8
G	5	3	5	7	5	7	9	7	G	Visus est Gregorius	PM 155	re	8
D	5	3	5	7	5	7	9	10	G	Testimonium perhibuit Joannes	LA 73	re	8
E	5	3	5	7	8	3	0	1	E	Exaudisti Domine orationem	LA 271 *WA 166	re	4
D	5	3	5	7	8	7	5	3	G	Magnum salutis gaudium	ST 439	hy	2 8
D	5	3	5	7	9	7	5	3	G	Felix per omnes festum mundi cardines	ST 447	hy	8
D	5	3	5	7	10	7	3	5	G	Alleluia: tu es sacerdos in aeternum	GR [4][33] LU 1183 1495B *SYG 38 *GB 272v	al	8
E	5	3	5	8	5	3	1	0	E	Ave maris stella Dei mater alma	ST 428	hy	4
A	5	3	5	8	7	5	7	8	D	Ad sacros virgo	AM 1132	hy	2
A	5	3	5	8	7	5	7	8	D	En adest pastor vigil et superno	LR 440	hy	2
A	5	3	5	8	7	5	7	8	D	Francicae lumen columenque gentis	LR 273	hy	2
A	5	3	5	8	7	5	7	8	D	Mira nocturnis modulante lingua	LR 455	hy	2
A	5	3	5	8	7	5	7	8	D	Norma tu vitae speculumque sanctae	LR 273	hy	2
D	5	3	7	3	5	7	3	0	D	Magnum salutis gaudium	ST 500	hy	2
D	5	3	7	5	2	3	0	3	G	Alleluia: sancte Michael archangele	GR 609 LU 1655	al	8
D	5	3	7	5	2	3	0	3	G	Alleluia: sancte Paule apostole praedicator	GR 535 LU 1526	al	8
D	5	3	7	5	3	5	3	2	E	O pastor apostolice	WA 290	re	4
G	5	4	0	-2	0	2	4	2		Pulchra facie sed pulchrior / In sanctitate fulgida	WA 431	rev	
G	5	4	0	-2	0	2	4	2		Virgo Dei N. rutilans / Pulchra facie	WA 433	rev	
G	5	4	0	-2	0	2	4	2		Visi sunt oculis / Justorum animae ... malitiae	WA 422	rev	
G	5	4	0	2	-3	0	2	0	E	Fili quid fecisti ... ecce	AR 693 *AM 891	an	3
G	5	4	0	2	4	2	0	4		Sic secum matrem / Ecclesiae sponsum	PM 269	rev	
G	5	4	0	2	4	2	4	5		Benedictus es Domine in firmamento / Benedicamus patrem	LA 477 *WA 160	rev	
G	5	4	0	2	4	2	4	5		Gloria Deo patri sit / Benedicamus patrem	LA 477	rev	

G	5	4	0	2	4	2	5	7		Cumque vidisset ventum Domine si tu es	LR 362 LA 414 WA 327	rev	
G	5	4	0	2	4	2	5	7		Ecce homo sine querela Iste homo ab adolescentia	LA 534 *WA 426	rev	
G	5	4	0	2	4	2	5	7		Et ego vidi et testimonium Testimonium perhibuit	LA 73	rev	
G	5	4	0	2	4	2	5	7		Ex quo omnia per quem omnia Unus est Dominus	WA 161	rev	
G	5	4	0	2	4	2	5	7		Genus electum gens sancta Laudem dicite	WA 396	rev	
G	5	4	0	2	4	2	5	7		In cujus adventu asportabuntur tibi Quam felix es Gallia	PM 347	rev	
G	5	4	0	2	4	2	5	7		In principio erat verbum Verbum caro	LR 67 *LA 34 WA 30	rev	
G	5	4	0	2	4	2	5	7		Iste est enim Joannes Iste est de sublimibus	LA 405	rev	
G	5	4	0	2	4	2	5	7		Juvenem quoque jam Caelestium minister	WA 294	rev	
G	5	4	0	2	4	2	5	7		Omnes montes qui in circuitu Montes Gelböe	LA 269 *WA 165	rev	
G	5	4	0	2	4	2	5	7		Proficiebat sapientia Descendit Jesus	LR 316	rev	
G	5	4	0	2	4	2	5	7		Quem unum caelestis Elegit Deus	PM 342	rev	
G	5	4	0	2	4	2	5	7		Tobias et Sara in tribulatione In illo tempore	PM 198	rev	
G	5	4	0	2	4	5	4	2	G	Cantabo Domino qui bona tribuit	WA 68	an	8
G	5	4	0	2	4	5	7	5	E	Sancta legio Agaunensium	WA 377	an	3
G	5	4	0	2	5	2	0	2	G	Accipe me ab hominibus	LA 500	an	8
G	5	4	0	4	5	2	0	2	G	Alleluia	AM 98	an	8
G	5	4	0	4	5	2	0	2	G	Audite et intelligite	AR 393 LU 1090 AM 367 WA 100 LA 155	an	8
G	5	4	0	4	5	2	0	2	G	Captabunt in animam justi	OHS 503 LU 708 WA 123 *LA 199	an	8
G	5	4	0	4	5	2	0	2	G	De fructu ventris tui	AR 272 LU 412 AM 247 *WA 272 *LA 39	an	8
G	5	4	0	4	5	2	0	2	G	Dedisti haereditatem timentibus	LR 136 WA 411 LA 506	an	8
G	5	4	0	4	5	2	0	2	G	In pace in idipsum dormiam	OHS 591 LU 752 WA 124 LA 201	an	8
G	5	4	0	4	5	2	0	2	G	Replevit et inebriavit me	LA 187	an	8
G	5	4	0	4	5	2	0	2	G	Venite adoremus eum	VP 92	an	8
G	5	4	0	4	5	2	0	2	G	Venite et videte locum	WA 138 LA 223	an	8
G	5	4	0	4	5	2	0	2	G	Videntibus illis elevatus est	AR 492 LU 851 AM 509 *WA 149 LA 250	an	8

G	5	4	0	4	5	2	4	2	G	Adjuva me et salvus ero	AM 94 96 WA 64 *LA 89	an	8
G	5	4	0	4	5	7	5	2	G	Sebastianus dixit Marcelliano	LA 326	an	8
G	5	4	0	4	5	7	5	7		Merito haec patimur Dixit Ruben fratribus	LA 150 *WA 97	rev	
G	5	4	0	5	7	9	5	2		Benedicat Israel Domino Benedictus es in firmamento	GS 44	trv	
G	5	4	0	5	7	9	5	4		Benedicat terra Domino Benedictus es in firmamento	GS 44	trv	
G	5	4	2	0	-3	-2	0	2	G	Sanctus	THAN #48		8
G	5	4	2	0	-2	0	2	0	G	Non intres in judicium	WA 439	an	8
G	5	4	2	0	-2	0	2	5	G	O Maria Jesse virga	PM 253 SYG 17	an	8
G	5	4	2	0	-2	2	0	2	G	Polycarpus presbyter dixit	LA 326	an	8
G	5	4	2	0	2	-2	0	-2	E	Alleluia	AR 19 LU 225 229	an	3
G	5	4	2	0	2	-2	2	5	G	Jam lucis orto sidere	ST 206	hy	8
G	5	4	2	0	2	0	-3	0	C	Salve mater misericordiae mater Dei	AR 139*		5
G	5	4	2	0	2	0	-2	-3	G	Comedi favum cum melle	WA 355 *LA 458	an	8
G	5	4	2	0	2	0	-2	0	G	Sancti angeli custodes	AR 869 LU 1667 *AM 1071	an	8
G	5	4	2	0	2	0	-2	0	G	Videntes autem turbae	WA 190	an	8
C	5	4	2	0	2	0	2	4	D	Alleluia: deus venerunt gentes	SYG 222	al	2
G	5	4	2	0	2	4	2	0		Benedictus es Domine Deus ... in saecula	GR 306 309 LU 904 911 *GS c *SYG 260 *GB 213	alv	
G	5	4	2	0	2	4	2	0		Crastina die delebitur	GR 25 LU 361	alv	
G	5	4	2	0	2	4	2	0	E	Magna opera Domini	AR 45 OHS 157 LU 253	an	3
G	5	4	2	0	2	4	2	0		Tanto tempore vobiscum sum ... credis	GR 489 LU 1465[C]	alv	
G	5	4	2	0	2	4	2	4	G	Kyrie alme domine (etc)	MEL #31		
C	5	4	2	0	2	4	2	7		Deus venerunt gentes	SYG 222	alv	
C	5	4	2	0	2	5	2	4	D	O lux beata trinitas	ST 271	hy	2
G	5	4	2	0	2	5	4	5	E	Ut autem sciatis	WA 157	an	3
G	5	4	2	0	2	5	7	5	G	Obaudite me divini fructus	PM 193	an	7
G	5	4	2	0	4	2	5	4	E	Haec est generatio	LR 383	an	3
C	5	4	2	0	5	7	4	2	D	A fructu frumenti	LR 121 LU 923	an	2
F	5	4	2	0	7	9	12	11	F	Agnus Dei	SCH #143		5
G	5	4	2	4	0	2	0	-2		Candor est lucis aeternae speculum	GR 572 LU 1586	alv	
G	5	4	2	4	0	2	0	-2		Caro mea vere est cibus ... qui	GR 314 [96] LU 944	alv	
G	5	4	2	4	0	2	0	-2		Concussum est mare	GR 609 LU 1655 *GS 198	alv	
G	5	4	2	4	0	2	0	-2		Levita Laurentius bonum opus	GR 579 LU 1595 *GS 194	alv	
G	5	4	2	4	0	2	0	-2		Minuisti eum Domine paulo	GR 451	alv	

G	5	4	2	4	0	2	0	-2	G	Regis immensi militis triumphis	ST 450	hy	8
G	5	4	2	4	0	2	0	-2		Solemnitas gloriosae virginis	GR 620 LU 1676[A]	alv	
C	5	4	2	4	0	2	4	2	D	Hodie sanctus Benedictus	AM 857 *LA 376	an	2
G	5	4	2	4	0	4	5	7	G	Alleluia	PM 236	an	7
G	5	4	2	4	2	0	-3	0		Ecce quam bonum et quam jucundum Haec est vera fraternitas	LA 517	rev	
G	5	4	2	4	2	0	-3	0		Gloria sit Deo patri Haec est vera fraternitas	LA 517	rev	
C	5	4	2	4	2	0	2	4	D	Isti sunt duae olivae	AR 745 LU 1510 *WA 333	an	1
C	5	4	2	4	2	0	2	4	D	Isti sunt viri sancti facti	AR 781 LU 1552	an	1
C	5	4	2	4	2	0	2	4	C	Kyrie	MEL #207		
G	5	4	2	4	2	0	2	4	G	Sanctus	THAN #47		8
C	5	4	2	4	2	0	2	5	D	Alleluia: deduc me Domine	AR 29 LU 237	an	2
G	5	4	2	4	2	0	4	5	G	Orabat Judas Deus	WA 309 *LA 398	an	8
G	5	4	2	4	2	0	4	5	G	Sanctus	THAN #46		8
G	5	4	2	4	2	0	4	5	G	Veni de Libano sponsa mea	PM 234	an	7
G	5	4	2	4	5	4	0	2	E	Tu puer propheta ... praeibis ... Dominum	AR 736 LU 1504 *AM 925 *WA 321 *LA 408	an	3
G	5	4	2	4	5	4	2	0	G	Intende in me	LA 92	an	8
G	5	4	2	4	5	4	2	0	G	Kyrie magne Michaele	MEL #30		
G	5	4	2	4	7	2	4	2	[G]	Agnus Dei	SCH #94		8
F	5	4	2	4	7	9	7	4	F	Kyrie	MEL #118		
G	5	4	2	5	4	0	2	4	E	Inter natos mulierum	AR 736 LU 1504 *AM 925 *WA 321 *LA 86 407	an	3
G	5	4	2	5	4	2	0	2	E	Iste cognovit justitiam	LR 151 LA 523 WA 417	re	3
G	5	4	2	5	7	5	2	0		Cibavit illum Dominus pane Misit me vivens	AR 116* LR 131 LU 938	rev	
C	5	4	2	5	7	5	4	2	C	Felix per omnes festum mundi cardines	ST 455	hy	6
G	5	4	2	7	5	7	5	0	E	Spiritus Domini super me propter	GR 564 LU 1579	int	3
G	5	4	5	2	-2	0	2	0	G	Dilectio Dei honorabilis	GR 603 LU 1645	int	8
G	5	4	5	2	0	-3	-2	0		Ecce tu Domine cognovisti Mihi autem	OTT 128 *GB 203 *SYG 201	ofv	
G	5	4	5	2	0	-2	0	2	G	Alleluia	WA 127	an	8
G	5	4	5	2	0	-2	0	2	G	Benedicta sit sancta Trinitas	GR 308 *SYG 260 *GB 212[V] *GS b	int	8
G	5	4	5	2	0	2	0	-2	G	Laetatus sum in his	LA 99	an	8
C	5	4	5	2	0	2	4	2	D	Vir Dei Benedictus signum crucis	AM 964	an	2
G	5	4	5	2	0	2	5	4	E	Angelus Domini apparuit in somnis Joseph	GR 4**	int	3

G	5	4	5	2	0	4	0	2		Confitemini Domino quoniam bonus	SYG 177	alv	
G	5	4	5	2	0	4	0	2	G	Deus meus es tu ne discedas	LA 167 *WA 106	re	8
C	5	4	5	2	4	0	2	4	D	Inito consilio fratres	LR 325 *LA 370	an	2
C	5	4	5	2	4	2	0	2	D	Et coegerunt illum dicentes	AR 476 *AM 490 *WA 132 LA *217 233	an	2
C	5	4	5	2	4	2	0	2	D	O Adonai et dux	AR 235 LU 340 AM 209 *WA 21 LA 27	an	2
C	5	4	5	2	4	2	0	2	D	O beata Radegundis	PM 176	an	1
C	5	4	5	2	4	2	0	2	D	O beatum virum cujus anima	AR 916 LU 1746 AM 1114 *WA 403 LA 480	an	2
C	5	4	5	2	4	2	0	2	D	O clavis David	AR 236 LU 341 AM 210 *WA 21 LA 28	an	2
C	5	4	5	2	4	2	0	2	D	O doctor optime ecclesiae	AR 577[17][66] LU 262[5] 1188 *AM 665 741	an	2
C	5	4	5	2	4	2	0	2	D	O Emmanuel rex	AR 237 LU 342 AM 211 *WA 22 LA 28	an	2
C	5	4	5	2	4	2	0	2	D	O mundi domina regis	PM 252	an	2
C	5	4	5	2	4	2	0	2	D	O oriens splendor lucis	AR 236 LU 342 *AM 210 *WA 21 LA 28	an	2
C	5	4	5	2	4	2	0	2	D	O qualem gloriam meruerunt	PM 43	an	2
C	5	4	5	2	4	2	0	2	D	O radix Jesse	AR 235 LU 341 AM 209 *WA 21 LA 28	an	2
C	5	4	5	2	4	2	0	2	D	O rex gentium	AR 236 LU 342 AM 211 *WA 22 LA 28	an	2
C	5	4	5	2	4	2	0	2	D	O rex gloriae Domine	AR 496 LU 853 AM 512 *WA 150 LA 252	an	2
C	5	4	5	2	4	2	0	2	D	O rex gloriae et tuorum	PM 346	an	2
C	5	4	5	2	4	2	0	2	D	O virgo virginum quomodo fiet	PM 246 *WA 22 LA 28	an	2
C	5	4	5	2	4	2	0	2	D	Sanctus Benedictus per viam	AM 858	an	2
C	5	4	5	2	4	2	0	2	D	Tua est potentia	LA 299	an	2
G	5	4	5	2	4	2	5	4	G	De illa occulta habitatione	WA 25	re	8
G	5	4	5	2	4	5	4	2	G	Kyrie	MEL #29		
C	5	4	5	2	4	5	7	5	E	Mediae noctis tempore	ST 448	hy	4
G	5	4	5	2	5	2	0	2		Ego diligentes me diligo Meum est consilium	GR 26**	trv	
F	5	4	5	2	5	2	0	2	F	In illa die suscipiam	WA 39 *LA 52	re	6
G	5	4	5	2	5	7	4	2	G	Christus resurgens ex mortuis	GR 252 OHS 799 LU 795 *SYG 158 *GS 121 *GB 137	co	8
C	5	4	5	2	5	7	5	4	D	Domine Jesu Christe magister	WA 237	an	2
G	5	4	5	2	5	7	5	7	G	Joseph fili David noli timere	GR 458 LU 1403	co	7
C	5	4	5	4	0	2	4	2	D	O Gregori dulcissimum	PM 141	an	2

C	5	4	5	4	2	4	2	0	D	O quam gloriosus est beatus	LA 48	an	2
C	5	4	5	4	2	4	2	0	D	O rex justitiae	WA 248	an	2
C	5	4	5	4	2	4	2	0	D	O sapientia quae ex ore	AR 234 LU 340 AM 208 WA 21 *LA 27	an	2
C	5	4	5	4	2	4	2	0	D	O Thoma Didyme	WA 247 *LA 28	an	2
G	5	4	5	4	2	5	7	5	G	Expandens manus suas	WA 39 *LA 51	an	8
G	5	4	5	4	5	7	2	-2		Ecce inimici tui Domine Bonum est confiteri	OTT 26 GB 57 *SYG 59	ofv	
C	5	4	5	7	0	2	4	2	D	Alleluia: Joannes est nomen ejus	GB 198^v	al	2
G	5	4	5	7	2	0	2	4	G	Exsultans in praeconio	ST 127	hy	7
G	5	4	5	7	2	4	5	4	G	Accipite spiritum sanctum	AR 507 LU 877 AM 523 LA 262	an	7
G	5	4	5	7	2	4	5	4	G	Alleluia: justi quasi virens folium	GR (21)	al	8
G	5	4	5	7	2	4	5	4	E	Tu Domine servabis ... a	GR 121 SYG 91 GB 80^v *GS 53	co	3
G	5	4	5	7	2	5	4	2		Non nobis Domine non nobis	GB 261^v	alv	
G	5	4	5	7	2	5	4	5	G	Alleluia: filii tui de longe venient	GR 46**	al	7
G	5	4	5	7	2	5	4	5	G	Alleluia: gloria et honore coronasti ... Domine et constituisti	GB 23 *SYG 201	al	7
G	5	4	5	7	2	5	4	5	G	Alleluia: haec est generatio quaerentium	GR 114**	al	7
G	5	4	5	7	2	5	4	5	G	Alleluia: jubilate Deo omnis terra	GR [127] LU 1294	al	7
G	5	4	5	7	4	5	2	0	G	Pontifices almi divina	WA 240	an	7
G	5	4	5	7	4	5	7	5	G	Sancti tui Domine mirabile	LR 182 LA 515 *WA 421	re	7
G	5	4	5	7	4	5	7	5	G	Verbera carnificum	LR 183 LA 516 *WA 421	re	7
G	5	4	5	7	4	7	9	5	G	Non lotis manibus	WA 100 *LA 155	an	7
G	5	4	5	7	5	2	0	2		Felix es sacra virgo Maria	GR 542 LU 1539	alv	
G	5	4	5	7	5	2	0	2		Spiritus sancti gratia	SYG 24	alv	
G	5	4	5	7	5	2	5	2	G	Quomodo fiet istud quia virum	WA 238	an	7
G	5	4	5	7	5	2	5	4	G	Congratulamini mihi quia inveni	WA 187	an	7
G	5	4	5	7	5	2	5	4	G	Cum autem sero	WA 75	an	8
G	5	4	5	7	5	2	5	4	G	Descendit angelus Domini	WA 325	an	7
G	5	4	5	7	5	2	5	4	G	Laetare alma mater ecclesia	PM 150	an	7
G	5	4	5	7	5	2	5	4	G	Octava decima die	WA 22	re	7
G	5	4	5	7	5	2	5	4	G	Sanctificamini hodie	LA 29 WA 25	re	7
G	5	4	5	7	5	4	2	0	G	Nemo te condemnavit mulier nemo	LA 156	an	7
G	5	4	5	7	5	4	2	4	G	Absterget Deus omnem lacrimam	AM 652 *AR [47] *LU 1156 LA 392	an	7

G	5	4	5	7	5	4	2	4	G	Benedicam te in vita mea	AR 3	an	7
G	5	4	5	7	5	4	2	4	G	Nemo te condemnavit mulier nemo	GR 138 *GB 89^v	co	8
G	5	4	5	7	5	4	2	4	G	Sancti tui Domine florebunt	LA 391	an	7
G	5	4	5	7	5	4	2	4	G	Sic benedicam te in vita	AR 365 AM 341 *WA 88 LA 132	an	7
G	5	4	5	7	5	4	2	5	G	Cum autem venerit	WA 145 *LA 242	an	8
G	5	4	5	7	5	4	2	5	G	Miserere Domine plebi tuae	GB 161	an	7
G	5	4	5	7	5	4	5	2	E	Laetare virgo Maria de te	PM 257 *SYG 18	an	3
G	5	4	5	7	5	4	5	4		Testimonium ergo perhibebat Cogitaverunt autem	WA 112 GS 83	rev	
G	5	4	5	7	5	4	5	7	G	Alleluia alleluia: hodie omnes apostoli	PM 88 *LA 264 SYG 182	an	7
G	5	4	5	7	5	4	5	7		Et in terra	BOS #24 GR 83* LU 86		
G	5	4	5	7	5	4	7	5	G	Moram faciente sponso	PM 139 LR 297	re	7
G	5	4	5	7	5	4	7	9	G	Congratulamini mihi omnes ... quia cum essem	PM 248 LR 248 WA 49	re	7
G	5	4	5	7	5	7	4	2	G	Benedictus es Domine Deus ... gloriosus	GR 16 *SYG 11 *GB 120^v 183 GS 9	hy	7
G	5	4	5	7	5	7	4	7	G	Alleluia: caeli enarrant gloriam Dei	SYG 239	al	7
G	5	4	5	7	5	7	4	7	G	Alleluia: exsultate Deo adjutori	GR 348 LU 1026 GS 150 SYG 244 GB 253	al	7
G	5	4	5	7	5	7	4	7	G	Alleluia: Jesus autem eo quod maneat	GR [101] LU 1283^B	al	7
G	5	4	5	7	5	7	4	7	G	Alleluia: nihil iniquinatum in eam	GR 51**	al	7
G	5	4	5	7	5	7	4	7	G	Alleluia: omnibus omnia factus sum	GR 68**	al	7
G	5	4	5	7	5	7	5	4	G	Audi filia ... et concupiscet	GR 583 LU 1602	gr	7
G	5	4	5	7	5	7	5	4	G	Audi filia ... quia concupivit	GR 655 LU 1755 GS 195 t SYG 228 GB 243^v	gr	7
G	5	4	5	7	5	7	5	4	G	Benedictiones patris tui	LR 307	re	7
G	5	4	5	7	5	7	5	4	G	Dignus es Domine accipere	LR 416 AM 1199 *LA 224 WA 139	re	7
G	5	4	5	7	5	7	5	4	G	Dum ingrederetur beata Agatha	LA 358 WA 273	re	7
G	5	4	5	7	5	7	5	4	G	Esuriente terra Aegypti	LR 306	re	7
G	5	4	5	7	5	7	5	4	G	Magnificate Dominum mecum	LR 269	re	7
G	5	4	5	7	5	7	5	4	G	Tribulationes civitatum audivimus	LA 291 WA 177	re	7
C	5	4	5	7	5	7	5	7	G	Cum jucunditate celebremus	LA 460 *WA 367	re	8
G	5	4	5	7	5	7	5	7		Si quae illi sunt Absolve Domine	WA 438	rev	
G	5	4	5	7	5	7	9	7	G	Adoremus victoriosissimum	WA 232	inv	7
G	5	4	5	7	5	7	9	7	G	Ave Maria gratia plena	LR 435 WA *238 301 LA 376	inv	7

G	5	4	5	7	5	7	9	7	G	Benedicta a filio tuo	WA 358 *LA 448	an	7
G	5	4	5	7	5	7	9	7	G	Christum Dei filium qui putari	LR 301	inv	7
G	5	4	5	7	5	7	9	7	G	Cum sanctus Benedictus post triduum	AM 816	an	7
G	5	4	5	7	5	7	9	7	G	Det tibi Deus de rore	LA 137 WA 91	re	7
G	5	4	5	7	5	7	9	7	G	Domum Dei decet sanctitudo	LR 231 *LA 547	inv	7
G	5	4	5	7	5	7	9	7	G	Exaudi Deus deprecationem meam	WA 66	re	7
G	5	4	5	7	5	7	9	7	G	Gaudeamus omnes in ... Agathae	WA 275	re	7
G	5	4	5	7	5	7	9	7	G	Ibant apostoli gaudentes	LR 166 LA 393 *WA 411	re	7
G	5	4	5	7	5	7	9	7	G	Isti sunt sancti qui pro testamento	WA 422	re	7
G	5	4	5	7	5	7	9	7	G	Lucia virgo quid a me	LA 320 WA 243	re	7
G	5	4	5	7	5	7	9	7	G	Memor Christus Dominus	LR 126	an	7
G	5	4	5	7	5	7	9	7	G	Praeoccupemus faciem Domini	WA 420	inv	7
G	5	4	5	7	5	7	9	7		Praeoccupemus faciem ejus Venite exsultemus	SYG 245 GS 154	alv	
G	5	4	5	7	5	7	9	7	G	Pretiosa in conspectu Domini	LR 166 *LA 386 WA 307	re	7
G	5	4	5	7	5	7	9	7	G	Pretiosa in conspectu Domini	WA 394	an	7
G	5	4	5	7	5	7	9	7	G	Qui persequebantur populum	LA 158 WA 101	re	7
G	5	4	5	7	5	7	9	7	G	Quoniam Deus magnus Dominus	LA 80 WA 72	inv	7
G	5	4	5	7	5	7	9	7	G	Sancta Maria Dei genitrix	LR 245	inv	7
G	5	4	5	7	5	7	9	7	G	Si vos manseritis in sermone	WA 90	an	7
G	5	4	5	7	5	7	9	7	G	Tres viri isti	WA 389	re	7
G	5	4	5	7	5	7	10	9		Requiem aeternam dona eis Domine Absolve Domine	LA 558	rev	
G	5	4	5	7	5	7	10	9		Sicque illi sunt Domine Absolve Domine	LA 558	rev	
G	5	4	5	7	5	9	7	5	G	Hic est vere martyr qui pro Christi	PM 218 LR 158 *WA 417	re	7
G	5	4	5	7	5	9	7	9	G	In sanctis suis alleluia	LA 387	re	7
G	5	4	5	7	5	9	7	9	G	Non sit vobis vanum	LA 127 *WA 85	inv	7
G	5	4	5	7	5	9	7	9	G	Venite exsultemus Domino jubilemus	LA 79	inv	7
G	5	4	5	7	5	9	7	9	G	Viri Galilaei quid admiramini	GR 285 LU 846 SYG 179 GB 178^{v} GS 135	int	7
G	5	4	5	7	9	5	4	5		Caeli enarrant gloriam Dei	SYG 239	alv	
G	5	4	5	7	9	5	4	5	G	Caritas pater est	WA 159	an	7
G	5	4	5	7	9	5	4	5	G	Cum Placidus ex aqua	AM 965	an	7
G	5	4	5	7	9	5	4	5		Filii tui de longe venient	GR 46**	alv	

G	5	4	5	7	9	5	4	5	G	Fulgebunt justi sicut lilium	LR 173	re	7
G	5	4	5	7	9	5	4	5		Jesus autem eo quod maneat	GR [101] LU 1283B	alv	
G	5	4	5	7	9	5	4	5		Jubilate Deo omnis terra	GR [127] LU 1294	alv	
G	5	4	5	7	9	5	7	2	G	Alleluia: non nobis Domine non nobis	GB 261v	al	7
G	5	4	5	7	9	7	4	5	G	Benedixit te Dominus in virtute	AR 872 LU 1679	an	7
G	5	4	5	7	9	7	4	5	G	Non enim misit Deus	WA 155	an	7
G	5	4	5	7	9	7	5	2	G	Alleluia: venite filii audite	GB 250v	al	7
G	5	4	5	7	9	7	5	2	G	Dixit paterfamilias operariis	AR 345 LU 503 AM 315 *LA 115	an	7
G	5	4	5	7	9	7	5	4	G	Dum paginae sacrae	AM 832	an	7
G	5	4	5	7	9	7	5	4	G	Ex odoris mira	WA 346	an	7
G	5	4	5	7	9	7	5	4	G	Exaudisti Domine orationem	AR 541 LU 988 AM 578	an	7
G	5	4	5	7	9	7	5	4	G	Glorificati hominis viderunt	WA 404	an	7
G	5	4	5	7	9	7	5	4	G	Lavit Maria lacrimis	WA 336	an	7
G	5	4	5	7	9	7	5	4	G	Nativitas est hodie ... pulchritudinem	WA 365	an	7
G	5	4	5	7	9	7	5	4	G	Orabat sanctus Joannes	WA 40	an	7
G	5	4	5	7	9	7	5	7	G	A Christo suscepta	WA 336	an	7
C	5	4	5	7	9	7	5	7	G	Adeste sancti plurimo	LR 451	hy	8
G	5	4	5	7	9	7	5	7	G	Dedit mihi Dominus pennas	AM 819	an	7
C	5	4	5	7	9	7	5	7	G	Deus tuorum militum	AR [13[1]] LR 148 LU 1126 AM 639	hy	8
G	5	4	5	7	9	7	5	7	G	In diebus illis mulier quae erat	AR 791 LU 1566 AM 975 WA 338 *GS 96	an	7
G	5	4	5	7	9	7	5	7	G	In jejuniis et orationibus	WA 343	an	7
C	5	4	5	7	9	7	5	7	G	Jam lucis orto sidere	ST 121	hy	8
G	5	4	5	7	9	7	5	7	G	Prudentes virgines aptate vestras	LR 222	re	7
G	5	4	5	7	9	7	5	7		Quem te petimus Pectore sincero	WA 337	rev	
C	5	4	5	7	9	7	5	7	G	Rex gloriose martyrum	AR [43]	hy	8
G	5	4	5	7	9	7	5	7	G	Salus nostra in manu ... respice	AR 8 (sup 1)	an	7
G	5	4	5	7	9	7	5	9	G	Benedicta es tu virgo Maria	AR 587 631 LU 1321 1381 AM 764	an	7
G	5	4	5	7	9	7	5	9	G	Cum jucunditate maternitatem	AR 882[2] LU 1683 AM 1081	an	7
G	5	4	5	7	9	7	5	9	G	Habet in vestimento	AR 894[13] OHS 832 LU 1718 AM 1097	an	7
G	5	4	5	7	9	7	5	9	G	In caelestibus regnis ... alleluia	AR [29] LU 1120 AM 633	an	7
G	5	4	5	7	9	7	5	9	G	Si cognovissetis me	AR 695 PM 152 LU 1465E AM 893 *WA 307 *LA 394	an	7

G	5	4	5	7	9	7	9	5	G	Adjutor et protector noster	GR 485 LU 1277^{A}	int	7
G	5	4	5	7	9	7	9	7	G	Alleluia: dedisti haereditatem	SYG 218	al	7
G	5	4	5	7	9	7	9	7	G	Christo cotidie sedulum	LA 324	an	7
G	5	4	5	7	9	7	9	7	G	Dixit autem dominus ad cultorem	LA 317	an	7
G	5	4	5	7	9	7	9	7	G	Novissime veniunt	WA 431	an	7
G	5	4	5	7	9	7	9	7	G	Qui regni claves	WA 278	an	7
G	5	4	5	7	9	7	9	7		Venite filii audite me	GB 250^{v}	alv	
G	5	4	5	7	9	7	9	10	G	Cum autem complacuit	WA 262 LA 346	an	7
G	5	4	5	7	9	7	9	10	G	Exhibeamus corpora nostra	AM 909	an	7
G	5	4	5	7	9	7	9	10	G	Hic est vere martyr qui pro Christi	WA 419 *LA 528	an	7
G	5	4	5	7	9	7	9	10	G	In matutinis Domine	WA 82	an	7
G	5	4	5	7	9	7	9	10	G	Pro quorum memoria	GS 233	co	7
F	5	4	5	7	9	7	9	11	F	In Domino Deo suo	WA 34	an	5
G	5	4	5	7	9	7	9	12	G	Beatus Vincentius cujus jam	WA 258	an	7
G	5	4	5	7	9	7	9	12	G	Benedicite Dominum omnes electi	LU 1831	an	7
G	5	4	5	7	9	7	9	12	G	Invocavi Dominum patrem	WA 435	an	7
G	5	4	5	7	9	7	10	9	G	Elegit te Dominus sacerdotem	LR 204 *LA 534	re	7
G	5	4	5	7	9	10	9	7	G	Confiteantur Domino misericordiae	GR 80**	co	7
G	5	4	5	7	9	10	9	7	G	Summum regem gloriae	LR 445	inv	7
G	5	4	5	7	10	9	10	7	G	Ibo mihi ad montem	WA 361	an	7
G	5	4	5	7	10	9	10	7	G	Ne derelinquas me ... Deus	GR 118 *SYG 88 GB 78 GS 50	int	7
G	5	4	5	7	10	9	10	9	G	Elegit Dominus sacerdotem	LA 534	re	7
G	5	4	5	9	7	5	7	10	G	Audivit Dominus et misertus	GR 91 GS 33 SYG 68 GB 63^{v}	int	7
G	5	4	5	9	7	9	7	5	G	Exspecta Dominum viriliter	GR 158 SYG 112 GB 99^{v} GS 73	int	7
G	5	4	5	9	7	10	9	10	G	Exsultet gaudio pater justi	GR 59 LU 470	int	7
G	5	4	5	9	7	10	9	10	G	Sicut portavimus imaginem	SYG 237	int	7
G	5	4	7	5	4	2	0	4	G	Sanctus	THAN #45		8
G	5	4	7	5	4	2	0	5	G	Kyrie	MEL #28		
G	5	4	7	5	7	9	7	12	G	Alleluia: Domine exaudi orationem	GR 367 LU 1049 *GB 256^{v}	al	7
G	5	4	7	5	7	9	10	12		Domine exaudi orationem meam ... veniat	GR 367 LU 1049 *GB 256^{v}	alv	
G	5	4	7	9	5	2	5	2		Et gratia tua illis Absolve Domine	GR 95* LU 1809	trv	

G	5	4	7	9	5	2	5	2		Et lucis aeternae beatitudine Absolve Domine	GR 95* LU 1809	trv	
G	5	4	7	9	5	2	5	2		Et sicut nix super foenum Attende caelum	GR 231 OHS 656 LU 776^{U} *GS 112 GB 119^{v} SYG 151	trv	
G	5	4	7	9	5	2	5	2		Et torcular fodit Vinea facta	GR 230 OHS 654 LU 776^{S} *GS 111 GB 120	trv	
G	5	4	7	9	7	5	2	5	G	Alleluia: venite exsultemus Domino	GR 358 LU 1038 *GS 154 GB 255 *SYG 245	al	7
G	5	4	7	9	7	5	4	5	c	Natura creans omnia	ST 310	hy	6
G	5	4	7	9	7	5	4	5	G	Terribile est Christe judicium	GB 161	an	7
G	5	4	7	9	7	5	7	10		Venite exsultemus Domino jubilemus	GR 358 LU 1038 GS 154 GB 255 SYG 245	alv	
G	5	4	7	9	7	9	5	4	G	Alleluia	AR 18 LU 224	an	7
G	5	4	7	9	7	9	5	4	G	Alleluia: confitemini Domino in saeculum	AR 18 LU 228	an	7
c	5	4	7	9	11	4	5	4	b	Sanctus	THAN #7		3
D	5	7	3	2	3	0	3	5	G	Fulgentibus palmis prosternimur	OHS 102 LU 589	an	8
G	5	7	4	5	2	0	5	2		Quoniam angelis suis mandavit Scapulis suis	OTT 32 *GB 66^{v} *SYG 74	ofv	
G	5	7	4	5	4	2	4	5		Liberasti in brachio tuo Tu es Deus qui facis	GR 81 LU 512 *GB 59^{v} *SYG 62 *GS 28	grv	
G	5	7	5	0	2	0	-2	2		Justi quasi virens folium	GR (21)	alv	
G	5	7	5	0	5	7	5	4		Conturbatus sum a voce inimici Exaudi Deus	OTT 36 *GB 84 *SYG 95	ofv	
G	5	7	5	2	-2	2	5	2		Quoniam iniquitatem meam Miserere mihi	OTT 35 *GB 77^{v} SYG 88	ofv	
G	5	7	5	2	5	7	5	2	E	Intret oratio mea ... inclina	GR 106 LU 541 SYG 81 *GB 73 GS 42	int	3
C	5	7	5	2	5	7	5	7		Qui cogitaverunt supplantare Custodi me Domine	GB 113	ofv	
C	5	7	5	2	5	7	9	5		Dixi Domino Deus meus Custodi me Domine	GB 113	ofv	
D	5	7	5	3	0	2	0	2		Sancte Michael archangele	GR 609 LU 1655	alv	
D	5	7	5	3	0	2	0	2		Sancte Paule apostole praedicator	GR 535 LU 1526	alv	
D	5	7	5	3	0	2	3	2	G	Hymnum cantate nobis alleluia	LA 239 *WA 145	re	8
D	5	7	5	3	0	5	3	5		Dominus regnavit decorem induit	GR 31 LU 405 SYG 16 *GB 15^{v} GS E	alv	
D	5	7	5	3	0	5	3	5		Propter veritatem ... et deducet	GR [67] LU 1237	alv	
E	5	7	5	3	1	3	5	7		Vix justus salvabitur Libera me Domine de morte	LA 597	rev	
E	5	7	5	3	5	3	0	1		Benedicta tu inter mulieres	SYG 216	alv	
E	5	7	5	3	5	3	0	1		Ite nuntiate fratribus meis	SYG 163	alv	

D	5	7	5	3	5	3	0	3	D	Domine ad adjuvandum me	GB 104^{v}	of	2
a	5	7	5	3	5	7	3	5	a	Christe sanctorum decus atque virtus	ST 395	hy	1
D	5	7	5	3	5	7	10	9	E	Tua est potentia	WA 180	an	3
G	5	7	5	4	5	7	9	7		Deus in nomine tuo salvum Deus exaudi	GR 156 *GS 73 *SYG 111 GB 99	grv	
G	5	7	5	4	5	7	9	7		Miserere mihi Domine quoniam conculcavit Deus vitam meam	GR 128 *GS 56 GB 83^{v} *SYG 94	grv	
G	5	7	5	4	5	7	9	7		Misericordias tuas Domine in aeternum Confitebuntur caeli	SYG 190	grv	
G	5	7	5	4	7	5	2	0	G	Alleluia: sicut oliva fructifera	GR 622^{4}	al	7
G	5	7	5	7	2	0	2	-2		Adorabo ad templum sanctum	GR [73] LU 1251 GS 175 k GB 174^{v} SYG 48 236	alv	
a	5	7	5	7	3	2	3	5	G	Sanctus Gamaliel per visum	WA 344	re	7
G	5	7	5	7	4	5	7	2		Dum clamarem ad Dominum Jacta cogitatum	GR 328 LU 982 GS 32 49 143 *GB 63^{v} *SYG 67	grv	
G	5	7	5	7	4	5	7	2		Ut probetis potiora ut sitis Testis mihi	GR 544 LU 1544	grv	
a	5	7	5	7	5	0	5	3		Ego dilecto meo et dilectus meus Nihil inquinatum	GR 48**	grv	
a	5	7	5	7	5	0	5	3		Lapidem quem reprobaverunt Haec dies	GR 253(241) LU 797(778) OHS 807(709) *SYG 158(152) *GB 137(125) *GS 121(117)	grv	
D	5	7	5	7	5	3	2	3	E	Oremus dilectissimi nobis	GB 158^{v} *WA 230	an	3
G	5	7	5	7	5	4	5	7	G	Populus Sion ecce Dominus	GR 4 LU 327 *SYG 3 *GB 2^{v} *GS 2	int	7
G	5	7	5	7	5	7	2	5		Super aspidem et basiliscum ... liberabo Scapulis suis	OTT 32 GB 66^{v} SYG 74	ofv	
G	5	7	5	7	5	7	4	5		Qui docet manus meas Deus qui praecinxit	GR 463 LU 1419	grv	
G	5	7	5	7	5	7	5	2	E	Filiae regum in honore tuo	GR [63] OTT 157 LU 1228 *SYG 39 *GB 43 GS 229	of	3
C	5	7	5	7	5	7	5	4	F	Laudemus Deum virginis	WA 310 *59	inv	6
D	5	7	5	7	5	7	5	7		Extendens caelum sicut pellem Emitte spiritum	OTT 77 GB 184 SYG 182	ofv	
G	5	7	5	7	5	7	5	9		Justitia ejus super filios Benedic anima mea	OTT 110 *SYG 80 GB 72	ofv	
G	5	7	5	7	5	7	9	7		Adorabo ad templum sanctum Si ambulavero	OTT 118 GB 86^{v} *SYG 97	ofv	

D	5	7	5	7	5	7	10	9	E	Maurus a teneris annis	PM 124 LR 275	re	3
G	5	7	5	7	5	9	7	9	G	Adorate Deum omnes Angeli	GR 70 LU 488 *SYG 42 GB 39 GS 23	int	7
G	5	7	5	7	9	5	2	3	c	Festa dies mundo	WA 350	re	6
C	5	7	5	7	9	5	9	12	F	O beatum virum qui spreto	VP 101	an	6
G	5	7	5	7	9	7	9	10	c	O diligens Christum	WA 337	re	6
D	5	7	5	7	10	7	5	3		Cantate Domino canticum ... cantate Exsultabunt sancti	OTT 143 GB 195 SYG 191	ofv	
D	5	7	5	7	10	9	5	7	G	Sanctus	THAN #169		8
D	5	7	5	7	10	9	7	9	E	Florem mundus protulit	ST 309	hy	3
D	5	7	5	7	10	12	10	9		O mira Christi regis Rex noster in cruce	WA 131 223	anv	
G	5	7	5	9	7	5	2	5		Sicut oliva fructifera	GR 622^{4}	alv	
G	5	7	5	10	9	7	0	3	G	Alleluia: salve virga florens	VP 53	al	7 8
D	5	7	5	10	9	7	5	7	E	Surge virgo et nostras	PM 209	re	3
D	5	7	5	10	9	10	7	5	G	Kyrie	MEL #168		
D	5	7	8	7	5	7	5	3	D	Panis quem ego dedero	GR 362 LU 1043 *SYG 80 GB 71^{v} *GS 41 158	co	1
G	5	7	9	5	0	5	7	9		Celsa omnipotentis In columbae specie	GB 54^{v}	trv	
G	5	7	9	5	0	5	7	9		Exsultabimus et laetabimur Inveni quem diligit	GR (11)	trv	
G	5	7	9	5	0	5	7	9		Sana contritiones ejus Commovisti Domine terram	GR 78 LU 507 GS 27 GB 58 SYG 60	trv	
G	5	7	9	5	0	5	7	9		Tota pulchra es Maria Tu gloria	GR 441 LU 1378	trv	
G	5	7	9	5	0	5	7	9		Vide quoniam tu laborem Exsurge Domine	GR [101] LU 1283^{B}	trv	
G	5	7	9	7	4	5	7	10		Exaltabitur sicut unicornis Bonum est confiteri	OTT 26 GB 57 *SYG 59	ofv	
C	5	7	9	7	5	4	2	4	D	Solemne tempus vertitur	ST 450	hy	2
G	5	7	9	7	5	4	5	7	G	Ne timeas Zacharia ... oratio	GR 521 *SYG 195 *GB 196 GS 188	int	7
G	5	7	9	7	5	4	5	7	G	Venite benedicti Patris ... quod	GR 250 OHS 795 LU 792 *SYG 157 *GB 135 GS 120	int	7
G	5	7	9	7	5	7	2	5	G	Exaudi nos Domine quoniam benigna	GR 84 LU 521 *AM 821 GB 61^{v} *SYG 64 *GS 29	an	7
G	5	7	9	7	5	7	5	2		Tibi gloria hosanna	GR [109]	alv	
G	5	7	9	7	5	7	5	4	G	Exclamemus omnes ad Dominum	WA 228 GB 154	an	8
G	5	7	9	7	5	7	5	4	G	Laetemur omnes in Domino	SYG 44 *GS h 177	int	7

G	5	7	9	7	5	7	5	4		Suscipiant montes pacem Benedictus Dominus	GR 64 LU 478 GS 20 GB 36 *SYG 32	grv	
G	5	7	9	7	5	7	5	9	G	Judicant sancti gentes	GR 645 (8) SYG 205 GB 210 GS 211	int	7
D	5	7	9	7	5	7	9	7	G	Alleluia: vox exsultationis et salutis	GB 269 *SYG 176 *GS 215	al	8
G	5	7	9	7	5	7	9	7		O quam pretiosum est regnum	GB 239[v]	alv	
G	5	7	9	7	5	7	9	10		Cumque intuerentur in caelum Viri Galilaei	LR 105 *LA 250 *WA 149	rev	
D	5	7	9	7	5	10	7	3		Cantate Domino benedicite nomen Confessio et pulchritudo	OTT 166	ofv	
D	5	7	9	7	5	10	7	3		Cantate Domino benedicite nomen Laetentur caeli	OTT 15 GB 15 SYG 15	ofv	
D	5	7	9	7	5	10	7	3		Cantate Domino canticum ... cantate Confessio et pulchritudo	OTT 166	ofv	
D	5	7	9	7	5	10	7	3		Cantate Domino canticum ... cantate Laetentur caeli	OTT 15 GB 15 SYG 15	ofv	
D	5	7	9	7	5	10	7	3		Inter apostolos vocatione Ingressus Paulus	SYG 45	ofv	
G	5	7	9	7	9	7	5	7	c	Qui me dignatus est	LA 361	re	6
G	5	7	9	7	9	10	12	10	G	Alleluia: o quam pretiosum est regnum	GB 239[v]	al	7
G	5	7	9	7	10	7	9	7		Specie tua et pulchritudine Audi filia ... quia concupivit	GR 655 LU 1755 GS t *GB 243[v] *SYG 228	grv	
G	5	7	9	7	10	7	9	7		Tota decora ingreditur filia Audi filia ... concupiscet	GR 583	grv	
G	5	7	9	7	10	7	9	10	G	Rex magnus natus est	WA 56	re	7
G	5	7	9	10	5	7	4	5	G	Cibavit illum Dominus pane	LA 54	re	7
G	5	7	9	10	7	5	7	5	G	Bethlehem civitas Dei	LA 13 *WA 14	re	7
G	5	7	9	10	7	5	7	5	G	Quam dilecta tabernacula	LR 240	re	7
D	5	7	9	10	9	7	5	3		Et in terra	BOS #56 *GR 15* *LU 26		
D	5	7	9	10	9	7	5	3		Imperatrix reginarum	VP 51	alv	
G	5	7	9	10	9	7	5	4		Fundata est domus Domini ... supra	SYG 264	alv	
D	5	7	9	10	9	7	5	7	E	A somno pigros excita	ST 338	hy	3
G	5	7	9	10	12	10	7	5		Ad te Domine clamavi Salvum fac populum	GR 119 *GS 43 50 171 GB 78 SYG 88	grv	
D	5	7	10	5	10	7	5	9		Intellexisti cogitationes meas Mihi autem	OTT 128 GB 203 SYG 201	ofv	
D	5	7	10	7	5	7	9	10		Ne avertas faciem ... ne Domine exaudi	OTT 53 GB 114[v] SYG 128	ofv	

D	5	7	10	7	5	7	9	10		Ne avertas faciem ... ne Exaudi Deus orationem	SYG 129	ofv	
G	5	7	10	9	5	7	5	7	c	Beatus Nicholaus jam triumpho	WA 241	re	6
D	5	7	10	9	7	5	3	5	E	Exsultemus et laetemur hodie	AR 170*		3
D	5	7	10	9	10	12	10	9	E	Benedictus sit Deus Pater	GR 309 LU 911 OTT 81 GS c SYG 262 *GB 215	of	3
D	5	7	10	9	10	12	10	9	E	Constitues eos principes	GR 534 LU 1520 OTT 131 SYG 203 *GB 206^{v} GS z 203	of	3
D	5	7	10	9	12	10	9	10		Plantatus in domo Domini Justus ut palma	OTT 150 *SYG 24 *GB 25^{v}	ofv	
G	5	7	12	10	12	14	10	7		Et requiescet super eum Egredietur virga	GR 622^{6} LU 1684	grv	
A	5	8	7	5	3	5	8	10	D	Gloria laus et honor	ST 485 GB 107^{v}	hy	2
D	5	9	7	5	0	5	7	10		Et animam sanctae Scholasticae In columbae specie	SYG 56	trv	
G	5	9	7	9	7	5	9	7		Quoniam quis in nubibus Confitebuntur caeli	OTT 138 *GB 153 *SYG 170	ofv	
D	5	10	7	5	0	5	7	10		Montes in circuitu ejus Qui confidunt	GR 139(40) LU 561 *GS 63 GB 90 *SYG 101	trv	
D	7	0	3	5	7	5	2	3	D	Agnus Dei	SCH #192		1
D	7	0	3	5	7	5	2	3	D	Sanctus	THAN #168		1
G	7	0	7	5	10	9	10	7	G	Factus est repente de caelo	GR 296 [94] LU 882 1281 GS 137 234 SYG 184 *GB 191	co	7
G	7	0	7	5	10	9	10	7	G	Quotiescumque manducabitis	GR 320 [99] LU 950	co	7
D	7	0	7	5	10	9	12	10		O admirabile pretium Dum fabricator	GS 103	anv	
a	7	2	3	2	3	2	3	2		Viam mandatorum tuorum Benedictus es ... in labiis	GB 60	ofv	
D	7	3	2	0	2	5	2	3	D	Gloria	BOS #49		I
D	7	3	5	3	2	0	-2	0	D	Haec tua virgo monimenta	ST 354	hy	1
D	7	3	5	7	0	12	10	7		Et in terra	BOS #50		
D	7	3	5	7	5	2	3	0		Mandavit Dominus benedictionem Ecce quam bonum	GB 201 *SYG 199 GS *n 214	grv	
D	7	3	5	7	5	3	0	-2		Fundamenta ejus in montibus Sapientia aedificavit	GR 398	grv	
D	7	3	5	7	5	3	2	3		Repleti fructu justitiae	GR 545 LU 1545	alv	
D	7	3	5	7	8	5	7	2	E	Acceptabis sacrificium justitiae	GR 347 SYG 67 GB 63^{v} GS 33 152 LU 1023	co	4
D	7	3	5	7	10	7	10	9		Viam veritatis elegi Confitebor tibi	OTT 44 GB 98 SYG 110	ofv	
G	7	4	5	7	2	0	5	4	G	Dirigatur oratio mea	GR 109 LU 1060 SYG 76 GB 68^{v} GS 38 163 171	gr	7

G	7	4	5	7	2	4	0	5	G	Michael praepositus paradisi	WA 380 *LA 465	an	7
G	7	4	5	7	9	7	9	7	G	Et ipse Jesus erat incipiens	AR 689 LU 1449 AM 887	an	7
G	7	4	5	7	9	7	9	7	G	Ipse Jesus erat incipiens	AR 655 AM 844	an	7
G	7	4	5	7	9	7	9	7	G	Surge propera amica mea	AM 820 *PM 140	an	7
G	7	4	7	5	7	9	5	4	G	Isti sunt duo viri	LA 409 *WA 324	re	7
G	7	4	7	9	7	4	7	9	G	Helena Constantini mater	WA 309 *LA 397	an	7
G	7	4	7	9	7	4	7	9	G	Tetradius cognita Dei	WA 400 *LA 481	an	7
G	7	4	7	9	7	5	4	5	G	Ingenua sum et exspectabilis	WA 273 *LA 356	an	7
G	7	4	7	9	7	5	7	5	G	Surrexit Odo plenus spiritu	AM 874	an	7
G	7	4	7	9	7	9	7	5	G	Argentum et aurum	AM 934 *AR 751 *LU 1515 LA 412 WA 328	an	7
G	7	4	7	9	7	9	7	5	G	Orante sancta Lucia apparuit	AM 769 *AR 592 *LU 1324 LA 322 WA 243	an	7
G	7	4	7	9	7	9	7	5	G	Orante sancto Clemente apparuit	AM 1145 *AR 927 *LU 1760 LA 496 WA 410	an	7
G	7	4	7	9	7	9	10	9	G	Viderunt oculi mei	WA 272	an	7
D	7	5	0	2	3	5	7	5	E	Jam Christus ascendit polum	ST 419	hy	4
D	7	5	0	3	7	5	2	3		Vox de caelis o vos Libera me de morte	WA 438	rev	
D	7	5	0	5	3	2	0	2	E	Sanctus V	GR 20* LU 30 THAN #167		4
D	7	5	2	3	2	0	[0	0]	D	Kyrie	MEL #167		
G	7	5	2	5	7	0	-2	2		In die resurrectionis ... praecedam	GR 262 LU 809 *GS 121 *SYG 169 GB 140	alv	
G	7	5	2	5	9	7	9	5	G	Datum est opus	WA 376	an	7
G	7	5	2	5	9	7	9	5	G	Praecursor Joannes exsultat	WA 59 LA 79 *VP 97	an	7
D	7	5	3	0	-2	5	3	5	D	Alleluia: cantantibus organis	SYG 228	al	1
D	7	5	3	0	2	3	2	0		Kyrie ... pater de caelis	PM 285 VP 35		
D	7	5	3	2	0	-2	0	-2	D	Alleluia: cantate Domino canticum novum	SYG 248	al	1
D	7	5	3	2	0	-2	0	2	D	Alleluia: veni Domine visitare	SYG 13	al	1
D	7	5	3	2	0	-2	3	2	D	Exsultet mentis jubilo	VP 121	hy	1
D	7	5	3	2	0	-2	3	2	D	Superna mater inclyta	ST 124	hy	1
D	7	5	3	2	0	-2	5	3	D	Alleluia: corona tribulationis effloruit	GR 15**	al	1
D	7	5	3	2	0	2	3	5	E	Amorem sensus erige	ST 224	hy	4
D	7	5	3	2	0	2	3	5		Constantes estote videbitis Judaea et Jerusalem	AM 1183 *PM 26 *WA 27	rev	
D	7	5	3	2	0	2	3	5	E	Gloria XII	GR 42* LU 49		4
D	7	5	3	2	0	2	3	7	E	Gloria	BOS #48		II

D	7	5	3	2	0	3	2	3		Cumque evigilasset Jacob Terribilis est	WA 317	rev	
D	7	5	3	2	0	3	2	5	D	Sanctus	THAN #166		1
D	7	5	3	2	0	3	5	2	D	Alleluia: fundata est domus ... super	SYG 264	al	1
D	7	5	3	2	0	3	5	3	D	De sacro tabernaculo	ST 351	hy	1
D	7	5	3	2	0	3	5	7	E	Agnus Dei	SCH #198		1
D	7	5	3	2	0	3	7	5		Assumpta est Maria ... angeli Hodie Maria	LR 379	rev	
D	7	5	3	2	0	3	7	5		Cernere divinum lumen gaudete Solem justitiae	AR 128* PM 185 VP 211 WA 366	rev	
D	7	5	3	2	0	7	5	3	D	Sanctus	THAN #165		1
D	7	5	3	2	3	0	3	5	D	Agnus Dei	SCH #197		1
D	7	5	3	2	3	2	0	-2	D	Agnus Dei	SCH #229		1
D	7	5	3	2	3	2	0	-2	D	Sanctus	THAN #164		1
D	7	5	3	2	3	2	0	2	D	Exorta a Bethsaida	ST 238	hy	1
D	7	5	3	2	3	2	0	12	D	Agnus Dei	SCH #228		1
D	7	5	3	2	3	2	0	12	D	Sanctus	THAN #163		1
D	7	5	3	2	5	3	2	0		Elongatus a nutrice Puer fletum	WA 299	rev	
D	7	5	3	2	5	7	5	7		Cum ambularent animalia Audiebam sonum	WA 375	rev	
D	7	5	3	2	5	7	9	10	D	Alleluia: concaluit cor meum	GR 502 LU 1473	al	1
D	7	5	3	5	2	0	5	7	D	Sanctus	THAN #162		1
D	7	5	3	5	3	2	0	-2		Cantata Domine canticum ... quia	SYG 248	alv	
D	7	5	3	5	3	2	0	-2		Surrexit Dominus et occurrens	SYG 163 *GS 120	alv	
D	7	5	3	5	3	2	0	2	[D]	Agnus Dei	SCH #196		1
D	7	5	3	5	3	5	7	0	D	Primus vocatione maximus	WA 278	an	1
D	7	5	3	5	7	0	2	3	D	Quicumque Christum quaeritis	ST 445	hy	1
D	7	5	3	5	7	0	3	5	D	Kyrie	MEL #165		
D	7	5	3	5	7	0	3	7	D	Angularis fundamentum	ST 107	hy	1
D	7	5	3	5	7	0	3	7	D	Urbs beata Jerusalem	ST 106	hy	1
D	7	5	3	5	7	3	2	0	a	Humili prece et sincera devotione	ST 492	hy	2
D	7	5	3	5	7	5	7	5		Statimque solutos a vinculis Audiens Christi	WA 240	rev	
D	7	5	3	5	7	5	7	8		Ideoque et quod nascetur ex te Quomodo fiet ... respondens	WA 302	rev	
D	7	5	3	5	7	5	7	10		In die tribulationis nostrae Angeli Dei qui	VP 225	rev	
D	7	5	3	5	7	5	12	10	D	Agnus Dei	SCH #195		1

D	7	5	3	5	7	5	12	10	D	Sanctus	THAN #161		1
D	7	5	3	5	7	8	7	5	D	Ego sum panis vivus qui	AR 533 LU 942 AM 553	an	1
D	7	5	3	5	7	8	7	5	D	Pax aeterna ab aeterno patre	PM 240	an	1
D	7	5	3	5	7	10	7	9	D	Alleluia: positis genibus	SYG 22	al	1
D	7	5	3	5	7	10	7	9	D	Alleluia: vado ad eum qui misit me	SYG 167 *GS 130	al	1
D	7	5	3	5	7	10	9	7	D	Agnus Dei	SCH #191		1
D	7	5	3	5	7	10	12	10	D	Kyrie	MEL #164		
D	7	5	3	7	5	3	2	0		Incessanter pro nobis supplica Pater insignis	VP 128	rev	
C	7	5	4	2	4	5	4	2		Beatus quem elegisti	GR 519 LU 1479	alv	
F	7	5	4	2	4	7	4	2	F	Kyrie	MEL #92		
G	7	5	4	2	5	7	0	-2		Levita Laurentius bonum opus	SYG 213	alv	
G	7	5	4	2	5	7	5	2		Qui tres pueros Summe Dei confessor	WA 241	rev	
G	7	5	4	2	5	7	9	7	G	Simile est regnum caelorum grano	AR 340 LU 1109 *AM 310	an	7
F	7	5	4	5	4	7	9	7	F	Gabriel angelus apparuit Zachariae	LR 356 *WA 321	re	5
G	7	5	4	5	7	5	2	0	G	Veni in hortum meum soror mea	PM 275 WA 355 *LA 458	an	7 8
G	7	5	4	5	7	5	4	5	G	Sanctus	THAN #44		7
G	7	5	4	5	7	5	12	10	G	Agnus Dei	SCH #67		7
G	7	5	4	5	7	9	7	4	G	Hosanna filio David	GR 166 OHS 91 LU 580 *WA 112 209 LA 179	an	7
G	7	5	4	5	7	9	7	5	G	Alleluia	AM 84	an	7
G	7	5	4	5	7	9	7	5	G	Esurientes humiles implevit	LA 106	an	7
G	7	5	4	5	7	9	7	5	G	Beata Lucia dixit	WA 244	an	7
G	7	5	4	5	7	9	7	5	G	Caro mea vere est cibus ... qui	LR 130	an	7
G	7	5	4	5	7	9	7	5	G	Confitebor Domino nimis in ore	LA 104	an	7
F	7	5	4	5	7	9	7	5	F	Diligamus in invicem	WA 214 *SYG 131 *GS 96	an	5
G	7	5	4	5	7	9	7	5	G	Ingressus Raphael archangelus	LA 293	an	7
G	7	5	4	5	7	9	7	5	G	Qui manducat meam carnem	LU 938 LR 131	re	7
G	7	5	4	5	7	9	7	9	G	Iste est frater vester	LA 150 WA 97	re	7
G	7	5	4	5	7	9	10	9	G	Gabriel angelus locutus ... ave	AR 670 LU 1417 AM 866	an	7
G	7	5	4	5	9	7	9	5	G	Alleluia	PM 225	an	7
G	7	5	4	5	9	7	9	5	G	Hic est sacerdos magnus	PM 224	an	7
G	7	5	4	7	9	5	7	0	G	Caput draconis salvator	WA 59 *LA 78 *VP 96	an	7
G	7	5	4	7	9	5	7	2	G	Cumque sibi conspicerent	LA 370	an	7
G	7	5	4	7	9	5	7	5	G	Aqua comburit peccatum	WA 59 LA 77 VP 96	an	7

G	7	5	4	7	9	5	7	5	G	Magnum mysterium declaratur	WA 59 LA 78 *VP 96	an	7
G	7	5	4	7	9	5	7	5	G	Pater de caelis	WA 59 LA 77	an	7
G	7	5	4	7	9	5	7	5	G	Te qui in spiritu	WA 58 LA 78 *VP 95	an	7
G	7	5	4	7	9	7	5	7	G	Baptista contremuit	VP 96 WA 59 *LA 78	an	7
G	7	5	4	7	9	7	5	7	G	Facta est cum angelo	AR 265 LU 398 *AM 241 *WA 32 *LA 37	an	7
G	7	5	4	7	9	7	5	7	G	Peccati aculeus conteritur	VP 96 WA 59 LA 77	an	7
G	7	5	4	7	9	7	5	7	G	Veterem hominem renovans	VP 95 *LA 78 *WA 58	an	7
D	7	5	7	0	3	2	0	-2	D	Agnus Dei	SCH #194		1
G	7	5	7	2	5	9	5	7	G	Dunstane pater inclyte	WA 312	an	7
E	7	5	7	3	1	0	1	0	E	Agnus Dei	SCH #163		4
E	7	5	7	3	1	0	1	0	E	Sanctus	THAN #132		3
D	7	5	7	3	2	0	2	0	D	Kyrie o Deus pater ingenite	MEL #163		
D	7	5	7	3	5	3	2	5		Admirandus cunctis O beatum praesulem	WA 295	rev	
D	7	5	7	3	5	7	5	3	D	Kyrie	MEL #166		
D	7	5	7	3	5	7	5	3	D	Qui sunt isti qui ut nubes	LR 146 WA 414	re	1
D	7	5	7	3	7	8	7	5		Auribus percipe Domine Salvum fac servum	GR 105 *GS 41 GB 72 SYG 80	grv	
D	7	5	7	3	7	8	7	5		Delectare in Domino et dabit Spera in Domino	GR 423 LU 1352^{v}	grv	
D	7	5	7	3	7	8	7	5		Dextera tua Domine glorificata Gloriosus Deus	GR [22] LU 1163 *GS 212 GB 43^{v} SYG 40	grv	
D	7	5	7	3	7	8	7	5		Misit de caelo Miserere mei Deus	GR 88 LU 526 *GS 31 GB 62 SYG 65	grv	
D	7	5	7	3	7	9	7	5		Quem ex Indorum Exsultemus cuncti in Deo	GB 227	grv	
D	7	5	7	5	0	3	2	5		Per te Dei genitrix	GR 552 LU 1557 *GS u	alv	
G	7	5	7	5	2	0	5	7	G	Ferculum fecit sibi	WA 163	an	7
D	7	5	7	5	2	3	2	0		Nos autem gloriari	GB 165 *GS v	alv	
G	7	5	7	5	2	5	7	5	G	Alleluia: magnus Dominus ... in civitate	GR 340 LU 1014	al	7
G	7	5	7	5	2	5	9	7	G	Misertus Dominus destitutae	WA 313	re	7
D	7	5	7	5	3	2	0	-2	D	Sanctus	THAN #160		1
D	7	5	7	5	3	2	0	2		O robur apostolice Pretiosus vir	WA 312	rev	
D	7	5	7	5	3	2	0	3		Aperti sunt oculi caecorum Sanctissimus monachorum	PM 168 LR 371	rev	
D	7	5	7	5	3	2	0	3		O quam dulcem vocem Dixit Dominus Mariae	WA 336	rev	

D	7	5	7	5	3	2	0	3		Petrus ergo et Paulus In visione	WA 312	rev	
D	7	5	7	5	3	2	0	5		Cherubim quoque et seraphim Te sanctum Dominum	AR 196* PM 109 VP 216 WA 282	rev	
D	7	5	7	5	3	2	0	5		Donetur nobis eorum Hodie martyrum	WA 46	rev	
D	7	5	7	5	3	2	0	5		Ecce sicut sol Beatus es care	WA 315	rev	
D	7	5	7	5	3	2	0	5		Pascha nostrum immolatus Immolabit haedum	AR 114* LR 122 LU 926	rev	
D	7	5	7	5	3	2	0	9	D	Agnus Dei	SCH #193		1
D	7	5	7	5	3	2	3	5		Liberator meus Deus Diligam te	LR 342	rev	
D	7	5	7	5	3	2	3	5	D	Quod chorus vatum venerandus olim	ST 184	hy	1
D	7	5	7	5	3	2	5	7	D	Auctor beate saeculi	AM 1255	hy	1
D	7	5	7	5	3	2	5	7		Benedictus venit in nomine Hic est dies	LR 370	rev	
D	7	5	7	5	3	2	5	7	D	Cor arca legem continens	AM 567	hy	1
D	7	5	7	5	3	2	5	7		Decursis omnibus poenis Gloriosus Dei	VP 199	rev	
D	7	5	7	5	3	2	5	7		Duplici doctrina fratribus praefuit N. praeesse	PM 231	rev	
D	7	5	7	5	3	2	5	7	D	En ut superba criminum	AM 563	hy	1
D	7	5	7	5	3	2	5	7		In omnem terram exivit sonus eorum Qui sunt isti	LR 146	rev	
D	7	5	7	5	3	2	5	7		Induit te Dominus vestimento Audi filia	VP 250 *WA 433	rev	
D	7	5	7	5	3	2	5	7		Jam quodammodo Dum vero adhuc	WA 239	rev	
D	7	5	7	5	3	2	5	7		Justorum semita quasi lux In Deo raptus	LR 281	rev	
D	7	5	7	5	3	2	5	7		Vigilate ergo quia nescitis Sint lumbi vestri	PM 228 LR 202 *LA 535 *WA 430	rev	
D	7	5	7	5	3	5	7	3	D	O crux admirabile ... effusus	SYG 141	an	1
D	7	5	7	5	3	5	7	3		Tres sunt qui testimonium dant Duo seraphim	PM 107 AR 179* LR 419	rev	
D	7	5	7	5	3	5	7	3		Vias tuas Domine notas Universi qui te	GR 2 LU 320 GS B 1 GB 1 SYG 1	grv	
D	7	5	7	5	3	5	7	5		Dum enim in corpore Translate ad caelestia	WA 315	rev	
D	7	5	7	5	3	5	7	5		Et cum appropinquasset Cum audisset turba	WA 112	rev	
D	7	5	7	5	3	5	7	5	D	Gloria laus et honor	PM 59 *GS 83	hy	1

a	7	5	7	5	3	5	7	8		Nativitas est hodie Nativitas gloriosae	LA 459 *WA 365	rev	
D	7	5	7	5	3	5	7	8		Nobis ergo petimus piis O constantia martyrum	PM 195	rev	
D	7	5	7	5	3	5	7	9		Candidiores nive Qui sunt isti qui ut nubes	WA 414	rev	
D	7	5	7	5	3	5	7	9		Constitues eos principes	SYG 221	alv	
D	7	5	7	5	3	5	7	10		Tibi junctus igitur Sanctissimi martyris Stephani	WA 36	rev	
D	7	5	7	5	3	5	8	7		Cum orasset Cornelius Cornelius centurio	PM 125 *WA 279	rev	
G	7	5	7	5	7	10	9	7	G	Summae trinitati simplici	WA 161	re	7
D	7	5	7	8	7	5	3	2		Tu gloria Jerusalem ... Bethlehem Salve virginale	PM 265 VP 41	rev	
D	7	5	7	8	7	5	7	3		Juravit Dominus et non paenitebit	GR [37] LU 1187 *SYG 189 *GB 41^v	alv	
D	7	5	7	8	7	5	7	3		Rogavi pro te Petre	GR 543 LU 1543	alv	
D	7	5	7	8	7	5	7	5	D	Kyrie rex saeculorum	MEL #162		
a	7	5	7	8	7	5	7	5		Laudibus gloriosus es O quam admirabilis vir	WA 390	rev	
D	7	5	7	8	7	5	7	5		Quoniam peccatorum mole Christi mater	VP 268 WA 303	rev	
D	7	5	7	8	7	5	7	5		Quoniam tribulatio proxima Circumdederunt me	PM 52 OHS 63 (nm) 303 (nm) LA 183 WA 113	rev	
D	7	5	7	8	7	5	7	5	D	Sanctus	THAN #159		1
D	7	5	7	8	7	5	7	8		Ad te clamaverunt patres Media vita	AR 152* PM 45 VP 106	rev	
D	7	5	7	8	7	5	7	8		In te speraverunt patres Media vita	PM 45 AR 152* VP 106	rev	
G	7	5	7	9	5	2	7	5		In Deo laudabimur Liberasti nos	GR 387 LU 1075 GS e *SYG 258 *GB 264^v	grv	
G	7	5	7	9	5	2	7	5		In Deo laudabimur Salvasti enim nos	GR 98**	grv	
G	7	5	7	9	5	2	7	5		Qui regis Israel intende Qui sedes	GR 7 LU 335 GB 5^v *SYG 6 GS 4	grv	
D	7	5	7	9	5	3	7	5		Ortus est sicut sol Dies sanctificatus	SYG 19	alv	
G	7	5	7	9	5	10	9	7	G	Mysterium ecclesiae	ST 40	hy	7
G	7	5	7	9	5	10	9	7	G	Vere gratia plena es	ST 40	hy	7
D	7	5	7	9	7	5	3	2		Veni Domine visitare	SYG 13	alv	
G	7	5	7	9	7	5	7	5		Dedisti haereditatem timentibus	SYG 218	alv	
D	7	5	7	9	7	5	7	5	E	Nisi diligenter perfeceris	WA 274 *LA 359	an	4
D	7	5	7	9	7	5	7	5	E	Sub tuam protectionem	WA 353	an	4

D	7	5	7	9	7	5	7	10	D	Gloria Libani data	AM 971	an	1
D	7	5	7	9	10	9	7	5	D	Apostolorum mystica	ST 451	hy	1
D	7	5	7	9	10	9	7	5		Et in terra	BOS #17		
D	7	5	7	9	10	9	7	5		Flores apparuerunt in terra	GR 442	alv	
G	7	5	7	9	10	9	7	9	G	Angelus ad pastores ait	AR 264 LU 397 AM 241 *WA 32 LA 37	an	7
G	7	5	7	9	10	12	10	9		Dunstanus columbae Dei Caelestium contemplator	WA 313	rev	
C	7	5	7	9	11	9	7	9	G	Marcellini atque Petri	ST 17	hy	8
D	7	5	7	9	12	10	9	7	D	Ave maris stella Dei mater alma	ST 40	hy	1
D	7	5	7	10	5	7	5	3		Et in terra	BOS #18 GR 45* LU 51		
D	7	5	7	10	7	5	3	2		Diriget mansuetos in judicio Dulcis et rectus	GR 324 [112] LU 971	grv	
GG	7	5	7	10	7	5	7	5		Ipse super Maria fundavit Tollite portas	OTT 14 SYG 14 GB 13	ofv	
D	7	5	7	10	7	9	5	3		Illuc producam cornu David Sacerdotes ejus	GR [36] LU 1187 *GS 225 *GB 212 SYG 209	grv	
D	7	5	7	10	7	9	5	3		Nihil proficiet inimicus in eo Inveni David	GR [3] LU 1130 *GS 221 *GB 41 *SYG 37	grv	
D	7	5	7	10	7	9	5	3		Timeat eum omne semen Qui timetis	GR 467	grv	
D	7	5	7	10	7	9	7	5	D	Agnosce o Vincenti	WA 259	re	1
G	7	5	7	10	7	9	7	5	G	Quandam vexatam demone	WA 293	an	7
D	7	5	7	10	7	10	5	3		Placita enim erat Deo Consummatus in brevi	GR 70**	grv	
D	7	5	7	10	7	10	5	3		Posuit os meum quasi gladium Inflammatum	GR 622[1] LU 1681[2]	grv	
D	7	5	7	10	7	10	5	3		Quoniam magnus es tu Omnes gentes	GR 78**	grv	
D	7	5	7	10	9	7	5	3	D	Ne timeas a facie ... ut eruam	WA 320	an	1
D	7	5	7	10	9	7	5	3		Separemur a sinistris Princeps sancte	WA 383	rev	
D	7	5	7	10	9	7	5	7	D	Quae in sinu beati patris	LR 282	re	1
G	7	5	7	10	9	7	5	7	G	Quantas habeo iniquitates	WA 171	an	7
D	7	5	7	10	9	7	5	7	D	Te lucis auctor personant	ST 288	hy	1
D	7	5	7	10	9	7	5	7	D	Te saeculorum principem	AM 1090	hy	1
D	7	5	7	10	9	7	5	7	D	Vexilla Christus inclyta	AM 1094	hy	1
G	7	5	7	10	9	7	9	7	G	Aperi mihi soror mea	WA 163	an	7
G	7	5	7	10	9	7	9	10	G	Et venerunt festinantes	AR 689	an	7
G	7	5	7	10	9	7	9	10	G	Pastores venerunt festinantes	AR 320 LU 468	an	7
D	7	5	7	10	9	10	7	5		Lex Dei ejus in corde Os justi	GR [38] LU 1191 *GS 204 *GB 53 *SYG 206	grv	

D	7	5	7	10	12	10	7	10	D	Alma Scholastica	LR 290	re	1
D	7	8	5	3	7	5	7	8	D	Ego elegi vos et posui vos	GR (6)	co	1
D	7	8	5	10	9	7	5	8		Domine Dominus noster Gloria et honore	OTT 133 *GB 23^{v} *SYG 34	ofv	
D	7	8	7	3	5	7	5	7	D	Domine nonne bonum semen	AR 339 LU 1109 AM 309 *LA 107	an	1
D	7	8	7	5	3	2	0	-2	D	Agnus Dei	SCH #190		1
D	7	8	7	5	3	2	0	2	E	Jesu redemptor omnium	ST 342	hy	4
D	7	8	7	5	3	2	0	3	D	Sanctus	THAN #157		1
D	7	8	7	5	3	5	0	3	D	Magne Pater Augustine	VP 208	hy	1
D	7	8	7	5	3	5	0	3	D	Sancte Dei pretiose protomartyr	VP 80	hy	1
D	7	8	7	5	3	5	3	5	D	Factus est Dominus protector	GR 320 LU 961 SYG 239 GB 247^{v} GS 142	int	1
D	7	8	7	5	3	5	3	5	D	Quam magna multitudo	GR 57**	of	1
D	7	8	7	5	3	5	7	0	D	Instet clara dies quo recolendus	ST 147	hy	1
D	7	8	7	5	3	5	7	3	D	Ibant parentes Jesu	AR 652 LU 1405	an	1
D	7	8	7	5	3	5	7	5	D	Domus mea domus orationis	LR 241	re	1
D	7	8	7	5	3	5	7	10	D	Justus es Domine et rectum	GR 365 LU 1047 SYG 250 GB 256 GS 160	int	1
D	7	8	7	5	3	5	7	10	D	Justus germinabit sicut lilium	LR 151 LA 522 *WA 416	re	1
D	7	8	7	5	3	5	8	7	D	Iste est Joannes	PM 33 *LA 53 WA 41	re	1
D	7	8	7	5	3	7	5	7	D	Dominus mihi adjutor non timebo	GR 35**	gr	1
D	7	8	7	5	3	7	5	7	D	Dulcis et rectus Dominus	GR 324 [112] LU 971	gr	1
D	7	8	7	5	3	7	5	7	D	Ecce quam bonum et quam jucundum	GR 384 455 LU 1071 SYG 199 GB 201 GS d n 214	gr	1
D	7	8	7	5	3	7	5	7	D	Tota formosa et suavis es	GR 60**	gr	1
D	7	8	7	5	3	7	5	8	D	Stabant juxta crucem Jesu	GR 595 LU 1633	int	1
D	7	8	7	5	7	2	3	5	E	Inventor rutili dux bone luminis	ST 478	hy	4
D	7	8	7	5	7	3	2	0	D	O mi pastor egregie	ST 329	hy	1
D	7	8	7	5	7	5	2	3		Deus virtuum convertere	GR [132]	alv	
D	7	8	7	5	7	5	2	3		Justi confitebuntur ... et habitabunt	GR 96**	alv	
D	7	8	7	5	7	5	2	3		Suscitans a terra inopem	GR 20**	alv	
D	7	8	7	5	7	5	3	2	D	Caeli enarrant gloriam Dei annuntiant	LR 289	an	1
D	7	8	7	5	7	5	3	2	D	Kyrie	MEL #160		
D	7	8	7	5	7	5	3	2	D	Novus athleta Domini	VP 195	hy	1
D	7	8	7	5	7	5	3	2	D	Quam pulchra es Maria	PM 272	an	1

D	7	8	7	5	7	5	3	2	D	Tunc praecepit eos	WA 309 *LA 397	an	1
D	7	8	7	5	7	5	3	5	D	Dedit mihi Dominus linguam	GR 28**	int	1
D	7	8	7	5	7	5	3	5	D	Dicit Dominus sermones	GR 656 LU 1758 SYG 228 GB 244^v GS 200	int	1
D	7	8	7	5	7	5	3	5		Reddam tibi vota mea Jubilate Deo	OTT 69 GB 38 SYG 36	ofv	
D	7	8	7	5	7	5	3	7	D	Concupivit rex decorem tuum	GR [65] LU 1230	gr	1
D	7	8	7	5	7	5	3	7	D	Spera in Domino	GR 423 LU 1352^v	gr	1
D	7	8	7	5	7	5	7	5	D	Alleluia: surrexit altissimus de sepulcro	SYG 168	al	1
D	7	8	7	5	7	5	7	5	D	Ave maris stella Dei mater alma	AR [126] AM 712	hy	1
D	7	8	7	5	7	5	7	5	D	Monstra te esse matrem	LU 1863	hy	1
D	7	8	7	5	7	8	7	5	D	Hi sunt qui cum mulieribus	AR 286 LU 426 AM 262 WA 47 LA 62	an	1
D	7	8	7	5	7	8	10	7	D	Novo decurrens lumine	ST 306	hy	1
D	7	8	7	5	7	8	10	8	D	Jesu nostra redemptio	ST 112	hy	1
D	7	8	7	5	7	9	10	7	D	Almi prophetae progenies pia	ST 42	hy	1
D	7	8	7	5	7	9	10	7	D	Assertor aequi non ope regia	ST 42	hy	1
D	7	8	7	5	7	9	12	10	D	Deus manens primordium	ST 161	hy	1
D	7	8	7	5	7	10	9	7	D	O grande cunctis gaudium	ST 37	hy	1
D	7	8	7	5	7	10	9	7	D	Optatus votis omnium	ST 36	hy	1
D	7	8	7	5	7	10	9	7	D	Sanctorum meritis inclyta gaudia	ST 43	hy	1
D	7	8	7	5	7	10	9	7	D	Simile est regnum caelorum fermento	AR 340 LU 495 AM 310	an	1
D	7	8	7	8	7	10	7	8	D	Da pacem Domine sustinentibus te	GR 372 [135] LU 1056 SYG 253 GB 259^v GS 161	int	1
D	7	8	7	10	7	5	7	5	D	Oculi mei ad fideles	GR (36)	of	1
D	7	8	7	10	7	5	7	8	D	Domine Dominus noster	LR 192 *WA 420 424 LA 530	an	1
D	7	8	7	10	7	5	7	8	D	Virgam virtutis tuae	WA 415 LA 512	an	1
D	7	8	7	10	7	5	9	7		Quid est homo quod memor Gloria et honore	OTT 133 GB 23^v SYG 34	ofv	
D	7	8	7	10	7	8	7	8	D	Statuit ei Dominus testamentum pacis	GR [3][32] LU 1182 SYG 37 GB 41 GS 220	int	1
D	7	8	7	10	7	9	10	7	D	Statuit Dominus supra petram	LA 91 *WA 65	re	1
D	7	8	7	10	9	7	5	7	D	Sacris solemniis juncta sint gaudia	PM 94 LR 120 VP 10	hy	1
D	7	8	7	10	9	7	5	8		Domine refugium factus es Repleti sumus	OTT 175 GB 163 SYG 171	ofv	
D	7	8	7	10	9	7	5	9		Priusquam fierent montes Repleti sumus	OTT 175 GB 163 SYG 171	ofv	

D	7	8	10	8	7	5	3	2		Inter haec manet Christi miles	WA 259	rev	
G	7	9	5	2	4	5	4	2	G	Ingressus angelus ad Tobiam	AR 891 LU 1701	an	7
G	7	9	5	4	2	4	0	2	G	Laudate Dominum quoniam confirmata	AR 76	an	7
G	7	9	5	4	5	7	5	7	G	Alleluia: exaudi orationem meam	GR 21**	al	7
G	7	9	5	4	5	7	9	7		Exaudi orationem meam	GR 21**	alv	
G	7	9	5	4	5	7	9	7	G	Surgens Jesus Dominus ... stans ... gavisi	OHS 812 *LR 92 *LA 210 WA 133	re	7
D	7	9	5	7	9	10	9	7	D	Aurea luce et decore roseo	ST 191 *AM 932	hy	1
D	7	9	5	7	9	10	9	7	D	Decora lux aeternitatis auream	AR 749 LU 1523	hy	1
D	7	9	5	7	9	10	9	7	D	Jucundetur et laetetur augmentetur	ST 110	hy	1
D	7	9	5	7	9	10	12	10	D	Ave maris stella Dei mater alma	ST 193	hy	1
D	7	9	5	7	9	12	10	9	D	Ave maris stella Dei mater alma	AR [117] PM 288 LU 1259 AM 704	hy	1
D	7	9	5	7	9	12	10	9	D	Lucis hujus festa colat plebs honesta	ST 107	hy	1
G	7	9	5	9	10	7	4	7	G	Ibant parentes Jesu	AM 841	an	7
G	7	9	5	9	10	9	7	9	G	Venerunt pastores festinantes	LR 303	an	7
G	7	9	5	9	10	12	10	9	G	Ave Katherina martyr et regina	ST 238	hy	7
C	7	9	7	2	4	2	4	5	D	Alleluia: tu es altissimus super omnem	GB 178^v	al	1
D	7	9	7	3	5	7	5	7	D	In omnibus exhibeamus	LA 127 *WA 85	re	1
F	7	9	7	4	2	4	5	4	F	Exsultet jam angelica ... caelestis	ST 345	hy	6
F	7	9	7	4	7	0	4	7		Exspectans exspectavi Dominum Domine in auxilium	OTT 106 *GB 80^v *SYG 91	ofv	
G	7	9	7	4	7	5	4	2	G	Alleluia: ascendo ad patrem	SYG 180	al	7
G	7	9	7	4	7	5	4	2	G	Alleluia: tolle puerum	SYG 30	al	7
G	7	9	7	4	7	5	4	2	G	Alleluia: tu gloria Jerusalem tu laetitia	GR 403	al	7
G	7	9	7	5	2	5	9	7	G	Puer qui natus est nobis	AR 741 LU 1505 AM 928 *LA 405	an	7
D	7	9	7	5	3	2	0	-2	D	Magnae dies laetitiae	ST 122	hy	1
D	7	9	7	5	3	2	0	-2	D	Sanctus	THAN #158		1
D	7	9	7	5	3	2	3	0	D	Sanctus	THAN #156		1
D	7	9	7	5	3	2	5	7	D	Quem terra pontus aethera	ST 122	hy	1
D	7	9	7	5	3	5	7	3	D	Alleluia	AM 108	an	1
D	7	9	7	5	3	5	7	5	D	Abiit Jesus foras	WA 89	an	1
D	7	9	7	5	3	5	7	5		In omnem terram exivit sonus apostolorum	SYG 209	alv	

D	7	9	7	5	3	5	7	5		Ingressus Zacharias templum	SYG 198	alv	
D	7	9	7	5	3	5	7	5	D	Kyrie theoricam practicamque (etc)	MEL #185		
D	7	9	7	5	3	5	7	5		Surgens Jesus Dominus ... stans	SYG 163	alv	
C	7	9	7	5	4	2	0	2	C	Gloria	BOS #55		III
G	7	9	7	5	4	2	5	4	G	Angelorum regi Deo	WA 379	inv	7
C	7	9	7	5	4	5	4	5		Viam iniquitatis Domine Benedictus ... in labiis	OTT 28 *GB 60 *SYG 62	ofv	
G	7	9	7	5	4	5	7	4	G	Bernardus inclytis ortus natalibus	ST 46	hy	7
G	7	9	7	5	4	5	7	5	G	Fatiscens corpus febribus	WA 252	an	7
G	7	9	7	5	4	5	7	5	G	Languor accrescens in dies	WA 296	an	7
G	7	9	7	5	4	7	9	10	G	Kyrie pater summe qui	MEL #26		
D	7	9	7	5	7	0	3	2	D	Agnus Dei	SCH #189		1
D	7	9	7	5	7	0	3	5		Fundata est domus Domini ... super	SYG 264	alv	
G	7	9	7	5	7	2	5	4	G	Surge propera amica mea	GR (9)	int	7
G	7	9	7	5	7	2	5	9	G	Aqua sapientiae potavit eos	GR 247 OHS 783 LU 789 *GS 119 *SYG 156 GB 133	int	7
G	7	9	7	5	7	5	2	4		Qui ad justitiam erudiunt	GR 497 LU 1467	alv	
G	7	9	7	5	7	5	2	5	a	Te decet laus te decet hymnus	AR 209* AM 1260 LR 42 *WA 6	hy	1
D	7	9	7	5	7	5	3	2	D	Agnus Dei	SCH #188		1
D	7	9	7	5	7	5	3	2		Et meritis tanti Aemula prosequitur	WA 284	rev	
D	7	9	7	5	7	5	3	2	D	Mittens haec mulier	WA 110 *LA 185	an	1
D	7	9	7	5	7	5	3	5	D	Fiat manus tua	AM 106 LA 89	an	1
D	7	9	7	5	7	5	3	5	D	Haec est clara dies	ST 496	hy	2
D	7	9	7	5	7	5	3	5	D	Praedicans praeceptum Domini	LR 149 LA 522 *WA 416	an	1
D	7	9	7	5	7	5	3	5		Qui ligandi et solvendi O princeps	WA 278	rev	
D	7	9	7	5	7	5	3	5		Speciosum fecit rex angelorum	SYG 219	alv	
G	7	9	7	5	7	5	4	5	G	Euge serve bone et fidelis ... intra	LR 193 LA 530 WA 425	re	7
G	7	9	7	5	7	5	7	5	G	Isti sunt dies quos observare	LA 166 WA 105	re	7
G	7	9	7	5	7	5	7	5		Tibi soli peccavi et malum Miserere mihi	OTT 35 GB 77v SYG 88	ofv	
G	7	9	7	5	7	5	9	7	G	Puer natus est nobis	GR 33 LU 408 SYG 18 GS G	int	7
D	7	9	7	5	7	9	7	3	E	Sanctorum meritis inclyta gaudia	ST 199	hy	4
D	7	9	7	5	7	9	7	5	D	Simile est regnum caelorum homini patrifamilias	AM 313 *AR 343 *WA 75 *LA 114	an	1

D	7	9	7	5	7	9	10	9	E	Panis angelicus fit panis hominum	AR 95* *VP 6		4
D	7	9	7	5	7	9	10	9	E	Sacris solemniis juncta sint gaudia	AR 106* GR 153* VP 9* LU 920	hy	4
G	7	9	7	5	7	9	10	12		Fundamenta ejus in montibus	SYG 263	alv	
D	7	9	7	5	7	10	7	5	D	Electus est a Domino	AM 779	an	1
G	7	9	7	5	7	10	9	7	d	Iste confessor Domini sacratus	ST 104	hy	2
D	7	9	7	5	7	10	9	7	D	Lucis creator optime	AR 51 LU 258	hy	1
G	7	9	7	5	7	10	9	7	d	Omnium Christe pariter tuorum	ST 98	hy	2
D	7	9	7	5	7	10	9	7	D	Optatus votis omnium	PM 84 VP 155	hy	1
D	7	9	7	5	7	10	9	10	D	Memor humanae conditionis	SYG 69	an	1
G	7	9	7	5	9	10	12	10	G	Mecum enim est maxima merces	WA 386	an	7
G	7	9	7	5	10	7	9	5		Virga recta est virga regni Filiae regum	OTT 157 GB 43 *SYG 39	ofv	
G	7	9	7	9	5	4	5	7	G	Simon Petre antequam de navi	LR 359 VP 181 LA 413 WA 277	re	7
G	7	9	7	9	5	4	5	7	G	Surge Petre et induc te	PM 172 LR 363 *LA 416 *WA 327	re	7
G	7	9	7	9	5	4	5	7	G	Tu es Petrus	LR 360 LA 414 WA 278	re	7
G	7	9	7	9	5	7	4	2	G	Oculi mei semper ad Dominum quia	GR 123 LU 552 SYG 92 GB 82 *GS 54	int	7
G	7	9	7	9	5	7	5	7	G	Solve jubente Deo terrarum	LR 364 *LA 418 WA 280	re	7
D	7	9	7	9	7	5	7	5		Stantes erant pedes Laetatus sum	SYG 3 *GB 3	alv	
D	7	9	7	9	7	5	7	10		Sit nomen Domini ... ex hoc Laudate pueri Dominum	*GS 123 SYG 206	alv	
G	7	9	7	9	7	9	7	9		Te decet hymnus ... ex tibi	GR 346 LU 1022 GS 148 SYG 242 GB 252	alv	
D	7	9	7	9	10	7	5	7	D	Ecce veniet Deus et homo	AR 222 LU 1081 AM 193 *WA 9 *LA 7	an	1
D	7	9	7	9	10	7	5	7	D	Puer Jesus crescebat	LA 62	an	1
G	7	9	7	9	10	9	7	5	G	Surge et accipe puerum	LR 312	re	7
D	7	9	7	10	7	5	7	5	D	Leva Jerusalem oculos	AR 220 AM 191 LA 7	an	1
D	7	9	7	10	7	5	7	9	D	Lauda et laetare	AM 1130	an	1
D	7	9	7	10	9	7	5	9		Omnes gentes plaudite manibus Ascendit Deus	OTT 75 SYG 179 *GB 177	ofv	
D	7	9	7	12	10	7	9	7	[D]	Agnus Dei	SCH #187		1
D	7	9	10	7	5	3	5	7	D	Nonne Moyses dedit	LA 164	an	1
D	7	9	10	7	5	3	5	7	D	Primo proscriptos patria	ST 307	hy	1
D	7	9	10	7	5	7	9	7	D	Dominus dedit Dominus abstulit	LA 287	an	1
G	7	9	10	7	9	5	7	9		Gloria sit patri summo creatori Impii super justum	WA 38(35)	rev	

D	7	9	10	9	7	5	7	5	D	Alleluia: cantabant sancti	SYG 26	al	1
G	7	9	10	9	7	9	5	7		Hebraeorum gens perfida Impii super justum	WA 38(35)	rev	
G	7	9	10	12	7	4	9	10	[G]	Agnus Dei	SCH #66		7
C	7	9	11	9	7	12	9	7		Disputabat enim cum Graecis Ingressus Paulus	SYG 45	ofv	
F	7	9	11	9	11	12	11	9	F	Katherinae solemnia sancta colat ecclesia	ST 49	hy	5
G	7	9	12	10	9	7	10	9	G	Amande praesul inclyte	ST 165	hy	7
G	7	10	7	5	2	0	2	-2		Conturbata sunt omnia ossa Miserere mihi	GR 133 GS 58 GB 85v SYG 96	grv	
G	7	10	7	5	2	0	2	-2		Quia non derelinquet Qui confidunt	GB 75	grv	
D	7	10	7	5	3	2	5	7		Audi filia Concupivit rex	GR [65] LU 1230	grv	
D	7	10	7	5	3	2	5	7		Benedixit te Dominus in virtute Tota formosa	GR 60**	grv	
D	7	10	7	5	3	2	5	7		Sicut unguentum in capite Ecce quam bonum	GR 384 455 LU 1071 GS *d *n 214 GB 201 *SYG 199	grv	
D	7	10	7	5	3	2	5	7		Viriliter agite et confortetur Diligite Dominum	GR 93**	grv	
D	7	10	7	5	3	5	7	3	D	Vado ad eum ... et nemo	AR 478 LU 825 AM 493 LA 241	an	1
D	7	10	7	5	7	2	3	5		Surrexit altissimus de sepulcro	SYG 168	alv	
D	7	10	7	5	7	3	2	0		Non vos me elegistis Vitone laudabilis	PM 204	rev	
D	7	10	7	5	7	3	2	0	D	Sancti qui sperant in Domino	PM 223 LR 177 *LA 514	an	1
D	7	10	7	5	7	3	5	3	D	Kyrie ad lib. II summe Deus qui cuncta	MEL #161 GR 76* LU 80		1
D	7	10	7	5	7	3	5	3	D	Sancti spiritus et animae	AR 743 LU 1510 AM 878 981 *WA 324 423 *LA 411 477	an	1
D	7	10	7	5	7	3	5	9	D	Hi qui linguis loquuntur	LA 266	an	1
G	7	10	7	5	7	3	7	5	G	Urbs fortitudinis nostrae	AR 224 LU 332 AM 195 WA 12 LA 11	an	7
D	7	10	7	5	7	5	2	3	D	Fontes et omnia quae moventur	AR 504 LU 884 AM 521 *WA 153 LA 261	an	1
D	7	10	7	5	7	5	2	3		In omnem terram exivit sonus eorum	GB 267	alv	
D	7	10	7	5	7	5	2	3	D	Juvenes et virgines ... quia	AR 302 LU 450 AM 280	an	1
D	7	10	7	5	7	5	2	3	D	Magna magnalia de Michael	LA 465	an	1
D	7	10	7	5	7	5	2	3		Quoniam praevenisti eum in benedictionibus Desiderium cordis	GR 82**	grv	

D	7	10	7	5	7	5	2	3		Surrexit Dominus de sepulcro	GR 248 LU 790 OHS 785 *GB 137^{v}	alv	
D	7	10	7	5	7	5	2	3	D	Vadam ad patrem meum	AR 386 LU 1088 AM 360 *WA 95 LA 146	an	1
D	7	10	7	5	7	5	3	2	D	Da fabricator noctis et diei	ST 332	hy	1
D	7	10	7	5	7	5	3	2	D	Libera me Domine et pone me	AM 6 *AR 82 WA 109	an	1
D	7	10	7	5	7	5	3	2		Veni sponsa Christi accipe palmam	SYG 208	alv	
D	7	10	7	5	7	5	3	2		Venite comedite panem meum	GR 627	alv	
D	7	10	7	5	7	5	3	5	D	Magnus Dominus ... et magnitudinis	AR 204 OHS 43 LU 310	an	1
D	7	10	7	5	7	5	3	5	D	Mulier quae erat ... stans	AR 548	an	1
D	7	10	7	5	7	5	3	5		Respice in me et miserere mei Ad te Domine	OTT 5 SYG 2 *GB 1^{v}	ofv	
D	7	10	7	5	7	5	3	5	D	Vado parare vobis locum	LA 254	an	1
D	7	10	7	5	7	5	3	5	D	Vos amici mei estis	AR [3] 511 LU 1111 AM 622 *WA 414 *LA 477	an	1
D	7	10	7	5	7	5	3	7		Verbo Domini caeli firmati Beata gens	GR 366 [91] LU 1048 GS 67 160 234 GB 93 SYG 105	grv	
D	7	10	7	5	7	5	7	2	D	Tantam gratiam ei	LR 324 *WA 298	an	1
D	7	10	7	5	7	5	7	5	D	Alleluia	AM 90	an	1
D	7	10	7	5	7	5	7	10		Dirige me in veritate tua Ad te Domine	OTT 5 *SYG 2 *GB 1^{v}	ofv	
D	7	10	7	5	7	8	7	5	D	Dixit Jesus discipulis suis venite	LA 220	an	1
D	7	10	7	5	7	8	7	5	D	Hi novissimi una hora	AR 346 AM 316 LA 115	an	1
D	7	10	7	5	7	8	7	5	D	Vim virtutis suae oblitus	AR 388 AM 362 WA 99 *LA 152	an	1
D	7	10	7	9	7	5	7	5	D	Hi sunt qui venerunt	AR 763 LU 1528 AM 949	an	1
D	7	10	9	5	3	2	5	7		Caelicus ordo sacram reveretur Virginitas caelum	AR 132* VP 203	rev	
D	7	10	9	5	7	5	3	0		Audivi vocem dicentem Oravi Deum	OTT 107 *GB 256^{v} SYG 250	ofv	
D	7	10	9	5	7	5	3	5		Assis nobis pater Ad occasum	WA 251	rev	
G	7	10	9	5	7	5	7	9		Et benedictum nomen Tibi laus tibi gloria	WA 160	rev	
D	7	10	9	10	7	5	3	7	D	Benedicat te hodie Deus	SYG 233	int	1
G	7	10	9	10	9	10	7	9	G	Oculus Dei respexit illum	GR 448 LU 1392	int	7
G	7	10	9	10	9	10	7	9	G	Respice Domine in testamentum	GR 354 LU 1032 SYG 247 GB 254 *GS 155	int	7
D	7	10	12	10	7	3	7	3	D	Angelis suis Deus mandavit	PM 193 *LA 130 WA 87	re	1
D	7	10	12	10	7	3	7	5	D	Hic est dies praeclarus in quo decus	LR 370	re	1
G	7	10	12	10	7	5	7	4	G	Gloria et honore coronasti ... et constituisti	SYG 200 GB 233^{v} *GS 204	int	7
D	7	10	12	10	9	7	5	7	D	Vadam ad montem myrrhae	AR 674 LU 1422	an	1